Social Work Practice
in **Healthcare**

Dedications

To Jim, for loving me enough to give me the time and support I needed to finish this part of the journey.

Karen M. Allen

To my father and mother (Dr. William C. and Violet Spitzer), who provided unfaltering support and serve as role models for me at every point of my life. At the same time, my son Colin has brought unbounded joy, love, and caring and in so doing has provided me with inspiration that has shaped and enriched my life. To these three, I will always be indebted. I would also happily say that being surrounded by a vast group of indulging friends who were always encouraging was a blessing.

William J. Spitzer

Social workers of Massachusetts General Hospital.

Source: Massachusetts General Hospital, Archives and Special Collections.

Social Work Practice in **Healthcare**

Advanced Approaches and Emerging Trends

Karen M. Allen | **William J. Spitzer**

Indiana University–Bloomington | *Healthcare and Social Service Consultant*

Los Angeles | London | New Delhi
Singapore | Washington DC | Boston

Los Angeles | London | New Delhi
Singapore | Washington DC | Boston

FOR INFORMATION:

SAGE Publications, Inc.
2455 Teller Road
Thousand Oaks, California 91320
E-mail: order@sagepub.com

SAGE Publications Ltd.
1 Oliver's Yard
55 City Road
London EC1Y 1SP
United Kingdom

SAGE Publications India Pvt. Ltd.
B 1/I 1 Mohan Cooperative Industrial Area
Mathura Road, New Delhi 110 044
India

SAGE Publications Asia-Pacific Pte. Ltd.
3 Church Street
#10-04 Samsung Hub
Singapore 049483

Acquisitions Editor: Kassie Graves
Editorial Assistant: Carrie Montoya
Production Editor: Libby Larson
Copy Editor: Allan Harper
Typesetter: C&M Pvt. Ltd.
Proofreader: Dennis W. Webb
Indexer: Terri Corry
Cover Designer: Edgar Abarca
Marketing Manager: Shari Countryman

Copyright © 2016 by SAGE Publications, Inc.

Printed in the United States of America

Library of Congress Cataloging-in-Publication Data

A catalog record of this book is available from the Library of Congress.

ISBN : 978-1-4833-5320-3

This book is printed on acid-free paper.

15 16 17 18 19 10 9 8 7 6 5 4 3 2 1

Contents

3. Knowledge and Theoretical Foundations of Healthcare Social Work Practice   69

Karen M. Allen and Mary Ruffolo

4. Healthcare Social Work Practice Skills and Competencies   95

Karen M. Allen and William J. Spitzer

5. Values and Ethics of Healthcare Social Work   127

Patricia O'Donnell

6. Practice-Based Research in Healthcare Social Work 145

PART II.   ADVANCED APPROACHES AND EMERGING TRENDS

7. Chronic Illness: Issues and Interventions 175

8. Transitional Planning Across the Continuum of Care 213

9. Social Work Practice in Oncology, Palliative, and End-of-Life Care 239

10. Community Health and Health Promotion 259

11. Gerontological Healthcare Social Work Practice 287

William J. Spitzer

12. Pediatric Healthcare Social Work Practice 315

Sarah Power and Melinda Gronen

13. Co-occurring Psychiatric and Substance Abuse Disorders in Medical Patients   357

Karen M. Allen

14. Supervision and Performance Evaluation   383

M. Carlean Gilbert and William J. Spitzer

SAGE was founded in 1965 by Sara Miller McCune to support the dissemination of usable knowledge by publishing innovative and high-quality research and teaching content. Today, we publish more than 750 journals, including those of more than 300 learned societies, more than 800 new books per year, and a growing range of library products including archives, data, case studies, reports, conference highlights, and video. SAGE remains majority-owned by our founder, and after Sara's lifetime will become owned by a charitable trust that secures our continued independence.

Los Angeles | London | Washington DC | New Delhi | Singapore | Boston

Preface

This text offers a comprehensive examination of social work practice in healthcare. Because it utilizes the advanced, contemporary knowledge and expertise of skilled practitioners and academics specialized in healthcare delivery, it is designed not only for graduate and undergraduate students but also for practicing professionals. Every effort was made to present content in a straightforward manner revealing not just the characteristics and competencies of practice, but the historic, current, and anticipated factors contributing to the shape and direction of healthcare social work. As administrative and academic social workers with 60 years of combined practice experience, the editors carefully considered the concepts, principles, methodologies, and operational dynamics that influence competent practice in the continuously evolving healthcare environment. Particular attention is devoted throughout on the impacts of the landmark Patient Protection and Affordable Care Act of 2010 (PPACA). Emphasis is placed on the integration of physical and behavioral healthcare, evidence-based practice, transdisciplinary care, and the increasing focus on primary health services associated with prioritized prevention, wellness, and chronic illness intervention.

This text has a singular intent—to promote competent healthcare social work practice. Competency is prescribed in the Council on Social Work Education Standards as well as the National Association of Social Workers' Standards for Practice in Health Care Settings. Contributing authors were selected on the basis of both their extensive patient care knowledge and ability to translate that in readily understood terms. The emphasis of the text is on conveying meaningful technical information in a manner that is logical, easy to understand, pragmatic, and readily applicable to healthcare professionals, regardless of present skill level. The goal is to advance social work practice to meet the current and anticipated needs of patients, families, and provider institutions. It is written in a style to not just hold the readers' attention, but more importantly, energize them to those vigorous, challenging professional opportunities associated with the healthcare environment.

Today's healthcare environment demands excellence. It expects the practitioner to not only be competent in their profession, but to understand the technological, social, political, ethical, and financial factors impacting patient care delivery. The introduction of managed care, alternately referred to by Munson (2002) as "managed cost," in the mid-1980s and 1990s and, more recently, the passage of the PPACA, provide clear evidence of concern about escalating healthcare costs, rising consumer expectations, evolving population demographics, and the challenge of un- and underinsured patient care. These and related factors place mounting pressure on institutional providers and individual practitioners alike to continuously adapt their patient care methodologies and priorities. This text addresses these issues by alerting readers to their bearing on current and future healthcare social work practice. It identifies the skills, ethical perspectives, techniques, and stresses associated with contemporary patient care. Using a systems approach to service delivery, significant emphasis throughout the text is placed on the importance of healthcare social workers being attentive to both individual patient and institutional provider needs.

This text has immediate applicability in the classroom, practicum, and by professionals in a wide range of patient care settings. With such use, the editors seek to enhance the integration of classroom and field by promoting a shared perspective on both pragmatic service delivery issues and professional orientation. It recognizes that learning accelerates and becomes more meaningful when students, academics, and practitioners share common ground. To facilitate this process, each chapter presents examples, exercises, and questions that challenge readers to translate theoretical concepts into competent practice.

ORGANIZATION OF THE TEXT

This text is organized in two parts. The first part consists of six chapters that provide a foundation in the knowledge, skills, and values associated with healthcare social work practice. Chapter 1 highlights the history of medical social work and the background for the development of healthcare delivery in the United States. Chapter 2 addresses the healthcare practice environment including organizational design, the continuum of patient care settings, and determining impacts on social work services. Chapter 3 introduces the knowledge and theoretical basis for contemporary healthcare social work practice. Chapter 4 delineates the requisite skills for competent practice, while Chapter 5 affords an overview of social work values and ethics in healthcare settings. Chapter 6 concludes the first part of the book by focusing on evidence-based practice and the considerations in evaluating such practice.

The second part of the book presents 10 chapters that describe advanced approaches and emerging trends in contemporary healthcare social work, including interventions with chronic illness, the characteristics of social work practice across the continuum of patient care settings, palliative and end-of-life care; community healthcare and health promotion, practice characteristics and issues associated with elderly patients, pediatric patient and family care, co-existing psychiatric and substance disorders, supervision and staff evaluation, and cultural competence in professional practice. Part 2 concludes with a final chapter on emerging trends in healthcare policy and delivery and projects the future of social work in healthcare. The statement given to students and practitioners alike is that the healthcare environment, while experiencing dramatic change, offers robust opportunities for social work practice.

ACKNOWLEDGMENTS

Development of this text involved considerable work on the part of many accomplished professionals. The editors are indebted to our 10 contributing authors for their commitment in the production of this text. Their expertise and perspectives reflect benchmark contemporary social work practice and offer experienced insight into the myriad of factors determining such practice.

The editors additionally wish to express their gratitude to those who contributed their time, interest, support, and expertise in commenting on the text. The information and perspective gained in that process was invaluable given their extensive leadership experience throughout the spectrum of healthcare services. Our distinguished colleagues included: Dr. Carolyn Watts, Chair, School of Health Administration, Virginia Commonwealth University; Dr. Frank Baskind, Professor and Dean Emeritus, School of Social Work, Virginia Commonwealth University and Past President, Council on Social Work Education; Dr. Kay Davidson, Professor and Dean Emeritus, School of Social Work, University of Connecticut; Michael Jurgensen, Senior Vice President for Health Policy and Planning, Medical Society of Virginia; Edward Woomer, LCSW, Associate Administrator, DuPont Hospital for Children and Past President, National Society for Social Work Leadership in Health Care; Barbara Farley, MSN, Senior Vice President for Patient Care Services and Chief Nursing Officer (retired), Virginia Commonwealth University/Medical College of Virginia Hospitals and Clinics; and Jeff Ruskin, Vice-President of Operations, Select Medical Corporation and previous Chief Executive Officer of HealthSouth Rehabilitation Hospital, Richmond, Virginia.

In addition, we wish to express our appreciation to SAGE Publications and to acknowledge the support, encouragement, and tangible assistance we received from Kassie Graves, Libby Larson, Carrie Montoya, and Allan Harper in completing this project. In addition, Karen Allen would like to recognize and acknowledge Michael J. Neuman and express her gratitude for the help and support received during her doctoral studies and dissertation. Further, she would like to acknowledge the support and mentoring she received early in her academic career by Dr. Andrew Weissman, a tremendous advocate for social work in healthcare. Finally, she would like to express her appreciation for Dr. Gary and Lauren Shepherd, for their unwavering loyalty, support and friendship.

REFERENCES

Munson, C. E. (2002). *Handbook of clinical social work supervision* (3rd ed.). New York: The Haworth Press, p. xviii.

About the Authors

Dr. Karen M. Allen, PhD, LCSW received her bachelor's degree in social psychology from Oakland University as well as an MSW in social work administration and a PhD in education from Wayne State University. She has nearly 20 years of experience in healthcare working as a medical social worker, department director, and administrator. Her clinical practice involved working with individuals and families affected with severe illnesses and traumas, including burns, spinal cord injuries, head injuries, cancer, and strokes. Most recently, her clinical work and research have been in trauma-infused cognitive behavioral therapy, especially as it relates to women who are recovering from interpersonal violence. She is a co-author with Danielle Wozniak of *Surviving Domestic Violence* and has written over 30 publications, including peer-reviewed papers, books, book chapters, and other publications.

Dr. Allen is currently Professor and Director of the Social Work Program at Indiana University Bloomington. She serves on the editorial review boards for *Social Work in Health Care, Social Work in Mental Health,* and *Advances in Social Work;* is a licensed clinical and macro-practice social worker; and teaches practice, policy, and research.

Dr. William J. Spitzer, PhD, DCSW earned his PhD in social work and business administration from the University of Illinois (Urbana-Champaign). His career extends over 30 years, with appointments as Department Director of Social Work Services for Virginia Commonwealth University/Medical College of Virginia Hospitals and Clinics, Oregon Health Sciences University Hospitals and Clinics, and the Sarah Bush Lincoln Health System. He served as State Manager of Licensing Operations for the Commonwealth of Virginia Department of Social Services, was acting Department Director of Human Resources for Sarah Bush Lincoln Health System and senior development partner for a proposed assisted-living community, and directed a staff private practice consulting extended-care facilities. Dr. Spitzer serves as Publications Editor and Communications Committee Co-chair for the National Society for Social Work Leadership in Health Care, was a National Board member, and served as President of the Virginia and Oregon Societies, Vice-President of the Central Illinois Society, and on the National Association of Social Workers Boards of Directors of Virginia, Oregon, and Michigan (Central).

Dr. Spitzer received the national Hy Weiner Social Work Health Care Leadership Award for administrative and academic achievement, the State Health Care Social Work Director of the Year Awards in Virginia and Oregon, two State Health Care Social Work Program of the Year Awards, and had his social work department honored as The Best Health System Patient Care Department by Virginia Commonwealth University/Medical College of Virginia

Hospitals administration. His academic appointments include Clinical Associate Professor of Social Work at Virginia Commonwealth University with prior appointments at Portland State University and the University of Illinois. Dr. Spitzer has served on numerous Council on Social Work Education (CSWE) university accreditation teams and journal editorial boards, presented at national and state conferences and has written 40 publications including articles in *Social Work in Health Care, Health and Social Work, Journal of Brief Therapy, the Social Work Desk Reference* (Oxford University), the *Journal of Prehospital and Disaster Medicine,* invitational social work healthcare text chapters, and the American Hospital Association publication on case management. He created and continues to edit the expanding 12-volume *Exemplars in Health Care Social Work Practice* text series of the National Society.

Contributing Authors

M. Carlean Gilbert, DSW, LCSW, ACM is Associate Professor at the Loyola University School of Social Work in Chicago. Practicing for 17 years as a pediatric social worker at The University of North Carolina at Chapel Hill and Duke University children's hospitals, she now teaches courses in social work practice in healthcare, group work, psychopathology, time-limited psychotherapy, and clinical supervision. Her scholarship has focused on health issues of children, clinical supervision, group therapy, and spirituality. She is editor of *The Clinical Supervisor: An Interdisciplinary Journal of Theory, Research, and Practice* and is an editorial board member of Social Work in Health Care.

Melinda Gronen, LCSW is an adjunct lecturer at the University of Illinois at Chicago Jane Addams College of Social Work and the University of Chicago School of Social Service Administration. Ms. Gronen received her Masters of Arts degree from the University of Chicago School of Social Service Administration with a clinical concentration. She has extensive experience in pediatric medical social work at Ann & Robert H. Lurie Children's Hospital of Chicago, where she provided services to children and families coping with chronic illness, trauma, and child maltreatment. As principal of a private practice, Ms. Gronen is a consultant and trainer on the assessment and intervention of child maltreatment for hospitals, schools, law enforcement, and community agencies.

Susan Hedlund, LCSW is Director of Patient & Family Services at the Knight Cancer Institute at Oregon Health & Sciences University and on the faculties of the OHSU School of Medicine and Portland State University School of Social Work. Ms. Hedlund has 30 years of healthcare social work practice experience, specializing in cancer, palliative, and end-of-life care. She is Past President of the Association of Oncology Social Work and recipient of the AOSW leadership award (1999), American Cancer Society Quality of Life Award (2009), and the Cambia Foundation Sojourn's Award in Palliative Care (2013).

Patricia O'Donnell, PhD, ACSW is the retired Director of the Center for Ethics of the Inova Health System, a non-profit healthcare system in Northern Virginia. In that role, she coordinated all systemwide ethics programming related to ethics consultation, policy, and education and end-of-life care. She received her MSW degree from the University of

Michigan and her PhD from the National Catholic School of Social Service (NCSSS) of the Catholic University of America with a concentration in Ethics and Clinical Practice. Her range of practice experience includes direct clinical and administrative social work in public health, university medical centers, and community hospital settings. Dr. O'Donnell taught social work ethics at the NCSSS, presented at local, national, and international social work and other professional conferences, and authored numerous chapters and articles in professional literature. She was a member of the national board of the Society for Social Work Leadership in Health Care, the Association for Oncology Social Work, and the District of Columbia Metro Chapter of NASW. Her research interests are in ethics issues and ethical stress in healthcare practice.

Sarah Power, LCSW is the Manager of Social Work in the Care Management Department at Oregon Health and Science University. She received her MSW degree from the University of Illinois (Urbana-Champaign) with a concentration in child welfare. As a pediatric social worker at Comer and Lurie Children's Hospitals, she served patients and families impacted by maltreatment with an emphasis on improving clinical assessment and community response. Ms. Power is responsible for supporting the design, development, and expansion of social work and transitional care programming in an academic, quaternary care setting. She advocates for vulnerable patient populations and is active in CMMI grant-funded healthcare reform initiatives.

Mary Ruffolo, PhD received her bachelor's degree in Social Work and Spanish from the University of Dayton, her MSW degree from the University of Illinois (Urbana-Champaign), and her PhD in Social Welfare from Ohio State University. She is a professor at the University of Michigan School of Social Work. Her funded research focuses on organizational factors that influence sustaining evidence-based interventions/programs in community mental health settings, adapting efficacious interventions for children and youth experiencing serious mental health challenges, and addressing ways to disseminate interventions with at-risk populations (e.g., families of children with serious mental illness, adults with severe mental illness). She is also involved in evaluating initiatives focusing on integrating behavioral health and primary care.

Sally Schmall, MSW, SPHR is a clinical faculty member at the University of Michigan Graduate School of Social Work specializing in integrated healthcare delivery. She received her MSW from the University of Michigan Graduate School and served as a medical social worker in Emergency Medicine, Spinal Cord Rehabilitation, and Hospice before joining the faculty in 2000. As the principal of Academy Coaching, Ms. Schmall provides coaching for faculty and customized organizational training for academic healthcare systems nationally.

Angela Schmidt, PhD, MNSc, RNP, RN is Associate Dean in the College of Nursing and Health Professions at Arkansas State University–Jonesboro. Dr. Schmidt received her D Lit et Phil degree from the University of South Africa, with an emphasis in physical rehabilitation and chronic illness. She serves as a consultant to healthcare agencies providing rehabilitation and chronic services, and has published on topics including chronic health, rehabilitation, ethics, health policy, and a variety of related health disorders. She is active as a Master Trainer in Chronic Disease Self-Management, certified by Stanford University.

Debbie Shelton, DNP, APRN, FNP-B.C. graduated from the University of Tennessee Science Center and received certification from the American Nursing Credentialing Center to practice as a Family Nurse Practitioner. Dr. Shelton has practiced in the role of advanced practice nurse in rural clinics for more than 20 years. She currently teaches in both didactic and clinic courses in the family nurse practice program and serves as the program coordinator for the Doctor of Nursing Practice program at Arkansas State University. Her research interests include the effects of childhood poverty on adult health behaviors, access to healthcare, and community health promotion.

Kristine Siefert, PhD, MSW, MPH is Professor Emerita of Social Work at the University of Michigan. Her research focuses on socioeconomic and racial/ethnic health inequities, including social and environmental contributors to racial/ethnic disparities in pregnancy outcome, the impact of household food insufficiency on physical and mental health, the social context of oral health disparities, and the impact of discrimination on African American women's mental health. Dr. Siefert has served in an advisory capacity or as an expert reviewer for numerous public health agencies and foundations and has served on the editorial board or as an occasional reviewer for more than 25 scientific and professional journals.

Introduction

Social work is the largest and most important social service profession in the United States (Whitaker, Weismiller, Clark, & Wilson, 2006), with healthcare representing one of the most significant fields of practice. The primary mission of the social work profession is to enhance human well-being and to help meet the basic needs of all people, with particular attention to those who are vulnerable, disenfranchised, oppressed, and living in poverty (NASW, 2005). Social workers assist people to better function in their environments, improve their relationships with others, and address personal and family problems through individual, social, and psychological counseling (Bureau of Labor Statistics, 2001; Volland, Berkman, Stein, & Vaghy, 2000).

As a field of practice, social work in healthcare is vibrant, exciting, and challenging. The extensive teamwork, sophisticated technology, intensity, and rapid pace of today's healthcare settings is highly stimulating, and the social worker's ability to contribute emotional support and tangible assistance to individuals and families facing health concerns is particularly rewarding. As an essential member of the service delivery team, social workers link together patients, families, and healthcare professionals by facilitating communication and ensuring that the psychosocial needs of patients are met during what frequently prove to be difficult life events.

Healthcare was one of the first arenas for social work practice as the profession emerged in the early 1900s. Social workers made significant contributions to the early public health movement, helping to limit the spread of communicable diseases such as tuberculosis by visiting and educating at-risk individuals in poor communities. From their earliest involvement, social workers provided insight to physicians and other healthcare team members about the impacts of social determinants, including lifestyles and the environment on patients' health, their self-care efforts, and compliance with medical instructions. Social workers played a crucial role in developing maternal and infant healthcare services and advocating for workplace safety laws.

Today, social workers are found in every arena of healthcare, from primary care clinics, hospitals, nursing home and continuing care retirement facilities, to home care and hospices. The National Association of Social Workers (NASW) 2007 membership workforce survey determined that 14% of social workers are employed in healthcare-related settings. When combined with an additional 9% who work with the elderly, health and aging are second only to mental health in the employment of social workers (Whitaker and Arrington, 2008). Health social workers are more prevalent in metropolitan areas (85%) than micropolitan areas (7%), small towns (6%), or rural areas (2%) (Whitaker et al., 2006).

Despite the strong presence of social work, the specialization has not been without its challenges. In 1983, the federal government eliminated the requirement that social work services be provided under Medicare, weakening the regulation and requiring only that the psychosocial needs of patients be addressed. As a consequence, many hospitals reduced hospital social work staffs and assigned some of their responsibilities to non-social work members of the healthcare team. The introduction of managed care in the mid-1980s and 1990s shifted the primary task of social work from providing psychosocial intervention to the more "concrete" aspects of discharge planning and coordinating post-hospital services for patients. Management models that became popular during the 1990s emphasized function and tasks rather than titles and identities and, as a result, many professions found themselves renamed. Over time, social workers became alternately known as discharge planners, case managers, care planners, and, most recently, "patient navigators" (Hart Health Strategies, 2010).

WHAT DO SOCIAL WORKERS IN HEALTHCARE DO?

The same factors that led to the introduction of social work in healthcare and shaped its practice at the turn of the century prevail today. Social workers serve as a bridge between patients, their families, and the healthcare team as well as the larger community. Arising from social casework, case management constitutes a principal function for most social workers, with the underlying intent that patients receive services to meet identified biopsychosocial needs. In acute care settings, social workers are characteristically responsible for continuity of care (or discharge) planning, in which they make sure that all necessary services, equipment, and arrangements are in place when a patient leaves the hospital. Because they have been trained to understand and negotiate the social welfare system, social workers also ensure that patients receive those benefits to which they are entitled. In many organizations, social workers provide medical information to patients' insurance companies and otherwise advocate so that payment for healthcare services is authorized. Because of their competence in establishing and maintaining strong networks with agencies providing crucial services, social workers are widely recognized as important liaisons or "boundary spanners" in the community. They identify patient and family care needs, locate resources, and communicate with providers to ensure that requisite services are delivered in a timely, competent manner.

In their clinical role, social workers help patients and families to cope with illnesses, injuries, and disabilities as well as the inevitable secondary adjustment issues associated with hospitalization or prolonged treatment. They often lead psychoeducational groups that combine emotional support with education about various illnesses. To illustrate, social workers frequently afford caregiver support, recognizing the stress experienced by caregivers as they assist patients with compromised health conditions. Counseling is a crucial component of case management and discharge planning as it addresses the inherent stresses of patients being ill, injured, or disabled and contemplating ongoing care needs, available resources, and future quality of life. Providing emotional support while formulating care plans with patients and families is a multifaceted process. In some healthcare settings, the counseling portion is separated from the discharge planning/case management functions, with a distinction made between clinical social workers and case managers.

Social work delivery of counseling often occurs in crisis situations, including emergency department admissions, "code blue" events, and those circumstances in which patients and families must contend with unanticipated and undesired changes in both physical condition and care. Not limited to patient and family care, social workers frequently intervene with healthcare and emergency "first-responder" professionals experiencing potentially debilitating critical incident stress arising from delivery of services in emotionally disturbing and potentially life-threatening patient care situations. In healthcare settings, these latter situations can extend from affording emotional support to staff grieving the unexpected death of a patient or being stressed with high volumes of complex patient cases to being thrust into actual danger—one of this text's two editors conducted multiple debriefings with physicians, nurses, and technicians following a gunfight that erupted *in* the emergency department of an urban trauma center.

Given the strong value base of the profession, and because social workers work closely with patients to ensure that their rights to self-determination are protected, social workers routinely engage when ethical issues arise. New medical technologies and procedures that save and extend lives can also trigger an array of potentially emotional dilemmas about whether and how to proceed with care. To address such issues, social workers often serve on or lead hospital ethics committees. On the individual patient level, they help patients to articulate and document their end-of-life wishes or advance directives. Social workers also engage with families and healthcare teams in their understanding and acceptance of patients' care decisions. In another context, healthcare social workers have been employed by funeral directors to help grieving survivors cope with their loss and re-establish their own capacities to function.

While social workers primarily serve on the individual patient level, there is an underlying professional expectation that social workers will exercise leadership in the delivery of patient care services. Reflective of their interpersonal communication and problem-solving skills as well as adeptness with group processes, social workers are often found chairing patient care committees, leading organizational task forces, directing departments, or otherwise contributing to system planning and service delivery efforts (Rosenberg & Weissman, 1995; Spitzer, 2004). Their value to the organization arises from being educated to have a global, "20,000 foot" perspective on difficult issues and complex, multifaceted situations—to accurately appraise priorities, relationships, and potentialities and propose realistic solutions.

While physicians are typically appointed as formal healthcare team leaders, social workers play important roles in guiding teams to recognize and ethically respond to the care needs and wishes of patients and their loved ones. In that context and based on knowledge of various racial and ethnic groups, social workers frequently educate healthcare professionals on the cultural practices and beliefs of patients in order to ensure that they are understood and respected. Depending on the hospital system, they may actively contribute in patient care rounds and/or present on the social determinants affecting patient quality of life, health status, and response to care. Recognition of social work as uniquely qualified to comment on the environmental impacts on patient medical compliance led to the creation of the very first hospital clinic social work position at Massachusetts General Hospital in 1905.

As patient advocates, social workers strive to ensure organizational policies and practices are non-discriminatory and adequately meet the needs of patients and families. When unmet needs or unfair practices are identified, social workers advocate for and design new policies and programs. Our roles as continuity of care planners and case managers position us to contribute to research and quality improvement activities that evaluate the outcomes and results of care. Promotion through the Patient Protection and Affordable Care Act of transdisciplinary practice and the integration of both physical and behavioral care increases the prospect that social work will be sought for input on community resources, benefits, and programs when personal and family needs arise.

A COMPETENCY-BASED APPROACH TO HEALTHCARE SOCIAL WORK

Healthcare social work practice is predicated on a core set of professional competencies. Regardless of the setting, healthcare social workers typically provide high-risk screenings and psychosocial assessments, counseling regarding patient/family adjustment to a health condition and its treatment, crisis intervention in emergent situations, patient/family education, case management, and/or discharge planning and resource referral for needed services, supplies, and/or equipment. With our aging population, advancing technologies that extend life and the prospect of less-affordable or available but still-needed care social workers are increasingly involved in ethical dilemmas faced by patients, families, and the healthcare team. Our core professional values that emphasize the dignity of each individual and their right to self-determination are particularly important in addressing these difficult situations.

Two sets of competencies pertain to healthcare social work practice. The 2015 Education and Policy and Accreditation Standards of the Council on Social Work Education (CSWE) identify 9 core competencies requisite for every graduate of an accredited social work program. Competent social work practice is characterized by CSWE as the ability to

- demonstrate ethical and professional behavior;

- engage diversity and difference in practice;

- advance human rights and social, economic and environmental justice;

- engage in practice-informed research and research-informed practice;

- engage in policy practice;

- engage with individuals, families, groups, organizations and communities;

- assess individuals, families, groups, organizations and communities;

- intervene with individuals, families, groups, organizations and communities;

- evaluate practice with individuals, families, groups, organizations and communities.

Social work practice is differentiated at the masters and bachelors educational levels. CSWE specifies that an individual with a BSW must demonstrate competency in all the above noted areas within the scope of *generalist* social work practice. The MSW "incorporates all of the core competencies augmented by knowledge and practice behaviors specific to a *concentration*" (Council on Social Work Education [CSWE], 2015). In this instance, the area of specialization or concentration is healthcare social work.

To understand the specialization of healthcare social work practice, we further reference standards for practice developed by the National Association of Social Workers. The NASW Standards for Social Work Practice in Health Care Settings (2005) were developed specifically to address the knowledge, skills, and values that are requisite for social workers in healthcare settings. The NASW standards overlap with the CSWE competencies but elaborate on how the core competencies are manifested in healthcare environments. Related standards have been promulgated by NASW that pertain to case management and practice involving palliative care and end-of-life issues. Additional efforts of the National Association of Deans and Directors of Schools of Social Work (NADD) in conjunction with CSWE are underway to produce a research-informed curriculum on competencies with the intent to promote the roles of social work in integrated behavioral health and primary care settings (Spitzer and Davidson, 2013).

GOING FORWARD: LOOKING TO THE FUTURE OF HEALTHCARE SOCIAL WORK

One of the important intents of this text is to offer inspiration to readers as to the future of healthcare social work practice. Although social workers are found throughout the continuum of care, the reduced presence of a centralized coordinating professional social work department and an increasing myriad of job titles have made them more difficult to locate. As we shall come to see, however, increasing patient care needs and volumes, changes in service delivery systems, enhanced technologies, and the reduced availability of physicians and other professionals are combining to significantly improve the potentials for future healthcare social work practice. U.S. Department of Labor projections for social work employment in healthcare are quite favorable, with distinct implications for new and expanded practices.

With the recent passage into law of the Patient Protection and Affordable Care Act (PPACA) and its hallmark Accountable Care Organizations, heightened emphasis is on "ramping up" the availability of healthcare and enhancing both the efficiency and effectiveness of health services. Integration of physical and behavioral healthcare, combined with the evolution of transdisciplinary service delivery, is dictating expanded use of allied healthcare professionals, including social workers. The challenge lies in being able to prepare sufficient numbers of appropriately trained and experienced practitioners. In particular, concern regarding the sufficiency of available geriatric practitioners in the future has prompted provision in the PPACA for financial grants to underwrite training and education of clinical social workers and social work educators focused on geriatric practice.

The PPACA focus on prevention, wellness, and intervention with chronic health conditions invites new opportunities for social work practice, particularly in an expanded array of outpatient settings. Emphasis on cost control and community care will further contribute to advancing historic social work roles in service brokerage, advocacy, and patient education. Our text lends credence to the interesting notion that "all things that go around, come around." The contemporary focus on the role of social determinants on health status and healthcare use is the same issue that contributed to the evolution of healthcare social work practice since the 1900s. With such recognition comes the opportunity for social work to flourish, using its patient-centered values, perspectives, experience, and knowledge to make substantial contributions to patient care. The information and views presented in this text provide a constructive basis on which to guide practitioners in making those contributions.

Karen Allen and William J. Spitzer
April 2015

REFERENCES

Bureau of Labor Statistics (2001). *Occupational outlook handbook, 2000–2001 Edition.* Washington, DC: author.

Council on Social Work Education. (2015). *Education policy and accreditation standards.* Retrieved from http://www.cswe.org/File.aspx?id = 79793

Hart Health Strategies. (2010). *Patient Protection and Affordable Care Act: A closer look. Patient navigator program.* Retrieved from http://www.primaryimmune.org/advocacy_center/pdfs/health_care_reform/Patient%20Navigator%20Program%20UPDATED_20101021.pdf

National Association of Social Workers. (2005). *Standards for Social Work Practice in Health Care Settings.* Retrieved from http://www.socialworkers.org/practice/standards/NASWHealthCareStandards.pdf.

Rosenberg, G., & Weissman, A. (1995). *Social work leadership in healthcare: Directors' perspectives.* New York: The Haworth Press.

Spitzer, W., & Davidson, K. (2013). Future trends in health and health care: Implications for social work practice in an aging society. *Social Work in Health Care, 52*(10), 959–986.

Spitzer, W. (2004). *Social work leadership in health care: Principles and practice.* The National Society for Social Work Leadership in Health Care. Petersburg, VA: The Dietz Press.

Volland, P., Berkman, B., Stein, G., & Vaghy, A. (2000). *Social work education for practice in health care: Final report.* New York: New York Academy of Medicine.

Whitaker, T., & Arrington, P. (2008). Social Workers at work. NASW membership workforce study. Washington, DC: National Association of Social Workers.

Whitaker, T., Weismiller, T., Clark, E., & Wilson. M. (2006). *Assuring the sufficiency of a frontline workforce: A national study of licensed social workers. Special report: Social workers in health care settings.* Washington, DC: National Association of Social Workers.

The Historical and Contemporary Context for Healthcare Social Work Practice

Karen M. Allen and William J. Spitzer

INTRODUCTION

This chapter examines the development of healthcare social work practice and provides a general overview of how healthcare in the United States evolved in the context of an emerging public health service. An overview of national healthcare reform efforts, including universal healthcare coverage, is presented along with the barriers impacting the passage of such legislation.

EVOLUTION OF MEDICAL SOCIAL WORK PRACTICE

Medical social work is acknowledged as the first subspecialty of the profession and the first venue for the delivery of organized social work services to people who were not poor. The emergence of medical social work can be traced to public health and social reform movements of the late 1800s, especially **Charity Organization Societies (COS)**. Although founded in Germany, these societies grew to particular prominence in England. In London, society director Sir Charles Loch perceived many patients attending the outpatient clinic to be in need of social support and assistance rather than medical treatment. That observation prompted Loch to advocate for a "charitable assessor" or "almoner" who would seek to reduce hospital crowding and focus on the non-medical needs of the patient population. A demonstration project initiated in 1895 by the London Charity Organization Society and the Royal Free Hospital led to the appointment of **Mary Stewart** as the "Lady Almoner." Charged with preventing abuse, Stewart referred patients to the appropriate Poor Law authority and local church parish while also administering the hospital's Good Samaritan Fund (Gleeson, 2006). This "Lady Almoner" is widely viewed as an early pioneer of the then-emerging medical social work profession.

Following the Civil War, the United States experienced an economic boom and industrialization coupled with both increased immigration and migration to the cities. Poverty and urban slums became national concerns as cities were unable to provide sufficient housing for the growing numbers of immigrant poor or even the most basic health and safety measures such as sewers, fire protection, and safe drinking water. Organized resistance to public relief programs, which many believed fostered dependency, forced states to create charitable agencies intended to serve the **worthy poor**—the disabled, elderly, children, and widows. The first Charity Organization Society appeared in the United States when *Reverend Stephen Humphreys Gurteens* began agency operations in December 1877 to fight widespread destitution in the manufacturing and shipping city of Buffalo, New York. By 1900, societies were operating under varying names in approximately 125 cities across the United States.

Rather than offering direct relief, the societies afforded moral and spiritual "uplifting" to **undeserving (or unworthy) poor,** who were able-bodied individuals believed to be impoverished as a result of moral failings (National Conference on Social Welfare, 1880; Nacman, 1977). The societies served as clearing houses for the operating charities in the communities. They maintained registries of those receiving relief, noted any assistance provided to the poor, and made referrals for additional help. Using **friendly visitors** modeled after English almoners, they visited the poor, investigated living conditions to determine the causes of destitution, and encouraged better nutrition, sanitary hygiene, and abstinence. As a friendly visitor in the Baltimore COS, **Mary Richmond**'s efforts in particular raised the prominence of the national charities movement. The organized curriculum she developed for training volunteers, including its detailed system for documenting case records, ultimately led to formal assessment and intervention procedures that were adopted by the emerging profession of social work.

In 1866, Dr. Elizabeth Blackwell created a role for **Dr. Rebecca Cole**, an African-American physician, as a **sanitary visitor** who visited the homes of women and children served by the New York Clinic. In 1889, increasing appreciation for the significant influence of social conditions on individual and community health status motivated Johns Hopkins Hospital to incorporate sanitary visitation into the training of some medical residents. At the same time, however, others were advocating for specially trained nurses to assess social conditions and promote health (Cannon, 1952; Nacman, 1977).

The appearance of social work in hospital settings is linked to the efforts of one physician, **Dr. Richard Cabot**. Prior to assuming the position of Medical Chief of Staff at Boston General Hospital in 1912, Cabot had already become convinced that living conditions impacted individual susceptibility to disease. Before entering medicine at Harvard, Cabot had studied philosophy with a commitment to identifying practical solutions to the problems of the day. By 1892, the widespread acceptance of the germ theory of disease had changed the understanding of the origins of infectious diseases and was included in Cabot's medical training along with bacteriology as well as early epidemiological and laboratory research methods. A social reformer, Cabot was an admirer of Jane Addams—the noted settlement house founder of Hull House in Chicago (see Johnson, 1989, for a superb photographic history). In an early career appointment as Executive Director of Boston's Children's Aid Society, Cabot advocated the approach of friendly visitors in assessment, recording, and presenting at case conferences. The friendly visitor was an opportunity to integrate information about social and environmental conditions into the practice of medicine.

Overseeing the dispensary at Massachusetts General Hospital (MGH) where "hopeless" cases (including those with tuberculosis and typhus) were seen, Cabot became further sensitized to how "nonsomatic" living conditions often created and exacerbated physical afflictions. Most dispensary patients were poor immigrants who were unable to speak English, and Cabot soon recognized that cultural and language issues detracted from clinic physicians' abilities to schedule and treat patients (Gehlert & Browne, 2006, p. 9). In an effort to address these concerns, Cabot created a new position for a recent nursing graduate, *Garnet Pelton*, as clinic social worker. Cabot believed that a home visit by a social worker could aid physicians in making more accurate and complete diagnoses by providing information about patients' personalities as well as their social and economic circumstances. Pelton was also positioned to both serve as a link between the clinic and other community agencies and to develop a system for recording and maintaining patient files. Pelton's tenure was unexpectedly cut short after only six months as a result of tuberculosis. Undaunted, Cabot remained committed to the notion of having a social worker in the clinic and moved to retain Ida Cannon as Pelton's successor. Working with Dr. Cabot, Cannon is widely acknowledged as the person most responsible for the early growth and development of medical social work (Gehlert & Browne, 2006; Nacman, 1977; Trattner, 1999).

Ida Maud Cannon began her career as a public health nurse in Saint Paul, Minnesota, but, after hearing a lecture by Jane Addams of Chicago Hull House fame, Cannon relocated to Boston for the purpose of studying social work. Not long thereafter, Cannon met Dr. Cabot though her older brother, and a lifelong friendship began. Cabot was deeply impressed with Cannon's interest in and understanding of social medicine. Following her internship at Boston General Hospital in 1907, Cabot used his own finances to hire her and others for the clinic.

Cannon and her staff served a patient population composed of nearly 50% immigrants, primarily Italian Catholics and Eastern European Jews. Many of these patients suffered with acute tuberculosis, and their inability to comprehend English prevented them from communicating with medical personnel. Although scientists identified the tuber-

Ida Cannon, first director of the Social Services Department at Massachusetts General Hospital.

Source: Massachusetts General Hospital, Archives and Special Collections.

culosis bacterium in 1882, widespread antibiotic treatment did not become available until the 1940s. As a result, tuberculosis remained a major public health issue, ranking second only to pneumonia as a leading cause of death. Cannon and her staff worked to educate physicians on how to communicate with their patients so that they could understand and follow the prescribed treatments of quarantine, rest, fresh air, and adequate nutrition. This meant that patients and families required support in coping with the emotional and financial effects of long periods of separation. Cannon and her staff also focused on countering the stigma of syphilis while encouraging patients to successfully endure the long course of required treatment. Of equal concern were the severe occupational injuries arising from the deplorable working conditions endured by many immigrants and the poor, particularly children. These issues as well as concern about the growing numbers of unmarried pregnant women motivated social workers to vigorously expand community resources and design prevention programs (Praglin, 2007; Nacman, 1977).

Cannon faced many obstacles in her efforts to professionalize medical social work services. Many physicians resisted the inclusion of social work, believing that it detracted from the medical or scientific mission of the hospital. Working conditions during this time left much to be desired, as record keeping was primitive and there was little regard for confidentiality. Cannon's efforts at developing formal case records and documentation guidelines were likely viewed as further intrusions. Cabot, sensing that nurses had compromised their mission by agreeing to "become mere implements" of the physician (Gehlert & Browne, 2006, citing Evison), argued that social workers should be recruited to address the social ills of patients.

Although Cabot envisioned an active "critique" of medical practice by social workers in an effort to humanize the patient–physician encounter, it is doubtful that most physicians welcomed this constructive criticism. Furthermore, Dr. Frederic A. Washburn, Jr., the Director of Massachusetts General Hospital at the time, was openly hostile to the inclusion of social work services. He refused to fund a social work department and attempted to restrain social work access to the outpatient clinics and dispensaries. When Cannon and her staff trespassed on the inpatient wards, they were "sharply rebuffed" (Cannon, 1952). Cannon's capacity to reframe these dictatorial activities in a positive light reflects her own level of professionalism. Cannon tried to appreciate Washburn's interest and curiosity about social work services and responded with "tact, patience and quiet determination" (Bartlett, 1975). Perhaps begrudgingly, Washburn was marginally won over and acquiesced to permitting social workers on the inpatient wards, albeit under his direct supervision. Although Cannon reluctantly accepted the position as Director of Social Services in 1914, it was not until 1918 that the Board of Trustees at Massachusetts General agreed to take over financing of the social work department from Dr. Cabot. Other hospitals followed in establishing their own hospital social work departments and, by 1924, the number of hospital social work departments had expanded to 420 (Bartlett, 1961 & 1975; Gehlert & Browne, 2006; Praglin, 2007).

Cannon is credited with establishing the first organized hospital social work department, defining the role of medical social work in outpatient and inpatient settings and negotiating the fine line for social workers serving in a "host," and at times hostile, setting. Rather than taking a radical position that challenged the medical model and the primacy of the physician in healthcare, she instead attempted to accommodate social work within the prevailing hospital culture. Such an approach put Cannon at odds with Dr. Cabot, who urged her to actively challenge and "socialize" medicine. The approach of advocating for patients and promoting organizational change while respecting the primary medical role of the physician in dealing with physical disease and the central position of the physician on the healthcare team remains today as a hallmark of contemporary social work healthcare practice.

Cannon and Cabot experienced other tensions as well that continue to be evident in professional practice today. Cannon, like Mary Richmond, believed that it was within the scope of practice for medical social workers to directly treat patients, intervene to alleviate social conditions, and improve the "mental attitude" of patients in order to improve health (Cannon, 1923, p. 15). Cabot, on the other hand, viewed the social worker as a liaison between the patient, physician, and community. He regarded the focus of social work direct treatment to be on patient/family adjustment to illness, hospitalization, and treatment rather than on efforts to alleviate any perceived causes of poor health.

Cannon wrote prodigiously and presented on behalf of medical social work at numerous national conferences for the emerging social work profession. Demonstrating both insightful leadership and professional advocacy, she was instrumental in establishing the American Association of Medical Social Workers in 1918. In 1928, Cannon and Dr. Cabot published the first practice standards for hospital social work departments with the American College of Surgeons (Cabot, 1928). Recognizing that medical social work emerged from a "friendly visiting" tradition that embraced moralism and paternalism to preserve the status quo, Cannon vigorously promoted professional training and developed model curricula for healthcare social work practice. In conjunction with teaching social work at Simmons College in 1929, Cannon initiated a national survey of university schools of social work that identified ten schools as offering specialized curricula in medical social work (Gehlert & Browne, 2006; Nacman, 1977).

Ida Cannon prominently served thirty-nine years at Massachusetts General Hospital before reluctantly retiring in 1945. She was the recipient of numerous professional and civic awards, including honorary doctoral degrees from the University of New Hampshire and Boston University in 1937 and 1950, respectively. In 1957, disabled by a stroke, she entered a nursing home, where she died on July 8, 1960.

During the period between 1920 and 1930, social work programs were initiated in the Army, Navy, and the Veterans Administration. In 1920, the American Hospital Association (AHA) sponsored the first formal survey of hospital social services. Recommendations from that survey prompted the establishment of a committee focusing on the training of hospital social workers. Eight years later, the first minimum standards for social service departments were promulgated by the American College of Surgeons.

Healthcare social work evolved from a focus on tuberculosis, syphilis, and the effects of the hazardous working conditions prevalent in the early 1900s to one in which psychiatric theory became prominent and the therapeutic relationship was regarded as the primary casework tool (Robinson, 1930). Psychoanalysis gained considerable status as an intervention in the 1940s, to the extent that many general hospitals ultimately divided their social work services into psychiatric and medical programs. Social workers assigned to the medical and surgical units were viewed less favorably as they were perceived to have only instrumental tasks, such as arranging various services (e.g., transportation, housing, etc.). In comparison, psychiatric social workers practiced analytically oriented therapy, concentrating less on environmental and social determinants than on psychodynamics of repressed fears, anxieties, and frustrations.

By the 1950s and continuing into the 1960s, group work became a fundamental component of healthcare social work practice. Family therapy was increasingly utilized in both psychiatric and medical settings. Groups were also valued as a means of intervening with patients experiencing similar medical problems, particularly those of a chronic nature. With the evolution of rehabilitative services and the development of increasingly sophisticated treatments for cardiac and cancer conditions, support groups became widespread.

The civil rights and welfare movements of the 1960s, along with expansion of the Social Security Act to include Medicare and Medicaid, had profound impacts on social work practice. Social workers had been actively involved with both aging and indigent populations, and the advent of Titles XVIII (Medicare) and XIX (Medicaid) generated millions of new patients for hospital and ambulatory healthcare. With social issues often being prominent among presenting problems among these patients, demand grew for healthcare social workers. Increasing numbers of graduate-trained social workers entered into practice, and social workers no longer waited for referrals from physicians and nurses but initiated their own "case-finding," high-risk screening efforts. The value of this activity persists today as early identification of problematic patient situations is crucial when short (and expensive) hospitalizations limit available intervention time. As we will see elsewhere in this text, the current configuration of healthcare social work carries the marks of these defining historical events but has now expanded into a broadened array of interventions conducted across the entire continuum of healthcare settings.

HISTORICAL CONTEXT OF HEALTHCARE IN THE UNITED STATES

The American social welfare and healthcare systems have their origins in England. The Elizabethan Poor Law of 1601 and subsequent poor laws made vagrancy a crime, associated disease with sinfulness, and mandated that local parishes provide for the poor and infirmed when families were unable to do so. Under the Poor Law, children, the able-bodied, and the impotent were identified as major categories of dependents and the authorities were directed to adapt their activities so as to address the needs of each. Colonists arriving in the New World unfortunately did not escape from the poverty and other social ills found in the Old World. Predictably, they turned to their prior customs and culture for examples of how to deal with the issue of providing relief to the growing numbers of needy. The harsh life in America was filled with deprivation and resulted in many colonists becoming impoverished and plagued with debilitating health problems. The colonies did acknowledge public responsibility for those unable to care for themselves and initially obligated families to assume care for a destitute person in their community during a part of the year.

Caring for the sick was generally provided in their own homes by a family or charitable townspeople. This type of charity was known as **outdoor relief** as it implied care that was delivered to individuals outside of institutions (Day, 2009). Institutions based on English alms and poor houses emerged over time, initially around seaport towns to quarantine incoming sailors with communicable diseases and then subsequently in communities to contain and care for infected colonists. Care provided in almshouses and later in asylums was called **indoor relief** as those receiving such care resided in an institution (Day, 2009). These early notions about indoor and outdoor relief eventually evolved into our contemporary distinction between institutional and community-based care. After a period of significant

Suffolk County Poor House.

Source: Longwood Public Library's Thomas R. Bayles Local History Room.

expansion from the mid-1800s to the 1950s, institutional (indoor) relief has now been largely replaced by community-based care. During the 1980s, a number of federal and state policy initiatives, known collectively as **deinstitutionalization,** prompted many of today's programmatic approaches that, under select conditions, enable chronically mentally ill and/or developmentally disabled individuals to reside in their local communities rather than in long-term care institutions.

Although some facilities were constructed to contain the sick during community epidemics, the first **almshouse** was established in Philadelphia in 1713 by William Penn to serve only Quakers. Other large cities in the colonies followed the example of Philadelphia, and, in 1736, New York founded the City Poor House. Later known as Bellevue Hospital, this facility continues to operate today. Early almshouses typically contained the sick, mentally ill, elderly, disabled, and vagrant together, making little if any distinctions between the circumstances and needs of their residents. By the mid-1700s, however, the sick began to be segregated from the other inhabitants of almshouses. Located in Philadelphia, the Pennsylvania Hospital opened in 1751 as the first institution in the United States to be singularly committed to caring for the sick. During the Revolutionary War, New York Hospital was the first institution to train medical students and, by the turn of the century, an emerging middle class demanded, and, importantly, was capable of paying for healthcare.

The Suffolk County Almshouse and Poorhouse in Suffolk County, New York, is one example of an institution in which the poor, ill, and mentally ill were housed together. Local historians have compiled detailed records of the "inmates" there as well as the history of the institution, which can be explored on http://www.poorhousestory.com/SUFFOLK.htm.

Inpatient institutional care for the sick in most major cities progressed through the 1840s with the establishment of voluntary hospitals that were funded by contributions from private and public foundations. The first mental asylums appeared during this period, and *dispensaries*, typically private clinics that provided medications and outpatient

Dorothea Dix and Iowa State Hospital

Sources: Bandholtz, F. J. (Frederick J.), 1877. Iowa State Hospital for Insane, Clarinda, IA. Panoramic photographs (Library of Congress). U.S. Library of Congress DIX, DOROTHEA LYNDE. Retouched photograph. [ND] Biographical File Reproduction Number: LC-USZ62-9797

services, also gained prominence. Most hospitals that emerged at this time were funded through private philanthropic contributions as neither the state nor federal government perceived an obligation to publically fund medical care. Although hospitals and charitable organizations continued to evolve by specializing in the treatment of particular client populations or diseases, the mentally ill, children, and poor more typically received care in the generic almshouses.

It was not until the mid-1800s that specialized care for the mentally ill became recognized as a social imperative. As a teacher and early reformer, **Dorothea Lynde Dix** inspected jails and almshouses that housed the mentally ill throughout the country. She documented abuse and maltreatment of residents and, as a prominent supporter of the **mental hygiene movement**, advocated for more humane forms of treatment, including care in institutions specializing in the treatment of the mentally ill. In 1854, Dix secured the passage of a federal land grant supporting the development of such a facility. The grant also established a role for the federal government in providing support for states and local communities that had assumed the sole burden of caring for the mentally ill. The bill was vetoed, however, by President Pierce. That decision was subsequently used to justify denial of federal assistance to states caring for the mentally ill and disabled until the 1930s (Nacman, 1977). In 1881, Dorothea Dix went on to oversee the construction of a state hospital in Trenton, New Jersey, that was dedicated to the humane and progressive treatment of the mentally ill (Muckenhoupt, 2003). A pioneer in the field of mental health, Dix is credited with the founding of state hospitals for mental patients in nine states (Trattner, 1999).

PUBLIC HEALTH IN THE UNITED STATES

The term *public health* implies a focus on the health of populations and emphasizes disease prevention, promotion of health, reporting and control of communicable diseases, responsibility for environmental factors such as air/water quality that affect health, and the collection and analysis of data identifying the current status of and emerging trends in public health. The role of public health agencies initially included quarantines to control diseases and the introduction and enforcement of sanitation principles. While some public health agencies offered limited direct services (like immunizations and treatment of sexually transmitted diseases), most agencies avoided direct competition with health services provided by the private sector (Barton, 1999).

The first efforts in public health in the United States involved the need to quarantine sailors and slaves who may have infectious diseases.

Source: US Library of Congress.

The origins of the public health service in the United States can be traced back to 1798, when President John Adams signed into law an act allocating federal funds to care for sick, disabled, and injured marines. Initially called the *Marine Hospital Service of the United States (MHS),* it primarily focused on affording health services to merchant seamen. The uncontrolled spread of the deadly yellow fever epidemic of 1877 along the Mississippi River corridor necessitated passage of the *National Quarantine Act* (1878). This act effectively shifted authority to quarantine individuals from individual states to the Marine Hospital Service, which had an already established network of marine hospitals and physicians in many port cities. In 1902, the MHS became the U.S. Public Health and Marine Hospital Service to reflect its expanded mission to provide medical care to certain populations and to continue quarantines as a protection against diseases introduced via the seaports (Barton, 1999).

The financial boom and wave of industrialization that followed the Civil War was without parallel in the history of the world, with consequences so great as to become known as an *economic revolution* (Trattner, 1999). Between 1865 and 1900, immigration into the United States greatly increased, as did the population shift from rural to urban areas. While the wealth of the country was greatly enhanced and the overall standard of living increased, the downside of the heralded revolution included cycles of depression and unemployment, unhealthy living conditions, and dangerous work environments. Urban areas in particular were filthy, disorderly, disease-ridden places with unsafe housing, inadequate sanitation, pest infestations, and toxic levels of pollution. Such conditions prompted deadly outbreaks of smallpox, cholera, and typhus, along with tuberculosis, diphtheria, and scarlet fever. It became increasingly apparent that addressing the public health issue was of paramount importance.

The "golden age of public health" from approximately 1890–1910 greatly contributed to our understanding of epidemiology and the factors influencing the spread of disease. During this period, hygienic laws and policies were implemented in an effort to contain disease. Laboratories were established, research evolved, and medical education improved. With greater understanding of the relationship between poverty and poor health, social workers (or charity workers as they were previously called) made significant contributions by working directly with communities to document, educate, and improve living conditions (Trattner, 1999). *The Progressive Era* (1880–1920) and its social reform movement improved working conditions and worker safety, regulated child labor, created the first industrial accident insurance, and created federal oversight and inspection of meat-packing plants and drug companies (Digital History, 2014). Together these reform movements improved overall health, decreased infant mortality, and contributed to increased longevity.

Reflecting its increasing assumption of healthcare to the general citizenry, the U.S. Public Health and Marine Hospital Service changed its name in 1913 to the **U.S. Public Health Service (PHS)**. State and county health departments and mental health clinics were formed and charged with overseeing the development and distribution of vaccinations as well as with preventing and managing various infectious disease outbreaks, including Spanish influenza, polio, tuberculosis, and venereal disease. In 1944, **The Public Health Service Act** consolidated all public health services into a single statute and made continued support available to the state and local health departments. The current **National Institutes of Health (NIH)** evolved from an early epidemiological laboratory operated by the PHS in 1887 (Parascandola, 1998).

As of 1996, The Office of Public Health Services operates as a division of the United States Department of Health and Human Services (DHHS). The public health service agencies within DHHS now consist of **the Centers for Disease Control and Prevention (CDC)**, the **Food and Drug Administration (FDA)**, the **Health Resources and Services Administration**, the **National Institutes of Health (NIH)**, the **Substance Abuse and Mental Health Services Administration**, the **Indian Health Services**, and the **Agency for Healthcare Policy and Research**. Operating ten regions and a uniformed corps of 6,000 service members in addition to the Office of the U.S. Surgeon General, the PHS does not focus on direct service delivery, but on shaping the national public health system to promote health and prevent disease (see http://www.hhs.gov/ophs/index.html). Information on the career opportunities that exist for social workers within public health may be found at http://www.socialworkers.org/research/naswResearch/PublicHealth/default.asp.

EARLY EFFORTS TO NATIONALIZE HEALTHCARE IN THE UNITED STATES

The United States has been unsuccessful in numerous attempts to create a national healthcare system that would guarantee that all citizens are provided with basic health insurance and/or medical care. A **nationalized healthcare system** is one in which healthcare providers are public sector employees paid by the government for their professional services. In a **single-payer system,** the government sponsors and administers a form of health insurance for all of its citizens. The insurance entity reimburses providers for services, but the providers do not necessarily have to be public employees. In both systems, the government pays for covered services, either directly or indirectly (through the single payer), with tax revenues and/or "premiums" paid for by individuals and businesses. The **multi-payer system** currently used in the United States is characterized by a significant array of insurance companies vying against one another in a highly competitive marketplace. The lack of a national healthcare system or nationalized health insurance makes the United States unique among first-world, industrialized nations.

By the turn of the 20th century, a number of industrialized countries were experimenting with national healthcare systems, or universal healthcare. In 1883, Germany became the first country to implement nationalized health insurance for industrial workers. By 1912, the United Kingdom, Austria, Norway, Hungary, Russia, and the Netherlands were in the process of developing systems of nationalized healthcare. In 1915, a coalition of labor unions, social reformers, and physicians under the auspices of the American Association of Labor drafted a model proposal for universal healthcare in the United States that was initially supported by the American Medical Association (AMA) (Palmer, 1999). The emerging private insurance industry and state medical societies, however, along with the funeral industry, did not support the proposal. When the outbreak of World War I generated anti-German sentiments, the proposal died in large measure as a result of unwarranted fears that the United States might become too much like its socialized enemy (Starr, 1983).

President Franklin D. Roosevelt sought to include universal healthcare as part of the New Deal legislation he was advancing. His advisors determined, however, that inclusion of any provisions for national health insurance would jeopardize passage of the Social Security Act of 1935. Roosevelt was not necessarily committed to universal health insurance that was compulsory for all citizens, but his support of care for the poor and elderly led to his attempt to pass the Wagner National Health Act in 1939. When first introduced, this act included a system of federal grants that would have funded a national health system. Later versions of the bill would have established compulsory health insurance funded by a payroll tax. Lacking the support of the AMA, however, it and subsequent iterations of the Act (The Wagner-Murray-Dingell Bill of 1943) failed despite strenuous efforts to reintroduce the bill for over fourteen years (Physicians for a National Health Program, n.d.).

In contrast, President Harry Truman supported a compulsory, egalitarian, universal system of health insurance afforded to all citizens, regardless of need, income, or status. When he introduced his proposal for nationalized health insurance in 1945, it was roundly decried by the press, the AMA, the American Bar Association, and the American Hospital Association, among many other groups. Physicians objected to government regulation, and along with many U.S. citizens feared communism and socialist-type programs in the wake of World War II.

The post-World War II economic boom saw a vibrant union movement that garnered health insurance benefits for workers through the collective bargaining process. However, while increasing numbers of individuals and families obtained health insurance through employer-sponsored insurance, the elderly, poor, and unemployed remained uninsured. Government programs to cover healthcare costs began to expand during the 1950s and 1960s as various benefits were incrementally added to the Social Security Act of 1935, including pensions for disabled workers and surviving spouses and children. It was not until 1965 that President Lyndon Johnson created the first national health insurance plan by amending the Social Security Act with the addition of the Medicare and Medicaid programs. At the time of its passage, private sources, including individuals and employers, paid for approximately three-fourths of all healthcare insurance premiums. By 1995, healthcare costs were split equally between the government and private payers. As **entitlement programs**, Medicare and Medicaid must be included in the federal budget (Palmer, 1999; also see Kaiser Family Foundation for timelines outlining the legislative process for the passage of Medicare and Medicaid at http://www.kff.org/medicaid/40years.cfm.

Medicare was inaugurated on July 1, 1966, and is considered to be a *social insurance program*. Created by Title XVIII of the Social Security Act, Medicare is a comprehensive program covering almost one in seven Americans. It was initially established as a basic hospital insurance program for persons 65 years of age and over. In 1972, the program was extended to disabled beneficiaries of any age under certain circumstances and to most persons with chronic kidney disease. Medicare has two major program components. Two optional components (Parts C and D) were subsequently made available. *Part A* provides coverage for inpatient hospital care, limited skilled nursing facility care, and home health and hospice care. Part A is financed through payroll deductions and employer contributions that are then deposited in a trust fund. *Part B* is supplementary medical insurance (SMI) that pays for certain costs of physicians' services and other medical expenses. Three-fourths of Part B financing comes from federal general funds, with the remainder made up from contributions that are voluntarily paid by beneficiaries (Kovner, 1995). Neither Part A nor Part B offers comprehensive coverage as there are deductibles, coinsurance, and limitations on the total amount of reimbursable charges. *Part C* is a **managed care** option that Medicare subscribers *may* purchase that covers the A and B benefits and may cover additional benefits of vision, hearing, dental, health and wellness programs, and prescription drug coverage if there are sufficient savings. As a prescription drug coverage plan, *Part D* was signed into law by President Bush in 2003.

Medicaid provides health insurance coverage for poor individuals, who must meet stringent eligibility requirements established by each state. Considerable variation exists among the states as to eligibility. Individuals, such as disabled children, are not required to have paid into the system in order to receive benefits. Although administered at the state level, it is funded through a combination of federal and state dollars. The federal government outlines services that all states must provide, such as payment of nursing home care for poor seniors and providing prenatal care to poor mothers. States can, however, request exemptions from these requirements through a **waiver** system. Waivers can also be used by the states to pilot new healthcare programs. The federal government also created the State Children's Health Insurance Plan (S-CHIP), to help provide care to children. With less-restrictive eligibility requirements (some states allow income in excess of 300% of the poverty level), S-CHIP afforded many more children of working-poor parents the opportunity to qualify for services. Medicaid is the largest health insurance program in the United States, covering over 66 million Americans, including the poorest individuals and families in the nation. The program also is the primary source of the country's long-term care financing. The Patient Protection and Affordable Care Act (PPACA) passed along with provisions for states to expand Medicaid beginning in 2014. The intent was for the expanded programs to serve as the foundation of the broader framework created by the PPACA to cover millions of previously uninsured low-income adults and children (Kaiser Family Foundation, 2013).

Debate over national healthcare escalated with concerns about seemingly uncontrolled rising costs, questionable quality (value), shifts in insurance funding (coverage) from the private to the public sector, and increasing difficulties with affordability (access). The United States spends more on health per capita than any other country in the world (Organization for Economic Cooperation and Development [OECD], 2013). While U.S. healthcare spending in the 1950s represented about 4% of the Gross National Product (GNP), health spending reached nearly 18% of the U.S. GNP in 2010 (Centers for Medicare and Medicaid Services [CMS], 2012). Put another way, this means that, in 2010, almost eighteen cents of every dollar spent in the United States was spent on healthcare. *Figure 1.1* compares U.S. healthcare expenditures as a percentage of GNP in the United States with those in other countries along with the average of over 200 countries reporting data to the OECD. Per-person expenditures increased from $356 per person in 1970 to

Figure 1.1   Total Healthcare Expenditures as a Percentage of Gross Domestic Products, 2009

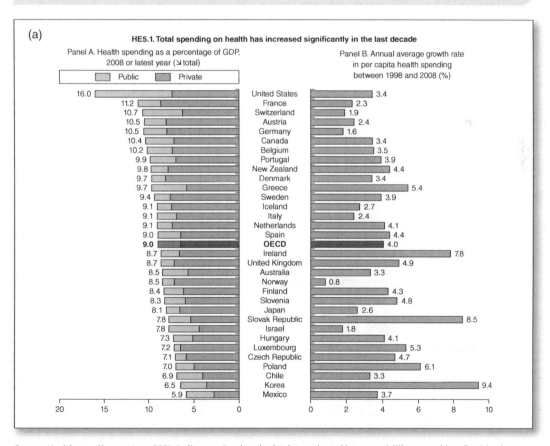

Source: Health at a Glance 2011: OECD Indicators. Retrieved 7/12/12 at: http://www.oecd-ilibrary.org/sites/health_glance-2011-en/07/02/g7-02-01.html?contentType=/ns/Book,/ns/StatisticalPublication&itemId=/content/book/health_glance-2011-en&containerItemId=/content/serial/19991312&accessItemIds=&mimeType=text/html

$8,160 in 2009. By 2012, expenditures reached a record level of $2.8 trillion, or $8,915 per person (Centers for Medicare and Medicaid Services [CMS], 2012). On average, healthcare premiums for a family in the United States equal the gross pay received at minimum wage.

Concern about healthcare costs was not limited to overall expenditures but also to disturbing trends in the sources of insurance funding and the extent of coverage. The percentage of individuals depending on government health insurance steadily *increased* to over 32% by 2011, whereas the percentage of those covered by employer-sponsored health insurance steadily *decreased* to 55% and the percentage of those directly purchasing healthcare insurance remained steady at about 10% (*Figure 1.2*) (United States Department of Health and Human Services, 2012).

Furthermore, an estimated 6 million **dual-eligible beneficiaries** accounted for about 30% of Medicare spending and 35% of Medicaid spending in 1995, although they represented only 16% of the Medicare population and 17% of the Medicaid population (Agency for Healthcare Research and Quality, 2013). Dual-eligible beneficiaries qualify for both Medicare and Medicaid. By 2009, the federal and state governments spent more than $250 billion on healthcare benefits for 9 million low income elderly or disabled people jointly enrolled in Medicare and Medicaid (Congressional Budget Office, 2013).

Concerns persist about whether the high rate of healthcare expenditures in the United States yields optimal health outcomes when contrasted with other countries. The CDC (2009) noted that while the average U.S. life expectancy in 2009 was approximately 78

Figure 1.2   Trends in Health Insurance, 1999 to 2011

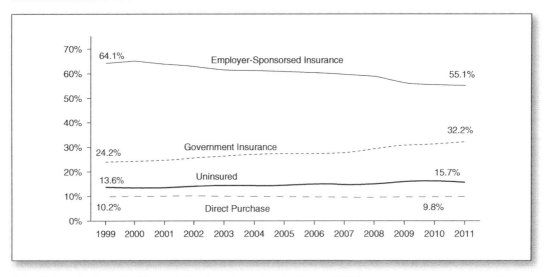

Notes: Data are for the entire U.S. population. Percentages do not add up to 100% because some people have more than one type of coverage. In 2010, the Census Bureau updated its coverage data for current and prior years to reflect changes in the methods used to impute health insurance for non-respondents. Government insurance includes military coverage.
Source: United States Census Bureau, *Income Poverty and Health Insurance Coverage in the United States: 2011.*

years, this figure has fallen from 11th to 50th in the world (*Figure 1.3*). Furthermore, large disparities exist in the health status of minorities in the United States. While life expectancy at birth increased more for the black population than for the white population and the gap narrowed between these two racial groups, life expectancy in 2010 was 78.9 years for whites and 74.6 years for blacks (Kaiser Family Foundation, 2014). In 2005, infant mortality rates were highest for infants of non-Hispanic black mothers (13.63 deaths per 1000 live births), American Indian mothers (8.06 per 1000) and Puerto Rican mothers (8.30 per 1000) compared with an overall infant mortality rate in the United States of 6.7% (Davis, Stremikis, Squires, & Schoen, 2014). The overall infant mortality rate placed the United States 28th in the world among developed countries, lagging behind Poland (twenty-sixth), and Slovakia (twenty-seventh). In addition, unlike in many other industrialized countries, many children in the United States fail to receive need services. For example, only 67% of

Figure 1.3   Top Ten Countries in Life Expectancy, 2009

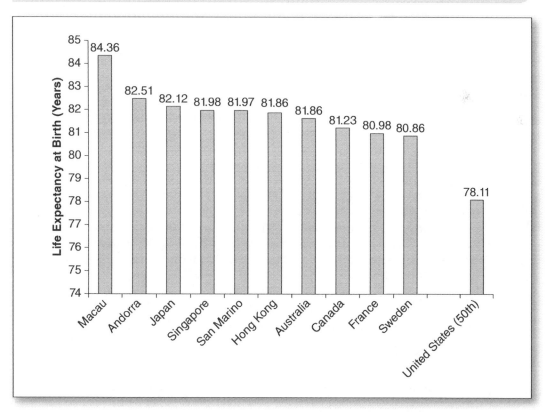

Source: CIA World Factbook. Retrieved from https://www.cia.gov/library/publications/the-world-factbook/rankorder/2102 rank.html

those aged 19 to 35 months of age receive the recommended vaccination series protecting them against seven infectious childhood diseases (CDC, 2009).

Despite the extent of its healthcare expenditures and health services, the United States ranked *last* overall of developed nations in terms of access to healthcare. Although the United States is the wealthiest nation in the world and is endowed with the most sophisticated healthcare system, prior to healthcare reform, nearly 16% of the U.S. population had no health insurance (United States Department of Health and Human Services, 2012). This equates to nearly one in six U.S. residents or the combined populations of 25 U.S. states. Affordability of healthcare limits its use and ultimately affects individual health status. The CDC (2009, p.4) reported that the percentage of adults ranging from 18 to 64 years of age who had not obtained needed medical care because of cost increased from 6% to 8% between 1997 and 2007. In 2007, 20% of people under 65 years of age who were uninsured did not receive needed medical care because of cost. Americans also have more difficulty paying for healthcare and healthcare insurance and are less satisfied with their healthcare system than individuals in other first-world countries (Davis et al., 2014; Science Daily, 2007). Being uninsured and not having access to needed healthcare delivered in a competent, timely manner poses significant risk to the individual. Approximately 18,000 preventable deaths each year are associated with a lack of health insurance (Universal Health Care Action Network, n.d.).

CONTEMPORARY HEALTHCARE REFORM: THE AFFORDABLE CARE ACT

The difficulty in creating universal access to healthcare services stems from a conflict of political, economic, and social values. This conflict in turn has been influenced at varying times by fears of Bolshevism during World War I and communism during World War II, Cold War politics during the 1950s and 1960s, and Reaganomics with its support of "small government" in the 1980s. Divisive, non-collaborative actions of the Republican and Democratic parties, particularly during the presidency of George W. Bush, slowed the process of healthcare reform. Political decision making is heavily influenced by various associations, organizations, and lobbyists representing the interests of physicians, hospitals, insurance companies, pharmaceutical companies, and innumerable other "special interest groups." Together, these interest groups spent more than $3.5 billion in the past decade in targeted efforts to impact proposed legislation. The healthcare industry doled out nearly $170 million in campaign contributions in 2007 and 2008, spending more than any other industry lobbying the federal government (Kapp, 2009). Lobbying by the AMA totaled nearly $263 million in 1998, an amount ranked second only to that of the U.S. Chamber of Commerce (Watts & Spitzer, 2014, quoting Collier, 2011). Although the interests and aims of these stakeholders often compete with each other, they can be seen as coalescing in a commitment to protect the profit-generating potential of the healthcare industry, which reached $200 billion in 2009 (Kapp, 2009).

The values of the right and left political sides appear in fundamental opposition to each other on the issue of providing healthcare for all citizens. Republicans, valuing a limited role for the government, view healthcare as a commodity that should be purchased in a marketplace free of government regulation and interference in order to maximize profits.

Despite claims avowing the value of competition in the marketplace, they are wary of any publically funded healthcare plan as private insurance companies would potentially find it difficult to compete while still generating a profit. In contrast, Democrats believe that the federal government has an obligation to provide healthcare to all citizens and is the only structure with the resources and capacity necessary to develop such a healthcare system (Monrone & Belkin, 1996).

In 1993, President William Clinton made another attempt at national healthcare reform. In addition to mandating employer-based health insurance, the proposed Health Security Act would have required every person to be enrolled in an insurance plan and would have offered various financial incentives and supports to that end. A National Health Board would have been created to oversee regional alliances designed to organize, regulate, and offer insurance options to individuals and employers. Minimum levels of health, mental health, and substance-abuse benefits were to be established, and insurance companies would have been prohibited from denying coverage or unenrolling recipients (Schroeder, 1993). Conservative opposition to "big government" effectively defeated the bill by criticizing it as unwieldy, too expensive, overly bureaucratic, and restrictive of patient choice and physician management.

President Barack Obama won the presidential election of 2008 based in large part on a platform that included healthcare reform. Earlier efforts, particularly during the Clinton administration, had brought reform issues to the public's attention and generated significant debate but failed to legislate changes. The Delegate Assembly of the National Association of Social Workers joined in support of reform, reaffirming its position of endorsing "a national healthcare policy that ensures the right to universal access to a continuum of health and mental healthcare throughout all stages of the life cycle" (National Association of Social Workers, 2008, p. 169). With his new electoral mandate, President Obama was able to push through Congress the **Patient Protection and Affordable Care Act (PPACA),** which he signed on March 23, 2010. Under the Act, 32 million more Americans are anticipated to gain insurance coverage, with individual membership increasing from 11 million today to nearly 20 million. Instead of cause for celebration, the Act has divided Americans. Having failed to create a single-payer system that would universally cover all Americans, Democrats were disappointed that the legislation did not offer a government-sponsored public option from which to choose. Republicans were outraged about the health insurance mandate for individuals and business and expanding Medicaid, believing that this was too intrusive a role for government. The Tea Party Movement, a group of ultra-conservative Republicans opposed to government regulation and interference, emerged during this debate and facilitated a number of misconceptions (including incorrectly asserting the PPACA created "death squads" to deal with end-of-life care) that clouded the real issues and inflamed the debate.

The PPACA sought to accomplish a fundamental transformation of health insurance in the United States by eliminating lifetime and unreasonable annual benefit limits, prohibiting healthcare policies from being rescinded, extending health insurance to those who were uninsured because of preexisting conditions, extending coverage of dependents to the age of 26 years, capping the extent to which insurance companies could charge for non-medical administrative expenses, offering consumer assistance when seeking health insurance or appealing claims, and establishing a delivery system that was simpler to administer and would lower costs. Extending coverage to 94% of U.S. citizens and other legal residents when fully phased in, the Act's important provisions include

- establishing an **individual mandate** that requires most U.S. citizens and legal residents to maintain a minimum level of health insurance coverage for themselves and their tax dependents beginning in 2014 or pay a tax penalty,

- expanding Medicaid eligibility to the working poor (138% of the federal poverty level [FPL]),

- requiring business with 50 or more employees to offer coverage or face penalties,

- creating Health Exchanges that offer qualified health plans to individuals and businesses,

- advance payment of tax credits to people with incomes between 100% and 400% of the federal poverty level to purchase health insurance through the exchanges,

- specifying the minimum benefit levels that plans must offer and establishing four tiers of coverage (Bronze, Silver, Gold, and Platinum). The lowest level of plan must cover 60% of costs and limit out-of-pocket expenses to $5,950 for individuals and $11,900 for families, and

- prohibiting insurance companies from (1) increasing premiums when an individual files a claim, (2) denying insurance to individuals with preexisting conditions, and (3) imposing lifetime limits on benefits (Kaiser Family Foundation, 2011, 2012).

The Act also mandates coverage for preventative healthcare and promotes the use of primary care physicians to coordinate and integrate care rather than specialists. It encourages physicians to use electronic records and creates incentives for evidence-based medical care. As we shall see in Chapter 2, new organizational designs, including Accountable Care Organizations and medical homes, are introduced to encourage innovation and integration in service delivery. Additional provisions support medical research and medical education. The law mandates tracking adverse complications and seeks to improve quality and patient safety. The law is financed by increasing Medicare taxes on the wealthy and by projected cost savings that are expected to result from improving quality of care and reduced duplication of services. The Congressional Budget Office (March 20, 2010) estimated that from 2010 to 2019, PPACA will reduce the federal deficit by 25 billion dollars.

Vehement national debate over passage of this Act, however, triggered its constitutional review by the United States Supreme Court. On March 23, 2010, the day that President Obama signed the PPACA into law, the state of Florida filed a lawsuit in federal district court challenging the constitutionality of the individual mandate and the Medicaid expansion. Currently, Florida is joined in this lawsuit by 21 other states with numerous cases proceeding through various state and federal courts. The National Federation of Independent Businesses (NFIB) and some individual plaintiffs, who did not have health insurance, also filed a lawsuit in Florida. Both cases were considered together by the Supreme Court (Kaiser Family Foundation, 2012).

In June 2012, a majority of the Court, including Chief Justice Roberts, joined by Justices Breyer, Kagan, Ginsburg, and Sotomayor, held that the individual mandate is a constitutional exercise of Congress's power to levy taxes. Following that decision, Congressional Republicans in the House of Representatives repeatedly (for the *50th time* on March 5, 2014) attempted to defund, delay, or repeal the Act. Those efforts failed. Time will tell how the Act is ultimately implemented, how challenges to the law are decided by the courts, the impact it has on everyday Americans, and whether the United States will step any closer to achieving universal health insurance.

SUMMARY

This chapter traced the history of healthcare social work as the first subspecialty of the profession in the United States, including the organized presence of social workers in hospital and clinic settings. The origin of public health services in the United States was described, along with the efforts made to nationalize healthcare and the creation of Medicare and Medicaid to serve the needs of the elderly, poor, and disabled.

Concern over escalating costs, quality care, and access to healthcare served as the major impetus for passing the Patient Protection and Affordable Care Act of 2010. The PPACA shifts focus to primary care, creates new health insurance exchanges to offer expanded care options to consumers and businesses, promotes evidence-based professional practice, and utilizes Accountable Care Organizations as mechanisms for aligning broad-based healthcare services. While the major provisions of the Act were upheld by the Supreme Court in 2012, additional court challenges have been initiated and the effects of the PPACA remain to be seen. As we will see, however, the Act is already influencing healthcare social work practice.

KEY TERMS AND CONCEPTS

- Indoor and outdoor almshouses relief

- Sanitary visitors

- Rebecca Cole

- Deinstitutionalization

- Friendly visitors/almoners

- Worthy poor unworthy (undeserving) poor

- Dorothea Lynde Dix/mental hygiene movement

- Mary Richmond/Charity Organization Societies (COS)

- Entitlement programs

- "Dual-eligible" beneficiaries

- Ida Maud Cannon/Dr. Richard Cabot

- Public health

- Nationalized healthcare
- Almshouse
- Centers for Disease Control
- Food and Drug Administration
- National Institutes of Health
- Substance Abuse and Mental Health Services Administration
- Indian Health Services
- Waiver
- Public Health Service
- Universal healthcare
- Single- and multi-payer insurance system
- Managed care
- Patient Protection and Affordable Care Act of 2010 (PPACA)
- Individual mandate

QUESTIONS FOR DISCUSSION

1. Historically a distinction has been made between the "worthy" poor and the "unworthy" poor. Do you think this distinction persists today? If so, who are the worthy and unworthy poor in today's society? Using this classification, how would Medicare and Medicaid patients be designated? Why?

2. What underlying values and political sentiments have prevented the development of a single-payer, nationalized healthcare system in the United States? Are these values still evident today? Would you support a single-payer, nationalized healthcare system? Why or why not? What would you be willing to sacrifice in order to achieve this kind of system?

3. How well do you think our healthcare system is working in the United States? How does it compare with those in other countries? Cite evidence to support your conclusions.

EXERCISES

1. Healthcare Reform Exercise

   Read a summary of the Patient Protection and Affordable Care Act of 2010 at: http://www.kff .org/healthreform/upload/8061.pdf. For an analysis of healthcare reform legislation along with other information on healthcare issues, visit the Kaiser Foundation Health Care Reform website at: http://healthreform.kff.org/.

Work in a small group to discuss the following:

- What issues prompted a growth in popular support for healthcare reform?
- What is the intent of the Patient Protection and Affordable Care Act?
- What provisions are enacted to achieve its goal(s)?
- What populations are most likely to be affected by the Act and how?
- What are your own reactions to the Act? Why?

2. Healthcare and Mental Health Pioneers

Two pioneers in healthcare and mental healthcare are Ida M. Cannon and Dorothea Dix. How are their legacies evident in the contemporary delivery of healthcare?

3. Professional history

Explore the proceedings from the 1880 National Conference on Social Welfare by going to http://quod.lib.umich.edu/cgi/t/text/pageviewer-idx?c = ncosw;cc = ncosw;idno = ACH8650.188 0.001;seq = 208

Work in a small group to discuss the following:

- What were some of the issues the profession of social work struggled with at the time?
- Are they similar or different from the issues the profession struggles with today?
- What does the language in the document tell you about how social workers viewed the people that they served? Has this changed?

4. How does the United States compare?

Go the interactive website for the Organization for Economic Cooperation and Development: http://www.oecd.org

Using the interactive graph link, explore how child health and wellness in the United States compares with other countries. Select three countries. Explore obesity rates and breast cancer survival rates for the same countries that you have selected. How does the United States compare?

REFERENCES

Agency for Healthcare Research and Quality. (2013). *Improving the health and health care of older Americans.* Retrieved from http://www.ahrq.gov/research/findings/final-reports/olderam/oldam2 .html

Bartlett, H. (1961). *Analyzing social work practice.* Silver Spring, MD: National Association of Social Workers.

Bartlett, H. (1975). Ida M. Cannon: Pioneer in medical social work. *Social Service Review, 49,* 208–229.

Barton, P. (1999). *Understanding the U.S. health services system.* Chicago, IL: Health Administration Press.

Cabot, R. (1928). Hospital and dispensary social work. *Hospital Social Service, 17,* 269–230.

Cannon, I. (1923). *Social work in hospitals: A contribution to progressive medicine.* New York: Russell Sage Foundation.

Cannon, I. (1952). *On the social frontier of medicine.* Cambridge, MA: Harvard University Press.

Centers for Disease Control and Prevention. (2009). *NCHS data brief: Death statistics.* Retrieved from http://www.cdc.gov/nchs/data/databriefs/db26.htm

Centers for Medicare and Medicaid Services (CMS). (2012). *National health expenditure data.* Retrieved from https://www.cms.gov/Research-Statistics-Data-and-Systems/Statistics-Trends-and-Reports/NationalHealthExpendData/NationalHealthAccountsHistorical.html

CIA World Fact Book. (2009). *Rank order of life expectancy by country.* Retrieved from https://www.cia.gov/library/publications/the-world-factbook/rankorder/2102rank.html?countryCode = #

Collier, R. (2011). American Medical Association membership woes continue. *Canadian Medical Association Journal, 183*(11), E713–E714.

Congressional Budget Office. (March 20, 2010). *Report to Speaker of the House, Nancy Pelosi.* Retrieved from http://www.cbo.gov/sites/default/files/amendreconprop.pdf

Congressional Budget Office. (2013). *Dual-eligible beneficiaries of Medicare and Medicaid: Characteristics, health care spending, and evolving policies.* Retrieved from http://www.cbo.gov/publication/44308

Davis, K., Stremikis, K., Squires, D., & Schoen, C. (2014). *Mirror, mirror on the wall, 2014 update: How the U.S. health care system compares internationally.* Retrieved from: http://www.commonwealth fund.org/publications/fund-reports/2014/jun/mirror-mirror.

Day, P. (2009). *A new history of social welfare* (6th ed.). Boston: Pearson.

Digital History. (2014). *The roots of progressivism.* Retrieved from http://www.digitalhistory.uh.edu/disp_textbook.cfm?smtID = 2&psid = 3134

Gehlert, S., & Browne, T. A. (Eds.). (2006). *The handbook of health social work.* Hoboken, NJ: John Wiley & Sons.

Gleeson, D. J. (2006). *The professionalization of Australian Catholic social welfare.*(Doctoral dissertation). Retrieved from http://primoa.library.unsw.edu.au/primo_library/libweb/action/search .do?vid = UNSWS

Johnson, M. (1989). *The many faces of Hull-House.* Urbana: The University of Illinois Press.

Kapp, M. (2009, September 24). The sick business of health-care profiteering. *Vanity Fair.* Retrieved from http://www.vanityfair.com/politics/features/2009/09/health-care200909

Kaiser Family Foundation. (2011, April). *Summary of new health reform law.* Retrieved from http://www.kff.org/healthreform/upload/8061.pdf

Kaiser Family Foundation. (2012, July). *A guide to the Supreme Court's Affordable Care Act decision.* Retrieved from http://www.kff.org/healthreform/upload/8332.pdf

Kaiser Family Foundation. (2013, March). *Medicaid: A primer—key information on the nation's health coverage program for low-income people.* Retrieved from http://kff.org/medicaid/issue-brief/medicaid-a-primer/

Kaiser Family Foundation. (2014). *Life expectancy at birth (in years) by race/ethnicity.* Retrieved from http://kff.org/other/state-indicator/life-expectancy-by-re/

Kovner, Anthony R. (1995). *Jonas's health care delivery in the United States.* New York: Springer Publishing Company.

Monrone, J., & Belkin, G. S. (1996). *The politics of health care reform: Lessons from the past, prospects for the future* (2nd ed.). Durham, NC: Duke University Press.

Muckenhoupt, M. (2003). *Dorothea Dix: Advocate for mental health care.* New York: Oxford University Press.

Nacman, M. (1977). Social work in health settings: A historical review. *Social Work in Health Care, 2,* 407–418.

National Association of Social Workers. (2008). *Social work speaks: NASW policy statements, 2009–2012*. (8th Ed.). Health Care Policy, 167–170. Washington, DC: National Association of Social Workers.

National Conference on Social Welfare. (1880). Retrieved from http://quod.lib.umich.edu/cgi/t/text/pageviewer-idx?c = ncosw;cc = ncosw;idno = ACH8650.1880.001;seq = 208

Organization for Economic Cooperation and Development. (OECD). (2013). *OECD Health Data 2013: How Does the United States Compare?* [Internet]. Retrieved from: http://www.oecd.org/united states/Briefing-Note-USA-2013.pdf

Palmer, K. S. (1999). *A brief history of universal health care efforts in the United States*. Retrieved from http://www.pnhp.org/facts/a_brief_history_universal_health_care_efforts_in_the_us.php

Parascandola, J. L. (1998). Public health service. In G. T. Kurian (Ed.). *A historical guide to the U.S. government* (pp. 487–493). New York: Oxford University Press.

Physicians for a National Health Program. (n.d.). *Our mission: A single-payer health system*. Retrieved from http://www.pnhp.org/

Praglin, L. J. (2007). Ida Cannon, Ethel Cohen and early medical social work in Boston: The foundations of a model of culturally competent social service. *Social Service Review*, 81, 27–46.

Robinson, V. (1930). *A changing psychology in social work*. Chapel Hill: University of North Carolina Press.

Schroeder, S. A. (1993). The Clinton health care plan: Fundamental or incremental reform. *Annals of Internal Medicine*, 119, 945–957. Retrieved from http://www.annals.org/content/119/9/945.full

Science Daily. (2007, May 16). *U.S. continues to lag on health care, according to new international comparison*. Retrieved from http://www.sciencedaily.com/releases/2007/05/070515074645.htm

Starr, P. (1983). *The social transformation of American medicine*. New York: Basic Books.

Trattner, W. I. (1999). *From poor law to welfare state: A history of social welfare in America* (6th Ed.). New York: The Free Press.

United States Census Bureau. (2011). *Income, poverty, and health insurance coverage in the United States: 2010*. Retrieved from http://www.census.gov/prod/2011pubs/p60–239.pdf

United States Department of Health and Human Services. (2012). *Overview of the uninsured in the United States: A summary of the 2012 current population survey report*. Retrieved from http://aspe.hhs.gov/health/reports/2012/uninsuredintheus/ib.shtml

United States Department of Justice. (1990). *Americans with Disabilities Act*. Retrieved from http://www.usdoj.gov/crt/ada/pubs/ada.htm#Anchor-Sec-11481

Universal Health Care Action Network. (n.d.). Retrieved from http://www.uhcan.org/

Watts, C. A. & Spitzer, W. J. (2014). *Full circle: U.S. health policy, social determinants of health and the organization of health care*. Paper delivered at the 2014 International Conference on Organisational Behaviour in Healthcare, Copenhagen, Denmark.

CHAPTER 2

The Organizational Context of Healthcare Social Work Practice

William J. Spitzer and Karen M. Allen

INTRODUCTION

This chapter provides an overview of the organizational contexts in which healthcare social work is practiced. It discusses the manner in which healthcare is delivered across a continuum of service contexts in the United States. The challenges to social work practice in these contexts are noted with reference to the profession's evolution in the healthcare arena. These challenges are related to the practice behaviors and competencies specified by the Council on Social Work Education (CSWE) and the National Association of Social Workers (NASW). The CSWE competencies may be found at http://www.cswe.org/File .aspx?id = 13780.

HEALTHCARE ORGANIZATIONS

An **organization** is a macro system that is goal-directed, consisting of units that are "deliberately structured" with coordinated activities and processes (Daft, 1998, p.11). A **system** is defined as an integrated whole, comprising subsystems with a common purpose and identity. Organizations are connected to, and interact with other systems, their external environments or communities. All organizations must establish what Levin and White (1961) referred to as a "domain." In their study of relationships among health agencies in a community, a domain consists of "claims which an organization stakes out for itself in terms of (1) diseases covered, (2) population(s) served, and (3) health care services rendered."

Systems and subsystems are defined by boundaries and roles. As portrayed in *Figure 2.1*, organizations may be perceived as taking resources (or "inputs") from the larger system (the environment in which it exists), processing these resources, and then returning them in changed form as "output" to the environment.

Figure 2.1

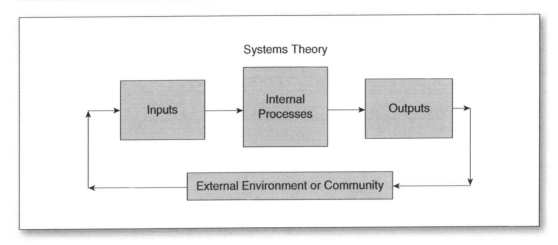

Source: Authors.

Organizations affect, and are affected by, their environments. The *macro environment* of healthcare organizations consists of "a set of systems including legal, political, cultural and sociological, publics (including the community at large, interest groups, media and constituents), economic, ecological and the health care environment" (Rakich, Longest, & Darr, 1985, p. 18). The *healthcare environment* consists of planning agencies, government regulators and regulations, accreditation associations and institutions, and professional licensure bodies that directly influence and regulate the delivery of services. Other forces include competition from other providers, the availability and competence of practitioners, available financing from payers, resources (equipment, technology, and materials) as well as health education/research, and the status of the public health (Figure 2.2). As we will see, these forces influence the design and functioning of the system and constitute the overall *organizational context* in which services are provided. At its broadest level in healthcare, this includes all layers of policy, including federal, state, local, and organization-specific economic forces that influence access, financing, and provision of services; scientific and technological resources and innovations; and both the broad social values and unique characteristics and needs of the communities served. Another important contextual factor in determining mission is an organization's place in the network of other community healthcare providers. Once established, the *organizational mission* then determines operational decisionmaking, goal setting, and ultimately patient care practices. The extent of an organization's influence, power, resources, range of services, and reputation in the community determine its place in the provider network.

Like all systems, healthcare organizations adapt to their external environments, become integrated with other systems, and eventually reach a stage in which they maintain their homeostasis, or balance (Friedman & Neuman Allen, 2011). Considering a hospital in terms of systems theory, the inputs of a hospital may be regarded as its physical plant, financial resources, equipment, supplies, and patients. The patients are "processed" by receiving the

Figure 2.2   The Healthcare Environment

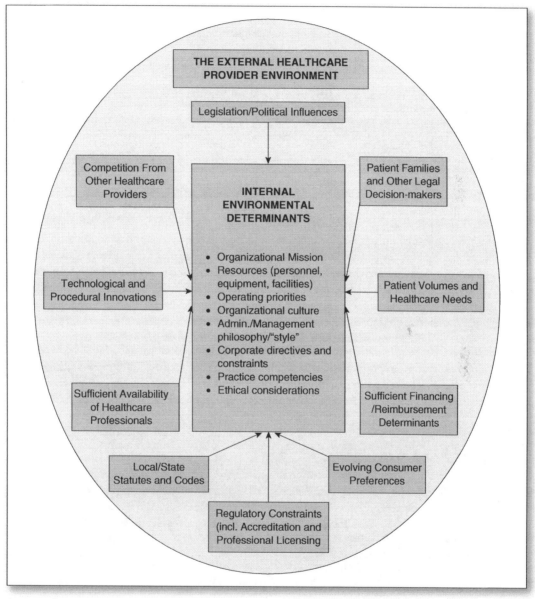

Source: Authors.

services available through the hospital. The output of the system are the treated patients. Organizational effectiveness is judged by evaluating the extent to which patients are restored to optimum levels of health given the severity of disease or injury from which they originally suffered. . The input-process-output variables for a hospital are summarized in *Table 2.1*.

Table 2.1 Systems Theory Applied to Hospitals

Inputs	Processes	Outputs
Patients Financial/physical resources Community engagement Environmental factors (i.e., locale and relation to other service providers)	Physical hospital characteristics (i.e.: size, capacity, services, treatments/interventions) Staff characteristics (skills/number) Practice policies and procedures	Patient care System management Research Training/education

Source: Authors.

Organizational design refers to the process for determining how tasks and authority will be delegated. Leatt, Shortell, and Kimberly (1988) noted that organizational design usually involves deciding the degree of complexity, formalization, and decentralization of a structure and ensuring effective coordination of the tasks necessary to achieve the organization's goals. One common framework for assessing the design of organizations is to examine its stucture, process, and oucomes. **Structure** describes the framework or skeleton of an organization and how its units are arranged, divided, and supervised. Structure also explains how roles and tasks are conceptualized and assigned. The structure of an organization is designed to enhance its effectiveness, efficiency, adaptability, and survival (Kilman, 1977). Most organizations are structured in such a way that there is some division of labor or specialization for each individual holding a position. Aspects of organizational structure include tallness or flatness (number of layers of staff); span of control (ratio of workers to supervisors or size of the superior-subordinate team); unity and chain of command; formal communication and reporting patterns; centralization or decentralization of decision-making and authority; professional specialization; and standardization of functions, tasks, and roles. **Process** describes the activities, services, tasks, and ways of doing things within the organization. Examples of healthcare processes include surgery, diagnostic testing, nursing care, rehabilitation services, and psychosocial counseling, among numerous other activities. **Outcomes** are the results of the services and/or products that are provided.

Table 2.2 Practice Behavior: Assessing Organizational Processes

List the resources available in your organization	Describe the inputs (patients) (i.e., where do they come from? what are their characteristics? what kinds of services are needed?) Identify any unmet needs	Describe the processes (services) provided Identify unique services and programs Identify strengths as well as opportunities for growth	Describe the outcomes (results) (i.e., how is success evaluated?)

Source: Authors.

Healthcare systems tend to be formal organizations that are often structured as bureaucracies. Weber (1947) referred to the term "**bureaucracy**" as a sociological concept that rationalized collective activities. This term describes a form or design of an organization that ensures the predictability of its employees' behaviors and activities. Bureaucracies are characterized by high degrees of specialization and clear divisions of labor. Authority and chain of command are also clear, typically with well-defined policies, procedures, and protocols governing operations of staff. Large health systems composed of multiple organizations might include one or more specialty hospitals, a home healthcare agency, a medical equipment supply company, and a nursing or rehabilitation facility functioning under the same organizational umbrella. The more complex a system, the greater the need for a bureaucratic structure to operate and sustain it.

Each organization strives to establish its own unique presence and manner of conducting business. **Organizational culture** describes the norms, values, customs, and behaviors with which employees are expected to comply. Members of organizations are also expected to observe and follow the ways that others typically act. **Organizational climate** describes the general atmosphere of an organization including the pace of work and level of trust that affect employee morale and attitude. Organizational cultures and climates can differ widely, depending on factors such as ownership, mission, staff composition, and geographic locale.

The patient-care operations of most healthcare systems (over 17,000) in the United States are accredited by the Joint Commission (2011) (see: http://www.jointcommission.org). The Commission on the Accreditation of Rehabilitation Facilities (CARF) (2011) also serves to establish organizational standards by accrediting nearly 6,000 rehabilitation and behavioral health facilities (http://www.carf.org). In addition to organizational accreditation, hospitals and nursing homes are regulated by the federal government through public law and code compliance and by state governments, which employ reviewers to routinely inspect for compliance with health and safety regulations. Social workers are an important part of the accreditation process because they contribute by ensuring compliance with patient care standards required by the government and accrediting agencies. Individual disciplines such as medicine, social work, and nursing are governed through standards oversight maintained by state and national professional licensing boards.

Like other major industries, our healthcare system operates in the competitive, capitalist marketplace of the U.S. economy. Healthcare organizations are either non-profit or for-profit and publically or privately owned. In "non-profit" (also referred to as "voluntary" or "not-for-profit") organizations, any additional income generated over expenses is not paid to individuals or stockholders, but "reinvested" by the organization to enhance the quality of services or to control costs. However, the presence of a profit-making motive in some organizations may lead to decisions to deny or limit care to people who are uninsured, underinsured, or present with costly conditions to treat. These patients may then seek treatment in public, non-profit institutions, increasing the burden of care and cost on public institutions, which are typically financed by taxpayers. Hospitals that provide uncompensated care often are forced to increase their charges on insured patients, a process called "**cost-shifting**." For-profit health insurers have historically denied coverage, increased rates, or cancelled coverage for individuals with costly diseases such as HIV-AIDs. For healthcare systems and insurers to remain economically viable, maintaining a balanced "pool" of patients is critical. The pool, or population served, must include an adequate number of healthy individuals to offset the costs of services for individuals in the pool who need expensive care. This is an important aspect of the PPACA and one of the reasons that younger persons and healthy individuals were mandated to obtain insurance. Their participation in the pool helps to generate the funds that will be use to pay for services needed by sicker people.

Fraze, Elixhauser, Holmquist, and Johann (2010) reported that, in 2008, there were 1,131 U.S. public hospitals, representing nearly 22% of all hospitals in the United States and providing care for over 14% of all inpatients. Approximately 5.6 million hospitalizations occurred in public hospitals. Nearly 25% of the patients in public hospitals were covered by Medicaid, compared with 17.3% in private, nonprofit hospitals. Public hospitals cared for over 75% more uninsured patients than did private nonprofit hospitals (8.3% compared with 4.7%) (Fraze et al., 2010, p. 3). In terms of location, 64% of public hospitals were in rural areas, 16.5% were in metropolitan areas (urban or suburban), and 19.5% were in small to medium-sized towns (Fraze et al., 2010, p. 2).

While Kovner (1995) noted that "there is insufficient evidence to make categorical statements regarding the effect of ownership per se on the cost or quality of medical care" (p. 431), much debate continues about the effects of ownership on healthcare delivery. As for-profit organizations concentrate on providing only those services that are profitable, they essentially leave the not-for-profit and public organizations to provide the preponderance of care for those who lack adequate insurance, live in rural or low-income areas, or require those procedures that, while medically necessary, are not profitable to deliver. Large urban public hospitals in particular have evolved as the primary provider of care for the poor (Haglund & Dowling, 1993), partly because of their accepting patients regardless of ability to pay and because they provide expensive, complex, and/or unprofitable services that for-profit hospitals do not finance or do not wish to offer (Haglund & Dowling, 1993, p.143). Arguments in support of for-profit providers focus on their increased efficiency prompted by the profit incentive, their contribution to the community through tax payments, and their ability to more rapidly respond to identified community needs.

Table 2.3 presents questions and concepts that should considered when assessing macro systems, organizational structures, culture, and climate.

SOCIAL WORK CHALLENGES IN CONTEMPORARY HEALTHCARE ORGANIZATIONS

In the decades since Ida Cannon established the first hospital social work department at Massachusetts General Hospital, social work has expanded, contracted, and reformulated itself to meet the needs of continuously evolving healthcare organizations. In addition to being the first identified subspecialty of the profession, health social work, or "medical social work" as it was initially known (Carlton, 1984, p. 5), also marked the first time social workers were employed in secondary **host settings**. As used here, the term *host setting* refers to an organization in which the primary purpose is something other than the provision of social work services. Examples of such contexts include hospitals, schools, and law enforcement agencies. As Cannon realized, the placement of social work in a host setting presents special challenges. In healthcare, the primary purpose is not to ameliorate psychosocial problems and conditions; historically, it has been to diagnose and cure disease.

Table 2.3   Practice Behavior: Assessing Macro Systems Organizational Structure, Culture, and Climate Exercise

Organization Structure	Organizational Culture and Climate
Review your organization's organizational chart and answer the following questions: • Describe the structure—Is it complex or simple? Static and stiff or fluid? • Can you tell anything about the organizational culture from the structure? • Is the chart clear? Are all major units represented on the chart? Is anyone/anything missing? • How many layers? • What is your estimate about span of control? Is this appropriate given the services provided by the agency? • Where are you/your department on the structure? • Follow chain of command—Who does your supervisor report to? Who does his or her supervisor report to? • What does the chart say about communication and processes?	Review your organization's organizational chart and answer the following questions: • Identify three expected norms or behaviors that reflect the culture. How did you learn these customs? • Can you think of a time when someone did not comply with the culture? What happened? • How do people dress at your organization? • How do people address each other—by first name or by title? • Would you describe the culture as informal or formal? • How would you characterize the organizational climate of your agency? • Are people energized or stressed? • What factors influence its climate? • How does the agency's leadership contribute to its climate? • What do you like/dislike about the climate? • How does the climate impact clients? • What could be done to improve climate?

Source: Authors.

To prevail in host settings, particularly during times of economic constraint, social work must be seen as directly contributing to the primary organizational mission. The intent is to contribute added value by effectively delivering competent, quality patient care while constructively impacting the organizational bottom line. Recognizing the reality that health services are economically driven, it is important that social workers be sensitive to impacting not just quality-of-life issues such as the patient's emotional adjustment to his or her treatment but also the financial conditions of both patients and provider institutions. Although often not fully recognized by organizations in this context, social work can have significant economic implications (see *Table 2.4*).

As emphasized by Rosenberg and Weissman (1995, p. 113), "social work needs to be flexible, able to respond to emerging patient care needs, medical program teams' needs, community needs, and health care system (needs)." The profession must strive " . . . to meet the needs of the health care system by defining a role to innovate, experiment, create and . . . produce creative programs that forward the mission of the health care system . . . " (p. 114) in which it practices.

To define a professional social work role and successfully innovate, it is not enough to be clinically competent. Social workers must understand the factors influencing their

Table 2.4   Organizational Fiscal Impacts of Healthcare Social Work Services

Intervention	Impact
Early intervention in emergency department	Reduction of costly and medically unnecessary admissions/use of ER as a non-emergency clinic
Rapid psychosocial assessment/care planning	Patient treatment compliance, with impacts on reduced length of hospitalization (LOS) and otherwise unnecessary readmissions while enhancing prospects of patient recovery and satisfaction with delivered care and health
Patient/family counseling	Knowledgeable compliance with treatment leading to enhanced prospects for recovery while performing a crucial *risk management function* by reducing potential patient/family litigation associated with miscommunication
Resource referral	Securing financial assistance for treatment reduces monetary burden to patient/family; contributes to organizational reimbursement. Use of available, less-expensive community resources reduces patient hospital reliance.
Outpatient clinic intervention	Patient treatment compliance; securing of outside resources needed for efficient, uninterrupted use of crucial healthcare; avoidance of unnecessary inpatient admissions

Source: Authors.

organization's environment and mission (Spitzer, Silverman, & Allen, 2015; Silverman, 2012; Spitzer & Nash, 1996). The historical impacts of the healthcare environment can be readily traced on hospital-based social work practice. From its beginnings in the early 1900s through the 1930s, social work practice expanded, with services typically directed toward lower economic and disadvantaged groups. Beginning in the 1930s and into the 1940s, the profession of social work went through a change process (Hubschman, 1983). As psychoanalytic theory grew in influence, psychiatric social work in hospitals also evolved to the point that many hospitals maintained two separate and distinct social work programs—one medical and one psychiatric. Following World War II, the work of Helen Harris Perlman in particular began to refocus hospital-based social work more on the patient's role in society and the impact of society on individuals' circumstances. The 1950s saw a significant expansion of social work services into new patient-care areas, including rehabilitation, transplantation, oncology, and cardiac service.

The activism of the 1960s contributed to social work practice becoming more independent and assertive in hospital settings, including a transition from requiring physician referral to initiating its own case-finding and intervention. A greater demand for social work services in hospitals resulted from the passage of the Social Security Act, with its Title XVIII **(Medicare)** and Title XIX **(Medicaid)** provisions (Hubschman, 1983, p.4). These two programs are a legacy of President Lyndon Johnson, resulting largely from previous failures to enact some form of national health insurance (Anderson, 1968). While both are **entitlement programs** (meaning that eligible individuals have legislative entitlement to all covered programs) and both are perceived by many as public insurance, only the Medicare program can be considered an insurance model as it was designed to conform to the structure of private health insurance

(Barton, 1999, p. 47). With greater numbers of patients 65 years of age and older being afforded care, along with increases in services to the medically indigent and permanently and totally disabled, social work intervention became crucial for dealing with the psychosocial issues that accompanied physical concerns. By the 1980s, recognition of the psychosocial impacts on health contributed to an increasing trend in healthcare to focus on preventive care. The impact on social work was to broaden the spectrum of its practice sites, ranging from primary care settings and outpatient clinics through tertiary care centers—the larger, complex teaching institutions providing the most technologically advanced care services available.

Prior to the **Omnibus Budget Reconciliation Act (OBRA)** of 1981, most social work departments in hospitals were centralized within traditional bureaucratic units or departments that afforded professional clinical supervision and administrative oversight by senior social workers, including department directors, supervisors, and/or lead staff. OBRA eliminated the Medicare requirement that professional social work services be provided to patients as a condition of Medicare participation, although it retained language that the psychosocial needs of patients must be addressed in some way by healthcare facilities (Beder, 2006). This exclusion, coupled with a fundamental financing shift in 1983 from a *fee-for-service* model (in which fees are collected after each service is provided) to a system of prospective-payment provider reimbursement, made social work services particularly vulnerable to service cuts during periods of organizational financial crises. The *Prospective Pricing System (PPS)* and its use of **Diagnostically Related Groupings (DRGs)** with predetermined reimbursement limitations for specific procedures and conditions were instituted as incentives for providers to curtail their use of costly interventions. The intent was to reduce burgeoning healthcare expenditures under Medicare and Medicaid as a result of their fee-for-service structure. The desired and actual effect was to have providers reevaluate their operations and find ways to cut costs, even if this meant cutting services. The implications were clear and not without concern. Social work services typically do not generate significant revenue, since reimbursement for inpatient social work is typically included in the hospital room rate charge (perdiem rate). Unfortunately, the recognition of the extent to which social workers reduce system operating costs while positively impacting patient care has not been well recognized in financial audits of hospitals. As a result, social work services may be cut during times of financial austerity.

The DRG system groups patients into approximately 500 diagnostic classifications based on similar costs and resource use. Under this system, hospitals are no longer paid on a fee-for-service basis in which a fee is charged and collected for each service. They are paid on predetermined rates of reimbursement that are based on the patient's DRG classification rather than on the actual cost of care (Inglehart, 1990; Mayes, 2007). To provide a much oversimplified explanation, the reimbursement rates use a formula to determine average cost that hospitals are paid regardless of the amount of care provided or the length of hospitalizations. Few exceptions are made, and when this occurs, it is referred to as an **"outlier."** The long-range effect of this system is that hospitals shifted from inpatient to outpatient services and sought to significantly shorten inpatient *lengths of stay (LOS)*. As Hubschman (1983, p. 5) accurately noted at the time, "The proposed changed regulations as well as the reductions in Medicare and Medicaid will be significant issues in hospital fiscal concerns as well as in hospital care for patient populations dependent upon these resources." Hospitals also placed increased attention on health service-utilization patterns, increasing the role for *utilization review departments* and staff to review each patient to determine if the severity of illness warranted the level of care planned.

The focus on cost containment, along with continuing efforts to maximize revenue, contributed to some management theorists becoming critical of traditional, hierarchical management structures. They believed that "overly" centralized organizations stifled innovation while creating arbitrary and rigid job-classification systems that contributed to inefficiency. Beginning in the 1990s and driven by advances in productivity gained in the manufacturing sector through *process reengineering* (see Hammer & Champy, 1994), accounting and management consulting firms aggressively promoted these concepts as applicable to healthcare delivery. Influenced by these recommendations and seeking new avenues to enhance revenue and/or reduce costs, numerous hospitals tried realigning employees together by medical service (alternately referred to as *service or product lines*) rather than by department, professional affiliation, or training. Operating under the unfounded assumption that centralized professional departments created artificial barriers to patient care and interfered with streamlining processes, social work services (and many other "ancillary" disciplines) were often decentralized. While such efforts could be and were construed as placing all services together as multidisciplinary teams working on similar patient populations or services, it also was commonly seen as a "simplifying" measure that effectively lowered operating costs. Payroll, equipment, space, and related support costs (including continuing education) were eliminated or substantially reduced as services were "realigned" and select departments were eliminated. Intradisciplinary oversight diminished as professional administrative, managerial, and supervisory positions were eliminated.

Several approaches were and are employed in decentralizing services. One approach assigned hospital personnel to a nursing unit or medical service (e.g., oncology, medicine, pediatrics, emergency, etc.) under the purview of a physician or nursing manager. In such a functional realignment, social work, nursing, and other disciplines were and are organized by a specific function or activity, such as discharge planning, case management, or reviewing utilization of services. In more dramatic models of this type, professional identities are abandoned, and new, idiosyncratic job classifications and titles are created on the basis of an activity or function. Post-implementation studies of such organizational redesigns have revealed decreases in employee morale with few, if any, improvements in patient care (Neuman, 2000). Alternative attempts to combine elements of centralization with decentralization resulted in adoption of the **matrix management** model, defined by "the existence of both hierarchical (vertical) coordination through departmentalism and the formal chain of command and simultaneously lateral (horizontal coordination) across departments (in a) patient care team." (Neuhauser, 1983; Spitzer, 1998). A matrix organization in a hospital is illustrated in *Figure 2.3.*

One difficulty with a matrix organization is that personnel in each discipline are placed in a position of responding to oversight both from their profession (through supervision) and from the "patient care unit or service line" manager who oversees their assignment area. That manager may be a physician, nurse, or member of another discipline. Issues become confounded when differences arise in priority, technique, ethical approach, interpersonal style, and staff availability. Responding to multiple lines of authority can prove untenable for staff as it creates the potential for conflicting expectations and ambiguity (Shortell and Kaluzny, 1988, p. 324). It is further complicated when a service such as social work is charged with coverage of an entire health system and temporary gaps associated with "peak" service demands and/or staff absence require personnel reassignment, involvement of substitute

Figure 2.3

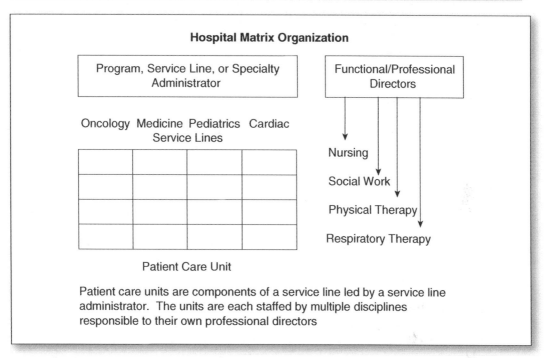

Source: Authors.

staff unfamiliar with a specific practice, or creation of response delays for previously unaffected units. Units predictably tend to attach singular importance to their specific interests and needs, notwithstanding their positioning within the larger delivery structure. Service modifications or differences in patient-care approach can and do negatively contribute to territorial responses, ultimately impacting future staff assignments, professional discretionary limits, budget expenditures, and the nature of ongoing collaboration.

The profession has tracked the extent and problematic impact of these trends in reorganization. Berger, Robbins, Lewis, Mizrahi and Fleit (2003), in a longitudinal study supported by the National Society for Social Work Leadership in Health Care, reported how the organization of social work services had changed in the six years between 1992 and 1998. Although the study is somewhat dated, by studying 1,221 healthcare systems, the authors found that, although most services (74%) continued to be provided through centralized departments, the number of departments that were decentralized or were now operating in a matrix environment had *steadily increased*. While the number of departments without a social work director at that time remained small (11%), the number *was increasing*. Although there was evidence that social work departments had been downsized, this was not commensurate with broader staffing decreases experienced in the institution. Over 79% of respondents indicated they had not experienced decreases at the time of the study.

Subsequent to the study by Berger et al. (2007), reports from professional conference and meetings suggest that social work services are being performed by various individual staff assigned to nursing units, medical practices, or work units who are not trained as social workers. These other non-social work staffs may include, but are not limited to, nursing, risk management, quality assurance, case management, and patient advocacy.

While Berger et al. (2003) noted "a continuing picture of the constant change in healthcare (that) creates a challenging and tumultuous work environment" (p. 13), the American Hospital Association (2002) reported that 76% of all psychiatric hospitals and 86% of acute-care hospitals provided social work services in some form and extent. These findings were echoed by Whitaker, Wilson, and Arrington (2008) in a major 2004 survey by the National Association of Social Workers (NASW), which found that approximately 38,500 (12%) of all sampled social workers were employed in some type of healthcare setting (p. 2). Compared to a 1982 NASW survey denoting a 6.1% decrease in the numbers of social workers in healthcare, the 2008 NASW study found healthcare to be the second most common specialty area after mental health (35%).

Most social workers in healthcare are credentialed at the MSW degree level (82%) and primarily provide direct services to patients and families. Healthcare social workers spend about half their time counseling patients and families and 17% of their time in continuity-of-care or discharge planning. The majority report working in hospitals (57%), followed by outpatient facilities (14%) and hospices (14%). Generally, social workers indicate that they are satisfied with their wages and benefits, which tend to be higher than those in the field at large. While they perceive they are effective with their patients, social workers also cite frustrations with their jobs, principally as the result of contending with large caseloads, increasing amounts of paperwork, and a sense that some of the required tasks are beneath their qualifications and training (National Association of Social Workers, Center for Workforce Studies, 2006; Cowles, 2003).

THE ADVENT OF MANAGED HEALTHCARE

Managed care in the United States can be traced back to the *Health Maintenance Organization Act of 1973 (PL 93–222)*. The Act as originally proposed was a means of promoting private-sector medicine through self-regulation while at the same time incorporating incentives to contain healthcare costs (Koch, 1993). The Health Maintenance Organization (HMO) Act sought to accomplish this end by providing funding for the planning and establishment of HMOs. The Act required employers with twenty-five or more employees to offer an HMO healthcare option and to make an employer contribution to the HMO premium. As Mezey and Lawrence (1995) pointed out, in classic **indemnity insurance**, enrollees pay a premium to a health insurer and the health insurer then contracts with separate providers to deliver healthcare services. Indemnity payment denotes a certain dollar value per procedure generally according to a "Table of Allowances." Providers can charge anything above a stipulated amount and collect the remainder directly from the patient. The table accords what can be charged on the basis of the complexity and time involved in the procedure (Koch, 1993).

Faced with escalating operating expenses and now federally predetermined limits on patient-care reimbursement, healthcare organizations and insurers shifted their focus to **managed healthcare** by creating organizational structures and staffing patterns called **Managed Care Organizations (MCOs)**. MCOs include **Health Maintenance Organizations (HMOs)**, Preferred Provider Organizations (PPOs), and competitive medical plans and managed indemnity-insurance programs. Their proliferation became so extensive that, by the mid-1990s, 85% of behaviorally managed care patients received their care from twelve MCOs (Davidson, Davidson, and Keigher, 1999). Some HMOs are unique in that they act as both the healthcare insurer *and* the service provider, delivering literally all needed health and mental health services in exchange for regular premium payments by service users (Gibelman, 2002, p. 17).

Rakich et al. (1985) identified HMOs as "a grouping of facilities, physicians, and other health personnel into a single system that provides a full range of medical services to a specifically enrolled population for a fixed fee, paid in advance" (p. 42). They typically employ salaried physicians and provide incentives to insured patients and providers alike to minimize the use of expensive inpatient services. HMOs focus on preventive healthcare as opposed to acute treatment services. Of fundamental importance, primary care physicians (PCPs) serve in **gatekeeper** roles, responsible for all patient primary care, initiating referrals to specialists only when needed, and then maintaining ongoing oversight for the patient's healthcare needs.

HMOs exist in varying forms. The original HMO form was the **staff-model physician group practice,** still exemplified by Kaiser Permanente and the Group Health Cooperative of Puget Sound. In this model, physicians are regarded as staff and are prepaid for services rendered to enrolled HMO members. **Individual Practice Associations (IPAs)** are composed of physicians who are paid on a discounted "fee-for-service" basis from an HMO rather than the salaried reimbursement characteristic of the staff-model physician group practice. Patients selecting an IPA as their service provider must use those physicians in office practices that participate in the IPA. **Preferred Provider Organizations (PPOs)** are typically third-party payers such as a self-insured business or union that contracts with selected physicians, hospitals, and other healthcare providers (called a "panel"). In return for the payers guaranteeing a certain volume of patients and assured payment, the providers will discount their conventional fees for service and establish utilization-review mechanisms to control costs. While PPO subscribers may use non-PPO healthcare providers, they do so at the expense of assuming copays and deductibles that would not have been charged had they utilized "in-network" providers. Koch (1993) noted that the popularity of PPOs has grown to the point that "many employers no longer even offer an indemnity option to their employees, thus forcing them to choose between PPOs and other forms of managed care" (p. 366).

HMOs have advantages and disadvantages to both consumers and providers. Emphasis on healthcare utilization results in cost savings, but often through restrictions in care access. Patient choice is limited as select services require asking the PCP for a referral and then services must be delivered only by select providers (or an extra charge will be leveled). Geographic availability and/or wait times may be additional issues in certain instances. For physicians participating in managed-care contracts, control through group practice *utilization review* is exercised over their use of services, particularly hospital care, and determining the numbers of patients they will serve. As a result, impacts are felt to their individual professional practice discretion and income.

THE AFFORDABLE CARE ACT
AND ACCOUNTABLE CARE ORGANIZATIONS

The major changes introduced in the healthcare delivery system as a result of managed care had only limited success in targeting service use, curtailing costs, and improving access. Escalating concern that non-healthcare personnel (notably insurance industry representatives) were "intruding" into medical decision making and negatively impacting reimbursement led to opposition of managed care by physician groups and other providers. At the same time, concern over the continuing growth of healthcare expenses, federal share of the expenses, numbers of uninsured, and quality of care prompted public and Congressional support for legislative change. The Institute of Medicine calculated that, in 2009 alone, the United States wasted more than one-third of the $2.5 trillion spent on healthcare through unnecessary use of high-cost services, defensive medicine, the duplicative costs of administering different health plans, inefficiently delivered services, uncoordinated care and medical errors, unreasonably high prices, Medicare/Medicaid fraud, and poor delivery of clinical prevention services (Regence, 2013). Furthermore, the federal government financed 28% of total health spending in 2011, a substantial increase from its share of 23% in 2007. In comparison, the shares of the total healthcare bill financed by households (28%), businesses (21%), state and local governments (17%), and other private revenues (7%) all declined (Centers for Medicare and Medicaid Services [CMS], 2012).

The **Patient Protection and Affordable Care Act of 2010 (PPACA)** seeks to broaden healthcare access by creating health insurance "marketplaces" (and separately expanding Medicaid eligibility) while controlling costs and enhancing clinical outcomes by fundamentally reshaping the service-delivery structure and adjusting provider reimbursement to encourage innovation. *Integrated care and collaboration* are hallmarks of the PPACA's management strategies that focus on concurrently addressing both physical and behavioral healthcare needs across a continuum of service-delivery sites, use of patient-focused transdisciplinary care, and reliance on *benchmarking* of evidence-based practices. Schrage (1990) once noted that "while virtually all of the leading management philosophers emphasize the need for effective communication in the work place; collaboration seems to be a conceptual afterthought" (p. 57). That is no longer the case.

Increasingly, all interventions will be evaluated by measuring their effectiveness in light of their costs. True service value (with maximized positive clinical outcomes and efficient delivery) will be attained only through the conscientious coordination of all relevant disciplines, organizational structures, and processes. Adoption of best practices, including achievement of such through integration and collaboration, will increasingly be the basis for determining provider reimbursement.

The PPACA established the Community-Based Collaborative Care Network Program to support consortia of healthcare providers to coordinate and integrate healthcare services for low-income uninsured and underinsured populations and the National Prevention, Health Promotion, and Public Health Council to coordinate federal prevention, wellness, and public health activities. The PPACA also established the Center for Medicare & Medicaid Innovation within the CMS to focus on research, development, testing, and expansion of innovative payment and delivery arrangements. CMS has identified 33 quality measures on care coordination and patient safety, appropriate use of preventive health services, improved care for at-risk populations, and patient and caregiver experience of care (U.S. Department of Health and Human Services, 2013a).

Along with the development of new consumer marketplaces in which to purchase lower cost health insurance, one of the most notable operational features of the PPACA is the creation of incentives that encourage the formation of public and private sector **Accountable Care Organizations (ACOs)** that take responsibility for the cost and quality of care received by patients. With a focus toward prevention, wellness, and intervention for patients with chronic conditions, ACOs promote patient-centered primary care and use of integrated services as central to coordinated healthcare delivery. Conceived as demonstration projects under the PPACA, ACOs offer physicians and hospitals incentives to provide quality care to Medicare beneficiaries while restraining costs. ACOs may include the following types of providers and suppliers of Medicare-covered services:

- ACO professionals (i.e., physicians and hospitals meeting the statutory definition) in group practice arrangements

- Networks of individual practices of ACO professionals

- Partnerships or joint venture arrangements between hospitals and ACO professionals

- Hospitals employing ACO professionals

- Other Medicare providers and suppliers as determined by the Secretary

The long-range implications of ACOs have been quickly recognized by both providers and payers, and a scramble is on to incorporate such models into existing provider delivery systems or to construct new systems consistent with recent federal regulations. Many types of entities may sponsor an ACO, but four major categories have emerged: hospital systems, physician groups, insurers and nonprofit organizations, and non-medical community-based organizations. The PPACA establishes a framework in which these provider groups agree to provide care for a population of patients with the goal of reaching or surpassing predetermined cost and quality benchmarks. The five key quality areas of patient care are (1) patient/caregiver experience of care, (2) care coordination, (3) patient safety, (4) preventive health, and (5) at-risk population/frail elderly health. If the ACO can meet the quality benchmarks and the cost of care is at or below established thresholds, the ACO is able to share in the "savings" (the difference between actual cost and benchmark cost) (Muhlestein, 2013).

ACOs agree to manage all of the healthcare needs for a minimum of 5,000 Medicare beneficiaries for at least three years. The U.S. Department of Health and Human Services (HHS) (2011) projected that ACOs could save Medicare up to $960 million in the first three years by creating savings incentives in the form of bonuses when providers keep costs down, meet the quality benchmarks, and focus on prevention and carefully managing patients with chronic diseases. In effect, the providers would get paid more for keeping patients healthy and out of hospitals. On the other hand, ACOs unable to save money would incur the costs of investments made to improve care. ACOs must meet quality standards to ensure that savings are achieved through improving care coordination and providing care that is appropriate, safe, and timely.

On January 10, 2013, the CMS announced that 106 Accountable Care Organizations (ACOs) were joining the Medicare Shared Savings Program (MSSP), bringing the total number of MSSP ACOs to more than 250 with coverage of up to 4 million Medicare beneficiaries (Muhlestein, 2013). When these public sector ACOs were combined with private sector ACOs, however, the national total reached 428 in 49 states. By December 2013, HHS announced that 360 Accountable Care Organizations (ACOs) had entered into agreements with the CMS and those ACOs were serving 5.3 million beneficiaries nationwide (Department of Health & Human Services, 2013b).

Efficiencies already achieved by ACOs are reflected in the fact that healthcare costs to their beneficiaries grew by only 0.3% in 2012, compared with nearly 1% for non-ACO beneficiaries. Thirteen of the first thirty-two "Pioneer ACOs" produced shared savings with CMS, generating a gross savings of $87.6 million in 2012 and saving nearly $33 million for Medicare Trust Funds. Pioneer ACOs earned over $76 million by providing coordinated, quality care. In comparison, only two Pioneer ACOs had shared losses totaling approximately $4.0 million. Program savings were driven, in part, by reductions that Pioneer ACOs generated in hospital admissions and readmissions (Centers for Medicare and Medicaid Services, 2013).

THE HEALTHCARE SYSTEM AS A SERVICE CONTINUUM

The "continuum" is a conceptualization of all healthcare-related services available to an individual. Evashwick (1987) defined a **continuum of care** as a "client oriented system composed of both services and integrating mechanisms that guides and tracks patients over time through a comprehensive array of health, mental health and social services spanning all levels of intensity of care" (p. 23). It is important to recognize that the continuum is not just envisioned as a broad array of services offered to a patient population, but as a systematic arrangement for organizing, connecting, and operating those services in a coordinated manner that maximizes their appropriate use. The goal is to facilitate patients' access to the most appropriate service meeting their needs and to do so as expediently and efficiently as possible.

There are different ways of creating a healthcare continuum. One way is to start with services designed to promote health and prevent disease and then move to disease-management strategies and conclude with end-of-life care. Another way is to think about where and how services are delivered. This continuum would start with services that are available to the person in his or her home and community, progress to more intensive or acute services provided by a hospital, and end with long-term-care services. In the past,

Table 2.5 The Health Service Continuum

Preventive/Primary Care		Acute Care		Long-Term Care		End-of-Life Care
Health Promotion and Disease Prevention	*Primary Care*	*Secondary Care*	*Tertiary Care*	*Rehabilitation Services and Long-Term Care*	*Chronic Disease Management*	*End-of-Life Care*
Smoking cessation programs	Early detection and routine care provided by private practice MDs or in settings associated with health organizations	General medicine and surgical services	Hospital-based advanced specialty, highly technical patient care	Home-based, inpatient and outpatient rehabilitation services including PT, OT, SW, speech and hearing	Home care including visiting nurses and home health aides	Hospice and palliative care is offered to patients and family when medical treatment is unlikely to cure/improve underlying medical conditions and the patient is considered terminal.
Family-planning services		Emergency treatment		Intervention follows serious illnesses or disabilities such as strokes or head injuries.	Care is provided over extended periods of time, for the duration of an illness or over the patient's life time.	
Weight loss programs		Critical care	Complex services including transplant, open heart surgery, and burn care			
Wellness activities	Managed-care organizations assign patients to primary care MDs who coordinate care and help control costs	Referred outpatient diagnostic testing		Services may include skilled care in nursing homes (covered 100 days by Medicare) or basic/custodial care.		
Nutritional programs		Services for outpatients requiring hospital equipment	Hospitals may be profit or nonprofit; religious, private, public, or military.			
Charge-based or free programs						
Neighborhood clinics, hospital outpatient departments, Community Mental Health Clinics, physicians' offices, poison control centers, school/university health clinics		General medical and surgical hospitals, hospital emergency departments and ambulatory care centers; specialty, trauma, and teaching hospitals		Sites include mental health clinics, HIV programs, substance abuse clinics, dialysis and other specialty clinics; may also include nursing home facilities (SNFs), day-care centers, and personal care homes		Services may be provided in patients' homes, designated hospital beds, or other inpatient programs

Source: Authors.

each unit of service along the continuum was often provided by a unique entity or health-care agency that offered that particular service. However, in the past twenty years, health-care systems have consolidated and incorporated so that many if not literally all of the possible services are available under the auspices of a single healthcare entity.

Continuity-of-care planning, or coordinating the care for patients and families as they move through the continuum, is a significant social work activity. To do this, social workers engage in the activity of case management and in some systems are called *case* or *care managers*. They often assist in coordinating the collaborative activities of the healthcare team as well as assess, facilitate, and evaluate healthcare services provided to patients as they receive services throughout the continuum. A derivative of social casework, **case management** evolved as a mechanism to address problems with continued fragmentation within larger health systems and across different service-delivery systems. Mandated by federal legislation such as Public Law (PL) 99–660, case management has become insepa-rable from the funding and delivery of public services (Rose, 1992). Social work can be found across the care continuum.

Conceptualized in relation to increasing levels of illness, *Table 2.5* presents a model for a continuum of care:

CONTINUUM COMPONENTS, FOCUS OF CARE, AND SOCIAL WORK SERVICES

Health-Promotion and Disease-Prevention Programs

Health promotion and disease prevention are strategies to intervene before an illness or disability occurs by educating and supporting individuals in making lifestyle choices that promote health and wellness. As we learned in Chapter 1, these strategies are often part of public health programs intended to improve the overall health status of a given population. To illustrate, the U.S. Department of Health and Human Services launched Healthy People 2010 (http://www.healthypeople.gov/2020/about/History-and-Development-of-Healthy-People), a national health-promotion program whose goals are to increase the quality and years of healthy life and to decrease the disparities in healthcare status between minority groups and Caucasians in the United States. The focus is to enhance health by addressing cancer, diabetes, substance abuse, sexually transmitted diseases, obesity, and prenatal care. Health-promotion efforts such as classes in stress management, smoking cessation, and weight reduction may be sponsored by hospitals, physician practices, neighborhood clin-ics, or organizations via their *employee assistance programs (EAPs)*. As a component of employee benefit packages, EAPs seek to reduce losses in worker productivity arising from illness and adverse lifestyles while also reducing business expenses related to decreased productivity and the funding of costly employee healthcare.

Community-based social workers have historically engaged in health-promotion and disease-prevention efforts in a broad array of independent and organizationally affiliated settings, notably including settlement houses such as Jane Addams's landmark Hull House in Chicago. From the time of Ida Cannon and the first hospital-based social work department, healthcare social work efforts have primarily been related to assessing and intervening with patients' problems that interfere with medical care, assisting in securing patient medical compliance with treatment, educating healthcare colleagues about patients' domestic and social conditions, and serving as a link between healthcare providers and the larger community (Dhooper, 1997, p. 172). Dziegielewski (1998) noted three benefits associated with social work involvement in health-promotion and disease-prevention programs. First, social workers have expertise in dealing with those bio-psychosocial factors that frequently affect individuals' health conditions. Second, social workers are skilled in counseling and understanding individual and family dynamics. They recognize and address issues, concerns, bias, and other factors affecting individuals' access and use of healthcare. Third, as they are familiar with making psychosocial assessments, making diagnoses, and providing supportive intervention, social workers can rapidly engage in situations where patients and families need assistance with problems beyond their control.

Primary Care

Based on a model developed by Roemer (1984), healthcare services are provided to patients at different levels (primary, secondary, and tertiary). Primary care is usually provided at a patient's first contact with the healthcare delivery system and involves the diagnoses of illnesses and diseases and provision of initial treatment. In addition, these outpatient, clinic, and physician-based services afford routine care for common illnesses and injuries and will refer patients for more complex secondary or tertiary care services, which are described later in this section.

Barton (1999) noted that primary-care services historically had been reimbursed at lower rates than more intensive services and that primary care and generalist physicians generally had lower incomes than their specialist counterparts. One effect of this differential was the implicit devaluing of primary care providers and a tendency for individuals to self-refer to a range of specialists rather than access specialty care through a primary provider (Barton, 1999, p. 299). As managed care evolved, the role of the primary care physician was strengthened as the person responsible for coordinating care and authorizing services. With the passage of the Patient Protection and Affordable Care Act of 2010, considerable attention is turning to the role of primary care in the delivery of health services (Horevitz & Manoleas, 2013). New care models including *patient-focused health or medical homes* emphasize early integrated intervention by physicians and other practitioners collaboratively addressing both health and mental healthcare patient needs. Regardless of setting, primary care professionals perform multiple roles beyond that of direct patient care. They serve in roles of advocate, advisor, and "gatekeeper" to the health system; they refer patients to sources for specialized care; they offer advice regarding various diagnoses; and they provide continuing care for chronic conditions (Williams, 1993, p.108).

With the increasing attention on primary care comes the prospect of a corresponding increase in the numbers of social workers shifting their focus from acute, hospital-based care and into primary-care settings. Some services provided by social workers in these environments can be billed to third-party insurers if the social worker is a licensed provider and the patient has a mental health diagnosis. In other scenarios, hospitals staff primary-care clinics with social workers and some progressive medical practices hire social workers to help physicians with complex cases. A principal role for primary-care social workers frequently involves organizational "boundary-spanning"—helping to negotiate the transaction of healthcare resources of multiple providers on behalf of patients and families. This may include dealing with service-coordination issues arising from lack of shared provider interests or differing approaches. Perceived competition among providers may also lead to problems of "turfmanship" (Rossi, Gilmartin, & Dayton, 1982) among providers. The social worker strives to negotiate such situations such that needed services are ultimately delivered to the patient.

Ambulatory (Outpatient) Care

Ambulatory care services are personal health services provided to individuals who are not inpatients in a healthcare institution (Jonas, 1992, p. 25). In the United States, ambulatory care traditionally was provided by individual medical practitioners working in their offices, patients' homes, and public clinics serving primarily poor and indigent patients (Williams, 1993, p. 108). Ambulatory care is offered in two principal categories. The largest category is that offered by physicians in solo, partnership, or group practices on a fee-for-service basis, whereas the second category is that associated with organizations such as hospital emergency rooms and departments, health promotion centers, "urgi- (urgent-care) centers," clinics, neighborhood health centers, school health services, and correctional institutions.

The use of ambulatory care expanded significantly with the advent of managed care and its focus on controlling the use and cost of healthcare. Service in ambulatory settings is less costly to provide, is more accessible to patients, and affords the opportunity for practitioners to make more careful analyses as to whether expensive inpatient hospitalization would be subsequently justified for medical treatment or other healthcare. Advances in medical procedures and equipment have made it increasingly possible to provide care on an outpatient basis that was historically available only onsite at hospitals. The origins of healthcare social work practice are thought to be associated with ambulatory care, in part traceable to Jane Addams establishing a free medical dispensary in Chicago's Hull House in the 1800s and the introduction of social work in the medical clinic of Dr. Richard Cabot at Massachusetts General Hospital in 1905.

CASE STUDY

Social Work in Ambulatory Care

The community hospital that Kay works in is developing an outpatient primary care clinic. It will be staffed by the medical staff and residents in order to provide care at a lower cost to patients. The clinic will also train medical students in primary care models. Kay asks to be involved to help assure that social work establishes a presence. She initially takes on the additional responsibility of being in the clinic two afternoons a week in addition to her regular duties.

Initially, things are slow and it takes a while for the physicians to get used to her being on site. Soon, though, the physicians are sending patients to her for help with medication assistance, Medicaid applications, and other community resources. Eventually, patients with psychosocial needs are scheduled for their visits on the afternoons when Kay is present. Mrs. Ryan is one such patient, with whom, after a number of months, Kay develops an ongoing case management relationship. Mrs. Ryan's doctor originally refers her to Kay because this patient takes quite a bit of his time and he is concerned that she is isolated and lonely. Kay recognizes that this is true but also that there are health-related goals that she and the patient can work on together.

Mrs. Ryan is a 56-year-old woman with multiple medical problems. She is obese, has difficulty breathing when she exerts herself, and has struggled with depression. She lives with an emotionally abusive husband who "causes stress"; however, there is no physical abuse, and Mrs. Ryan assures Kay that she loves him. Kay sees her and makes sure that she has a source of income and refers her for food stamps when she sees how low her income is. She also explains to Mrs. Ryan that, although she has too much income to qualify for full Medicaid, she might qualify for a Medicaid spend-down. Although complicated, Mrs. Ryan can save her medical bills and expenses and apply for Medicaid assistance every six months when her expenses reach a certain level. This would then help her to pay the balance of her medical bills.

Kay also discusses nutrition and smoking cessation options with Mrs. Ryan, who agrees to complete the hospital's smoking-cessation class. Kay calls her in between clinic visits to see how she is doing with her exercise, nutritional, and quitting smoking goals. Although Mrs. Ryan does not quit smoking completely, she does cut down and is proud to report that she is trying to "walk a couple of blocks each day" in an effort to get more exercise. Kay hopes that she and the primary care doctor can encourage Kay to continue on this path and provide feedback to her as her conditions improve.

After six months, Kay has established a strong presence in the clinic as well as excellent relationships with the staff. The clinic is established in the community and is running well. She submits a proposal to fund a social worker for two days a week in the clinic, which is approved by the Medical Director.

Questions:

In this case, Kay is working organizationally as well as clinically. Describe her strategy to develop social work services in ambulatory care.

What do you think about Kay's willingness to take on the responsibility of the clinic? Is this a good strategy? Could it have backfired?

Discuss ways in which the relationship between the social work and clinic staff might have evolved.

Acute Care

Acute care refers to healthcare interventions including emergency services, hospitalization, and more involved outpatient or specialty care. These services are rendered by and generally within a hospital. Acute care often begins with a patient entering through the emergency room. Acute care that is provided by a community-based hospital and that is fairly routine is considered secondary care. Medical care that is provided by specialists and at specialty clinics is also considered secondary care.

The American Hospital Association (AHA) identifies hospitals by their size (based on the numbers of beds or cribs regularly maintained) or by type. *Medical/surgical hospitals* utilize medical and professional staff to offer inpatient care and medical and nursing services to diagnose and treat both surgical and non-surgical conditions. *Specialty hospitals* offer services limited by medical specialty, such as obstetrics and gynecology, rehabilitation medicine, or psychiatry. Hospitals may also be distinguished by their *length of patient stay (LOS)*, being deemed either "short-term" when the patient's average length of stay is 30 days or less or "long-term" when stays exceed 30 days (Jonas, 1992, p. 51).

Taken together, nonfederal short-term hospitals, whether for-profit, nonprofit, or public, are commonly referred to as **community hospitals** because they are typically available to the entire community and meet most of the public's needs for hospital services. Community hospitals represent over 80% of the nation's hospitals (Haglund and Dowling, 1993, p. 146). These hospitals provide **secondary care** characterized by routine medical or surgical unit hospitalization and specialized outpatient care. In contrast with primary care, secondary care is continuing care for sustained or chronic conditions (Barton, 1999) and, in addition to being delivered by hospitals, may be provided in a wide range of specialty centers, including ambulatory surgery centers, radiology centers, urgent care centers, and renal dialysis centers. "Free-standing" surgical centers that are not associated with a hospital inpatient or outpatient service have experienced particular growth in recent years as a result of their ability to deliver services more economically than is possible in conventional inpatient hospitals.

Inpatient hospital services are organized by units, medical diagnoses, departments or services, medical specialties, and/or types of procedures. Acute-care hospitals provide many sublevels of care, including emergency services, general medicine, cardiac, critical care, and intensive care. Physicians are primarily organized along the lines of the medical specialties. As hospitals get larger in size, they have more specialized services and larger numbers of medical departments. There is no universal logic in categorizing the medical departments, with some separated by the age or sex of their patients, some by organ or organ system in their primary purview, and others delineated by their type of practice skill (Kovner, 1995).

CASE STUDY

Social Work in Acute Care

Ms. Jones is admitted to the 400-bed community hospital in her city with acute shortness of breath, weakness, and fatigue. She asks her significant other to let Kay know that she is there, and Kay goes to see her. Ms. Jones has pneumonia and congestive heart failure and will be in the hospital for a few days for antibiotic therapy, a cardiac workup, and respiratory therapy. Kay documents the patient's social history in the chart and asks to be notified when the patient is being discharged. On the day of discharge, Ms. Jones is feeling better but is still weak and is unable go up and down the stairs. She has a split-level home, and there is no bedroom on the same floor as the bathroom. She will also need oxygen and physical therapy. The doctors have assumed that her boyfriend will assist with her care, but he is intoxicated when he arrives to pick her up. He becomes quite belligerent when the doctor confronts him, and Kay is called.

Kay tries to calm the staff and situation a bit and takes the boyfriend aside. She explains that the hospital cannot permit him to drive Ms. Jones home as he appears to have been drinking. He denies this, and Kay points out that there is a smell of alcohol about him, he is slurring his words, and his eyes are bloodshot. She is not confrontational or judgmental. The approach she takes is one of just making observations. Initially, he continues with his denial, but eventually he concedes that he had a "few beers with lunch." Kay then talks to him about his feelings about having to take care of Ms. Jones. He admits that he does not know how to take care of her, and Kay recognizes that he is ambivalent and anxious about taking care of her. She also asks him about his drinking and whether he is interested in any referrals or information on alcohol abuse, but he declines.

Kay is aware of the DRG for this patient and the financial pressures to avoid extending the admission. Still, she feels that the discharge home is unsafe, and she asks the physician to delay discharge until the next morning. He agrees, and Kay goes back to Ms. Jones, who is quite upset and embarrassed about her boyfriend's behavior. Kay is reassuring that the staff understands the stress that they are under but is firm that there are problems with her going home without assistance. Kay asks if there are any other options for care and suggests a skilled nursing home facility for rehabilitation for a few weeks, but Ms. Jones declines. Instead, Ms. Jones contacts her daughter, who agrees to have her come to her home. A visiting nurse and outpatient physical therapy are ordered. The daughter is able to drive Ms. Jones to her appointments. A bedside commode and a walker are also arranged to minimize the risk of falling until the patient's strength returns.

Kay continues to see Ms. Jones in the clinic. Six months later, the boyfriend accompanies Ms. Jones to the clinic and asks to see Kay alone. Kay is surprised but talks with him privately. He asks for help with his drinking, which has now reached the point that he is having blackouts. Kay asks one of the doctors in the clinic to see him. The physician concludes that the boyfriend is at risk of severe withdrawal symptoms if he stops drinking suddenly and outlines a detoxification program that includes a prescription for a benzodiazepine (tranquillizer), which will be used when withdrawal symptoms emerge. The physician then makes arrangements to see the boyfriend every day for the next week to manage the withdrawal. Kay refers the boyfriend to Alcoholics Anonymous and explains that a group meets regularly at the hospital. She also makes arrangements for the boyfriend to be seen in the mental health clinic for assistance during his recovery.

Questions:

1. Who is the "patient" in this case?

2. Discuss how a doctor might view a situation as a simple discharge while a social worker might view the same situation differently.

3. What does this case demonstrate about the continuum of care and the benefits of social work spanning boundaries across the continuum of care?

4. What skills and abilities does Kay demonstrate in this situation?

Academic Tertiary Hospital System. This view of the Oregon Health and Science University system in Portland, Oregon, shows the complexity of a tertiary healthcare facility. There are multiple hospitals and specialty clinics and services within the same organization.

Source: Oregon Health & Sciences University.

Tertiary care is the apex of healthcare services. It represents the most complex diagnostic and therapeutic services, including organ transplants, burn treatment, and cardiac or other organ surgery. These services are provided by large regional healthcare centers that are most often teaching hospitals affiliated with universities (also referred to as *academic medical centers/systems*). Teaching hospitals that are qualified by the Council of Teaching Hospitals (COTH) offer secondary and tertiary level care, either have or are affiliated with a medical school, and have at least two of the approved residency programs in medicine, surgery, obstetrics and gynecology, pediatrics, family practice, or psychiatry. They provide the most complex services, typically are designated as trauma centers, and have significant involvement in medical/healthcare research. Because these services represent the most specialized of all healthcare services, patients are often referred and transferred to tertiary centers from primary and secondary care providers seeking highly skilled medical personnel who are knowledgeable about the most sophisticated diagnostic and therapeutic interventions and who have access to very costly leading-edge medical equipment that is not typically found in community hospitals.

Tertiary care facilities are also often designated *trauma centers* because of their ability to handle particularly complex emergent patient care situations. In the United States, a hospital can receive trauma center verification by meeting specific criteria established by the American College of Surgeons (ACS) and passing a site review by the Verification Review Committee. Official designation as a trauma center is determined by individual state law provisions. Trauma centers vary in their specific capabilities and are identified by "Level" designation, with Level I (Level 1) being the highest and Level III (Level 3) being the lowest. Higher levels of trauma centers will have trauma surgeons available, including those trained in such specialties as neurosurgery and orthopedic surgery as well as highly sophisticated medical diagnostic equipment. Lower levels of trauma centers may only be able to provide initial care and stabilization of a traumatic injury and arrange for transfer of the victim to a higher level of trauma care. Academic medical centers frequently are designated Level-I trauma centers (see photo above) because of their size and resources, whereas community hospitals, if approved, tend to be designated as Level II on the basis of their more limited expertise, equipment, and physical plants.

Most hospitals have social workers on staff who provide services in some capacity to inpatients. Larger hospitals and hospital systems may afford a centralized social work department headed by a senior social worker. As discussed, however, facilities are increasingly likely to staff individual social workers as members of a particular service, team, or medical unit in which they specialize or are otherwise specifically designated.

CASE STUDY

Social Work in Tertiary Care

Jason is a six-year-old boy who is sent to the emergency room (ER) after his mother brings him to the doctor because of abdominal pain. He is admitted to the pediatric unit from the ER. He is a lovely little boy who is feverish and lethargic. The nurse on the unit asks him what happened, and he replies that his tummy hurts. She asks if he has eaten anything that tasted funny and Jason says "no" but explains that he and his dad were wrestling and he fell off the bed. In the next few days, Jason presents a number of stories about how he hurt his tummy, including one in which he says his father punched him in the tummy. There is no sign of injury, and the medical team is unable to determine what is wrong with Jason.

The nurse refers the case to the social worker, insisting that a referral then be made to protective services. The social worker, Amber, goes up to the floor and talks to Jason, who tells her he just doesn't know why his tummy hurts. He says his father didn't punch him and denies that he has ever been spanked. Amber talks to the parents (separately) as well as the grandparents. There is no history of abuse or neglect, but the parents share that they have just initiated divorce proceedings. Jason's mother assures Amber that although there are plans to divorce, it is a sad but amicable situation and her husband is a wonderful and devoted father. The social worker is concerned that an unjustified report to protective services might affect the family in the long run and affect future custodial decisions.

Amber talks to Jason's doctor and the Medical Director, who is a pediatrician. Both concur that there seems no basis for the referral, especially since the team has been unable to make a definitive diagnosis. Amber also talks to the nurse and explains her reservations about making the referral. The nurse is very angry and accuses Amber of not doing her job, and Amber reminds the nurse that she also is obligated to report suspicions of child abuse. Amber provides the nurse with the number for protective services and reassures her that if she does report the case, Amber will be support and assist in any way. The nurse does not report the case.

After a week, the patient is transferred by ambulance to a tertiary care facility. The children's hospital is affiliated with a large university. Many of the doctors there are pediatric specialists, including the doctor who takes Jason's case, who is a pediatric immunologist. A series of body scans and blood tests demonstrate that the boy has an autoimmune response that mimics rheumatoid arthritis and that can cause inflammation of internal organs. He is treated with steroids and intravenous antibiotics and recovers. Amber knows this because she has followed up on the case, given her concerns about not referring the child to protective services. She informs the nurse of the outcome so that the nurse is aware that this was the right call.

(Continued)

(Continued)

Questions:

1. Did Amber do the right thing in holding back the protective service referral?

2. Were her concerns about making the referral reasonable, or should she have reported them?

3. What precautions did she take to make sure that her decision was justified? Do you think that these steps were adequate?

4. What would you have done?

Long-Term Care

More than 21 million individuals 70 years of age and over will need help with activity limitations by the year 2030 (National Academy on an Aging Society, 2000). Of further concern, increased numbers of women in the work force, increased instances of cross-country family relationships, and lifestyle/schedule conflicts, coupled with the increasing care needs of the elderly, threaten to reduce the availability of family care givers (Spitzer & Neuman, 2004). With decreased availability of family care and increasing numbers of those needing assistance, the prospects increase for necessary placement of dependent seniors (Stone, 2000). It has been estimated that, by 2018, there will be 3.6 million elderly persons in need of a nursing home bed, 2 million more than in 1997 (National Academy on Aging, 1997).

Long-term care "is one of the greatest challenges facing the health care delivery system and (it) will be a dominant issue during the coming decades." (Evashwick, 1993, p. 177) Long-term care encompasses a range of services designed to meet the physical, emotional, and social needs of people with chronic illnesses or disabilities that interfere with their independence and ability to perform activities of daily living (Schneider, Kropf, & Kisor, 2000). Long-term care may be offered in one's own home using home health services or in a broad range of outside settings extending from nursing homes and hospital swing beds or "step-down units" through acute and rehabilitative care, ambulatory sites (such as physician offices and clinics), and hospice programs to various forms of housing such as continuing-care retirement communities, assisted-living facilities, independent senior housing, and adult family homes.

Nursing homes (also referred to as *extended-care facilities*) provide services at two levels: skilled and basic. Skilled nursing home care services are covered by Medicare for up to 100 days. The first 20 days are covered at 100%, whereas the remaining 80 days require copayments. A three-day acute care hospital stay is required to qualify under very specific conditions. Examples of *skilled nursing facility (SNF) care* being warranted include instances in which patients need rehabilitation, wound care, and intravenous or feeding tube care requiring the skills of a nurse. Basic nursing home care is considered "custodial" care in a nursing home. This form of care can be covered by Medicaid, private insurance, or private funds. Nursing homes are regulated by state public health departments, which periodically inspect the nursing homes and track violations and complaints. Federal oversight exists to ensure compliance with Medicare reimbursement and other regulations. *Intermediate care facilities (ICFs)* must provide nursing services in accordance with the needs of residents and must offer restorative care so as to allow residents to maintain the highest possible degree of function, self-care, and independence. In comparison, *residential care facilities (RCFs)* have no nursing care available and are essentially a sheltered environment (Rakich et al., 1985, p. 40).

The anticipated growth in demand for long-term care has prompted forecasts for increases in opportunities for social work practice (Dziegielewski, 1998; Feinberg, 2002; Getzel and Mellor, 1983; Klein, 1998; Schneider et al., 2000; Spitzer, Neuman, & Holden, 2003). Federal law recognizes medical social services in home healthcare, whereas laws in many states require nursing homes of a certain size to have social workers on staff. Michigan, for example, requires nursing homes with 100 or more beds to employ at least one social worker at the BSW or MSW level. Social workers in nursing homes complete psychosocial assessments of new patients, assist patients and families with their adjustment to the nursing home, facilitate visits, lead patient and family groups, provide patient counseling, and conduct discharge planning (Brody, 1974; Conger & Moore, 1981; Silverstone & Burack-Weiss, 1983). Social work roles in long-term care also exist in policy development, home health, hospice, assisted-living care, and other housing contexts and in independent professional practice ranging from counseling to long-term care facility consultation.

Home healthcare is one of the oldest of the service contexts in the continuum of care. Home healthcare is a preferred modality as it strives to contain costs and reduce healthcare expenditures while allowing patients to reside in their own familiar surroundings. Use of home healthcare can deter unnecessary institutionalizations, including rehospitalization, rehabilitative hospital stays, and nursing home placement.

Home healthcare can consist of skilled nursing care, home health aide care, provision of durable medical equipment **(DME)**, homemaker services, and various high technology therapies. Home health services may be delivered by hospitals, visiting-nurse associations, governmental agencies such as public health departments, proprietary and private non-profit agencies, or independent practitioners such as private practice nurses or other healthcare professionals. **Skilled home health services** covered by Medicare include nursing care provided by registered nurses; respiratory therapy; physical, occupational, and speech therapy; and, notably, medical social services. Levande, Bowden, & Mollema (1988) regarded home health social work intervention as both cost-effective and valuable as it provides timely long-range planning for the elderly by linking these patients with resources, informal networks, and potential family-care options. In comparison with skilled home healthcare, the less intense **homemaker/home health aide care** includes personal care and assistance with bathing, grooming, meal preparation, transportation, shopping, and those tasks that do not warrant trained healthcare professionals (Evashwick, 1993).

CASE STUDY

Long-Term Care

Mrs. Smith is a 78-year-old, widowed woman who is admitted to a skilled nursing home for rehabilitation services following a stroke. She is a thin, frail woman with dyed red hair and ruby lipstick. She is alert; is oriented to person, place, and time; and is able to participate in her care and decision making. The stroke, which occurred on the right side of her brain, has resulted in left-side hemiparalysis. She lives alone in a second-floor apartment with no elevator. She has no family or close friends, although she does know a few of the neighbors in her building.

Mrs. Smith's stay in the skilled nursing home is covered by Part B of her Medicare as long as she is receiving skilled care. This includes her physical therapy. Medicare will cover this care at 100% for the first twenty days and then at 80% for the next eighty days as long as she needs skilled services and is making progress. Because she has no other insurance to cover the balance of the 80 days that Medicare will not cover, the social worker initiates a Medicaid application. Medicaid will also cover her stay if she needs to remain in the nursing home for more than 100 days.

Many large nursing homes are required by state laws to provide social work services to their residents. The social worker for this facility, John, has a BSW degree. He completes a psychosocial assessment on Mrs. Smith and sees her regularly to provide support and encouragement during her stay. When it is time for discharge, Mrs. Smith is able to perform some of her activities of daily living with adaptive equipment from the occupation therapist, but she is unable to walk and must use a wheelchair. She also has difficulty transferring from a bed or chair into the wheelchair. The doctor recommends twenty-four-hour supervision, but Mrs. Smith has no funds for this service and no one is available to serve. She insists on going home alone, despite John's efforts to help her accept the risks involved. The doctor wants John to petition for a guardian, but John and the psychiatrist agree that the patient is competent to make her own decisions. John orders a visiting nurse, Meals on Wheels, and a hospital bed, commode, and chair. John also completes a chore grant application with the Department of Human Services to pay for some housekeeping and personal-care assistance. Because Mrs. Smith is unable to get into her home on her own, John orders a wheelchair van to transport her.

Because he is so concerned about Mrs. Smith, John takes the rare step of accompanying the patient to her home at discharge. When he is confident that she is settled and seems safe, John leaves. A neighbor will bring her dinner in the evening , and the visiting nurse will check on her in the morning. John feels that he has done his best in this case.

The next morning, John comes into work to find a tearful message from Mrs. Smith. During the night she attempted to use her commode and fell while transferring from the bed. She is back in the hospital, and it appears that she has broken her hip. John contacts the social work department at the hospital and asks them to see her and checks on her himself on his way home from work. Mrs. Smith now accepts that she cannot manage alone at home and will need to move into a basic nursing home or a home for the aged when she has completed treatment for her broken hip. John tells her that he recognizes how difficult this is for her to accept and says that he admires her strength and courage. He asks Mrs. Smith for permission to talk to the social worker so that she may know the efforts and arrangements that had been made. The hospital and social worker collaborate, and Mrs. Smith is placed in a nursing home with skilled care for therapy while her hip heals as well as a home for the aged unit, which will accept her Medicaid and Social Security when the therapy is done.

John reflects back on the case, wondering if he had done everything he could. On the one hand, he felt like he had put a great deal of work into making arrangements that lasted less than twenty-four hours. However, he also felt that trying to live at home even for one night helped Mrs. Smith more realistically accept her situation.

Questions:

1. Do you think that John did everything that he could have done?

2. What might you have done?

3. Think about all the services John put in place. Are there more services that you might have considered? Do you think this is a complex or routine case?

4. Do you think that our social system provides adequate care and support for people like Mrs. Smith? What policy/program innovations are needed?

5. What do you think are the emotional issues that Mrs. Smith was dealing with? How would you help her to deal with these issues?

End-of-Life Care

End-of-life care includes **hospice and palliative care** that refrain from providing patients with aggressive medical treatments. The intent of these interventions is to promote comfort, quality of life, and function during the course of a terminal illness. The care is primarily supportive and neither hastens nor postpones death (Rakich et al., 1985, p. 45). Social workers play a critical role by providing emotional support to the patient and family. While preferably delivered in the patient's own home, hospice services also may be rendered in a variety of organizational settings such as hospitals, hospice agencies, home health agencies, and nursing homes. Services are made available on a continuous on-call basis and involve skilled and homemaker home care, respite care for families, use of palliative drugs, patient and family counseling, use of volunteers, and bereavement follow-up care for family and friends. Hospice benefits are covered by Medicare Hospital Insurance (Part A) when services are provided by a Medicare-certified agency. Patients are generally eligible for hospice care when they have been diagnosed with a terminal illness that is expected to be fatal within 90 to 180 days. The patient, with the family, must acknowledge the pending death and desire palliative care.

Researchers have identified end-of-life issues as the most common basis for ethical dilemmas faced by social workers. The most frequently cited end-of-life issues include Do Not Attempt Resuscitation (DNAR) orders; confusion or conflict about advance directives; withdrawal or withholding of treatments such as artificial nutrition and hydration, dialysis, and mechanical ventilation; physician-assisted suicide; and futility (Farrar & O'Donnell, 2003, p. 71). Futile treatment is commonly defined as treatment that will not alter the natural course of the disease and may, in fact, add additional physical, social, and/or emotional burdens to the patient (Schneiderman, Jecker, & Jones, 1990). Protocols for dealing with futile treatment and other ethical concerns increasingly call for deliberate consultation among involved professionals and may, when available, engage institutional resources such as ethics consultation teams to stimulate and guide such discussion (American Society for Bioethics and Humanities, 1998). Such consultations characteristically focus on maintaining the care and comfort of patients rather than on financial considerations. Safeguarding patient autonomy, including self-determination and informed consent, is crucial but also can be problematic in circumstances in which conflict exists among healthcare team members as to the capacity of patients to make responsible, viable care plans (O'Donnell, 2014).

CASE STUDY

Social Work in Hospice/End-of-Life Care

Mr. Jones is a sixty-eight-year old, widowed gentleman who is admitted to the hospital with late-stage pancreatic cancer. He is informed that his cancer has metastasized throughout his body. Mr. Jones is a beloved patient in the hospital. His family is supportive and has been involved throughout his care. Because he has been in and out of the hospital so much, he has supportive relationships with many of the hospital staff. He has undergone four rounds of chemotherapy, and his oncologist, who is known for not wanting to "give up" on his patients, would like to try a different type of chemotherapy. This treatment is experimental, and it is uncertain if it will generate any positive results.

The social worker, Angela, also knows Mr. Jones well. Before seeing him, she talks to his primary care doctor, who believes that hospice care would be the most appropriate course of action. She visits him and is shocked at his appearance. He has lost a great deal of weight and his coloring is yellow. She notes that talking has become difficult and that he tires very easily. He is also seems to be in a great deal of pain.

Mr. Jones tells her that he is in fact, tired. He is ready to "give up and let go," but he worries that his family will not understand this. He says that "they are not ready to give up and let go." Angela talks about what stopping the treatment would mean and explains hospice care.

Under Medicare, a patient entering hospice care changes from traditional Medicare benefits to hospice benefits. The expectation is that the condition is terminal, and the prognosis is generally limited to six months or less. Benefits that normally would go toward traditional medical treatments are then used to pay for additional nursing care, personal care, and social work services. The goal of hospice care is to make the patient and family comfortable and to provide a good quality of life during the patient's last days.

Occasionally, individuals receive hospice care on an inpatient basis, either in a unit at the hospital or nursing home or at an inpatient hospice center. Regardless of the site, the goal is to have the patient be in comfortable surroundings along with his or her family and loved ones.

Mr. Jones and Angela discuss hospice care, and Mr. Jones feels that it is time. He worries that his family is not ready to accept this decision. Angela calls a family meeting and meets briefly with the family apart from Mr. Jones to see where everyone is at with the issue. She gives them time to talk about their feelings about the patient and to remember him when he was strong and healthy. She explains hospice care and talks a bit about the grieving process and then shares that while Mr. Jones says that he is ready for hospice, he is concerned about his family's acceptance of this decision. As expected, his oldest daughter resists the idea and accuses the social worker and medical team of "giving up on him." The family and the social worker talk further and, when the other family members seem to accept hospice, Angela suggests that the daughter meet with her and Mr. Jones. Prior to this meeting, the social worker prepares Mr. Jones and offers suggestions about how to help the daughter accept the situation.

The meeting is held, and Mr. Jones explains that he is tired. He asks his daughter for permission to let go and stop the treatment. When asked in this way, the daughter tearfully agrees. It is decided that Mr. Jones will go to her home and that she will assume the role of primary caregiver. She feels positive but is scared and states that she feels grateful for being able to spend this time with her father.

The social worker talks to the physician and initiates the hospice referral. The hospice nurse comes to the hospital to see Mr. Jones and begins to make arrangements for the discharge. The social worker also discusses her concern about Mr. Jones' pain, and the hospice nurse requests that he be sent home with a morphine pump for pain management.

Angela also spends some time talking with the treatment team as they have feelings about this patient. She gives them a chance to talk about how his disease progressed and how he faced each step with courage and without complaint. Angela also approaches the oncologist, who, while initially gruff with her, admits that there was probably little that he could do at this point. Angela acknowledges that it must be frustrating when there are no further treatments available for a patient like Mr. Jones. This triggers something in the oncologist, who talks at length about how he hates giving up on patients and how he sees cancer as a war that he is fighting. Angela is surprised by this show of emotion but lets him ventilate. She notices that their relationship has changed following this meeting and that the oncologist is much more approachable and engaging with her on the unit.

(Continued)

(Continued)

Mr. Jones goes home with his daughter with hospice care, pain management, and the necessary durable medical equipment. Once home, he rallies and becomes noticeably stronger for a period of time. This improvement lasts for about two months, when he suddenly starts to decline and then falls into state of near unconsciousness. The hospice nurse works with the family to prepare them for the death. The nurse worries the daughter will panic and call an ambulance, which will then by law be required to start CPR and other life-saving measures.

As Mr. Jones's death approaches, the daughter calls his family around him and notifies the hospice nurse. When Mr. Jones dies, they are all there and grieve together. Later, the daughter calls the hospital social worker to let her know that the time that she spent with her father was the most meaningful time in her life. During the two months that he rallied, they grew very close and had an opportunity to resolve some outstanding personal issues.

Questions:

1. What are the issues and dynamics involved in reaching the decision to implement hospice care?

2. How does the social worker address and resolve these issues?

3. What do you think about the social worker's intervention with the treatment team and oncologist?

4. How did hospice care help this patient and family?

SUMMARY

In this chapter, we have explored the characteristics of organizations, including their environments, design, structures, cultures, and climates. We have identified how hospitals are classified by service, target population, and/or ownership. We have examined the challenges presented to healthcare social work practice, particularly as the result of changes in legislation, reimbursement strategies (such as prospective pricing and managed care), and evolving management concepts ranging from service (product) line management through Accountable Care Organizations and their emphasis on integrated, transdisciplinary care. The continuum of care was introduced, with discussion on the focus of care and the characteristics of social work practice in the myriad of inpatient and outpatient settings comprising the contemporary healthcare environment. Examples of practice in these settings offered insight into the differing experiences and responsibilities of healthcare social workers.

KEY TERMS AND CONCEPTS

- Organizational structure, process, and outcomes

- Organizational climate and culture

- Centralization of services vs. matrix management

- Host setting

- Omnibus Budget Reconciliation Act (OBRA)

- Entitlement program

- Prospective pricing system (PPS)

- Diagnostically related groupings (DRGs)

- Continuum of care

- Primary, secondary, and tertiary care

- Community hospitals

- Managed healthcare

- Skilled home healthcare

- Skilled home health services

- Hospice and palliative care

- Homemaker/home health aide

- Skilled Nursing Facilities and Intermediate Care Facilities

- MCOs: HMOs, PPOs, and IPAs

- Indemnity insurance

- Patient Protection and Affordable Care Act of 2010 (PPACA)

- Accountable Care Organizations

QUESTIONS FOR DISCUSSION

1. What makes healthcare organizations a host setting for social workers? What is the primary mission of healthcare organizations? How do social workers help organizations to achieve this mission? Why could social work services in host settings be vulnerable when budget crises occur? What strategies can be adopted to try to prevent service cutbacks in host settings?

2. How have social work services in hospitals been reduced since the 1980s? What do you think might be some of the effects of these reductions on patients? On social work staff?

3. Working in small groups, discuss your field-placement agencies. Describe the organizational structure, climate, and culture. Would you describe the agency as formal or informal? What makes an organization's climate positive or negative? What are cultural aspects of the agency?

EXERCISES

1. Continuum of care

   Working in groups, identify agencies in your community that represent each level of the continuum of care. Go out and visit a social worker who works in each of the levels and learn about the services they provide, the patients they see, and their role and working conditions.

2. Hospital utilization and costs

   Visit the website for the Agency for Health Research and Quality. Search the site for information about hospitals by examining the report "HCUP Facts and Figures: Statistics on Hospital-Based Care in the United States, 2009," which can be retrieved from

   http://www.hcup-us.ahrq.gov/reports/factsandfigures/2009/highlights.jsp

   Determine the following:

   - What trends occurred in hospitalization lengths of stay (LOS) in 2009?
   - What were the aggregate costs of hospital care?
   - What were the top three reasons for hospitalization?
   - What were the most common conditions for uninsured hospital stays?
   - What conditions incurred the highest aggregate costs?
   - Who was the highest single payer for hospitalizations in 2009?

3. Organizational structure

   Contact a hospital social worker in your community or invite him or her to class as a guest speaker. Ask how many social workers work at the facility? What is the role of the social worker at that facility? Is there is a centralized social work department or are social workers assigned to a nursing unit? How are they supervised? How do these conditions affect the work that they do? What are the pros and cons of these arrangements?

REFERENCES

American Hospital Association. (2002). *Hospital statistics*. Chicago: Health Forum.

American Society for Bioethics and Humanities. (1998). *Core competencies for health care ethics consultation*. Glenview, IL: author.

Anderson, O. W. (1968). *The uneasy equilibrium*. New Haven, CT: College and University Press.

Barton, P. (1999). *Understanding the U.S. health services system*. Chicago: The Health Administration Press.

Beder, J. (2006). *Hospital social work: The intersection of medicine and caring*. New York: Routlege.

Berger, C., Robbins, C., Lewis, M., Mizrahi, T., & Fleit, S. (2003). The impact of organizational change on social work staffing in a hospital setting: A national, longitudinal study of social work in hospitals. *Social Work in Health Care, 37*, 1–18.

Brody, E. (1974). *A social work guide for long-term facilities*. Washington, DC: U.S. Government Printing Office.

Carlton, T.O. (1984). *Clinical social work in health settings: A guide to professional practice with exemplars*. New York: Springer Publishing Company.

Centers for Medicare and Medicaid Services (CMS). (2012). *National health expenditure data*. Retrieved from http://www.cms.gov/Research-Statistics-Data-and-Systems/Statistics-Trends-and-Reports/NationalHealthExpendData/NationalHealthAccountsProjected.html

Centers for Medicare and Medicaid Services (CMS). (2013). *Pioneer accountable care organizations succeed in improving care, lowering costs*. Retrieved from http://www.cms.gov/Newsroom/MediaReleaseDatabase/Press-Releases/2013-Press-Releases-Items/2013-07-16.html

Commission on the Accreditation of Rehabilitation Facilities (CARF). (2011). Organizational website: www.carf.org

Conger, S. A., & Moore, K. D. (1981). *Social work in the long-term care facility*. Boston, MA: American Health Care Association/CBI Publishing Company, Inc.

Cowles, L. A. F. (2003). *Social work in the health fields: A care perspective*. Binghamton, NY: Haworth Press.

Daft, R. L. (1998). *Organizational theory and design*. (6th ed.). Cincinnati, OH: South-Western College Publishing.

Dhooper, S. (1997). *Social work in health care in the 21st century*. Thousand Oaks, California: SAGE.

Davidson, T., Davidson, J. R., & Keigher, S. M. (1999). Managed care: Satisfaction guaranteed not! *Health and Social Work, 24*, 163–171.

Dziegielewski, S. F. (1998). Managed care principles: The need for social work in the health care environment. *Crisis Intervention and Time-Limited Treatment, 3*, 97–100.

Evashwick, C. (1993). The continuum of long-term care. In S. Williams & P. Torrens (Eds.). *Introduction to health services* (pp. 177–218). Albany, NY: Delmar Publishers, Inc.

Evashwick, C. (1987). Definition of the continuum of care. In C. Evashwick & L. Weiss (Eds.). *Managing the continuum of care: A practical guide to organization and operations* (p. 23). Rockville, MD: Aspen Publishers.

Farrar, A., & O'Donnell, P. (2003). Biomedical issues and social work: The state of practice and research. In W. Spitzer (Ed.). *Ethics in health care: A social work perspective*. Petersburg, VA: The Dietz Press.

Feinberg, R. K. (2002). The increasing need for social workers in assisted living. *Journal of Social Work in Long-Term Care, 1*, 9–12.

Fraze, T., Elixhauser, A., Holmquist, L., & Johann, J. (2010). *Public hospitals in the United States, 2008: Statistical brief #95. Healthcare Cost and Utilization Project (HCUP) statistical brief*. Rockville (MD): Agency for Health Care Policy and Research (U.S.); 2006–2010. Retrieved from http://www.ncbi.nlm.nih.gov/pubmed/2141320

Friedman, B., & Neuman Allen, K. (2011). Systems theory. In J. Brandell (Ed.). *Theory and Practice of Clinical Social Work* (pp. 3–18). New York: The Free Press.

Getzel, G. S. & Mellor, J. M. (Eds.). (1983). *Gerontological social work practice in long-term care*. New York: The Haworth Press.

Gibelman, M. (2002). Social work in an era of managed care. In A. Roberts & G. Greene (Eds.), *Social workers' desk reference*. New York: Oxford University Press.

Haglund, C. L., & Dowling, W. L. (1993). The hospital. In S. Williams & P. Torrens (Eds.), *Introduction to health services* (pp. 134–176). Albany, NY: Delmar Publishers, Inc.

Hammer, M., & Champy, J. (1994). *Reengineering the corporation: A manifesto for business revolution.* New York: HarperBusiness.

Horevitz, E., & Manoleas, P. (2013). Professional competencies and training needs of professional social workers in integrated behavioral health in primary care. *Social Work in Health Care, 52,* 752–787.

Hubschman, L. (1983). *Hospital social work practice.* New York: Praeger Scientific Publishers.

Inglehart, A. P. (1990). Discharge planning: Professional versus organizational effects. *Health and Social Work, 15,* 301–309.

Joint Commission. (2011). Organizational website: www.jointcomission.org

Jonas, S. (1992). *An introduction to the U.S. health care system.* New York: Springer Publishing.

Kilman, R. (1977). *Social systems design.* New York: North-Hillard.

Klein, S. M. (Ed.). (1998). *A national agenda for geriatric education: White papers (Vol. 1).* Health Resources and Services Administration, Bureau of Health Professions. Washington, DC: U.S. Government Printing Office.

Kovner, A.R. (1995). *Health care delivery in the United States.* New York: Springer Publishing Company.

Koch, A. L. (1993). Financing health care services. In S. Williams & P. Torrens (Eds.), *Introduction to health services* (pp. 299–331). Albany, NY: Delmar Publishers, Inc.

Leatt, P., Shortell, S. M., & Kimberly, J. R. (1988). Organizational design. In S. Shortell & A. Kaluzny (Eds.). (1988). *Health care management: A text in organization theory and behavior* (2nd ed.) (pp. 307–343). Albany, NY: Delmar Publishers, Inc.

Levande, D., Bowden, S., & Mollema, J. (1988). Home health services for dependent elders: The social work dimension. *Journal of Gerontological Social Work, 11,* 5–17.

Levin, S., & White, P. (1961). Exchange as a conceptual framework for the study of interorganizational relationships. *Administrative Science Quarterly, 5,* 583–601.

Mayes, R. (2007). The origins, development and passage of Medicare's revolution prospective payment system. *Journal of the History of Medicine and Allied Sciences, 62,* 21–55.

Mezey, A. P., & Lawrence, R. S. (1995). Ambulatory care. In A.R. Kovner (Ed.), *Jonas's health care delivery in the United States* (pp. 122–161). New York: Springer Publishing Company.

Muhlestein, D. (2013). *Continued growth of public and private accountable care organizations.* Retrieved from http://healthaffairs.org/blog/2013/02/19/continued-growth-of-public-and-private-account able-care-organizations/

National Academy on Aging. (1997). *Facts on long-term care.* Washington, DC: Gerontological Society of America.

National Academy on an Aging Society (2000). Caregiving: Helping the elderly with activity limitations. *Challenges for the 21st Century: Chronic and Disabling Conditions, 7,* 1–6. Washington, DC: Author.

National Association of Social Workers, Center for Workforce Studies. (2006). *Licensed social workers in health.* Retrieved from http://workforce.socialworkers.org/studies/health/health_chap1.pdf

Neuhauser, D. (1983). The hospital as a matrix organization. In A. Kovner & D. Neuhauser (Eds.), *Health services management: Readings and commentary* (2nd ed.) (p. 256). Ann Arbor, MI: Health Administration Press.

Neuman, K. (2000). Understanding organizational reengineering in health care: Strategies for social work's survival. *Social Work in Health Care, 31,* 19–33.

O'Donnell, P. (2014). Futility: Proactive intervention. In W. Spitzer, (Ed.). *Ethics in health care social work practice: Issues and directions* (pp. 15–28). Philadelphia, PA.: National Society for Social Work Leadership in Health Care.

Rakich, J. S., Longest, B. B., & Darr, K. (1985). *Managing health service organizations* (2nd ed.). Philadelphia, PA: W.B. Saunders Company.

Regence Blue Cross/Blue Shield. (2013). *Why does U.S. health care cost so much?* Retrieved from http://www.regence.com/transparency/regence-and-reform/what-drives-up-health-care-costs.jsp

Roemer, M.I. (1984). Analysis of health services systems--a general approach. In Pannenborg C., van der Werff, A., Hirsch, G. B., & Barnard, K. (Eds.). *Reorienting health services*. New York: Plenum Press

Rose, S.M. (1992). *Case management and social work practice.* White Plains, NY: Longman.

Rosenberg, G., & Weissman, A. (Eds.). (1995). *Social work leadership in healthcare: Directors' perspectives.* New York, NY: The Haworth Press.

Rossi, R. J., Gilmartin, K. J., & Dayton, C. W. (1982). *Agencies working together: A guide to coordination and planning.* Beverly Hills, CA: SAGE.

Schrage, M. (1990). *Shared minds: The new technologies of collaboration.* New York: Random House.

Schneider, R. L., Kropf, N. P., & Kisor, A. J. (2000). *Gerontological social work: Knowledge, service settings, and special populations* (2nd ed.). Stamford, CT: Brooks/Cole.

Schneiderman, L. J., Jecker, N. S., & Jonsen, A. R. (1990). Medical futility: Its meaning and ethical implications. *Annals of Internal Medicine, 112*, 949–954.

Shortell, S., & Kaluzny, A. (Eds.). (1988). *Health care management: A text in organization theory and behavior* (2nd ed.). Albany NY: Delmar Publishers, Inc.

Silverman, E. (2012). Organizational awareness and health care social work: Enhancing a profession and environmental fit. In W. Spitzer, (Ed.). *Education for health care social work practice: Issues and directions* (pp. 1–18). National Society for Social Work Leadership in Health Care. Petersburg, VA: The Dietz Press.

Silverstone, B., & Burack-Weiss, A. (1983). The social work function in nursing homes and home care. In G. Getzel & J. Mellor (Eds.), *Gerontological social work practice in long-term care* (pp. 7–34). New York: The Haworth Press.

Spitzer, W. (1998). Reengineering integrated patient care in an academic medical center. In *Readings in Case Management* (pp. 43–48). Chicago, IL: American Hospital Association. Also appears in *Continuum: An Interdisciplinary Journal on Continuity of Care, 16*(4), 10–15.

Spitzer, W., & Nash, K. (1996). Educational preparation for contemporary health care social work practice. *Social Work in Health Care, 24*(1/2), 9–34. Co-published in Mailick, M., & Caroff, P. (1996), *Professional social work education and health care: Challenges for the future.* New York: The Haworth Press, 9–34.

Spitzer, W., & Neuman, K. (2004). The evolution of assisted living and implications for social work practice. In W. Spitzer (Ed). *Selected proceedings—38th annual meeting and educational conference.* The National Society for Social Work Leadership in Health Care. Petersburg, Virginia: The Dietz Press.

Spitzer, W., Neuman, K. & Holden, G. (2003). The coming of age for assisted living care: New options for senior housing and social work practice. *Social Work in Health Care, 38*, 21–45.

Spitzer, W., Silverman, E. & Allen, K. (2015). From organizational awareness to organizational competency in health care social work: The importance of formulating a "Profession-in-Environment" fit. *Social Work in Health Care, 43:3*, 193–211.

Stone, R. (2000*). Long term care for the elderly with disabilities: Current policy, emerging trends and implications for the twenty-first century.* Milbank Memorial Fund.

United States Census Bureau. (2011). *Income, poverty, and health insurance coverage in the United States: 2010.* Retrieved from www.census.gov/prod/2011pubs/p60-239.pdf

United States Department of Health and Human Services (2000). *Healthy people 2010.* Washington, DC: U.S. Government Printing Office. Retrieved from http://www.healthypeople.gov/2010/Sitemap/

United States Department of Health and Human Services. (November 2, 2011). Medicare Program; Medicare Shared Savings Program: Accountable Care Organizations. *Federal Register, 76*(2), pp. 67802–67990.

United States Department of Health and Human Services (January 10, 2013a). *More doctors, hospitals coordinate care for people with Medicare*. Retrieved from http://www.hhs.gov/news/press/2013 pres/01/20130110a.html

United States Department of Health and Human Services (December 23, 2013b). *More partnerships between doctors and hospitals strengthen coordinated care for Medicare beneficiaries*. Retrieved from http://www.hhs.gov/news/press/2013pres/12/20131223a.html

Weber, M. (1947). *The theory of social and economic organization*. New York: Oxford University Press.

Whitaker, T., Wilson, M., & Arrington, P. (2008). *Social workers at work: NASW membership workforce study*. Washington, DC: National Association of Social Workers.

Williams, S. (1993). Ambulatory health care services. In S. Williams & P. Torrens (Eds.). *Introduction to health services* (pp. 108–133). Albany, NY: Delmar Publishers, Inc.

CHAPTER 3

Knowledge and Theoretical Foundations of Healthcare Social Work Practice

Karen M. Allen and Mary Ruffolo

INTRODUCTION

Social workers actively engage on healthcare teams to address the social and emotional needs of patients and families across the continuum of care. Their expertise is increasingly being recognized with the contemporary focus on "whole-person" care, including wellness and preventive counseling as well as acute and chronic care (Berry & Mirabito, 2009).

This chapter explores how the evolving healthcare system is creating new opportunities for social workers to address the mental health and emotional well-being of patients and families. It identifies key components of promising, evidence-based psychosocial interventions that can be delivered in a broad spectrum of healthcare settings and addresses the challenges and opportunities for social workers in providing such care. Attention is focused on social workers engaging with patients and families primarily because of physical health issues but also because of mental health conditions (e.g., depression, anxiety, post-traumatic stress disorder, etc.) that either preexisted or developed in response to physical health crises and that are impacting patient functioning.

THE CHANGING HEALTHCARE SYSTEM

The United States healthcare system will experience rapid change as a result of healthcare reforms currently being implemented that will increase access to care and improve the quality of services. These reforms are prompting a shift from a disease-driven to a primarily wellness-driven system (Berry & Mirabito, 2009) with increased emphasis on care coordination, patient outcomes research, disease prevention and health promotion, primary care, community-based care, and integrated behavioral and physical health services (Kaiser Family Foundation, 2013). Increasingly, patients and families will be encouraged to become active, full-fledged members of healthcare teams. Patient-centered medical homes are emerging in primary care in which every person has a consistent source of medical care and access to integrated healthcare teams that address the "whole person," providing a continuum of wellness, preventive, acute, chronic, and end-of-life care. For social workers providing health services, the implication is that delivery and coordination of services for the behavioral health needs of patients and families will be central to improving health outcomes. Furthermore, social workers are increasingly likely to have roles coordinating patient care across the healthcare continuum.

DEFINITIONS OF HEALTH, WELLNESS, DISEASE, AND DISABILITY

What does it mean to be healthy? If being healthy means the absence of disease or disability, then few of us can be considered "healthy." All of us, if we are lucky to live long enough, will at some point in our lives encounter a disability or disease. More and more of us are living with chronic diseases that, until not long ago, would have caused our deaths. Many different definitions of health, wellness, illness, and disability exist in contemporary healthcare.

The World Health Organization (WHO) constitution (2009) defines **health** as "a state of complete physical, mental and social well-being and not merely the absence of illness." It further defines mental health as "a state of well-being in which every individual realizes his or her own potential, can cope with the normal stresses of life, can work productively and fruitfully, and is able to make a contribution to her or his community." The WHO emphasizes that social justice and advocacy are essential in promoting health by ensuring that "equal opportunities and resources are available to all individuals so that they may achieve their fullest health potential" (World Health Organization, 1986, p. 2). This means that achieving an optimum state of health and quality of life for individuals may involve the use of supports, services, and adaptive equipment.

Movement toward a system of health services that recognizes the importance of a whole-person perspective supports the manner in which social workers utilize multi-system, ecological, person-in-environment interventions in health settings. A wellness-driven system affords the prospect of opportunities for more preventive mental health interventions in primary care and other emerging healthcare settings. To function on integrated healthcare teams and provide crucial mental health interventions, social workers must demonstrate they are engaging in evidence-based "best practices" that contribute to positive outcomes for patients and families experiencing mental health challenges.

A major incentive for the health system to adopt a whole-person focus and wellness framework is the high cost of healthcare. As reported in the Medical Expenditures Panel Survey (Soni, 2009), the five largest categories for U.S. healthcare expenditures between 1996 and 2006 were heart disease, trauma-related disorders, cancer, asthma, and mental disorders. Mental disorders, such as depression, bipolar disorders, and anxiety, are among the twenty leading causes of disability worldwide (WHO, 2008), and it is projected that, by 2020, *behavioral health disorders will surpass all physical diseases as a major cause of disability worldwide* (Bloch, 2011).

With increasing appreciation for physical and emotional well-being, new conceptualizations of wellness stress an individual's awareness, choice, and capacity to reach to an optimum level of functioning regardless of health status or disability. The National Wellness Institute (2007) identified six dimensions of wellness: emotional, intellectual, physical, cultural, occupational, social, and environmental. **Wellness** is an integrated and holistic approach to living that requires balance and purpose in order to enable an individual to reach his or her potential. It is a dynamic and ever-evolving state of being that involves a conscious and deliberate approach to advancing physical, psychological, and spiritual health (Dunn, 1971; Ardell, 1979). Wellness (and by inference, health) exists on a continuum and involves a process of continual improvement that is unique for each individual. Health, then, is a "state of being and wellness a process of being" with disease prevention and intervention distinct from health and wellness promotion (Jonas, 2000).

Disease is a more discrete term, referring to a pathological, biomedical condition that interferes with the body's capacity to regulate itself and perform essential functions. According to Webster's Medical Dictionary, disease "is an impairment of the normal state of the living animal or plant body or one of its parts that interrupts or modifies the performance of the vital functions and is a response to environmental factors (as malnutrition, industrial hazards, or climate), to specific infective agents (as worms, bacteria, or viruses), to inherent defects of the organism (as genetic anomalies), or to combinations of these factors." The term *illness* is much broader and more personal, incorporating social and emotional dimensions in addition to biomedical components. Illness describes an individual's subjective experience of disease. As Cassell explained, "a disease is something an organ has; illness is something a man has" (as cited by Jonas, 2000, p. 11).

In today's world, **disability** is a socially constructed term that is highly dependent on culture, politics, resources, and values. As defined by the Americans with Disabilities Act (1990), a disability is a "physical or mental impairment that substantially limits one or more of the major life activities of such individual." The disability rights movement cautions against making assumptions based on simple categorizations of visible and invisible disabilities. More importantly, the movement emphasizes that many instances of impairment result from limitations in the environment rather than limitations in the individual.

Health status describes an individual's or community's state of health, wellness, and risk factors at a given point in time. The U.S. Department of Health and Human Services has compiled data on the health status of all counties in the United States on its Community and Health Status Indicator website (www.cdc.gov/communityhealth). The website provides information on average life expectancy and health status, among other variables, and enables one to compare prevalence and mortality rates for one's county relative to national averages.

Healthcare social workers intervene with individuals and families when there is an illness, injury, or disability, but these workers are increasingly involved in health promotion, health maintenance, disease prevention, and wellness programs. As an illustration, social workers have responded in a variety ways to the present obesity epidemic, particularly as it affects children. Beyond conventional counseling interventions, social workers are also creatively integrating alternative healing approaches into their practice, including meditation, yoga, creative visualization, Reiki, and other techniques.

THE MEDICAL MODEL OF PRACTICE

The traditional practice paradigm of physicians is referred to as the **medical model**. Although imprecise, this term, originally coined in 1961 by the sociologist Erving Goffman, describes a general orientation of physicians and their assumptions about patients, diseases, and treatment. It espouses that a patient is someone who is sick or diseased and as such requires the interventions of a physician to diagnose, treat and, if possible, cure disease. The benefit of the model is that it provides focus and organization to the process of delivering care. In the model, physicians provide leadership to the healthcare team and oversee the medical care provided to patients. Their advanced training permits them to diagnose medical conditions, order diagnostic tests, perform procedures, and prescribe medications.

The criticism of the model is that historically physicians have often acted in isolation, disregarding the individual patient as a person at times and failing to acknowledge cultural, social, and spiritual dimensions (Kroenke, 1996). The medical model can act as a "lens" that encourages physicians to see all conditions as a disease requiring diagnosis, medication, and intervention even when the patient is unlikely to benefit from such treatment. Expecting patients to passively accept their care, physicians may discourage interaction, questioning, or active participation in decision making. The result may be that patients feel dehumanized and treated as if they were the disease. Furthermore, if a physician is functioning in the role of team leader and is lacking in communication and leadership skills, the impact may be to marginalize other involved professionals' opinions and influence on decision making.

Beyond minimally recognizing the impact of stress on the body, traditional Western medicine and the medical model often fall short in appreciation of the mind–body connection. For example, the model fails to acknowledge the roles of ethnicity and culture as they affect the experience of illness and disability. People from different cultures will vary in how and from whom they seek help, how they experience and communicate pain, how they interpret and label diseases and symptoms, how they understand the causes of illness, and how they select treatments (McGoldrick, 1982, p. 6).

Figure 3.1 presents a visualization of the medical model, showing the focus on impairments, disease, and symptoms rather than on the individual. There is no recognition of the strengths or adaptive capacities of individuals or their social systems, and the director of care is a physician rather than the patient. Although this model is evolving in medicine, with increased recognition of patient self-determination and inclusion, some institutions and individuals are entrenched in this model. Social workers play a particularly important role in advocating for patients in order to ensure that they understand their conditions and treatments and are empowered to make decisions and direct their own care. In addition, culturally sensitive biopsychosocial-spiritual histories and assessments completed by healthcare social workers can offer important and valuable insights into patients' emotional states as well as uncover ethnic or alternative healing practices that are often ignored in care based on the tradition medical model. With this understanding, social workers can guide the medical team in recognizing the importance of patients' faith, religious, and healing practices as they influence care.

Figure 3.1   The Medical Model

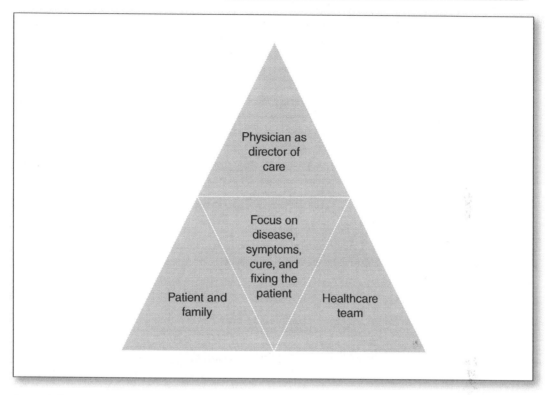

Source: Authors.

ADJUSTMENT TO ILLNESS COUNSELING

Healthcare social workers typically do not function as therapists from the standpoint of providing long-term counseling that addresses personality disorders, chronic mental illness, and other types of persistent mental and emotional disorders. More characteristically, social workers offer problem-oriented interventions, including counseling focused on the patient's (and family's) adjustment to illness or other health condition. **Problem-oriented interventions** are employed to resolve problems or issues related to a health condition, such as the need to make a decision about treatment or to secure placement in a care facility. In the latter instance, the process involves locating and ultimately selecting an appropriate facility, determining finances and coverage for care, and addressing the emotional issues surrounding placement. Dealing with the emotions arising from a serious illness, injury, or disability can be overwhelming, even for otherwise stable, resilient patients. The individual may not have underlying mental health needs, but the experience of a health crisis may well exceed his or her coping capacities. In these instances, social workers provide a specific type of intervention referred to as **adjustment to illness counseling**. This intervention assists patients and families in understanding a health condition, its prognosis, and its treatment. Such counseling is a blended approach that includes emotional support, education about the health condition, and community resources that can help with coping, including crisis intervention and/or psychotherapy.

While adjustment to illness counseling frequently occurs as an intervention in the context of discharge and continuity-of-care planning or case management, social workers continuously strive to be sensitive regarding how individuals and families cope with health conditions (Mizrahi & Abramson, 2000). Learning that you have a serious disease or that you will have limits in your functional abilities as a result of an injury understandably generates feelings of loss of control, uncertainty, and confusion. These feelings may in turn trigger anger, resentment, bitterness, and despair. Individuals often feel anxious and overwhelmed and experience grief as they realize that they have lost their identity as a "healthy" individual as well as their body's prior integrity or wholeness.

There is no single model for understanding how individuals accept and adapt to an illness. To illustrate, Antonak and Livneh (1995) studied this process in the context of individuals' adjustment to a diagnosis of multiple sclerosis. They identified eight reaction stages that patients commonly go through when initially told that they have a serious condition: shock, anxiety, denial, depression, internalized anger, externalized hostility, acknowledgement, and adjustment. Although individuals do not necessarily progress through the stages in a strictly linear fashion, the stages can be grouped into three global phases: early reactions (shock, anxiety, and denial), intermediate reactions (depression, internalized anger, and externalized hostility), and later reactions (acknowledgement and adjustment). Antonak and Livneh explained that *acknowledgment* refers to one's cognitive or intellectual understanding of a disease, whereas true *adjustment* includes an emotional and intellectual acceptance of the disease as well as an internalization of "the functional implications of an impairment into one's self concept coupled with behavioral adaptation and social integration into the newly perceived life situation" (p. 1100).

Age, personality configuration, social support, employment (or ability to perform other customary social roles), education, and spiritual well-being have all been shown to influence how well people adjust to an illness, injury, or disability (Commerford & Reznikoff, 1996, Masakazu et al., 2007; Northouse, Laten, & Reddy, 1995; McIvor, Riklan, & Reznikoff,1984; Anema, Johnson, Zeller, Fogg, & Zetterlund, 2009). An important factor in one's adjustment is how the individual perceives his or her condition. Individuals and/or families who perceive the condition as less disabling than it actually is (when objectively measured by rehabilitation specialists) are likely to better cope with the disease. This suggests that helping patients reframe and reconstruct their perceptions can aid their psychological adjustment and management of their condition (Crawford & McIvor, 1985).

A THEORETICAL FRAMEWORK FOR INTERVENTION

Some healthcare systems employ clinical social work staff to provide individual and family counseling. Other systems have social workers who provide counseling in the context of case management or continuity-of-care planning. In either case, social workers use a variety of clinical approaches to enhance patient coping skills. We have combined a number of key approaches used in healthcare social work counseling into a model that we refer to as the *Theoretical Framework for Transitions in Health Counseling.* This framework emphasizes the role that healthcare social workers play in assisting patients and families negotiate transitions—life stage transitions, transitions through stages of behavioral change, transitions across the continuum of care, transitions from healthcare crisis to resolution, and transitions that integrate the concept of a chronic illness or health condition into a newly evolved sense of self and lifestyle. The use of the word "transitions" further denotes the universal nature of changing health status over the course of one's lifetime. All of us, if fortunate to live long enough, will be faced, at some point in our lives, with a serious illness or disability requiring us to make some kind of transition.

The theoretical framework is an integrative approach embracing aspects of systems theory (ecological model and family systems theory); human development theory (individual and family life cycle development, grief theory, and crisis theory); cognitive behavioral interventions (cognitive behavioral, problem-solving, motivational interviewing, narrative, and existential therapies), and contemporary, integrative approaches. We have found that a clinical approach incorporating basic elements from each of these theories facilitates patients' and families' decision making by enhancing their ability to make sense and meaning of serious health circumstances. An overview of basic concepts in these theories follows.

Systems-Based Theories

Systems transcend our lives. Social workers are employed in healthcare systems, the families that we work with are systems, and the ecological model that frames our practice is a representation of a person-in-environment system. A **system** is a set of related or interrelated elements or units that function together as a whole in order to achieve a purpose (Friedman & Allen, 2011; Kirst-Ashman & Hull, 2009). Our designation of client systems by size (e.g., micro, mezzo, and macro) is drawn from systems theory. Examples of units or elements in a system include departments in healthcare systems or the individuals in a family system. The primary purpose of a healthcare system is to offer services that help individuals to maintain health. One primary purpose of a family is to care for and socialize children. Each of the units in a system contributes in some manner toward achieving its goals and purpose.

In social work, the approach to systems theory essentially evolves from the work of Ludwig von Bertalanffy (1968) and Uri Bronfenbrenner (1969), who were interested in how individuals interact with social systems. **Systems theory** recognizes individuals as subsystems of a larger system, which in turn, are subsystems of still larger systems. Bronfenbrenner (as cited by Friedman & Allen, 2011) used the metaphor of "nested" Russian dolls, one inside of another to describe the layer of social systems that surround and influence an individual. Systems, and the elements within them, are defined by *boundaries,* which von Bertalanffy described as the parameters and demarcations of a system or a unit that set it apart from other systems and units. Systems can be open or closed. An *open system* exchanges inputs and outputs with its environment, whereas a *closed system* is self-contained. The social systems in which social workers interact are open systems because interaction occurs between the system and its broader environment. One *input* of healthcare systems are the individuals with health conditions whom they receive from the community; the system *through-put or processes* are the services offered by the health system to affect the *output* of, hopefully, healthy patients back into the social environment (see *Figure 3.2*). Systems seek a state of *equilibrium* or **homeostasis** with their environment. This means the capacity to remain stable and balanced during and after change rather than being rigid, unchangeable, and not evolving (Friedman & Allen, 2011). Systems enhance their performance by modifying their practice based on continuously sought feedback from those providing and receiving care.

Because units in a system interact in some way to achieve a particular purpose, changing one aspect of a system can affect other units. When a patient comes to the hospital with a serious illness, the other members in his or her family system are also affected. Systems also interact with other systems in the environment. In addition to other individuals in the family being affected by an individual's illness, employers and co-workers can also be affected if an absence from work is prolonged.

Social workers conceptualize and interpret human development and behavior within the context of one's environment by using the biological, social, psychological, and spiritual perspective of the *ecological model* (i.e., the "person-in-environment" model) (Germain & Gitterman, 1996). In order to understand biopsychosocial-spiritual development, one must consider culture, history, and community and social forces. Germain (1991) viewed

Figure 3.2 Systems Model Example: Healthcare Provider

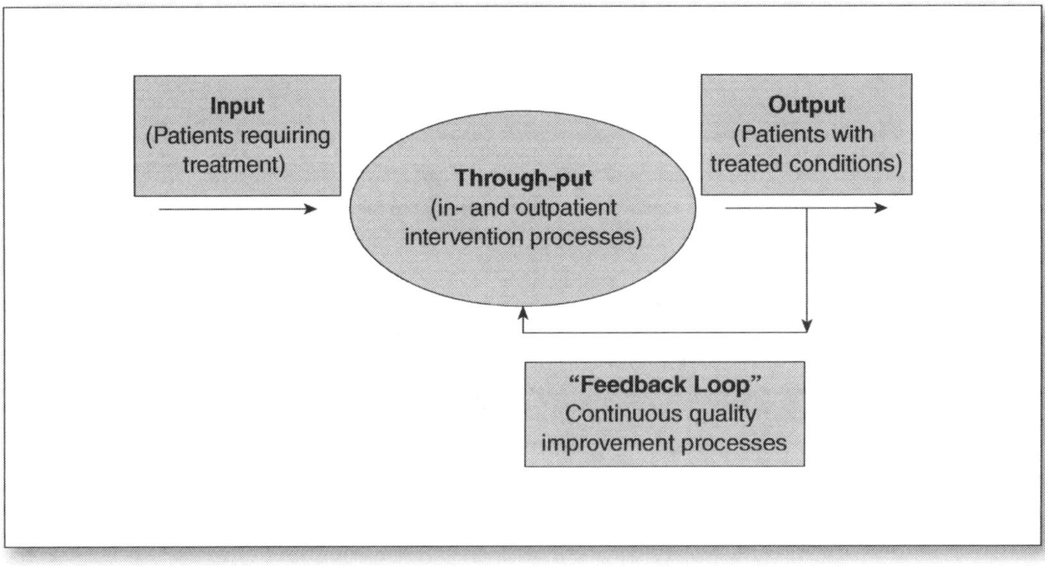

Source: Authors.

the relationships between individuals and their social environments as "reciprocal exchanges" and interactions that are cyclical in nature (p. 16). She identified adaptation, stress, coping, power, and human relatedness as key concepts within the ecological model. *Coping* describes the ability to problem-solve and modulate feelings, and *adaptation* occurs when an individual changes in order to respond to the environment or when the environment is changed so that it is more responsive to human needs (p. 17). While there is normally tension between the person and his or her environment when change and adaption are occurring, stress occurs when an individual's coping capacities are overwhelmed by new, unique, multiple, or large-scale events.

Recognition of **family systems theory** is essential to healthcare social workers. While not family therapists, social workers do employ key concepts and principles of family therapy to understand the patient and family. According to Bateson (1979), family systems theory acknowledges the mutual influence of family members on each other within the context of the broader social environment. We evaluate families with regard to how members communicate with one other, how individuals contribute to problems and problem-solving, the strengths and limitations of the family system, the organization and roles of the family, who has power, and whether the family is cohesive or not (Walsh, 2011). Bowen (1978) viewed family cohesion as a continuum, with disengagement and disinterest at one end of the continuum and enmeshment at the other. Knowing where a family falls on the continuum becomes valuable when involving family members in the care of the patient as unresolved issues can impact decision making and ultimately the patient's care.

Throughout the assessment and intervention process, it is crucial to maintain focus on the person within his or her environment. Social workers are trained to implement change strategies with individuals by recognizing their broader social environment, including their family, the health system where they are receiving care, and their neighborhood and larger community. The intent is to enhance the "goodness of fit" between a patient and his or her environment by working on both sides of the person-in-environment equation. To illustrate, when we engage with a patient who is experiencing depression as a result of a cancer diagnosis, we intervene by providing support, counseling, and education around the diagnosis of cancer and depression. We explore the patient's environment to determine if he or she is safe in the home, to assess the availability of family support, and to ensure that there is adequate food and income. If warranted, we arrange for community services such as a caregiver or Meals-on-Wheels. We assess whether the patient qualifies for additional benefits and facilitate applications to Social Security Disability, Medicare, and/or Medicare if warranted.

Social workers are sensitive to how changes and challenges in one part of a system affect other elements of that system. At the same time, we recognize the importance of limiting the scope of any intervention so that it is both manageable in its execution and appropriate in meeting patient needs. Typically, interventions are at the level of the patient within the context of his or her family system. In addition to affording counseling and education to patients, with patient consent, we make an effort to include family members in the treatment and to address their emotional needs as well. While appropriate and even necessary in many cases, this focus can prove daunting at times. For example, we would recognize a newborn and its mother as a single system or unit within a larger family system. In contrast, a healthcare system may recognize only the newborn as the patient and therefore the focus of care. In that scenario, and recognizing the importance of congruence in the approach of the delivered health services, focus shifts to the patient as recognized by the system. Interventions may be offered to the mother, but in ways that support her capacity to provide care to the infant. Ongoing psychotherapy, for example, would be outside the purview of offered services. Confidentiality and privacy concerns must be carefully considered, and social workers must act in accordance with HIPAA (Health Insurance Portability and Accountability Act) guidelines that prevent the sharing of information without patients' expressed permission.

Human Developmental Theories

Erik Erikson's life-cycle model of development is particularly crucial to healthcare social workers as they engage with individuals at all stages of the human life cycle, and a brief model overview therefore follows.

Erikson delineated a theory of human development in which specific stages of development are thought to constitute the life cycle of all individuals (Erikson, 1997). He suggested that each stage evolves as part of an overall and universal life cycle, which he called the *epigenetic principle*. Each stage involves a specific challenge, or developmental turning point, called an **epigenetic crisis**, which, if resolved successfully, results in the development of positive *ego strength* (Schriver, 2011). The challenge presented by each stage must be resolved successfully if healthy development is to continue. Successful resolution requires that the potential negative and positive outcomes of the development challenge of the stage (such as trust or mistrust) are resolved. This resolution results in the individual attaining a "psychosocial virtue," or desired ego strength. To illustrate, in the first stage during infancy, healthy individuals generally learn to trust their caregivers and to understand that their basic needs will be met. Eventually, they learn that there may be some times when needs are not immediately met, and so they learn to delay gratification. However, in some cases in which needs are rarely met, infants understandably fail to learn how to trust, which is essential for attachment, bonding, and the development of healthy relationships. As attachment theorists have shown, failing to develop healthy attachments and to bond during infancy can have lifelong consequences. (Ainsworth, 1979; Bowlby, 1982). Should a serious illness occur within the context of an individual's life cycle, it has the potential to impact the individual's ability to successfully move through that stage of development. Parents can also respond in ways that impede the progress of the child's psychological development, as often happens when parents overprotect a child with a serious illness or disability.

Interestingly, although the eight-stage life-cycle model is most commonly referenced, it was Erikson's wife Joan who returned to his work after his death and suggested a ninth stage of development in response to increased longevity and extended life span. This stage for the "old-old" or those in "elder adulthood" as we have called it, involves the challenge of withdrawing from the world and becoming preoccupied with loss and failing health. She viewed this stage as a synthesis of all of the other stages and "selfs" and felt that successful resolution involved a connection to or understanding of being a part of a greater whole. We have used the term "self-realization" to describe the positive resolution of this final stage; Tornstam (2005) called it **gerotranscendence**. This resolution is attained by maintaining supportive relationships sustained reflection, and introspection that ultimately helps an individual accept and prepare for death (Erikson, 1997). Tornstam believed that, in order for gerotranscendence to emerge, a contemplative process is necessary, which requires some withdrawal from the busy world but which also may be part of a natural aging process. We caution that withdrawal and isolation can also be indicators of depression and dementia and do not necessarily believe that social withdrawal is required for deep contemplation and successful resolution of this stage. While we find Erikson's life-cycle model useful, we recognize criticism that is predicated on a Eurocentric model of human development that may not necessarily reflect the experience of women and individuals in other cultures. We have integrated the work of the Erikson along with Tornstam's to create *Table 3.1*, which presents a nine-stage life-cycle development model. Note that we have refrained from inserting the typically indicated age marker for each of the stages to acknowledge wide variations in human development.

Table 3.1   Life Cycle Stages of Development

Stage	Epigenetic Crisis	Ego Strength
Age: Infancy Experiencing the trustworthiness and dependability of others	**Trust vs. Mistrust** Not being able to establish trust, necessary for forming relationships and a sense of security	Hope
Age: Toddlerhood Establishing self-control, understanding rules; learning right from wrong	**Autonomy vs. Shame** Excessive or lax parental control inhibits the development of an appropriate sense of autonomy	**Will**
Age: Early Childhood Development of a sense of responsibility and conscience, being able to connect with peers as part of a group	**Initiative vs. Guilt** Parental and authority figures' responses to trying new things and showing in can provoke guilt	Purpose
Age: Middle Childhood Demonstrating mastery, self-esteem, achievement; testing self and abilities	**Industry vs. Inferiority** Parental and peer responses can promote competition and/or sense of failure inhibiting self-esteem	Competence
Age: Adolescence Developing a personal sense of identity as well as learning expected social and gender norms and roles; testing social limits.	**Identity vs. Role Confusion** Not establishing a sense of self that is distinct but still connected to others (identity confusion or diffusion) or prematurely accepting identity (identity foreclosure)	Fidelity

(Continued)

Table 3.1   (Continued)

Stage	Epigenetic Crisis	Ego Strength
Age: Young Adulthood Developing intimate relationships, establishing a family and/or having children	**Intimacy vs. Isolation** Potential of losing oneself in a committed relationship or inability to form and maintain intimate relationships	Love
Age: Middle Adulthood Raising family, providing for them, leading a productive life, assisting others even beyond the immediate family	**Generativity vs. Stagnation** Risking or failing to risk personal investment and involvement in others outside the family, for example, over-involvement with career	Care
Age: Late Adulthood Reflection, life assessment, acceptance of the life one has lived	**Integrity vs. Despair** Loss of integrity as one ages, development of regrets, increasing isolation	Wisdom
Age: Elder adulthood Acceptance and synthesis of all stages of the self and life cycle into a unified construct; acceptance and preparation for death, including preparing loved ones for their impending loss	**Self-absorption vs. Self-realization** Preoccupation with loss of loved ones and of health; despair	Gerotranscendence

Source: Adapted from Erikson, J. M. (1997). *The life cycle completed: Extended version.* New York: Norton; Tornstam, L. (2005). *Gerotranscendence: A developmental theory of positive aging.* New York: Spring Publishing. Schriver, J. M. (2011). *Human behavior and the social environment: Shifting paradigms in essential knowledge for social work practice.* (5th ed.). Boston: Allyn & Bacon.

From a systems perspective, individual and family development co-evolve over the life cycle and across individuals and generations (McGoldrick, Carter, & Garcia-Preto, 2010). Relationships, roles, and tasks of individuals and their families change over time. Stress and tension often occur as individuals move through their developmental challenges or when people exit and enter families. Depending on circumstances, the life-cycle stages as well as life events of one individual may conflict with those of another. A health condition or challenge occurring in the context of an individual's life cycle may potentially affect his or her ability to successfully transition from one stage to another. That health challenge intersects and impacts the life cycle of the family as a unit as well as with the individual life cycles of each family member. For example, a woman in mid-life with breast cancer may also be faced with the developmental challenge of productivity in her career while supporting her adult children as they establish themselves in life may be further challenged if she is called on to be a primary caregiver for an aging parent. It is crucial then to explore how to address the needs of the patient while simultaneously recognizing the developmental needs of other individuals in the family.

Grief and Loss

The experiences of grief and loss are universally encountered by all human beings, and, as such, may be conceptualized as an inevitable developmental event occurring as we all traverse the life cycle. As an individual ages and transitions through life stages, he or she loses others, especially in the later stages of the life cycle. Grief, however, is not restricted to mourning the loss of a loved one. Individuals with serious illnesses, injuries, and disabilities grieve in ways that are similar to the grief that occurs after the loss of a loved one.

Rando (1993) described losses as both physical and psychosocial. *Physical losses* are tangible and include the loss of a loved one or home. *Psychosocial losses* are intangible and may not be as obvious, like the loss of health or functional abilities. Physical losses are more likely to be recognized by others, whereas less apparent psychosocial losses may fail to be acknowledged or appreciated. Furthermore, the timing of a loss within the context of the life cycle impacts how it is experienced by individuals and perceived by others. The loss of one's parents, as one example, is expected at some point during mid-life and therefore is viewed as a **normative loss.** The loss of one's children, in comparison, is perceived as occurring outside of the expected evolution of the life cycle and is therefore viewed as a **non-normative loss** and is understood as being more traumatic (Brunhofer, 2011).

Kubler-Ross (1975) identified the five stages of grieving as denial, bargaining, anger, depression, and acceptance. Individuals may not go through the stages in a strict sequence and often return to earlier stages. Although the Kubler-Ross model described the process of adjusting to terminal illness, it is also relevant to many other circumstances that provoke a grief response, including serious illness. Patients grieve the loss of their health as well as their identity as a "healthy" individual. They experience a loss of control, order, and predictability that they previously experienced in their lives. If the condition is fatal, they will grieve the loss of time and the experiences that they were anticipating. Individuals may be angry and feel that their body has betrayed them or let them down, and this anger is often displaced on loved ones and/or the healthcare team. Guilt may be experienced as it may bring into question whether or not, for example, having a diagnostic test earlier would have made a difference in one's health status. Similarly, when functional abilities are impaired to the point that individuals must leave their home and transition into living with family or supported living environments, feelings of grief regarding the loss of previous familiar contexts (home and community) develop.

Rando (1993) conceptualized grieving in three stages: avoidance, confrontation, and reestablishment. In the avoidance stage, individuals experience shock and disbelief in the face of loss. The confrontation phase often evokes intense and painful feelings such as despair as individuals begin to accept the reality of loss. Finally, in the reestablishment phase, individuals begin to reestablish their lives, returning to customary activities and interests. Both Kübler-Ross and Rando stressed that individuals rarely move through the stages of grief in a linear fashion but rather move in and out of stages throughout the grieving process.

For older individuals encountering multiple losses, grief can have a cumulative effect that results in prolonged depression. Furthermore, for some older adults, emotional "lability" (frequently shifting moods) associated with aging processes can increase feelings of confusion and anxiety that exacerbate grief and/or depression. There also can be an associative aspect to grief as individuals find themselves reminded of past losses while facing new losses. Rando (1993) explained that it is not uncommon for individuals to experience subsequent temporary upsurges of grief (STUGs) that can occur periodically, long after the loss has occurred. These "normal" demonstrations of grief potentially leave individuals with the sense that they lack control or are not moving on as expected. These perceptions unnecessarily complicate the grieving process.

In our culture, we have established rituals for grief when someone dies. However, we do not typically understand grief when it is associated with something other than death. Social workers help patients to recognize that grieving is a normal reaction to illness, which we understand as a potential loss of health, body integrity, and physical capacity. We help individuals interpret their feelings in the context of a grief process. We intervene if we observe that a normal grief process has become emotionally paralyzing to patients and is preventing them from enjoying the positive aspects of their lives. If grief becomes too prolonged or severe, we facilitate discussions between patients and their physician or psychiatrist to determine if treatment for depression is warranted. In particular, weight loss or gain, disrupted sleep patterns, excessive guilt for actions not taken, suicidal thoughts, and an impaired ability to carry out day-to-day functions can signal a shift from an expected grief reaction to serious depression.

Crisis Intervention

Social workers regularly intervene with individuals in crises. According to James (2008), a **crisis** is a "perception or experiencing of an event or situation as an intolerable difficulty that exceeds the person's current resources and coping mechanisms" (p. 3). While a crisis can present danger and the possibility of becoming emotionally overwhelmed, it also affords opportunities to grow and mature. James identified four types of crises: developmental crises, situational crises, existential crises, and ecosystemic crises (pp. 13–14). A **developmental crisis** occurs when an abnormal reaction occurs in response to events and transitions that are considered to be within the normal flow of the life cycle. A **situational crisis** describes an uncommon and extraordinary event that can be foreseen and prepared for by an individual. An **existential crisis** describes inner conflicts and anxieties around the issues of life's meaning and purpose. An **ecosystem crisis** describes a natural or human-caused disaster that overcomes an individual, group, or community. A serious healthcare crisis can be composed of developmental, situational, and existential crises.

Individuals respond to crises differently. Some individuals in crisis become immobilized or "frozen" in the sense of not being capable of adapting to the situation or coping with the emotions triggered by the event. Others remain mobile and flexible in their capacity to respond to the crisis. James (2008) presented a six-step model of crisis intervention (pp. 39–40):

1. **Define the problem.** This step involves developing an understanding of the crisis and the challenges that it presents from the patient's perspective.

2. **Ensure client safety.** It is essential to ensure the patient's emotional and physical safety by assessing and then responding to those conditions that could jeopardize the physical and psychological safety of the patient and others.

3. **Provide support.** It is fundamentally important that the patient perceive that he or she is valued and that care is available.

4. **Examine alternatives.** This step involves exploring situational supports and resources, coping mechanisms, and positive, constructive thinking patterns in order to identify a range of appropriate choices and options available to the patient.

5. **Make plans.** At this stage, concrete steps are taken to address the crisis. The goal is to resolve the crisis, to ensure continued support of the patient, and then to access and enhance coping mechanisms. Patient autonomy and self-determination are central considerations. Typically a short-term plan is established, while longer-term plans evolve from ongoing supportive interventions.

6. **Obtain commitment.** If all of the previous steps have been developed appropriately and patient self-determination has been respected, commitment to carry out the plan should follow. Whenever possible, it is important to follow-up with patients once they are discharged. The intent is to support them in implementing the plan and, if necessary, to help modify the plan if difficulties arise. If it is beyond the role of the clinician to provide follow-up or continued support to the patient, then a referral to a professional and/or agency that can provide this service should be included as part of the plan.

Social workers characteristically employ crisis intervention when individuals present in emergency departments following accidents or other traumatic events. These strategies, however, can be initiated when crises occur at any point during serious health events. Significantly, social workers have extended beyond "lay" patient populations and have utilized critical incident stress management to address crises experienced by healthcare and "first-responder" professionals contending with traumatic events (Spitzer, 2001; Spitzer & Neely, 1992; Spitzer & Burke, 1993).

Cognitive-Behavioral Approaches

Cognitive-behavioral interventions are often utilized by healthcare social workers dealing with individuals experiencing anxiety, depression, mood disorders, or other mental health conditions. Pioneered by Albert Ellis and Aaron Beck, these approaches prompt the patient to take an active role in collaborating and working with the therapist; involve education about the intervention and health concerns; use a Socratic method of questioning to explore underlying beliefs; are empirically based; and are time-limited but provide guidance regarding relapse prevention (Granvold, 2011). The interventions typically address cognitive distortions that influence behavioral choices. Patients who are faced with an uncertain health prognosis or diagnosis will often develop cognitive distortions such as catastrophizing, selectively abstracting and focusing on one piece of information, all-or-nothing thinking, and overgeneralizing. The social worker challenges these distortions by exploring the evidence for the patient's beliefs and pointing to where there is faulty, incomplete, or inconsistent information that does not support the patient's conclusions. With the social worker and patient working together, alternative reality-based cognitions are then developed.

Cormier, Nurius, and Osborn (2009, p. 348) described six steps in cognitive-behavioral treatment (CBT) that we have modified slightly for healthcare practice:

1. Provide a brief overview of CBT and how it will be employed with the patient

2. Identify client perceptions, beliefs, and feelings related to the healthcare concern

3. Select and challenge perceptions, distortions, and beliefs by exploring for evidence and exceptions

4. Explore alternative perceptions, cognitions, and conclusions

5. Work to internalize and reinforce modified perceptions, cognitions, and conclusions related to health

6. Provide homework and follow-up to promote behavioral change, such as improved decision making regarding healthcare and improved emotional adjustment

CASE STUDY

CBT Use With Mother of a Newborn

CBT might be employed with a mother of a toddler who experienced breathing problems due to prematurely developed lungs at birth. In this instance, because of the success of current treatments, the toddler is no longer at risk for serious breathing problems. The mother, however, continues to not sleep well, as has been the case since the child was born. She finds that whenever she falls asleep briefly, she wakes up and runs to the toddler's room to make sure that everything is okay. CBT is employed to help the mother examine her beliefs and the lack of evidence for sustaining them. The social worker focuses on changing her behavior on the basis of corrected and modified cognitions. As "homework," the mother is asked to track the frequency of her checking on the child during the night and then at a point is asked to wait thirty minutes longer before engaging in subsequent checks. The time frame could then be extended to an hour, two hours, etc. The lack of any negative event as a result of her changing her behavior is then used to reinforce the cognitions and beliefs that were unwarranted and prompted the initial problem behavior.

Self-management and **stress management** strategies are often used as part of CBT, especially to help reduce anxiety levels. Stress-management strategies often involve relaxation exercises such as deep breathing, creative visualization, and body relaxation. Gradual, controlled exposure to an anxiety-producing stimulus also can be employed. Self-management strategies include effective management of behaviors and feelings and are used to help patients to control impulsive behavior and to regulate and control emotions that are out of proportion to actual circumstances. **Scaling** describes the use of a 10-point scale by patients to describe and chart the severity of stress or anxiety before and after stress-management interventions (with 1 representing low severity and 10 representing extremely high severity). Homework provides the opportunity for the patient to monitor changes and maintain improvements over time.

Motivational interviewing is an effective evidence-based intervention that is used with patients who are experiencing mental health concerns. Motivational interviewing aids in restoring emotional balance by eliciting patients and family members to introduce change in their lives. This technique recognizes a "stages of change" approach (Prochaska, Norcross, & DiClemente, 1994) in which individuals cycle through a series of steps when making challenging behavioral changes, such as complying with a cardiac diet, exercising more, or maintaining sobriety. It is considered "**trans-theoretical**" because it can be integrated into a number of theoretical approaches for work with a variety of clients and problems. This model recognizes that many individuals will implement behavioral changes and maintain these changes for a period of time, but then will give up and "relapse" at some point. Maintaining a nonjudgmental perspective, the social worker helps the patient to explore the motivations and reasons for the changes and his or her relapse and then, if desired by the patient, facilitates the changes once again. The progressive stages of change in this model are

1. *Pre-contemplation*: Not fully acknowledging or accepting problem behavior

2. *Contemplation*: Beginning acknowledgement of problem behavior but without commitment yet to change

3. *Preparation*: Exploring possibilities for change; preparing to change

4. *Action/Willpower*: The point of changing the behavior

5. *Maintenance*: Sustaining behavioral change over time

In recognition of the difficulty of maintaining behavioral changes over time, some stages of change model recognize a sixth stage--relapse. The goal is to encourage individuals to begin the process of change again to resume positive behaviors. Motivational interviewing facilitates transitioning through the stages of behavioral change. Delivered in a brief intervention format, it can be effectively used in a range of contexts to move patients and their families to a place of wellness. Rollnick, Miller, and Butler (2008, p. 7) identified four guiding principles of motivational interviewing:

1. To resist the "righting reflex"

2. To understand and explore the patient's own motivations

3. To listen with empathy

4. To empower the patient, encouraging hope and optimism

The first principle addresses the tendency that many healthcare professionals have to "make things right." It actively discourages the interventionist from seeking to "fix" or persuade a patient to make a change based on the professional's perception that the patient's current path is the wrong one. This principle focuses the professional on listening to gauge where the individual wants to go with change. The second principle encourages the professional to determine the individual's reasons for change, whereas the third principle underscores the importance of active listening. The fourth principle is an expectation that the individual will be aided in exploring ways to change and how to change. It involves a "can-do" approach arising from a perspective that the individual *wants* to make constructive change. Motivational interviewing helps an individual address the ambivalence that often makes change difficult.

One application of this intervention occurs when a patient experiences depression following major surgery and becomes apprehensive of leaving the hospital to return home. The patient's ambivalence toward returning home is addressed, as are his or her efforts to contend with their depression and change in physical status. When patients are ambivalent about making a change or have been inconsistent with medical treatment compliance, motivational interviewing may prove useful in eliciting change by helping to identify why the patient wants to (or does not want to) change and how he or she can effectively initiate change.

Another approach that is useful when patients are experiencing health crises is **narrative therapy**. Narrative therapy is based on a belief that every individual makes sense out of life by creating a story or narrative in which events are linked together by themes, beliefs, and understandings. Through the construction of personal narratives, we make sense of our lives and the world around us. This approach honors and respects patients' perspectives by recognizing that there are many plausible interpretations of events and innumerable points of view that shape our experiences. Narrative therapy pioneers White and Epston (1990) put forth that the nature of our stories are either oppressive or inspiring. Oppressive stories are "problem saturated" and are focused on the inevitability of repetitious problems, whereas inspiring stories involve overcoming problems or finding meaning and purpose in problems that seem insurmountable.

White and Epston (1990) identify the following essential features of narrative therapy:

1. The person is never the problem; the problem is the problem.

2. The focus of the work is the story created; the story is the unit of experience.

3. People use stories as a filter which determines which information is focused on or ignored. Narrative therapy attempts to refocus the lens for the widened perspective necessary to reshape a person's life.

4. Identity and meaning are co-created with others.

5. Narrative therapy involves exploring the stories that have shaped a person's life and determining which stories have the most meaning. It involves building a new plot to connect life events in a way that enriches experiences and opportunities.

6. There are multiple stories, plots, characters, meanings, and metaphors in every person's life.

7. The social worker's role is to actively collaborate with patients in a respectful, non-judgmental partnership to create preferred stories and meanings.

For individuals in a serious health crisis, narrative therapy can be helpful for determining how an illness or other health condition fits into the context of one's life story. It is then used to explore choices about how we will live and act with the reality of our current health status. Pennebaker and Seagal (1999) found that spending as little as fifteen minutes a day writing a narrative about personal challenges can bring about improvements in mental and physical health and that these benefits have been found across age, gender, culture, social class, and personality types.

When patients experience a serious, perhaps life-threatening illness, they often ask deep philosophical questions about the meaning of life and death and the purpose of suffering. **Existential therapy** explores these questions and assists patients in finding their own answers. It holds that an individual's emotional and psychological distress reflects his or her inability to cope with the realities of existence. The focus is then to work with the patient so that he or she is able to be fully present in the here and now, to be authentic and true to themselves in every unfolding minute and choice (Krug, 1999).

A branch of existential therapy, **logo therapy**, is particularly useful in helping people cope with health crises (Frankl, 1959). Frankl was a professor of philosophy and psychiatry in Vienna when he was sent to a concentration camp by the Nazis during World War II. While there, he developed logo therapy as a psychotherapeutic approach focused on healing, wholeness, and finding will and purpose during challenging, difficult circumstances. The Greek word "logos" is interpreted to mean *will* or *meaning*. Frankl believed that every individual has a healthy core that includes a spiritual dimension with resources for healing and wholeness. Three basic assumptions are made: (1) life has meaning under all circumstances, (2) people have a will to make meaning, and (3) people have freedom under any condition to find and create meaning. Logo therapy involves accepting that we may not have choices about certain conditions in our life. We do, however, have the freedom and will to find purpose and meaning as we deal with these challenges.

CASE STUDY

"Logo Therapy" Intervention

Mr. R was a 78-year-old man entering the last stages of cancer. He had undergone multiple treatments and, while some experimental options remained available to him, he was considering stopping his treatment. His children loved him very much but were having difficulty supporting his decision. The social worker spent time with him reviewing his life and its important events. She learned that the patient had been married for 60 years, served in World War II, established a small business that provided for his family, and sent four children to college. He was a church deacon and, until recently, had volunteered at a local senior center.

(Continued)

(Continued)

In describing his life, Mr. R explained that he believed there was a "quiet dignity" in providing for his family and in serving his church and community. He accepted his cancer and said that he found comfort in his faith. In stopping treatment, he wanted his children to understand that he was not afraid of dying, and he did not want them to be afraid when their time came. Building on this important theme of dignity that was evident throughout his life, he wanted to die with dignity. He hoped that his children would understand that he was able to accept death because he had lived a good life based on service, faith, and commitment. The narrative of his life and its themes were clear to him. In a family meeting facilitated by the social worker, Mr. R asked his children to accept the meaning of his life as he had constructed it and hoped that they would find meaning in their own lives by doing so. The family came to appreciate this view, which helped them accept his decision to forego treatment. For them not to accept his decision would have compromised the fundamental message of Mr. R's life.

Integrative Approaches

Recently, the biopsychosocial framework has been expanded to more deliberately acknowledge spiritual dimensions of the human experience, and many social work educators now refer to the **biopsychosocial-spiritual** approach. Whereas in the past when the spiritual aspects of client's experiences might be thought to be the purview of the clergy and/or pastoral care, there is increased recognition of the importance of acknowledging this dimension of the human experiences from a values-neutral position with our clients (Canda & Furman, 2010). This more holistic model also bridges Western and Eastern philosophy by stressing wellness and "whole" personhood (Lee, Ng, Leung, & Chan, 2009). Spirituality, life values, culture, and personal meaning provide a foundation for the dynamic interplay between the mind and body and should be explored as part of the assessment process (Lee et al., 2009). *Figure 3.3* is a visual representation of the integrated self.

This integrative perspective fits well with the increased appreciation in healthcare systems of the patient as an active member of the healthcare team. Empowering patients and families to be decision-makers and informed consumers of healthcare services is an important perspective for healthcare social workers who are engaged in providing mental health services. While partnering in assessment and treatment is of fundamental importance, it may challenge traditional medical intervention models.

In the body-mind-spirit framework, key therapeutic tasks in the initial phase involve

1. Developing a collaborative therapeutic relationship

2. Understanding problems and assessing lethality

3. Accessing and appreciating client strengths

4. Expanding awareness and perspectives

5. Facilitating body-mind-spirit connections

6. Assessing the "person in their environment"

7. Accessing balance and dynamic flow and assessing goals

This ecological, life-model framework and its body-mind-spirit perspective can prove useful for social workers who are engaged with patients and families across a continuum of provider settings. Allen and Wozniak (2014, 2013, 2011, 2010) have integrated a holist approach to working with women traumatized by domestic violence. Allen and Wozniak determined that persistent post-traumatic symptoms could be reduced using art, music, poetry, journaling, and "body work" such as yoga and meditation in a group modality. For women who had participated in the group therapy, traditional forms of psychotherapy and counseling through domestic violence shelters had been used to help the women through the initial stages of recovery, such as leaving the abuser; finding housing; and dealing with legal, financial, and employment-related concerns. Later stages of healing identified by Wozniak and Allen include (1) reclamation of self and identity, (2) resumption of one's life trajectory, (3) the restoration of future hope, and (4) reconnection with the patient's community. Part of the healing process required exploring existential questions related to being victimized by an abuser and reestablishing the ability to trust and have hope, similar to the first stages of Erikson's model.

Figure 3.3   Mind-Body-Social–Spiritual Integrated Self

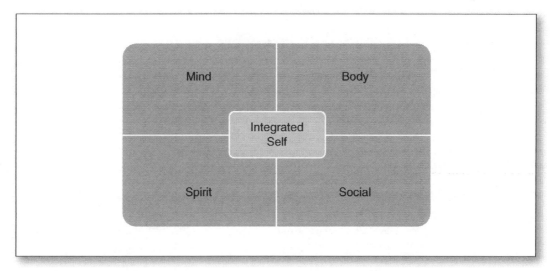

Source: Authors.

SUMMARY

This chapter examined the knowledge and theory foundations of healthcare social work practice. It identified the effects of the medical model historically used in patient care and noted the implications of the recent Patient Protection and Affordable Care Act of 2010. The importance of social work intervention was stressed in the context of assisting patients and families with their adjustment to medical conditions and the planning of ongoing care.

The theoretical framework for transitions in health counseling practice was presented as it is influenced by systems and human-development theories as well as cognitive-behavioral, crisis intervention, and integrative approaches to care. Emphasis was placed on considering the responses of patients and families to their health conditions and treatment as influenced by their environments and life experiences.

KEY TERMS AND CONCEPTS

- Health

- Wellness

- Disease

- Illness

- Disability

- Health status

- Medical Model

- Problem-oriented interventions

- Adjustment to illness counseling Boundaries

- System, systems theory

- Equilibrium, homeostasis

- Epigenetic crisis

- Motivational interviewing

- Stages of change; trans-theoretical model

- Narrative therapy

- Logo therapy

- Existential therapy

- Family systems theory

- Gerotranscendence

- Normative loss

- Non-normative loss

- Situational crises

- Biopsychosocial-spiritual

- Existential crisis

- Ecosystem crisis

- Situational crisis

- Self-management

- Stress management

QUESTIONS FOR DISCUSSION

1. What unique perspectives does a social worker bring to an integrated healthcare team? How can social workers document the contributions they make to improving health outcomes for individuals and families living with a mental health problem and a physical health condition?

2. How might you more actively include mind-body and spirit assessments in your work with individuals living with a health condition (e.g., cancer, heart disease) and a behavioral healthcare condition (e.g., anxiety, depression)? What evidence exists to support these assessment methods?

3. You are a health social worker working in an integrated healthcare clinic. You have been getting several referrals from the team to address the needs of caregivers dealing with family members living with bipolar disorders. You want to develop a group for these caregivers. What evidence-based approaches might be used to help you in developing a group intervention that can be delivered successfully in an integrated healthcare clinic? What steps would you take to search for evidence-based models and how might you adapt and evaluate these models in your setting?

4. How might you employ motivational interviewing or cognitive-behavioral approaches in your work with youth, adults, and families across healthcare settings?

   Additional website resources of interest for social workers delivering mental health services:

- Case Management Society of America: http://cmsa.org

- National Association of Social Workers: http:/www/naswdc.org

- National Council for Behavioral Health Care: http://www.thenationalcouncil.org

- Substance Abuse and Mental Health Services Administration (SAMHSA): http://www .samhsa.gov

- World Health Organization: http://www.who.int/en/

REFERENCES

Ainsworth, M. S. (1979). Infant-mother attachment. *American Psychologist, 34*(10). doi:10.1037/0003-066X.34.10.932

Allen, K., & Wozniak, D. (2010). The language of healing: Women's voices in healing and recovering from domestic violence. *Social Work in Mental Health, 9*(1), 37–55.

Allen, K., & Wozniak, D. (2014). The integration of healing rituals in group treatment for survivors of domestic violence. *Social Work in Mental Health, 12*(1), 52–68.

Americans with Disabilities Act. (1990). Retrieved from http://www.usdoj.gov/crt/ada/pubs/ada.htm#Anchor-Sec-11481

Anema, C., Johnson, M., Zeller, J. M., Fogg, L., & Zetterlund, J. (2009). Spiritual well-being in individuals with fibromyalgia syndrome: Relationships with symptom pattern variability, uncertainty, and pychosocial adaptation. *Research and Theory for Nursing Practice, (23)*1, 8–22.

Antonak, R. F., & Livneh, H. (1995). Psychosocial adaptation to disability and its investigation among persons with multiple sclerosis. *Social Science Medicine, 40*(8),1099–1108. Retrieved from http://www.sciencedirect.com/science/article/pii/027795369400167R/

Ardell, D. B. (1979). *High level wellness: An alternative to doctors, drugs and disease.* New York: Bantam Books.

Bateson, G. (1979). *Mind and nature: A necessary unity.* New York: Dutton.

Berry, L., & Mirabito, A. (2010). Innovative healthcare delivery. *Business Horizons, 53*(2), 157.

Bertalanffy, L. von. (1968). *General systems theory: Foundations, development, applications.* New York: Braziller.

Bloch, C. (April 2011). *Addressing behavioral health.* Retrieved from http://telemedicinenews.blogspot.com/2011/04/addressing-behavioral-health.html

Bowen, M. (1978). *Family therapy and clinical practice.* New York: James Aronson.

Bowlby, J. (1982). *Attachment.* New York: Basic Books.

Bronfenbrenner, U. (1969). *The ecology of human development: Experiments by nature and design.* Cambridge, MA: Harvard University Press.

Brunhofer, M. (2011). Loss and mourning: A life cycle perspective. In J. R. Brandell (Ed.). *Theories & practice in clinical social work* (2nd ed., pp. 665–664). Thousand Oaks, CA SAGE.

Canda, E., & Furman, D. (2010). *Spiritual diversity in social work practice.* New York: Oxford University Press.

Cormier, L. S., Nurius, P., & Osborn, C. J. (2009). *Interviewing and change strategies for helpers: Fundamental skills and cognitive behavioral interventions.* Belmont, CA: Brooks/Cole Cengage Learning.

Commerford, M. C., & Reznikoff, M. (1996). Relationship of religion and perceived social support to self-esteem and depression in nursing home residents. *The Journal of Psychology, Interdisciplinary and Applied, 130*(1), 35–50.

Crawford, J. D., & McIvor, G.P. (1985). Group psychotherapy: Benefits in multiple sclerosis. *Archives of Physical Medicine and Rehabilitation, 66*(12), 810–813.

Dunn, H. L. (1961). *High-level wellness.* Arlington, VA: Beatty Press.

Erikson, J. M. (1997). *The life cycle completed: Extended version.* New York: Norton.

Frankl, V. (1959). *Man's search for meaning.* Boston: Beacon Press.

Friedman, B. D., & Allen, K. N. (2011). Systems theory. In J. R. Brandell (Ed.). *Theory and practice in clinical social work* (2nd ed., pp. 3–20). Thousand Oaks, CA: SAGE.

Germain, C. B. (1991). *Human behavior in the social environment: An ecological view.* New York: Columbia University Press.

Germain, C. B., & Gitterman, A. (1996). *The life-model of social work practice: Advances in theory and practice.* New York: Columbia University Press.

Granvold, D. K. (2011). Cognitive-behavioral therapy with adults. In J. R. Brandell (Ed.). *Theory and practice in clinical social work* (2nd ed., pp. 179–212). Thousand Oaks, CA: SAGE.

Hine, C., Howell, H., & Yonkers, K. (2008). Integration of medical and psychological treatment within the primary health care setting. *Social Work in Health Care, 47*(2), 122.

James, R. K. (2008). *Crisis intervention strategies.* (6th ed.). Belmont, CA: ThomsonBrooks/Cole.

Jonas, S. (2000). *Talking about health and wellness with patients: Integrating health promotion and disease prevention into your practice*. New York: Springer Publishing Company.

Kaiser Family Foundation. (2013, April 23). *Focus on health care reform: Summary of the Affordable Care Act*. Retrieved from http://kaiserfamilyfoundation.files.wordpress.com/2011/04/8061-021 .pdf

Kirst-Ashman, K., & Hull, G. (2009). *Generalist social work practice*. Belmont, CA: Brooks/Cole, Cengage Learning.

Kroenke, K. (1996). Review and notes: A critique of the medical model. *Annals of Internal* Medicine, *24*, 7, 697.

Kübler-Ross, E. (1975). *Death: The final stage of growth*. Englewood Cliffs, NJ: Prentice Hall.

Krug, O.T. (1999). James Bugental and Irvin Yalom: Two masters of existential therapy cultivate presence in the therapeutic encounter. *Journal of Humanistic Psychology*. Advance online publication. doi:10.1177/0022167809334001

Lee, M.Y., Ng, S., Leung, P., & Chan, C. (2009). *Integrative body-mind-spirit social work: An empirically based approach to assessment and treatment*. New York: Oxford University Press.

Masakazu, N., Masatoshi, O., Masashi, U., Masami, A., Toshiharu, Y., Tetsuichiro, M., & Keiko, K. (2007). The influence of life stage on colorectal cancer patients. *Journal of Psychosocial Oncology, 25*(4), 71–87.

Merriam-Webster's Medical Dictionary. (2012). Retrieved from http://www2.merriam-webster.com/ cgi-bin/mwmedsamp/

McGoldrick, M. (1982). Ethnicity and family therapy: An overview. In M. McGoldrick, J. K. Pearce, & J. Giordano (Eds.). *Ethnicity and family therapy*. New York: Guilford Press.

McGoldrick, M., Carter, B., & Garcia-Preto., N. (Eds.). (2010). *The expanded life cycle: Individual, family and social perspectives*. (4th ed.). Needham Heights, MA: Allyn & Bacon.

Mizrahi, T., & Abramson, J. S. (2000). Collaboration between social workers and physicians: Perspectives on a shared case. *Social Work in Health Care, 31*(3), 1–24.

National Wellness Institute. (2007). *Six dimensions of wellness*. Retrieved from http://www.national wellness.org/?page = Six_Dimensions&hhSearchTerms = %22six + and + dimensions + and + we llness%22

McIvor, G. P., Riklan, M., and Reznikoff, M. (1984). Depression in multiple sclerosis as a function of length and severity of illness, age, remissions, and perceived social support. *Journal of Clinical Psychology, 40*:1028–1033.   doi:10.1002/1097-4679(198407)40:4 < 1028::AID-JCLP2270400427 > 3.0.CO;2-1

Northouse, L. L., Laten, D., & Reddy, P. (1995). Adjustment of women and their husbands to recurrent breast cancer. *Research in Nursing & Health, 15*(6), 515–524. doi:10.1002/nur.4770180607

Pennebaker, J. W., & Seagal, J. D. (1999). Forming a story: The health benefits of narrative. *Journal of Clinical Psychology, 55*(10), 1243–1254.

Prochaska, J. O., Norcross, J., & DiClemente, C. (1994). *Changing for good: A revolutionary six-stage program for overcoming bad habits and moving your life positively forward*. New York: Avon.

Rando, T. (1993). *Treatment of complicated mourning*. Champaign, IL: Research Press.

Rollnick, S., Miller, W. R., & Butler, C. (2008). *Motivational interviewing in health care: Helping patients change behavior*. New York: Guilford Press.

Schriver, J. M. (2011). *Human behavior and the social environment: Shifting paradigms in essential knowledge for social work practice*. (5th ed). Boston: Allyn & Bacon.

Soni, A. (2009). *The five most costly conditions, 1996 and 2005: Estimates for the U.S. civilian non-institutionalized population*. Statistical Brief #248. July 2009. Agency for Healthcare Research and Quality, Rockville, MD. Retrieved from http://meps.ahrq.gov/mepsweb/data_files/publications/ st248/stat248.shtml

Spitzer, W. (2001). Critical incident stress management. In Albert Roberts and Gil Greene (Eds.). *Social workers' desk reference*. New York: Oxford University Press.

Spitzer, W., & Burke, L. (1993). A critical stress debriefing program for hospital based healthcare personnel. *Health and Social Work, 18*(2), 149–156.

Spitzer, W., & Neely, K. (1992). Critical incident stress among emergency service personnel: The role of hospital-based social work in development of a statewide intervention system. *Social Work in Health Care, 18*(1), 39–58.

Tornstam, L. (2005). *Gerotranscendence: A developmental theory of positive aging*. New York: Springer Publishing Company.

Walsh, F. (2011). Family therapy: Systemic approaches to practice. In J. R. Brandell (Ed.), *Theory and practice in clinical social work* (pp. 153–178). Thousand Oaks, CA: SAGE.

White, D., & Epston, M. (1990). *Narrative means to therapeutic ends*. Adelaide, South Australia: Dulwhich Center.

World Health Organization. (1986, November). *Ottawa charter for health promotion*. Retrieved from http://www.who.int/hpr/NPH/docs/ottawa_charter_hp.pdf

World Health Organization. (2008). *The global burden of disease: 2004 update*. Retrieved from http://www.who.int/healthinfo/global_burden_disease/2004_report_update/en/index.html

World Health Organization. (2009). *Mental health: A state of well-being*. Retrieved from. http://www.who.int/features/factfiles/mental_health/en/

Wozniak, D., & Allen, K. (2011). Ritual and performance in domestic violence healing: From survivor to thriver through rites of passage. *Culture, Medicine and Psychiatry*. doi:10.1007/sl11013-011-9236-9

Wozniak, D., & Allen, K. (2013). *Surviving domestic violence*. Avon, MA: Adams Press.

CHAPTER 4

Healthcare Social Work Practice Skills and Competencies

Karen M. Allen and William J. Spitzer

INTRODUCTION

The specialized skills of a healthcare social worker are built on a foundation of knowledge and values that can be applied to a wide variety of psychosocial problems at the micro-, mezzo- and macro-system levels. This chapter identifies the characteristic roles and tasks associated with contemporary healthcare social work practice. Using a model initially formulated by Hepworth, Rooney, Rooney, Strom-Gottfried, and Larsen (2010), the primary elements of practice are presented, including patient high-risk screening, psychosocial evaluation, and subsequent intervention methodologies. Ethical considerations in patient care are introduced. Case management is noted as the predominant contemporary service-delivery model. The integration of behavioral and physical health is explained, and practice competencies are outlined.

DEFINITION OF HEALTHCARE SOCIAL WORK PRACTICE

Healthcare social work describes the activities, services, roles, and functions of a social worker who is employed at any point in the healthcare continuum (prevention, primary care, acute care, long-term care, and end-of-life care). Thus, the term describes a field of practice as well as a special configuration of knowledge, skills, abilities, and values that form the foundation for practice. Holosko (1994) underscored the unique and challenging nature of social work in healthcare by noting that it is different from other forms of social work practice in three profound ways: "it is more costly; its practitioners are held more accountable; and the likelihood of an intervention contributing directly to people either living or dying is implicit in each and every decision made" (p. 23). The National Association of Social Workers (NASW) (2011) identified the four primary functions of healthcare social work as

1. Encouraging behavior contributing to physical and emotional health, while preventing disease

2. Addressing psychosocial conditions that negatively impact on health and well-being

3. Intervening to ensure that patients receive necessary care and services required to improve and/or maintain health and quality of life as they transition through service levels

4. Helping individuals affected by health concerns to emotionally adjust and manage their condition in order to achieve maximum social functioning

Social work practice in healthcare encompasses all levels of social systems: micro, mezzo, and macro. At the macro level, social workers engage in formulating healthcare-related policies; develop, administer, and evaluate healthcare programs; assist in the educational preparation of social workers for health practice; and conduct research (Carlton, 1984). According to the U.S. Department of Labor, healthcare social workers "provide individuals, families, and groups with the psychosocial support needed to cope with chronic, acute, or terminal illnesses. Services include advising family care givers, providing patient education and counseling, and making **referrals** for other services. [Healthcare social workers] may also provide care and case management or interventions designed to promote health, prevent disease, and address barriers to access to healthcare" (United States Department of Labor, Bureau of Labor Statistics [BLS], 2013, p. 1).

The Department of Labor reported in 2013 that 141,830 healthcare social workers were employed in the United States (United States Department of Labor, 2013). The largest proportion of these social workers were practicing in general medicine and surgical hospitals (40,710), followed by home healthcare services (16,770), individual and family services (16,180), nursing care facilities (15,480) and outpatient care centers (8,650). The states with the highest employment levels of healthcare social workers were California (13,260), New York (11,150), Massachusetts (10,430), Texas (8,410), and Pennsylvania (8,040).

THE ROLES AND FUNCTIONS OF HEALTHCARE SOCIAL WORK PRACTICE

Healthcare or medical social work services were historically offered through hospital-based departments, which primarily focused on inpatient discharge planning. Over the past twenty years, however, there has been a dramatic shift away from hospital-based care to care provided in the home or community. Economic factors are one important force propelling this shift. Evolving medical technologies have contributed to making hospital-based care very costly but at the same time have enabled a greater array of procedures and services to be safely provided in settings outside of the hospital. Hospital-based care can also actually introduce patient risks. Medicare and other insurers have begun to implement financial penalties to providers for failing to reduce and/or eliminate negative or adverse consequences of care, such as hospital-acquired infections and falls.

Changes in population demographics are also impacting healthcare delivery and the nature of social work healthcare practice. The aging population and increased life expectancy of individuals living with chronic health conditions increase the potential number of patients needing medical care, particularly in-home and long-term care. Such increasing care needs prompt greater demand for providers, including social workers. At the same time, patient and family expectations for timely, unimpeded access to care and direct participation in medical decision making are changing the culture of medicine away from the traditional physician-dominated "medical model" to models that are more available, participatory, responsive, and inclusive (Williams & Torrens, 1993). Social work has evolved from its singular focus on discharge planning to one of fulfilling multiple, highly visible roles that span a continuum of service settings (Blumenfield & Rosenberg, 1988). The Patient Protection and Affordable Care Act (PPACA) in particular is prompting both opportunities and challenges in disease prevention, health promotion, the integration of behavioral and physical healthcare services, and new models of primary care, such as the patient-centered medical home (PCMH).

A general way to think about the competencies of social work in healthcare is by identifying four general domains, which include the ability to (1) provide *care* addressing the psychosocial needs of patients and families; (2) *collaborate* with other members of the healthcare team; (3) understand *complexity* in social and organic systems in the human body, healthcare system, families, and organizations; and then (4) negotiate the social, cultural, historical, and organizational *context* in which healthcare services are provided. Each of these domains is demonstrated consistently throughout the variety of roles performed by the social worker.

In demanding contemporary healthcare settings, however, it is crucial to appreciate that competent practice is predicated not only on sharpened clinical skills, but tact, timing, creativity, initiative, and, importantly, overall perspective. Perspective and context determine the manner in which skills, technologies, and processes are applied. Social workers must understand the mission, priorities, and values of the organizations in which they practice. In turn, they must recognize how those factors have been influenced by the larger, external healthcare provider environment in their communities. The mission and behavior of any healthcare provider such as a hospital is affected by federal and state regulations and statutes, the directives of any corporate "parent," the management style of administrators, facility policies and procedures, contractual stipulations with payers, its financial viability, and the social/cultural/economic dynamics of the community in which the provider resides.

To effectively plan and implement care, social workers must be knowledgeable about the continuum of service options that are available and acceptable to patients and families in specific communities. They must also be resourceful enough to construct an alternative "Plan B" when needed resources are not available. They must be able to efficiently coordinate care for patients as they move across that continuum, potentially utilizing services from multiple specialty providers at varying times and in differing locales. Importantly, social workers must recognize the organizational implications of their decision making. Care must be exercised in executing interventions that are ethical and therapeutically appropriate to patient needs but that also demonstrate recognition of the priorities and/or constraints that may prevail within the service-delivery system.

The following section lists and describes the essential roles common in healthcare social work. Social workers may find that they are charged with any or all of these roles, depending on the provider context (organizational/management expectations) and patient-care needs.

Care (Case) Coordinator/Manager

Beginning in the 1970s, escalating costs, emerging technologies, and an interest in coordinating care were catalysts for the evolution of **case management** (Raiff & Shore, 1993; Rubin, 1992; Henderson & Collard, 1992). Case management has now evolved into the predominant healthcare service-delivery model. It attempts to balance two potentially conflicting goals: optimizing patient-care outcomes and minimizing operating expenses. It may also be viewed as an effort to efficiently contend with burgeoning numbers of patients with complex needs and an increasing appreciation for the effects of social factors (including support and social networks) on patients' health conditions and their use of health services.

Social work case management is a "method of providing services in which a professional social worker assesses the needs of a client and family and when appropriate, arranges, coordinates, monitors, evaluates and advocates for a package of multiples services to meet the specific client's complex needs" (Kirst-Ashman & Hull, 2012, p. 548, citing NASW). As defined by the Case Management Society of America (CMSA), case management is " . . . a collaborative process of assessment, planning, facilitation, care coordination, evaluation and advocacy for options and services to meet an individual's and family's comprehensive health needs through communication and available resources to promote quality cast effective outcomes" (CMSA, 2010, p.8). The following are guiding principles for case management practice:

- use a client-centric, collaborative partnership approach;

- whenever possible, facilitate self-determination and self-care through the tenets of advocacy, shared decision making, and education;

- use a comprehensive, holistic approach;

- practice cultural competence with awareness and respect for diversity;

- promote the use of evidence-based care, as available;

- promote optimal client safety;

- promote the integration of behavioral change science and principles;

- link with community resources;

- assist with navigating the healthcare system to achieve successful care;

- pursue professional excellence and maintain competence in practice;

- promote quality outcomes and measurement of outcomes; and

- support and maintain compliance with federal, state, local, organizational, and certification rules and regulations.

Source: CMSA, 2010, pp. 9–10.

Case management is a core function of social workers in healthcare and will likely be even more critical as healthcare systems evolve in response to the PPACA. A similar term in use is **care coordination,** which has been defined as a "person centered, assessment-based, interdisciplinary approach to integrating healthcare and social support services in a cost-effective manner in which an individual's needs and preferences are assessed, a comprehensive care plan is developed and managed and monitored by an evidence-based process which typically involves a designated lead care coordinator" (The New York Academy of Medicine, n.d., p. 1). We use these terms interchangeably, although arguably, care coordination reflects a more contemporary and comprehensive approach. Case management and care coordination are used to develop a transitional care plan for the patient moving from one level of healthcare to another, which is the focus of Chapter 8 in this book.

Rose (1992) characterized case management as a system reform strategy that is necessary because of an absence of integrated, comprehensive, and client-centered care that fosters healthy, stable lives of patients and families. He further emphasized that "case management . . . belong(s) in the realm or domain of social work, but not because we simply declare this to be self-evidently true. Social work potentially can best construct and implement a client-driven, systems impact paradigm for case management practice. The stated values of human dignity and social justice, along with expressed commitments to clients' self-determination and a dual focus on individuals or families and on social contexts, grant social work the right to leadership in case management policy and practice" (pp. v–vi).

A central feature of case management is its client or "person-centered" emphasis in which social workers have an important role in ensuring that patients' rights to self-determination are respected and understood by the healthcare team. This often involves sensitizing members of the team, including the physician, to the cultural, religious, and ethnic values and beliefs influencing patient/family emotions and behaviors (Spitzer, 2005a). Social workers help patients contend with frequently complicated healthcare systems and help them to understand the different titles and roles of treatment team staff, the types of available care, and whether and how costs for care will be covered. Social workers also explain various options for care, work with the patient and team to determine the appropriate level care, investigate resources for care, and facilitate decision making on the part of the patient and other involved parties in advance of securing the needed services. In addition, the unique characteristics of the patient and family, including age, race, gender and sexual orientation, socioeconomic status, religion and belief system, are considered and reflected in the care planning. Often, social workers serve as a bridge between the patient and the healthcare team, helping to improve communication and understanding.

Regardless of practice setting or context, social workers engage in continuous *collaboration* with other service providers about their assessment of patient and family needs. Collaboration occurs when the principal service providers are in agreement with one another regarding a client's care and are working harmoniously rather than at cross-purposes (Goldstein, 1981; Moxley, 1989). This collaboration may occur internally (e.g., within teams) and externally (e.g., between agencies or providers). Collaborative relationships occur when participants are "being cooperative on common issues, recognizing and appreciating the critical relationship of interdependence to goal achievement, and establishing an explicit, mutually agreed-on partnership with well-identified outcomes as the driving force" (Stetler & Charns, 1995, p. 4).

Because of their community-based focus and ecological perspective, including the use of a "person-in-the-environment" model, social workers are often regarded as community-relations specialists. In this way, social workers often represent their agencies to the public. As *service brokers* arranging care, social workers must interact and negotiate with a myriad of practitioners and provider organizations to implement ongoing (post-hospitalization) care plans. This **boundary-spanning** role is increasingly valued by healthcare institutions striving to deliver safe and appropriate, but expedited, patient care in conjunction with various community service providers (Schwaber, 2002).

Case management may take different forms, including models developed to support chronically mentally ill patients who remain in the community or "in place." These situations require a long-term relationship between the social worker/case manager and patients, who are followed across time and across the service continuum. While this model is practiced in some healthcare systems, particularly in comprehensive managed care organizations (MCOs) in which most services are performed within the network, a more prevalent form of healthcare case management is **transitional care planning** or discharge planning. *Transitional care planning involves collaboration between the patient, family, and treatment team and any other key decision-makers so as to facilitate the patient's transition from one level of care to another or to move in and out of various types of care.* The goal of a transitional care plan is to ensure that necessary services are pre-arranged and in place so that the patient's health status can be maintained or improved. Both social work and nursing engage in transitional care planning, with many health systems deploying both professions as part of the patient-care team.

Regardless of provider or context, the underlying principles of case management are that care is individualized to meet the unique needs of patients, services are comprehensive, duplication of services is avoided, ineffective services are discontinued, patient autonomy is fostered, and continuity of care is ensured (Kirst-Ashman & Hull, 2012, pp. 548–549). The American Hospital Association standards for transitional care planning require (1) early identification of patients who may need post-hospitalization care; (2) indication of patient preferences for post-hospital care; (3) patient and family education; (4) patient and family assessment and counseling; (5) planning, development, and coordination of community resources needed to ensure continuity of care after discharge; and (6) post-discharge follow up to ensure services and plan outcome (Beder, 2006).

Orchestrating satisfactory ongoing care plans can be challenging when patient healthcare needs are complex, finances are limited, and/or availability of resources is of concern. Social workers who are responsible for developing and implementing transitional care plans consider patients' medical needs; physical, cognitive, and emotional functioning; and the resources and supports necessary for care. Members of the interdisciplinary treatment team individually and collectively contribute their assessments of patients' needs, strengths, and abilities. Functioning in a "broker" capacity, social workers connect patients and families to needed community resources and ensure that all necessary instructions and provisions for ongoing care are provided in advance of hospital discharge.

Counselor/Therapist

Once identified through pre-admission planning or high-risk screening upon admission, social workers meet with patients, families, and/or other significant parties and conduct a psychosocial assessment to determine present and potential care needs. Needed services may include *information and referral, crisis intervention, problem-oriented counseling, adjustment to illness counseling, education, transitional care planning and counseling, or various combinations therein.* One common need focuses on assisting patients and families with their psychological adjustment to their illnesses, injuries, and/or disabilities as well as with secondary adjustment issues frequently associated with treatment and/or hospitalization and the prospect of needing and arranging ongoing care. Family members or other involved parties may also warrant counseling related to their ability or willingness to assume new roles in providing care to dependent patients and/or contending with changes in the patient's persona and relationships as a result of his or her altered health status.

Patients experiencing changes in their health are often understandably overwhelmed by unanticipated and frequently painful circumstances that may be without precedence. The equilibrium of both the patient and family is disturbed. Anxiety surrounds the prognosis for recovery, fear of recurrence, and any debilitations that may detract from self-care, the ability to work, the need to maintain care for (or now be cared by) any dependents, and/or the maintenance of satisfactory personal relationships. At the same time, the patient and any significant others must contend with hospitalization and treatment, experiences that can also be unsettling because they include unfamiliar and often uncomfortable procedures, sophisticated and intimidating equipment, non-home-like institutional surroundings, and a seemingly endless multitude of practitioners whose roles may be unclear and anxiety-provoking.

Further exacerbating these circumstances, the patient, family, and other involved loved ones may experience significant and potentially long-term disruptions in personal schedules as a result of hospitalization and ongoing treatment. Patients may have their sleep disrupted by necessary procedures; uncomfortable and unfamiliar surroundings; the actions of other patients, staff, and visitors; the insertion or use of equipment (e.g., intravenous lines, braces, or masks); and/or the pain associated with a condition. Patients with employment may find additional stress from being detached from and unable to communicate about work. Being separated from loved ones, having limited visiting hours, and being confined to a bed or unit often contribute to stress beyond that associated with the medical condition itself. Those living at a distance from the patient may find the cost of travel, schedule conflicts, concurrent responsibilities, or other competing factors make visiting an unwell patient difficult. Invariably, stresses are introduced to both patient and loved ones when sought-after contact does not occur. Almost universally, concern exists with regard to the payment for both immediate and ongoing patient care. Stress rises as patients and caregivers are expected to assume new roles that they did not anticipate and/ or for which they lack experience. These factors can and often do negatively impact on one's sense of self-worth, self-confidence, and image (Bartlett, 1961; Shevlin, 1983).

To address some of these stresses, social workers often serve as educators in addition to counselors. Education can be offered on an individual level or in groups of people with similar health conditions or treatments (e.g., dialysis, transplant, or radiation treatment). The goal is to help patients understand their conditions and treatments as well as to provide support and to promote new coping skills for patients and other affected parties contending with health and lifestyle changes. A **psychoeducational group** is one that provides information, sometimes with a structured curriculum or outline of topics along with time to discuss feelings and concerns. Frequently, other members of the interprofessional team present information to the group as part of the educational process and the social worker helps the group process the information and their reactions to it.

Advocate

Advocacy has historically been a fundamental role of healthcare social work (Carlton, 1984; Dziegielewski, 1998; Holosko & Taylor, 1994; Schneider & Lester, 2001; Shevlin, 1983). This function similarly is a key component of case management. As noted by Raiff and Shore (1993), McGowen (1987) defined **advocacy** as "an activity designed to secure or enhance needed services, resources or entitlements" (p. 92), while Cohen, Nemec, Farkas, & Forbes (1988) regarded it as a process designed to address deficiencies that clients encounter "when choosing, accessing, or using service providers" (p. 12). Schneider & Lester (2001, pp. 59–64) summarized the key dimensions of advocacy as including

- Pleading or speaking on behalf of another

- Representing another

- Taking action

- Promoting change

- Accessing rights and benefits

- Serving as a partisan

- Demonstrating influence and political skills

- Securing social justice, empowering clients

- Identifying with clients

- A legal base

In the context of serving as advocates, healthcare social workers have increasingly been involved in the identification and resolution of biomedical ethical issues (Reamer, 1985) and "more so than social workers in any other professional setting" (Reamer, 2003, p.8). Farrar and O'Donnell (2003) noted that the range and complexity of these issues has grown with technological advancements that significantly impact quality of life, the increasing desire for individual self-determination in health decisions, and the growing fiscally-driven constraints affecting the availability and use of needed interventions (p. 71). Because they have been trained to understand social welfare systems, social workers advocate for patients by striving to maximize patients' receipt of any benefits and aid to which they are legitimately entitled (for an example of patient financial assistance, see Spitzer and Kuykendall, 1994). They help patients to articulate and document care preferences and facilitate patients and/or families in communicating these wishes such that they are accepted and acted upon by the healthcare team.

The delivery of healthcare elicits a multitude of ethical challenges to service providers, whether at the individual or organizational level. Because healthcare delivery exists in environments recoiling from escalating costs, Raiff and Shore (1993) noted that " . . . some settings have interpreted case management as synonymous with 'managed care' or 'cost containment,' as a program with a system-oriented, fiduciary focus, and as a macro-level intervention designed to alter the profile of community, region or state services" (p. 7). It is important to emphasize that advocacy for patients and families must occur with an aware-ness of operational limitations, policy directives, institutional missions, priorities, and legal constraints. As such, the compelling issue becomes the ethical application of sanctioned organizational policies and practices in a manner consistent with the best interests of patients and families.

Kane (1992) perceived principal ethical challenges to healthcare providers within three macro-categories: (1) advocacy vs. resource control, (2) autonomy vs. **beneficence**, and (3) justice (or fair decision making). In the first instance, social workers serve as "gate-keepers" to the provider system and have a responsibility to sensitively advocate for the needs of patients in the face of frequent limitations on available healthcare resources. Social workers also face the prospect of needing to reconcile the principle of autonomy (the right to be protected from unwanted force or interference) with the principles of benefi-cence or **nonmaleficence**—the moral obligation to do good and not do harm. For the social worker, the issue is one of determining the extent to which one defers to family preferences before questioning their competence, the potential negative impacts to other affected par-ties, and the benefits derived from influencing decision making on the basis of professional expertise, experience, and judgment. Justice is served when fair decisions are rendered about who will receive care, when benefits and services are appropriately allocated, and when patient-care decisions are made in an equitable manner.

Reflecting Rose's (1992) concerns about the justification for case management, social workers advocate at individual, organizational, and social (community) levels to correct perceived inequities in healthcare delivery systems. While advocating for ethically just treatment, social workers also utilize their familiarity with legal procedures and protections on behalf of patients and families. For example, an understanding of the criteria for appointing legal guardians for patients and familiarity with the processes to initiate such protection aids rapid, appropriate action when needed for incapacitated patients. Conversely, guardianship would not be sought for a patient who is competent as doing so would constitute a violation of the patient's rights. Within the context of case management,

Rose (1992) noted that "none of the value-based issues can be more significant than the commitment to clients' self-determination, autonomy or empowerment" (p. 2). From the initial needs assessment through goal determination and selection of prioritized services requisite for care, the patient right and ability to participate in decision making must be promoted and validated by staff (Rose, 1992, p. viii). Rosenberg and Katz (2004), Rosenberg (1994), and Simmons and Bixby (1989) put forth that, as social policy advocates, social workers ultimately have an ethical responsibility to link formal healthcare systems to community-based agencies in order to create healthier communities and increase the quality of life of its members by improving their social conditions.

Leader

Given the unique nature of their professional evolution, interpersonal skills, and balanced healthcare-delivery perspective, social workers are often thrust into formal and informal *leadership* roles benefitting patients, families, colleagues, and organizations alike. Abundant examples of such leadership exist in arenas extending from policy development, program management, consultation, practice education, and organizational development to patient/family advocacy and resource creation (Carlton, 1984; Rosenberg & Weissman, 1995; Spitzer, 2004; Wilson, 1980). Social workers' knowledge of psychosocial dynamics, sensitivity to ethical decision making, familiarity with community resources, understanding of operational systems issues, concern for patient/family rights, and recognition of the need for prudent resource utilization contributes to their participation in diverse roles and frequent leadership of crucial functions within and among provider organizations. Given this diversity of roles, Rosenberg and Katz (2004) noted the need for the effective social work leader to possess vision, ethical reasoning, a calculated risk-taking ability, strong interpersonal skills (including competence in mediation, negotiating, collaboration, and participatory management), knowledge of business administration/design, and the capacity to effectively address the conflict between the social-action agenda of social work and the organizational and structural needs of the organization employing social work.

Researcher and Evaluator

Increasing disparities in health and healthcare delivery are a prompt for social workers to participate in *research and outreach activities* focusing on underserved groups. When unmet needs are identified, social workers advocate for, often design, and then lead new programs and services that address these gaps. By engaging in **continuous quality improvement (CQI)** efforts that evaluate the effectiveness of their own practice, social workers contribute to enhanced outcomes for patients and service-delivery systems. At the hospital provider level, CQI analyses generally focus on admission rates, providers, and delivered services; the appropriateness of inpatient admission and LOS; and the frequency of providing certain diagnostic and other therapeutic procedures (Williams & Torrens, 1993). For social work, CQI studies typically focus on, but are not limited to, the rapidity with which patient contact was initiated and pertinent problems identified, the degree to which established patient goals were accomplished, intervening variables that deterred discharge and/or contributed to readmission, the extent of delayed discharges and readmissions, and specific patient service complaints. These analyses may lead to subsequent research into mechanisms that promote patient recovery, reduce obstacles to service delivery, and enhance patient/family satisfaction with care. This process may entail examination of internal provider processes for delivering care and submission of proposals for new, expanded, or otherwise revised services.

The elements or characteristics of a healthcare social worker's role will inevitably vary by the employing organization's mission, priorities, and perspective of the social work contribution. The latter variable amounts to the perceived worth of the service and is largely determined by historical and current performance. Competence is viewed in terms of making timely and substantial contributions that achieve meaningful goals both for patients and for the provider organization. Collegial, results-oriented leadership styles and constructive, collaborative staff personnel positively influence organizational perceptions. With regard to role delineation, Levin and Herbert (1995) noted there are not clear guidelines about what constitutes the tasks of healthcare social workers at the MSW and BSW levels. Generally speaking, if both levels exist in an employing provider organization, the MSW more likely will be engaged in service areas with complex cases involving more extensive counseling and/or resource negotiation (e.g., transplantation, burn units, critical care, emergency departments, or pediatrics), whereas BSW assignments in areas such as general medicine or surgery will tend to focus on the identification and provision of "*concrete services*" such as transportation, housing, and/or financial arrangements. In some systems, medical and psychiatric social work services are separate, and MSWs provide mental health services to patients.

A position description for a master's level healthcare social worker at a large, tertiary, acute-care hospital is presented at the end of the book (see *Appendix A*). It notes the principal objectives of the position, clinical activities of patient care, the manner in which interdisciplinary collaboration occurs, expectation and avenues for the social worker to enhance his or her own professional development, mechanisms for accountability in the position, and those decisions/actions that are characteristically initiated without prior approval.

THE HELPING PROCESS APPLIED
TO HEALTHCARE SOCIAL WORK PRACTICE

The helping process is initiated once a determination is made to open a patient case. The three-phase model of the helping process described by Hepworth et al. (2010, pp. 34–41) can be modified to serve as a general framework for healthcare social workers. For example, as the numbers of patients in healthcare systems typically exceed the capacity of social work resources, initial identification of patients potentially benefitting from services becomes an ever-more-important activity. We have therefore added this step to the helping model (*Table 4.1*).

Care planning does not necessarily occur in a strictly linear manner as patients' health conditions may intermittently change, the timing of certain medical procedures may be altered, key decision-makers (e.g., family members, guardians, healthcare team members) may or may not be available or agree with one another, and required resources may not be available. These factors often compel social workers to reevaluate the needs of patients and the adequacy of their plans. The phases of the helping process and essential tasks for patients and social workers are introduced below and then are described more fully along with applications and considerations for healthcare social workers.

Table 4.1 Helping Process Phases

Phase I Identification, engagement, assessment, and care planning	Phase II Implementation and goal attainment	Phase III Evaluation and termination
• Establish rapport and relationship • "Start where the patient is" • Determine roles and who will be involved in helping process • Identify problem(s) and needs • Identify patient and family strengths • Evaluate patient commitment to problem solving • Consider patient attitude, including sociocultural variables • Explore problems in the ecological context • Formulate multidimensional (biopsychosocial-spiritual) assessments • Consult with healthcare team members • Develop plan • Establish initial goals and agreement to collaborate on plan	• Refine/clarify goals • Prioritize tasks • Select strategies and interventions • Plan task implementation • Identify community service providers for needed follow-up care • Assess resources for care; initiate referrals • Monitor progress on plan implementation • Identify and address barriers • Modify plan and interventions as warranted	• Reassess patient needs and capacities prior to discharge • Assure needs are addressed • Reinforce patient strengths, positive learning, and problem-solving capacity • Complete implementation of plan or revise • Initiate additional referrals to community resources for follow-up care as needed • Terminate with patient • As warranted/feasible, follow up to assess for unmet and/or new needs or concerns

Source: Authors.

Phase I. Identification, Engagement, Assessment, and Care Planning

Initial Patient Need Identification and Prioritization

When patients are hospitalized in an acute-care setting, transitional care planning is initiated at the first opportunity to ensure that suitable plans are expediently developed for post-hospitalization care and recovery. A multitude of factors drive such behavior. Efforts are made to reduce unwarranted provision of expensive services, including days of hospitalization, use of expensive equipment, and deployment of specialized personnel. Not only is the effort made to avoid having the patient incur unnecessary costs, but unneeded utilization of resources may prohibit their accessibility when needed in legitimate patient-care circumstances. Furthermore, there is recognition of the psychological and practical implications to all involved parties of extended care. If hospitalization is anticipated and scheduled in advance, the initial stages of such planning may actually commence in the physician's office or clinic *prior to* admission (referred to as **pre-admission planning**). The intent is to address any identifiable issues that would serve to delay an otherwise appropriate discharge. Once the patient has been hospitalized, and if not already identified through any pre-admission planning, the first step in initiating services is a screening to prioritize which patients require attention. Assessment of outpatients begins at the first physician's office or clinic contact, at which time inquiries are made about health condition and actual/potential needs in relation to available resources (financial, potential caretakers, transportation, etc.). The focus in this instance is to address any factors that would disrupt ongoing clinic appointments or compliance with medical regimens.

In many institutions, the number of patients potentially needing services exceeds the capacity of social work staff resources. Therefore, a **high-risk screening** is characteristically initiated to help the social worker determine which patients are most in need of services. A broad range of options for high-risk screening exist, from a shared, computer-based patient screening form that automatically triggers electronic referrals to specified disciplines including social work (Boutin-Foster et al., 2005; Spitzer, 1997) (see *Appendix B*) to participation in rounds, care conferences, and/or other unit and service meetings in which patient conditions and needs are revealed and intervention plans formulated. *High-risk screening is crucial as it is essentially the work of prioritizing all subsequent work.* In some organizations, social workers may initiate their own screening process and independently determine who they contact and in what prioritized order (Spitzer, 1997). In this *open referral* scenario, the social worker additionally responds to physicians' requests or orders to provide services. In contrast, in other organizations, social workers may need a physician's order or a request from some other member of the team (such as the nurse manager) to consult with patients. This is referred to as a **closed referral** system.

A **high-risk screen** identifies certain patient characteristics or circumstances that potentially place the patient at risk of poor health outcomes or of encountering problems either prior to or subsequent to inpatient discharge. While single factors may be sufficient to trigger initial social work contact, more often than not, multiple, interwoven issues or problems exist and support the need for sustained intervention. The concern is that if a patient's adjustment to his or her health condition and hospitalization is tenuous, treatment consequently may become unnecessarily extended, the discharge delayed in the absence of a viable post-hospitalization care plan, and, absent patient/family cooperation and sufficient ongoing care resources, the patient ultimately may be vulnerable to re-hospitalization. In addition to a patient's lack of understanding of, and adjustment to, his or her health condition and treatment, other examples of potentially high-risk, problematic circumstances likely to trigger special attention upon admission include

- New, concurrent and/or significant medical diagnoses

- Recurrences of previous health conditions

- Multiple hospitalizations within six months

- Readmission within thirty days of last hospitalization

- Marked changes in patient's cognitive and/or functional status

- Patient has no known prior address or is homeless

- Patient over 75 or under 18 years of age

- Non-English-speaking; otherwise unable or unwilling to communicate

- Family, caregiver system, and/or other significant decision-makers unavailable or non-existent

- Potential discharge target (e.g., own/relative home or formal placement such as assisted living or nursing facility) unavailable or non-existent

- Citizenship or guardianship issues (including legal competency)

- Adult or child protective service intervention warranted

- Potential or actual financial concerns (lack of or limited insurance)

- Necessary resources such as transportation unavailable

- Patient is at actual/potential risk to self and/or others

- Patient refuses treatment for significant condition

- Patient has history of engaging in substance abuse

Source: Spitzer, W. (1997) Psychosocial high-risk screening: Enhancing patient care through rapid social work engagement. *Continuum: An Interdisciplinary Journal on Continuity of Care, 17*(1), 1,3–9.

Although there is no nationally agreed-upon best-practice model for high-risk screening, Medicare guidelines note that at least three general dimensions of the patient should be assessed. These dimensions are the patient's functional status, which includes his or her capacity for self-care and mobility, level of cognitive functioning, and extent of family support (Center for Medicare Advocacy, n.d.). Holland, Harris, Leibson, Pankratz, and Krichbaum (2006) noted that, of Medicare recipients readmitted for hospitalization within thirty days after discharge, 64% had not received discharge-planning services or arrangements for continued care. They concluded that the majority of these readmissions could have been prevented with proper transitional-care planning. They developed a high-risk screening process that involved an evaluation of patient age, walking limitations, living arrangements, and disabilities upon admission and then reassessed these factors along with self-perceived health status, caregiver ability, number and severity of comorbid conditions, and depression later during the admissions process.

Whatever the screening process, social workers typically engage other members of the team in identifying patients with actual or potential needs for assistance with their current and ongoing (post-discharge) care. It is crucial that team members understand the reasons why a patient is identified as being at high psychosocial risk, the implications to treatment and discharge of such patients, the use of screening processes in place, and the importance of engaging social work services in a timely (i.e., early) manner. Such insight can prove invaluable to other professionals as they render treatment and seek patient/family compliance in formulating post-hospitalization care plans. Given these dynamics, it is understandable that social work CQI analyses of patient screening typically concentrate on accurate, rapid identification rates of at-risk patients and any impacts on the appropriate, but expedited, discharge of these hospitalized patients.

Engagement

In this phase, the social worker engages with the patient to identify problems and goals that will become the focus of intervention. The patient and social worker also determine other individuals who will or may potentially need to be included in the intervention process. To do this, the social worker consciously works to develop a constructive, positive relationship with the patient (as well as the family and any other significantly involved decision-makers). In many healthcare settings, however, shortened lengths of hospital stay **(LOS)** and limited outpatient contact typically result in social workers having very limited time to build the rapport essential for such relationships. Unfortunately, patient contact may be as little as one session that is measured in minutes, not hours. To work within these constraints, social workers must maintain a dual focus on relationship-building while concurrently managing the case, completing the assessment, and developing and implementing the intervention plan (Kanter, 1989; Morrow-Howell, 1992).

Essential to patient rapport and relationship is the need to empathically convey concern for the patient while maintaining a non-judgmental attitude (Hepworth et al., 2010; Kanter, 1989; Morrow-Howell, 1992). The high levels of stress and emotional discomfort experienced by patients, however, also serves to facilitate development of the patient–social worker relationship. *For the relationship to develop quickly, patients must have confidence in the social worker's professional competency, emotional capacity, and technological knowledge to help them negotiate their health and healthcare circumstance.* By reviewing the patient medical record, consulting with the physician and other involved staff (e.g., nurses, physical and occupational therapists, dieticians, respiratory therapists, clergy, etc.) and doing any research indicated prior to meeting with the patient, the social worker can more readily demonstrate his or her familiarity with the patient's circumstances. A sensitive, understanding, and consoling approach to the patient, coupled with possession of factual knowledge regarding the patient's situation, effectively conveys an aura of professional competency and preparedness. Concrete assistance in the form of offering to initiate telephone calls, obtaining needed information, and guiding the patient in organizing his or her questions for the physician can further cultivate the constructive, positive relationship needed for decision-making.

Assessment

Assessment is the process by which the professional(s) and the client cooperate in the collection, analysis, prioritization, and synthesis of information concerning the needs of the client (Hepworth & Larsen, 1982). The assessment further legitimates a particular course of helping designed to ameliorate identified problems (Kisthardt & Rapp, 1992;

Wilson, 1980). Dating from its catalytic role in the inception of the original social work service in hospitals, the psychosocial assessment (or evaluation) remains a critical tool used to understand patients and plan for their care. In describing the key attributes of assessment in the context of case management, Moxley (1989, pp. 27–32) noted that assessment is (1) client need-based; (2) holistic and comprehensive; (3) interdisciplinary; (4) participatory; (5) a dynamic, changing process; 6) systematic; and (7) a written document that analyzes the type, nature, and extent of client needs with a statement about the related factors that support or hinder the fulfillment of client needs.

Given the historic tendency among human service professionals to be preoccupied with pathology or dysfunction of clients (Moxley, 1989; Spitzer, 2005b; Weick, 2005; Weick, Rapp, Sullivan, Patrick, & Kishardt, 1989), Moxley (1989, p. 26) made the point that "assessment is a positive concept that recognizes the client's limitations while seeking to identify the strengths of the situation that can lead to client growth and development." This view is congruent with Weick's (2005) and Saleebey's (2002) recognition of social work's continuing development of the "**strengths perspective,**" a practice approach that builds on patients' strengths (talents, knowledge, capacities, resources) as they work toward an enhanced quality of life. Kisthardt and Rapp (1992, p. 113) emphasized that "in the strengths perspective, reluctance and a modicum of suspicion on the part of the consumer are not understood as symptoms of paranoia. These responses are expected as a normal reaction to an uncertain and somewhat invasive interpersonal situation." The responsibility of the social worker is to establish a nonthreatening, supportive context in which the patient can disclose information and constructively participate in decision making.

In some situations, individual patients may be unable to fully participate in the assessment or planning process because of physical and/or cognitive impairments. Dependent on their availability, familiarity with the patient, legal competence and relevance to the circumstances, family members or other parties may be encouraged to participate in assessment, planning, and implementation activities. Caution is exercised, however, in guarding against reliance on secondary information from those who may have limited understanding or history of the patient's problems and/or harbor outright conflicts of interest. Such conflict can occur, for example, when challenges arise during the discharge process regarding the estates of incapacitated patients, the discharge target, or who will provide ongoing care.

There are two prevalent types of psychosocial assessment. A **problem-oriented assessment** focuses on immediate problems that directly affect patients' health and well-being. Although the assessment is limited in scope to variables and conditions that intersect with a problem, the social worker still assesses the problem by identifying the fundamental biopsychosocial conditions that impact it. Intervention plans then directly address the problem and its related concerns. The number of admitted hospital or clinic patients and/or limitations on available time generally necessitate case prioritization. In these instances, social workers focus on those problems with the actual or potentially greatest impact on the patient and his or her care. This impact may be partially reflected in how the patient (and family) is psychologically responding to the patient's health condition and its treatment. It may also suggest that resolution of an issue is sufficiently complex as to require considerable time and, in turn, constitutes a potential risk to a timely discharge. Examples of such problems include the need to secure nursing home or assisted-living care following hospital discharge; obtain Medicaid or initiate a claim for Social Security Disability; arrange for home healthcare, rehabilitation services, or other ongoing assistance; investigate patients with unknown identities; and locate family members or other decision-makers regarded as crucial to complete the actual hospital discharge and/or participate in the patient's ongoing, post-hospitalization care. Circumstances can be confounded with other issues, such as when the patient is unable or unwilling to communicate and/or has cognitive limitations, lives in an area where needed healthcare resources are scarce, has no or limited financial or familial assistance, or lives in a setting in which suspected abuse, neglect, or exploitation may be an issue.

The **biopsychosocial assessment** represents a more detailed, in-depth evaluation of the patient, including his or her social history. It is used to increase the healthcare team's awareness and understanding of complicated, high-risk problems that impact the patient's care and health status. While potentially useful in any medical or surgical service area, these assessments are more often a characteristic service component in specialty areas such as organ transplantation. Because of their intensity, these assessments take longer to complete. Key elements of patient biopsychosocial assessments include:

- Demographic information (age, sex, race, address, marital status, telephone numbers)
- Religious affiliation, if any
- Mobility status
- Functional status (degree of mobility, activities of daily living, transportation)
- Mental and cognitive status, particularly whether the patient is capable of making his or her own decisions and directing plans for transitional care
- Current/historical substance (alcohol, drug and tobacco) use
- Social history, including:
    - Significant developmental history
    - Family health history
    - Educational and employment history
    - History of personal abuse, neglect, and/or financial exploitation
    - Presence of mental illness (current and/or past)
- Current emotional state (calm, agitated, detached, depressed, etc.)
- Current risk factors for abuse, neglect, and/or financial exploitation
- Social support system profile, including membership and degree of available support
- Living arrangements, current adequacy, and potential need for accommodation
- Financial resources, employment status
- Insurance for healthcare. If inadequate, does patient qualify for Medicaid?

- Educational literacy. Extent to which patient understands medical information

- Cultural considerations related to healthcare beliefs, values, and practices

- Understanding/perception of presenting health problem(s) and care implications

- Goals of treatment and discharge; needed steps/resources to achieve these goals

- Strengths and barriers in achieving goals

The social worker may directly assess each of these areas, but collaboration with other team members and involved parties is always recommended to obtain information producing a truly comprehensive assessment. An occupational therapist, for example, will contribute an assessment and report on a patient's willingness and ability to perform **activities of daily living (ADLs)**, which include bathing, toileting, dressing, cleaning, and meal preparation. If long-term impairments exist, the social worker can contribute additional information as to how the patient managed these problems in the home prior to his or her current circumstance and evaluate factors in the current home that would either contribute or deter the patient from satisfactorily performing ADLs.

Genograms represent another useful tool for guiding patient assessments. They depict the patient's family tree, describing relationships between individuals and generations. In recording family health histories, data are characteristically obtained for a minimum of three generations (McGoldrick and Gerson, 1985). Data gathered can aid patients in visualizing patterns of health and behavior in family systems that provide insight into their personal behavior and conditions (Friedman & Allen, 2011). To adapt genograms for use in healthcare settings, it is useful to inquire about the cause of death for family members and the existence of any health, substance abuse, or mental health conditions. *Figure 4.1* presents a genogram of four generations in a family history, including select health issues.

Planning/Goal Development

The development of a service and support plan is a critical function of case management. Moxley (1989) regarded this function as a systematic process of identifying meaningful goals, developing activities, and services in response to these goals and ensuring that the delineated goals are linked to patient needs. With the patient's adjustment to his or her health condition and care is noted during the initial assessment process, the planning phase focus then becomes one of determining (1) the impacts on the patient's immediate and future health and quality of life and (2) establishing a viable action plan to address needs and concerns. Any problems need to be broken down into basic terms, which, once identified, establish the groundwork for the development of concrete goals and objectives (Dziegielewski, 1998, p. 107).

Establishing goals provides direction and structure for the social worker's intervention and permits the practitioner to determine if he or she has the skills or desire to work with the patient (Cormier & Cormier, 1991). The goals have to be clear, specific, measureable, and achievable. To maximize the likelihood that they will be accomplished, care plan goals should be mutually agreed upon by the patient (and/or family or other significant decision-maker) and the social worker. Companion objectives also need to be developed that serve to further quantify the goals. If patients are hospitalized and/or incapacitated, patient

Figure 4.1   Example—Family Genogram

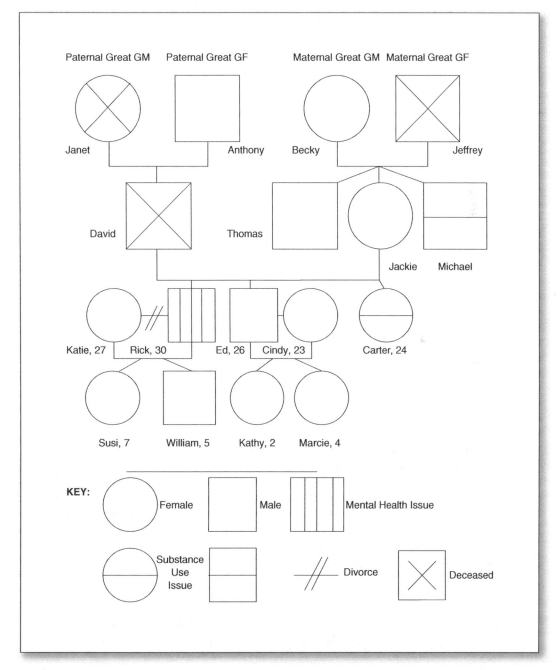

Source: Authors.

consent is obtained as feasible and family decision-makers are engaged. Informal and/or formal contracting processes may be used to guide care planning, which may include written contracts (Kerson, 1997).

Planning may be viewed as both a process and a product (Moxley, 1989). On one hand, planning is a series of purposeful activities leading to the development of a viable action plan for ongoing patient care. Planning also produces a physical document identifying the specific goals to be accomplished, the objectives of how the goals will be accomplished, a timetable for achievement, and notation of who will deliver which services, where, and at what point. Timing quickly becomes significant as every effort is made to ensure compliance with the specified hospital discharge date and time unless agreement is secured from the physician(s) and healthcare team members that the date can be adjusted. Timing becomes a further issue when multiple services must be engaged for post-hospitalization care. Each community provider is affected by his or her own protocols for accepting and responding to service referrals. Availability of necessary professionals and/or equipment may also prove a constraint that negatively impacts on a timely discharge. These factors make it necessary for social workers to maintain continuously updated familiarity with available community agency resources and to have established relationships with "vendor" liaison staffs who are prepared to answer questions and trigger agency-specific actions that make the discharge a "seamless process." Continuity of care is important as it contributes to patient safety, cost-containment, and the emotional tranquility of the patient and other involved parties.

As part of the planning process, some patient-care needs may fall outside the conventional scope of the healthcare social worker's role. The social worker will explore these with the patient and family or other decision-makers, particularly as they affect the patient's health and the patient's motivation to work on addressing the issue. Developing an understanding of patient concerns from the patient's point of view and accurately communicating them to the healthcare team is crucial. Because of differing professional perspectives, team members may have varying goals for the patient, and these may or not be shared with or understood by the patient. If an attempt is made to impose the goals without having secured patient and family concurrence, it likely will result in resistance during the planning stage and stymie successful implementation of any proposed plan.

Patients experiencing a serious illness, injury, or disability typically need more extensive follow-up care subsequent to hospital discharge. This care may range from outpatient rehabilitative therapy to skilled nursing home care or arrangements for home healthcare and transportation to clinic and/or lab appointments. Terminally ill patients may benefit from palliative care. Planning for follow-up care requires involvement of all pertinent disciplines to ensure that post-hospitalization care plans are complete and understood, including the specific roles that family members may play in providing any care. An assessment of finances, including insurance, is also required to establish which specific options for care may be affordable.

Importantly, if the patient is without insurance and/or sufficient individual funds, it is appropriate for the social worker to take the steps necessary to trigger an application for Medicaid and/or to investigate the patient's Medicare status. While the details of these two major "safety net" programs are beyond the scope of this text, the following is provided for basic reference:

Medicare, passed in 1965 as Title XVIII of the Social Security Act, provides health insurance for the elderly (adults over the age of 65 years) and disabled (adults who have been disabled for a period of two years and who qualify for Social Security Disability). The Centers for Medicare and Medicaid Services (CMS) (2014) estimated that 52.2 million aged and disabled individuals received Medicare benefits in 2013.

- Part A covers inpatient care, home health, hospice care, and skilled nursing home care.

- Part B covers outpatient and physician services; it requires individuals to enroll and pay a monthly premium ($96.40 per month in 2008).

- Part C is a private-policy Medicare that subscribers **may** purchase to cover vision, hearing, dental, health and wellness programs, and prescription drug coverage.

- Part D is the prescription drug coverage plan passed by President Bush in 2003.

If a patient's condition warrants it, Medicare covers home healthcare services, including a visiting nurse, a home health aide, and, often, physical therapy and social work services. For individuals discharged from hospitals and in need of additional inpatient care, Medicare Part A will cover up to 100 days of skilled nursing home care. Skilled nursing home care includes physical therapy to improve mobility, intravenous drug therapy, and specialized wound care. Medicare will cover the first 20 days at 100%; Days 21–100 are covered at 80%. Individuals will need additional insurance or funds to cover nursing home care if their stay exceeds 20 days, a need that is assessed as part of the discharge plan. Part B is used to cover physician services that are provided to patients in nursing homes.

Medicaid (Title XIX to the Social Security Act) provides health insurance for low income/indigent individuals. Over 62 million people participated in 2012. Medicaid covers all individuals receiving Temporary Assistance to Needy Families (TANF) funds. Fourteen percent of Medicaid recipients are disabled, and less than 8% are elderly. While half of Medicaid recipients are children, 22% are elderly or disabled and 66% of Medicaid funds are spent on their care (Segal, 2009).

Medicaid covers skilled care as well as basic care in a nursing home. There is no limit to the number of days Medicaid will cover in a nursing home. However, because the cost of care in a nursing home is so high, Medicaid has initiated a number of demonstration projects (such as the Money Follows the Person [MFP] program) to help individuals transition from care facilities to the community (Centers for Medicare and Medicaid Services, n.d.). Medicaid is administered by each state and is funded through a combination of federal and state revenues.

Because Medicaid is an **entitlement program** that must be funded to cover all individuals who qualify, states have some latitude in establishing criteria and services. Typically, individuals are allowed to own a home, an automobile, and a pre-purchased burial plot, but they must have very limited financial assets to qualify (in Michigan, $2,000 or less in savings). If income and/or financial assets exceed the Medicaid eligibility requirement but an individual has incurred healthcare expenses that he or she cannot pay, the individual may qualify for a *Medicaid "spend-down,"* during which he or she expends some of his or her financial assets to pay for care and then qualifies to receive Medicaid payments. Spouses needing to place a dependent spouse in a nursing home are entitled to apply for spousal protection of financial assets. This permits them to retain a portion of the couple's accumulated assets while they use a portion for the patient's care. Once the patient has exhausted his or her share of the assets, he or she may be eligible for Medicaid.

Medicaid application can be a complicated and time-consuming process in its own right as there must be irrefutable verification of citizenship status and patient assets before a determination is reached. If the Medicaid application is initiated but not completed, reimbursement will not be authorized to any providers, regardless of whether the provider has delivered services and incurred costs. Because of the combined application complexity and time-limited hospitalizations, it consequently becomes imperative that referrals for Medicaid applications, when warranted, be taken at the earliest possible moment. These referrals may be made to specialists within social work units (Spitzer & Kuykendall, 1994), hospital financial services, or admitting departments or to state Medicaid Services intake staff. Again, if the application is initiated but not completed during the period of hospitalization, it must be finalized by the patient following discharge. Provider reimbursement becomes contingent on the ability and willingness of the patient to fulfill his or her responsibility. Social workers must be influential in prompting such completion. Significant credence is given to social work intervention when it simultaneously demonstrates being able to secure reimbursement for the provider while facilitating uninterrupted healthcare coverage to meet the ongoing needs of eligible patients.

Phase II. Implementation and Goal Attainment

Activities in this phase of the helping process reflect a final reassessment of patient needs and capacities, along with assurances from the social worker, physician(s), and other involved health professionals that the patient's needs are addressed in the care plan. The patient's strengths and capacity to contend with his or her health and care needs are acknowledged and reinforced. The patient, family, and other significant decision-makers are invited to express any remaining questions, concerns, or opinions about current (pre-discharge) care, the post-hospitalization care plan, health prognosis, or related issues.

With confirmation from the physician(s) of the patient's medical readiness for discharge, the social worker modifies the care plan in response to any remaining issues that have been identified and then triggers the final implementation steps of the care plan. This may involve initiating any additional referrals to community resources for needed follow-up care. The benefits of having established, constructive relationships are ever-more apparent at this stage of the care process. Finalizing potentially complex plans for ongoing care of a patient is facilitated by having the understanding and agreement of all involved parties. This understanding is predicated on mutual trust, patient/family confidence in the social worker's competence, and the social worker's positive relationships with other healthcare team members as well as with community agency personnel to whom services will be shifted upon patient discharge.

Patient and family education, while important throughout the entire care process, becomes particularly crucial at the point of discharge. It must be remembered that, to the extent that family members may now be called upon to deliver or help orchestrate care, they likely are not familiar with the unique duties or procedures they may have to correctly execute in their new roles as caregiver. At the same time, they understandably are still contending with their own reactions to the patient's health condition. The patient and family have experienced a set of demanding, often unprecedented challenges associated with the onset of the condition and its treatment. The impact on patient and family life is often disruptive and disturbing and further triggers trepidation about the patient's and family's future. Previous roles and relationships may be permanently altered by changes in the patient's health condition and need for ongoing care. Recognizing these dynamics, healthcare social workers will, as feasible, follow-up with care providers after discharge to assess the ongoing status of the patient and to provide both emotional support and additional resource referrals as warranted.

Collaboration, coordination, patient/family education, and the overall discharge process are characteristically monitored frequently by healthcare providers because of the profound impact of these processes on overall patient care. In addition, outside evaluative and regulatory agencies focus on these processes in their formal reviews. Of these agencies, The Joint Commission (JC) is most well-known and utilized. Founded in 1951, JC seeks to continuously improve healthcare for the public, in collaboration with other stakeholders, by evaluating healthcare organizations and inspiring them to excel in providing safe and effective care of the highest quality and value. As an independent, not-for-profit organization, JC evaluates and accredits more than 19,000 healthcare organizations and programs in the United States, including approximately 88% of hospitals as well as ambulatory care services, behavioral healthcare services, home healthcare services, laboratories, and long-term-care facilities in the United States (The Joint Commission, 2014).

JC standards for discharge planning contain essential components of assessment, communication, education, and coordination. The standards specify that hospitals must have a process for discharge planning that addresses patients' needs for continuing care, treatment, and services after discharge or transfer. The process, often written as a policy or protocol, must establish when and how discharge planning starts, who is involved in the process, responsibilities for development and implementation of the plan, and an outline of the assessment process with periodic reassessment of patient needs.

Central to this process, hospitals must coordinate follow-up care of patients and have a mechanism for sharing essential information with other agencies and providers involved in the patient's ongoing care. A **transfer form** is a document that is often employed by hospitals to provide patient information upon institutional transfer from the hospital to a nursing home or other type of care center. While this document is increasingly an element of the patient's electronic medical record, it remains a practice to provide the patient and/ or transferring parties (including ambulance squads) with a hard-copy of the transfer form. When patients are discharged to their own or other care-providers' sites, it is particularly crucial that specific care instructions be complete and clearly stated with contact numbers for additional assistance as needed. A challenge exists, however, when care instructions become more complicated because of the complexity of the patient's health condition. In such instances, it is likely that multiple medical services and disciplines were involved in the patient's hospital care, and each service may well have specific recommendations for the patient's ongoing post-hospital care. The *Discharge Information Form* (Spitzer, Burger, & Farley, 1998) found in *Appendix C* is an example of how consolidated multidisciplinary information can be compiled in a permanent electronic medical record with a hard copy of customized instructions then provided to the patient and/or family upon inpatient discharge. Another resource, the Re-Engineered Discharge (RED) Toolkit, is a project between the Boston University Medical Center and the Agency for Healthcare Research and Quality (AHRQ, 2014) that, in addition to providing evidence-based approaches that improve continuity of care planning, offers a number of templates that can be used for creating patient-discharge instructions, patient-education materials, and continuity-of-care plans.

CASE STUDY

Nursing Home Placement

An 88-year-old widowed woman was admitted to the hospital after a stroke, which left her paralyzed and unable to speak. After two weeks of inpatient rehabilitation services, including physical, occupational, and speech therapy, the patient's condition remained nearly unchanged. The social worker facilitated a meeting between the team, the patient, and the patient's daughter, during which it was decided to seek a nursing home placement. The social worker then met privately with the daughter, provided her with a list of possible facilities, and began the process of applying for Medicaid to supplement Medicare, which would only pay for care for a limited period of time. The daughter indicated her intentions to visit nursing homes in order to select one for her mother. After a number of days, the daughter had failed to visit any nursing homes or to obtain financial paperwork necessary for the Medicaid application process.

During the next meeting, the social worker explored the daughter's reasons for not following through on the steps of the plan. Through non-judgmental and empathic counseling that explored resistance to the plan, it became clear that the problem was not one of locating a nursing home. Rather, the daughter was grieving the loss of her mother as she had known her and was emotionally unable to accept placing her mother in a nursing home. As a result, the intervention became one of helping the daughter come to terms with the realities of having her mother live with her at home. This process involved educating the daughter on the mother's care and making arrangements for home care and support. It also involved helping the daughter grieve the loss of independence and privacy that would occur with having her mother live with her. Additional referrals to a caregiver support group were made, and the patient was discharged to the daughter's home the next day. In this case, the social worker and team identified the problem as one of nursing home placement and after initially agreeing to this approach, the daughter had second thoughts.

Our case study illustrates the importance of eliciting an ongoing plan and understanding the placement issue from the patient and family perspective, rather than imposing a plan that has been unilaterally developed by the treatment team. The social worker's intervention enhanced the daughter's ability to contend with her mother's new health condition and need for placement. It also served to prompt the patient transfer and thereby conclude an unnecessary and expensive hospitalization. In so doing, it demonstrated sensitivity to the input of the patient and daughter, reduced the financial liability of the patient (and/or potentially the hospital), and, importantly, made an inpatient bed available that might have been needed by another patient with legitimate care needs.

Phase III. Evaluation and Termination

Termination describes the process of ending the patient–social worker relationship. In healthcare situations, termination will likely involve ending other types of supportive medical care in addition to those of the social worker. Termination occurs when either party decides to end services, when treatment is completed, or when constraints such as time and distance prevent services from continuing. Because of situational constraints, medical social workers may have only a few, limited encounters with their patients and families. However, a strong bond can still be built that warrants attention to the feelings associated with termination. The need to identify additional resources for longer term interventions and emergency situations is particularly important when work is brief and time-limited. It is our opinion that even if the social worker has a single encounter with a patient and/or family, building in a few moments to discuss termination or the feelings associated with an impending transition to another level or type of care is critical. In traditional therapeutic situations, clients often feel a sense of accomplishment but may also experience some anxiety when services end because goals have been achieved. For the medical patient, recovery and reaching goals often require continued work beyond the healthcare encounter and identifying patient strengths, supports, and resources is helpful in reassuring and motivating the patient as well as promoting adherence to the continuity of care plans.

An integral part of effective termination involves an evaluative process of reviewing the treatment outcomes and outlining goals and hopes for continued recovery. This can be an informal discussion between the patient and social worker or part of a more formal practice evaluation process. For example, many social work departments institute follow-up phone calls or emails to patients and ask if the patient is following the transitional care plan that was developed and if it was adequate and comprehensive in meeting his or her needs. If additional needs have emerged, they can be identified through follow-up and addressed. Evaluation is critical for the continued professional development of the social worker, improving patient care, and demonstrating the value of social work services. Chapter 6 of this text is dedicated to strategies for evaluating practice interventions at the case, program, and organizational levels.

SUMMARY

Healthcare social work is a sophisticated, challenging practice that is conducted in complex, multidisciplinary, fast-paced environments. Practice expectations are high, but so are the rewards from engaging in often life-and-death situations, collaborating in a knowledge-driven setting, and making contributions to the enhanced health and safety of one's community. In this chapter, we have identified the core characteristics and functions of healthcare social workers as being

- Pre-admission assessments or high-risk screening upon admission
- Patient/family psychosocial evaluation
- Crisis intervention (emergency room, critical care, or other emergent situations)
- Short-term supportive counseling for health condition/treatment adjustment
- Longer-range counseling (post-hospitalization; clinic or office-based)
- Post-hospitalization care planning (case management)
- Patient/family advocacy with other health-team members/community agencies
- Patient/family education regarding condition, adjustment issues, and care plan
- Information/resource referral for immediate and post-hospitalization care needs
- Collaboration/education with other healthcare providers regarding patient and family adjustment issues, home conditions affecting ongoing care, and available versus needed ongoing care resources
- Research continuously enhancing practice (CQI) and positive patient outcomes

Using a modified version of the model described by Hepworth et al. (2010), this chapter identified the **three phases of the helping process** and, in discussing the roles of the social worker, presented the tasks and responsibilities associated with contemporary healthcare practice. Ethical issues included the dilemma of advocating for patient access to needed resources while recognizing their limited availability and conserving them through prioritized use. Also challenging is the need for healthcare social workers to balance their commitment to the patient's active role in decision making (autonomy) about his or her care versus pursuing care recommendations based on their professional knowledge, skills, and experience (beneficence). Finally, we are reminded that social work exists in host or secondary settings in which the primary mission is not the provision of social work services, but delivery of medical services, the treatment of diseases and illnesses, and the promotion of health and wellness. It is crucial that social workers be conscientious in appropriately communicating those contributions made to patient care, provider-system operations, and, ultimately, the health of the larger community.

KEY TERMS AND CONCEPTS

- Healthy care social work
- Care coordination
- Case/care management

- Transitional care planning

- Boundary-spanning/resource "brokering"

- Psychoeducational group advocacy

- Pre-admission screening

- Roles of the social worker in healthcare

- Beneficence

- Nonmaleficence

- Roles of healthcare social work

- Three phases of the helping process

- Ethical patient care challenges

- High-risk screening

- Open and closed referral systems

- Strengths-based practice perspective

- Biopsychosocial assessment

- Genograms

- Activities of Daily Living (ADLs)

- Continuity of care

- Medicare and Medicaid

- Entitlement programs

QUESTIONS FOR DISCUSSION

1. Healthcare social workers provide their services in settings in which the primary purpose is not necessarily to provide social services. This can put social work services at risk when budget cuts must be made. What steps can social workers take to document and communicate the impact of their services?

2. Social workers often walk a tightrope, balancing the needs of the patient/family with the wishes of the institution. How would you handle a situation when you think a decision that the hospital or medical team has made negatively impacts your patient?

3. Discuss the helping process. Is it difficult to follow a sequential model of helping when patients come in and out of the healthcare system on the basis of their physical/medical needs rather than psychosocial needs. How can the social worker adapt the helping process to these situations?

EXERCISES

1. The roles of healthcare social workers are as follows:

   - Care/case coordinator/manager

   - Counselor/therapist

   - Advocate

   - Leader

   - Researcher and evaluator

   Define each role and provide an example of something a social worker would do when performing this role.

2. Complete a genogram for the following family:

   You are seeing a patient, Jim, who is admitted after breaking his leg while falling down stairs. He had been drinking, and laboratory results show the beginning stages of liver disease. He had a concussion, and there may be some mild cognitive impairments that may or may not resolve.

   - Jim and Barb have been married since 1996. Jim is 31, Barb is 30.

   - They have two children, Tommy (age 2) and Megan (age 1).

   - Jim is an electrician, Barb stays home with kids.

   - The marriage is the second for Jim, whose first wife's name is Sue. The couple divorced in 1994 after having one child, Jimmy Jr. (age 6).

   - Jim's parents are Paul and Mary (age 56 and 54). Paul is a recovered alcoholic. Mary has cancer.

   - Jim has two brothers and a sister, all of whom married. One brother committed suicide eight years ago; this brother had been addicted to drugs and alcohol.

   - All of Jim's siblings have two children (a boy and girl).

   - Barb's parents, Mike and Kathy, were divorced. Mike has died. Kathy has remarried to Pete.

   - Barb has a sister, who is married with two boys.

REFERENCES

Agency for Health Care Research and Quality. (May 2014). Reengineered Discharge (RED) Toolkit. Rockville, Maryland: AHRQ. Retrieved from http://www.ahrq.gov/professionals/systems/hospital/red/toolkit/index.html

Bartlett, H. M. (1961). *Social work practice in the health field*. New York: National Association of Social Workers.

Beder, J. (2006). *Hospital social work: The interface of medicine and caring*. New York: Taylor & Francis.

Blumenfield, S., & Rosenberg, G. (1988). Towards a network of social health services: Redefining discharge planning and expanding the social work domain. *Social Work in Health Care, 13,* 31–49.

Boutin-Foster, C., Euster, S., Rolon, Y., Motal, A., BeLue, R., Kline, R., & Charlson, M. E. (2005). Social work admission assessment tool for identifying patients in need of comprehensive social work evaluation. *Health and Social Work, 30,* 117–125.

Carlton, T. O. (1984). *Clinical social work in health settings*. New York: Springer Publishing Company.

Case Management Society of America. (2010). *Standards of practice for case management—revised 2010*. Little Rock, AK: Case Management Society of America.

Center for Medicare Advocacy. (n.d.). *Discharge planning*. Retrieved from http://www.medicareadvocacy.org/medicare-info/discharge-planning/

Centers for Medicare & Medicaid Services. (n.d.). *Money follows the person (MFP)*. Retrieved from http://www.medicaid.gov/medicaid-chip-program-information/by-topics/long-term-services-and-supports/balancing/money-follows-the-person.html

Centers for Medicare & Medicaid Services. (2014). *Medicare enrollment reports*. Retrieved from http://www.cms.gov/Research-Statistics-Data-and-Systems/Statistics-Trends-and-Reports/MedicareEnrpts/index.html?redirect = /medicareenrpts/

Cohen, M., Nemec, P., Farkas, M., & Forbes, R. (1988). *Planning for services: Training module*. Boston, MA: Boston University Center for Psychiatric Rehabilitation.

Cormier, W. H., & Cormier, L. S. (1991). *Interviewing strategies for helpers* (3rd ed.). Pacific Grove, CA: Brooks/Cole.

Dziegielewski, S. F. (1998). *The changing face of health care social work*. New York: Springer Publishing Company.

Farrar, A., & O'Donnell, P. (2003). Biomedical issues and social work: The state of practice and research. In W. Spitzer, (Ed.,) *Ethics in health care: A social work perspective*. The National Society for Social Work Leadership in Health Care. Petersburg, VA: The Dietz Press, 71–84.

Friedman, B., & Allen, K. N. (2011). Systems theory. In J. Brandell, (Ed.), *Theory and practice of clinical social work* (pp. 3–18). New York: The Free Press.

Goldstein, H. (1981). Generalist social work practice. In N. Gilbert, & H. Specht, (Eds.), *Handbook of the social services*. Englewood-Cliffs, NJ: Prentice Hall.

Henderson, M. G., & Collard, A. (1992). Measuring quality in medical case management programs. In S. M. Rose (Ed.), *Case management and social work practice* (pp. 170–184). New York: Longman Publishing Group.

Hepworth, D., & Larsen, J. (1982). *Direct social work practice: Theory and skills*. Homewood, IL: Dorsey Press.

Hepworth, D. H., Rooney, R. H., Rooney, G. D., Strom-Gottfried, K., & Larsen, J. A. (2010). *Direct social work practice: Theory and skills* (8th ed.). New York: Brooks/Cole.

Holland, D. E., Harris, M. R., Leibson, C. L., Pankratz, V. S., & Krichbaum, K. E. (2006). Development and validation of a screen for specialized discharge planning services. *Nursing Research, 55,* 62-71.

Holosko, M.J. (1994). Social work practice in health care: Daring to be different. In M. Holosko, & P. Taylor, (Eds.). *Social work practice in health care settings* (pp. 21–32) (2nd ed.). Toronto: Canadian Scholars' Press, Inc.

Holosko, M. J., & Taylor, P. A. (1994). *Social work practice in health care settings* (2nd ed.). Toronto: Canadian Scholars' Press, Inc.

Kane, R. (1992). Case management: Ethical pitfalls on the road to high-quality managed care. In S. M. Rose (Ed.), *Case management and social work practice* (pp. 219–228). White Plains, NY: Longman Publishing Group.

Kanter, J. (1989). Clinical case management: Definitions, principles and components. *Hospital Community Psychiatry, 40,* 361–368.

Kerson, T. S. (1997). *Social work in health settings: Practice in context.* New York: Haworth.

Kirst-Ashman, K., & Hull, G. (2012). *Understanding generalist social work practice.* (6th ed.). Belmont, CA: Brooks/Cole Cengage Learning.

Kisthardt, W. E., & Rapp, C. A. (1992). Bridging the gap between principles and practice: Implementing a strengths perspective in case management. In S. M. Rose (Ed.). *Case management and social work practice* (pp. 112–125). New York: Longman Publishing Group.

Levin, R., & Herbert, M. (1995). Differential work assignments of social work practitioners in hospitals. *Health and Social Work, 20,* 21–30.

McGoldrick, M., & Gerson, R. (1985). *Genograms in family assessment.* New York: W. W. Norton and Company.

McGowen, B. G. (1987). Advocacy. In A. Minahan (Ed.), *Encyclopedia of social work* (pp. 89–96). Silver Springs, MD: National Association of Social Workers.

Morrow-Howell, N. (1992). Clinical case management: The hallmark of gerontological social work. *Journal of Gerontological Social Work, 18,* 119–131.

Moxley, D. (1989). *Practice of case management.* Thousand Oaks, CA.: SAGE.

National Association of Social Workers. (2011). *Social workers in hospitals and medical centers, occupational profile.* Washington, DC: author.

New York Academy of Medicine. (n.d.). *Policy brief: Implementing care coordination in the Patient Protection and Affordable Care Act.* New York, NY: author.

Raiff, N. & Shore, B. (1993). *Advanced case management.* Newbury Park, CA: SAGE.

Reamer, F. (1985). The emergence of bioethics in social work. *Health and Social Work, 10,* 271–281.

Reamer, F. (2003). Social work ethics in health care: Past, present and future. In W. Spitzer, (Ed.). *Ethics in health care: A social work perspective.* Petersburg, VA: The Dietz Press.

Rose, S. M. (Ed.). (1992). *Case management and social work practice.* New York: Longman Publishing Group.

Rosenberg, G. (1994). Social work, the family and the community. *Social Work in Health Care, 20,* 7–20.

Rosenberg, G., & Katz, A. (2004). Characteristics of effective leadership for clinical health care social work practice. In W. Spitzer, (Ed.). *Leadership in health care social work: Principles and practice* (pp. 9–26). National Society for Social Work Leadership in Health Care. Petersburg, VA: The Dietz Press.

Rosenberg, G., & Weissman, A. (1995). *Social work leadership in healthcare: Directors' perspectives.* New York: The Haworth Press.

Rubin, A. (1992). Case management. In S. M. Rose, (Ed.). *Case management and social work practice.* New York: Longman Publishing Group.

Saleebey (2002). *The strengths perspective in social work practice.* Boston: Pearson, Allyn & Bacon.

Schneider, R., & Lester, L. (2001). *Social work advocacy: A new framework for action.* Belmont, CA: Brooks/Cole.

Schwaber, T. (2002). *Boundary spanning. An ecological reinterpretation of social work practice in health and mental health care systems.* New York: Columbia University Press.

Segal, E. (2009). *Social welfare policies & social welfare programs: A values perspective.* Belmont, CA: Brooks/Cole.

Shevlin, K. M. (1983). Why a social service department in a hospital? In L. Hubschman, (Ed.), *Hospital social work practice* (pp. 1–14). New York: Praeger Publishers.

Simmons, W. J., & Bixby, N. (1989). A model for leadership in administrative practice. *The Mount Sinai Journal of Medicine, 56,* 429–434.

Spitzer, W. (1997). Psychosocial high-risk screening: Enhancing patient care through rapid social work engagement. *Continuum: An Interdisciplinary Journal on Continuity of Care, 17*(1), 1,3–9.

Spitzer, W. (Ed.). (2003). *Ethics in health care: The social work perspective.* National Society for Social Work Leadership in Health Care. Petersburg, VA: The Dietz Press.

Spitzer, W. (Ed.). (2004). *Leadership in health care social work: Principles and practice.* National Society for Social Work Leadership in Health Care. Petersburg, VA: The Dietz Press.

Spitzer, W. (Ed.). (2005a). *Cultural competence in health care social work practice.* National Society for Social Work Leadership in Health Care. Petersburg, VA: The Dietz Press.

Spitzer, W. (Ed.). (2005b). *Strengths-based perspective on social work practice in health care.* National Society for Social Work Leadership in Health Care. Petersburg, VA: The Dietz Press.

Spitzer, W., Burger, S., & Farley, B. (1998). Promoting patient/family education through use of automated interdisciplinary discharge information. *Continuum: An Interdisciplinary Journal on Continuity of Care, 18*(1), 3–7.

Spitzer, W., & Kuykendall, R. (1994). Social work delivery of hospital-based financial assistance services. *Health and Social Work, 19*, 294–297.

Stetler, C., & Charns, M. (Eds.). (1995). *Collaboration in health care: Hartford Hospital's experience in changing management and practice.* Chicago: American Hospital Publishing, Inc.

The Joint Commission. (2014b). *Joint commission requirements.* Retrieved from www.jointcommission.org/standards_information/joint_commission_requirements.aspx

United States Department of Labor, Bureau of Labor Statistics. (2013). *Occupational Employment Statistics: Occupational Employment and Wages, May 2013 (Healthcare Social Workers).* Washington, DC: Author. Retrieved from http://www.bls.gov/oes/current/oes211022.htm

Weick, A. (2005). Being well: A strengths based approach to health and healing. In W. Spitzer, (Ed.). *Strengths-based perspective on social work practice in health care.* National Society for Social Work Leadership in Health Care. Petersburg, VA: The Dietz Press, 1–14.

Weick, A., Rapp, C., Sullivan, W., Patrick, W., & Kishardt, W. (1989). A strengths perspective for social work practice. *Social Work, 34*, 350–354.

Williams, S. J., & Torrens, P.R. (1993). Assessing and regulation system performance. In S. J. Williams, & P. R. Torrens, (Eds.), *Introduction to health services.* (4th ed.). Albany, NY: Delmar.

Wilson, S. J. (1980). *Recording: Guidelines for social workers.* New York: The Free Press.

Values and Ethics of Healthcare Social Work

Patricia O'Donnell

INTRODUCTION

"The primary mission of the social work profession is to enhance human well-being and help meet the basic human needs of all people, with particular attention to the needs and empowerment of people who are vulnerable, oppressed, and living in poverty. A historic and defining feature of social work is the profession's focus on individual well-being in a social context and the well-being of society. Fundamental to social work is attention to the environmental forces that create, contribute to, and address problems in living." (National Association of Social Workers [NASW], 2008, p.1)

The mission statement of the profession of social work reflects the profession's core values from which the Code of Ethics' ethical principles, **obligations**, and practice standards are derived. The mandates for ethical practice apply to all social workers but are particularly relevant to practice in the healthcare field. Healthcare social workers confront complex ethical issues in their clinical practice in a variety of organizational settings. The complexity of the issues is related to the plurality of professional and personal values among healthcare providers, patients and their families, and society in general; differing ethical perspectives and practice priorities of the healthcare team members; and the ongoing advances in biomedical technology that affect clinical practice and decision-making by both clinicians and patients. Reamer (1985) noted that the rise of bioethics-based issues in healthcare social work requires both a thorough knowledge of the problems and knowledge of ethical principles and training in ethical reasoning to prepare the social worker to manage ethical issues in a consistent, thoughtful manner and to generalize learning and experience from one situation to another instead of just responding to the situation at hand.

SOCIAL WORK VALUES

Values are generally defined as preferences, perceptions, and evaluations of worth. They can be concrete or abstract, permanent or situational, and general or specific to a group or society. Social work attends to a variety of values, including those that are particular to the patient and family, the personal values of the professional, the practice setting, the profession, and society in the management of ethical dilemmas in healthcare social work practice (Joseph, 1983). Patient and family values may include privacy, protection from harm, and freedom to make decisions. The professional's personal values may mirror the client's values or may conflict with them, leading to conflict. The practice setting may be guided by values of service, compassion, and stewardship of resources. Professional values may include integrity, competence, and wisdom, whereas societal values may focus on the general welfare, altruism, and safety. The examination of all values, whether congruent or conflicted, that are involved in the ethical dilemma and their ranking in the perspective of all the involved parties is a key component of ethical problem solving.

The social work profession is grounded in a set of core values that serves as the foundation for the ethical principles that mandate social work ethical obligations and practice standards to our patients and their families, our colleagues and practice settings, our profession, and society as a whole (NASW, 2008). These values include service, the dignity and worth of the individual, integrity, the importance of human relationships, social justice, and competence as delineated in the introduction to the NASW Code of Ethics. Reamer (2009) aligned the delineation of social work values with the shift of focus in social work practice from the morality of the client to the morality, values, and ethics of the profession and its practitioners. Perlman (1976, p. 389) noted that "It is the distinguishing mark of a professional helper that he not only is knowledgeable, that he is not only skillful, but that he is constantly striving for a 'fit' between what he believes in and what he tries to make happen." She supported the examination of professional and personal values in the context of practice as a basic task in managing value complexity and value conflict.

In examining social work values and ethics, Reamer (1999) identified social work pioneers and scholars (Gordon, 1965; Hamilton, 1940; Pumphrey, 1959; Vigilante, 1974) who contributed to the designation of the values of dignity, individuality, self-determination, respect, justice, and equality as core values for the social work profession. Levy (1973) framed these values and others to serve as the base for actualizing values into ethical principles to guide practice *(Exercise 5.1)*. He categorized social work major orientation values as preferred conceptions of people, preferred outcomes for people, and preferred instrumentalities for dealing with people. These dimensions provided a base for the codifying of ethical principles and obligations in social work practice as seen in the NASW Code of Ethics (2008).

ETHICAL DILEMMAS

Dolgoff, Loewenberg, and Harrington (2009) described **ethical dilemmas** as those situations in which social work practitioners question the right thing to do when confronted with a moral question. The source of these questions originates in conflicts related to

Exercise 5.1   Match Levy's dimensions as described above with the ethical principles and obligations that are listed in the boxes below.

Value	Ethical Principle	Obligation
Service	Social workers' primary goal is to help people in need and to address social problems.	Place interests of clients first. Utilize skills and knowledge to help people. Offer volunteer services.
Social Justice	Social workers challenge social injustice.	Promote social change to address social injustice. Educate on cultural diversity. Ensure access.
Dignity and Worth of the Person	Social workers respect the inherent dignity and worth of the person.	Respect all and be sensitive to cultural diversity. Encourage capacity to change. Maintain professional boundaries.
Importance of Human Relationships	Social workers recognize the central importance of human relationships.	Use of self in professional relationships as agent for change. Strengthen relationships for well-being of people and society.
Integrity	Social workers behave in a trustworthy manner.	Awareness of professional values and mission in practice. Respect ethical standards in organizational practice settings.
Competence	Social workers practice within their areas of competence and develop and enhance their professional expertise.	Increase knowledge and skills and apply to practice. Contribute to the knowledge base of the profession.

competing values, duties, and rights of the individuals involved in the dilemma. Competing values, duties, and rights create dilemmas that concern how to decide which value, duty, or right takes priority when all appear to have equal standing in an ethical quandary (Beauchamp & Childress, 2001). The hierarchy of decision making proposed by Dolgoff, et al., presented below, is to be used when the Code of Ethics does not provide specific instructions as to a right course of action:

- Principle of the protection of life
- Principle of equality and inequality
- Principle of autonomy and freedom
- Principle of least harm
- Principle of quality of life
- Principle of privacy and confidentiality
- Principle of truthfulness and full disclosure

This is a hierarchical system in which the principles are presented in rank order. Thus, the highest principle, that involving the protection of life, trumps all other ethical principles. The principle of privacy and confidentiality is lower on the list, which is appropriate. We would break the principle of confidentiality to protect an individual's life if the individual indicated a plan and intent to commit suicide. The authors described this as an ethical values screen rather than a model for strict and rigid adherence. The circumstances of each case must be considered individually. Although no absolute rules can be applied to the resolution of an ethical dilemma, which by definition has more than one morally acceptable outcome, practitioners are expected to examine relevant factors in a systematic manner in order to ensure that all issues are addressed during the decision-making process.

Reamer (1985) first reported the emergence of bioethical issues in social work resulting from the increasing complexities of medical decisions regarding quality of life, use of technology, and end-of-life issues that encompassed value conflicts for patients, families, and healthcare team members. Reamer's "Social Values Hierarchy" is described below.

- Rules against basic harm to an individual's survival take precedence over rules against harms such as lying or revealing confidential information or threats to additive goods.

- An individual's right to basic well-being takes precedence over another individual's right to self-determination.

- An individual's right to self-determination takes precedence over his or her right to basic well-being.

- The obligation to obey laws, rules, and regulations to which one has voluntarily and freely consented ordinarily overrides one's right to engage voluntarily and freely in a manner that conflicts with these.

- Individuals' rights to well-being may override laws, rules, regulations, and arrangements of voluntary associations in cases of conflict.

- The obligation to prevent basic harms and to promote public goods such as housing, education, and public assistance overrides the right to complete control over one's property.

Patients and families have increasingly turned to social workers to help them in their ethical reflection process. A survey of social workers' responses to bioethical issues and perceived training needs as reported by Foster, Sharp, Scesny, McLellan, and Cotman (1993) reinforced the observation that social workers encounter bioethical issues on a routine basis in practice situations, with quality-of-life issues being cited as the most common. The authors recommended increased education for social workers in how to recognize bioethical problems, how to increase their ability to engage and reflect on the issues, and how to differentiate bioethical issues from practice problems. O'Donnell et al. (2008) reviewed previous studies (Black, 2004; Csikai & Bass, 2000; Egan & Kadushin, 1999; Gellis, 2001; Mackelprang & Mackelprang, 2005; Manetta & Wells, 2001; Miller, Hedlund, & Murphy 1998; Proctor, Morrow-Howell, & Lott, 1993; Walsh-Bowers, Rossiter, &

Prilleltensky, 1996; and Yen & Schneiderman, 1999) and outlined a number of recurring ethical issues in healthcare practice. These included establishing and following Do Not Attempt Resuscitation (DNAR) orders; confusion or conflict about advance directives; withdrawal or withholding treatment such as artificial nutrition and hydration, dialysis, and mechanical ventilation; physician-assisted suicide; the concept of futility; and managing conflict related to patient self-determination and team practice.

ETHICAL DECISION MAKING

CASE EXAMPLE

Liz is employed in a long-term-care center for ventilator-dependent patients. One of her patients is Mike, a 50-year-old man who suffered severe injuries in a motor-vehicle accident three years ago. Initially, he recovered well enough to be transferred to a rehabilitation facility, but he then suffered a stroke and became paralyzed and ventilator-dependent. Mike has been in long-term care for a year and a half. His physician, in consultation with the neurologist, has recently determined that he is in a permanent vegetative state (PVS) and will not recover consciousness.

Liz has been working with Mike's wife, children, and parents to help with their adjustment to his initial injury and now to his diagnosis of PVS. The patient's wife and parents have a fragile relationship. Mike is an only child, and the parents objected to his marriage. Mike's wife has maintained the children's relationships with their grandparents out of respect for her husband's wishes. She and Mike made all their decisions together, and now she feels very alone in decision making. She has come to depend on her husband's former boss for direction. Mike's parents resent this dependence and do not understand why the wife does not consult them. With the new diagnosis of PVS, the physician reviewed a variety of care options, including a terminal wean from the ventilator for the patient. In reflecting on the options, Mike's wife and Mike's boss both agree that the patient would choose to be removed from the ventilator if there was no hope of recovery. The parents are absolutely adamant that there is always hope and have told the social worker and the facility's administrator that they will fight the decision. The administrator has asked the social worker to arrange for an ethics consultation. The wife and parents have agreed to the consultation.

There are a number of stepwise models for the resolution of ethical problems that the social worker may apply in addressing ethical dilemmas (Dolgoff et al., 2009; Joseph, 1983; Reamer, 1999). The model described by Joseph (1983) enhances examination of ethical dilemmas through consideration of the context of the dilemmas. Reflecting on the mission and values of the organizational setting as well as a review of relevant literature and legal and regulatory mandates, her model utilizes applicable ethical perspectives, principles, and standards in the codes of ethics of social workers and other professionals to identify options for resolving dilemmas. The general model described by Dolgoff et al. (2009) is particularly applicable to healthcare workers as it focuses attention to the missions and values of institutions and the values of multiple parties that often are involved in complex medical cases.

Utilizing the components of the models described above, the ethics consultation team would begin with a clarification of the dilemma to be resolved. The dilemma to be addressed is the right of the surrogate (wife) to make decisions for the patient versus the parent's right to refuse a decision that they believe is not in the best interest of their son as it will shorten his life. The mission of the facility where Mike is placed is to provide rehabilitative services to ventilator-dependent patients, including restoring the patient's ability to breathe independently so that the patient eventually can be discharged to home. In Mike's case, the facility's secondary goals of care and compassion would support finding a resolution that will relieve the patient's suffering and protect him from harm. This goal could be interpreted to support the options to resolve this dilemma, which include terminal weaning from the ventilator as opposed to maintenance on the mechanical ventilator.

The staff of the facility has identified continuing maintenance on a ventilator as **futile treatment**. Referrals related to concerns about futile treatment represent some of the most vexing and time-consuming challenges faced by the Ethics Committee. Schneiderman, Jecker, and Jonsen (1990) explored the quantitative and qualitative roots of the concept of futility. According to those authors, a futile treatment can be defined *quantitatively* as a treatment that has not been effective in the last 100 cases but that may be effective on the 101st attempt. In comparison, a futile treatment can be defined *qualitatively* as a treatment that merely preserves permanent unconsciousness and cannot end dependence on intensive medical care. This definition gives rise to concern related to the professional's judgment of quality of life being imposed on patient-care decisions. Schneiderman et al. (1990) rejected these definitions and suggested that the definition of futility focus on the expected benefit to the patient based on clinical criteria. They recommend the analyis ask two questions. How probable is successful recovery, and how will the patient benefit?

The American Medical Association (1999) defined **futility** as the use of life-sustaining or invasive interventions for patients who are in a persistent vegetative state or who are terminally ill with no prospect of recovery. There is concern that the treatment may only prolong the dying process while increasing the physical suffering of the patient and the emotional stress of the family. Fin and Solomon (2001) suggested that futility disputes are fueled by suboptimal communication that erodes family trust. We do not know how involved Mike's parents have been in the conferences with the physicians. Are they dependent on second-hand information, or do they feel excluded from the decision-making process?

When there is no consensus among the parties involved in the dilemma, a stepwise process is recommended beginning with an evaluation of the patient's history and prognosis. A second or third opinion may help to clarify the patient's status. The process utilizes a mediation approach whereby the ethics consultant ensures that all parties' concerns and viewpoints are considered to promote joint decision making. If the process fails, the patient may be transferred to another care provider or facility that is willing to provide the treatment. In Mike's case, a second opinion from a neurologist who is not already involved in his care may promote the parent's understanding of his overall poor prognosis.

In addition to the ethical principles of service, the importance of human relationships, and the dignity and worth of the individual, the social worker also would consider the principles of bioethics in examining this dilemma. Beauchamp and Childress (2001) identified the bioethical principles of autonomy, beneficence, nonmaleficence, and justice as the primary principles in determining professional practice at the bedside and in the organization. The principle of **autonomy** supports the patient's right to participate in all aspects of and decisions related to his or her treatment and, in this case, would mandate that the wife as the patient's primary surrogate decision maker has the right to her decision if fully informed and understanding of its consequences. Autonomy can be the source of conflict in the provider–patient relationship. The imbalance of power inherent in the provider–patient relationship requires that the professional work toward an enhanced autonomy for the patient whereby ideas are exchanged, differences are explicitly negotiated, and power and influence are shared (Quill & Brody, 1996).

The principle of **beneficence** directs the professional to place the interests of the patient first in making any recommendations for intervention and care. Pellegrino and Thomasma (1988, p. 73) stated that "acting for the good of the patient is the most universally acknowledged principle in medical ethics." This principle would support both Mike's wife's right and Mike's parent's right to advocate for what each party feels and believes is in the best interest of Mike. The principle of **nonmaleficence** guides the professional to take actions that will prevent the patient from being harmed and also to assess the potential burden associated with recommended treatments in terms of pain, cost, suffering, and discomfort. The professionals believe that continuing Mike's dependence on the ventilator is extending his burden of suffering and will not result in the positive outcome for which his parents are hoping. The principle of **justice** directs the professional to treat all patients equitably and to be attentive to the just allocation of resources. There may be some concern on the part of the facility that providing treatment considered futile is a poor use of resources that could be used to benefit other patients.

The ethical perspectives of deontology, consequentialism, virtue ethics, and the ethics of care inform this dilemma in several ways. The **deontological perspective** holds that ethical rules are self-evident and should be upheld under all circumstances (Dolgoff et al., 2009). Mike's parents believe in the sanctity of life. The deontological perspective of the principle of nonmaleficence would support interventions that preserve life and prevent harm. However, it would also support the wife's and staff's efforts to prevent Mike's further suffering. The **consequentialist perspective** states that ethical decisions may consider the expected outcomes of a decision in the determination of whether the decision is morally acceptable (Dolgoff et al., 2009). Consequentialism would justify removing Mike from the ventilator to relieve his suffering. The **virtue ethics perspective** states that ethics constitute the basis for moral virtues in us and our communities (Manning, 2003). The professional virtues of compassion, integrity, and wisdom may be enhanced by choosing the option that promotes the best interest of the patient. The **ethics of care perspective** proposes that decisions include consideration and promotion of the relationship needs of all parties involved in the dilemma (Dolgoff et al., 2009). In this case, the ethics of care perspective would support the option that would strengthen family relationships over the long term. Mike's wife wants what is best for her husband, but she also wants to maintain the children's relationship with their grandparents.

Legal mandates and regulatory agencies may also have some influence on the options for resolution of this dilemma. When a patient is not capable of participating in the decision-making process, he or she has the right to have a surrogate speak for his or her choices

(Kass, 1993), including the right to refuse treatment. In most state laws, the surrogate is mandated to make the decision on the basis of the values and beliefs of the patient and not on the wishes of the surrogate. The Joint Commission (2009) has directed all healthcare facilities to develop and enforce policies that inform staff and patients of the facilities' commitment to honor patients' advance directives and other statements of care preferences made by patients. In this case, Mike had not completed a written advance directive but had talked in general with his wife and friends about what he would want if he was terminally ill. The ethics consultant reviewed the options for resolution of the dilemma and the ethical justification for each option with Mike's wife, parents, and care providers. The social worker talked extensively with the parents about their potential loss and was able to help them think about what they wanted for Mike and his family. The physician and respiratory therapist reviewed the process of weaning, with emphasis on how Mike's comfort would be maintained. Within a few weeks of the consultation, the parents supported the option of a terminal wean. Mike died peacefully with his family at his side. Schneiderman et al. (2003), in a study on the potential benefit of ethics consultations in cases of disputes regarding the continuance of non-beneficial life-sustaining treatments, found that 87% of the physicians, nurses, and patients/surrogates agreed that the ethics consultation facilitated resolution of treatment-decision conflicts.

This case illustrates that social workers must have a fundamental understanding of the history, values, principles, and standards of professional social work ethics and utilize "disciplined, critical thinking" to apply to complex practice situations (Strom-Gottfried, 2007). Grady et al. (2008) reported that social workers with a strong educational base in ethics are more able and willing to take moral action when they are faced with an ethical dilemma. The resolution of this case also reflects the standards for ethical principles in professional practice, particularly that social workers "apply strategies of ethical reasoning to arrive at principled decisions" as outlined in the Council on Social Work Education's *Educational Policy and Accreditation Standards* (2008).

ETHICS COMMITTEES

O'Donnell (1998), in a study of Ethics Committees and the factors that influence the satisfaction of committee members, included a review of the origins and the purpose of the Ethics Committee and the role of the social worker on the committee. Cranford and Doudera (1984, pp. 6-7) defined the **Ethics Committee** as "a multidisciplinary group of healthcare professionals within a healthcare institution that has been specifically established to address the ethical dilemmas that occur within the institution." The Ethics Committee emerged in response to numerous social and cultural factors that have influenced and changed the provision of healthcare and the perspective of its providers at both the individual and institutional levels. O'Donnell et al. (2008) described McCormick's (1984) summary of the most influential factors as including

1. the increasing complexity of problems related to the rise in technology and an increased ability to offer miracle care;

2. the expanded range of options available to the patient, family, and physician, complicated by issues of best interests and self-determination;

3. the professional's fear of litigation if all options for treatment are not provided on demand;

4. the influence of values held by not only the physician but also by the patient and others in reaching clinical decisions;

5. the emergence of patient autonomy over the traditional paternalism in physician–patient relationships;

6. the view that health is a commodity to be managed and sold as a market good;

7. the potential conflict of religious convictions with individual and institutional values of healthcare providers; and

8. the impact of multiple outsiders on previously private decisions between the physician and patient.

Fletcher (1991) added that the rise of bioethics was rooted in the expanding pluralism and individual rights of American society in the 1960s and paralleled the emergence of the factors that have changed the paradigm of healthcare delivery. More recently, Aulisio and Arnold (2008, p. 420) affirmed that the formal mechanism of ethics consultation is required to manage "the complex value laden nature of clinical decision making, a pluralistic societal context, and a growing appreciation or the rights of individuals to live by their values and the relevance of those values for medical decision making."

The Ethics Committee is expected to approach decision making in ethical dilemmas in a systematic and principled manner; to link societal values with the actual developments related to caring for patients in healthcare settings; to channel information related to patient care and ethical issues to physicians, staff, patients/families, and the community at large; and to identify areas of consensus and non-consensus for continuing study (Cranford & Doudera, 1984). Veatch (1977) noted that the key activities of the Ethics Committee include the review of ethical and other values in decisions, the development of policy that reflects institutional and community values, the provision of counsel and support to those involved in difficult decisions by acting as a sounding board rather than as the decision-maker, and the confirmation of prognosis. Ross , Glaser, Rasinski-Gregory, Gibson, and Bayley (1993) noted that the Ethics Committee often is one of the few places within the facility where values and their meaning to clinical practice are still actively discussed as legitimate areas of focus for an Ethics Committee.

The professional social worker has been a core member of the Ethics Committee since its inception. The social workers' frontline experience with patients, families, staff, and the community in managing ethical issues such as quality of life; skills in gathering, assessing, and presenting data to and from patients, families, staff, and the community; skills in communication and group process; knowledge of systems and community resources; and identification with the values supported by the work of the Ethics Committee are essential to the work of the Ethics Committee (Foster 1993; Furlong, 1986; Joseph & Conrad, 1989; Reamer, 1985; Rues & Weaver, 1989).

Joseph and Conrad's (1989) study of social workers in healthcare confirmed that social workers participate in bioethical issues at the individual, committee, and administrative levels in the ethics-related roles and functions described by Furlong (1986), with particular emphasis on serving as the presenter on psychosocial issues in ethics case consultations and interpreting ethical information to patients and families. Skinner (1991) found that social workers on the Ethics Committees had roles in establishing and chairing the Ethics Committee, in leading discussions, and in providing education to patient, families, staff, and the community on ethical issues. Csikai (1997) evaluated social workers with regard to their level of participation in the activities of the Ethics Committee as well as their satisfaction with their role on the Ethics Committee. Csikai found that high participation in case consultation and increased satisfaction levels were influenced by the level of involvement with the Ethics Committee. She suggests that the social worker's satisfaction is linked to the challenge of thinking through the difficult issues that routine work does not provide (Csikai, 1997, p. 11).

In an another study, Csikai (2004) noted that Ethics Committees provide the ideal forum for discussion of difficult cases, for policy formulation, and for staff and community education about difficult bioethical issues. She found that the committee membership is multi-disciplinary and that Ethics Committees were fairly widespread in hospitals, although this is not the case in many other types of healthcare settings (Csikai, 2004). Additionally, social workers identified their peers as being their chief, although informal, resource in dealing with ethical dilemmas. They also consulted with team leaders, interdisciplinary team members (Csikai, 2004), or other colleagues external to the hospital (Walsh-Bowers, et al., 1996).

CHALLENGES

Social workers who specialize in healthcare or are employed in healthcare settings face unique ethical challenges in clinical practice. Even when they are well educated to recognize and address ethical issues, social workers may face barriers in taking ethical action to resolve ethical dilemmas. Jansson and Dodd's (2002) examination of ethical activism, or the degree to which social workers in hospitals were involved in ethical deliberations with patients and professionals, demonstrated that many social workers do engage in ethical activism, particularly in the areas of seeking multidisciplinary ethics training, promoting norms to encourage social work participation in multidisciplinary ethical deliberations, and educating physicians about the role of social workers in these deliberations. Those who participated at the micro level were more likely to also do so at the institutional level. However, the researchers found that ethical activists needed skill in diagnosing the institutional context from both a political and power perspective.

O'Donnell et al. (2008) noted Landau's (2000) report that perceptions of powerlessness when dealing with ethical issues may be due to the roles played by the social worker and the locus of decision-making authority found in each of these positions. Social workers may perceive themselves as less-powerful members of the medical hierarchy and be treated as such by physicians (Gellis, 2001), decreasing their participation and influence in ethical decision making (Walsh-Bowers et al., 1996). Organizational support in a positive work environment strengthens social workers' ability to manage work-associated stress. As Manning (2003) pointed out, when social workers have the opportunity to influence the organization, they have an ethical responsibility to take on moral leadership. The study by

O'Donnell et al. (2008) indicated that this is most likely to happen when the organizational climate is supportive and useful resources are available.

Even when social workers have a strong educational base in ethical problem solving and are employed in an ethically supportive environment, the range of ethical issues they encounter can be daunting. Earlier in this chapter, the issues of the establishment of and compliance with Do Not Attempt Resuscitation (DNAR) orders; the continuing confusion or conflict about advance directives; the decisions related to the withdrawal or withholding of treatments such as artificial nutrition and hydration, dialysis, and mechanical ventilation; the disputed concept of futility; and the management of conflict related to patient self-determination were identified as social workers' most commonly encountered ethical issues. Other ethical practice issues are related to more global issues, such as the provision of services to undocumented aliens and team-based practice conflicts concerning boundaries, conflicts of interest, and sharing information.

The provision of healthcare services to undocumented aliens is a segment of the general debate about immigration reform. The World Health Organization (2000) stated that the right to healthcare means that governments must generate conditions in which everyone can be as healthy as possible. The four elements of the provision of healthcare include *availability, access, acceptability, and quality*. In providing healthcare, the state meets its obligation to respect, protect, and fulfill the lives of its citizens. Healthcare systems, especially those with budget gaps, look to cost-control measures, which may result in targeting the uncovered costs of services to undocumented aliens. The dilemma for professional caregivers arises from trying to honor their professional obligation to not discriminate in the provision of care for social reasons while meeting their obligation to contribute to the financial stability of their facility.

Jennings, Callahan, and Wolf (1987, p. 9) described the public duty of the profession of social work as "mak(ing) the invisible visible" on the basis of the profession's espoused values of altruism, mutual aid, and social justice. Social work serves as the voice of these values in the social conscience. The NASW Code of Ethics (2008) promotes general societal values of well-being, stewardship, justice, and integrity. The obligations derived from these values include promotion of the overall well-being of society, including the provision of basic human needs such as healthcare, to achieve social justice as outlined in Standard 6.01. Other duties related to supporting societal well-being include positively influencing social policy and institutions and active engagement in advocating for expansion of opportunity to ensure equity and access to services for all members of society, particularly those who are disadvantaged because of their status in society, including their immigration status.

The legalistic view of the issue focuses on the legal status of immigrants as the deciding factor for society's responsibility to the immigrant, believing that those who have no right to be in the country correspondingly have no right to the country's benefits. The humanist perspective declares that all people should have access to care on the basis of the worth and dignity of the individual—a core value of social work. Social workers help members of society to avoid loss of function due to disease and disability in order to secure the full range of opportunity for their patients by avoiding the inequalities associated with illness. If the medical community establishes excellence in standards of care for all without equity of access for all, a human rights dilemma is created (Farmer, 2001). The NASW Code of Ethics (2008) also recognizes, in Standard 3.09 ("Commitments to Employers") that social workers should adhere to organizational policies, procedures, regulations, and administrative orders. If social workers believes that any of these considerations impedes their ethical practice of social work, they have a duty to improve them. In no instance is it ethically acceptable for social workers to promote and support discrimination.

Teamwork is an essential methodology for healthcare service delivery. The knowledge and skills of each profession on the team addresses the total care needs of the patient. Ethical issues of collective responsibility are a core concern in interdisciplinary settings involving care teams and generate questions related to how best to resolve ethical conflicts among individual team members (Abramson, 1984). It is critical that the team and its members have a sense of individual as well as group accountability in service provision and are able to accept that compromise may be the best thing for the patient but not for the individual team member. Holland and Kilpatrick (1991) identified social work's interpersonal approach to ethical problems as one focused on the mutual and common goal of promoting client autonomy and independence. At the same time, this goal may not be the team's priority. The authors recognized that other team members may have differing approaches to ethical problems based on their unique professional codes of ethics and their perspectives as specialist clinicians and suggested that social workers require a strong base in ethical reflection and judgment when practicing on teams. Social workers may be concerned at times that team members are engaging in dual relationships with patients and families.

The NASW Code of Ethics (2008) Standard 1.06 ("Conflicts of Interest") cautions that a dual relationship can interfere with the exercise of professional discretion and impartial judgment and should be avoided. A dual relationship is defined as having a professional relationship with a patient as well as a personal or business relationship. The personal or business relationship has the potential to negatively affect the personal relationship. Reamer (2010) posed the ethical question of whether a professional violates a professional relationship when he or she accepts a "friend" invitation from a patient on Facebook. What are the risks associated with boundary crossings and violations? Ultimately, it is the responsibility of the professional to assess the risks and to advise the patient of real or potential conflicts.

OPPORTUNITIES

The gap between what the patient-care team communicates to the patient and family and what the patient and family understand about the patient's condition is an ongoing issue in end-of-life care (Keating et al., 2010; Lo, Quill, & Tulsky, 1999; Quill, Arnold, & Back, 2009; Truog, 2007). These authors pointed to physician reluctance to initiate the "conversation," patient reaction to awkward phrasing of decisions ("Do you want us to do everything?"), and a failure to elicit goals of care from patients to help frame their end-of-life decisions. In response, Back, Arnold, and Tulsky (2009); Casarett and Quill (2007); and Pantilat (2009) identified process-based guides on how professionals should approach communication with seriously ill patients. Questions include when conversations should be held, how much information should be shared, with whom the information should be shared, and why these conversations promote trust for the patient in the professional. All of the authors recognized that the emotions attached to the context of the situation adds to the complexity of the decisions for all parties.

Mizrahi (1992) asserted that social workers' demonstrated strength remains in our ability to adapt through reclaiming our competence, reframing our goals, reconfiguring our roles, redefining expected outcomes, reconnecting our links to the community, rebuilding our coalitions, and reasserting our vision and values. The need for education and support for other members of the care team to improve their communication skills is an ideal opportunity for social work to reaffirm its leadership role in addressing the total needs of the patient and family. Csikai and Sales (1998) found that ethics committees valued the contribution of social work to the committee activity and desired increased participation from social workers.

Bern-Klug, Gessert, and Forbes (2001) described the role of social workers in end-of-life care as "context interpreters" promoting the understanding of patients and families of the natural course of their illness, the process of dying, and the benefits and risks of continuing medical intervention. Cagle and Kovacs (2009) reinforced that education is a key social work intervention in the provision of end-of-life care. An important feature of the education intervention utilized by the social worker is giving patients and families an opportunity to share their story in the context of the experience of a serious illness and then attending to the importance of their story with the care-team members. Social workers are sensitive to the values imbedded in the patient's story and are open to the range of emotions attached to the story. Utilizing a balanced viewpoint of the stories of the care-team members and the patients and families, social workers help to avoid an adversarial aspect to ethics conflicts in end-of-life decision making, which can mar the process for all parties (Cohn, Goodman-Crews, Rudman, Schneiderman, & Waldman, 2007). In both inpatient and nursing-home settings, social workers can assume a leadership role in helping patients and families to manage the complexity of the system and treatment options, but only with adequate training and support from their facilities (Lacey, 2006; Snow, Warner & Zilberfein, 2008).

SUMMARY

This chapter has reviewed the role of ethics in healthcare social work practice, including the value base of the profession, common ethical dilemmas and ethical problem-solving models, the role of ethics committees, challenges to ethical practice at the individual and organizational levels, and opportunities for social work to assume a stronger leadership role in the ethical care of the patient and in promoting an ethical environment within the organization.

Ethical practice is enhanced by education to recognize ethical issues and how to take action to resolve them, the availability of ethical resource services such as an active ethics consultation service, and an overall perceived duty among all professionals to place the interests of the patients above their own. This grounding will prepare social workers for the continuing and developing ethical challenges related to quality patient care and the ethical implications of the advances in technology to expand care.

KEY TERMS AND CONCEPTS

- Ethics

- Values

- Obligations

- Ethical decision making

- Futile treatment

- Do not resuscitate

- Autonomy

- Beneficence

- Nonmaleficence

- Justice

- Deontological perspective

- Consequentialist perspective

- Virtue ethics perspective

- Ethics of care perspective

QUESTIONS FOR DISCUSSION

Discuss Beauchamp and Childress's four principles of **biomedical ethics**. How do they correspond to social work values and ethics? What is the difference between beneficence and nonmaleficence? Are their limits to patient autonomy? If so, what kinds and why?

Consider deontological and consequential ethics. Which approach is most consistent with your personal values and ethical beliefs? Why? How might this affect your work with patients and other team members?

In what ways should principles of justice be considered in making decisions about medical care? Does the effort to ensure a more equitable distribution of healthcare resources lead to healthcare rationing? Why or why not?

EXERCISES

1. You are the social worker on a pulmonary care unit. The patient is 75 years old, has lung cancer, and is on a ventilator in a comatose state. The patient's family, medical team, and ethics committee have determined that keeping the patient on a ventilator is futile care, and they order the patient to be slowly withdrawn from the ventilator. Furthermore, the cost of caring for this patient in now in excess of $300,000 and a shortage of available beds in the hospital has meant that some patients have had to be referred to other hospitals.

   - How would you feel about being involved in this process?
   - Apply a decision–making model to determine if this is an ethical course of action or not. What values are involved?
   - What other information would you want to know?
   - How do justice and the distribution of resources figure into this case?

2. Your hospital has decided to close its outpatient dialysis center to deal with a largely undocumented alien population. The hospital has agreed to cover the costs of six months of services in a private community-based outpatient clinic with which you have formed a close relationship as you often refer patients with full insurance coverage. The dialysis center has asked you to identify the clinic patients who are undocumented. You want to maintain your good working relationship with this service as they often make special arrangements for some of your insured patients but are concerned that the undocumented patients will face discrimination. How do you balance the interests of all parties?

   OR

   The situation is the same as the one described above, but the hospital has asked to identify where the undocumented patients are originally from and to work with a contractor who will fly the patients back home and arrange for dialysis services in their homeland. You have read that these companies fail to follow through with their patients and in fact that many patients have died because of access to services. How would you work with administration to ensure that the patients actually receive the services promised?

3. You are working in an outpatient women and children's clinic that has a large immigrant population. You learn from one of your young African patients that her family has arranged for her marriage and that, in preparation, they have scheduled a clitorectomy, which is a custom in their country and family. A local practitioner will perform the procedure in her home. Your patient believes she should have the procedure but is frightened. She has asked that you maintain her confidentiality and not disclose her concerns to her family or other professionals in the clinic. Would you maintain her confidentiality? If yes, what ethical principles and sections of the Code of Ethics would justify your choice? If no, what ethical principles and sections of the Code of Ethics would justify your choice, and how would you intervene?

REFERENCES

Abramson, M. (1984). Collective responsibility in interdisciplinary collaboration: An ethical perspective for social workers. *Social Work in Health Care, 10*, 35–43.

American Medical Association. (1999). Medical futility in end-of-life care. *JAMA, 281*, 937–941.

Aulisio, M. P., & Arnold, R. M. (2008). Role of ethics committees: Helping to address value conflicts or uncertainties. *Chest, 134*, 417–424.

Back, A., Arnold, R., & Tulsky, J. (2009). *Mastering communication with seriously ill patients.* New York: Cambridge University Press.

Beauchamp T. L., & Childress, J. F. (2001). *Principles of biomedical ethics* (5th ed.). New York: Oxford University Press.

Bern-Klug, M., Gessert, C., & Forbes, S. (2001). The need to revise assumptions about the end of life: Implications for social work practice. *Health and Social Work, 26*, 38–47.

Black, K. (2004). Advance directives communication with hospitalized elderly patients: Social worker's roles and practices. *Journal of Gerontological Social Work, 42*, 131–145.

Cagle, J. G., & Kovacs, P. J. (2009). Education: A complex and empowering social work intervention at the end of life. *Health and Social Work, 34*, 17–27.

Casarett, D. J., & Quill, T. E. (2007). "I'm not ready for hospice": Strategies for timely and effective hospice discussions. *Ann Intern Med, 146*, 443–449.

Cohn, F., Goodman-Crews, P., Rudman, W., Schneiderman, L. J., & Waldman, E. (2007). Proactive ethics in the ICU: A comparison of value perceived by healthcare professionals and recipients. *The Journal of Clinical Ethics, 18*, 140–147.

Council on Social Work Education. (2008). Educational Policy and Accreditation Standards. Alexandria, VA: CSWE.

Cranford, R. E., & Doudera, A. E. (1984). The emergence of institutional ethics committees. In Cranford, R. E., & Doudera, A.E. (Eds.). *Institutional ethics committees and health care decision making* (pp. 5–21). Ann Arbor, MI: Health Administration Press in cooperation with the American Society of Law and Medicine.

Csikai, E. L. (1997). Social worker participation on hospital ethics committees: An assessment of involvement and satisfaction. *Arete, 22*, 1–13.

Csikai, E. L., & Sales, E. (1998). The emerging social work role on hospital ethics committees: A comparison of social worker and chair perspectives. *Social Work, 43*, 233–242.

Csikai, E. L., & Bass, K. (2000). Health care social workers' views on ethical issues, practice and policy in end-of-life care. *Social Work in Health Care, 24*, 1–22.

Csikai, E.L. (2004). Social workers' participation in the resolution of ethical dilemmas in hospice care. *Health and Social Work, 29*, 67–76.

Dolgoff, R., Loewenberg, F. M., & Harrington, D. (2009). *Ethical decisions for social work practice* (8th ed.). Belmont, CA: Thomson Brooks/Cole.

Egan, M., & Kadushin, G. (1999). The social worker in the emerging field of home care: Professional activities and ethical concerns. *Health and Social Work, 24*, 43–55.

Farmer, P. (2001). The major infectious diseases in the world—To treat or not to treat. *NEJM, 345*, 208–210.

Fin, J. J., & Solomon, M. Z. (2001). Communication in intensive care settings: The challenge of futility disputes. *Critical Care Medicine, 29*(Supplement), N10–N15.

Fletcher, J. C. (1991). The bioethics movement and hospital ethics committees. *Maryland Law Review, 50*, 859–894.

Foster, L. W., Sharp, J., Scesny, A., McLellan, L., & Cotman, K. (1993). Bioethics: Social work's response and training needs. *Social Work in Health Care, 19*, 15–38.

Furlong, R.M. (1986). The social worker's role on the Institutional Ethics Committee. *Social Work in Health Care, 11,* 93–100.

Gellis, Z. (2001). Job stress among academic health center and community hospital social workers. *Administration in Social Work, 25,* 17–32.

Gordon, W.E. (1965). Knowledge and value: Their distinction and relationship in clarifying social work practice. *Social Work, 10,* 32–39.

Grady, C., Danis, M., Soeken, K., O'Donnell, P., Taylor, C., Farrar, A., & Ulrich, C. (2008). Does ethics education influence the moral action of practicing nurses and social workers? *American Journal of Bioethics, 8,* 4–11.

Hamilton, G. (1940). *Theory and practice of social casework.* New York: Columbia University Press.

Holland, T. P., & Kilpatrick, A. C. (1991). Ethical issues in social work: Toward a grounded theory of professional ethics. *Social Work, 36,* 138–144.

Jansson, B. S., & Dodd, S. J. (2002). Ethical activism: Strategies for empowering medical social workers. *Social Work in Health Care, 36,* 11–28.

Jennings, B., Callahan, D., & Wolf, S. M. (1987). Professions: Public interest and the common good. *Hastings Center Report, 17*(Special Suppl.), 1–20.

Joseph, M. V. (1983). Ethical decision-making in clinical practice: A model for ethical problem solving. In C.B. Germain (Ed.), *Advances in clinical practice* (pp. 207–217). Silver Spring, MD: NASW Press.

Joseph, M. V., & Conrad, A. P. (1989). Social work influence on interdisciplinary ethical decision making in health care settings. *Health and Social Work, 14,* 22–30.

Kass, L. R. (1993). Is there a right to die. *Hastings Center Report, 23*(1), 34–43.

Keating, N. L., Landrum, M. B., Rogers, S. O., Baum, S. K., Virnig, B. A., Huskamp, H. A., . . . & Kahn, K. L. (2010). Physician factors associated with discussions about end-of-life care. *Cancer, 116*(4), 998–1006.

Lacey, D. (2006). End of life decision making for nursing home residents with dementia: A survey of nursing home social services staff. *Health and Social Work, 31,* 189–199.

Landau, R. (2000). Ethical dilemmas in general hospitals: Differential perceptions of direct practitioners and directors of social service. *Social Work in Health Care, 30,* 25–44.

Levy, C. S. (1973). The value base of social work. *Journal of Education for Social Work, 9,* 34–42.

Lo, B., Quill, T., & Tulsky, J. (1999). Discussing palliative care with patients. *Ann Intern Med, 130,* 744–749.

Mackelprang, R. W., & Mackelprang, R. D. (2005). Historical and contemporary issues in end-of-life decisions: Implications for social work. *Social Work, 50*(4), 315–323.

Manetta, A. A., & Wells, J. G. (2001). Ethical issues in the social worker's role in physician-assisted suicide. *Health and Social Work, 26,* 160–167.

Manning, S. S. (2003). *Ethical leadership in human services: A multi-dimensional approach.* Boston: Pearson Education, Inc.

McCormick, R. A. (1984). Ethics committees: Promise or peril? *Law, Medicine, and Health Care, 12,* 150–155.

Miller, P. J., Hedlund, S. C., & Murphy, K. A. (1998). Social work assessment in end of life. Practice guidelines for suicide and the terminally ill. *Social Work in Health Care, 26,* 23–36.

Mizrahi, T. (1992). The direction of patient's rights in the 1990s: Proceed with caution. *Health and Social Work, 17,* 247–252.

National Association of Social Workers. (2008). *Code of Ethics of the National Association of Social Workers.* Washington, DC: NASW.

O'Donnell, P., Farrar, A., BrintzenhofeSzoc, K., Conrad, A. P., Danis, M., Grady, C., Taylor, C., & Ulrich, D. M. (2008). Predictors of ethical stress, moral action and job satisfaction in health care social workers. *Social Work in Health Care, 46,* 19–38.

O'Donnell, P. A. (1998). *The experience of institutional ethics committee membership: A survey* (Unpublished doctoral dissertation) Catholic University of America, Washington, DC.

Pantilat, S.Z. (2009). Communicating with seriously ill patients. *JAMA, 301*(12), 1279–1281.

Pellegrino, E. J., & Thomasma, D. (1988). *For the patient's good: The restoration of beneficence in health care.* New York: Oxford University Press.

Perlman, H. H. (1976). Believing and doing: Values in social work education. *Social Casework, 57,* 381–392.

Proctor, E. K., Morrow-Howell, N., & Lott, C. L. (1993). Classification and correlates of ethical dilemmas in hospital social work. *Social Work, 38,* 166–177.

Pumphrey, M. W. (1959). *The teaching of values and ethics in social work education, Vol. 13.* New York: Council on Social Work Education.

Quill, T. E., Arnold, R. M., & Back, A. L. (2009). Discussing treatment preferences with patients who want "everything." *Annals of Internal Medicine, 151,* 345–349.

Quill, T. E., & Brody, H. (1996). Physician recommendations and patient autonomy: Finding a balance between physician power and patient choice. *Annals of Internal Medicine, 125,* 763–769.

Reamer, F. G. (1985). The emergence of bioethics in social work. *Health and Social Work, 10,* 271–281.

Reamer, F. G. (1999). *Social work values and ethics* (2nd ed.). New York: Columbia University Press.

Reamer, F. G. (2009). *The social work ethics casebook: Cases and commentary.* Washington, DC: NASW Press.

Reamer, F. G. (2010). Novel boundary challenges: Social networking. *Social Work Today.* Retrieved from http://www.socialworktoday.com/news/eoe_111309.shtml

Ross, J. W., Glaser, J. W., Rasinski-Gregory, D., Gibson, J. M., & Bayley, C. (1993). *Health care ethics committees: The next generation.* Chicago, IL: American Hospital Association.

Rues, L. A., & Weaver, B. (1989). Membership issues for hospital ethics committees. *HEC Forum, 1,* 127–136.

Schneiderman, L., Jecker, N. S., & Jonsen, A. R. (1990). Medical futility: Its meaning and ethical implications. *Annals of Internal Medicine, 112,* 949–954.

Schneiderman, L., Gilmer, T., Teetzel, H. D., Dugan, D. O., Blustein, J., Cranford, R., Briggs, K. A., Komatsu, G. I., Goodman-Crews, P., Cohn, F., & Young, E. W. (2003). Effect of ethics consultations on nonbeneficial life-sustaining treatments in the intensive care setting: A randomized controlled trial. *JAMA, 290,* 1166–1172.

Skinner, K. W. (1991). A national survey of social workers on institutional ethics committees: Patterns of participation and roles. *Dissertation Abstracts International, 53,* 623.

Snow, A., Warner, J., & Zilberfein, F. (2008). The increase of treatment options at the end of life: Impact on the social work role in an inpatient hospital setting. *Social Work in Health Care, 47,* 376–391.

Strom-Gottfried, K. (2007). *Straight talk about professional ethics.* Chicago, IL: Lyceum Books, Inc.

The Joint Commission. (2009). *2009 Joint Commission Hospital Accreditation Program Standards.* Chicago: Author. Retrieved from http://www.jointcommission.org/standards/

Truog, R. D. (2007). Tackling medical futility in Texas. *NEJM, 357,* 1–3.

Tulsky, J. A. (2010). Interventions to enhance communication among patients, providers, and families. *Journal of Palliative Medicine, 8*(Supplement 1), S-95.

Veatch, R. M. (1977). Hospital ethics committees: Is there a role? *Hastings Center Report, 7,* 22–25.

Vigilante, J. L. (1974). Between values and science: Education for the profession: Or is proof truth? *Journal of Education for Social Work, 10,* 107–115.

Walsh-Bowers, R., Rossiter, A., & Prilleltensky, I. (1996). The personal is the organizational in the ethics of hospital social workers. *Ethics and Behavior, 6,* 321–335.

World Health Organization (2000). *The right to health.* Retrieved from http://www.who.int/mediacentre/factsheets/fs323/en/index.html

Yen, B. M., & Schneiderman, L. J. (1999). Impact of pediatric ethics consultations on patients, families, social workers, and physicians. *Journal of Perinatology, 19,* 373–378.

Practice-Based Research in Healthcare Social Work

Karen M. Allen and William J. Spitzer

INTRODUCTION

Research informs and advances social work practice in two ways. The first benefit occurs when we use empirical studies to help select and evaluate clinical interventions and strategies or to learn more about a disease, its causes, and its prognosis. **Evidence-based practice** describes the process of inquiry that begins when we turn to published, scholarly research to answer questions about the type of treatment shown to be most effective with a given patient population or problem (Giles, 2004; Jackson, 1998; McNeece & Thyer, 2004). We identify research on the problem, critically evaluate it, assess its applicability to our situation, and, after integrating it into our practice or program, evaluate the effectiveness of the intervention (Drake, et al., 2001; Straus, Richardson, Glasziou, & Haynes, 2005.). **Best practice standards** are published protocols or steps that should be followed in certain circumstances. These standards arise from research findings that support their effectiveness.

Best practice models incorporate the most efficient and effective *standards of care* in treating problems. When social workers design new programs and look to the literature and/or agencies in the community to learn about state-of-the art programs, their effort is to identify a best practice model that can be applied to the new program. The landmark Patient Protection and Affordable Health Care Act that was passed in 2010 supports the use of evidence-based medicine and best practice standards as a means of standardizing care across the country, thereby reducing costs and variations while improving overall quality.

The second benefit of research occurs when we evaluate our own practices, programs, and services. **Practice evaluation** involves integrating basic research methodologies and evaluation strategies into our own professional practice so that questions about the effectiveness of our interventions can be answered. Particularly during periods of financial constraint, all human-service providers, including social workers, are challenged to demonstrate that their interventions are effective and that their services make a positive difference in the lives of their clients. Funding sources understandably require data that justify research or operating expenditures, and, particularly during times of decreasing government resources, administrators need a sound basis for making decisions about maintaining or eliminating programs and services. Documenting how problems have been successfully addressed serves to educate decision-makers about the important contributions made by social work (Bloom, Fisher, & Orme, 2009).

Practice-based evaluation typically describes the research activities of a social worker relative to delivering services to patients on their own caseload. When we expand the scope of evaluation and collect data from the caseloads of multiple social workers, we engage in *program, department, and/or agency evaluation*, similar to our conceptual model of micro-, mezzo- and macro-level client systems. Micro-evaluation is focused on individual workers' practice, whereas mezzo-evaluation aggregates data from multiple workers at a program, service, or department level and macro-evaluation examines the composite results of multiple workers, services, and programs at the agency level. Employing all three levels of evaluation is crucial for assessing the overall effectiveness of social work services and value of the professional contributions added to an agency.

The process of integrating research, evidence, and empirical data into practice overlap and can be conceptualized as a circle. The beginning of the circle starts when one explores existing research to determine the best clinical approach or best practice standard to use with your patient population. You read and critique the literature, determine the best studies and model approaches based on your goals or focus, design a program or intervention incorporating the findings in the literature, and then evaluate the effectiveness of your program. When you analyze and summarize your evaluation data, you close the circle as shown in *Figure 6.1* below.

This chapter takes you through each step of evidence-based practice and the practice evaluation cycle described above. Each chapter in Part II of this book presents an overview of a theoretical or treatment approach that can be utilized in given situations. Research is cited to justify each approach and to demonstrate its effectiveness. The practice approaches described in this book are therefore evidence based.

EVIDENCE-BASED PRACTICE

Evidence-based practice (EBP) is an approach that was introduced into medicine during the 1980s and that has now been adopted in many professional contexts. EBP in medicine is defined as the "integration of best researched evidence and clinical expertise with patient values" (Institute of Medicine, 2001, p. 147). This broad definition recognizes the importance of professional experience and knowledge in consideration of patient values and preferences when selecting treatment options. Evidence-based practice is a decision-making process that uses established evidence to design, select, implement, and evaluate practice interventions (NcNeece & Thyer, 2004; Mullen, 2004). Empirical evidence is established through testing in formal research studies.

Figure 6.1   Evidence-Based Practice and Practice Evaluation Cycles

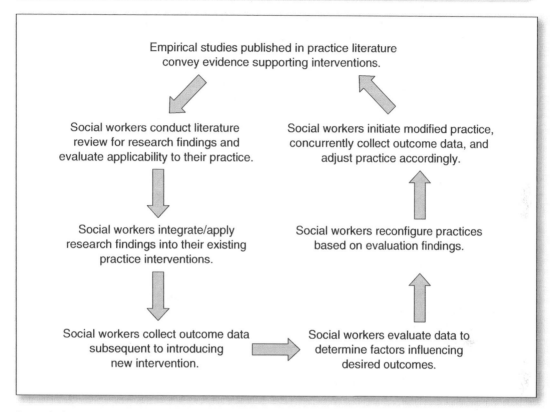

Source: Authors.

One way of integrating best-practice standards in healthcare is through the use of **critical pathways** or *clinical practice guidelines* based on empirical evidence. These treatment protocols are standardized and implemented most frequently as a tool for intervening with chronic, complex, and/or high-cost diseases. A critical pathway affords a methodology or "map" that can be used by healthcare team members to focus on particular patient problems or populations. Pathways list and sequence times for "critical" steps during patient-care interventions (Rotter et al., 2010). Pathways seek to increase consistency in care by reducing any variation between provider interventions. This consistency is achieved by articulating step-by-step patient-care guidelines based on demonstrated research and best practice approaches. Healthcare organizations select or develop critical pathways for patient problems and then scrutinize any reasons for varying from these pathways. At the same time, attention is focused on determining the effectiveness of the pathways and identifying factors that influence outcomes.

Social workers benefit from being aware of, and being part of, critical pathways. Our services may represent one component of a path, for example, when certain patients warrant a psychosocial assessment on a particular day of care. It is fundamentally important that social workers be active participants on interdisciplinary teams responsible for developing critical pathways used by our facilities, particularly when mental health, psychosocial, or continuity-of-care issues affect patient care. Such participation is important as it affords opportunities for social workers to define the optimal manner for using our services and thereby deriving maximum benefit for both the patients and the facility. We effectually determine when, how, and by whom particular services will be initiated. Dienemann, Campbell, Landenburger, and Curry (2002) developed an illustrative critical pathway for use with patients admitted to the hospital as the result of interpersonal violence.

Although there may be evidence documenting their effectiveness, some interventions may transgress sensitive cultural, religious, social, and/or personal values of patients. To illustrate, while a legitimate and usually effective medical intervention, the ordering of a blood transfusion would violate the fundamental religious beliefs of any practicing Jehovah's Witness. Healthcare professionals must strive to be aware of and respect patient wishes. Colleagues and/or hospital ethics committees should be readily consulted when questions arise about the appropriateness of any intervention. Gambrill (1999) defined EBP as "the effective use of professional judgment in integrating information regarding each client's unique characteristics and circumstance, including their preferences and actions, and external findings. The steps in the process are

1. Identify a practice decision that needs to be made.

2. Formulate a question that can be answered by exploring the research.

3. Locate the best evidence and information available to answer the question.

4. Critically evaluate the evidence.

5. Apply the results of this appraisal to the practice decision.

6. Evaluate effectiveness and seek ways to improve intervention in the future

(Straus et al., 2005, p. 3–4)

Evidence-based practice is based on an expectation that practitioners will critically evaluate information discovered during the exploration of patient-care issues (Gibbs, 2003; Gibbs & Gambrill, 2002). Gibbs (1989) and Cournoyer (2004) developed resources and guidelines for social workers to use when looking at empirical and evaluation studies on practice interventions. These guidelines can be used to critique the study and to consider factors such as the sample size, whether or not random assignment and controls were used, and the extent to which study findings can be generalized to other populations.

While Internet sources on diseases and treatments can be useful to patients when they are learning about their condition and its management, practitioners need to systematically review current scholarly and empirical research studies published in *peer-reviewed* professional journals. Literally all hospitals feature medical libraries that are available for staff researching patient conditions and treatment. A thorough analysis of research studies is necessary to determine which interventions yield the most desirable or "best" outcomes. Even the most carefully conducted research contains some margin of error, so professional experience dictates caution in using a given treatment approach, even when supported by evidence.

Clinical experience also can guide us in taking an approach used and tested with one group of patients and then making appropriate modifications so that another group might benefit from its application. In all instances, social workers and other healthcare professionals have an ethical responsibility to inform patients of any known limitations in research guiding their interventions and recommendations. Patients and families are in a better position to make informed decisions about their care when they understand the basis for and implications of involved professionals' opinions and actions. Importantly, informed consent also increases the prospect for the patients' subsequent compliance with any treatment directives.

Depending on the presenting issues, healthcare social workers most often review articles in social work, nursing, and/or medical journals. When addressing complex problems, research into the literature of disciplines beyond social work is recommended. The more extensive the literature review, the greater the likelihood of achieving a fuller understanding of both the presenting problem(s) and the interventions. Since disciplines vary in their patient-care approaches because of unique perspectives, methodologies and expertise, it is valuable to be aware of the factors that influenced the selection of any one approach. Such knowledge enhances your understanding of other professionals' actions, can guide your interaction with them, and can influence your recommendations about maximizing your contribution to patient care. Regardless of literature, some consistent criteria exist for evaluating articles:

- Is the article a scholarly publication in a peer-reviewed journal?

- Are the authors identified with their professional affiliations and credentials?

- Is an abstract provided that summarizes the content of the article? Does it assist in deciding whether to read the article?

- Is the problem or topic clearly defined? Does the author outline research questions, study purpose, approach, theoretical framework, or hypothesis?

- How would you classify the article? Is the article conceptual or theoretical, empirical or research?

- Is a description provided of a best-practice model or program?

- What supportive or clarifying literature is cited in the article? Are the articles recent and appropriate to the topic?

- Are the research methods clearly identified?

- How were the participants selected?

- Is a control (comparison) group included to contrast or aid in explaining findings?

- Are variables operationalized and appropriately measured? If data-collection instruments are used, are they found elsewhere in the literature or were they created by the author(s) for the current study? Was the reliability and validity of the data collection instruments ascertained?

- Are study findings clearly summarized and conclusions clearly presented?

- Are study limitations discussed? Can study findings be generalized to other populations?

- Is the article written in language that is appropriate to the professional discipline, and is it free of bias?

The case study below provides an example of how research can be used in the everyday practice of a hospital-based healthcare social worker.

CASE EXAMPLE

Susan is a medical social worker in an acute-care community hospital. Because the staff size is small, the social workers are not able to contact every patient. In addition to seeing patients when they are referred by other team members, Susan reviews the admission information for every patient who is admitted to her unit in order to identify those who potentially would benefit from social work services. On reviewing the admissions records one morning, Susan notices that a 35-year-old man was admitted to intensive care the previous night with a diagnosis of scleroderma.

From her knowledge of medical terminology, Susan is able to partially discern his medical condition as his diagnosis contains the suffix "derma," which relates to the skin. She is curious as to what skin condition would cause a young man to require intensive care. On her way to the unit, she stops at the medical library for a quick reference. She learns that scleroderma actually means "hard skin" and that it is an autoimmune disease affecting connective tissue. In some patients the condition is localized and can be treated, but in others it can affect all tissues and organs in the body, hardening the tissues and potentially resulting in death. She prepares herself as this latter category probably describes the patient who has been admitted to the intensive care unit. She realizes that she needs to prioritize visiting the patient as she will likely need to address end-of-life as well as grief and loss issues.

During her quick search of the literature in the MEDLINE database, Susan learns that there is no known cure for the disease, but best-practice standards indicate that the use of steroids and immunosuppressant drugs can be helpful. A number of articles indicate that patients often experience depression and may develop a substance-abuse disorder. Susan reads in one article that alternative approaches, including Vitamin E, can be beneficial, and that detoxified patients may be particularly sensitive to chemicals in the environment. She notes, however, that the article does not appear to be peer-reviewed and is not published in a scholarly or scientific journal. Furthermore, the author does not cite any empirical evidence justifying the use of these alternative approaches. Now suspect of the article's findings, Susan decides to ask the patient's attending physician, a rheumatologist, if he is aware of any indications for using alternative treatments.

When Susan arrives on the unit, the nurse manager eagerly approaches her and asks her to see this patient, who is in fact, dying from scleroderma. Susan recognizes from her research that she needs to screen the patient for depression and substance abuse. While saddened by the patient's prognosis, she is grateful that she researched the patient's condition so that she was prepared to provide the appropriate support needed by the patient and his family.

Because of the potential harm to patients and families from practitioners acting on the basis of poorly designed studies, the field of medicine developed criteria for evaluating research and the legitimacy of any study findings. These criteria include expecting large sample sizes and the random assignment of subjects into control and treatment groups. These studies, referred to as **clinical trials**, are divided into specific phases.

The National Institutes of Health (www.clinicaltrials.gov), which provide substantial funding for medical and healthcare research projects, define four phases of clinical trials. *Phase I trials* investigate the use of experimental drugs or treatments on small groups of people (usually numbering 20 to 80 subjects). The goal is to determine if the interventions are safe to use, identify potential side effects, and determine effective dosage levels. In *Phase II*, treatments are rendered to larger samples ranging from 100 to 300 subjects. In *Phase III*, between 1,000 and 3,000 participants are engaged in an effort to confirm treatment effectiveness, monitor side effects, and compare any new treatment to existing treatments. Permission to move from one phase to another must be given by the Institutional Review Board (IRB), an oversight committee that approves research projects and ensures that human subjects in the study are protected from unreasonable risks. A research study can be halted at any point if a treatment produces serious side effects. The final stage, *Phase IV*, occurs after the treatment is introduced to the market. Phase IV trials seek to delineate serious risks, benefits, and most appropriate use. Studies that have proceeded through all phases of clinical trial, including random assignment of patients to experimental and control groups, are referred to as the "gold standard" of medical research. These trials represent the most carefully conducted research studies, yielding the most reliable findings available to guide practice.

A **Meta-analysis** is a technique used to synthesize and evaluate findings of multiple research studies that address a particular problem. In the analysis, investigators establish criteria for judging research and then summarize all of the study findings. Bradley, Greene, Russ, Dutra, and Westen (2005), for example, conducted a meta-analysis of treatment for Post-Traumatic Stress Disorder (PTSD). To be included in this meta-analysis, studies had to have tested established psychotherapeutic approaches, used a validated instrument to examine PTSD (the dependent variable), and employed an experimental design with random assignment into treatment and control groups. With 26 studies meeting the criteria, the meta-analysis revealed that while psychotherapy seemingly improved initial recovery from PTSD, patients were often left with residual symptoms over the long term.

FROM RESEARCH TO QUALITY IMPROVEMENT

Healthcare organizations expend considerable time, money, and energy evaluating the quality of their services. This effort evolves from a commitment to providing quality care but also reflects the fact that the costs and risks of delivering poor care can be significant and impact the life or death of patients. Severe negative consequences arising from care or lack of care are referred to as **adverse outcomes or occurrences** and are customarily reviewed by a healthcare team of the facility or health system. Beginning in 2008, the federal government elected to deny or reduce provider reimbursement for 10 preventable complications found to occur in hospitals. These complications include hospital-acquired infections, pressure ulcers (Stages III and IV), and patient injuries sustained as result of falls (U.S. Department of Health and Human Services, 2008).

To assist tracking these occurrences, most healthcare organizations maintain a philosophy and practice of **continuous quality improvement (CQI)** or **total quality management (TQM)**. Originally designed by Edward Deming (Walton & Deming, 1986) for use in business, TQM has been widely applied in the healthcare arena. TQM seeks to create a culture in which all staff members continuously engage in activities that evaluate and improve upon patient satisfaction and service quality. The following principles are crucial in TQM (Kirst-Ashman & Hull, 2009):

1. The centrality of the patient and family as customers is critical to all improvement activities.

2. Customer feedback is essential to improving services.

3. Quality is a primary goal of the institution.

4. Employee empowerment is essential in creating a culture of quality. This requires providing adequate training and support to employees.

5. Teamwork is essential for improving quality.

6. Leadership is critical for establishing a culture of quality.

7. TQM assumes a long-term perspective based on a continuous cycle of process improvement requiring determination of where we are now, where we want to be, and what specific action steps are necessary to get there, followed by an ongoing evaluation of progress.

Although quality-improvement efforts are typically centralized and overseen by one department such as an Outcomes Management or Quality Improvement Department, every professional providing patient care contributes in some way to this effort. Social work and nurse case managers in Quality Management Departments frequently provide leadership and administrative oversight to quality-improvement efforts.

Fundamental to quality improvement is a *continuous* cycle of monitoring. Important performance variables called **indicators** are identified for study, and a minimum standard or **benchmark** is set. To illustrate this process, let's say we want to examine patient satisfaction with the continuity-of-care planning provided by social work. Patient satisfaction with this planning may be identified as one indicator. As satisfaction with care planning is necessary to promote patient compliance with treatment, patient satisfaction becomes a particularly important variable. We accordingly set a benchmark that 90% of all patients surveyed will report they are "very satisfied" or "somewhat satisfied" with social work services. When we first do our study, we learn that only 80% of our patients are satisfied. As we did not reach our desired benchmark performance, we set out in sequence to (1) identify the contributing factors that detracted from patient satisfaction, (2) implement procedural changes in response to those factors, (3) repeat the study, and (4) continue introducing practice changes until we determine that patient satisfaction with care planning has reached our desired benchmark performance level.

TQM is predicated on teamwork and utilizes tools to understand and remedy quality concerns. *Flow charts* are often used to outline major patient-care processes. When a problem develops, flow charts aid in identifying the point(s) in the overall process where things went wrong. An example of a flow chart developed to assess how to prevent patient falls in hospitals can be found at http://www.ahrq.gov/professionals/systems/hospital/fallpxtoolkit/fallpxtk-tool3a.html.

Fishbone diagrams are another quality-improvement tool that is used to identify the causes and effects of problems. *Figure 6.2* demonstrates how a fishbone diagram might be utilized to reveal potential contributing factors to delayed discharges of hospitalized patients in a particular health system. To create this diagram, optimally an interdisciplinary team would be assembled to explore factors complicating the discharge of patients. The main spine of the diagram represents the essential process under study. The "fish bones" on the top and bottom of the main spine (e.g., personnel, the operating environment, patient-care processes, and relevant resources) reflect contributing factors that impact the patient-discharge process.

"Fishboning" can be used to focus brainstorming discussions when teams are convened for *critical incident debriefings*. Following a patient-care incident with negative implications, debriefings are often employed to analyze problems and to propose corrective steps that minimize or eliminate reoccurrence of those problems. The Joint Commission defines **sentinel events** as "unexpected occurrences involving death or serious physical or psychological injury, or the risk thereof." Serious injury specifically includes loss of limb or function. The phrase "or the risk thereof" includes any process variation for which a recurrence would carry a significant chance of a serious adverse outcome (see http://www.jointcommission.org/sentinel_event.aspx). Hospitals and **regulatory agencies** require that sentinel events be tracked and systematically studied in an ongoing effort to protect patient safety and promote optimal care.

To best analyze the issue or problem, all parties relevant to the process are convened and are given the opportunity to provide input on the steps, roles, or functions, and

Figure 6.2   Select Factors Affecting Delayed Hospital Discharges

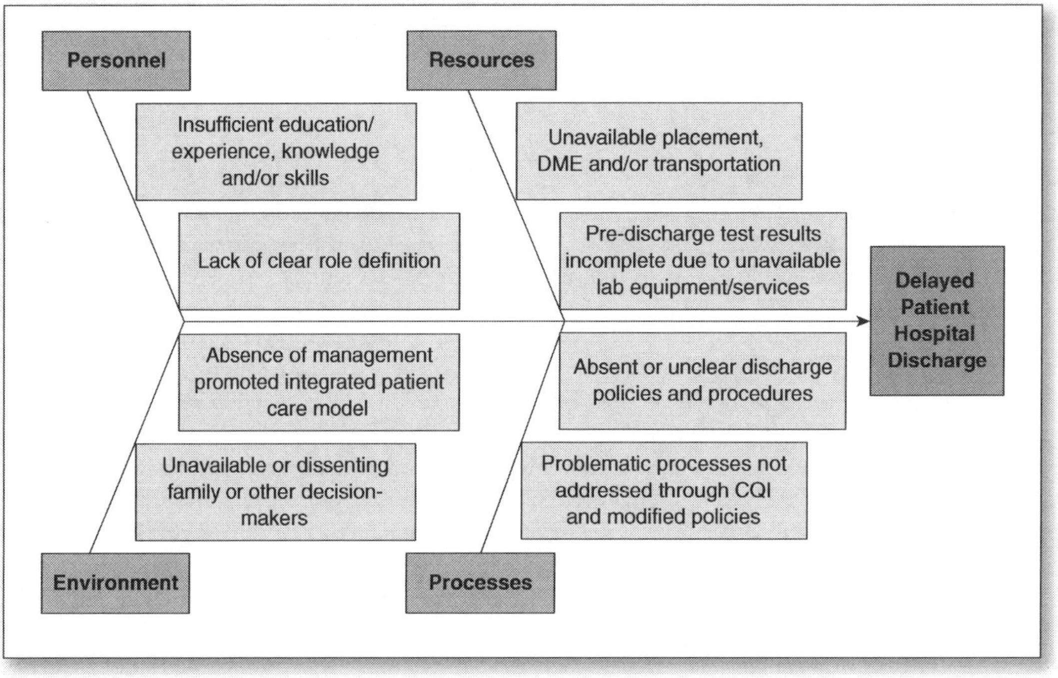

Source: Authors.

outcomes related to their patient-care effort. The intent is to reveal at what point and in what manner certain factors that led to an adverse outcome developed. As patient-care processes are most generally intertwined and interdependent on one another, one negative factor can have a compounding impact on yet other factors and trigger a sentinel or otherwise undesired event. Through discussion, these compounding factors can be mapped and then steps can be initiated to remedy identified concerns.

PRACTICE-BASED EVALUATION

Social workers are ethically obligated to evaluate their practice with attention to the success and appropriateness of their interventions. Practice-based evaluation is a systematic, continuous process for posing and answering important questions about the services, programs, and treatments provided by a facility, a work unit such as a department, or individual staff. Practice evaluation is also referred to as **practice-based research**, and here the terms are used interchangeably. Research, as you know from your research classes, strives to eliminate bias and to achieve rigorous control over the variables being studied. In true research, those providing patient care would not serve as researchers because serving in the dual roles of provider and researcher could bias any study. In comparison, practice-based research or evaluation often involves service providers directly evaluating their own work. Despite the risk of introducing bias, the intent is to encourage professionals to knowledgeably self-critique their practice and consequently implement service changes that better meet patient needs.

Evaluation differs from research in several ways. Although a report is compiled, evaluation findings are treated in confidence and remain internal to the facility. They generally do not appear in the literature, although public dissemination of results could potentially benefit the profession and overall patient care. Studies destined for publication require approval by the facility's Institutional Review Board before the project is started. This requirement ensures that protections for human subjects are in place and are followed. Evaluations tend to be naturalistic in that they typically examine something that we are doing and how we are doing it. Evaluations rarely involve random assignment into groups or study the impact of withholding specific treatment from patients. Exceptions are made when naturally occurring comparator groups are available for study, such as patients on service waiting lists.

Crucial ethical issues must be considered when engaging in practice evaluation. These include potential bias toward wanting to study and report successes; contending with managers, funders, and clinicians who may seek to influence findings (whether positive or negative); using evaluation to highlight conflicts between the needs of an organization, its patients, and its workers; recognizing actions that can influence the dissemination or suppression of evaluation findings; and avoiding the use of information gathered for one purpose (such as program improvement) for different purposes (such as performance evaluation). Additional ethical challenges arise when evaluation designs are changed midstream or at the time of formal reporting and/or when weak findings are used as the basis for making critical service decisions. Responsible evaluations require that designs be developed in consultation with staff, be written in advance with approval from administration, and be executed according to stated plan; they also require that the findings be reported and used as initially proposed (Bloom et al., 2009).

Posavac (1980) put forth a definition of evaluation that remains relevant to healthcare social workers. Evaluation was regarded as "a collection of methods, skills and sensitivities necessary to determine whether a human service is needed and likely to be used, whether it is conducted as planned, and whether the human service actually does help people" (p. 6). While social work services should be examined to determine if they are *effective* in accomplishing stated goals, *utilized* by clients, and *compliant* or consistent with established plans and policies, it is crucial that productivity and efficiency be evaluated. Such analysis simultaneously contributes to advancing benchmark professional practice and maximizing positive patient-care outcomes.

Productivity can be measured by using frequency counts of the services provided, patients seen, and problems addressed. Social workers should routinely collect such data as well as select patient profile characteristics including, but not limited to, age, income, educational level, residence, and type of insurance coverage. Incorporating such data affords a more comprehensive, updated client profile for program oversight and service planning. It provides insight into factors that may account for differential results in service delivery.

Efficiency is related to the amount of time required to render a unit of service and/or the cost of delivering that service. While always an important dimension, determining efficiency in service delivery becomes particularly important when resources are limited. To maximize the use of valuable resources (e.g., staff, equipment, physical plants, etc.), we must responsibly ensure that services are offered in the most efficient and cost-effective manner. One methodology for calculating efficiency utilizes time studies in which staff document the length of time necessary to perform select activities, such as assessments, counseling, family meetings, referrals, nursing home placements, and so on. An average is calculated and is used for projecting the time required to provide a planned service with an assumed number of staff and clients. Studies are typically performed for a specified period of time (e.g., day, week, month, or year) and then are repeated as warranted when workloads or other operational changes occur.

Studies that involve assessing the results of interventions measure effectiveness. Immediate results are often labeled outputs, while long term results are called outcomes. For example, passing a class is an immediate outcome of an educational activity. Using the material learned in class with clients is an outcome.

To illustrate the use of a time study, let's assume that the average initial psychosocial assessment by a social worker in a healthcare system takes 40 minutes. Three years later, as a result of an increase in patient turnover and decrease in patient length of stay (LOS), the social work department was found to have intervened with approximately 20% more patients without a staffing increase. How was it possible to have decreased assessment times by such an amount? While one can argue whether or not this change represents a service improvement, the data were presented to hospital administration as evidence that social work had responsibly self-adjusted its operations to contend with the challenging increase in patient admissions and reduced LOS times experienced by the healthcare system. The following general framework can be used for evaluation of patient-care services:

- **Productivity:** What services do we provide and how much are we providing?

- **Efficiency:** How much does it cost in dollars and/or time to provide services?

- **Utilization:** Who needs and receive our services?

- **Compliance:** Are we doing what we are supposed to do?

- **Effectiveness:** Does what we do make a difference? Do we achieve desired outcomes?

Table 6.1 provides a basic template for recording social work productivity measures. The patient name and admitting diagnoses are entered, and a key is developed for listing problems, delivered services, and the outcomes associated with social work intervention. Problem lists identify contributing factors such as inadequate home support, substance abuse, inadequate health insurance, and inadequate income. Social work services provided in healthcare settings typically include high-risk screening, psychosocial assessments, patient/family education, counseling, and continuity-of-care (or discharge) planning. The referral list of other facility and community professionals is tracked as evidence of perceived/actual patient

Table 6.1 Service Provision Record

Patient Name	Diagnosis	Identified Problems	Services Provided	Referral initiated to:	Intervention Outcome

Source: Authors.

needs. Listed outcomes can include whether problems were resolved and/or the discharge target of the patient (e.g., own home, nursing home, home healthcare, assisted-living facility, etc.). If a time series study is conducted, time per service category can be calculated and productivity can then be deduced. Other categories can be added, such as referral sources (how patients came to the attention of social work), type of health insurance, and patient admission and discharge dates.

Systematic, ongoing collection of data about delivered services is crucial, whether by an individual professional or organized operational unit like a department. Such statistics reflect the efficiency and effectiveness of the service contribution, thereby addressing the relative worth of the professional operation. On a micro-level, they allow for determination of individual staff performance, whereas on a macro-level, aggregated performance statistics can influence decisions to shift unit staffing on the basis of changes in patient volumes and needs or to concretely support the need for additional staff.

An example of an actual inpatient social work statistical data collection form is found in *Appendix D*. This form, utilized at a large academic tertiary medical system, focuses on the most significant factors in assessing the "value-added" contribution of social work to overall patient care:

- What services were rendered?

- Were the services efficiently delivered (was service promptly initiated and then executed)?

- Were the intended service goals accomplished?

- Were there barriers that deterred efficient, effective service delivery and what were the implications of these barriers?

- What was the complexity (or "acuity") of the service need?

- Who had responsibility for the satisfactory delivery of each afforded service?

- What was the ultimate patient outcome; i.e., what happened to the patient?

Several crucial features are integrated into this form. *First,* by collecting the dates of the high-risk screening along with the patient's admission date, an analyst is able to determine the *rapidity* of problem identification. An accompanying analysis of medical-record charting would then allow assessment of both the prompt initiation of service following identification of the problem and the extent of necessary involvement (one potential measure of service *intensity and/or competence*). *Second,* not only are the specific services listed but, by obligating the social worker to indicate the extent to which he or she satisfactorily provided that service ("goal accomplishment"), there is a measure of at least *staff-perceived* effectiveness. *Third,* by noting systemic (hospital), community, patient, and/or family barriers to service, insight is provided into possibilities for addressing such issues in future circumstances while also emphasizing social work's role in *solving* rather than contributing to service-delivery problems. The *fourth* feature, noted at the bottom of the form, is a recording of the patient acuity level.

This department used four specifically designated levels of increasing problem complexity (acuity) based on the numbers and nature of presenting medical and psychosocial issues. Provision for form completion by multiple social workers reflects the prevalence of patient intra-hospital unit transfers (e.g., emergency department admission with transfer to intensive care and subsequent transfer to a medical or "step-down" unit). With the form being provided to subsequent social workers who receive the patient on transfer, the initial (opening) social worker formally conveys what was done with the patient to that point. When those social workers complete and submit the form, there is then one complete statement of all presenting issues and what was attempted and accomplished with that patient. This information was utilized in supervision as one means of assessing staff intervention as well as generating recommendations for needed process change.

One potential drawback of evaluations is that the process can become political, with staff and administrators reluctant to embark on studies that would reveal service shortcomings or highlight issues with negative repercussions. Examining the impact of service reductions, for example, could prove to be a painful process for individual practitioners or professions potentially negatively impacted by the study findings. It is important to remember, however, that any self-study by practitioners or professions, even if addressing contentious issues, still places them in the *proactive* position of identifying key patient-care issues and initiating their own recommendations or remedies. Reflecting responsible action, it is far more advantageous than passive reliance on *others* to assess the extent of a problem, its contributing factors, and what potential solutions or alternative future courses of action are most viable or appropriate.

BEST PRACTICE IN EVALUATION DESIGN

Evaluation strategies should be empowering. They should be simply constructed, accomplishable in their execution, and capable of producing meaningful results. If evaluation becomes an overly complex or irrelevant process, staff will resent the additional work and may subvert or otherwise negate the legitimacy of any findings and recommendations. Evaluation plans, like a research study, should be prepared as a proposal or protocol, with the purpose of the study and its steps being clearly stated. Supervisory input should be sought, followed by approval from an appropriate facility committee or administrator(s). The design should minimize intrusions on patients and families who are directly involved in the study. Only pertinent questions should be used, and efforts must be made to protect the confidentiality of both the data and the participants. If there is a prospect that the study findings will be published or otherwise made available to outside audiences, consultation regarding the dissemination of the study and its findings should be sought from the healthcare facility's Institutional Review Board, Human Subjects Protection Committee, or equivalent body within the larger organization.

There are seven steps in the **evaluation process**: *designing, planning, implementing, data analysis and interpretation, reporting, data utilization,* and *follow-up.* The *design phase* determines the purpose of the evaluation as well as its scope, target, and questions. The methodology for the evaluation is identified along with the type of data that will be collected and the sampling techniques. Data-collection instruments unique to the study may be designed, or, alternately, standardized instruments may be employed because of their proven track records and the desire to avoid additional time in preparing new instruments. *Planning* calls for establishing realistic timelines for data collection, methodologies, and interpretation. The need for any resources must be outlined. The study proposal must be clearly written and presented with regard to the manner in which data will be used to evaluate and improve patient-care services.

In the *implementation phase*, data are gathered, coded, and entered. The data are then analyzed, and the results are summarized and interpreted. In the *reporting phase*, an initial report is prepared and then is shared with all key stakeholders for their review and response. Incorporating stakeholder recommendations in the final study report enhances both the prospect of a more comprehensive assessment of the problem(s) as well as inclusion of all potentially viable corrective actions. Of particular importance, such collaboration furthers the prospect for subsequent "buy-in" to any future service changes by affected parties in the organization. The *utilization phase* takes the proposed recommendations and integrates them into operations by changing policies, practices, and services. Steps for further evaluation are identified, including assessment of any operational changes that will be initiated as a result of the study.

The term **evaluation target** refers to the focus of an evaluation. We can study an individual patient, a caseload, a service or program, the facility as a whole, a community, or specific policies. The strategies presented here are generally appropriate for most evaluation problems, although they may have to be modified depending on the intended evaluation target. When we begin an evaluation project, we ask *evaluation questions*, which are formulated like the questions in a research study. The wording of evaluation questions is exceedingly important. Questions that are ambiguous, leading, or misunderstood will invalidate the evaluation by generating responses that are inappropriate and irrelevant. Questions should be posed broadly enough to yield complex findings but narrow enough to focus the study. Examples of suitable evaluation questions include "How well are we doing at providing this particular service?", "Are we doing what we set out to do?", "What do patients need?", "Are they getting what they need?", "Are we reaching our goals or benchmark?", and "What is achieved as a result of providing specific services?"

After deciding what we need to evaluate, the next step is to determine how we will get the answers to our questions. This determination in turn impacts the design of the evaluation. We can gather quantitative data, qualitative data, or both. Evaluation designs must be spelled out in terms of the type of data that will be collected, how the data will be collected, and how the data will be analyzed. The sample must be identified in terms of who will be questioned and why they were selected for study. We can sample patients, family members, other members of the healthcare team, and members in the community (such as referral agencies). Often, convenience samples are used to expedite data collection. An example of such a sample would be the surveying of every patient on our caseload for a given period of time. We do need to make sure that our sample is representative, meaning that our sampled population is the one that is most relevant for responding to our questions, and that we have sampled enough of our population that we can reasonably generalize or apply our findings to others outside of our sample. If we cannot generalize, the applicability and usefulness of our study will be limited to only those we sampled.

Sometimes it is not necessary to ask questions of patients directly. Instead, we can elect to review patient medical records or computer files and seek answers there. This method is called **data mining**, or conducting a **retrospective audit**. This process entails obtaining data about a service *after it has been rendered*, as opposed to engaging in a **concurrent monitor** to collect information from recipients of a service *while it is still being provided*. A retrospective audit is exemplified by a review of 200 randomly selected medical records that was performed for the purpose of determining if there were adverse outcomes among high-risk hospitalized patients who *had not* received social work services. For purposes of the audit, "high-risk patients" were defined as those aged 75 years or more, who lived alone, were uninsured or under-insured, and who were experiencing three or more chronic illnesses. The medical records department randomly selected patients' medical records based on the desired sample criteria provided. Upon review, 30% of the sampled inpatients were found more likely to be readmitted to the hospital within 90 days after discharge if they did *not* see a social worker for discharge-planning services. The medical records were also reviewed to determine compliance with protocol and policies, such as the standard that patient assessments be completed within a specified period of time following referral to the social worker. The representative sample size meant that the study findings could be generalized to that hospital inpatient population and those of similar hospitals.

The finding that nearly a third of inpatients who did not receive social work were readmitted is significant both from the standpoint of unmet patient-care needs and from the standpoint of the negative financial impacts to patients and institutions experiencing potentially avoidable and costly re-hospitalizations. This finding revealed a particularly meaningful value added contribution by social work not only in promoting patients' safe, expedient recovery (a quality-of-life issue) but also in minimizing unnecessary healthcare expenditures to patients and the prospect of incurred losses arising from non-reimbursed care to provider facilities and involved professionals. Such a dual-focus undeniably underscored the systemic importance of maintaining sufficient social work resources and promoting their timely introduction upon patient admission.

When we involve patients, family members, or other involved parties in completing surveys or focus groups, **informed consent** must be obtained. Informed consent simply means that those who would be questioned agree to participate on the basis of their understanding of the study, their role, and how the information will or will not be used. The voluntary nature of participation must be stressed, with an assurance that there will be no penalties for refusing or withdrawing. A survey introductory paragraph can address such issues by providing the following information:

- The purpose of the study

- Basic participant instructions and information (such as time required)

- Any potential risks and benefits

- How confidentiality will be assured

- How data will be handled

- How results will be used and shared

- The voluntary nature of the study, with no penalties for opting out of all or part of the study

Formative and Summative Evaluations

Two overarching strategies are available to evaluate practice. In a **formative evaluation,** concurrent monitoring collects data *during the time of service* that is used to measure how a service is being delivered and received. The advantage of this strategy is that the identification and remedying of existing service problems can immediately benefit the patient and family. The intent is to determine how a program or service is currently operating, the extent to which it is reaching the appropriate target population, whether or not the service is being implemented as designed, and whether or not resources are appropriate to deliver the service (Rossi & Freeman, 1993).

To illustrate the use of a formative evaluation, we could ask patients and families currently receiving hospice care if they perceive that they are receiving adequate support from their social worker during the dying process, if their questions are being adequately answered in a timely manner, and if they perceive that their wishes are being respected. We can then intervene to modify a patient's treatment plan or our approach on the basis of the responses to our questions. While we frequently engage in such questioning, systematically collecting respondent data allows us to incorporate this information as part of a formative practice-evaluation strategy.

When counseling patients and families, we may use a task or goal-attainment scaling to measure progress. Patients would periodically be asked to rate their progress on achieving goals by using a scale with a range of positive and negative values or numbers. A score of 0 would indicate that the patient had not made progress toward a goal, whereas a positive score would indicate progress and a negative score would mean the patient had fallen behind in reaching his or her goal. When we integrate this kind of simple tool into our practice and track progress from week to week, the social worker and the patient openly discuss the results of treatment and make ongoing adjustments to the intervention plan and approach as indicated.

The other type of general evaluation approach is called **summative evaluation** because it is done at the conclusion of services. The word "sum" means the total or the act of totaling. Summative evaluations may be conducted when a patient is being discharged and is asked to complete a patient-satisfaction survey or when patients attend a group and complete an evaluation at the end of the session(s). There are four levels to consider in summative evaluation. A *Level-I evaluation* asks patients to report their overall satisfaction with, or appreciation of, a service. An illustrative Level-I question is "To what extent did you enjoy the program?" *Level-II evaluation* questions are more specific and ask patients to subjectively report on whether they learned something from an experience or service. An example of a Level-II question response might be "As a result of this program, I learned how to use the food pyramid to plan meals." A *Level-III evaluation* occurs when patients are objectively tested on their knowledge after an intervention. When you take a final examination in a course, your instructor is using a Level-III evaluation to determine what you learned from the course. Level-I, II, and III evaluations are also called one-group, post-test only designs (Kirst-Ashman & Hull, 2009). If your instructor pre-tested you in the first class period and then repeated that test at the end of the course, he or she was using a *Level-IV* evaluation. As a Level IV evaluation requires a pre-test and post-test design to measure changes as a result of the intervention, it is also referred to as a *pre-test/post-test design* (Kirst-Ashman & Hull, 2009).

CASE STUDY

Patient Evaluation

As a pediatric social worker, Carly was concerned about the number of her patients who were obese. The unit recently initiated a peer-support group for obese children and teens in addition to a weight-loss and exercise program. Unfortunately, interventions remained unavailable for the parents. Carly reviewed the research and learned that parental involvement is a key component to all successful childhood obesity intervention programs. Working with the unit interdisciplinary team, Carly developed a psychoeducational support group for parents of teens in the weight-loss program. A primary care physician interested in health promotion and disease prevention was invited to consult with the group.

The team identified a variety of topics that parents would benefit from knowing and understanding about childhood obesity. These topics included health risks and obesity, the role of genetics in obesity, developmentally appropriate nutrition, creative options to promote activity and exercise, emotions and food, and behavioral management strategies for children participating in weight-loss programs. For each of topics, the team created three multiple-choice questions from material covered in class. The parents were tested on the first and last nights of class, and the difference between the test scores was computed. Items were then analyzed to determine if there were gaps in covered material. The curriculum was then revised to provide additional content in areas reported by parents as problematic.

What kind of evaluation is this?

After reviewing the data, Carly wondered if the participants enjoyed being in the group, felt supported, and thought their time was well spent. She designed a satisfaction survey for the group that was then distributed to group members for completion on the last night of class.

What level is this evaluation?

EVALUATION DESIGNS

Both formative and summative designs can be used to gather quantitative and qualitative data. **Qualitative research designs** typically explore the experiences of small samples of subjects. While the data gathered can be measured numerically and thus quantified, the emphasis in qualitative research is on analyzing the words of respondents in order to understand common themes, beliefs, perceptions, knowledge, or impressions of an issue, service, or problem. In comparison, **quantitative research designs** use larger samples and gather objective, numerical data such as test scores, recidivism, and relapse and drop-out rates to measure relationships between variables or the impact of interventions (Kirst-Ashman & Hull, 2009). Utilizing data from both sources can prove to be beneficial when we summarize quantitative data about patient satisfaction with social work services and then add narrative comments from patients or family members to clarify the manner in which the intervention proved valuable. Focus groups of recipients may also prove valuable in gathering qualitative data about impact and other impressions of rendered or planned services.

To gather data for statistical analysis, we can develop our own unique survey questions or select from a broad array of existing and proven standardized data-collection instruments and surveys. We can also create surveys that combine our questions with those of previously prepared surveys that are available in the public domain. Many physicians, for example, routinely use *the Beck Depression Inventory* to screen patients for depression. Another common instrument, *the Quality of Life Survey*, is used to measure the general emotional and physical well-being of patients. The RAND Foundation makes a number of frequently used survey instruments available on their website at http://www.rand.org/health/surveys_tools.html/. Corcoran and Fisher (2007) developed a valuable compendium of frequently used assessment tools for social workers and mental healthcare providers.

When designing your own survey, it is important to ensure that each question is relevant to the study. Survey-response instructions should be provided with an introductory paragraph clearly explaining the study purpose and the voluntary nature of participation. The researchers and bodies sanctioning the study as well as the provisions for confidentiality and protection of the data should be identified. Contact information regarding the study should be provided, and, if the survey is mailed, the return address and requested data submission date should be noted.

Whenever a survey data-collection instrument is being used for the first time, a "pilot" (preliminary) study should be undertaken with a small, separate test group of respondents to ensure that the study instructions and questions are clear. The goal is to create an easily understood instrument that minimizes any misinterpretation of questions. Confusing questions may go unanswered, or respondent answers may not address the intended issue or topic. To avoid introducing potential bias into responses, care should be taken to ensure that questions are neutrally stated in terms that cannot be interpreted as culturally or socially inappropriate.

Questions should only address *one* issue. "Double-barreled" questions that simultaneously address multiple issues are apt to prompt inappropriate, inaccurate, or otherwise unusable responses. An example of a double barreled-question is "Overall, I felt the hospital social worker was knowledgeable and available to me." This item simultaneously asks the respondent about both the social worker's knowledge and availability—two different things that could easily warrant two completely different responses. What if the respondent perceived the social worker as available but not knowledgeable? If the respondent answers "no" or provides a Likert-scale response like "strongly disagree," is that in relation to both the worker's knowledge and ability, just the ability, or just the availability? The answer becomes unclear and therefore unusable.

Two categories of questions can be asked on a survey. *Open-ended questions* allow respondents to choose their own words and length when answering. Because of the infinitely unique array of possible answers, content analysis is required during survey-response analysis. In comparison, *closed-ended questions* ask individuals to state their responses on some form of a scale, such as being able to choose among answers that range from "strongly agree" to "strongly disagree" in response to specific statements about an issue. Both open- and closed-ended questions can be utilized on the same survey.

A variety of scales are available to organize study-questionnaire responses. *Anchored scales* assign increasingly large positive or negative numbers to reflect the intensity of response to a question. A value of -5, for example, could be assigned to show that respondents "Strongly Disagree" with a statement, whereas a value of $+5$ would denote that respondents "Strongly Agree" with the statement. By providing a continuum, respondents are afforded the opportunity to more accurately convey their individual reactions to a statement. "On a scale of 1 to 10, with 1 being the lowest score and 10 being the highest, how would you rate your experience?" is an example of *continuum scaling.* To ensure enough variation for statistical data analysis (e.g., mean, median, mode, standard deviation), provide at least five and up to seven possible response options, or data points. Scales should be evenly balanced with the same number of negative and positive responses. Scales may provide respondents with a "neutral point" ("neither agree nor disagree") or with a "not applicable (n/a)" option. There are pros and cons to providing respondents the option of being "neutral" in their answer. If a neutral point is not provided, the scale is considered to be a *"forced-choice scale"* as respondents are forced to indicate a positive or negative answer. One advantage of selecting a forced-choice scale is that it compensates for *"regression to the mean,"* or the tendency of respondents to select a midpoint in answering questions in order to avoid taking an extreme position.

The following are examples of *Likert-type scales* that can be considered when creating survey instruments. Note the modifiers at the beginning of the questions that encourage respondents to answer in ways that are generally, rather than absolutely, true or false.

1. **Rosenberg Self-Esteem Scale**

   Question: How true is this statement? "All in all, I am inclined to feel that I am a failure":

   - Almost always true
   - Often true
   - Sometimes true
   - Seldom true
   - Never true

2. **Post-Workshop Evaluation**

   Question: " Overall, I would rate the material provided in this workshop as . . . ":

   - Excellent
   - Good
   - Average
   - Fair
   - Poor

3. **Market Survey**

   Question: "In rating this product, my reaction was to . . . ":

   - Dislike it completely
   - Dislike it somewhat
   - Dislike it a little
   - Like it a little
   - Like it somewhat
   - Like it completely

4. **Performance Assessment**

   Question: "Overall, my supervisor lets employees know what is expected":

   - Never
   - Seldom
   - Sometimes

- Often
- Always

5. **Attitude Index**

   Question: To what degree do you agree with this statement . . . "Overall, I think staff morale has improve":

   - Strongly Agree
   - Agree
   - Neither Agree nor Disagree
   - Strongly Disagree
   - Disagree

Single-Subject Designs

Evaluations may also employ a **single-subject design**. Single-subject designs are case-specific and measure the progress of *one* client or patient over time. The presenting problem, whatever it may be, is measured *before treatment* to establish a *baseline*. The problem is then repeatedly measured and graphed to create a visual representation of changes in the patient's condition or problem over time. The problem behavior is counted or measured along the vertical (or "Y") *axis* (the left hand side of the graph) and the time elapsed on the horizontal ("X") *axis* (the bottom of the graph). Time may be measured in increments of minutes, hours, days, weeks, months, or beyond.

The following exercise uses a continuum scale to assess a presenting problem for a single subject. Each week, the patient rates the severity of his or her concerns, with responses recorded on a graph to illustrate progress.

Exercise: Creating a Single-Subject Design

Single-Subject Design Exercise

Directions: Think of problems, issues, needs, etc. that you commonly face in your practice. Select a case that best represents a "typical case scenario" for you. What would the patient/ family describe as their present concerns or stressors? List them below.

1. Present concern:

2. Using the scale below, how would you rate the severity of their concerns?

0	1	2	3	4	5	6	7	8	9	10

   Not severe   Extremely severe

3. What would constitute adequate coping for this situation?

4. How would you rate the patient/family's current coping ability?

| 0 | 1 | 2 | 3 | 4 | 5 | 6 | 7 | 8 | 9 | 10 |

No coping difficulties   Extreme coping difficulties

5. To integrate this with single subject design techniques, you would create a line graph documenting the change in stressors and coping ability. You would plot a point for each time you saw the patient/family and/or took a measurement. You would use one line and/or color for each of the measurements.

Scores
10
9
8
7
6
5
4
3
2
1

Sessions   1   2   3   4   5

Source: Authors.

Representative Case Studies

Representative case studies are a form of single-subject design with particular relevance to healthcare social workers. This study type is popular when patient and/or family characteristics and presenting problems are the most commonly seen in a given situation. Often used for training and evaluation purposes, case studies are written as complete narratives with essential variables or characteristics highlighted. The presenting problems are identified, and then initiated interventions are reviewed and the outcomes are discussed. An invitation is generally made for any plausible alternative approaches to such patient-care situations.

Illustrating the usefulness of single-subject designs, a young woman with multiple sclerosis is presented as a representative case study in an in-service training program of a hospital social work department. The case is selected because the following issues are involved: financial concerns because the woman can no longer work, relationship issues with her spouse, sexual dysfunction, substance abuse secondary to inadequate pain management, grief and loss issues due to decreased functional ability, and inadequate health insurance coverage for treatment. As these issues are prevalent among many patients experiencing progressive, degenerative neuromuscular diseases, this case became a representative study. The intervention of the social worker was also regarded as representative of the services and skills used in this kind of practice. The social worker assisted the patient in applying for Social Security Disability, initiated a spend-down and spousal protection of assets as part of the process of applying Medicaid, found a community resource that would donate needed medical equipment and build a needed wheelchair ramp, initiated family and substance-abuse counseling, made a referral to a community mental health agency so that counseling could be continued post-discharge, and requested consultation by appropriate medical specialists to evaluate the patient's sexual dysfunction and pain.

Cost-Benefit Analysis

Generally speaking, social work services in healthcare institutions do not directly generate revenue through fees. Hospital reimbursement for inpatient social work services is characteristically derived from the room rate charge. While insurance may be directly billed in some instances for counseling or crisis intervention, our services more often are viewed as enhancing the quality of patient care and life by addressing psychosocial needs identified during case management, discharge, or continuity-of-care planning. These interventions are potentially significant cost-saving contributions to health systems. Cost savings are achieved when inpatient discharges are not delayed due to inadequate post-hospitalization care plans or when inappropriate readmissions, emergency department use, and/or extended outpatient care result from patient incomprehension of or inability or unwillingness to comply with crucial medical instructions. Of importance, health system savings resulting from reduced patient litigation may also evolve from social work interventions that clarify patient and family understanding of healthcare interventions and options and the implications of treatment compliance.

Cost savings may be difficult to isolate because numerous coexisting factors may interact to affect any potential financial gain. It is relevant to note, however, that beginning with changes in hospital reimbursement during the 1980s, many services, including social work, were eliminated or substantially changed because accounting and design consultants focused only on the "bottom line" financial impacts of any patient-care service. This meant that the service had to demonstrate that it generated revenue, reduced incurred costs, or otherwise afforded some strategic operational gain to the healthcare system. Insufficient evidence of those contributions can be thought to have partially contributed to organizational redesigns that negatively impacted social work. **Cost-benefit studies** represent one important strategy for documenting and analyzing the financial impacts achieved by a service. In a cost-benefit study, the costs of providing a service are compared with the financial benefits that are derived to the system or its users.

To generate a cost-benefit study or analysis, all resources and costs associated with a particular service are examined. These costs include personnel salaries and benefits as well as costs arising from facility space and administrative "overhead transfer" charges, equipment, supplies, and staff education. The amounts of these costs must be determined and then combined to arrive at the total service-delivery cost for a designated time period. At the same time, benefits resulting from providing the service during that specified time period must be identified, and then an analysis of the costs associated with achieving the benefit(s) must be performed. The goal is to demonstrate either that an intervention brought in revenue exceeding the cost of providing the service (thereby contributing a system profit) or that the system experienced savings that were greater than the costs incurred in delivering the service.

While appearing to be a straightforward process, linking dollar amounts to results achieved by social work may require considerable effort. While we may be able to measure a reduction in patient anxiety as a result of seeing a social worker for discharge planning before the patient goes home, how do we assign an economic value to this benefit? In many situations, doing so is not possible. However, since patients' decreased anxiety contributes to the prospect of them being discharged on time or earlier, we can compute cost savings from not having the expenses associated with a hospital room and associated services (including housekeeping, dietary services, utilities, debt servicing, and any or all involved professional charges). As shown in the case studies below, accurately measuring the financial impacts of any one service or procedure dictates close collaboration with fiscal services.

CASE STUDY [1]: COST-BENEFIT ANALYSIS

Unnecessary Emergency Admissions

An example of a cost-benefit study was conducted by one of the authors at a community hospital where unnecessary emergency room admissions were costing the institution $300,000 in uncompensated care per year. Area physicians were directing their elderly patients and families to the hospital ER for a 3-day admission to qualify them for skilled nursing-home coverage under Medicare. The patients, however, had no legitimate need for skilled nursing-home care, nor had they any medical condition to warrant hospital admission. Rather than being turned away, the patients were held in observation until a social worker could see them to assist with the nursing home-placement process. This process resulted in the loss of revenue to the health system when Medicare denied coverage for the hospital stay.

To address the problem, the hospital social work director met with the Medical Director and Chief Financial Officer (CFO). A part-time social worker with an MSW was hired with the goal of preventing three unnecessary emergency room hospital stays. The CFO calculated the cost savings derived from reducing unnecessary admissions by determining that each uncompensated hospital day cost the system incurred approximately $1,000. Based on that figure, if the social worker were able to reduce hospital stays by three days per month, the savings would offset the payroll costs of the social worker and any further reduced hospital stays would represent real operational savings to the hospital. The social worker proved to be an important resource to the hospital by successfully reducing hospitalizations and contributing to overall system savings.

CASE STUDY [2]: COST-BENEFIT ANALYSIS

Patient Medicaid Application Intervention

Another cost-benefit study reflecting the significant impact of targeted social work intervention was conducted at a major academic tertiary health system in the Northwest. In this instance, profound amounts of reimbursement were not being realized by the health system when potentially Medicaid-eligible inpatients were discharged from the hospital with little or no social work contact to assess either their financial status or ability to subsequently follow-up in a timely manner to complete a Medicaid application.

Recognizing the implications to patients and the health system, the social work director approached hospital administration, fiscal services, and state Medicaid program officials with a plan to initiate early social work contact with this patient population for the purpose of establishing eligibility status and actually opening Medicaid cases with hospitalized patients when appropriate. As such permission had never been delegated by the state to a hospital or outside entity, the social work director convinced the Medicaid agency and hospital to initiate a pilot study with the hiring of a full-time staff in the health system social work department. On the specific request of social work, fiscal services then conducted two cost-benefit analyses that produced significant findings. "One revealed that the first 32 cases (with social work intervention) analyzed generated $122,272 in revenue on hospital charges of $1,291,650, and the other concluded that the annualized program effect of the new social work intervention was **$2,322,513.00.** Fiscal services formally identified this revenue as otherwise unrealized if not for the intervention of the social work department." (Spitzer & Kuykendall, 1994, p. 296)

Beyond the addition of *four* new staff, the social work department experienced widespread recognition and enhanced organizational stature for what was regarded as its major contribution to the university during an otherwise difficult financial period. It should be emphasized that the derived benefit was not only to the health system by virtue of the revenue stream, but importantly, the quality of life of the patients and their families was enhanced as a result of their now having available reimbursement for basic healthcare services. Of consequence, the social work intervention brought not only initial but *ongoing* coverage for needed healthcare. The clearly documented success of this program led to its subsequent adoption by other hospitals with the endorsement of the state Medicaid program.

OUTCOMES AND QUALITY EVALUATION

The ultimate study question focuses on the effectiveness of our intervention. *Did it make a difference? Is the patient and/or family better off as a result of our intervention?* In healthcare, a number of outcome studies are required by various oversight bodies including Medicare and accrediting organizations such as the Joint Commission (http://www.jointcommission.org) and the Commission on Accreditation of Rehabilitation Facilities (www.CARF.org). National patient-safety goals have been developed, including reducing hospital acquired infections, improving communications between patients and providers, reducing patient injuries from falls, and reconciling medications as patients transition from one level of care to another (http://www .jointcommission.org/PatientSafety/NationalPatientSafetyGoals). Healthcare providers submit their data, and publically available reports are generated for review.

One important source of public-safety information that is relevant for social workers are those reports detailing the safety and quality inspections of nursing homes and other licensed community-care providers. These reports are prepared by the federal and many state governments. A Medicare website offers quality data on every Medicare and Medicaid-certified nursing home in the United States (http://www.medicare.gov/NHCompare). Since social workers (in deference to client self-determination and to avoid potential conflicts of interest) do not typically recommend patients and families to specific nursing homes, this resource is invaluable for families seeking data on which to base needed placement decisions. In addition to the federal site, select states such as Virginia provide websites providing basic data and inspection findings that reflect the quality of care in assisted-living communities, and adult day-care and respite-care homes (http://www.dss.virginia.gov/facility/search/alf.cgi). Social workers and others seeking inpatient and outpatient hospital care can make comparisons of providers in their communities by utilizing the United States Department of Health and Human Services website (http://www.hospitalcompare.hhs.gov/hospital-search.aspx).

Utilization review (UR) is an integral function of quality-care assessment and regulatory compliance. Utilization review coordinators or case managers are responsible for making sure that patients meet specified criteria for the services that they are receiving, ranging from inpatient hospitalization to skilled nursing or rehabilitation care. UR personnel review patients' medical records and work closely with insurance companies to get initial approval for services and then continuations, if justified. Social workers often serve in UR and case-management functions, particularly in behavioral health.

CREATING A POSITIVE CULTURE FOR EVALUATION

Carefully planned and executed evaluation is critical to ensure that patients and families receive the best healthcare possible. At the same time, providing data that denotes efficiency, including the numbers and types of patients served, crucial issues or care problems addressed, and the quality of rendered services is of vital interest to social work and health systems. Substantiating that the profession made positive impacts on patients' quality of life by economically delivering effective services makes an impressive statement about the "value" and soundness of social work operations.

Evaluation can be risky, however, when complex, expensive, or recurring problems are explored and accountability is assigned. To address such problems, it is important to create work environments that actively promote continuous service evaluation. Practitioners should be expected to engage in self-assessment and collaborative reviews toward the goal of benefiting those who receive their services by continuously refining their own interventions and competence. Regular, constructive staff supervision should be augmented by opportunities to update practice knowledge through continuing education, including conference attendance. While service evaluations should be integrated into existing practice whenever possible, care should be taken to avoid over-evaluation. Evaluations should conclude once problems are found to have low risk of adverse outcomes, are infrequent events, and/or lead to findings that are not useful in understanding or reshaping practice. While collaboration among all levels of staff is critical, quality studies must be kept clear from performance evaluations, which are a separate management activity. Most importantly, evaluations should be kept simple and meaningful (Mullen, 2004; Proctor, 2004; Wade & Neuman, 2007).

SUMMARY

This chapter examined the significance of practice research and evaluation in contemporary healthcare social work. It highlighted the importance of evidence-based practice and discussed use of clinical pathways and clinical practice guidelines. The concepts of continuous quality improvement and total quality management were introduced as mechanisms for tracking outcomes both at the individual practitioner level and the organizational level.

Evaluation of practice was considered in terms of patient outcomes, productivity, and efficiency. The seven evaluation process steps (designing, planning, implementing, data analysis and interpretation, reporting, data utilization, and follow-up) were introduced. The use of retrospective audits and concurrent monitors are employed to collect data, followed by formative or summative evaluations to present findings. Qualitative and quantitative research designs were discussed as well as the use of single-subject designs, representative case studies, and cost-benefit analyses. The importance of creating a positive culture for evaluation was underscored. While risks exist, carefully planned and executed evaluations are fundamental to maximizing positive patient-care outcomes either at the individual patient level or the overall operational level.

KEY TERMS AND CONCEPTS

- Best practice models
- Best practice standards
- Practice evaluation
- Evidenced-based practice
- Meta-analysis
- Adverse outcomes or occurrences
- Critical pathways
- Continuous quality improvement
- Sentinel events
- Indicators
- Benchmarks
- Output and outcome
- Practice-based evaluation and research

- Productivity, efficiency and effectiveness
- Data mining
- Retrospective audit
- Formative and summative evaluation
- Qualitative and quantitative designs
- Evaluation process
- Evaluation target
- Concurrent monitor
- Informed consent
- Single-subject design
- Representative case study
- Cost-benefit studies
- Utilization review

QUESTIONS FOR DISCUSSION

1. Why is evaluation important in social work practice?

2. What activities are you doing in your field agency that might be interesting to evaluate? How might you go about beginning to evaluate them?

3. What are the barriers to conducting evaluation studies in our agencies?

EXERCISES

1. You are running a psychoeducational support group for cancer survivors in your organizations. Design a Level-3 evaluation for the group.

2. Review the evaluation and assessment data at your agency. What is currently being studied? How is it being studied? What are the results? How are the results used to make program improvements?

3. Present a representative case study for an individual who is coping with multiple sclerosis or some other chronic, progressive disease. Go to the literature and determine who is mostly to be affected? How many are affected? What is the typical disease progression? What are the physical and emotional effects of the disease? What are the treatments? What supports and strengths can help people cope with the illness. After doing the research, create a "case study" of an individual who demonstrates the conditions and characteristics that you have identified. How can social work assist the person/family?

REFERENCES

Bloom, M., Fischer, J., & Orme, J.G. (2009). *Evaluating practice: Guidelines for the accountable professional.* (6th Ed.). Boston, MA: Allyn & Bacon.

Bradley, R., Greene, J., Russ. E., Dutra, L., & Westen, D. (2005). A multidimensional meta-analysis of psychotherapy for PTSD. *American Journal of Psychiatry, 162,* 214–227. Retrieved on-line from http://ajp.psychiatryonline.org/doi/full/10.1176/appi.ajp.162.2.214

Corcoran, K., & Fisher, J. (2007). *Measures for clinical practice. Volumes I & II.* (4th ed.). New York: Oxford University Press.

Commission on Accreditation and Rehabilitation Facilities. (n.d). CARF accreditation focuses on quality results. Retrieved from http://www.carf.org/home/

Cournoyer, B. (2004). *The evidence-based social work skills book.* Boston, MA: Allyn & Bacon.

Dienemann, J., Campbell, J., Landenburger, K., & Curry, M. A. (2002). The domestic survivor assessment: A tool for counseling women in intimate partner violence relationships. *Patient Education and Counseling, 46*(3), 221–228.

Drake, R. E., Goldman, H., Leff, H. S., Lehman, A. F., Dixon, L., Mueser, K. T., & Torrey, W.C. (2001). Implementing evidence-based practices in routine mental health service settings. *Psychiatric Services, 52,* 179–182.

Gambrill, E. (1999). Evidence-based practice: An alternative to authority-based practice. *Families in Society, 80,* 341–350.

Gibbs, L. E. (1989). Quality of Study rating form: An instrument for synthesizing evaluation studies. *Journal of Social Work Education, 25,* 55–67.

Gibbs, L. E. (2003). *Evidence-based practice for the helping professions.* Pacific Grove, CA: Brooks/Cole.

Gibbs, L., & Gambrill, E. (2002). Evidence-based practice: Counterarguments to objections. *Research on Social Work Practice, 12,* 452–476.

Giles, S. (2004). Establishing evidence-based renal social work practice guidelines. *Journal of Nephrology Social Work, 23,* 48–52.

Institute of Medicine. (2001). *Crossing the quality chasm: A new health system for the 21st century.* Washington, DC: National Academies Press.

Jackson, C. A. (1998). *Evidence-based decision-making for community health programs.* Santa Monica, CA: Rand.

Kirst-Ashman K., & Hull, G. (2009). *Understanding generalist social work practice.* (5th ed.). Belmont, CA: Brooks/Cole.

McNeece, C. A., & Thyer, B. A. (2004). Evidence-based practice and social work. *Journal of Evidence-Based Social Work, 1,* 7–25.

Mullen, E. J. (2004). Facilitating practitioner use of evidence-based practice. In A. R. Roberts, & K. Yeager K. (Eds.). *Evidence-based practice manual: Research and outcome measures in health and human services.* New York: Oxford University Press, 205–210.

Posavac, E. (1980). *Program evaluation: Methods and case studies.* Boston, MA: Prentice Hall.

Proctor, E. K. (2004). Leverage points for implementation of evidence-based practice. *Brief Treatment and Crisis Intervention, 4,* 227–242.

Rossi, P. H., & Freeman, H. E. (1993). *Evaluation: A systematic approach.* Thousand Oaks, CA: SAGE.

Rotter, T., Kinsman, L., James, E., Machotta, A., Gothe, H., Willis, J., & Kugler, J. (2010). *Clinical pathways: Effects on professional practice, patient outcomes, length of stay and hospital costs.* Cochrane Database of Systemic Reviews, 3(3). doi: 10.1002/14651858.CD006632.pub2

Spitzer, W., & Kuykendall, R. (1994). Social work delivery of hospital-based financial assistance services. *Health and Social Work, 19,* 295–297.

Straus, S. E., Richardson, W. S., Glasziou, P., & Haynes, R. B. (2005). *Evidence-based medicine: How to practice and teach EBM.* (3rd Ed.). Edinburgh: Churchill Livingstone, UK.

The Joint Commission. (2014). *Sentinel Event.* Retrieved on-line from http://www.jointcommission.org/sentinel_event.aspxm

U.S. Department of Health and Human Services: Office of the Inspector General. (2008, Dec.) *Adverse events in hospitals: Overview of key issues.* Retrieved from http://oig.hhs.gov/oei/reports/oei-06-07-00470.pdf

Wade, K., & Neuman, K. (2007). Practice-based research: Changing the professional culture and language of social work. *Social Work in Health Care, 44*(4), 49-64.

Walton, M., & Deming, W. E. (1986). *The Deming management method.* New York: Berkeley Publishing.

CHAPTER 7

Chronic Illness

Issues and Interventions

Sally Schmall and Angela Schmidt

INTRODUCTION

Chronic disease is the nation's greatest problem shaping contemporary healthcare. While chronic disease refers to the pathophysiology of the condition, chronic illness is the human experience of symptoms and suffering, referring to how the disease is perceived, lived with, and responded to by individuals, their families, and their healthcare providers (Lubkin & Larsen, 2013). Chronic disease can appear suddenly or through an insidious process, with periods of exacerbation and remission affecting the illness experience.

The characteristics of chronic diseases were identified by the Commission on Chronic Illness in 1949 as all impairments or deviations from normal that included one or more of the following: permanency, residual disability, nonpathologic alteration, required rehabilitation or a long period of supervision, observation, and care (Mayo, 1956). Disability depends not only on the kind of condition and its severity but also on the implications that it holds for the person and family. The degree of disability and altered lifestyle may relate more to the client's perceptions and beliefs about the illness than to the disease itself. In addition, long-term and iatrogenic effects of some treatments may be identified as chronic conditions. Lifestyle changes in persons on dialysis for end-stage renal disease and life-saving procedures for cancer can, for example, result in chronic illness. More recently, chronic illness has been defined as, "the irreversible presence, accumulating, or latency of disease states or impairments that involve the total human environment for supportive care and self-care, maintenance of function, and prevention of further disability" (Curtin & Lubkin, 1995, pp. 6–7).

Americans are living longer than ever before but are spending fewer years of their lives without disease. The prevalence of chronic disease has risen with the lengthening of the life span and the increasing availability of advances in medical technology. In 2005, it was estimated that 133 million persons were living with at least one chronic disease (CDC, 2010) and seven of 10 Americans who die each year (more than 1.7 million people) will die of a chronic disease. Influencing this extreme growth in chronic illnesses, the number of persons greater than 65 years old is expected to increase from 35 million in 2000 to an estimated 71 million in 2030 and the number of persons greater than 80 years old is expected to increase from 9.3 million in 2000 to 19.5 million in 2030 (U.S. Census Bureau, 2008). Medicare data indicate that 83% of beneficiaries have at least one chronic condition, with 23% having five or more chronic conditions, accounting for 68% of the program's funding. On the basis of these reports, it is expected that 49% of the population will have a chronic illness by 2025 (Stanhope & Lancaster, 2008).

While life expectancy has steadily increased, longer living has not equated with improved health. Average *morbidity*, or the period of life spent with chronic disease or loss of functional mobility, has actually *increased* in recent decades. While individuals can expect to live more years with chronic conditions simply as a result of living longer in general, the average number of healthy years has decreased since 1998 (Crimmins & Beltrán-Sánchez, 2011). To quantify the burden of disease from mortality and morbidity, one **DALY (Disability-Adjusted Life Year)** can represent one lost year of healthy life. The sum of the DALYs across the population, or the burden of disease, can be thought of as a measurement of the gap between current health status and an ideal health situation where the entire population lives to an advanced age free of disease and disability often associated with chronic disease. The recent GBD (Global Burden of Disease) Project published by IHME (Institute for Health Metrics and Evaluation) in 2012 used an updated life expectancy standard for the calculation, based on prevalence rather than incidence, and applied social value weights (WHO, 2014).

The World Health Organization identifies chronic diseases as the leading cause of death in the world, accounting for 60% of all deaths worldwide (WHO, 2011). Similarly, in the United States, chronic diseases are the leading causes of death and disability, prompting chronic illness to become the number one national health issue. Chronic diseases account for 70% of all deaths in the United States, according to the National Center for Health Statistics (CDC, 2007). In fact, six of the seven leading causes of death among older Americans are chronic diseases (Federal Interagency Forum on Aging-Related Statistics, 2010). Chronic diseases also contribute to major limitations in daily living for almost one of every 10 Americans, or about 25 million people. This reality is in contrast to what had been expected, specifically, that the same forces contributing to a longer lifespan, including better health behaviors and medical advances, would also delay the onset of disease, allowing people to spend fewer years of their lives with debilitating or chronic health conditions.

HEALTH DISPARITIES AND ASSOCIATED COSTS OF CHRONIC ILLNESS

Disparities in the U.S. healthcare system are evidenced by indicators of cost, access, and quality of care. The Institute of Medicine (IOM) (2003) defined disparities in healthcare as "racial or ethnic differences in the quality of care that are not due to access-related factors or clinical needs, preferences, and appropriateness of intervention" (pp. 3–4). The term **"disparities"** refers to lower-quality care or poorer outcomes and may result from patient-level factors such as mistrust, provider factors such as stereotyping or prejudice, or health-system factors such as lack of insurance coverage or under-insurance (IOM, 2003). Additionally, social and political factors can influence disparities.

The growing incidence of chronic illness and the aging population in the United States are acting to reshape the structure of the healthcare system. The anticipated increase in chronic disease to 49% by 2025 is also expected to increase healthcare costs. This expectation prompts particular concern as the growth rate of healthcare spending has historically outpaced the growth of the overall economy. According to Medical Expenditure Panel Survey (MEPS) data (Rhoades & Cohen, 2007), *of the five conditions proven the most costly in the non-institutionalized population, four are chronic conditions.* Heart disease generated the highest medical expenditures, followed by trauma-related disorders, cancer, and mental disorders. *Currently, more than two-thirds of healthcare expenditures are attributable to the treatment of chronic illnesses; almost 95% of healthcare expenditures among older Americans are for chronic diseases* (CDC & The Merck Company Foundation, 2007).

The Organization of Economic Cooperation and Development (OECD) annually trends and reports on more than 1,200 health system measures in 30 industrialized countries. The cost of chronic disease is compounded among the uninsured or underinsured, with those in fair to poor health being the most likely to be uninsured (Rhoades & Cohen, 2007). Geographically, 42.4% of the uninsured lived in the South, 26.2% live in the West, and 12.8% live in the Northeast (Roberts & Rhoades, 2010). Government programs such as Medicare, Medicaid, and the State Children's Health Insurance Program (SCHIP) afford assistance in meeting the needs of the uninsured with chronic illness.

Individuals with chronic illnesses face significant barriers when seeking to obtain and keep health insurance. About 25 million people with chronic health conditions are uninsured, including 2 million children. An estimated 50% of uninsured people with chronic illnesses delay care because they cannot afford it. Continued growth in the numbers of uninsured or underinsured has resulted in gaps in coverage. One goal of the Patient Protection and Affordable Care Act (PPACA) of 2010 was to improve the health of those experiencing chronic illnesses and to decrease the costs of treating their health conditions. Those decreases are anticipated to occur as the result of the PPACA redefining insurance coverage to eliminate "preexisting conditions," encouraging the use of less expensive generic drugs, placing limits on out-of-pocket medical expenses, removing "lifetime caps" from insurance policies, and making subsidies available for health coverage purchased through state health-insurance exchanges. Essential health benefits offered by the exchanges are anticipated to lessen existing disparities among those with chronic illness.

Disparities in access to care and quality of service exist with respect to race and ethnicity. Smedley, Stith, and Nelson (2003), in their report entitled *Unequal Treatment: Confronting Racial and Ethnic Disparities in Health Care,* concluded that disparities in healthcare remain across a range of chronic illnesses, with racial and ethnic minorities experiencing higher rates of morbidity and mortality than non-minorities. *Healthy People 2010* (Centers for Disease Control, 2011a), the compendium used to set the nation's health priorities each decade, acknowledges that race and ethnicity correlate with persistent and often increasing health disparities among U.S. populations and consequently warrants national attention. *Healthy People 2020* focuses on identifying, measuring, tracking, and reducing health disparities through a determinants-of-health approach (Healthy People 2020, 2011).

Considering health disparities in the context of social justice, it is important to note that differences in health among minority populations are often associated with factors beyond individual control. Disparity not only means difference but also implies inequality. The root causes of health disparities are systemic and institutionalized, evolving over decades or even centuries. The root causes of health disparities are multifactorial and directional and hence require intervention at every level.

Although the healthcare system treats both single and multiple chronic conditions, it has not fully adapted existing acute-care service-delivery models to include comprehensive management of chronic conditions. Instead, the system is often characterized by fragmentation and lack of service coordination. While this affects individuals of all ages, the elderly are especially challenged. Those suffering from conditions such as hypertension and congestive heart failure are often difficult to treat as each condition requires simultaneous ongoing care from multiple providers. In addition, older patients often suffer from anxiety and depression that are reactions to functional losses and cognitive impairments.

Complicating matters, weakened or strained social support networks of vulnerable elderly people are not dependable resources for navigating health-delivery systems. Older adults with chronic conditions visit healthcare providers, fill prescriptions, and are hospitalized more often than the general population. They are also more likely to experience poorly coordinated care with diminished health outcomes, repeated hospitalizations, caregiver stress, dissatisfaction with care, and higher service costs.

The IOM (2003) identifies care coordination as one strategy to enhance patient care in six dimensions, including safety, effectiveness, patient-centeredness, timeliness, equity, and efficiency. Social work can and does represent a significant care-coordination resource, frequently performing principal roles in such models. Uncoordinated care is inefficient and therefore more costly, particularly when it involves treatment of chronic conditions. Despite the fact that chronic diseases are both costly and preventable, many communities lack sufficient chronic disease-prevention resources that are included in a coordinated-care model.

The American healthcare system is evolving with the prospect of important roles for social work. The IOM (2007) identified three principles designed to guide healthcare system changes relative to care of older adults:

1. Healthcare needs of the elderly should be addressed comprehensively. For example, preventive services should be provided side-by-side with social services.

2. Services should be provided efficiently. For example, multidisciplinary services should be provided in a coordinated, integrated manner across the continuum of healthcare settings (e.g., acute, outpatient clinic, long-term care, etc.).

3. Caregivers should be sensitive to engaging older patients (and their families) as active partners in their own care. With the prospect of greater care needs, both patients and caregivers benefit from timely provision of targeted health-education, preventive, and follow-up services.

While healthcare costs for those aged 65 years or older is *three to five times greater* than the cost of providing care to younger individuals, chronic health problems experienced by people aged 55 to 64 years suggest the prospect of greater functional decline in later years. In 2003, 42% of adults in this age group had high blood pressure and 56% of them did not meet recommended guidelines for physical activity. Importantly, 12.5% were diagnosed with Type-2 diabetes, an important factor associated with obesity. These statistics suggest that preventing or delaying disease and disability among older adults not only enhances individuals' quality of life but deters avoidable healthcare costs as well.

Longer productive lives rather than lives characterized by dependency and disability can only occur with the effective management and coordinated care of the chronic illnesses that often accompany old age. Uncontrolled diets and tobacco/alcohol consumption, limited physical activity, psychological stress, and exposure to unhealthy work environments impact health; these factors are linked to illness, disability, and premature death arising from chronic disease (CDC & Merck Company Foundation, 2007). The capacity to manage these conditions and thereby maintain health is also influenced by social supports and timely access to healthcare. Encouragement of positive health behaviors and provision of assistance in adapting to chronic illnesses are fundamentally important and constitute central components of healthcare social work practice. Assessment and care coordination are two principal social work roles associated with chronically ill patients and their caregivers.

Chronic illness requires a shift in perspective compared with the rapid onset and focus on curing of an acute problem. Development of self-management skills is encouraged, with attention to the individual's self-concept and self-esteem as well as to those resources that will be needed to manage the disease and illness outside the medical system. The focus is on healing (a unique process resulting in a shift in the body-mind-spirit system) rather than on curing or eliminating signs and symptoms of disease.

Chronic health conditions and psychosocial well-being are interrelated. Three important characteristics of chronic illnesses among older adults in particular must be considered as they affect the social work role and function:

1. The trajectories for many serious illnesses evolve from an acute terminal illness to a chronic illness with episodes of exacerbations, remissions, altered abilities, and reductions in overall functioning.

2. Advanced chronic illness is often highly stressful for patients and their families.

3. The increase in the total number of older people with advanced chronic conditions will require more in-home care, with the prospect of greater reliance on provision by family members, requiring life-care planning.

The IOM stresses that psychosocial factors must be considered in the design and delivery of healthcare services. Health and disease are determined by dynamic interactions among biological, psychological, behavioral, and social factors (IOM, 2001, p. 16). Social factors regarded as determinants of health include, but are not limited to

- Socioeconomic status (SES)

- Transportation

- Housing

- Access to services

- Discrimination by social grouping (e.g., race, gender, or class)

- Social or environmental stressors

Social determinants have a major impact on health disparities associated with chronic diseases, such as cardiovascular disease, cancer, and diabetes. Projected demographic changes over the next decades underscore the importance of addressing disparities in health status, particularly with regard to chronic diseases. *Figure 7.1* illustrates that older minorities will grow to over 44% of the population aged 65 years and older by 2050. The number of African American elders is projected to grow to 12% of the population in 2050, whereas the number of Hispanic elders is projected to grow to 18%.

Figure 7.1   Population Aged 65 and Over in 2006 and 2050

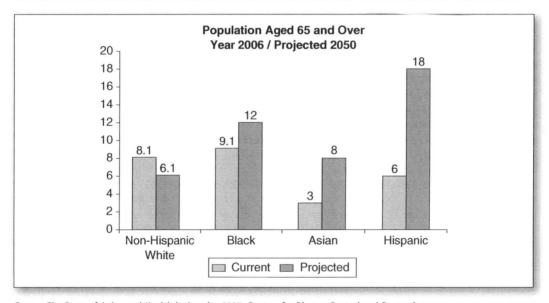

Source: The State of Aging and Health in America 2007. Centers for Disease Control and Prevention.

African Americans, Hispanics, American Indians, Alaska Natives, Asian Americans, and Pacific Islanders are particularly susceptible to chronic disease compared with the overall U.S. population. Current examples of ethnic health disparities in chronic disease include

- *Cardiovascular disease*—Racial and ethnic populations have higher rates of hypertension, tend to develop hypertension at an earlier age, and are less likely to undergo treatment to control their high blood pressure.

- *Cancer*—For men and women combined, African Americans have a cancer death rate about 35% higher than that for whites (171.6 vs. 127.0 per 100,000). The death rate for cancer for African American men is about 50% higher than it is for white men (226.8 vs. 151.8 per 100,000).

- *Diabetes*—The prevalence of diabetes in African Americans is approximately 70% higher than that in whites, and the prevalence in Hispanics is nearly double that in whites.

The **Chronic Care Model (CCM)** is relevant when examining how care is provided to those with chronic disease. Wagner's (1998) solution was to replace the physician-centered office with a structure that supported a team of professionals collaborating with patients in their care. *Improving Chronic Illness Care* (2006–2011), a national program that was launched by the Robert Wood Johnson Foundation in 1998, uses the CCM at its core. Multifaceted professional interventions can enhance the performance of healthcare professionals, including the social worker, in managing clients with a variety of chronic illnesses.

Healthcare and social care processes become complex when there are barriers to partnering roles. Application of an *ecosystems perspective* defines a role for social work to work collaboratively with other health professions within a chronic care model (Findley, 2014). A *reciprocal perspective* diminishes emphasis on cause, instead emphasizing the effect of what has occurred (Gitterman & Germain, 2008). For example, if a patient does not adhere to a prescribed medication regimen, the reciprocal perspective suggests focus should be on what has occurred that might be changed in the person's environment and encourage him to acquire and take his medications. *Table 7.1* presents a crosswalk between CCM with the ecosystem perspective for social work intervention proposed by Findley (2014, p. 91):

Table 7.1 Chronic Care Model and the Ecosystems Perspective

Chronic Care Model Key Areas	Area Focus	Level of Social Work Intervention
• Self Management Support	• Patients participating in the management of their own healthcare	• Microsystem
• Health Systems/ Organization of Care	• Creating and fostering an environment that values quality and system change to promote high quality care	• Mezzosystem
• Delivery Systems Design	• A team focus with interventions that are evidence-based and includes regular follow up by the team	• Macrosystem
• Decision Support	• The use of evidenced-based guidelines on care delivery, and sharing these guidelines with patients and specialists to encourage collaborative care	• Macrosystem
• Clinical Information Systems	• Timely reminders for care activities and the monitoring of care delivery to assess team and care system performance	• Macrosystem
• Community Resources and Policies	• Help patients engage with community-based services as well as develop partnerships on the provider level to support advocacy	• Macrosystem

Source: Findley, P.A. (2014). Social work practice to the chronic care mode: Chronic illness and disability care. *Journal of Social Work*, 14(1):83–95.

Using the CCM as a basis, researchers at Johns Hopkins University developed a **Guided Care Model (GCM)** to improve the quality of life and efficiency of resource utilization for older adults with multiple chronic conditions. The GCM uses the principles of chronic care, disease management, self-management, case management, lifestyle modification, transitional care, caregiver education and support, and geriatric evaluation and management (Boyd et al., 2007, p. 697). Clinical activities of the GCM include

1. *Assessment.* Initial assessments include medical, functional, cognitive, affective, psychosocial, nutritional, and environmental. Other tools used may include the Geriatric Depression Scale and the CAGE alcoholism scale. The client is asked to list his or her priorities for improved quality of life.

2. *Planning.* The electronic health records system merges assessment data with evidence-based practice guidelines to create a care guide that manages and monitors the patients' health condition(s).

3. *Chronic disease self-management (CDSM).* Self-efficacy in the management of the chronic condition(s) by the person is encouraged and taught using a 15-hour CDSM course that operationalizes patients' action plans.

4. *Monitoring.* The GCN monitors each person at least monthly by telephone to address any issues and respond to questions.

5. *Coaching.* Motivational interviewing is used to facilitate the patient's participation in care along with reinforcing adherence to the action plan.

6. *Coordinating transitions between sites and providers of care.* The GCN is the primary coordinator of care for persons in this program and is responsible for the care transitions that occur between home, the emergency room, the hospital, long-term care facilities, and other healthcare settings.

7. *Educating and supporting caregivers.* The GCN works with family or other informal caregivers to educate and support by individual or group efforts.

8. *Accessing community resources.* Determining appropriate community resources for the person, referring to available community resources without duplicating services is the goal.

Evidence suggests that the GCM model improves quality of care, reduces medical care costs, and results in high satisfaction among healthcare providers, patients, and the GCN (Boult et al., 2008).

Competencies for chronic disease practice were developed by the National Association of Chronic Disease Directors (NACDD) to assist healthcare programs develop competent workforces and effective programs (Lubkin & Larsen, 2013). The NACDD competencies are organized within domains congruent with the WHO competencies (i.e., partnering, evidence-based interventions) and are summarized in *Table 7.2*.

Table 7.2   Competencies in Building Chronic-Disease Practice

• Domain 1: Build Support	• Chronic-disease practitioners establish strong working relationships with stakeholders, including other programs, government agencies, and nongovernmental lay and professional groups, to build support for chronic disease prevention and control.
• Domain 2: Design & Evaluate Programs	• Chronic-disease practitioners develop and implement evidence-based interventions and conduct evaluations to ensure ongoing feedback and program effectiveness.
• Domain 3: Influence Policies & Systems Change	• Chronic-disease practitioners implement strategies to change the health-related policies of private organizations or governmental entities capable of affecting the health of targeted populations.
• Domain 4: Lead Strategically	• Chronic-disease practitioners articulate health needs and strategic vision, serve as catalysts for change, and demonstrate program accomplishments to ensure continued funding and support within their scope of practice.
• Domain 5: Manage People	• Chronic-disease practitioners oversee and support the optimal performance and growth of program staff as well as themselves.
• Domain 6: Manage Programs & Resources	• Chronic-disease practitioners ensure the consistent administrative, financial, and staff support necessary to sustain successful implementation of planned activities and to build opportunities.
• Domain 7: Use Public Health Science	• Chronic-disease practitioners gather, analyze, interpret, and disseminate data and research findings to define needs, identify priorities, and measure change.

Source: National Association of Chronic Disease Directors. (n.d.). *Competencies for Chronic Disease.* Retrieved from http://c.ymcdn.com/sites/www.chronicdisease.org/resource/resmgr/workforce_development/competenciesforchronicdiseas.pdf

BIOPSYCHOSOCIAL ASSESSMENT OF HEALTH NEEDS AND SERVICES

Chronic illnesses have differing effects on patients, and adaption to such conditions can vary widely among patients. Social work interventions are designed and developed with consideration to the psychodynamics of the individual as well as the specific characteristics of the illness and its effect on the patient. The *Social Status Examination in Health Care* (Falck, as cited by Carlton, 1984) identifies a number of variables that, when taken together as whole, provide a balanced perception of pertinent biological, psychological, and social elements affecting a patient. In this model, health and social conditions are recognized as mutually affecting each other and are thus a system. Management of an illness then is seen as a social process. *Table 7.3* provides an updated version of the social status examination. It affords social workers the basis for determining the current status of the patient as well as identifying potentially needed services and interventions.

Table 7.3 Social Status Examination in Healthcare

1. **Life stage**
   - What is the developmental stage of the patient?
   - What level of psychosocial functioning have they achieved?
   - What are the challenges they face in successfully resolving this life stage and preparing for the next?

2. **Health Condition**
   - What is the patient's illness, disability, health condition and/or problem?
   - How well do they understand their condition?
   - How does it affect them?
   - How does the patient express concern over their circumstances?
   - What is adaptive capacity of the individual in coping with this health condition?
   - How well does the patient interact with healthcare providers?

3. **Family/Other Supports**
   - What family and/or other supports are linked to this condition and how does this affect the social management of the condition?
   - Who is available to assist the patient in activities of daily living?
   - Upon whom does the patient depend?

4. **Racial/Ethnic/Cultural Memberships**
   - To what racial/ethnic/cultural group does the patient belong?
   - Are issues of gender or sexual identity involved?
   - How does this affect social management of the condition?

5. **Social Class**
   - What is the social, economic, and educational class of the patient?
   - How does this impact the social management of the health condition?

6. **Occupation**
   - How does the health condition/problem influence the patient's occupation?
   - Did occupationally-related factors affect the physical condition?

7. **Financial Condition**
   - How does the health condition influence the patient's financial condition?
   - What income maintenance efforts are being made?
   - Are sufficient financial supports available?

8. **Benefits and Entitlements**
   - Is health insurance available to pay for care? What costs will the patient incur?
   - What other benefit might the patient be eligible for?

9. **Transportation**
   - How will the patient be transported to appointments?
   - Will transportation services be needed?

10. Housing

- What is the patient's current housing situation?
- Is the patient able to function within the home or is alternative housing needed?
- Are modifications needed? How will these be arranged for?

11. Mental functioning and cognition

- Is the patient able to participate in medical decision making and plan for the future?
- Are they alert and oriented to time, place and person?
- Does the patient have a healthcare proxy or patient advocate in place?
- Is the patient capable of following medication and other care instructions?
- How capable/inclined is the patient to request help or use it when offered?

Source: Adapted from Carlton, T. (1984). *Clinical social work in health settings: A guide to professional practice with exemplars.* New York: Springer Publishing Company, pp. 79–82.

SOCIAL WORK ROLE IN CARE COORDINATION

Care coordination is a key strategy to deal with the growing problems in the treatment of chronic conditions (IOM, 2003). Care coordination is the deliberate organization of patient-care activities between two or more participants (including the patient) involved in a patient's care to facilitate the appropriate delivery of healthcare services (McDonald et al., 2007). In 2007, the Agency for Healthcare Research and Quality (AHRQ) issued a review and synthesis of the evidence base for the effectiveness of these approaches to intervention (McDonald et al., 2007). These findings are used to develop care-coordination plans for ongoing services based on the biopsychosocial needs of patients and families. The assessment process identifies factors that are (or may be) issues contributing to ill-health and/or that may inhibit patients' participation in disease-management programs. Social workers' value orientation and expertise in collaboration, resource management, and advocacy make them particularly well positioned to provide care coordination. Patient and family needs may be addressed by

1. Conducting prompt, thorough screenings and assessments of functional impairment, pain, depression, and anxiety of patients with chronic illnesses

2. Advocating for delivery of culturally tailored chronic disease-management programs in conjunction with coordination of care in health facilities and non-traditional settings that focus on underserved populations.

3. Collaborating in developing and implementing enhanced outreach, screening, and assessment strategies for use with vulnerable and underserved populations (e.g., people of color, low-income individuals, and frail older adults with few social supports).

4. Educating patients about diagnoses and prognoses and adhering to medical regimens.

FACILITATING ADHERENCE TO MEDICAL REGIMENS

Patient and/or family responsibility for managing chronic conditions has increased with concerns about medical outcomes and costs. Most patients deal with a loss of independence, the threat of disease progression, and the challenge of modifying their behavior to adhere to the prescribed treatment regimen. Adherence to modifications has a direct effect on treatment success and decreased disease progression. Failure to adhere can result in increased disease complications, increased hospitalizations, and greater treatment costs as well as disruptions in lifestyle, family function, and coping skills. Studies indicate that adherence rates in chronic illness are approximately 50% (Dunbar-Jacob et al., 2000; Haynes, McDonald, Garg, & Montgomery, 2002), with ranges in non-adherence rates to be 20%–40% for acute illness, 20%–60% for chronic illness, and 50%–80% for preventive regimens (Bosworth, 2010; Lubkin & Larsen, 2013).

Concern about chronic disease has prompted a paradigm shift from regarding individuals as consumers of healthcare to partners with their healthcare providers. Responsibility for prevention and daily management of chronic diseases increasingly resides with patients and their families. Correspondingly, there is increased interest in determining how to best facilitate patient awareness and adherence to the necessary adaptive demands of living with chronic illnesses.

Patients' abilities and willingness to collaborate with healthcare professionals, family members, and community support systems are crucial to managing often complicated medical regimens (Auslander & Freedenthal, 2006). Adherence to treatment for heart disease, for example, involves diet, regular exercise and medication, and blood pressure and lipid monitoring. Routine visits to cardiologists, who may not be conveniently located, are also necessary. For diabetes, strict adherence to a meal plan, consistent exercise, and regular blood glucose testing (sometimes multiple times per day) is required, often in conjunction with medications. Type-1 diabetes further involves daily insulin injections or the use of insulin-infusion pumps. For cancer patients, adherence to treatment such as self-medication, monitoring blood glucose levels, and engaging in healthy self-care behaviors is crucial to slow disease progression and to minimize potential complications.

The health beliefs of a person with chronic illness and their family can facilitate adherence to treatment regimens. The **Health Belief Model (HBM)** explains the relationships of attitudes and behaviors to adherence behavior. According to the HBM (Becker, 1976), the likelihood of an individual taking recommended health actions is based on the perceived severity of the illness, the individual's estimate of the likelihood that a specific action will reduce the threat, and perceived barriers to following recommendations. The degree to which people attribute accountability to themselves (internal control) such as personal behavior or characteristics as opposed to uncontrollable forces (external control) such as fate or luck is referred to as their locus of control (Rotter, 1966). The outcome of seeking and gaining a sense of control over a chronic illness is linked to one's overall physical health (Bandura, 1989).

Cognitive and learning theory combines environment, cognition, and emotion in the understanding of health behavior change (Bandura, 2004). Necessary requirements to altering health behavior are the recognition that a lifestyle component can be harmful, that a change in behavior would be beneficial, and that one has the ability to adopt a new behavior (self-efficacy) (Lubkin & Larsen, 2013). This self-efficacy is an important predictor of self-management behaviors required for the adherence to treatment regimens in cases of chronic illness.

Education and emotional support are catalysts for patient motivation, including medical **treatment compliance**. Auslander and Freedenthal (2006) proposed a systematic cognitive-behavioral adherence-counseling approach for patient populations that include children with Type-1 diabetes, adolescents with poorly controlled diabetes, and adults diagnosed with Type-2 diabetes. The universal basis of this approach gives it applicability to other patient populations and disease entities. The counseling model is comprised of four distinct phases.

Phase 1

A patient and family biopsychosocial assessment is conducted to determine

- Health beliefs

- Lifestyle and daily routine

- Psychological factors prior to diagnosis

- Social support systems

- Prior treatment satisfaction and adherence history

Phase 2

A treatment plan is developed in relation to the necessary medication regimen. Emphasis is on facilitating a clear understanding of the need for a plan, affording an opportunity for expression of feelings about the regimen and promoting participation in decisions about how the plan will be implemented.

Phase 3

Treatment goals are translated into concrete, accomplishable behavioral goals for the patient. The emphasis is on promoting self-management strategies and proactively planning for high-risk situations in which treatment compliance might be compromised. Family involvement is encouraged, with recognition of the shared responsibilities for carrying out the plan. Effort is made to enhance the patient's ability to utilize medical and social supports.

Phase 4

Strategies are developed for long-term success of the care plan, including identifying the skills needed by the patient to maintain adherence to the medical regimen and sustain positive health behaviors.

This approach for enhancing adherence to potentially complicated medical regimens acknowledges and builds on the influence of patients' social contexts, such as personal and cultural beliefs about health and the utilization of healthcare services. It can be employed as a preventative strategy for newly diagnosed patients by proactively addressing potential barriers to adherence. In order to be effective in adherence counseling, it is necessary that healthcare professionals understand chronic diseases, their treatment, and their impact on patients, families, and caregivers.

THE IMPACT OF CHRONIC ILLNESS ON FAMILY FUNCTIONING

Adaptation to chronic illness is a dynamic process that warrants special attention during assessments and subsequent intervention. Patients and family members experiencing chronic illness face the daunting challenge of simultaneously focusing on the present and the future. Families must become adept in managing the immediate needs of patients' illnesses while also planning a course for coping with the complexities and uncertainties of the future.

The National Alliance for Caregiving (NAC) and the American Association of Retired Persons (AARP) estimated that 28.5% of the American population serves as unpaid family caregivers to an adult or child with special needs. This translates into approximately 65.7 million caregivers in the United States (NAC & AARP, 2009). Most chronically ill, dependent persons have their long-term care needs met in the home or with community-based care arrangements. Approximately two-thirds of dependent persons in the community rely solely on informal caregivers such as family or extended family members (Mittelman, 2003). Motivation for caregiving, such as love, duty, or obligation, can be based on ethnicity, culture, and spiritual beliefs. Adding to the complexity of caregiving, the dynamics of the family or other close personal relationships that existed before the chronic illness can influence caregiving relationships after the illness.

The stage of a **family life cycle** will significantly influence, and in turn be influenced by, the onset of an illness as well as the developmental stages of individual family members. Family-centered interventions that focus on life stages and relationships are particularly well-suited to assist adherence to complex medical regimens and aid patients in leading fulfilling lives while managing changing health conditions. Familiarity with life cycles is crucial to understanding both individual and family development. As originally postulated by Erikson (1959) life unfolds in a predictable order with major events such as the onset of chronic illness and the loss of independence occurring at expected points within an anticipated evolution (McGoldrick, Giordano, & Garcia-Preto, 2005; Rolland, 2012). Life is planned to a great extent in expectation of, and preparation for, this evolution. Beginnings, transitions, and endings are expected to unfold at specific times within one's life. Individual, family, and chronic illness development share the unspoken notion of phases marked by different developmental tasks. Unexpected, unwanted, and untimely events such as the onset of a chronic disease can distort the "normal" trajectory of life as well as the rhythm of family life cycles.

The concept of the family life cycle is not new. William Shakespeare's play *As You Like It* depicted the developmental stages of individuals as their lives progress from birth to death. Haley (1976) identified six Family Life Cycle stages involving different emotional and physical processes often experienced by families:

- Establishing independence

- Creating a commitment to a couple relationship

- Parenting the first child

- Living with an adolescent

- Launching the children

- Reinvestment in later life

Life cycle stages do not occur in the same way for all families. Some families can be in multiple stages at any one time. The same family, for example, could be living with an adolescent while launching an older child. The life stages are fluid, lack rigid boundaries, and encompass the emotional, intellectual, physical, social, and spiritual aspects of life.

It is important to consider the onset of a chronic illness in terms of the collective family life stage and the individual developmental stage of the patient and family. The illness and disability of one family member can significantly impact the developmental goals of another. For example, a life-threatening illness in a young adult can interfere with his or her partner's desire to launch into parenthood. No two individuals will respond and adjust to an illness within the same family at the same pace, direction, or time. Each family member's manner and ability to adapt is directly related to his or her own developmental stage, personality, belief system, and role within the family (McGoldrick et al., 2005). At no stage in the life course does human development unfold independently outside of the family system.

As with individual and family life cycles, one can conceptualize the time phases of illness in terms of progressing from the initial crisis to a period of chronic maintenance and potentially to a terminal stage. Rolland (2012) characterized chronic diseases according to four dimensions impacting family systems: onset, course, outcome, and degree of incapacitation. The onset of a chronic condition (which may precede the actual diagnosis by months) often forces the individual and family into a transition that is out of sync with the period in an individual's or family's life cycle. For instance, a significant early adulthood task is to establish independence by pursuing personal goals that differentiate oneself as unique from his or her family. Early adulthood is generally not a time when one anticipates being diagnosed with a chronic illness and moving back home for needed support.

In the initial crisis phase, it is useful to explore the key beliefs that shape families' illness narratives and coping strategies. Family belief systems are shared constructions of reality. These belief systems reinforce family identities as well as support families in making sense of everyday complexities, including crises associated with the onset and progression of chronic disease. When a serious health issue arises, it is predictable that one wonders "Why me (or why our family)?" and "Why now?" We create explanations that help us make sense of experiences.

Families' beliefs about the cause of an illness need to be assessed separately from their beliefs about what can influence outcomes. These are two very distinct belief systems, each significant in its own right. To begin this dialogue in a neutral manner that invites each member to share his or her personal perspective, one might comment, "All of us have ideas about how or why something happens in our life, yet often we don't have a chance to talk about it. I am interested in what each of us has thought about why Jane had a stroke at such a young age." Responses will highlight both individuals' understanding of the medical condition as well as their own beliefs about why something has happened. The key is to assist family members in exploring different perceptions while providing clarification, acceptance of differing perspectives, and promoting a sense of cohesiveness. The ability to support a family as it navigates the onset and progression of a chronic illness often requires sensitive exploration into family core beliefs, including how family members define themselves. The social worker aids the family in making sense of the illness while helping them muster resilience and unity.

Chronic diseases vary greatly in that some are progressive, becoming worse over time (e.g., amyotrophic lateral sclerosis [ALS]), or are constant and relatively stable (e.g., osteoarthritis). Some chronic illnesses entail periods of stability interspersed with sudden physical setbacks (e.g., multiple sclerosis). If the illness is progressive and the disease outcome is a rapid decrease in independent functioning, family members may find their roles rapidly changing as they adapt to the shifting and increasing care needs of the patient. A state of uncertainty keeps the illness in the forefront of the family's consciousness and works against attempts to regain "normalcy." It becomes crucial to continuously assess the family's capacity to organize itself around adaptive demands of the illness such as accommodating numerous clinic appointments, dietary restrictions, losses in functional capacity, and the difficult role changes experienced by family members.

Unlike fatal diseases, chronic diseases are not necessarily life-ending, although they are life-altering and in some cases may contribute to shortened independent life spans. Chronic diseases may entail moving from a crisis state to a chronic state. The transition from the crisis to chronic phase of the illness life cycle occurs when the family is better able to incorporate normal day-to-day activities that are in alignment with their family life stage. That does not necessarily mean, however, that the family does not need to continue altering its course along the way. When caring for a child with cerebral palsy who may have a significant degree of incapacitation, family responsibilities and tasks need to shift in response to the child's ever-changing medical condition and care needs. As a result, family coping and adaptation may differ when the child and the family are in different life cycle stages. Coping strategies that families use to manage daily events in a certain stage may differ as well. A useful question at this stage is "Tell me about your child's illness and what it has meant for you and your family."

Forward-thinking clinical approaches incorporate individual, family, and illness life cycle perspectives as a way of encouraging families to envision different dimensions of their life. Relationships, family, work, and recreation are likely to change during the progression of a family member's illness. These factors are impacted by the individual's degree of functional independence or degree of incapacitation. It is useful to consider the following exploratory questions once the acute crisis stage has subsided and the chronic long-term nature of the illness has become apparent:

- What individual, family, or illness milestones and transitions are anticipated in the next six months to a year? In two years?

- What do you think are the normal developmental tasks for your children/self/ partner at that time? (These tasks should be assessed for a realistic understanding of developmental tasks versus an ideal.)

- How will those important transitions be impacted by the health condition? (Check for consistency across affected parties.)

- Whose life might be most affected at that time? (Consider all family members, including young children.)

These questions address how much or how little life cycle planning is wrapped around the status of the family member's condition. Understanding individual and family expectations is crucial as it provides insight into family dynamics, ethnic and cultural practices, and underlying beliefs that will affect decision making during future transitions. When the future is ambiguous, as, for example, when cancer is in remission, it is beneficial to explore hypothetical questions such as "If your brother were cured tomorrow, what would each person do differently in terms of making plans for next week?" "What would it look like if . . . ?" These queries elicit the extent to which individual and family life cycle tasks have been affected by the illness. They prompt conversation regarding how each aspect has been positively or negatively affected by the illness. There is no substitute for understanding individual family members' beliefs about what has happened as a result of the illness and what will happen in the future.

The manner in which a chronic illness impacts a family system is dependent in part upon

- the onset, course, and outcome of the condition,

- degree of the individual's incapacitation,

- the family belief system(s),

- the convergence of the roles the family member with the illness fulfills in the family (primary parent, caregiver to extended family members, significant other, financial contributor, day-to-day organizer of family events), and

- the extent by which treatment modalities and illness symptoms, illness course, and related functional limitations affect an individual's ability to fulfill his or her preexisting roles.

SPECIAL CONSIDERATIONS: CHRONIC ILLNESS IN CHILDHOOD

Chronic illnesses are often associated with the aging process but in reality, they may appear at any age and point in the family's life cycle. Taking care of a child with an ongoing health problem can be one of the most difficult tasks a parent can face. An estimated 20% of the school-age population experiences a chronic medical illness or disabling condition, putting the number of children under the age of 18 years with chronic conditions at 12 million (Child Study Center, 2001).

Parents experience grief around the loss of a healthy child when they realize that there will be an ongoing impact on their child's life that may preclude the child from enjoying the lifestyle that they have imagined for the child. Relationships within the family will be altered and sometimes strained as everyone adjusts to the situation and perhaps takes on additional responsibilities and concerns. One major task for parents of chronically ill children is to aid the child in coping with his or her condition while simultaneously managing their own worries as the parents. Issues of parental concern include the prospect of diminishing control, not being able to help one's child, and apprehension about making appropriate treatment decisions. Additional issues that warrant attention and support include

- challenges of shifting care of the child to others and trusting the healthcare team;
- stress over making medical decisions for their child with limited understanding of events or not perceiving that they are heard and/or believed by medical caregivers;
- struggles with emotions of anger/guilt as well as physical/mental exhaustion;
- stress on the marriage or partnership associated with a child's chronic illness falling outside of the anticipated normal sequence of family life;
- consumption of so much time at the hospital that employment becomes impossible and family income is negatively affected;
- fear of an emergency situation and knowing how to respond;
- not understanding how the condition will evolve and if or when it might worsen;
- monitoring the child's symptoms and knowing a condition may be worsening despite the best efforts of the parents to intervene;
- knowing how to parent a chronically ill child and whether to discipline the child;
- meeting overall family needs while caring for a chronically ill child, and
- defining a new "normal" for the family and its individual members.

CHRONIC DISEASES OVERVIEW

Chronic heart disease, cancer, and diabetes are among the most common, costly, and preventable of all health problems in the United States (*Table 7.4*). Although chronic diseases are more common among older adults, they affect people of all ages and are now recognized as a leading health concern of the nation. The Centers for Disease Control and Prevention noted that the percentage of U.S. children and adolescents with a chronic health condition increased from 1.8% in the 1960s to more than 8% in 2006. The WHO estimated that 60% of deaths around the world in 2005 were due to chronic diseases, with 80% of the total occurring in low- to middle-income countries. *Chronic diseases are currently the leading cause of death in every country in the world, except for those with the lowest levels of income.* Four modifiable health risk behaviors—lack of physical activity, poor nutrition, tobacco use, and excessive alcohol consumption—are responsible for much of the illness, suffering, and early death associated with chronic diseases.

Table 7.4 Major Chronic Disease in United States Risk Factors/Prevention

	Heart Disease	**Cancer**	**Diabetes**
Deaths (in 2008)	616,000	562,000	78,705
Risk Factors	• Inactivity • Obesity • High blood pressure • Smoking • High cholesterol • Diabetes • Approximately 37% of adults reported having two or more of the risk factors listed (American Heart Association, 2012)	• Smoking • Prolonged exposure to secondhand smoke • Exposure to pesticides • Exposure to ultraviolet rays • Excessive alcohol consumption	• Obesity • Physical inactivity • High blood pressure • Family history
Preventative measures	• Exercise • No smoking • Diet rich with fiber, fruits & vegetables • Control blood pressure and cholesterol	• No smoking • Protective measures for pesticide exposure • Avoid ultraviolet rays • Limit alcohol intake • Diet rich with fiber, fruits & vegetables • Maintain healthy body weight	• Weight control • Physical activity • Manage blood pressure • Early screening if family history exists

Source: Major Chronic Diseases in the United States. Centers for Disease Control and Prevention.

Social workers impact our national health and well-being by intervening with chronically ill patients across the continuum of healthcare settings, including in emergency departments, hospitals, outpatient centers, rehabilitation facilities, nursing homes, and palliative care programs and hospices. An overview of chronic illnesses, including risk factors, gender differences, racial and ethnic disparities, cultural considerations, and successful interventions is shown below.

- *Heart disease* and stroke are the first and third leading causes of death, accounting for more than 30% of all deaths annually in the United States.
- *Cancer* is the second leading cause of death, claiming more than half a million lives each year.
- *Diabetes* is the leading cause of kidney failure, non-traumatic lower extremity amputations, and new cases of blindness each year among U.S. adults aged 20–74 years.
- *Arthritis* is the most common cause of disability, limiting activity for 19 million U.S. adults.
- *Obesity* has become a major health concern for people of all ages. One in every three adults and nearly one in every five young people aged 6–19 are obese.

HEART DISEASE

The term "**cardiovascular disease**" embraces a number of conditions affecting the structures or function of the heart.

- Coronary artery disease (including heart attack) occurs when arteries become hardened and narrowed by plaque, decreasing blood flow to the heart and oxygen to the heart muscle.
- Congestive heart failure is characterized by the inability of the heart to effectively pump blood, resulting in shortness of breath, fluid retention, and excessive fatigue.
- Heart muscle disease (cardiomyopathy) is a weakening of the heart muscle.
- Congenital heart disease is a type of defect or malformation in one or more structures of the heart or blood vessels that occurs before birth. Congenital heart defects may produce symptoms at birth, during childhood, and sometimes not until adulthood.

Epidemiology

Cardiovascular disease, known more simply as "heart disease," is the number one killer in America, affecting more than 13 million Americans. Heart disease accounted for 29% of all deaths in Michigan in 2005 (CDC, 2008). Coronary heart disease, the most common type of heart disease, accounted for 405,309 deaths in 2008 (American Heart Association, 2012). About 550,000 people are diagnosed with heart failure each year, prompting it to be the leading cause of hospitalization for people aged 65 years or older (American Heart Association, 2010). As life expectancy increases, so will the incidence of heart disease. About 500,000 adults in the United States have congenital heart disease.

Gender and Heart Disease

Although heart disease is sometimes thought of as a man's disease, nearly the same number of women and men die each year of heart disease in the United States. Unfortunately, 36% of women do not perceive a risk for heart disease and when seeking treatment, may encounter a gender bias among providers (Mosca, Appel, Benjamin, et al., 2004).

- Heart disease is the leading cause of death for women in the United States, with 315,930 women dying from it in 2006.

- Heart disease accounted for 26% of female deaths in 2006, representing one out of every four women.

- Heart disease is the leading cause of death for women of most racial/ethnic groups in the United States, including African Americans, American Indians, Alaska Natives, Hispanics, and Caucasians. For Asian American women, heart disease is second only to cancer as a cause of death.

Racial and Ethnic Disparities in Heart Disease Management

Disparities in cardiovascular health are among the most serious public health problems in the United States. Despite declines in cardiovascular mortality over the last three decades, many population subgroups defined by race, ethnicity, gender, socioeconomic status, educational level, or geography show striking, and often widening, disparities in cardiovascular health. Heart disease is the leading cause of death for people of most ethnicities in the United States, including African Americans, Hispanics, and whites. For American Indians or Alaska Natives and Asians or Pacific Islanders, heart disease is second only to cancer. Similar studies have found racial differences in the quality of care for comorbid conditions, including both testing and treatment for hypertension and dyslipidemia among Hispanics and African Americans compared with non-Hispanic whites (Arday et al., 2002; Hertz, Unger, & Ferrario, 2006). *Figure 7.2* displays the percentage of all deaths caused by heart disease in 2008 as listed by ethnicity.

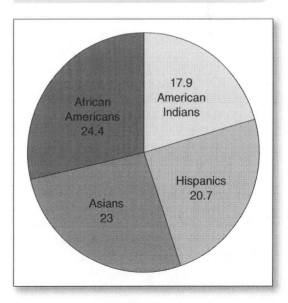

Figure 7.2 Percentage of Deaths Due to Heart Disease by Race/Ethnicity

Source: Race of Ethnic Groups by Percentage of Deaths. Centers for Disease Control and Prevention (2012).

Cultural Variations and Considerations

People are shaped by cultural forces and those cultural forces significantly affect numerous (if not all) communication behaviors. Health behaviors, including regular participation in screening exams and imaging, blood tests, and physician visits, are a form of communication. However, willingness to comply with recommended health behaviors and regimes varies between cultures and genders. The American Heart Association notes that ethnic minority groups, especially women minorities, face the greatest risk of death due to heart disease and stroke, yet they have the lowest risk-factor awareness of any racial or ethnic group. Given such concern, the National Heart, Lung, and Blood Institute (NHLBI) and partner organizations sponsor a national campaign called *The Heart Truth* to increase awareness and action among women about their risk of heart disease. *The Red Dress*—the centerpiece of *The Heart Truth*—was introduced as the national symbol for women and heart disease awareness in 2002 by NHLBI. *The Red Dress* is intended to remind women of the need to protect their heart health and serves as an inspiration to take action.

Interventions

Self-management is critical in managing chronic conditions, particularly heart disease. Knowledge, attitudes, and beliefs relating to illness and wellness are influenced by culture and ethnicity, which in turn impact individuals' capacity to engage in self-care behaviors. Effective management of heart disease is largely dependent on patient adherence to both pharmacological and non-pharmacological care strategies. For patients with heart disease, self-management education is usually provided as a component of a cardiac rehabilitation program or through more generic chronic-disease initiatives commonly referred to as *Chronic Disease Self-Management Programs*. However, low enrollment is a problem for these programs, and concerns have been raised over whether they are reaching those who are most in need (Baum, Begin, Houweling, & Taylor, 2009).

Delivering culturally tailored self-management interventions over the Internet (Web-based interventions) may reduce disparities in access by overcoming many of the practical barriers that hinder attendance to programs using one-on-one approaches (Kerr, Murray, Stevenson, Gore, & Nazareth, 2006). Web-based interventions can additionally overcome educational barriers by presenting complex information in a more easily accessible manner, for example, through animations or video. Gilmour (2007) cited evidence that web-based interventions achieve health benefits in patients with chronic diseases and that patients see the potential of Web-based interventions in meeting their information and support needs.

Despite the relative lack of Internet access among disadvantaged groups, individuals in these groups make relatively high use of the Internet for their health-information needs. Women and chronically ill individuals are more inclined to use the Internet as a health information resource, and Atkinson, Saperstein, and Pleis (2009) noted that these individuals make particular use of the Internet to increase awareness of self-management strategies for heart disease. Available on demand anytime and anywhere, Web-based interventions are a transformative technology, conveniently delivering education and guidance to affected patients and caregivers as appropriate.

While important, individual responsibility and behaviorial change must be supplemented with widespread policy and operational changes in healthcare systems. Substantial barriers impede the implementation and dissemination of these programs. Barriers to self-management occur at multiple levels, including the levels of patients (and their environment), providers, and the system. *Patient-level challenges* include difficulties in prioritizing multiple demands, acquiring individualized care plans, and using new technologies to optimize self-management. *Provider-level barriers* to facilitating self-management include inadequate staffing, time, and resource, as well as a lack of appropriate treatment guidelines for complex chronic illnesses. *Barriers linked to systems* may include a lack of reimbursement from third-party payers for specific self-management support tasks. Successful implementation of complex chronic disease self-management processes is linked to the extent that these multilevel barriers have been recognized and addressed. Social workers, in their boundary-spanning and advocacy roles, are well qualified to collaborate with policymakers, providers, and health-professional organizations in these endeavors.

CASE STUDY

Social Work Intervention: Chronic Illness and a Family

Mrs. Maria Costello is a 62-year-old woman who was initially referred to a community family practice clinic after a fainting episode that occurred during her afternoon shift at work. A nonsmoker and moderately overweight, Maria describes having experienced bouts of shortness of breath yet is adamant that it "doesn't slow her down" and is proud to be working outside the home. Together, she and her husband provide day-care for their four grandchildren while the parents are at work, and Maria works at Meijer's three evenings a week. Because she works more than twenty hours a week, she is eligible for healthcare insurance (with large copays); however, if she were to decrease her hours, she would lose her eligibility.

Maria and her husband must survive on her limited income as her husband, who worked for decades as a mechanic, is a non-citizen and is not eligible for Social Security. Maria is a naturalized citizen who emigrated from Mexico thirty-three years ago. Her four adult children are citizens. While she and her husband speak English as a second language, they are functionally illiterate. They depend upon their oldest daughter (and sometimes their 11-year-old granddaughter) to interpret written directions regarding medications and physician appointments.

During this physician appointment, Maria is diagnosed with hypertension and is being evaluated for congestive heart failure. The prescribed anti–hypertensive medications cost roughly $250 under her current insurance plan, with a $20 co-pay. The potential diagnosis of congestive heart disease, however, creates the possibility that she will not be able to continue working long hours on her feet and therefore may lose her health insurance.

(Continued)

(Continued)

Maria does not believe her diagnosis is accurate as she has been healthy all her life, and she cannot understand how her heart would suddenly fail. The primary-care physician from the clinic refers her to the social worker because of concerns about her ability to manage her heart disease effectively.

Questions:

In conducting your psychosocial assessment, what areas should be explored?

What are the critical elements of information related to the patient's beliefs about diagnosis, treatment recommendations, and disease management?

How might the patient's beliefs influence adaptation to the specific demands necessary to manage congestive heart failure?

How might you engage the family in the assessment and planning process?

What resources and healthcare system access might be warranted?

What potential tensions could develop between the patient and the healthcare team, and what role could social work play in preventing or alleviating such tensions?

What is the impact of multiple chronic diseases on the lives of caregivers?

What new roles and supportive services are needed to relieve their burden?

CANCER

Epidemiology

Cancer is the second leading cause of death in the United States, exceeded only by heart disease. About 577,190 Americans are expected to die of cancer in 2012, amounting to more than 1,500 people per day. Another 1,638,910 new cancer cases are expected to be diagnosed in 2012 (American Cancer Society [ACS], 2012). The term *cancer* refers to diseases in which abnormal cells divide without control and are able to invade other tissues. Cancer cells can spread to other parts of the body through the blood and lymph systems. Cancer is not one disease, but many diseases. There are more than 100 types of cancer; however, the most common type is lung cancer.

The five-year relative survival rate for all cancers diagnosed between 2001 and 2007 is 67%, up from 49% in the period from 1977 to 1979 (American Cancer Society, 2012). The improvement in survival is associated with both diagnosing certain cancers at an earlier stage and improved analysis of tumor-registry data. Also, improved follow-up care after cancer treatment, fewer deaths from other causes, and an aging U.S. population contribute to the larger number of cancer survivors who now live with cancer as a chronic illness. In January 2007, about 11.7 million people with a diagnosis of cancer were living in the United States (CDC, 2011a).

The cost of cancer extends beyond the number of lives lost and new diagnoses each year. Cancer survivors, as well as their family members, friends, and caregivers, face physical, emotional, social, and spiritual challenges as a result of their cancer diagnosis and treatment. The overall financial costs of cancer are profound. As noted by the ACS (2012), the National Institutes of Health (NIH) estimated that the over-all costs of cancer in 2007 were $226.8 billion: $103.8 billion for direct medical costs (total of all healthcare expenditures) and $123.0 billion for indirect mortality costs (cost of lost productivity due to premature death).

Gender and Cancer Mortality Perceptions

Lung cancer is the leading cancer-related cause of death, with an estimated 173,200 cancer deaths in 2012 thought to be associated with tobacco use (American Cancer Society, 2012, p. 1). Most media and research attention is devoted to breast cancer and, more recently, prostate cancer. Given the widespread focus on these two types of cancer, social science theories of media influence such as the *Cultivation Hypothesis* (McCreary & Sadava, 1999) predict that people overestimate men's likelihood of dying from prostate cancer and women's likelihood of dying from breast cancer. Furthermore, because the media focus on prostate cancer is relatively new and there has been a relative absence of men in cancer-prevention marketing campaigns, these theories also predict that people will believe women are at greater risk than men for being diagnosed with cancer and experiencing a cancer-related death. In actuality, U.S. men have slightly less than a 1 in 2 lifetime risk of developing cancer; for women, the risk is a little more than 1 in 3 (American Cancer Society, 2012, p. 1). In the case of breast cancer, incidence rates began to decline in 2000 after peaking at 142 per 100,000 women in 1999. The dramatic decrease of almost 7% from 2002 to 2003 has been attributed to reductions in the use of menopausal hormone therapy (MHT), previously known as hormone replacement therapy (American Cancer Society, 2012, p. 9).

Racial, Ethnic, and Socioeconomic Disparities in Cancer Management

Cancer can affect men and women of all ages, races, and ethnicities, but it does *not* affect all groups equally. African Americans, for example, are more likely to die of cancer than people of any other race or ethnicity. According to the CDC (2011a) the age-adjusted death rate per 100,000 people for all types of cancer combined was 216 for African Americans, 177 for Caucasians, 119 for American Indians/Alaska Natives, 117 for Hispanics, and 108 for Asians/Pacific Islanders.

Persons with lower socioeconomic status (SES) have disproportionately higher cancer death rates than those with higher SES, regardless of demographic factors such as race/ethnicity. People with lower SES are more likely to engage in behaviors that increase cancer risk, such as tobacco use, physical inactivity, and poor diet, in part because of marketing strategies that target these populations and in part because of environmental or community factors that provide fewer opportunities for physical activity and less access to fresh fruits and vegetables. Lower socioeconomic status (SES) is also associated with lower literacy rates as well as financial, structural, and personal barriers to healthcare, including inadequate health insurance, reduced access to recommended preventive-care and high-quality treatment services. Disparities in healthcare access and use impact survival. Individuals without health insurance are more likely to be diagnosed with advanced cancer and less likely to receive standard treatment and survive their disease (American Cancer Society, 2012, p. 43).

Cultural Considerations

Culture influences how a diagnosis of cancer (or any illness for that matter) is perceived and how symptoms are expressed and discussed, healthcare information is received, the type of care afforded, and how rights and protections are exercised. It is therefore crucial that healthcare professionals have an understanding of the sociocultural backgrounds of patients, including their beliefs about health and use of healthcare. Perceptions of personal health and how decisions are made with regard to use of healthcare are influenced by factors such as level of education, socioeconomic status, geographic region (urban, rural), and time spent in the United States.

Patient and family interpretations of illness and treatment are often different than those of the healthcare team. In some cultures, "illness" is perceived as spiritual rather than physical and cancer is regarded as a punishment for past sins—vastly different concepts than those held by Western medicine. Being unaware or in denial of the presence of diabetes also may thwart prompt initiation of treatment, with negative health consequences. Concepts of family structure often extend beyond the definition of the traditional nuclear family. Because patient decision making may extend to members of the patient's extended family and community, social workers should consider familial influence on healing practices and treatment decisions.

Interventions

A diagnosis of cancer typically has a profound psychological impact on the individual and involved parties. It constitutes a traumatic life event that threatens one's physical, emotional, and social existence (Holland & Lewis, 2000). It challenges one's core existence, equilibrium, and sense of normalcy. Overwhelming fear, sadness, anger, uncertainty, and isolation are not uncommon responses to cancer. Some patients experience a sense of isolation, with friends and family not knowing what to say or do. A cancer diagnosis potentially affects all aspects of social and emotional functioning. The themes of the cancer experience for many patients are those of vulnerability and uncertainty coupled with fear of recurrent disease. Cancer survivors are at greater risk for recurrence of the initial cancer and for the development of second cancers due to the effects of treatment, unhealthy lifestyle behaviors, underlying genetics, or risk factors that contributed to the initial cancer. To reduce the emotional impacts of cancer, healthcare social workers (1) address the possible long-term and late effects of cancer and its treatment on survivors' physical and psychosocial well-being, (2) provide patients with coordinated care, and (3) promote healthy, culturally appropriate coping behaviors. Cognitive and behavioral interventions are among the most widely used as they can be applied to a broad range of patient populations. Hypnosis, progressive muscle relaxation, and autogenic training to induce relaxation are techniques that are commonly employed as adjuncts to pain management. These techniques serve to reduce anxiety, particularly in anticipation of a frightening experience or procedure.

DIABETES

People with diabetes have high blood sugar because their body cannot move sugar into fat, liver, and muscle cells to be stored for energy. This is because either their pancreas does not make enough insulin and/or their cells do not respond to insulin normally. Over time, diabetes can have a profound impact on an individual's quality of life and overall health status. Common complications from unmanaged diabetes include vision problems, nerve damage, kidney failure, cardiovascular disease, and stroke. In fact, two of three people with diabetes ultimately die of heart disease or stroke (NIH, 2011).

There are three major types of diabetes, each of which has unique causes and risk factors:

- *Type-1 diabetes* can occur at any age, but it is most often diagnosed in children, teens, or young adults. Type-1 diabetes accounts for approximately 5% of all diagnosed cases of diabetes. In this disease, the body makes little or no insulin, so daily injections of insulin are needed, sometimes before every meal, using injections or an insulin pump. The exact cause is unknown, but risk factors for Type-1 diabetes may be autoimmune, genetic, or environmental (CDC, 2011c, p. 11).

- *Type-2 diabetes* is the most prevalent form of diabetes, representing 90% to 95% of all diagnosed cases of diabetes. Type-2 diabetes is associated with older age, obesity, family history of diabetes, history of gestational diabetes, impaired glucose metabolism, physical inactivity, and race/ethnicity (CDC, 2011c, p. 11). Teenagers and young adults are increasingly being diagnosed because of high obesity rates and low activity levels. Those who are diagnosed with Type-2 diabetes often are unaware that they have the disease because the onset of symptoms is gradual. Many patients with Type-2 diabetes can control their blood sugar by managing their diet, losing weight, exercising several times a week, and remaining on medications to control blood sugar levels. In the absence of these actions, patients with Type-2 diabetes will require insulin, either by itself or in conjunction with medication.

- *Gestational diabetes* is high blood sugar that develops at any time during pregnancy in a woman who does not have diabetes. Pregnancy hormones can block the effect of insulin, and, consequently, glucose levels may increase in a pregnant woman's blood. High blood sugar (glucose) levels often subside to normal after delivery. Women with gestational diabetes, however, have a 35%–60% chance of developing Type-2 diabetes within five to ten years after delivery (Hillier et al., 2008; Kitzmiller, Dang-Kilduff, & Taslimi, 2007).

Epidemiology

According to the CDC, diabetes is reaching epidemic levels as a result of the greater prevalence of obesity and sedentary lifestyles. Diabetes affects nearly 26 million people, or 8.3% of the U.S. population, with 18.8 million diagnosed cases and 7 million undiagnosed cases (CDC, 2011c, p. 1). In Michigan alone, the number of adults between the ages of 45 and 65 years who were diagnosed with diabetes more than doubled from 150,000 in 1994 to 325,000 in 2009 (CDC, 2011b). The number of people diagnosed with diabetes is escalating so rapidly, both nationally and worldwide, that the WHO considers it to be an epidemic, with a rate of premature deaths similar to that associated with HIV/AIDs. In 2007, diabetes was the seventh leading cause of death (CDC, 2011c) and accounted for an estimated $116 billion in direct medical costs and another $58 billion in indirect costs, including disability, work loss, and premature mortality (CDC, 2011c, p.7).

Gender and Diabetes

Of the 16 million Americans who have diabetes, approximately 55% of them are women. More people with Type-2 diabetes mellitus are women (58.4%) compared with men (41.6%), whereas about 47% with Type-1 disease are women (CDC, 2008). Among different studies, prevalence rates of diabetes are not consistently higher for women, with the ratio of the prevalence in women versus men varying among populations studied, probably because of different distributions of risk factors such as body mass index, physical activity, and genetic differences.

Racial and Ethnic Disparities in Diabetes Management

The burden of diabetes is much greater for minority populations than the Caucasian population. Compared with non-Hispanic white adults, the risk of diagnosed diabetes was 18% higher among Asian Americans, 66% higher among Hispanics, and 77% higher among non-Hispanic blacks. When compared with non-Hispanic whites, the risk of diagnosed diabetes was about the same for Cubans and for Central and South Americans, but 87% higher for Mexican Americans, and 94% higher among Puerto Ricans (CDC, 2011c, p. 3).

Cultural Considerations

The unfavorable consequences of diabetes in African Americans and Hispanics do not seem to be due to inherent biological differences. Rather, it appears that differences in awareness and perceptions of one's own health condition, use of professional medical care, and self-management of diabetes may be the major factors. Fewer minorities with diabetes are aware of their diagnosis: for example, of the estimated 2 million Latinos with diabetes, only half are aware of their condition (Tripp-Reimer, Choi, Kelley and Enslein, 2001). Such failure to be initially aware of diabetes may detract from the effectiveness of subsequent treatment and impact survival; certain minorities also have much higher rates of diabetes-related complications and death, in some instances by as much as 50% more than the total population (CDC, 2008).

Beyond initial awareness of diabetes, cultural bias may impact whether and how one seeks treatment. For example, Tripp-Reimer et al. (2001) pointed out that many Native American tribes believe that diabetes is a new disease introduced by the "white man." Typically, diabetes is believed to result from a state of imbalance caused by consuming too much sugar, consuming too much food in general, drinking alcohol, or behaving immorally. Because one should strive to follow the right path, a diagnosis of diabetes may indicate a failure to live properly and a lack of spiritual strength. As a result, a person may feel shamed by a diagnosis of diabetes and reluctant to tell family or friends.

The provision of lower quality care may also be an important contributor to the current state of diabetes disparities. An IOM literature review identified that, while healthcare access and demographic variables account for some of the racial disparities in health status, there is a persistent residual gap in outcomes attributed to differences in the quality of care received (Smedley, et al., 2003).

Culture, health beliefs, socioeconomic status, and psychosocial factors such as social support, self-efficacy, and coping skills play a large role in explaining diabetes self-care and health outcomes (Chipkin & de Groot 1998; Anderson et al., 2003). Bach, Pham, Schrag, Tate, and Hargraves (2004) noted that many low-income African American and Latino patients limited diabetes care because of financial concerns. In addition, limited access to recreational facilities and stores with recommended diabetes food items also disproportionately limits participation of racial/ethnic minorities in recommended physical activity and healthy nutritional habits.

Although there has been progress in identifying specific approaches for diabetes treatment among African Americans and Hispanic Americans, much work remains to more thoroughly understand other minority groups. Batts et al. (2001) reported that the illness concerns of African Americans and Hispanic Americans include

- diabetes-management techniques that include use of ethnic foods and participation in social gatherings involving food;

- access to proper instruction about disease management;

- methods for dealing with concerns about the trustworthiness of healthcare providers;

- accommodation of preferences for more familiar traditional remedies versus insulin therapy, and

- enhanced knowledge about the financial consequences of diabetes.

The family is regarded with special significance by African Americans and Hispanic Americans. The valuing of interdependence, cooperation, collectivism, and synergism in African American and Hispanic American life suggests the importance of the family to disease management (Tillman, 2002). Given the predisposition of these populations, intervention with use of a multidimensional model of family life and a biopsychosocial conceptualization of health appears particularly appropriate for patients with Type-2 diabetes.

Interventions

Continuously evolving assessment and treatment interventions for diabetic patients have improved health outcomes, with the potential to reduce health disparities among racial/ethnic minorities. Increasingly, these approaches seek to integrate patients, families, providers, and healthcare organizations into a coordinated continuum of care in which all parties participate in timely, culturally sensitive decision making.

Successful minority patient-targeted interventions tend to utilize interpersonal skills and social networks such as family members, peer support groups, interactive or one-on-one education, and social work case coordination (Peek, Algernin, & Haung, 2008). Culturally tailored interventions take into account participants' unique cultural preferences or orientations about health and healthcare use. These programs are an important component of "cultural leverage," which Peek et al. (2008) promoted as a strategy for enhancing health in racial and ethnic communities by using their cultural practices, philosophies, or environments as opportunities to facilitate behavioral change.

The IOM (2001) identified family relationships as prime targets for interventions that might produce more enduring changes in health behavior than those achieved in individual behavioral interventions. These interventions seek to develop positive family-interaction skills, including conflict resolution. Family members are encouraged to stay involved in relative care, to interact supportively rather than critically, and to be realistic about patient diet, exercise, and glucose control. Positive family involvement affects patient (and family) morale and supports disease-management behaviors among patients with Type-2 diabetes.

Interventions targeting providers should include a focus on identifying and addressing potential provider biases, refining patient/provider communication, and promoting culturally sensitive service delivery. As suggested by Tripp-Reimer et al. (2001), addressing barriers arising from the healthcare system involves

> locating services within the targeted community to maximize access, offering a broad array of health and social services to increase efficiency and continuity, maintaining a consistent staff, hiring and retaining bilingual, bicultural staff, expanding hours of operation, and emphasizing family and community involvement with regard to graphics, posters and pictures, music, and seating arrangements. To address areas of practitioner culture competencies, diabetes health professionals need cultural knowledge and a repertoire of culturally competent skills. (p. 20)

Stewart (1995) emphasized the correlation between positive health outcomes, including diabetes control, with enhanced communication and shared decision making. Evidence supports the role of community-based initiatives such as *REACH Detroit* as being particularly effective for improving diabetes health outcomes (Lorig, Ritter, & Gonzalez, 2003; Wang & Chan, 2005; Two Feathers et al., 2005; Rodondi et al. 2006). Tripp-Reimer et al. (2001) emphasize the consistent need for involvement of community leaders in the identification of community health needs and in the planning, delivery, and evaluation of health services, including diabetic care.

REACH Detroit findings suggest that culturally tailored, community-based healthy lifestyle interventions delivered by trained community residents can significantly improve diabetes self-care and reduce Type-2 diabetes complications among African American and Latino populations. Integrated care achieved through community health centers and larger health systems' partnerships offer promise at reducing health disparities, a dynamic encouraged in the PPACA. The already strained U.S. healthcare system faces an unprecedented influx of patients in 2014, when 32 million Americans will have health insurance for the first time. Constrained budgets, increased population diversity, intensified patient-care needs, and the prospect of insufficient numbers of healthcare providers make development of new delivery models essential. There is ample opportunity for social work to infuse clinical and administrative leadership in this scenario based on its competence in biopsychosocial health and healthcare issues.

SUMMARY

This chapter defined and examined the significance of chronic disease and illness. The implications to patients and families were underscored along with the repercussions of chronic disease and illness on the nation's overall health and economy. The disparities that exist among age and socioeconomic groups were discussed, and both the Chronic Care and Guided Care Models were reviewed as means of providing intervention to those experiencing chronic conditions. The role of social work in care coordination was emphasized. The epidemiology, disparities, and interventions associated with heart disease, diabetes, and cancer were presented.

A profound change is occurring in our perception of what should constitute healthcare. Rather than a vision of illness based on episodes involving a time-limited series of interventions of greater or lesser intensity, patients (and healthcare practitioners) are now often faced with chronic health problems extending over years. In many cases, aging individuals will experience several chronic diseases simultaneously, making care especially complex, particularly if these conditions are not addressed from an interdisciplinary, biopsychosocial perspective. Intervention for patients with multiple chronic diseases requires a set of methodologies different from those that earlier served as the basis for our health systems and traditional treatment processes. The forthcoming era of integrated care offers social workers the opportunity to collaborate in shaping these systems and contributing their clinical and leadership expertise in dealing with chronic-disease management.

KEY TERMS AND CONCEPTS

- Cardiovascular disease
- Care coordination

- Health Belief Model

- Chronic Care Model (CCM)

- Chronic disease

- DALY

- Disability

- Disparities (in health and care)

- Guided Care Model (GCM)

- Healthcare literacy

- Family life cycle

- Treatment compliance (adherence)

QUESTIONS FOR DISCUSSION

1. Will providing self-management programs over the Internet help reduce health disparities by reaching a greater number of patients? What factors might impact their effectiveness?

2. Age and race are examples of factors that contribute to differences in health outcomes that are unavoidable, but behaviors, actions, and access to preventive and primary care are examples of factors that can be changed by the individual, system, or society. Do you think that patients who are overweight or who smoke should pay more for their healthcare insurance and services? Why or why not?

EXERCISES

1. **Cultural and Health Belief Exercise**

   Think of a time when someone in your family faced a serious illness. Examine how cultural and personal differences, including communication barriers, health beliefs, attitudes toward pain, chronic disease, and use of unconventional therapies affected disease management. Were there any tensions between the patient, family, and healthcare team? What were the sources of these tensions? What is the role of social work in these situations?

2. **Patient Adherence Exercise**

   Read *Needles; A Memoir of Growing Up With Diabetes* (Dominick, A., 1998) an autobiography about the author's struggle adapt to Type-1 diabetes and her family's response. Analyze the author's ability to cope with the diagnosis throughout her childhood, adolescence, and young adulthood using the Adherence Counseling model outlined in this chapter. Describe the disease onset and progression, symptoms, progression, and treatment experienced. Assess and explain how various factors, such as family health beliefs, medical history, and experiences within the healthcare system, impacted their perceptions and trust of providers and subsequent adherence to treatment recommendations. Based on this assessment, how might a social worker facilitate behavioral changes, improve communication and advocacy skills, and maximize effective coping?

3. **Social Determinants of Health Exercise**

Research reveals that the economic and social conditions under which people live also affect their health and well-being. The WHO published a final report and recommendations for creating health equity through action on the social determinants of health. Discuss those factors impacting individual health and pursuit of healthcare (see http://www.who.int/social_determinants/en/).

4. **Myths of Chronic Disease**

The *World Health Organization. Preventing Chronic Diseases: A Vital Investment* report and website contain fact sheets, country-based information, and technical papers on projections of morbidity, mortality, and impact of chronic diseases. Review these documents and watch the short video (seven minutes) related to the myths of chronic diseases and their prevalence around the world. Review the information and contrast international experiences with that of the United States (see http://www.who.int/chp/chronic_disease_report/en/index.html).

Health Statistics Websites

Centers for Disease Control and Prevention, Center for Health Statistics, Trends in Health and Aging. Available at http://www.cdc.gov/nchs/agingact.htm

Centers for Disease Control and Prevention & the Merck Company Foundation. The State of Aging and Health in America 2007. White House Station, NJ: The Merck Company Foundation. Available at http://www.cdc.gov/aging.

Council on Social Work Education—The Role of Social Work in Managing Chronic Illness Care. Available at http://www.cswe.org/CentersInitiatives/GeroEdCenter/Programs/MAC/Reviews/Health/22419/22454.aspx

REFERENCES

American Cancer Society. (2012). *Cancer Facts and Figures, 2012*. Retrieved from http://www.cancer.org/acs/groups/content/@epidemiologysurveilance/documents/document/acspc-031941.pdf

American Heart Association. (2010). Heart disease and stroke statistics—2010 update: A report from the American Heart Association. *Circulation,* 121: e46-e215. doi: 10.1161/CIRCULATIONAHA.109.192667. Retrieved from http://circ.ahajournals.org/content/121/7/e46.short#

American Heart Association. (2012). Heart disease and stroke statistics—2012 update: A report from the American Heart Association. *Circulation,* 125: e2-e220. doi: 10.1161/CIR.0b013e31823ac046. Retrieved from http://circ.ahajournals.org/content/125/1/e2.short?rss = 1&amp%3bssource = mfr

Anderson, R., Musch, D., Nwankwo, R., Gillard, M., Fitzerald, J., & Hiss, R. (2003). Personalized follow-up increases return rate at urban eye disease screening clinics for African Americans with diabetes: Results of a randomized trial. *Ethnicity and Disease, 13,* 40–46.

Arday, D., Fleming, B., Keller, D., Pendergrass, P., Vaughn R., Turpin, J., & Nicewander, D. (2002). Variation in diabetes care among states: Do patient characteristics matter? *Diabetes Care, 25*(12), 2230–2237.

Atkinson, N., Saperstein S., & Pleis J. (2009). Using the Internet for health-related activities: Findings from a national probability sample. *Journal of Medicine Internet Research, 11*(1), e4.

Auslander, W., & Freedenthal, S. (2006). Social work and chronic disease: Diabetes, heart disease and HIV/AIDs. In S. Gelhert & T. Arthur Browne (Eds.), *Handbook of health social work* (532–567). Hoboken, NJ: John Wiley & Sons.

Bach, P., Pham, H., Schrag, D., Tate, R., & Hargraves, J. (2004). Primary care physicians who treat blacks and whites. *New England Journal of Medicine, 351*(6), 575–584.

Bandura, A. (1989). Human agency in social cognitive theory. *American Psychologist,* 44, 1175–1184.

Bandura, A. (2004). Swimming against the mainstream: The early years from chilly tributary to transformative mainstream. *Behavior Research and Therapy,* 42(6), 613–630.

Batts, M., Gary, T., Huss, K., Hill, M., Bone, L., & Brancati, F. (2001). Patient priorities and needs for diabetes care among urban African American adults. *Diabetes Education, 27,* 405–412.

Becker, M. H. (1976). Socio-behavioral determinants of compliance. In D. L. Sackett, & R. Haynes, (Eds.), *Compliance with therapeutic regimens.* Baltimore, MD: Johns Hopkins University Press.

Baum F., Bégin, M., Houweling., T., & Taylor, S. (2009). Changes not for the fainthearted: Reorienting health care systems toward health equity through action on the social determinants of health. *American Journal of Public Health, 2009 Nov, 99*(11), 1967–1974.

Bosworth, H. B. (2010). *Improving patient treatment adherence: A clinician's guide.* New York: Springer Publishing Company.

Boult, C., Reider, L., Fre, K., Leff, B., Boyd, C.M., Wolff, J.L., et al. (2008). Early effects of "guided care" on the quality of health care for multimorbid older persons: A cluster-randomized controlled trial. *Journal of Gerontology:Medical Sciences, 73A*(3): 321–327.

Boyd, C. M., Boult, C., Shadmi, E., Leff, B., Brager, R., Dunbar, L., et al. (2007). Guided care for multi-morbid older adults. *The Gerontologist, 45*(5), 697–704.

Carlton, T. (1984). *Clinical social work in health settings: A guide to professional practice with exemplars* (pp. 79–82). New York: Springer Publishing Company.

Centers for Disease Control and Prevention. (2007). *The state of aging and health in America 2007.* Retrieved from http://www.cdc.gov/Aging/pdf/saha_2007.pdf

Centers for Disease Control and Prevention. (2008). *Healthy aging: Preserving function and improving quality of life among older Americans.* Retrieved from www.cdc.gov/nccdphp/publications/aag/pdf/healthy_aging.pdf

Centers for Disease Control and Prevention. (2010). *Chronic Disease and Health Promotion.* [Internet]. Retrieved from www.cdc.gov/chronicdisease/overview/index.htm

Centers for Disease Control and Prevention. (2011a). *Healthy people 2010.* Retrieved from http://www.cdc.gov/nchs/healthy_people/hp2010.htm

Centers for Disease Control and Prevention. (2011b). *National diabetes surveillance system.* Retrieved from http://apps.nccd.cdc.gov/DDTSTRS/default.aspx

Centers for Disease Control and Prevention. (2011c). *National diabetes fact sheet, 2011.* Retrieved from http://www.cdc.gov/diabetes/pubs/pdf/ndfs_2011.pdf

Centers for Disease Control and Prevention. (2012). Heart disease facts. Retrieved from http://www.cdc.gov/heartdisease/facts.htm

Child Study Center. (2001). *Children with chronic illnesses: The interface of medicine and mental health.* Retrieved from http://www.aboutourkids.org/files/articles/mar_apr_3.pdf

Chipkin S., & de Groot, M. (1998). Contextual variables influencing outcome measures in minority populations with diabetes mellitus. *Diabetes Spectrum, 1998, 11*(3), 149–160.

Commission on Chronic Illness. (1949). *American Journal of Public Health & the Nation's Health, 39* (10), 1343–1344. doi: 10.2105/AJPH.39.10.1343

Crimmins, E. M., & Beltrán-Sánchez, H. (2011). Mortality and morbidity trends: Is there compression of morbidity. *The Journals of Gerontology: Series B, 66B*(1), 75–86. doi:10.1093/geronb/gbq088

Curtin, M., & Lubkin, I. (1995). What is chronicity? In I. Lubkin (Ed.). *Chronic illness: Impact and interventions* (3rd ed.). Sudbury, MA: Jones Bartlett Publishing.

Dunbar-Jacob, J., Erlen, J. A., Schlenk, E. A., Ryan, C. M., Sereika, S. M., & Dowell, W. M. (2000). Adherence in chronic disease. *Annual Review of Nursing Research, 18*, 48–90.

Erikson, E. H. (1959). Identity and the life cycle: Selected papers. *Psychological Issues, (1)*, 1–171.

Federal Interagency Forum on Aging-Related Statistics. (2010). *Older Americans 2010: Key indicators of well-being.* Retrieved from http://www.agingstats.gov/main_site/data/2010_Documents/docs/Introduction.pdf

Findley, P. A. (2014). Social work practice to the chronic care mode: Chronic illness and disability care. *Journal of Social Work, 14*(1), 83–95.

Gilmour, J. (2007 Sept). Reducing disparities in the access and use of Internet health information: A discussion paper. *International Journal of Nursing Studies, 44*(7), 1270–1278.

Gitterman, A., & Germain, C. (2008). *The life model of social work practice*. New York, NY: Columbia University Press.

Haley, J. (1976). *Problem-solving therapy: New strategies for effective family therapy.* San Francisco: Jossey-Bass Behavioral Science.

Haynes, R. B., McDonald, H., Garg, A. X., & Montgomery, P. (2002). Interventions for helping patients to follow prescriptions for medications. *Cochrane Database of Systematic Reviews*, (2), CD000011.

Healthy People 2020. (2011). *Topics and Objectives*. Retrieved from http://healthypeople.gov/2020/topicsobjectives2020/default.aspx

Hertz, R. P., Unger, A. N., & Ferrario, C. M. (2006). Diabetes, hypertension and dyslipidemia in Mexican Americans and non-Hispanic Whites. *Journal of Preventative Medicine, 30*(2), 103–110. doi: http://dx.doi.org/10.1016/j.amepre.2005.10.015

Hillier, T., Vesco, K., Pedula, K., Beil, T., Whitlock, E., & Pettitt, D. (2008 May). Screening for gestational diabetes mellitus: A systematic review for the U.S. Preventive Services Task Force. *Annals of Internal Medicine 148*(10), 766–775.

Holland, J., & Lewis, S. (2000). *The human side of cancer*. New York: HarperCollins Publishers.

Improving Chronic Illness Care. (2006–2011). *Chronic Care Model*. Retrieved from http://www.improvingchroniccare.org/index.php?p = The_Chronic_Care_Model&s = 2

Institute of Medicine. (2001). *Health and behavior: The interplay of biological, behavioral, and societal influences*. Washington, DC: National Academies Press.

Institute of Medicine. (2003). *Unequal treatment: Confronting racial and ethnic disparities in healthcare*. Washington, DC: National Academies Press.

Institute of Medicine, Committee on Psychosocial Services to Cancer Patients/Families in a Community Setting. (2007). *Cancer care for the whole patient: Meeting psychosocial health needs*. Washington, DC: National Academies Press.

Kerr, C., Murray, E., Stevenson, F., Gore, C., & Nazareth, I. (2006). Internet interventions for long-term conditions: Patient and caregiver quality criteria. *Journal of Medical Internet Research, 8*(3), e13.

Kitzmiller, J. L., Dang-Kilduff, L., Taslimi, M. M. (2007). Gestational diabetes after delivery: Short-term management and long-term risks. *Diabetes Care, 30*, S225–S235.

Lorig, K., Ritter, P., & Gonzalez, V. (2003). Hispanic chronic disease self-management: A randomized community-based outcome trial. *Nursing Research, 52*(6), 361–369.

Lubkin, I. M., & Larsen, P. D. (2013). *Chronic illness: Impact and intervention*. Burlington, MA: Jones and Bartlett Learning.

Mayo, L. (Ed.). (1956). *Guides to action on chronic illness*. Commission on Chronic Illness. New York: National Health Council.

McDonald, K. M., Sundaram, V., Bravata, D., Lewis, R., Lin, N., Kraft, S., et al. (2007). Care coordination (vol. 7). In K. G. Shojania, K. M. McDonald, R.M. Wachter, & D. K. Owens, (Eds.). *Closing the quality gap: A critical analysis of quality improvement strategies*. AHRQ Publication No. 04(07)-0051-8. Rockville, MD: Agency for Healthcare Research and Quality.

McCreary, D. R., & Sadava, S. W. (1999). Television Viewing and Self-Perceived Health, Weight, and Physical Fitness: Evidence for the Cultivation Hypothesis1. *Journal of Applied Social Psychology*, 29(11), 2342–2361.

McGoldrick, M., Giordano, J., & Garcia-Preto, N. (2005). *Ethnicity and family therapy* (3rd ed.). New York: Guilford Press.

Mittelman, J. S. (2003). Community caregiving. *Alzheimer's Care Quarterly*, 4(4), 273–285.

Mosca, L., Appel, L. J., Benjamin, E. J., Berra, K., Chandra-Strobos, N., Fabunmi, R. P., ... & Williams, C. L. (2004). Evidence-based guidelines for cardiovascular disease prevention in women 1. *Journal of the American College of Cardiology*, 43(5), 900–921.

National Alliance for Caregiving & American Association of Retired Persons. (2009). *Caregiving in the U.S. 2009*. Retrieved from http://www.caregiving.org/data/Caregiving_in_the_US_2009_full_report.pdf

National Association of Chronic Disease Directors. (n.d.). *Competencies for chronic disease*. Retrieved from http://c.ymcdn.com/sites/www.chronicdisease.org/resource/resmgr/workforce_development/competenciesforchronicdiseas.pdf

National Institute of Diabetes and Digestive and Kidney Diseases (NIDDK). National Institutes of Health *Publication No. 11-3892 (2011)*. Retrieved from http://diabetes.niddk.nih.gov/dm/pubs/statistics/#fast

Peek, M., Algernin C., & Haung, E. (2008). Diabetes health disparities; A systematic review of health care interventions. *Medical Care Research and Review, 69,* 1015–1565.

Rhoades, J. A., & Cohen, S. B. (2007). *The long-term uninsured in America, 2002–2005: Estimates for the U.S. population under age 65* (Statistical Brief #183). Rockville, MD: Agency for Healthcare Research and Quality. Retrieved from http://www.meps.ahrq.gov/mepsweb//data)files/publications/st183/stat183.shtml

Rodondi, N., Peng, T., Karter, A., Bauer, D., Vittinghoff, E., Tang, S., Pettitt, D., Kerr, E., & Selby, J. V. (2006). Therapy modifications in response to poorly controlled hypertension, dyslipidemia, and diabetes mellitus. *Ann Intern Med*, 144(7), 475–484.

Rolland, J.S. (2012). Mastering family challenges in serious illness and disability. In Walsh, F. (Ed.), *Normal family processes*. (4th ed., pp. 452–482). New York: Guilford Press.

Roberts, M., & Rhoades, J. A. (2010). *The uninsured in America: First half of 2009: Estimates for the U.S. civilian noninstitutionalized population under age 65 (Statistical Brief #291)*. Rockville, MD: AHRQ. Retrieved from http://meps.ahrq.gov/data_files/publications/st291/stat291.pdf

Rotter, J. P. (1966). Generalized expectancies for internal versus external control of reinforcement. *Psychological Monographs, 80,* 1–28.

Selby, J. (2006). Therapy modifications in response to poorly controlled hypertension, dyslipidemia, and diabetes mellitus. *Annals of Internal Medicine, 144*(7), 475–484.

Smedley, B., Stith, A., & Nelson A. (Eds.) (2003). *Unequal treatment: Confronting racial and ethnic disparities in health care*. Washington, DC: The National Academies Press.

Stanhope, M., & Lancaster, J. (2008). *Public health nursing: Population-centered health care in the community*. St. Louis, MO: Mosby Elsevier.

Stewart, M. (1995). Effective physician-patient communication and health outcomes: A review. *Canadian Medical Association Journal, 152*(9), 1423–1433.

Tillman, L. (2002). Culturally sensitive research approaches: An African American perspective. *Education Research, 31,* 3–12.

Tripp-Reimer, T., Choi, E., Kelley, L., & Enslein, J. (2001). Cultural barrier to care: Inverting the problem. *Diabetes Spectrum, 14*(1), 13–22.

Two Feathers, J., Kieffer, E., Palmisano, G., Anderson, M., Sinco, B., Janz, N., Heisler, M., Spencer, M., Guzman, R., Thompson, J., Wisdom, K., & James, S. (2005). Racial and Ethnic Approaches to Community Health (REACH) Detroit Partnership: Improving diabetes-related outcomes among African American and Latino adults. *American Journal Public Health, September, 95*(9), 1552–1560.

U.S. Census Bureau, Population Estimates and Projections. (Also see CDC. The State of Aging and Health in America, 2007 http://www.cdc.gov/Aging/pdf/saha_2007.pdf)

U.S. Census Bureau. (2008). *Facts and features. 2008.* Retrieved from http://www.census.gov/Press-Release.html

Wagner, E. H. (1998). Chronic disease management: What will it take to improve care for chronic illness? *Effective Clinical Practice, 1,* 2–4.

Wang, C., & Chan, S. (2005). Culturally tailored diabetes education program for Chinese Americans: A pilot study. *Nursing Research, 54*(5), 347–353.

World Health Organization. (2005). *Preventing chronic diseases: A landmark investment, the World Health Organization (WHO).* Retrieved from http://www.who.int/chp/chronic_disease_report/en/

World Health Organization. (2011). *Chronic disease and health promotion.* Retrieved from http://www.who.int/chp/en/index.html

World Health Organization. (2014). *About the Global Burden of Disease (GBD) Project.* Retrieved from http://www.who.int/healthinfo/global_burden_disease?metrics__daly/en/

CHAPTER 8

Transitional Planning Across the Continuum of Care

Karen M. Allen

INTRODUCTION

Changes and transitions are often difficult, but even more so when individuals are frail, ill, elderly and vulnerable. **Transitional care planning** is an important service provided by social workers to help patients and families cope with these transitions, understand the services available, facilitate transfers and access benefits to help with the cost of care. Transitional care planning [bold term] is defined as:

> a set of actions designed to ensure the coordination and continuity of health care as patients transfer between different locations or different levels of care within the same location. Representative locations include (but are not limited to) hospitals, sub-acute and post-acute nursing facilities, the patient's home, primary and specialty care offices, and long-term-care facilities. (The American Geriatrics Society, 2003, p. 556).

> Transitional care is based on a comprehensive plan of care developed by health care practitioners who are well-trained in chronic care and have current information about the patient's goals, preferences, and clinical status. It includes logistical arrangements, education of the patient and family, and coordination among the health professionals involved in the transition. Transitional care, which encompasses both the sending and receiving aspects of the transfer, is essential for persons with complex care needs Coleman, (2003); (Coleman & Boult, 2003).

Transitional care planning is often a primary responsibility of social workers in health-care institutions. Historically, this activity was referred to as discharge planning, and, in many facilities, it still is. However, the term discharge planning implies that the job of the social worker is finished once a patient has been discharged. Because the healthcare needs of patients and the structure of healthcare systems have both grown increasingly complex, more patients are requiring ongoing support from a transitional care planner as they move from one type of care to another over an extended period of time. With that in mind, for the purposes of this chapter, we use the term *transitional care planning*.

Patients, particularly the elderly, are most vulnerable when transitioning from one setting to another (Brooten et al., 2002). Each year, Medicare patients experience 13 million transitions from hospital to home (Jencks, Williams, & Coleman, 2009) and one in five patients returns to the hospital within 30 days after discharge (Forster, Murff, Peterson, Gandhi, & Bates, 2003; Perry, Golden, Rooney, & Shier, 2011). Kripalani, Jackson, Schniper, and Coleman (2007) found that, after discharge, nearly half of hospitalized patients experienced at least one "medical error" (p. 314) in post-acute care. Examples included problems with medications or in completing medical appointments and tests. Some of these problems are potentially life-threatening, and many can be prevented. Research (Coleman, Perry, Chalmers, & Min, 2006; Shepperd et al., 2010) has shown that individualized transitional care planning can decrease complications and rehospitalization rates while improving overall patient satisfaction.

Interprofessional Care Coordination

The emphasis of the Patient Protection and Affordable Care Act (PPACA) on care integration and coordination is increasing interest and reinvestment in interprofessional care teams or interprofessional collaborative care. An interprofessional team is a multidisciplinary group of healthcare professionals who collaborate together to coordinate and deliver care to a common group of patients. This type of care is called collaborative care. Members of effective interprofessional teams collaborate together and with the patient to develop common goals and regularly share information, monitor the carrying out of plans, and evaluate the outcomes of their interventions. Members understand and respect the discipline, appropriate roles, functions, and expertise of other team members. An interdisciplinary or interprofessional team differs from a "transdisciplinary team," in which fluid professional boundaries between disciplines are created or new roles that combine two or more professions are developed (Interprofessional Education Collaborative, 2011).

The Canadian Health Services Research Foundation (2006) found that the benefits of collaborative care included increased access to healthcare, improved outcomes for individuals with chronic diseases, decreased tension and conflict among caregivers, better use of clinical resources, and improved recruitment and retention of healthcare providers. Reeves, Perrier, Goldman, Freeth, and Zwarenstein (2013) studied the impact of interprofessional teams in emergency rooms and found improved organizational culture and patient satisfaction, reduction in errors, improved care of women seen for domestic violence, and improved knowledge and skills among mental health professionals.

To prepare social workers for interprofessional teamwork, educational initiatives in interprofessional education are emerging. The federal government's Health Resources and Services Administration has launched major grant-funding initiative to support the development of programs that educate healthcare providers for interprofessional education and collaborative practice (Health Resources and Services Administration [HRSA], n.d.). A number of schools of social work are partnering with nursing programs and public health to design learning experiences and curricula that include interprofessional education. The Interprofessional Education Collaborative (2011) identified four general domains of competencies in interprofessional collaborative teamwork for which students in health fields should be trained. The first domain involves values and ethics and requires that practitioners "work with individuals of other professions to maintain a climate of mutual respect and shared values." The second domain requires "the use of knowledge of one's own role and those of other professions to appropriately assess and address the healthcare needs of patients and populations served." The third domain requires team members to "communicate with patients, families, communities, and other health professionals in a responsive and responsible manner that supports a team approach to the maintenance of health and the treatment of disease." The fourth domain requires practitioners to "apply the relationship building values and principles of team dynamics to perform effectively in team roles to plan and deliver patient/population-centered care that is safe, timely, efficient, effective and equitable" (pp. 15–25). Like the Council on Social Work Education (CSWE), the Interprofessional Education Collaborative Expert Panel identifies practice behaviors that are used to operationalize and assess the competencies identified for collaborative team work.

As the PPACA rolls out, the population ages, and the number of individuals living with chronic diseases expands, the need for collaborative care that extends and supports the care traditionally provided by physicians will also increase. The use of interprofessional teams is an exciting and emerging approach in which social workers can contribute significantly.

Medical Gatekeepers

One important development in transitional care planning is the development and extension of the role of medical **gatekeepers**. Social workers who are involved in transitional care planning will encounter these professionals at multiple points along the continuum. Case managers, nurses, and social workers employed by insurance companies serve a gatekeeping role when they are contacted to approve a request for patient services. Similarly, physicians in certain types of managed-care organizations will also authorize and approve services for patients to determine if the required services are medically justified and cost-appropriate. Gatekeepers will ascertain patient acuity, diagnoses, the rationale for services, and patients' insurance benefits before they authorize services such as psychiatric care, rehabilitation services, and home healthcare. In addition, in many cases, contractual "preferred provider" arrangements have been established by the insurance company. In these arrangements, providers agree to accept lower reimbursement rates, which are then compensated for through increased volume. In these cases, social workers or discharge planners will be instructed as to which agency should be contacted for services. Social workers should anticipate communicating with gatekeepers and ensure they have all the necessary information available to justify referring a case for post-discharge services.

Reimbursement mechanisms have historically rewarded face-to-face encounters, episodes of inpatient care, and outpatient visits rather than care coordination and follow-up. In contrast to these arrangements, the evolving **medical home** model has patients' primary-care physicians or groups of physicians focusing on longitudinal care and, rather than employing gatekeepers to restrict service access, affords a personal physician advocate who leverages resources of the medical home to coordinate care and helps patients navigate often confusingly complex healthcare delivery systems. Using advanced technology, care is integrated across inpatient, outpatient, in-home, or nursing home settings with ongoing guidance from the physician or physician-directed medical home team. The care team might include nurses, social workers, physical and occupational therapists, pharmacists, dieticians, and other consultants (Moreno, Gold, & Mavrinac, 2014). In 2011, the National Committee for Quality Assurance (NCQA) established best practice and accreditation standards for Patient Centered Medical Homes (NCQA, 2011).

TRANSITIONAL CARE PLANNING THROUGH THE CONTINUUM OF CARE

The diagram below presents a modified version of the continuum of care initially presented in Chapter 2. Individuals move up and down through various levels of care, although not necessarily in a linear fashion. *Figure 8.1* is a visualization of the complexity or acuity (and therefore the relative costs) of the medical interventions provided at each stage. It also reflects how patients can go back and forth across the continuum. Hospice care is located at the end of the table not to disparage the level or complexity of care provided to patients but rather because such care occurs at the end of traditional medical treatments. Professionals who provide transitional care planning services may be employed by an organization at any point along the continuum, or, in the case of managed-care case managers who work for insurance companies, may be employed "outside" of the continuum of providers and may coordinate care through all levels and stages.

Failure to provide for a smooth patient transition following discharge from an acute-care hospital can result in unplanned readmissions, falls, medication problems, and poor compliance in follow-up care. Consequently, patients who request services, who meet high-risk criteria, or who are referred by their physician or other provider should be seen for assessment. In Chapter 4, we discussed **high-risk screening** as a tool to identify patients potentially needing post-hospitalization care planning or other social work services. Once those patients are identified, the next step is to initiate a planning assessment.

According to the Center for Medicare Advocacy, all healthcare facilities that accept Medicare and Medicaid insurance must provide **transitional care planning** or **discharge planning** (the terms are used interchangeably throughout this book) to all patients who meet criteria or request services. Transitional care planning not only helps to ensure the continued recovery of patients, it also reduces costs by preventing unnecessary readmissions that might have been avoided through the provision of follow-up care. Because of the **Diagnostically Related Groupings** (DRG) based payment system used by Medicare, preventable readmissions may not be reimbursed. The DRGs "bundle" most routine hospital services (nursing, room and board, common diagnostic and supportive care) used to treat a patient into a single fee for reimbursement. The rate is calculated based upon the average cost required to treat a patient with a particular diagnosis, and, in 2002, there were 499 DRG categories. The system does build in some mechanisms to revise the cost based on case complexity and complications but essentially establishes a flat fee for reimbursing (Office of Inspector General, 2001).

Figure 8.1 The Continuum of Care by Medical Complexity

Preventive care	Physician based care
Primary care	Physician based care
Community based care	Home care / Equipment / Support services
Rehabilitative care/restorative care	PT, OT, Speech / Skilled nursing care
Acute care	Hospitalization / Outpatient diagnostic / Clinics
Tertiary care	Specialized medical care
Acute care	Hospitalization / Outpatient diagnostic / Clinics
Rehabilitative care/restorative care	PT, OT, Speech / Skilled nursing care
Community based care	Home care / Equipment / Support services
Primary care	Physician, nursing based comfort care
Hospice end of life care	Physician, nursing based comfort care

Source: Author.

Beginning in 2012, the Affordable Care Act reduces payments to hospitals with high readmission rates for heart attacks, heart failure, and pneumonia. In many instances, readmission for these conditions can be prevented through good transitional care planning.

The Agency for Healthcare Research and Quality (AHRQ), a unit of the Department of Health and Human Services, endorses a system called *Re-Engineered Discharge* planning (RED), which is a model that was developed and tested by the Boston Medical Center as a best practice for comprehensive discharge planning. RED consists of "twelve mutually reinforcing actions" (AHRQ, 2013, p. 1) that were shown to be effective in achieving the following outcomes:

- **Improved clinical outcomes.** The RED system was shown to decrease 30-day readmission rates by 25% and emergency room use by 8% and to improve patient "readiness for discharge" and follow-up with primary-care providers.

- **Improved patient safety.** The system helps to meet national patient-safety standards, including those required by the Joint Commission and the Center for Medicare and Medicaid Services (CMS).

- **Improved documentation.** The system improves documentation of the discharge plan, patient needs, post-discharge follow-up services, and patient understanding of the discharge plan.

- **Improved cost-effectiveness.** The system decreases patient-care costs and increases the amount paid to physicians for quality discharge planning.

- **Enhanced hospital reputation.** The system enhances the hospital's reputation as a high-quality provider, improves patient and family satisfaction, and improves relationships with primary-care and other service providers.

AHRQ recognizes that the "hospital discharge is a complex process requiring integrated communications among the inpatient care team, primary care team, community services, the patient, and the patient's caregivers" (AHRQ, 2013, p. 1) and that improving the process could significantly reduce the almost 20% readmission rate of Medicare patients. While some readmissions are unavoidable, four factors that contribute to complications can be addressed, including (1) delays between the time a patient is released and the time when the primary-care physician receives the discharge summary, (2) discharge prior to receiving pending test and laboratory results, (3) lack of follow-up care (partially due to inadequate patient understanding), and (4) failing to reconcile medications.

The RED project emphasizes patient diversity, the need for language assistance when working with non-English-speaking patients, and the importance of being able to work effectively with Gay, Lesbian, Bisexual, Transgendered and Queer (GLBTQ) patients. The project resulted in a user-friendly "RED Toolkit," available from AHRQ, which identifies the model components in detail and provides a plan for implementation in healthcare systems:

Components of the RED Model

1. Ascertain need for and obtain language assistance.

2. Make appointments for follow-up care (e.g., medical appointments, post-discharge tests/labs).

3. Plan follow-up for test results that are pending at discharge.

4. Organize post-discharge outpatient services and medical equipment.

5. Identify the correct medicines and a plan for the patient to obtain them.

6. Reconcile the discharge plan with national guidelines.

7. Provide a written discharge plan that the patient can understand.

8. Educate the patient about his or her discharge plan, diagnosis, and medicines.

9. Review with the patient what to do if a problem arises.

10. Assess the degree of the patient's understanding of the discharge plan.

11. Expedite transmission of the discharge summary to clinicians accepting care of the patient.

12. Provide telephone reinforcement of the discharge plan.

RED provides a useful framework for approaching the process of discharge planning. It stresses the importance of leadership in implementing a coordinated system as well as in developing discharge plans for individual patients. The social worker's assessment skills; knowledge of social systems and resources; ability to apply the ecological perspective to understand the interactions, resources, and barriers in the patient's environment; and values promoting self-determination are a natural fit for this role. Advocating for a coordinated system of quality discharge planning requires an understanding of the many potential positive clinical and financial outcomes.

Bull and Roberts (2001) identified four general stages in the discharge-planning process: (1) determining the current status, resources, needs, preferences, and limitations of the patient and his or her family or caregivers, (2) establishing the initial discharge plans and selected resources for care, (3) actively preparing and educating the patient/family for the return home, and (4) implementing services and assessing the transition back to the community following an acute hospital stay. The process for assessing patients from initial discharge screening and high-risk screening to comprehensive assessment is shown in *Figure 8.2* as developed by the state public health department of New York (New York State Department of Health, 2008).

Whenever possible, **preadmission planning** for surgical or other types of hospitalization can occur in the primary-care clinic. Preadmission planning can occur at the primary-care clinic, the surgical clinic, or the hospital. Preadmission planning can be conducted in a group format or even on-line. Examples of planned admissions suitable for a group format include joint replacement, back surgeries, some cardiac surgeries, bariatric surgeries, and

Figure 8.2 Discharge Assessment Flow Chart

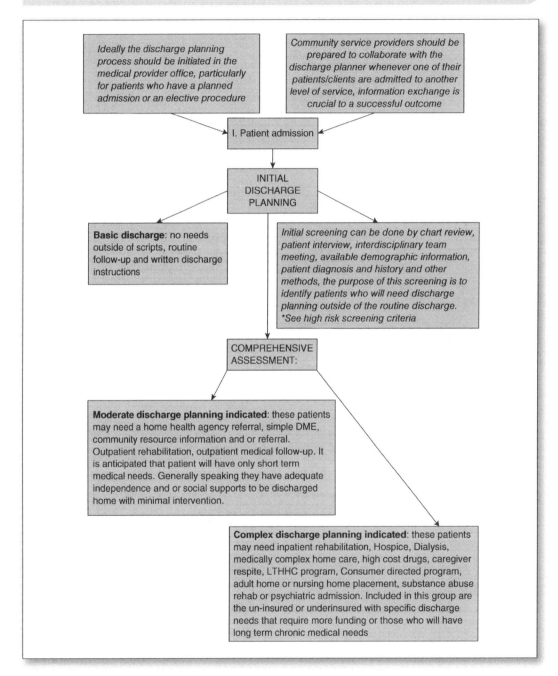

Source: Discharge Assessment Flow Chart. New York State Department of Health, 2008.

so on. It is crucial for information to follow the patient throughout the healthcare system, and it is ideal if members of the preadmission planning team follow the patient during hospitalization.

Preadmission planning has three purposes: (1) to assess that the patient is stable and medically appropriate for the admission, (2) to provide information and education about the planned hospitalization that emotionally supports the patient and family, and (3) to gather current information so that it can be shared with the hospitalization team and thereby avoid any miscommunications about the patient's condition or treatment. In some instances, the preadmission planning visit is conducted by an interdisciplinary team and may include an anesthetic assessment as well as a medication assessment. In addition, any preadmission treatments or instructions are implemented, such as stopping blood thinners. Patient-consent forms are also explained and completed.

The social work role in preadmission planning is to determine if the patient has adequate support for follow-up care and to begin the process of making arrangements for any necessary rehabilitation or home-care services. This role includes evaluating financial and insurance resources and restrictions for care. For example, in some cases, patients may require inpatient rehabilitation services in a skilled-nursing facility. Planning ahead can allow the social worker to locate a suitable facility (i.e., one that is close to home, that meets patient/family needs and expectations, that accepts the patient's insurance), to arrange safe patient transport, and to ensure that a bed is available on the tentative day of discharge. If a patient is targeted for discharge to his/her own home, the physical characteristics of the home are considered and any necessary medical equipment is ordered. Furthermore, if additional community services are warranted, such as Meals on Wheels, these services can be discussed and arranged for ahead of time.

Equally important is the need to address any anxiety that the patient may have about hospitalization. Hospitalization can be an overwhelming event filled with concern, apprehension, and a sensed loss of control. Patients with depression or mild cognitive impairment require special support to help them contend with a pending hospitalization. Social workers can identify specific concerns that can be addressed prior to hospitalization in order to help the patient feel more comfortable. For example, should a patient be a primary caregiver for a spouse, he or she may be reluctant to pursue his or her own medical treatments because no one else is available to care for his or her partner.

One effective strategy for preadmission screening (and preadmission support through education) is psychoeducational groups that provide information, answer questions, introduce team members, and orient patients to the hospital and upcoming treatment procedures. These groups are commonly utilized with cardiac, cancer, and orthopedic patients as well as numerous other patient groups. Such groups are often coordinated by social workers in partnership with nurses who specialize in the involved diagnostic group and procedure. *Table 8.1* reflects a sample outline of topics covered in a 90-minute preadmission group session for scheduled orthopedic surgeries (Liebergall et al., 1999).

As length of stay has decreased and more and more procedures are being done on an outpatient basis, one-session group interventions are increasingly being used. Gibbons and Plath (2009) found that skilled practitioners are able to establish rapport, demonstrate empathy, facilitate non-judgmental exploration of concerns, and offer meaningful practical assistance in a single encounter. Bixby and Naylor (2009) present a ten criteria

Table 8.1   Sample Outline: 90-Minute Preadmission Orthopedic Patient Group Session

Topic	Speaker	Time
Introduction and welcome "Who's who" in the hospital Logistics: parking, meals, etc.	Social Worker	10 minutes
Preadmission paperwork Consent forms Durable Power of Attorney Patient Advocate forms	Admissions Nurse	20 minutes
Medication records Medication assessments	Pharmacist	10 minutes
About anesthesia	Clinical Nurse Anesthetist	10 minutes
About orthopedic surgery	Orthopedic Resident	10 minutes
Rehabilitation following orthopedic surgery	Physical Therapist	10 minutes
Post-hospitalization care options: rehabilitation unit, skilled nursing unit, home care, outpatient services Other community resources	Social Worker	10 minutes
Questions and concerns	Social Worker	10 minutes

Source: Author.

screening tool to identify older patients most in need of transitional care or discharge planning services. The criteria include aged 85 or older; moderate to severe functional impairments; behavioral or psychiatric conditions; multiple medications and health conditions; low literacy and poor social supports. Sulman, Savage, and Way (2001) addressed the challenge of providing social work services in an era in which lengths of stay have been dramatically shortened and more services are being provided on an out-patient basis. They recommended that social workers reexamine their roles on interdisciplinary teams in order to provide services in outpatient clinic settings; develop mechanisms for preadmission screening and early transitional care planning; streamline documentation procedures and ensure that information follows patients as they move through the healthcare system; sharpen skills in brief, short-term, solution-focused interventions; and develop community partnerships with services that offer sustained intervention to patients post-discharge.

The Center for Medicare Advocacy (2009) developed a *Discharge Planning Checklist* of elements that should be considered as part of the transitional care/discharge-planning assessment. The checklist underscores the need to talk to healthcare providers, patients, and family members to determine how follow-up care will be provided.

Concerns that are typically addressed during a discharge-planning assessment include

- where care will be provided and who will assist after discharge;

- the patient's level of understanding of the health condition, identified problems, and recommendations on how to handle them;

- the patient's level of knowledge about the drugs that have been prescribed, including how and when to take them;

- whether medical equipment (e.g., a walker) will be needed and the patient's instruction and comfort in use;

- whether the patient will need help with various activities, such as bathing, dressing, grooming, using the bathroom, shopping for food, making meals, doing housework, paying bills, getting to physicians' appointments, and picking up prescriptions;

- the patient's comfort level with self-care tasks such as using medical equipment, changing bandages, or self-administering a shot;

- the identification of family members or other caregivers who are able to assist the patient and their understanding of the help needed from them;

- assessment of how well family members are coping with the patient's illness;

- whether the patient knows which physician or other healthcare provider to contact if there are questions or problems;

- the patient's understanding of follow-up appointments and tests needed in the weeks following discharge;

- the provision of written discharge instructions, including instructions for medications and a current health-status summary, that are understood by the patient and/or caregiver;

- the determination of whether the patient needs home health, nursing, hospice services, or other supportive services and the arrangements for those services or instructions on how to make such arrangements;

- the patient and/or caregiver's knowledge about available community resources; and

- the patient's or caregiver's level of understanding of what insurance will cover for needed prescription drugs, equipment, and services, as well as the beneficiary copays, deductibles, and maximum "out-of-pocket" expenses.

Coleman and Boult (2003) identified a framework for determining patient complexity relative to discharge-planning needs. Their conceptualization involves two general dimensions: medical complexity and patient functional ability. We have added a third dimension to recognize the crucial importance of social support and resources for care. In our experience, strong social supports (family care givers in conjunction with reliable resources for care) are necessary to successfully manage patients, particularly those with high medical needs and low functional ability.

Medical complexity *(Figure 8.3)* is determined on the basis of current diagnoses, prognoses, impact, and treatments required. **Functional ability** is determined by the interplay of a variety of social and personal characteristics, which include social/environmental complexity, functional/cognitive complexity, and behavioral/psychiatric complexity. The patient who is medically complex is likely to have multiple conditions, to require medications, and to have complex follow-up plans for care and is unlikely to be able to manage the post-hospital transition independently (e.g., as a result of deficits in one of the other domains). The patient with social/environmental complexity is at risk of not having his or her medical needs managed appropriately because of a suboptimal living environment or suboptimal/absent caregiver support. The patient with functional/cognitive complexity cannot perform activities of daily living (ADLs) independently because of physical or cognitive impairments, may have had falls at home recently, and/or has dementia or other types of cognitive impairments such as stroke. The patient with behavioral/psychiatric complexity is noncompliant, refuses the recommended treatment or level of care at discharge, and/or has a co-occurring substance-abuse issue or mental diagnosis that impedes the ability or desire to manage health. Using this model, the social worker looks at the interaction of medical complexity, functional capacity, and social support to determine the degree of post-discharge risk for an individual patient.

Figure 8.3   Medical Complexity vs. Functional Ability

Low medical complexity High functional ability High social support	High medical complexity High functional ability High social support		
Low medical complexity Low functional ability Low social support	High medical complexity Low functional ability Low social support		
Likely Vulnerability	Low		High

Source: Adapted from Shackelford, J. R., Sirna, M., Mangurian, C., Dilley, J. W., & Shumway, M. (2013). Descriptive Analysis of a Novel Health Care Approach: Reverse Colocation—Primary Care in a Community Mental Health "Home." *The Primary Care Companion for CNS Disorders, 15*(5).

CASE STUDY

High/Low Vulnerablity

Mr. Jones is a 79-year-old widowed gentleman who was admitted to the hospital with a degenerative spinal stenosis that is gradually impacting his ability to use his arms and legs. Before long, Mr. Jones will essentially be functioning as a quadriplegic, with limited mobility in all of his extremities. He is admitted to the hospital because a urinary tract infection has caused a systemic blood infection that required intravenous antibiotics. He is alert and is able to participate in his care and decision making. He is not able to perform any activities of daily living without assistance and is able to walk with assistance. Because of the impaired mobility in his arms, he cannot use a walker or a wheelchair for independent mobility.

Knowing this much, would you consider Mr. Jones at high or low vulnerability or risk for post-discharge complications?

Mr. Jones lives with his daughter, who is a retired nurse. She is very devoted to her father and will not consider nursing-home placement as an option.

Knowing this much, would you consider Mr. Jones at high or low vulnerability or risk for post-discharge complications?

Mr. Jones is a retired banking executive. He is quite wealthy, has Medicare and Blue Cross insurance, and has an additional nursing-home insurance policy that includes an option for additional home care in place of a nursing home.

Knowing this much, would you consider Mr. Jones at high or low vulnerability or risk for post-discharge complications?

Transitioning Home

Home healthcare services represent an important post-discharge intervention for patients with additional medical needs that continue following hospitalization. Two levels of care can be considered: skilled home care and basic and personal assistance. Significant technological advances in medicine have made it possible for many treatments that were once only offered in a hospital or clinic to now be safely performed in patients' homes. Home healthcare is usually less expensive, more comfortable, and just as safe and effective as inpatient care. Frequently chosen when medically appropriate, approximately 12 million individuals receive home healthcare services from nearly 33,000 providers because of illness, disability, or terminal care. In 2009, the cost of providing these services was approximately $72.2 billion (National Association for Homecare & Hospice Association, 2010). The goal of home healthcare is to help patients with complex medical treatments involving nursing care (such as wound care and intravenous medications) or rehabilitation services to regain independence through physical therapy. Typically, the services are provided on an intermittent basis and are not adequate for individuals requiring 24-hour care or supervision.

To be considered for home healthcare, it must be unsafe and/or physically taxing for the patient to leave home and/or the patient must require the physical assistance of another person and/or specialized transportation services to leave his or her domicile. Infrequent absences for non-medical reasons (e.g., religious services) and for medical reasons (e.g., physician appointments) are acceptable. According to the American Health Care Association (2011a) under Medicare, services are typically authorized in 60-day increments called **episodes of care** and are covered if the patient

- is under the care of a physician who certifies the need for home healthcare;

- requires skilled nursing care, physical therapy, speech-language pathology services, and/or occupational therapy; and

- is certified by a physician as being home-bound.

In addition to skilled care provided by a nurse and therapist, home health aide services may be covered. **Home health aides** provide assistance with bathing and dressing and can help with light meal preparation and housekeeping. To qualify, the need for a home health aide must be related to a medical diagnosis, illness, or injury. Medicare will not cover home health aides unless the patient also qualifies for skilled care such as nursing care or other physical therapy, occupational therapy, or speech-language pathology services from the home health agency. A typical referral form utilized to trigger home healthcare is located in *Appendix E* at the end of this book.

Often, healthcare systems include certified home healthcare agencies within their network. Reflecting the presence of established financial and service-delivery contracts, there can be considerable pressure on social workers and discharge-planning teams to only refer to agencies identified as providers within a network. Referring parties, however, must recognize their ethical responsibilities to ensure medically appropriate, competent, and economical provider services and avoid referring cases that are potentially beyond the capacity of an agency to successfully manage. It is important to be aware that insurance companies similarly have established home healthcare provider arrangements and that the failure to use a contracted agency may result in a denial of payment for services rendered.

As part of their assessment, social workers should determine if the patient is now receiving or has previously received services from a particular provider. If the services met the patient's needs and consent is obtained, services should be coordinated with the pre-existing agency to ensure continuity of care. In situations in which there is no identified preference for a home-care agency, social workers will customarily rely on a maintained list of acceptable providers. Patients are invited to select from the list, thereby avoiding any potential conflict of interest by the professional in the referral process. Social workers typically discuss home healthcare services and with the patient, family, or existing care provider(s) and physician(s) to determine appropriate care plans for the patient. Working with a nurse, the home healthcare referral form is then completed.

Individuals who qualify for Medicaid also may be eligible for chore and companion services that are necessary to help them remain in their own home. These provisions vary state by state and are referred to as **chore grants, chore services,** or **adult home help services**. To qualify, individuals must be eligible for Medicaid and must live at home or an unlicensed community setting. These services assist the elderly, blind, disabled, and other functionally limited individuals with necessary daily activities that they are unable to perform independently. Chore or service providers can help patients with their **activities of daily living (ADLs)** including eating, bathing, transferring, toileting, and meal preparation.

Initiation of these services is accomplished by special application through the local department of human (or social) services. Once the application is received, a worker contacts the patient and family, evaluates their income and eligibility, and conducts a thorough needs assessment. An individualized service plan is developed and must be certified by a physician. The worker then assists with locating providers and authorizes payment. Individuals can retain their own chore service providers, with payments being negotiated between the patient and the service provider. In some instances, family members can be hired by the patient to provide chore services. The amount of the grant is determined by examining the services necessary, the amount time required, and other special circumstances. Service payments vary but are typically around $333 per month. In very complex situations, however, up to $999 can be authorized with special approval by the state (Michigan Department of Community Health, n.d.).

Waiver programs, which provide more extensive services and supports in order to allow individuals to remain in their home, are available in some states. A waiver is granted by the federal government to states to permit them to be exempted from various requirements and regulations in order to develop new programs and initiatives. Through a waiver program, eligible adults who meet income and asset criteria can receive Medicaid-covered services like those provided by nursing homes. However, these services are provided to them in their own home or another community-based setting. Services that may be covered through a waiver program include homemaker assistance, transportation, adult day care, home modifications, and private-duty nursing. Some states have been very creative in designing waiver programs and support services to help individuals remain in their homes, and a listing of these programs is available at the Medicaid website (http://www .medicaid.gov/Medicaid-CHIP-Program-Information/By-Topics/Waivers/Waivers .html?filterBy = (b)(c)#waivers).

Durable medical equipment (DME), when ordered by a doctor, also may be covered up to 80% by Medicare. DME includes wheelchairs, walkers, bedside commodes, and other types of adaptive devices that can help the patient's mobility and functioning. This equipment must meet certain criteria to be covered. Medicare usually pays 80% of the Medicare-approved amount for certain pieces of medical equipment, such as wheelchairs or walkers. Typically, the physical therapists will recommend equipment to help with the patient's mobility, and the occupational therapist will recommend equipment to help with ADLs such as bathing and toileting. Sometimes, a home visit to assess for equipment needs is conducted by these therapists.

Transitioning Into an Extended-Care Facility

The number of people who enter **extended-care facilities** (skilled and basic nursing homes) has increased since 1994, and most are admitted after having been hospitalized. Approximately 1.4 million Americans were residing in nursing homes in 2011. **Skilled care** involves the provision of physical therapy or complex nursing services and may be covered for up to 100 days by Medicare (with Days 21–100 being covered at 80%). **Basic care** is routine, custodial care and is paid for privately, by Medicaid, or by nursing-home insurance plans. A number of patients are admitted to nursing homes temporarily, and a total of 2.4 million individuals are discharged to home, to hospice, or to the hospital from nursing homes each year. In 2011, about 63% of these patients were covered by Medicaid insurance, and about 21% were covered by Medicare. The remaining patients were covered by other insurance or were paying privately. The average length of stay for residents was 835 days, with a median length of stay of 463 days. Because Medicare typically covers approximately 27 days of skilled care in a nursing home per benefit period, Medicaid soon becomes the primary payer in most cases, covering 65% of total resident days (Center for Medicare Advocacy, 2012).

Almost half of all nursing home residents are over the age of 85 years, and 72% are women, most often widowed. Typically, some type of health condition impairs residents' ability to perform activities of daily living and more than 50% of residents are *incontinent*, or unable to control their bowel and/or bladder. Dementia affects somewhere between 50% and 70% of all nursing home residents, and one-third of patients demonstrate problem behaviors. General risk factors for being admitted to a nursing home include advanced age, low income, poor family support, low activity level, and cognitive and mental disorders. Impaired ability to perform three or more activities of daily living was found to be highly correlated with the need for nursing-home placement (The American Geriatric Society Foundation for Health in Aging, 2005).

It is important that patients be engaged in the decision-making process as much as their physical and cognitive capacities permit. Social workers may need to ask for a psychiatric evaluation to evaluate competency and then pursue legal guardianship if cognitive impairments are severe enough to preclude the patient from making rational decisions. If the patient is competent to make decisions, he or she has the right to refuse placement and to determine where to live, even if, in the judgment of others, going home might be unsafe. In such instances, following hospital treatment policy and risk-management practices, it may be necessary to facilitate a discharge that the hospital perceives as being risky or unsafe. These circumstances invariably pose ethical dilemmas. It becomes important to carefully evaluate the scenario, making sure to advise the patient and other involved parties of any perceived risks and documenting offers for follow-up care and information so that a placement may be implemented from home if necessary.

Social workers can have an important role to play in helping individuals and families select a nursing home for care. States inspect nursing homes, and reports listing care violations are often publicly available. Social workers should encourage families to visit more than one nursing home and to check the inspection reports, which many states post online for consumer convenience. The American Geriatric Society Foundation for Health Aging (2005) provides the following *Nursing Home Check List* as another resource for families to use:

- Is the nursing home clean? Are there any unpleasant smells?

- Is it well maintained?

- Do the residents look well cared-for?

- Are the rooms adequate?

- What recreational and private space is available?

- Are there safety features, such as railings and grab bars?

- Is the home licensed by the state and certified by Medicaid? Is the license posted?

- How many nurses/nursing assistants are there relative to the numbers of residents?

- Do the administrators and medical professionals have special training in geriatrics or long-term care?

- Are key professionals full-time or part-time?

- How long have the administrators and medical professionals been with the nursing home?

- What type of medical coverage is provided?

- How close is the nursing home to family members? How close is it to the nearest hospital?

- What is the food like?

- How much do basic services cost? What services are covered?

- What additional services are available? How much do they cost?

- What happens if a person runs out of money and needs medical assistance?

Upon identifying the nursing home, social workers will ensure that the required patient information is shared, in accordance with HIPPA guidelines.

The **deinstitutionalization** revolution of the 1980s and 1990s resulted in the discharge of a number of mentally ill and developmentally disabled from nursing homes to community-based care settings. In order to comply with federal guidelines (Omnibus Reconciliation Act of 1987 or *OBRA*; Code of Federal Regulations, Title 42; Part 483), additional screening may be necessary to ensure that a patient is not inappropriately institutionalized or to determine if he or she has a developmental disability or mental illness that may be amenable to treatment other than nursing-home care. State procedures vary on how these screenings are conducted.

The role of long-term care has evolved along with the increased longevity of elderly individuals who live with chronic diseases and/or experience periodic acute health crises that require time to recover in long-term care facilities. In 2012, 15,683 nursing homes participated in the Medicare and Medicaid programs to provide care to over 1.4 million long-term and post-acute care to individuals. Although the number of individuals in nursing home equals only about 0.5% of the total U.S. population, it represents almost 11% of those 85 years of age and older (Center for Medicare and Medicaid Services, 2013). The average length of stay for all residents is 2.8 years; however, many patients use Medicare's short-term benefit (100 days of coverage) for skilled nursing care and rehabilitation services after a hospitalization. As the length of stay in hospitals decreased, the severity of illness in care facilities increased to the point that over half of all patients were rated "extremely serious" by Medicare's Severity of Illness criteria. From 2005 to 2009, the percentage of Medicare patients with nine or more conditions increased to over 50%. The most common conditions are atrial fibrillations, renal failure, congestive heart failures, urinary tract infections, and hypertension (American Health Care Association, 2011b). Many individuals who enter a nursing home typically experience feelings of uncertainty and anxiety when unsure if they will be able to return home and feelings of grief and loss if it becomes clear that they cannot. In addition to harboring concerns about the health issues that have necessitated nursing home care, families are often fraught with myriad feelings, including guilt, when it becomes necessary to place a loved one in a long-term care facility.

When discharged from acute care to a nursing home or other potentially long-term-care setting is anticipated, hospital-based social workers will facilitate placements by helping individuals begin to identify and explore these feelings. Things to consider in helping the patients and families adjust to placement include exploring how they have dealt with other losses in their life, their overall emotional stability and resilience, and past coping strategies and abilities. Individuals who have historically been more independent through life, who have a good sense of self-esteem, who tend towards optimism, who have had a positive support network, and who have a strong sense of faith may adjust better to the placement.

Social workers may also assist families in easing patient adjustment to nursing-home placement by planning ahead and selecting nursing-home options before they are needed. They may assess financial resources for such care, including the purchase of long-term-care insurance, encourage family visiting of the nursing home ahead of placement, and attempt to ascertain if transitional activities and services are offered.

While exploration of the patient's adjustment is typically initiated during the acute-care (hospitalization) stage, nursing home social workers have a fundamental role in addressing the emotional and psychological reactions of the individual to placement as well as the impacts of these factors and aging on the individual's ability to sustain his or her activities of daily living (Silverstone & Burack-Weiss, 1983, p. 9). It is important to ensure that family bonds are preserved during the placement process and any anger expressed by the patient and/or family members is expressed and resolved. Studies have shown that family members avoid nursing home placement as long as possible, making the decision only after they have exhausted all other alternatives and the individual's health condition has progressed beyond their capacity to care for the individual (Ryan & Scullion, 2000). For those involved, there may be feelings of abandonment, a sense of impotence and frustration associated with the deterioration of a patient's health condition, apprehension about the future, and even pensive reactions by family members regarding their own health and mortality in the face of witnessing a patient's changing physical condition.

Once the placement has occurred, the nursing home social worker will typically try to meet with family members to identify potential issues, concerns, and unmet needs, while alerting them to what they and the patient can expect in terms of changing routines (Conger & Moore, 1981). It is helpful for family members to be available as much as possible for the first day or two and then withdraw gradually as the patient becomes integrated into nursing home activities. Family members can help make sure the staff knows the patient and their needs and address any communication problems, if present. Familiar objects and pictures brought from home may also be comforting to the patient during the transition. The prospect of a successful placement increases when family members and staff work collaboratively in identifying individual strategies to aid the residents' adjustment to the nursing home setting and routines.

For the resident of the nursing home, intervention represents a two-pronged approach that involves helping the individual adjust to the new facility and helping him or her resolve any existing grief and loss issues. Many nursing homes utilize new-resident support groups to smooth transitions into care, connecting new residents with other, more established residents as a means of helping them take steps toward engaging in activities (Bitzan & Kruzich, 1990). In addition to helping residents adjust, nursing home social workers also serve an important advocacy function in bridging communication between the patient, family, and healthcare team to ensure that residents' needs are understood and respected (Brody, 1974; Conger & Moore, 1981, p. 93). Nursing home social workers are typically involved in coordinating resident's rights activities, including facilitating a resident's council or group.

Nursing home social workers also contribute to and often coordinate processing the **Minimum Data Set** (currently version 2.0)—an interdisciplinary patient-assessment form that is required by the federal government for each nursing home resident (Center for Medicare and Medicaid Services, n.d.). The Minimum Data Set is used to justify nursing home care, to ensure that the patient's care is appropriate to his or her needs, and to gather data on the characteristics of nursing home patients. An example of a position description for a nursing home social worker is contained in *Appendix F* of this book.

ALTERNATIVES TO NURSING HOME CARE

In 1947, more than a quarter of U.S. households comprised three or more generations. The number of seniors living with their children decreased as women entered the workforce and as Social Security and pensions contributed to the financial stability of seniors. However, as longevity has increased, elder resources have become exhausted and the economic downturns of the 1980s have reduced pension and healthcare benefits. Medical care and housing costs have also increased.

Since 1990, the number of **multigenerational households** has increased by over 40%, and, in 2007, 3.6 million seniors (6.5%) were living with family members. While these arrangements can be mutually rewarding and beneficial, they can also become stressful as the health status and functional abilities of seniors change over time. Again, helping seniors and their families plan ahead is critical to ease the adjustment and to make any home modifications that may be necessary. Many of these discussions are sensitive, particularly those surrounding financial arrangements (As You Age, n.d).

Nearly 66 million caregivers make up the 29% of the U.S. adult population providing care to someone who is ill, disabled, or aged (National Alliance for Caregiving and AARP, 2009). The value of these caregiver services was estimated to be $450 billion per year in 2009, up from $375 billion in 2007 (AARP Public Policy Institute, 2011). Furthermore, studies have suggested that the cost of informal caregiving in terms of lost productivity to U.S. businesses is $17.1 to $33 billion annually. Costs reflect absenteeism ($5.1 billion), shifts from full-time to part-time work ($4.8 billion), replacing employees ($6.6 billion), and workday adjustments ($6.3 billion) (MetLife, 2010). Two-thirds of caregivers are women 50 years of age and older; over half of all caregivers remain simultaneously employed in their own jobs. Women in this age group may still be raising children and teens in addition to caring for an elder, and, as a result of lost work hours, is at risk of reduced wages and pension. In fact, the national total estimated aggregate lost wages, pension, and Social Security benefits of caregivers of parents is *nearly $3 trillion,* or a lifetime financial loss for men of nearly $284,000 and nearly $304,000 for women (MetLife, 2011).

Physical and emotional stress can have an impact as well, and the typical caregiver experiences chronic diseases more frequently than non-caregivers. Thirty-one percent of adult caregivers report stress, anxiety, or depression (National Alliance for Caregiving and AARP, 2009), and 15% of working women and 17% or working men who provide care report that they are in "fair or poor health" (MetLife, 2011). To help with caregiver stress, social workers frequently facilitate caregiver support groups (Galinsky & Schopler, 1995) for individuals providing care to disabled or frail family members. In describing best-practice models, The Family Caregiver Alliance (www.caregiver.org) recommends that group leaders determine a focus for the group; establish contact persons, collaborate with other professionals to recruit participants and as potential speakers, consult the literature and topic experts, engage community agencies providing services to seniors, and develop marketing strategies.

Social workers employ traditional group work skills and outline curriculum, structure, goals, and group processes when providing caregiver support groups. In some groups, the social worker will serve as facilitator, whereas other groups may be led by participant members. Standardized instruments are available to evaluate the levels of stress and strain experienced by caregivers and may be used in the context of such groups to measure their effectiveness (Kaufer et al., 1998; Robinson, 1983). New approaches using technology to deliver a group experience to caregivers who are unable to leave their home to attend traditional meetings are also being piloted (Brown et al., 1999; Finn, 1995; Maier, Galinsky, & Rounds, 1995).

Adult Day Care

Adult day-care centers and homes offer recreational, nutritional, and some basic nursing care services to frail seniors. Caregivers can arrange for full-day or half-day care and can use these centers daily if necessary, depending on the extent of their own respite or work-related needs. Seniors using this service may be dropped off or picked up each day but spend their evenings and nights at home. Typically, insurance does not cover the cost of adult day care, but this does represent an important care option for dependent individuals who have family supports *partially* available to assist with care needs.

Adult Foster-Care Homes (AFHs)

Adult foster-care homes are residential homes in the community, much like those that provide reimbursed care to non-related foster children. Foster-care homes are typically run by private providers and licensed or otherwise regulated by the state. Insurance does not usually cover foster care, although state funding can be obtained for care for low-income seniors.

Continuing-Care Retirement Communities (CCRCs)

Continuing-care retirement communities have proven increasingly popular for the full continuum of options that they afford, ranging from independent and semi-independent apartment living, through support living to basic and skilled nursing-home care. The fundamental benefit of these programs is their commitment to providing care to seniors for the balance of their lives. Often, an endowment, or one-time entrance fee, is required and may range from $35,000 to $300,000 or more. Additional monthly fees are also required. These communities are designed to accommodate increasingly higher levels of patient acuity and service intensity while permitting the resident to essentially stay on the same site—a concept frequently referred to as "aging in place." Additional information on CCRCs and other placement options may be found at http://www.alfa.org/alfa/Senior_Living_Options.asp.

Senior Apartment and Assisted-Living Facilities (ALFs)

Many larger towns and cities offer congregant housing options that include apartments and co-ops, which may be partially subsidized by the federal government. These domiciles vary greatly in terms of services, space, and costs but typically provide nutritional and transportation services. Residents can live in an apartment, small studio, or single room and can choose to cook meals, to have their meals delivered, or to eat in a dining room with other residents. Assisted-living facilities are semi-independent options that emphasize a residential rather than the medical models of care characteristic of nursing homes. These facilities stress resident autonomy and privacy but create a homelike atmosphere through carefully selected architectural designs and features. These programs frequently offer specialized care for individuals experiencing dementia. Assisted-living facilities are not typically covered by conventional health insurance, but specialized riders (long-term-care insurance) can be found, albeit with higher premiums (Spitzer, Neuman, & Holden, 2004).

CASE STUDY

Care Planning

Mrs. Albertson is an 88-year-old widowed woman who is a breast cancer survivor, has chronic obstructive pulmonary disease (COPD) after years of smoking, and severe arthritis. She has some beginning signs of dementia, but these are very mild. She is having more difficulty with her arthritis, and has trouble bathing and dressing. She also has difficulty getting up from a chair and transferring to a wheelchair.

Mrs. Albertson has Social Security. Her Medicare is her primary insurance, and when her medical bills have reached a certain amount, she qualifies for a Medicaid "spend-down." She currently lives alone in a large home that she can no longer maintain. She has a daughter who is married with three teenage daughters and who works full-time.

(Continued)

(Continued)

Last week, Mrs. Albertson fell at home and fractured her shoulder. She lay on the kitchen floor all day until her daughter stopped by on her way home from work to check on her, as she always does. It is clear that Mrs. Albertson can no longer live alone.

What alternative housing options might you consider for Mrs. Albertson?

What services might help Mrs. Albertson if she were to move in with her daughter?

What adjustment issues might develop in creating a multi-generational household?

How would you counsel Mrs. Albertson and her family?

SUMMARY

This chapter has examined transitional care planning across the continuum of healthcare settings. The importance of such planning has increased with the growing number and vulnerability of the elderly in our population as well as the complexity of the healthcare needs of patients and structure of our healthcare system. With the emphasis of the Patient Protection and Affordable Care Act (PPACA) on care integration, attention is being focused on the value of interdisciplinary and transdisciplinary coordination in service delivery. The evolving medical-home model presumes such coordination in wrap-around, inclusive patient care that combines both physical and mental healthcare provided across the full continuum of inpatient and outpatient settings.

Preadmission and high-risk screening, along with needs assessment, patient/family education, counseling, and resource procurement constitute fundamental components of transitional care planning. The medical complexity of the patient's condition, coupled with his or her functional abilities, will impact the nature of necessary services, including placement options. The unique issues associated with patients transitioning either from acute to home or long-term care were identified along with the range of available patient-care services and placements and the role of social work in facilitating such transitions.

KEY TERMS AND CONCEPTS

- Transitional care planning
- Gatekeeper
- Preadmission planning
- Four stages of discharge planning

- Medical home

- Interprofessional teams and education

- Diagnostic related groups (DRGs)

- Deinstitutionalization

- Medical complexity

- Functional ability

- Home healthcare

- Episodes of care

- Chore grants and services

- Waiver program

- Durable medical equipment

- Minimum data set

- Multigenerational households

QUESTIONS FOR DISCUSSION

1. Most long-term residents of nursing homes have their care paid for by Medicaid. It is illegal for a senior to divest and spend his or her savings in order to eventually qualify for Medicaid. Yet, some estate planners and lawyers advise seniors on how to do this legally. Do you think it is ethical for seniors to legally spend down their assets (for example, by giving children their inheritance early) in order to eventually have the state and federal government pay for their nursing home care? Why or why not?

2. Medicaid will pay family members, through the form of a chore grant, to provide personal care and assistance to another family member. Do you think the state should pay family members to provide care? Why or why not? Why do you think the state does this? How might it be cost-effective? How might it be abused?

EXERCISES

1. Medicare has a Nursing Home Compare website that that compares the quality of nursing homes on the basis of public health inspections and Medicare reports. Go to the website at http://www.medicare.gov/Quality-Care-Finder/?utm_source = Weber&utm_ medium = CPC&utm_campaign = QCF#nursing-home-compare and find the report for your state. According to Medicare, what are the best nursing homes in your state? In your city?

2. Go to the Centers for Medicare and Medicaid website (https://www.cms.gov/) and locate the Minimum Data Set form for nursing homes. Review the sections on the form. Which sections should a social worker complete? What other kinds of data are collected? Why do you think this kind of data is collected by the federal government?

3. Interview three different professionals on a healthcare or mental healthcare team. Ask the individual to describe what he or she does. Ask about his or her educational experiences and why he or she chose this field. What are some key values and ethics of his or her profession? Describe the role of the social worker and compare how the other professions are different and similar. Do social workers work in a team with other healthcare providers? If so, who leads the team and how do they communicate?

REFERENCES

Agency for Healthcare Research and Quality. (2013, March). *Re-Engineered Discharge (RED) toolkit.* http://www.ahrq.gov/professionals/systems/hospital/red/toolkit/redtool1.html

American Geriatrics Society. (2003). Improving the quality of transitional care for persons with complex care needs. American Geriatrics Society position statement. *Journal of the American Geriatrics Society, 51*(4), 556–557.

The American Geriatric Society Foundation for Health Aging. (2005, March 15). *Aging in the know: Nursing home care.* Retrieved from http://www.healthinagingfoundation.org/

American Association of Retired Persons Public Policy Institute. (2011). *Valuing the invaluable: 2011 Update. The economic value of family caregiving in 2009.* Washington, DC: author.

The American Health Care Association. (2011a). *2011 annual quality report: A comprehensive report on the quality of care in America's nursing and rehabilitation services.* Retrieved from http://www.ahcancal.org/quality_improvement/Documents/2011QualityReport.pdf

American Health Care Association. (2011b). *Long term care statistics.* Retrieved from http://www.ahcancal.org/research_data/oscar_data/Pages/default.aspx

As You Age. (n.d). *Seniors and adult children aging at home together.* Retrieved from http://www.asyouage.com/Seniors_Living_With_Adult_Children.html

Bitzan, J. E., & Kruzich, J. M. (1990). Interpersonal relationships of nursing home residents. *The Gerontologist, 30*(3), 385–390.

Bixby, M. B., & Naylor, M. D. (2009). *The transitional care model (TCM): Hospital discharge screening criteria for high risk older adults.* New York: The Hartfold Institute for Geriatric Nursing, New York University College of Nursing. Retrieved from consultgerirn.org/uploads/File/trythis/try_this_26.pdf

Brody, E. (1974). *A social work guide for long-term care facilities.* Rockville, MD: U.S. Department of Health, Education & Welfare, National Institute of Mental Health.

Brooten, D., Naylor, M. D., York, R., Brown, L. P., Munro, B. H., Hollingsworth, A. O., Cohen, S. M., Finkler, S., Deatrick, J., & Youngblut, J. M. (2002). Lessons learned from testing the quality cost model of advanced practice nursing (APN) transitional care. *Journal of Nursing Scholarship, 34*(4), 369–375. Doi: 10.1111/j.1547-5069.2002.00369.x

Brown, R., Pain, K., Berwald, C., Hirschi, P., Delehanty, R., & Miller, H. (1999). Distance education and caregiver support groups: Comparison of traditional and telephone groups. *Journal of Head Trauma Rehabilitation, 14*(3), 257–268.

Bull, M. J., & Roberts, J. (2001). Components of a proper hospital discharge for elders. *Journal of Advanced Nursing, 35*(4), 571–581.

Canadian Health Services Research Foundation. (2006). *Teamwork in healthcare: Promoting effective teamwork in healthcare in Canada*. Retrieved from http://www.cfhi-fcass.ca/Migrated/PDF/team work-synthesis-report_e.pdf

Center for Medicare and Medicaid Services. (n.d.). *Medicare and home health care*. (Government pamphlet). Washington, DC: Department of Health and Human Services.

Center for Medicare Advocacy. (2009). *Medicare and discharge planning: Thinking through your needs*. Retrieved from http://www.medicareadvocacy.org/medicare-discharge-planning-think-through-your-needs/

Center for Medicare Advocacy. (2012). *What happens to current nursing home residents if current budget resolution becomes law?* Retrieved from http://www.medicareadvocacy.org/what-happens-to-current-nursing-home-residents-if-the-house-budget-resolution-becomes-law/

Centers for Medicare & Medicaid Service. (2013). *Nursing home data compendium, 2013*. Retrieved from http://www.cms.gov/Medicare/Provider-Enrollment-and-Certification/Certificationand Complianc/downloads/nursinghomedatacompendium_508.pdf

Coleman, E. A. (2003). Falling through the cracks: challenges and opportunities for improving transitional care for persons with continuous complex care needs. *Journal of the American Geriatrics Society*, 51(4), 549–555.

Coleman, E. (2011). *Care transitions intervention®*. Care Transitions Program, Denver, CO. Retrieved from http://www.caretransitions.org/index.asp

Coleman E. A., & Boult, C. E. (2003). Improving the quality of transitional care for persons with complex care needs. *Journal of the American Geriatrics Society, 51*(4), 556–557.

Coleman, E. A., Parry, C., Chalmers, S., & Min, S. J. (2006). The care transitions intervention: Results of a randomized controlled trial. *Archives of Internal Medicine*, 166(17), 1822–1828.

Conger, S., & Moore, K. (1981). *Social work in the long-term care facility*. Boston, MA: American Health Care Association/CBI Publishing Company.

Department of Health and Human Services. (n.d.) *Affordable Care Act: Coordinating Center for Interprofessional Education and Collaborative Practice*. Retrieved from https://www.cfda.gov/inde x?s = program&mode = form&tab = core&id = 697258a496b9583c5195d57b5afcbaf1 https:// www.cfda.gov/index?s = program&mode = form&tab = core&id = 697258a496b9583c5195d57b5 afcbaf1

Finn, J. (1995). Computer-based self-help groups: A new resource for support groups. In M.J. Galinsky, & J. H. Schopler, (Eds.), *Support groups: Current perspectives on theory and practice* (pp. 109–188). Binghamton, NY: Haworth Press.

Forster, A. J., Murff, H. J., Peterson, J. F., Gandhi, T. K., & Bates, D. W. (2003). The incidence and severity of adverse events affecting patients after discharge from the hospital. *Annals of Internal Medicine, 138*(3), 161–167.

Galinsky, M. J., & Schopler, J. H. (1995). *Support groups: Current perspectives on theory and practice*. Binghamton, NY: Haworth Press.

Gibbons, J., & Plath, D. (2009). Single contacts with hospital social workers: The clients' experience. *Social Work in Health Care, 48*, 721–735. doi: 10.1080/00981380902928935

Health Resources and Services Administration. (n.d.). *Coordinating Center for Interprofessional Education and Collaborative Practice*. Retrieved from http://www.hrsa.gov/grants/apply/assistance/ interprofessional

Interprofessional Education Collaborative Expert Panel. (2011). *Core competencies for interprofessional collaborative practice*. Washington, DC: Interprofessional Education Collaborative. Retrieved from http://www.aacn.nche.edu/education-resources/ipecreport.pdf

Jencks, S. F., Williams, M. V., & Coleman, E. (2009). Rehospitalizations among patients in the Medicare fee-for-service program. *New England Journal of Medicine, 14*(360), 1418–1428.

Kaufer, D., Cummings, J. L., Christine, D., Bray, T., Castellon, S., Masterman, D., MacMillan, A., Ketchel, P., & DeKosky, S. T. (1998). Assessing the impact of neuropsychiatric symptoms in Alzheimer's disease: The Neuropsychiatric Inventory Caregiver Distress Scale. *Journal of the American Geriatrics Society, 46*(2), 210–215.

Kripalani, S., Jackson, A. T., Schnipper, J. L., & Coleman, E. A. (2007), Promoting effective transitions of care at hospital discharge: A review of key issues for hospitalists. *Journal of Hospital Medicine*, 2, 314–323. doi: 10.1002/jhm.228

Liebergall, M., Soskolne, V., Mattan, Y., Feder, N., Segal, D., Spira, S., Schneiderman, G., Stern, Z., & Israel, A. (1999). Preadmission screening of patients scheduled for hip and knee replacement: impact on length of stay. *Clinical Performance in Quality Health Care, 7*(1), 17–22.

Moreno, G., Gold, J., & Mavrinac, M. (2014). Primary care residents want to learn about the patient-centered medical home. *Family Medicine, 46*(7), 539–543. Retrieved from https://www.stfm.org/Portals/49/Documents/FMPDF/FamilyMedicineVol46Issue7Moreno539.pdf

MetLife. (2010, February). *The MetLife study of working caregivers and employer health care costs.* Westport, CT: Author.

MetLife. (2011, June). *The MetLife study of working caregivers and employer health care costs.* Westport, CT: author.

Michigan Department of Community Health. (n.d.). *Choices for older or disabled persons who may need help caring for themselves.* Retrieved from http://www.michigan.gov/mdch/0,4612,7-132-2943_4857_5045-16263--,00.html

National Alliance for Caregiving and American Association of Retired Persons. (2009). *Caregiving in the U.S.* Bethesda, MD: Author.

National Association for Homecare & Hospice. (2010). *Basic statistics about homecare.* Retrieved from http://www.nahc.org/assets/1/7/10HC_Stats.pdf

National Committee for Quality Assurance. (2011). *Patient-centered medical home.* Retrieved from http://www.ncqa.org/Programs/Recognition/Practices/PatientCenteredMedicalHomePCMH.aspx

New York State Department of Public Health. (2008). *Suggested model for transitional care planning.* Retrieved from http://www.health.ny.gov/professionals/patients/discharge_planning/discharge_transition.htm

Office of Inspector General. (2001). *Medicare hospital prospective payment system: How DRG rates are calculated and updated.* Report OEI-09-00-00200. Retrieved from https://oig.hhs.gov/oei/reports/oei-09-00-00200.pdf

Perry, A., Golden, R., Rooney, M., & Shier, G. (2011). *Best practice: Rush University Medical Center's Enhanced Discharge Planning Program. Comprehensive Care Coordination: Community Care of Chronically Ill Adults.* Chichester, West Sussex, UK: Wiley-Blackwell, 277–292.

Reeves, S., Perrier, L., Goldman, J., Freeth, D., Zwarenstein, M. (2013). Interprofessional education: Effects on professional practice and healthcare outcomes (update). *Cochrane Database of Systematic Reviews, 2013*(3). doi:10.1002/14651858.CD002213.pub3.

Robinson, B. C. (1983). Validation of a caregiver strain index. *Journal of Gerontology, 38* (3): 344–348. doi:10.1093/geronj/38.3.344

Ryan, A. A., & Scullion, H. F. (2000). Nursing home placement: An exploration of the experiences of family caregivers. *Journal of Advanced Nursing, 32*(5), 1187–1195.

Shepperd, S., McClaran, J., Phillips, C. O., Lannin, N. A., Clemson, L. M., McCluskey, A., Cameron I. D., & Barras, S. L. (2010). Discharge planning from hospital to home. *The Cochrane Collaboration.* Hoboken, NJ: John Wiley & Sons, Ltd.

Silverstone, B., & Burack-Weiss, A. (1983). The social work function in nursing homes and home care. In G. Getzel, & M. J. Mellor, (Eds.), *Gerontological social work practice in long-term care.* Binghamton, NY: The Haworth Press.

Spitzer, W. J., Neuman, K., & Holden, G. (2004). The coming of age for assisted living care. *Social Work in Health Care, (38)*3, 21–45

Sulman, J., Savage, D., & Way, S. (2001). Retooling social work practice for high volume, short stay. *Social Work in Health Care, 34*(3–4), 315–332.

CHAPTER 9

Social Work Practice in Oncology, Palliative, and End-of-Life Care

Susan Hedlund

INTRODUCTION

Social work practice in oncology has changed radically in the last thirty years. In the mid-1980s, treatment options included surgery, high-dose radiation treatments, and the beginning of chemotherapy. The side effects experienced by patients were difficult, including protracted nausea and vomiting, and pain was difficult to control. Of note, the hospice movement reached the United States during that time, initially beginning as a "grass roots" volunteer-driven movement utilizing the talents of passionate volunteers and volunteer nurses. Hospice was well in place in the United Kingdom and Canada, driven largely by the efforts of Dame Cicily Saunders, an RN, MD, and social worker. Dame Saunders pioneered efforts to care for the dying in facilities, and her goals were to relieve pain and suffering while reducing the isolation of patients and families at the end stage of life. Beginning with an exploration of how cancer care evolved in the United States, this chapter will address the nature of interventions with patients and families, focusing on the role of social workers in oncology, palliative, and end-of-life care. Later in this section, the hospice movement in the United States will be described, including its differences from the origins of hospice in the United Kingdom.

EVOLUTION OF CANCER CARE

The first writings about social work practice in oncology are attributed to Ruth Abrams in her work *Not Alone With Cancer* (1974), in which she described the experience of patients with cancer and her attempts to alleviate their suffering. Because little was known at the time about cancer or its etiology, widespread fear of contagion resulted in the stigmatization and isolation of cancer patients (Sontag, 1990). Abrams wrote: "The fears and anxieties generated by this disease erect a wall of silence around the patient and those who are involved, frequently presenting barriers to management, adjustment, and rehabilitation" (p. xviii).

Early treatment options were limited, management of side effects was difficult, and patients often experienced isolation and shame, not wanting to publically disclose their cancer diagnosis. The "*Big C*" was code for a cancer diagnosis, and early writings in the nursing literature described the experience of cancer patients as being "roomed at the end of the corridor, drapes closed, and very isolated" (Haylock, 2008, p. 187). There was a tendency to answer patient-call lights more slowly, perhaps reflecting the helplessness that providers felt in caring for people with cancer. While early stages of treatment were marked by optimism, quite often in the advanced stages, after all efforts to cure or arrest the disease had failed, frustration and an absence of further care options often led medical staffs and even families to turn away from patients. For the sake of continued treatment, patients would often repress their feelings of abandonment and fear, with the patient's plight, as well as that of their family, both obvious and tragic (Weisman, 1979).

With increased disclosure about patients' experiences with cancer and the stages of their adjustment to the disease (see Weisman, 1979), greater attention became focused on the "human side of cancer," including the need for emotional support, patients' ability to cope, and the impacts of cancer on families and others involved with the patient. Weisman noted that the diagnosis of cancer was not the same as being a cancer patient and that psychosocial "**cancerology**" was barely in its infancy (Weisman, 1979).

Project Omega (Weisman, 1976–1977) represented one of the first efforts both to understand the stages of life experienced by cancer patients and to formulate principles of coping and vulnerability pertaining to the "completeness" of life. In the early work, *Coping with Cancer*, Weisman (1979) wrote

> Cancer is not just another chronic disease. It evokes many of the deepest fears of mankind. Despite assiduous, skillful, and intelligent treatment, it can spread throughout the body. It can also spread into social and emotional domains, drastically disrupting families and challenging the very values that make life worth living.

Mukherjee (2010), in *The Emperor of All Maladies,* furthered understanding by writing a "biography" of the disease in which he put forth the epic battles of the 20th century to cure, control, and conquer the disease. He described the history of cancer as a story of human ingenuity, resilience, and perseverance but also one of hubris, paternalism, and misperception. Recounting centuries of discoveries, setbacks, victories, and deaths, Mukherjee sought to demystify much of what we understood, then and now, about cancer.

Influenced by the nation's success in putting a man on the moon, President Richard Nixon made the bold announcement in 1971 that cancer would be cured by the nation's Bicentennial in 1976. However, as 1976 came and uneventfully went without significant research findings into the identification and treatment of cancer, the date for a cure was further put off. Meanwhile, the fears, stigma, and conspiracy of silence pervasive in the post-World War II "baby boomer" years continued such that it was not until the 1970s that the stigma of cancer diminished to the extent that patients were advised of a cancer diagnosis. Further contributing to the late development of the field was the stigma attached to mental illness and psychological problems, even in the context of medical illness. It has only been in the last 40 years that the subspecialty devoted to cancer-related psychosocial care (i.e., psycho-oncology) became firmly established, with its own journals, scientific meetings, and professional societies (Holland & Rowland, 1989; Christ, 1989).

By the 1980s, support groups began to emerge as a resource for information and emotional support as well as a venue in which patients and families could share their experiences in dealing with cancer. These groups were not always well received, particularly by the medical profession, which was initially skeptical about the information and content shared in the meetings. At the same time, the role of social work in healthcare settings became more pronounced, including the role of social work with cancer patients and their families.

Over the next 10 to 20 years, treatment options for individuals with cancer continued to expand and improve. Childhood cancers were more successfully treated and cured; treatment for breast cancers, colon cancers, lymphomas, and other cancers continued to be successful; and the management of side effects drastically improved. Importantly, awareness of the psychological impact of cancer also increased, including a dramatic rise in the availability of support groups, education, advocacy, and community resources such as the American Cancer Society and the Leukemia and Lymphoma Society. By providing needed education and support services to patients and families, these resources sought to reduce both the isolation and stigma previously associated with cancer. No longer regarded as an automatic death sentence, cancer began to be seen as a more treatable, sometimes curable, cluster of diseases.

By the 1990s, the awareness and treatment of cancers evolved to the point that patients were assuming more active roles in contending with their disease. Side effects were more effectively managed with the development of new anti-emetic (anti-nausea) medications, more precise radiation treatments, and better management of pain. The availability of information about the etiology, nature, and treatment of cancer took a quantum leap with the introduction of the Internet. With increased knowledge about their disease, patients were able to be more assertive in asking questions of care providers about their individual circumstances and treatment options.

SURVIVABLILITY FACTORS

Between 1970 and the 1980s, the five-year survival rate for all cancers was 52% (National Cancer Institute, 2012). By 1995, the five-year survival rate had risen to 66% and was continuing to climb. For breast cancer, the five-year survival rate in the 1970s was at 75%, but by 2002, it had improved to 90% (Jemal et al., 2004). In the 1990s, the view of cancer increasingly shifted from one of an acute, life-threatening disease to that of a chronic disease, with greater emphasis correspondingly placed on the issues of maintaining a quality of life and living with chronic illness (Rosenbaum & Rosenbaum, 1998). Our understanding of the mechanisms of cancer also changed dramatically with the introduction of new medications (such as Herceptin and Tykerb) that target pathways for tumor growth. Other "smart" drugs emerged that effectively interfered with cell growth by blocking cancer cells' link to crucial proteins. Still other breakthroughs inhibited the formation of blood vessels supporting cancer growth. A new generation of tests have emerged that have enhanced diagnosis and, in some cases, cancer containment. One such test is Oncotype Dx, which looks at 21 genes to determine if chemotherapy will be helpful.

Unfortunately, despite the progress and enhanced recovery prognosis for many cancer patients, mortality from cancers is still significant. While new treatment approaches offer promise to those with advanced disease, the death rate for all cancers adjusted for the size and age of the population dropped only 5% from 1950 to 2005 (Kolata, 2009). In contrast, the death rates associated with heart disease, influenza, and pneumonia dropped 64% during the same period of time. The good news is that patients whose cancer has not spread have a better survivability rate, with many cancers controlled for years with new medications. Significantly, cancer treatments today tend to be less harsh. Surgery is less disfiguring; chemotherapy less disabling. Still, cancer remains a dauntingly complex "number of diseases," and although recent progress in cancer molecular biology is encouraging, there is still a long way to go.

CULTURAL ISSUES

Haynes and Smedley (1999), citing a report by the Institute of Medicine, *The Unequal Burden of Cancer*, substantiated the fact that ethnic minorities and medically underserved populations face cultural, socioeconomic, and institutionalized barriers to cancer prevention and treatment. It also noted that these groups experienced poorer cancer survival rates than Caucasians. Complex and interrelated factors contribute to the observed disparities in cancer incidence and death rates among racial, ethnic, and underserved groups. The most obvious are lack of healthcare coverage and low socioeconomic status. Although cancer deaths have declined for both Caucasians and African Americans in the United States, African Americans/Blacks continue to suffer the greatest burden from common types of cancer. American Caucasian women have the highest incidence rate of breast cancer, but African American/Black women are most likely to die of the disease. African American/ Black men have the highest incidence rate of prostate cancer and are more than twice as likely as Caucasian men to die of the disease (National Cancer Institute, 2012). Stigmatism and fatalism as well as isolation, lack of social supports, and mistrust of the medical and scientific establishment often act as further barriers regarding a cancer diagnosis in some ethnic minority communities (Haynes & Smedley, 1999).

In his investigation of cultural barriers to access of care, Dr. Harold Freeman, a medical oncologist in Harlem, New York, proposed a model of "**patient navigation**" to assist particularly people of color whose healthcare use often entailed facing numerous socioeconomic challenges (Freeman, 1989). The concept of patient navigation seeks to eliminate barriers to timely cancer screening, diagnosis, treatment, support, and end-of-life care. These obstacles include *financial barriers* (e.g., including being uninsured or underinsured), *communication barriers* (e.g., lack of understanding, language/cultural factors), *medical system barriers* (e.g., fragmented system structure, missed appointments, lost results), *psychological barriers* (e.g., fear and distrust), and *logistical barriers* (e.g., transportation, need for child care).

Oncology social workers represent a particularly valuable resource in addressing barriers to care. Competent, culturally sensitive social work practice becomes crucial given the significant diversity of our population and continuing influx of immigrants. Leigh (1997) noted that a culturally competent social worker "is aware that any helping situation must be consistent and consonant with the historical and contemporary culture of the person, family, and community, and take into account the nature of the exchange relationships which characterize and give objective and subjective meanings to helping encounters" (p. 173). Oncology social workers serving on healthcare teams give voice and meaning to the social and cultural issues that cancer patients experience and struggle to reconcile within mainstream healthcare systems. Armed with advocacy skills and an understanding of cultural diversity and biomedical ethics, social workers influence the more effective provision of healthcare to ethnically diverse cancer patients. The significance of cultural competence and the reality of social diversity make them a part of the NASW *Code of Ethics* (NASW, 2008) and an essential component of oncology social work practice.

CURRENT TRENDS IN PSYCHOSOCIAL CARE: FUNCTIONS AND ROLES

Psychosocial needs have become increasingly complex in recent years as treatment has shifted to the outpatient setting, as patients are presented with more treatment choices, and as the patient and family bear increasing responsibility for managing their own care. Patients and families spend significantly less time with healthcare providers than in the past and are consequently expected to manage complex treatment regimens on their own. Improvements in symptom management have had the effect of allowing many more patients to continue to work. While these changes have lessened the debilitating aspects of cancer, they have created new challenges and burdens for families. Wolff et al. (2005) reported that 32% of cancer survivors perceived a lack in advancement opportunities at work, whereas 34% felt trapped because of health insurance and 81% stated they were unable to make career changes.

Cancer has always been expensive. Between 1995 and 2004, the cost of treating cancer increased by 75%. In recent years, the unprecedented development of outpatient pharmaceuticals has benefitted care by increasing treatment options; however, many of these pharmaceuticals are not reimbursable under insurance plans and the subsequent effect is to shift the financial burden to the patient and family. For patients receiving care for long periods of time, navigating insurance and financial issues can become very complex and requires patients to function as strong advocates for their own needs. The potentially dramatic financial impact of a cancer diagnosis is revealed in the findings of a study by the Kaiser Family Foundation (2006), which indicated that 25% of patients used up all or most of their savings, 13% borrowed money from relatives, 13% were contacted by collection agencies, 11% sought the aid of a charity or public assistance, and 11% borrowed money or had to secure a loan.

At the same time, the psychological impact of cancer on families is profound. In the 2006 Kaiser Foundation study, 32% of families stated that cancer caused someone in the family to have psychological problems, 25% indicated that cancer prompted severe strains with other family members, 22% indicated that cancer contributed to someone in the family having a lower income, and 19% indicated that someone had lost or changed jobs because of cancer. Fortunately, psychosocial support has become increasingly available, particularly in major cancer centers in the United States. These centers offer psychoeducational programs, support groups, counseling, and a range of support services to patients and their families.

Research on the psychosocial issues for patients with cancer has emerged (Jacobsen & Wagner, 2012) and has influenced program development for cancer centers. One particularly significant report, the 2008 publication by the Institute of Medicine (IOM) entitled, *Cancer Care for the Whole Patient: Meeting Psychosocial Health Needs,* reflected the work of a multidisciplinary panel that sought to evaluate how best to translate research findings about psychosocial care into practical applications to improve the quality of cancer care. The panel found evidence for the effectiveness of an array of formal psychosocial services, including counseling and psychotherapy, pharmacological management of psychological symptoms, self-management and self-care programs, family and caregiver education, and health-promotion interventions. The panel also determined that despite this evidence, many individuals who could benefit from these services did not receive them. This was in part due to the barriers that some patients experience in accessing comprehensive care, be it distance from major cancer centers, poverty, lack of awareness, and/or health-literacy issues.

In the United States, the National Comprehensive Cancer Network (NCCN) was among the first organizations to propose guidelines related to psychosocial care. The guidelines, first issued in 1999, focus on the recognition and management of distress in patients with cancer (NCCN, 2004). The rationale for the guidelines' focus on distress, even though it is not a precise clinical term, is that it is easily understood by the layperson and does not carry the stigma that is often associated with more formal psychiatric terminology.

In 2011, the College of Surgeons initiated new standards for all accredited cancer programs that impact the role of psychosocial support services. Establishing a new national benchmark, these standards require all accredited cancer centers to implement three components of psychosocial care by 2015: (1) patient navigation that is designed to assess, identify, and eliminate barriers to access for cancer treatment, (2) **distress risk screening** for all newly diagnosed cancer patients being treated at the cancer center, and (3) **survivorship care planning** at all accredited cancer centers. The IOM report entitled *From Cancer Patient to Cancer Survivor: Lost in Transition* (2005) revealed that, at the end of their treatment, many cancer patients felt "lost," confused about follow-up recommendations, and generally abandoned. The new American College of Surgeons' *Cancer Program Standards* are a specific attempt to address these undesirable outcomes, and they have significant ramifications for social workers practicing in these settings (American College of Surgeons Commission on Cancer, 2012). Social workers are often the professionals assisting in patient navigation in addition to identifying barriers to access. Additionally, in most cancer treatment settings, it is the oncology social workers who implement distress screening and follow-up with patients who indicate high levels of distress. Many survivorship issues are psychosocial in nature and thus warrant social work assessment and intervention.

As the field of psycho-oncology continues to evolve, an array of different models now exists with regard to clinical skills and services offered. In smaller, community-based healthcare systems, the role of social workers engaged with cancer patients in hospitals characteristically consists of discharge planning, coordination with community agencies such as the American Cancer Society or the Leukemia and Lymphoma Society, and/or facilitating cancer-support groups. In large metropolitan cancer centers, social work roles may include psychosocial screening, crisis intervention, short- and long-term counseling, advocacy, facilitation of support groups, and program development.

While variations in practice can be expected depending on the particular context (large/small hospital, clinic, in-home care, etc.), oncology social workers typically address a broad range of patient needs. These needs routinely include

- patients' understanding of their illness, treatments, and services;

- coping mechanisms for dealing with the emotions surrounding illness/treatment;

- management of the illness and health condition;

- behavioral change options to minimize disease impact;

- management of disruptions in work, school, and family life; and

- provision of financial assistance.

PSYCHOSOCIAL SCREENING AND ASSESSMENT

As greater understanding about the psychosocial impacts of cancer diagnosis and treatment emerges, the development and employment of screening, assessment, and subsequent interventions become crucial to clearly delineate patients' response to life-threatening conditions. Given the significant variations that exist in patients' and families' attempts to adapt to and manage life-threatening diagnoses, practice models that apply brief and effective methods of psychosocial screening followed by evidence-based assessments and interventions are necessary (Kilbourn et al., 2011).

Significant evidence indicates that the majority of newly diagnosed cancer patients, patients with recurrent diseases, and even patients with terminal diagnoses gradually adapt to these crises (Zabora, 1998). **Adaptation** begins when patients are able to incorporate the diagnosis or the new transition into their daily lives and then effectively address problems or concerns created by their changed health status. The ability of most patients to adapt to the diagnosis and treatment of cancer is documented, with approximately 75% of patients indicating the ability to cope with the diagnosis and treatment with some or little support (Fawzy, Fawzy, & Canada, 2001). For these patients and their loved ones, psychoeducational models, which include a combination of education and support, appear to be most helpful (Fawzy et al., 2001). As more information is gained about the experience of distress among cancer patients, social workers will be tasked to identify the interventions (and their timing) that most appropriately address patient concerns.

The National Comprehensive Cancer Network chose the term "distress" to describe the cancer patient's experience because it found the term to be more acceptable to patients and less stigmatizing. Psychological **distress** is defined as

> . . . an unpleasant emotional experience of a psychological, social, and/or spiritual nature that interferes with the ability to cope effectively with cancer and its treatments. Distress extends along a continuum ranging from common normal feelings of vulnerability and sadness to problems that can be disabling such as depression, anxiety, and social isolation. (NCCN, 2010)

All patients experience some level of distress as they attempt to normalize their reactions to a cancer diagnosis, a recurrence, or the anticipation of death. Estimates regarding the prevalence of distress indicate that 40% patients report significant distress (Zabora, BrintzenhofeSzoc, Curbow, Hooker, & Pianadosi, 2001). Individuals with certain cancers, such as lung, brain, and pancreatic cancers, are more likely to be distressed, but differences by cancer type are somewhat modest. More powerful predictors are reduced quality of life, disability, and ongoing unmet needs.

Cancer patients often describe periods of grief reactions, demoralization, hopelessness, or times of despair while undergoing treatment. For social workers, distress has been correlated with numerous concepts of importance to clinical practice (Weisman, 1979). For example, distress is correlated with feelings of vulnerability such as pessimism, high anxiety, low ego strength, social isolation, and substance abuse (Weisman, 1979, p. 67). Conversely, Anderson (1982) identified that increased social support contributes to lower levels of patient distress and determined that higher levels of spirituality were associated with lower levels of distress. Similar correlations have been found between distress and performance status, family functioning, problem-solving skills, symptoms, and quality of life.

Distress can be measured with a high level of reliability and validity. Of the numerous tools available to measure patient-experienced distress, the *Brief Symptom Inventory (BSI)* has been used more frequently than any other instrument (Gotay & Stern, 1995). Investigators developed cancer norms for the BSI-18 in order to use this shorter form as a screening instrument to correctly identify patients at elevated risk for significant distress. *The Distress Thermometer*, a patient self-report evaluation developed by NCCN, is being widely piloted in cancer centers in the United States. The Distress Thermometer asks cancer patients to self-report their level of distress using a 1 to 10 scale, with 10 being the highest level of distress. The *NCCN Guidelines for Distress Management* (NCCN, 2004) consist of recommendations for psychosocial screening, evaluation, treatment, and follow-up, presented primarily in the form of clinical pathways. According to the guidelines, all patients should undergo brief psychosocial screening, with patients who are found to have moderate to severe distress being referred to psychosocial care professionals. If patients display signs and symptoms of a mood disorder, the initial recommendation is further evaluation, diagnostic studies, and the modification of factors potentially contributing to symptoms, such as adverse medication interaction and pain.

The NCCN guidelines offer important opportunities for the involvement of oncology social workers in assessing and treating the distress and other psychosocial concerns of cancer patients. Programs can be developed to intervene at many points along the treatment continuum to support and, when appropriate, treat patients and families. Oncology social workers assist by providing counseling and support as well as by facilitating support groups that reduce isolation and offer peer support.

DEPRESSION AND ANXIETY IN CANCER PATIENTS

Some patients will experience psychological disruption to the extent that a Diagnostic Statistical Manual (DSM)-IV diagnosis becomes applicable. Major depression has been found to occur in approximately 16% of people with cancer, with the incidence increasing as the disease progresses. Minor depression combined with dysthymia has been reported in almost 22% of cancer patients (Mitchell, Chan, & Bhatti, 2011). *These rates are at least three times as common as those found in the general population.* Depression in people with cancer may range in severity from nonpathologic sadness to marked distress and disability. More severe symptoms of depression are of concern because of their association with a reduced quality of life and increased desire for hastened death or suicide. These patients also have the prospect of incurring more frequent and prolonged hospital stays, experiencing physical distress, and exhibiting poorer treatment compliance.

For a majority of people with cancer who have depression with symptoms that are "subthreshold," conditions may go unrecognized and untreated. Cancer-related depression can be very difficult to diagnose because of the often ambiguous boundaries between realistic sadness, sub-threshold depression, and major depression. There may be uncertainty about the significance of physical and psychological symptoms. Many symptoms of cancer and its treatment, such as fatigue, anorexia, insomnia, and cognitive impairment, overlap with symptoms of depression. Patients who are not clinically depressed may still experience a sense of being demoralized (Walsh & Hedlund, 2011). More than one-third of cancer patients experience significant anxiety as a result of a cancer diagnosis or come to the cancer experience with preexisting anxiety (Traeger, Greer, & Fernandez-Robles, 2012). Patient anxiety levels can range from mild to severe and can fluctuate at particular points, such as before or after learning test results.

Treatment of depression in cancer patients should address not only the depressive symptoms but also the disease-related and psychosocial factors that contribute to depression in this context. These factors may include pain and other distressing symptoms, the relationship with the oncologist and other healthcare providers, the social support system, and the individual experience of the illness. Antidepressant medications are most effective for patients with more severe depression, whereas psychotherapeutic approaches may be of value in cases of both milder and more severe depression. Counseling techniques that include cognitive-behavioral or existential therapies, often in combination with antidepressant therapy, have been found to be most effective (Li, Fitzgerald, & Rodin, 2012). Other frequently employed interventions include relaxation training and problem-solving approaches.

Data on the time-course of specific disorders for patients with cancer are limited. Anxiety is more likely to be a reactivation of a preexisting disorder than the development of a new disorder (Traeger et al., 2012). Panic and anxiety disorders typically have onsets earlier in adulthood, often before a cancer diagnosis. Post-traumatic stress disorder (PTSD) can occur throughout the lifespan as a result of experiencing trauma, including cancer-related traumatic events.

Stiefel and Razavi (1994) suggested that anxiety in people with cancer consists of four different types: situational, psychiatric, organic, and existential. *Situational anxiety* is an understandable reaction to anticipated treatment and/or medical procedures. *Psychiatric anxiety* refers to a history of anxiety or trauma that predates the cancer diagnosis. *Organic anxiety* may be precipitated by medication side effects, metabolic disorders, central nervous system metastasis, or substance withdrawal. *Existential anxiety* is related to uncertain disease course and/or fear of suffering or death. Another issue to consider is *pre-morbid anxiety,* which is associated with high risk for clinically significant depression in the year after a cancer diagnosis. Disease and treatment-related risk factors can exacerbate or mask anxiety. These factors include adverse effects from anti-emetics, corticoid steroids, neuroleptics, metabolic disorders, or abrupt substance withdrawal. Anxiety also can be difficult to separate from other symptoms such as fatigue, pain, appetite disturbances, dyspnea, nausea, and insomnia.

With this population in particular, behavioral techniques such as mindfulness-based stress reduction, guided imagery, and meditation have proven helpful. Psychoeducational approaches such as patient orientation and teaching prior to the onset of treatment can assist in reducing pre-treatment anxiety. Cognitive behavioral approaches, supportive-expressive therapies, and mind-body approaches are very effective for the treatment of anxiety in cancer patients, with potential further benefit derived from prescribed medications. Emerging literature suggests that individuals who are treated for cancer may experience symptoms of post-traumatic stress disorder, either as a result of the disease and treatment or as the result of previous traumatic events that are re-triggered as a result of treatment (Kangas, Henry, & Bryant, 2005). Additional risk factors for post-traumatic stress disorder include a history of trauma, avoidant coping, and social isolation (Gurevich, Devins, & Rodin, 2002). Counseling approaches that include cognitive behavioral techniques and other interventions such as Eye Movement Desensitization Reprocessing (EMDR) may be helpful.

Existential approaches or use of "meaning-centered" work may prove to be useful for patients who have advanced cancers and are entering a noncurable stage. **Dignity therapy** has been effectively utilized by patients at the end of life to help them create a legacy as they conduct a life-review and anticipate life's close. Early studies on dignity therapy suggested that patients who are initially more distressed (as reflected on measures on quality of life, dignity, suffering, and suicidality) seem to be those most likely to find the intervention beneficial (Chochinov et al., 2005). The data also suggest that although quality of life and sense of well-being inevitably deteriorate as physical decline ensues, suffering, depression, and sense of dignity (all facets of the patient's internal psychological and spiritual life) may have resilience, or the capacity to improve, independent of bodily deterioration (Chochinov et al., 2005). It is often beneficial to consider the addition of palliative care as well.

CHARACTERISTICS OF ONCOLOGY SOCIAL WORK PRACTICE

Oncology social work is largely guided by the scope of practice promulgated by the Association of Oncology Social Work (AOSW). Their *Standards of Practice* (2012) include

- **services to cancer survivors, families, and caregivers,** including clinical practices providing comprehensive psychosocial services and programs through all phases of the cancer experience;

- **services to institutions and agencies,** including services designed to increase their knowledge of the psychosocial, social, cultural, and spiritual factors that impact coping with cancer and its effects and to ensure provision of quality psychosocial programs and care;

- **services to the community,** including education, consultation, research, and volunteering efforts designed to utilize, promote, or strengthen the community services, programs, and resources available to meet the needs of cancer survivors; and

- **services to the profession**, including services designed to support the appropriate orientation, supervision, and evaluation of clinical social workers in oncology; to increase participate in and to promote student training and professional education in oncology social work; and to advance knowledge through clinical or other research.

Social work practice in oncology comprises a broad array of interventions, the selection of which is determined largely by the specific circumstances and needs of the individual patient and other involved parties. These interventions include the following;

- **Individual counseling** can range from insight-oriented approaches to supportive and cognitive-behavioral interventions.

- **Family counseling** is principally aimed at easing the distress of the family system while dealing with members' coping with the patient's disease. Counseling components may include education and support as well as communication training.

- **Behavioral techniques** can include guided imagery, mediation, mindfulness-based stress reduction, and progressive muscle relaxation.

- **Psychoeducation** offers combinations of education and support for patients and/or family members.

- **Group counseling** benefits patients and/or families by seeking to reduce isolation, "normalizing" the cancer experience, and assisting in the development of coping techniques.

- **Dignity therapy** provides a meaning-centered, existentially based approach that seeks to assist patients at the end of life by helping them to identify their legacy while reducing distress.

- **Problem-solving** aims at assisting patients and families in developing self-efficacy and self-reliance in dealing with cancer.

The role of oncology social work in palliative and end-of-life care is multifaceted. The knowledge and expertise that social workers bring to the oncology setting have lasting positive impacts on the care of persons with cancer throughout the cancer experience, ranging from the time of initial diagnosis to end-of-life care and bereavement follow-up. The ability of oncology social workers to assist with both practical and existential concerns can be of tremendous reassurance to patients and families facing loss and experiencing overwhelming grief. The social worker's ability to offer a calming, reassuring presence while focusing on how to normalize the grief process at the end of life can significantly influence a healthy recovery from grief.

Oncology social work practice offers numerous opportunities not only to impact the patient and family experience but also to influence program development, community outreach, and policies determining patient services. This potentially broad-based practice can involve hospital committees and boards of community agencies, liaisons with community services, and efforts to influence legislation and public policy. At a national level, the Association of Oncology Social Work and the Association of Pediatric Oncology Social Workers are often invited to participate in professional liaisons with other oncology professional societies. Opportunities exist to serve in leadership capacities at the national offices of the American Cancer Society, the Leukemia and Lymphoma Society, the National Cancer Institute, and the College of Surgeons in addition to the Society for Social Work Leadership in Health Care and the National Association of Social Workers. Through their research and teaching, social workers contribute to the understanding of the psychosocial impacts of cancer and the design of new patient-intervention models.

PATIENT AND FAMILY INTERVENTION

Individual Counseling

A wide range of specific treatment approaches have been used for patients with cancer. As previously noted, these approaches include psychoeducation (which provides information designed to increase knowledge and to reduce uncertainty for patients), problem-solving therapy, **cognitive-behavioral therapy**, interpersonal therapy, and supportive-expressive therapy (Li et al., 2012). The issues that generally occur for individuals with cancer include coping with the diagnosis and changes brought about by treatment; rearranging family priorities to adapt to the disease; and managing fear, anxiety, or physical symptoms while also preparing for an uncertain future or possible death (Rolland, 1994). Points of specific vulnerability for cancer patients include diagnosis, beginning of treatment, changes of treatment, the development of complicated side effects, end of treatment, recurrence of disease, and terminal illness. The oncology social worker should be aware of these specific points of vulnerability and be ready to intervene at any of these points. For patients who indicate an interest in counseling or who experience high rates of distress, counseling can be beneficial throughout the course of disease treatment. Other patients benefit from counseling after treatment is completed, indicating that they have more emotional energy to finally deal with the issues and changes that occur as a result of a cancer diagnosis (Rolland, 1994).

Group Counseling

Group counseling is frequently employed as an effective intervention for cancer patients and their families. Individuals with cancer consistently speak of a sense of isolation and feelings of being unprepared for coping with this unexpected crisis in their lives. The ability to interact with others in similar circumstances, to share methods of coping, and to develop new relationships at a time of perceived isolation all factor into the decision to participate in a group. Groups also play an important role by enhancing participants' knowledge of cancer and by offering specific techniques for dealing with a complex healthcare system. Support groups, which are helpful at all stages of the disease, focus on coping with, adapting to, and living with cancer (Cella & Yellen, 1993). These groups may be open-ended, with constantly changing membership, or they may be time-limited, ranging from six to twelve sessions.

Family Counseling

Abrams (1974) was an early pioneer in recognizing the effect of cancer on the entire family. Spouses, parents, children, and siblings are affected by the disease, particularly when it becomes a chronic illness, and the equilibrium of the family is disrupted for extended periods. Rolland (1994) maintained that it is crucial to determine at what point in life, in what form, and with what intensity cancer occurs and how long it persists. Some families experience a deterioration in the quality of life, whereas other families are resilient and thrive. Rolland further maintained that we need to consider the family or care-giving system ("health-related unit"), rather than the ill person, as the central unit of care (Rolland, 1994, p. 2).

Family members frequently express concerns that are remarkably similar to those of the patient. These feelings may include helplessness, confusion, and anger. Spouses and children may experience guilt because they may become impatient with the person who is sick. Caring for the person with cancer may also burden a family financially and exhaust them physically, a problem that is more and more common with decreased hospitalizations and extended survival. Family systems or individual family members may bring dysfunctional coping systems to the cancer experience. Social workers can effectively engage by offering family counseling to assist in understanding, coping with, and communicating with the patient about the cancer experience.

Survivorship Issues

The Centers for Disease Control and Prevention and the National Cancer Institute (NCI) estimated that, as of 2007, there were 11.7 million cancer survivors, with the number expected to grow with continued advances and the aging of the population. As noted, the

2005 Institute of Medicine Report, *From Cancer Patient to Cancer Survivor: Lost in Transition,* highlighted patients' special needs arising from late-occurring health problems from cancer and its treatment as well as financial, legal, logistical, and psychological challenges. The IOM recommended the use of survivorship care plans, and the implementation of such plans is mandated by the College of Surgeons for accredited cancer centers by 2015. These care plans, which are generated at the end of active treatment and are created by the primary oncologist or nurse practitioner, are personalized documents that summarize the patient's diagnosis and treatment; provide information on possible late effects and other challenges commonly faced by survivors; recommend ongoing care; and offer resources to support patients in the survivorship transition.

For oncology social workers, there is an opportunity to assist patients by offering emotional support that acknowledges the psychosocial challenges that can occur at this stage of the transition. Social work intervention often encompasses providing practical information about insurance, exploring financial/legal issues, and, importantly, addressing relationship issues, including communication, intimacy, and sexuality. Wellness programs such as yoga, mindfulness-based stress reduction, exercise, nutrition, and rehabilitation are often coordinated by oncology social workers.

Hospice and Palliative Care

As noted, the hospice movement in the United States evolved during the late 1970s and early 1980s as a primarily volunteer-driven, "grass roots" program. In 1982, the Centers for Medicare approved payment for hospice services on a per-diem basis to patients predicted to be in the last six months of life as determined by their physician. At that time, most patients were individuals with cancer who were cared for on a visiting basis at home or in a care facility by nurses, social workers, volunteers, chaplains and hospice aides. Patients usually would forego life-prolonging treatment in favor of measures aimed at treating pain and promoting comfort.

Since that time, the trajectory of how people die in the United States has changed dramatically, with an increasingly older population with multiple comorbidities constituting the rolls of hospice programs. A century ago, the majority of adults died fairly quickly from infections or accidents and death was construed as a relatively straightforward part of life. In comparison, dying has now evolved into a complex phenomenon. Death may come more slowly, either because medical advances slow the progression of disease or because the moment of death is postponed as a result of medical technologies that allow one to stay alive in situations that previously would have resulted in the patient's certain demise. Today, dying is so influenced by medical technology, social science, and economics that there is no universally accepted medical definition for the terms *dying* and *terminal condition* and no consensus about how soon before death one should be considered dying (Hedlund & Clark, 2001).

While an elongated dying process may offer a degree of satisfaction for patients whose quality of life remains high, patients experiencing a poor quality of life may find their suffering prolonged. Ironically, it has become harder to die. Through antibiotics, transfusions, artificial feedings, and other interventions, dying can be extended well beyond the point where living has much meaning for either the individual or the family. Alternatively, for those who are dying "well" and whose symptoms are well managed, the dying process offers a time of introspection, resolution, and meaning. The extended period may be a time for saying goodbye to family and friends and for achieving the completion of life's tasks (Byock, 1998).

The criteria for hospice, designed 30 years ago with cancer patients in mind, are now in need of revision. For a person to be eligible for hospice care, his or her physician must determine that the person has a life expectancy of approximately 6 months and the patient must forego active treatment. Individuals with incurable cancer may continue to pursue active treatment, even though it entails more active pain and symptom management. Because cancer, even in its advanced stages, may be considered a chronic illness, many patients continue treatment, which makes them ineligible for hospice services. As noted, today, cancer patients make up a smaller number of hospice patients, with the rolls of hospice made up primarily of older patients with chronic illnesses and often comorbid conditions. Because these diseases are often more difficult to prognosticate, it is difficult to know when a referral to hospice might be appropriate. Alternate models such as **palliative care** are increasingly more appropriate for patients with a wide range of chronic illnesses. Unlike care that is oriented toward cure or remission of disease, palliative care comprises medical and support services that are designed to help alleviate pain and other symptoms of illness. Patients receiving palliative care may have a grave prognosis but may not be terminal. Therapy aimed at remission or cure may still be appropriate and desired. Comprehensive palliative-care programs provide for mental health and spiritual needs in addition to physical comfort. Recognizing the evolving care options, the Health Care Financing Administration (HCFA) created a diagnostic-related group (DRG) that allows payment for end-of-life care for people who die in hospitals or require hospitalization for the palliation of symptoms. Comprehensive coverage for palliative care, however, particularly in the outpatient sector, is still needed (Cassel & Fiedl, 1997).

SUMMARY: THE CHALLENGE OF ONCOLOGY PRACTICE

To effectively practice in the oncology field, social workers must recognize the impact that their career work has on their personal lives. They must regularly engage in self-assessments, contemplate the means to establish a balanced life, and practice healthy self-care. Given the emotional dimensions of interacting with those suffering from cancer, it becomes crucial that the professional identifies and contends with prospective burnout, compassion fatigue, and vicarious traumatization.

To witness suffering is difficult. Sharing of such significant events, however, can enrich rather than diminish caregivers and professionals alike. Observing the strength, courage, and resilience of patients and their loved ones can serve to magnify the social worker's own resilience. As one of the foremost experts on loss and grief, C. Murray Parkes (1986), once noted, "With proper training and support, we shall find that repeated grief, far from undermining our humanity and our care, enables us to cope more confidently and sensitively with each succeeding loss" (p. 7).

Oncology social work practice is firmly rooted in comprehensive patient care. The Institute of Medicine's intervention recommendations further promote the oncology social work role in supporting patients and families who must contend with the frequently overwhelming psychosocial and physical dimensions of this disease and do so while navigating complex healthcare-delivery systems. While challenging, the opportunity to assist these individuals provides the greatest reward of professional practice, and, if the professional is receptive to it, he or she may gain renewed perspective on one's own life as well.

KEY TERMS AND CONCEPTS

- Cancerology

- Adaptation

- Patient navigation

- Distress

- Distress risk screening

- Survivorship care planning

- Palliative care

- Hospice care

- Dignity therapy

QUESTIONS FOR DISCUSSION

What would constitute an ideal program of psychosocial support for cancer patients and their families? What key elements would be included?

EXERCISES

Clinical Intervention

A 38-year-old woman with two young children (4 and 6 years of age) is diagnosed with advanced lung cancer. Her husband and children are frightened and struggling to understand what this diagnosis means, how to help, and how to keep the family's normal routines going. You are the oncology social worker who is called in to help. What interventions might you use?

Cultural Issues

You are an oncology social worker who is asked to see a woman of Southeast Asian descent who was recently diagnosed with leukemia. She is non-English-speaking, and her family asks that the healthcare team not tell her that she has cancer. How might you intervene with both the patient and family and also the healthcare team? What principles will be important to uphold in this situation? How can you interpret the family's preferences to the healthcare team?

Public Policy

Palliative care is currently minimally reimbursed by Medicare and other insurers. How might you, as an oncology social worker, advocate for the inclusion of palliative care as a reimbursable service for oncology patients?

REFERENCES

Abrams, R., (1974). Not alone with cancer: A guide for those who care—what to expect, what to do. Springfield, IL: Charles C Thomas Publisher.

American College of Surgeons Commission on Cancer. (2012). *Cancer program standards 2012: Ensuring patient-centered care (*v1.2.1). Retrieved from https://www.facs.org/ ~ /media/files/quality%20programs/cancer/coc/programstandards2012.ashx

Anderson, C. M. (1982). The community connection: The impact of social networks on family and individual functioning. In F. Walsh (Ed.). *Normal family processes* (1st ed.). New York, NY: Guilford Press.

Association of Oncology Social Workers (2012). *Standards of Practice in Oncology Social Work.* [Internet]. Retrieved from: http://www.aosw.org/aosw/Main/professionals/standards-of-practice/AOSWMain/Professional-Development/standards-of-practice.aspx?hkey = 51fda308-28bd-48b0-8a75-a17d01251b5e

Bradley, C., & Bednarek, H. (2002). Employment patterns of long-term cancer survivors. *Psychooncology, 11*, 188–198.

Byock, I. (1998). *Dying well.* New York, NY: Riverhead Books.

Cassel, C., & Fiedl, M. (Eds.). (1997). *Approaching death: Improving care at the end of life.* Washington, DC: National Academy Press.

Cella, D., & Yellen, S. (1993). Cancer support groups: The state of the art. *Cancer Practice, 1*, 56–61.

Chochinov, H., Hack,T., Hassard, T., Kristijanson, L., McClement, S., & Harolos, M. (2005). Dignity therapy: A novel psychotherapeutic intervention for patients near the end of life. *Journal of Clinical Oncology, 23*(24), 5520–5525.

Christ, G. (1989). Social work in oncology. In J. Holland, & J. Rowland, (Eds.), *Handbook of psychooncology: Psychological care of the patient with cancer* (pp. 670–677). New York, NY: Oxford University Press.

Fawzy, F. I., Fawzy, N. W., & Canada, A. L. (2001). Pyschoeducational intervention programs for patients with cancer. In A. Baum, & B. L. Andersen, (Eds.), *Psychosocial interventions for cancer* (pp. 235–267). Washington, DC: American Psychological Association.

Freeman, H. (1989). Cancer and the economically disadvantaged. *CA: A Cancer Journal for Clinicians., 64*(1), 324–334.

Gurevich, M., Devins, G. M., & Rodin, G. M. (2002). Stress response syndromes and cancer: Conceptual and assessment issues. *Psychosomatics, 43*, 259–281.

Gotay, C., & Stern, J. (1995). Assessment of psychological functioning in cancer patients. *Journal of Psychosocial Oncology, 13*(1/2), 123–160.

Haylock, P. J. (2008). Cancer nursing: Past, present, and future. *Nursing Clinics of North America, 43*(2), 179–203.

Haynes, M., & Smedley, B. (1999). *The unequal burden of cancer: An assessment of NIH research and programs for ethnic minorities and the medically underserved.* Washington, DC: National Academy Press.

Hedlund, S., & Clark, E. (2001). End of life issues. In M. Lauria, E. Clark, J. Hermann, & N. Stearns, (Eds.), *Social work in oncology: Supporting survivors, families, and caregivers.* Atlanta, GA: American Cancer Society.

Holland, J., & Rowland, J. (Eds.). (1989). *Handbook of psychooncology: Psychosocial care of the patient with cancer.* New York, NY: Oxford University Press.

Institute of Medicine. (1999): *The unequal burden of cancer: An assessment of NIH research and programs for ethnic minorities and medically underserved.* Washington, DC: National Academies Press.

Institute of Medicine. (2005). *From cancer patient to cancer survivor: Lost in transition.* Washington, DC: National Academies Press.

Institute of Medicine. (2008). *Cancer care for the whole patient: Meeting psychosocial health needs.* Washington, DC: National Academies Press.

Jacobsen, P., & Wagner, L. (2012). A new quality standard: The integration of psychosocial care into routine cancer care. *Journal of Clinical Oncology, 30*(11), 1154–1159.

Jemal, A., Clegg, L. E., Ward, L., Reis, L. A., Wu, X., Jamison, P. M., Wingo, P. A., Howe, H. L., Anderson, R. N., & Edwards, B. K. (2004). Annual report to the nation on the status of cancer, 1975–2001, with a special feature regarding survival. *Cancer, 101*(1), 3–27.

Kangas, M., Henry, J. L., & Bryant, R. A. (2005). The course of psychological disorders in the 1st year after cancer diagnosis. *Journal of Consulting and Clinical Psycholology, 73,* 763–768.

Kaiser Family Foundation/Harvard School of Public Health. (2006, Nov. 19). *National survey of households affected by cancer.* Retrieved from http://kaiserfamilyfoundation.files.wordpress.com/2013/01/7590.pdf

Kilbourn, K., Bargai, N., Durning, P., Madore, S., Deroche, K., & Zabora, J. (2011). Validity of psychooncology screening tool (POST). *Journal of Psychosocial Oncology, 29,* 475–498.

Leigh, J. (1997). *Communicating for cultural competence.* Needham Heights, MA: Allyn & Bacon.

Li, M., Fitzgerald, P., & Rodin, G. (2012). Evidence-based treatment of depression in patients with cancer. *Journal of Clinical Oncology, 30*(11), 1178–1187.

Mitchell, A. J., Cahn, M., & Bhatti, H. (2011). Prevalence of depression, anxiety and adjustment disorder in oncological, haematological, and palliative-care settings: A meta-analysis of 94 interview-based studies. *Lancet Oncology, 12,* 160–174.

Mukherjee, S. (2010). The emperor of all maladies: A biography of cancer. New York, NY: Scribner.

National Association of Social Workers. (2008). *NASW Code of Ethics.* Washington, DC: Author (also retrieved from: http://www.socialworkers.org/pubs/code/code.asp).

National Cancer Institute. (2012). *Cancer trends progress report.* Retrieved from www.cancer.gov

National Comprehensive Cancer Network. (2004). *Distress: Treatment guidelines for patients.* Fort Washington, PA: Author. (Retrieved from http://www.nccn.org/patients/guidelines/default.aspx)

National Comprehensive Cancer Network. (2010) *Annual Report.* Fort Washington, PA: Author.

Kolata, G. (2009, April 24). Advances elusive in the drive to cure cancer. *The New York Times,* p. A1.

Parkes, C. M. (1986). The caregivers' griefs. *Journal of Palliative Care, 1,* 5–7.

Rolland, J. (1994). *Families, illness, and disability: An integrative treatment model.* New York, NY: Basic Books.

Rosenbaum, E. H., & Rosenbaum, I. R. (1998). *Cancer supportive care: A comprehensive guide for patients and families*. Kansas City, MO: Andrews McNeel Publishers.

Sontag, S., (1990). *Illness as metaphor.* New York, NY: Picador.

Stiefel, F., & Razavi, D. (1994). Common psychiatric disorders patients: Anxiety and acute confusional states. *Support Care Cancer, 2,* 233–237.

Traeger, L., Greer, J., & Fernandez-Robles, C. (2012). Evidence-based treatment of anxiety in patients with cancer. *Journal of Clinical Oncology, 30*(11), 1197–1206.

Walsh, K., & Hedlund, S. (2011). Mental health risk in palliative care: The social work role. In T. Altilio T., & S. Otis-Green, (Eds.), *Oxford textbook of palliative care social work* (pp. 181–190). New York, NY: Oxford University Press.

Weisman, A. (1979). *Coping with cancer.* New York, NY: McGraw-Hill.

Weisman, A (1976-1977) The existential plight in cancer: Significance of the first 100 days. *International Journal of Psychiatry in Medicine, 7*(1), 1–15.

Wolff, S., Nichols, C., Ulman, D., Miller, A., Kho, S., & Armstrong, L., (2005). Survivorship: An unmet need of the patient with cancer-implications of a survey of the Lance Armstrong Foundation. *Journal of Clinical Oncology, 43*(11), 1253–1259.

Zabora, J. (1998). Screening procedures for psychosocial distress. In J. Holland, (Ed.), *Psychooncology* (pp. 389–397). New York, NY: Oxford University Press.

Zabora, J., BrintzenhofeSzoc, K., Curbow, B., Hooker, C., & Piantadosi, S. (2001). The prevalence of psychological distress by cancer site. *Psychooncology, 10,* 19–28.

CHAPTER 10

Community Health and Health Promotion

Kristine Siefert and Debbie Shelton

INTRODUCTION

Social work has long been active in community health—in fact, social workers were among the first to recognize the influence of community factors on health and well-being. In 1919, Julia Lathrop, the first Chief of the Children's Bureau, published a pioneering study in the *American Journal of Public Health* detailing the Bureau's investigation of the high rate of infant mortality in the United States. These innovative studies in epidemiological research did not approach infant mortality as a medical question but rather investigated the "economic, social, civic, and family conditions" associated with higher or lower infant mortality (Lathrop, 1919, p. 270). The Bureau found that the majority of infant deaths were associated with preventable causes, including poverty, lack of education, unfavorable location of the home, poor housing conditions, and lack of prenatal care. Social workers used the findings of their research to advocate for passage of the Sheppard-Towner Act of 1921, which established the first federally funded preventive-health services for women and children and established prenatal and child-health centers in almost every state (Siefert, 1983). Today, social workers practice in all aspects of community health, including prevention, health promotion, health education, community outreach, community organizing, advocacy, health program planning and administration, and research and evaluation (Otis-Green, 2008; Ruth & Sisco, 2008).

THEORETICAL FRAMEWORK

The Spectrum of Health Promotion and Preventive Intervention

Consistent with the profession's person-in-environment and systems-based perspectives, social work practice in community health and health promotion draws on epidemiological theories of health and disease and the spectrum of preventive intervention. Gordis (2014) defines **epidemiology** as the "the study of how disease is distributed in populations and the factors that influence or determine this distribution" (Gordis, 2014, p. 2). However, the definition from Kipling in 1902 is much broader and applicable to social work. Kipling described epidemiology as "the study of the distribution and determinants of health-related states or events in specified populations and the application of this study to control of health problems" (Kipling, 1902, p. 79). Epidemiologists seek to understand the causes of disease in order to prevent reccurrence; to that end, they use both original data that were collected for a specific purpose as well as secondary data, such as birth and death certificates, disease registries, administrative data on healthcare use, case reports, and surveys (Roberts, 2009). An exemplar of epidemiologic research is the study of infant mortality that was carried out by the social workers of the Children's Bureau. The Bureau prospectively examined the contribution of the social environment to infant mortality by interviewing the mother of each child born in a given calendar year in eight cities and several selected rural areas. An illustration of the rigor of these studies can be seen in the concern for accuracy demonstrated by the interviewers; maternal answers to questions about income were verified with information from other sources, including fathers and employers (Lathrop, 1919; Siefert, 1983).

Classic epidemiologic theory views the "natural history" of a disorder as a progression from a pre-disease period, during which the person is in a state of equilibrium but is vulnerable to personal, environmental, and causal risk factors that interact to produce a threat to health (Krieger, 2004). If the risk factors for vulnerability are not reduced or eliminated, the next stage is a period in which disease is early but can be detected and treated before it progresses (i.e., a period of pathogenesis). If recovery does not occur, the process progresses to a chronic condition, disability, or death.

Passive and active surveillance are used in epidemiology to monitor for changes in disease frequency and changes in risk factors. **Passive surveillance** includes the usage of data that have been previously collected. These data are often required or mandated by the healthcare system, and the accuracy of the data is solely dependent upon the individual who is collecting the information. An example may include the use of data from the local health department to determine the number of H1N1 influenza cases in the county. The individual who entered the data may not have been trained to ask questions that would differentiate between other types of influenza and the H1N1 virus. Therefore, the mandatory data may or may not be accurate. Interviewing and collecting data from individuals by healthcare workers is called active surveillance (Gordis, 2014). **Active surveillance** tends to be more accurate as trained individuals are collecting data through an approved process for gathering the information that is needed. Data collectors ask and report the same information from all involved individuals. Passive surveillance is used more frequently for reasons related to cost and availability as there is an abundance of recorded data that can be utilized (Gordis, 2014). During the H1N1 epidemic in 2008, active surveillance was employed by the Centers for Disease Control to interview individuals who were suspected of having the H1N1 virus with regard to signs, symptoms, and outcomes. Since there were no existing data to be utilized, active surveillance was necessary to protect the population. The Children's Bureau in China interviewed each child born in a given calendar year prospectively to examine social environment in relation to mortality rates as an active surveillance method (Lathrop, 1919; Siefert, 1983). In measuring known diseases, such as heart disease among females between the ages of 35 and 55 years, passive surveillance is more likely to be used as these data are available through medical records, hospital admissions, and death certificates and this process for obtaining the data is less expensive than interviewing each female with heart disease.

Passive and active surveillance are both used to gather information to measure morbidity and mortality rates. **Mortality rates** measure cause of death for all individuals and are instrumental for measuring the severity of disease processes and the success of treatment of diseases (Gordis, 2014). **Morbidity rates** measure how often a disease occurs within a population. There are two measurements of morbidity that include incidence and prevalence rates. Incidence rates are instrumental in the prediction of risk. **Incidence** refers to the number of new cases of a disease that occur during a certain time frame within a *population of people at risk* for developing the illness (Gordis, 2014). For example, the number of new cases of influenza among middle-school children who were not immunized during the 2013–2014 school year at a certain school.

Prevalence does not measure risk but rather measures the number of individuals with a specific disease in a *population* at a specific point in time. Risk cannot be measured as all cases of the disease in all stages of the illness are included in the measurement of prevalence (Gordis, 2014). Using the example for incidence given earlier, an example of prevalence would include all middle-school children who were infected with the influenza virus at a certain school during the 2013–2014 school year. In this case, the difference between incidence and prevalence is clear. Incidence takes into account those students who were at risk (not immunized), whereas prevalence includes the total number of cases in the school during the time frame.

Mortality rates are good indicators of disease within a population; however, the **Global Burden of Disease (GBD)** (*Figure 10.1*) is a more thorough predictor of health and disability. The GBD is an indicator that measures disability and losses from a healthy life combined with premature death (Stanhope & Lancaster, 2012). Premature death is calculated by subtracting the difference 'between the actual age at death and life expectancy at that age in a low-mortality population" (Stanhope & Lancaster, 2012, p. 81). Contribution to the family home and economy is minimized when an individual suffers a disability that prevents self-care and employment. When premature death occurs, an individual's future contributions to society must be taken into account. The GBD is represented by *disability adjusted life-years (DALYs)*, which was previously discussed in Chapter 10 (Stanhope & Lancaster, 2012).

Epidemiologists use the global burden of disease indicator and disability adjusted life-years to allocate resources and make predictions on future healthcare needs. Prevalence rates are necessary to measure disease within a population while incidence rates are best utilized to identify a potential relationship between exposure to a disease and risk of developing a disease (Gordis, 2014). A strong knowledge of risk and risk factors is necessary to decrease the incidence and prevalence of disease in a society and to reduce the global burden of disease.

To reduce the incidence of disease within a community, an effort must be made to reduce risk. Health promotion and disease prevention programs aim to reduce risk of certain diseases at varying levels.

- **Primary prevention** refers to interventions at the pre-disease stage. These interventions include general health promotion and specific protection against disorders for which a preventable cause is known. An example of health promotion is having a healthy diet and/or exercise regime. An example of specific disease prevention is vaccination to prevent measles, mumps, and rubella.

- **Secondary prevention** is applied during the period of pathogenesis and includes early detection and prompt intervention to prevent permanent damage. Examples are screening for breast or colon cancer and crisis intervention following exposure to violence or trauma.

- **Tertiary prevention** includes rehabilitation services, efforts to limit disability, and interventions to maximize functioning and quality of life. Examples include diabetes-education classes, physical therapy following stroke, and chronic disease management.

This classic model of health promotion and prevention originated in the study of infectious disease and is more difficult to apply to non-infectious conditions, which involve the complex and often poorly understood interplay of multiple risk and protective factors. Mrazek and Haggerty (1994) described an alternative classification system for health promotion and prevention that was developed by Gordon (1983, 1987). In Gordon's system, **universal prevention** refers to interventions that benefit the entire population, such as prenatal care and seat belt use. **Selective prevention** refers to interventions that target a specific subset of the population who are deemed to be at higher risk than the general population because of their membership in a group, such as a family with a history of genetic vulnerability to a specific disease. **Indicated prevention** includes interventions directed to those with early signs or symptoms of a disorder, such as hypertension. Building on Gordon's work, the Institute of Medicine (IOM) adapted this model for the prevention of mental disorders (Mrazek & Haggerty, 1994).

Social Production of Disease and Eco-social Theories

Two recent theories that are relevant to social work in community health and health promotion are the social production of disease theory and **eco-social theory**. These theories, which focus on the **social determinants of health**, are important because they emphasize environmental and contextual factors that influence health and well-being rather than focusing solely on individual behavior in explaining health status and outcomes. As Moniz (2010) noted, this perspective fits well with social work's biopsychosocial approach to social problems and the profession's commitment to social justice. The **social production of disease theory** proposes that one's social and economic position (e.g., gender, race/ethnicity, and social class) determines one's exposure to health-damaging risk factors as well as the presence or absence of health-protective factors (Link & Phelan, 1995; Krieger & Zierler, 1995; Williams, 1997; Braveman, et al., 2011). Therefore, effective health promotion interventions must target the social determinants of health and health disparities rather than focusing on individual behavior alone.

To fully understand the factors that influence health, one must appreciate the factors that discourage health. Health disparities and social determinants of health increase risk of decreased health, increased disability, and premature death, thereby increasing the global burden of disease. Healthy People 2020 defined a **health disparity** as ". . . a particular type of health difference that is closely linked with economic, social, or environmental disadvantage" (Healthy People 2020, 2014). According to the World Health Organization (2010), the social determinants of health are the conditions in which people are born, grow, live, work and age. Access to and the quality of care provided by the available health care system are also social determinants. Social determinants are the primary cause of health care disparities or health inequalities (the terms are often used interchangeably) which are considered to be unfair and avoidable differences affecting the health of individuals, groups, communities, and within and between countries (WHO, 2010).

Successful efforts to increase health promotion and disease prevention decrease the global burden of disease for a population. Within populations, social determinants of health must be considered. *Social gradient* (a shorter life expectancy and more disease processes occur as an individual moves down the social ladder), *social exclusion* (resentment and discrimination), and *social support* (lack of social support systems) accumulate to further separate an individual from health. Early life experiences (lack of early education), stress (anxiety and inability to cope), work (stress in the workplace), unemployment (unable to find means to support self or family), food (inability to pay for or find food sources), transport (lack of transportation), and addiction (use of alternative methods to cope) are other social determinants of health (WHO, 2010). Social determinants of health are far reaching into the economy and environment and are often non-modifiable by the individual although they can directly affect health status and result in health disparities.

Health promotion and disease prevention services must begin with measures to assess and decrease health disparities that exist for individuals and communities. Understanding the social determinants of health for a population is vital for successful health promotion program development.

Figure 10.1   Conceptual Model—Health Impacts

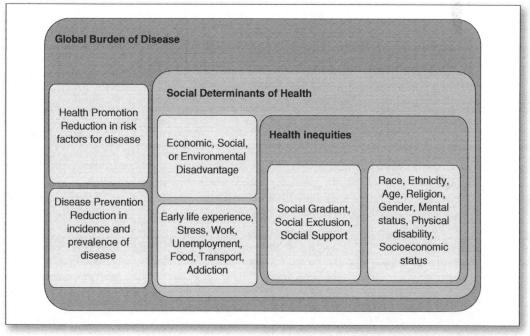

Source: Author (D. Shelton).

SKILLS AND COMPETENCIES

Social work in community health and health promotion requires a broad range of knowledge, skills, and competencies. In addition to core social work competencies, social workers need to have knowledge and skills in health promotion, health education, and disease prevention. Importantly, social workers must be able to recognize and intervene in health disparities and inequities and to provide culturally competent, participatory, evidence-based interventions. Some specific skills that are needed include the ability to

- Engage and build partnerships with key community constituencies for the purposes of health promotion, disease prevention, and elimination of health disparities

- Conduct comprehensive community-based assessments of risk and protective factors for health and disease

- Plan, implement, and evaluate culturally competent health promotion, health education, and preventive interventions at multiple levels

- Engage in advocacy, community organizing, social action, and administrative, organizational, and policy approaches to promote health and prevent disease and overcome barriers to equity, access, and quality of care

- Incorporate social work values and ethical principles in planning, developing and implementing, and evaluating healthcare social work interventions

VALUES AND ETHICS

The core social work values of *service, social justice, dignity and worth of the person, importance of human relationships, integrity*, and *competence* should be reflected in every aspect of social work practice in community health and health promotion (NASW, 2008). As Otis-Green (2008) noted, healthcare social workers must consider the ethical implications of everything they do. Social workers in community health must adhere to the NASW *Code of Ethics* and should also consider ethical issues that have been specifically defined in relation to community interventions (KU Work Group for Community Health and Development, 2012). This includes adhering to ethical guidelines around *confidentiality of information* from participants in a community intervention or program; *consent,* including consent to sharing information, informed consent, and community consent to the program or service; *disclosure,* including disclosure to participants about the conditions of the program, information about disclosure of participant information to others, and disclosure of any conflict of interest; and *competence* of the services offered. In addition, the guidelines include eliminating *conflicts of interest* and *enforcing sanctions for unethical behavior* such as exploitation, defrauding funders, or discriminating in service delivery; as well as *actively striving to do what is right* for program participants, staff members, and the community (Kansas University [KU] Work Group for Community Health and Development, 2012).

HEALTH PROMOTION AND WELLNESS MODELS

The Health Belief Model

It is well documented that adherence to recommendations to promote health and prevent disease has been consistently poor, and many models have been developed to address the problem (Clark & Houle, 2009). An early and widely used model, the **Health Belief Model (HBM)**, was developed to understand why people fail to engage in preventive behavior or utilize screening tests (Rosenstock, 1974, cited in Clark & Houle, 2009). Based on well-established psychological and behavioral theory, the HBM includes the following dimensions: *perceived susceptibility,* or the person's perception of vulnerability to a disease, *perceived severity*, or the person's assessment of the seriousness of developing the disease; *perceived benefits*, or the person's perception of the likelihood of avoiding the disease by engaging in preventive actions; *perceived barriers* to taking the recommended actions; and *cues to action*, such as media campaigns, medical advice, or the illness of a family member (Becker, Drachman & Krischt,1974, cited in Clark & Houle, 2009).

Upon application of the HBM to individual or community health-behavior change, it is important to acknowledge health disparities and social determinants of health that may exist. An individual's perceived susceptibility to an illness can be affected by health disparities such as a religious affiliation or belief that a higher authority would not allow such an illness to occur or the mental incapacity to appreciate the risk of the disease state. Ethnicity and age can be factors associated with the perceived severity of the disease. Examples may include the increased risk of diabetes among the Hispanic population or hypertension among African Americans. Does the individual expect to have these illnesses because of the health disparity that is present?

Likewise, the availability of employment, transportation, and food choices as social determinants of health must be assessed and may be instrumental in perceiving benefits and cues to action in receiving prevention or health promotion services. Many of the social determinants of health could present as barriers to improving health outcomes for an individual or a community.

The HBM provides a framework to analyze how behavioral change occurs. Interventions aimed at the reduction of health disparities and social determinants of health can be developed, applied, and evaluated on the basis of the dimensions of the HBM. Although the HBM is supported by a substantial body of research, it is limited in that it only explains health behavior to the extent that such behavior is determined by the value that the person places on health and by the person's attitudes or beliefs. More recent research indicates that health behavior is also significantly influenced by habit, non-health-related reasons such as concern about appearance, and economic or environmental factors (Clark & Houle, 2009).

The Transtheoretical Model

Another widely used model, discussed previously in this text as the basis for motivational interviewing, is the **Transtheoretical Model (TTM),** which uses stages of change to integrate leading theories of health-behavior change in individuals and populations (Prochaska, Johnson, & Lee, 2009). The TTM involves progress through five stages, from *pre-contemplation* of action, through *contemplation, preparation, action,* and finally to *maintenance* of the desired behavior or *termination* of an unhealthy behavior. Some models include a sixth stage: Relapse, because it is often difficult for individuals to permanently maintain behavioral change. The inclusion of this step is an effort to avoid the stigma often associated with relapse in order to encourage individuals to re-enter the stages of change cycle and resume positive change related behaviors. If progress is to occur, interventions must be matched to each individual's stage of change.

In the pre-contemplation stage, the individual does not plan to change behaviors. This action may be due to many health disparities or social determinant of health that may be present. An example may include instructing a diabetic patient that exercise is important in controlling blood sugars. The individual may not understand (mental status) that exercise is an important intervention to control blood sugars. Through the next stage of contemplation, the individual learns that exercise is important (health promotion/disease prevention) and begins to consider the change. Adding a segment of time onto the daily calendar that includes 30 minutes of walking per day occurs in the preparation stage. The individual will need to consider the pros and cons of the action. For example, the individual may need to consider whether he or she has social support at home to babysit while the exercise takes place or whether the work schedule is flexible to allow an additional half hour for the regime to occur. The action stage begins with the first walking exercise, and maintenance occurs when the action becomes a ritual for the patient. Termination of an unhealthy, sedentary lifestyle for the individual has now occurred according to the TTM (Stanhope & Lancaster, 2012).

Although research findings with respect to individual behavior in clinical settings are encouraging, the TTM model has only recently begun to be tested with diverse populations and communities (Prochaska et al., 2009). Health disparities and social determinants of health must be considered with any application of behavioral change to individuals and/ or communities.

Social Marketing

Social marketing is a process that uses information about a population to promote the adoption or acceptability of ideas or practices in that population (Green & Kreuter, 2005). Research has shown that effective health promotion media campaigns feature well-designed messages that are delivered to their target audience frequently enough and with enough "reach" that they are seen, heard, and remembered (Abroms & Maibach, 2008). In an effort to vaccinate young girls against the human papillomavirus (HPV), the campaign of "One Less" was developed by the pharmaceutical company and manufacturer Merck (Grantham, Ahern, & Connolly-Ahern, 2011). Merck used a direct-to-consumer approach in advertising to reach the target audience of young women. (Grantham et al., 2011). The "One Less" campaign was simple and easy for the audience to understand. The use of young girls in the ads "reached" the target population that consisted of young females as well as parents. Risk and benefits of the vaccine were provided via the campaign and supported by the CDC as well as many popular television physicians. This television commercial was represented on all major networks frequently, so most consumers of aired television knew the purpose of the ad.

With the advent of ecological models of health and disease, it is now recognized that effective mass-media campaigns must also target social networks, communities, and the local and distal places that influence health behavior, such as neighborhoods, schools, workplaces, and grocery stores, as well as laws and policies and their enforcement (Abroms & Maibach, 2008). This approach requires multilevel interventions that target the larger social system as well as the individual.

Many disciplines of health and education have forged together to develop ecological models that are useful in health promotion (Green, Richard, & Potvin, 1996; Richard, Gauvin, & Raine, 2011). Health promotion and disease prevention are no longer believed to be influenced by the individual alone. Social determinants of health along with disparities heavily impact an individual's ability to seek or participate in better health practices. In the past, epidemiology has had a strong focus on the linear causation of disease that has broadened with the emergence of social factors and their effect on health (Richard et al., 2011). It is well known that a virus is the causative agent of influenza. Based on epidemiological studies, we know that the virus mutates yearly and the most appropriate vaccination is formulated for the public in an effort to prevent an influenza epidemic. If a vaccination for influenza exists and is readily available for the public, then why do influenza cases add to the global burden of disease annually? Perhaps an individual has a belief system that does not value the influenza vaccine or is opposed to vaccinations. Individuals may not have the financial resources and/ or transportation methods to get to the site for vaccinations. Many factors beyond the virus itself are responsible for influenza cases. Understanding the many social and environmental factors that are present has led to the development of multilevel models of health that have shown success with health promotion interventions (Richard et al., 2011).

The PRECEDE-PROCEED Model

PRECEDE-PROCEED is a participatory educational and ecological model for health promotion and wellness that has been used successfully in communities, schools, workplaces, and healthcare settings for more than 30 years (Green & Kreuter, 2005). A thorough community assessment is necessary before undertaking a new health promotion program (Bracht, 1999). A community assessment reveals the members of the community, the geographical boundaries of the community, and the characteristics of the members of the community (Stanhope & Lancaster, 2012). Stanhope and Lancaster noted that "community assessment helps identify community needs, clarify problems, and identify strengths and resources" (Stanhope & Lancaster, 2012, p. 407). Through the community assessment, target interventions and programs will be designed that possess a greater potential for successful behavioral change.

The first part of the model, PRECEDE, is a series of four planned phases or assessments that provide information to guide decisions about priorities, goals, and objectives for intervention. The acronym stands for **P**redisposing, **R**einforcing, and **E**nabling **C**onstructs in **E**ducational **D**iagnosis and **E**valuation. Green and Kreuter (2005) describe the phases as follows:

Phase 1: Social Assessment

According to Green and Kreuter (2005), this phase assumes that people will support health-related issues if they can see how they are related to the social and economic concerns that affect their overall quality of life. Participatory planning is critical as it builds capacity and sustainability and promotes evaluation and diffusion. Total community participation is not usually feasible, but it is important to have broad representation, not just token involvement. It is also important to think in terms of a partnership—a collaboration between planners, agencies, community leaders, and the lay community. The involved community leaders, agencies, and lay people become stakeholders in the program (Stanhope & Lancaster, 2012). Given representation at the onset of a health promotion program, stakeholders become important as they influence other community members of the importance of the intervention.

Strategies for social assessment include *social reconnaissance,* an assessment process that uses community leaders at multiple levels as informants; *focus groups,* which are usually 60- to 90-minute sessions that eight to twelve representatives of the target population along with a trained moderator; *central location intercept interviews,* which are face-to-face interviews held in a place that is likely to yield broad representation of the target population, such as a shopping center; and *community surveys.*

CASE STUDY

A community health center received a grant to develop an outreach program to reduce the high rate of obesity among children and adolescents in a large public housing project in the predominantly African American neighborhood served by the center. Obesity is an urgent public health problem in the United States; more than 30% of adults and almost 17% of children are obese, with significantly higher rates among African Americans and Hispanics (Flegal, Carroll, Ogden, & Curtin, 2010; Ogden, Carroll, Kit, & Flegal, 2012). Obesity is associated with numerous adverse health consequences, including diabetes, hypertension, cardiovascular disease, and some cancers.

The social worker at the center was asked to conduct an assessment to identify community perspectives on the problem and to engage residents in efforts to combat obesity in the community. Her first step involved social reconnaissance, during which she met with representatives from key community organizations, including the president of the housing project's Tenant's Organization, representatives from local service agencies, the pastor from the church attended by many of the housing project residents, and leaders from local businesses—all stakeholders in the community. She presented detailed information about the health consequences of childhood obesity, such as diabetes and hypertension, and also presented the findings of the community assessment, which revealed that many children in the local school had higher mass body indexes than in other local communities. Many of the community representatives were unaware of the extent of the problem and the seriousness of the health consequences and agreed to form a Community Advisory Committee to the outreach program.

With the help of the Tenant's Organization, which provided volunteers, the social worker also conducted focus groups with project residents. Participants' views of the causes of the problem varied considerably, but some important findings emerged. Many of the residents were knowledgeable about the importance of diet and exercise but reported that healthy food was hard to find in local stores. Residents complained about outdated meat and expensive produce, often not very fresh, and about the abundance of fast-food restaurants offering tasty and inexpensive but calorie-laden food. The local elementary and middle schools sold soft drinks and junk food through vending machines supplied by companies that made donations to school programs. In addition, because of budget constraints, after-school athletic programs had been cut. At the same time, mothers reported being afraid to let their children play outside because of gang activity. Parents complained that the police often failed to respond to calls and related an incident in which a young man had been shot to death and no one came to pick up the body for several hours. Some described unsuccessfully trying to shield their children from the sight. Interviewees reported that drugs were sold openly and that the stairwells were unsafe for their children.

It became clear from the social assessment, which included both focus groups and interviews, that parents and children needed to be educated about healthy food and exercise and that project residents needed access to better quality, affordable food, and a safe physical environment. Armed with these findings, the Community Advisory Committee successfully recruited representatives from the local police department and the elementary and middle school administration to serve as members of the Committee. Becoming stakeholders in the health promotion intervention enforces the commitment of the police department and school leaders. The Committee recommended increasing police surveillance and ensuring safety in the housing project; improving access to fresh, healthy, and affordable food; and reducing the availability of unhealthy food as key goals for the program.

Phase 2: Epidemiological Assessment

Green and Kreuter (2005) described the tasks of this phase as identifying and prioritizing the problems on which the health promotion program will focus, identifying the environmental and behavioral factors that are most likely to influence the problems that have emerged, and translating this information into measurable objectives. Objectives should describe *who* will benefit, *what* benefit they should receive, *how much* of the benefit should be received, and *by when* the benefit should be received. In setting priorities and objectives, it is important to determine which problems have the largest impact or disproportionately burden certain subpopulations or communities, and which problems are most amenable to intervention. In addition, it should be determined which problems are not currently being addressed, and which, if effectively addressed, with yield the greatest benefits.

Once a health problem has been identified as a priority, behavioral and environmental assessments are conducted. The steps in *behavioral assessment* are to (1) list potential behavioral risks for the problem, (2) rate behaviors on importance, (3) rate behaviors on changeability, (4) choose behavioral targets for intervention, and (5) state behavioral objectives. *Environmental assessment* steps are to (1) identify environmental factors likely to influence the health problem directly or indirectly, (2) rate the factors on their relative importance, (3) rate the factors on changeability, (4) choose environmental targets, and

(5) state the environmental objectives in quantitative terms. Clear, concise objectives provide measurable indicators that can be used to evaluate the effectiveness of health promotion efforts.

From the above case study, the behavioral and environmental assessment includes confirming the risks that lead to the behavioral concern. The unsafe environment for outdoor activity and the unavailability of fresh fruits and vegetables are identified risks for increased obesity in children in this community. Prioritizing the recommended behavioral changes occurs next. Protecting the children by increasing police awareness in the neighborhood would be of upmost importance and would be instrumental in increasing outdoor play. Second, compiling a plan to increase the availability of fresh produce would be in order. A community garden or an invitation to local farmers to set up produce stands would aid in increasing the amounts of fresh food to the neighborhood. At this time, a more detailed plan can be established through focus groups. Interviewees would need to be asked such questions as "Would you spend money at a farmer's market?", "Would you be willing to work in a community garden that would be shared by the neighborhood?", and "Would you be willing to be a part of a neighborhood watch program after school so children could play?". Answers to these questions would reveal the changeability of behaviors of the community, allowing measurable objectives to be recorded. Objectives need to be measurable and time-limited; for example, "Police surveillance will be increased by 30% during the hours of 3 P.M. to 9 P.M. in the community." Another measurable objective would be a decrease in the incidence of childhood obesity from the preceding school year to the following school year as measured by body mass indices of children at the end of each school year.

Phase 3: Educational and Ecological Assessment

This phase identifies the interacting factors that influence behavior and the environment. Green and Kreuter (2005) identified three general categories of factors that can affect behavioral or environmental change, individually or collectively: (1) *Predisposing factors*—antecedents to behavior that provide the rationale or motivation (e.g., knowledge, beliefs, attitudes, confidence); (2) *enabling factors*—antecedents to behavioral or environmental change that permit or facilitate motivation or environmental policy (e.g., availability and accessibility of resources, laws and policies, priorities); and (3) *reinforcing factors*—post-behavior factors that provide reward or incentive for maintenance or repetition (e.g., family, peers, teachers, employers, community leaders, policymakers). Behavioral change—of politicians, for example—influences the environment, but the environment can also be changed independently through enabling factors.

In the case study from above, the predisposing factor would be increased knowledge of the problem. Knowledge given from the community assessment to the stakeholders increases awareness of increased childhood obesity rates and an unsafe environment for play. Increasing police surveillance or the addition of a community garden or farmer's market would constitute enabling factors. Last, a reinforcing factor may consist of a community picnic to which community members bring freshly prepared foods with recipes for exchange.

The second part of the model is PROCEED—Policy, Regulatory, and Organizational Constructs in Educational and Environmental Development. PROCEED includes the phases described below.

Phases 4 and 5: Intervention Alignment and Administrative and Policy Assessment, and Implementation

In these phases, the components of the health promotion program are matched to changes from earlier assessments at the individual, organizational, and/or community level. Specific evidence-based interventions are then "mapped" to the specific determinants that were identified in previous phases as priorities. Program components are aligned at two levels: (1) the macro, or ecological, level (policy, regulatory, and/or organizational changes needed) and (2) the micro level (individual, behavioral, family, small group, classroom, etc.). The resources needed are assessed, and organizational and policy supports for and barriers to the proposed program are identified, as are the settings in which program activities will take place and any modifications that may be needed. An important task in the intervention process is reviewing and pooling information from best prior attempts to address the problem. Numerous sources of information are available for seeking out evidence-based interventions, such as journal articles, reports, meta-analyses, books and monographs, conferences, clearinghouses, and funding agency websites. It is also important to acknowledge, coordinate with, or integrate existing programs and activities in the community or other setting for the proposed intervention or program.

Interventions to increase police surveillance and implement a community garden would begin the PROCEED process. An evidence-based literature review would be assembled to give confirmation that these activities are interventions that have shown success when implemented. Next, city policy would need to be examined for the recommended interventions. Is there funding to allow for increased police surveillance to the community? Is there available land that can be used for the garden? Are farmers who bring in fresh produce required to buy permits to sell their products, and are they required to pay taxes on sold products? City policy may need to be updated to allow for interventions to occur. Community members and stakeholders would need to be present at city council meetings to address concerns and to offer solutions.

Phases 6, 7, and 8: Process, Impact, and Outcome Evaluation

Green and Kreuter (2005) emphasized that evaluation is integrated throughout the PRECEDE-PROCEED model. During and following implementation, ongoing monitoring is used for continuous quality improvement and for evaluation. *Process evaluation* focuses on implementation of the health promotion program or intervention; this is usually done through observations and interviews. *Impact evaluation* assesses the immediate effect of the program on target behaviors and their antecedents or on environmental factors. *Outcome evaluation* focuses on the health status and quality-of-life indicators of the community that have been identified through earlier planning.

Process evaluation would be evident through focus groups with the community. Evaluating the receptiveness of a community garden on the basis of how many community members would support the initiative or how many would agree to work in order to supply fresh foods to the community would be a process evaluation that would occur very early in the program development. Thus, further monitoring of how many individuals actually began the land cultivation and planting would also be necessary. Working in the garden would demonstrate the beginning efforts of an individual behavioral change, and the benefits would be twofold—increasing outdoor activity and consuming more fresh produce. Outcome evaluation may include qualitative and quantitative measures. Quality-of-life assessment tools could be employed to assess life satisfaction before and after the community garden intervention. Body mass indices for children may be recorded at the local school one year, two years, and five years after the beginning of the community garden to assess for a decreased incidence of childhood obesity. Qualitative data could be obtained through focus groups to assess whether stakeholders perceived the garden to be of benefit to the community.

Table 10.1 illustrates how a local health department could use the PRECEDE-PROCEED model to develop a program to promote oral health in low-income African American and Hispanic preschool children, a population with a high rate of early childhood caries (ECC), or "baby bottle" tooth decay. ECC affects children's growth, behavior, and functioning and can cause considerable pain as well as long-term treatment needs (Chattopadhyay, 2008). Low-income preschool children are twice as likely as higher-income children to have poor oral health and to lack dental care, and Mexican American and African American children are at especially high risk (Fisher-Owens et al., 2008) (for detailed information about using the model, see Green & Kreuter [2005]; Dr. Green's website, http://lgreen.net/precede.htm; Kansas University's Community Toolbox website, http://ctb.ku.edu/en/tablecontents/sub_section_main_1008.aspx [KU Work Group, 2012] and Crosby & Noar [2011]).

Table 10.1   PRECEDE-PROCEED Model: Oral Health Program Example

Phase	Tasks	Examples
Social Assessment	Gather key information related to health issue	Perform a community assessment of the target community to assess for needs, strengths/weaknesses, clarify problems, and locate resources.
		Recruit a Community Advisory Board that includes community leaders, dental professionals, and representatives from state and local health and social service agencies to serve as stakeholders. Gather data on the prevalence of ECC and complications stemming from ECC such as rheumatic fever and bacterial endocarditis, availability of dental insurance, and number of local dental providers.
		Use key informant interviews, surveys, and focus groups to gather information about the value placed on oral health by the community, including cultural beliefs, risk and protective factors such as diet and oral hygiene practices, and access to dental care.
		Clarify behavioral changeability interventions from interviews. Identify other health disparities and/or social determinants of health that reside within the target community that influence behavior.

Phase	Tasks	Examples
Epidemiological Assessment	Establish measurable, time-limited objectives that can be used to evaluate the program and identify the most important and most changeable behavioral and environmental factors influencing the objectives.	Literature review to assess for evidence-based interventions that have proven success in decreasing ECC in communities. Example of overall program objective: "By 2017, the number of low-income Mexican American and African American preschool children affected by dental caries will be reduced by 50%." Behavioral risk factors, listed in terms of importance and changeability, include inappropriate bottle feeding by mothers who put their children to bed with a bottle of sweetened fruit juice at night to help them sleep, not brushing their children's teeth at bedtime, and not taking preschool children to the dentist for preventive care. Environmental risk factors include lack of dental insurance and no regular source of dental care. Example of behavioral sub-objective: "Inappropriate baby bottle use will be reduced by 50% in 12 months and will be measured in repeat interviews with parents." Example of an environmental sub-objective: "Safety-nets will be established to provide preventive care for uninsured preschool children within 12 months. Efforts to change insurance procedures and policy may be needed to insure safety-nets. Select key community leaders to support policy changes."
Educational and Ecological Assessment	Identify and select the predisposing, reinforcing, and enabling factors that have the largest impact on the behavioral and environmental targets identified in the previous phases.	For the "reduction in inappropriate baby bottle use" sub-objective, the following predisposing, reinforcing, and enabling factors are identified: • Predisposing factors—lack of knowledge about the effects of prolonged exposure to sugary beverages on children's teeth, belief that decay in baby teeth is not important because these teeth fall out, and the belief that very young children do not need dental care. • Enabling factors: Increasing the community knowledge on the effects of baby bottle tooth decay, increasing access to dental care through safety-nets and dental insurance reform. • Reinforcing factor: Rewarding families with small gift cards for child supplies with each kept dental appointment reinforcing positive behavioral change. • Enabling factors—Seeking available grants to assure adequate funding for children's oral health and provide an increased number of dental providers in the community. • Reinforcing factors: Community award program to thank local dentist and community leaders for support.

(Continued)

Table 10.1 (Continued)

Phase	Tasks	Examples
Intervention Alignment and Administrative and Policy Assessment	Determine the program components and interventions needed to achieve the program objectives and assess resource availability, organizational capacity, and the policy changes required.	To achieve the "safety nets" sub-objective, the following intervention strategies are identified: providing knowledge to the community and stakeholders on the harmful effects of ECC, recruiting volunteer dental providers, securing the donation and/or grant writing to provide a mobile dental van, and advocating for the allocation of local government funds for pediatric preventive dental care through policy change. Some of the resources available include the local dental society and members of the Community Advisory Board members, who can serve as organizers and advocates, and local politicians.
Implementation	Develop a detailed plan to implement and evaluate the interventions identified.	Some of the strategies for implementation of the "safety-nets" sub-objective include: The president of the local dental society will recruit dentists and dental hygienists to donate 4 hours per month to provide free dental care for children. Two business leaders on the Community Advisory Board will ask a local auto dealership to donate a van, and a local foundation will be approached for funding to equip the van with needed supplies. A citizen coalition will be organized to lobby for the policy changes needed to provide preventive dental care for low-income children.
Process Evaluation	Monitor fidelity to program plan and make adjustments as needed.	For the "safety-net" sub-objective: Is the community receptive to change as evidenced by vocal commitment by parents to have their children evaluated by local dentist for preventive care? Has the president of the local dental society been successful in recruiting dental providers? Has a van been donated? Is the citizen coalition lobbying for the needed changes in policy?
Impact Evaluation	Assess whether sub-objectives have been met.	Are parents inquiring about dental services? Has inappropriate baby bottle use been reduced by 50% as assessed through focus groups and further interviews?
Outcome Evaluation	Determine whether the program has accomplished its intended goal.	Has the number of low-income Mexican American and African American preschool children affected by dental caries been reduced by 50%?

Source: Adapted from Crosby, R. & Noar, S. (2011). What is a planning model? An introduction to PRECEDE-PROCEED. *Journal of Public Health Dentistry, 71*, S7-S15; Green, L.W., and Kreuter, M.W. (2005). *Health program planning: An educational and ecological approach* (4th edition). New York: McGraw-Hill; KU Work Group for Community Health and Development. (2012). Chapter 19, Section 5: Ethical Issues in Community Interventions. Lawrence, KS: University of Kansas. [Internet]. Retrieved January 20, 2012, from the Community Tool Box: http://ctb.ku.edu/en/tablecontents/sub_section_main_1165.aspx

CULTURAL CONSIDERATIONS

Cultural competence is one of the NASW standards for practice in healthcare, and social workers play a critical role in assuring that community health programs and health promotion efforts are effective in meeting the needs of the diverse populations that they serve. A widely used definition of cultural competence is that adapted by the Office of Minority Health (2001) from Cross, Bazron, Dennis, and Isaacs (1989) in its final report on *National Standards for Culturally and Linguistically Appropriate Services in Health Care*:

> Cultural and linguistic competence is a set of congruent behaviors, attitudes, and policies that come together in a system, agency, or among professionals that enables effective work in cross-cultural situations. "Culture" refers to integrated patterns of human behavior that include the language, thoughts, communications, actions, customs, beliefs, values, and institutions of racial, ethnic, religious, or social groups. "Competence" implies having the capacity to function effectively as an individual and an organization within the context of the cultural beliefs, behaviors, and needs presented by consumers and their communities. (Office of Minority Health, 2001, p. 4)

Related concepts include **cultural targeting**, a cultural competence strategy that seeks to reach group members who share certain values, beliefs, and practices, and **cultural tailoring**, which focuses on individual preferences (Fisher et al., 2007).

A recent systematic review of health promotion interventions adapted for racial/ethnic minority communities identified five principles that can be used to guide practice (Netto, Bhopal, Lederle, Khatoon, & Jackson, 2010). These principles are listed below.

1. Use community resources, such as ethnic-specific media and community events and leaders, to increase the accessibility of interventions.

2. Identify and address barriers to access and participation, such as cost, transportation, and child care.

3. Develop communication strategies that overcome language and literacy barriers.

4. Identify and work with participants' cultural or religious values that either encourage or inhibit healthier lifestyles.

5. Take into account differing degrees of cultural identification and acculturation in the target population when planning and evaluating interventions.

CASE STUDY

A social worker in a local health department was asked to help develop a preventive program to address the high number of deaths from breast cancer among the growing population of Arab American women in the community, most of whom were Muslim. She learned that many of the

(Continued)

(Continued)

deaths were due to delay in diagnosis: women were presenting with advanced disease, i.e., cancers that had progressed to a stage at which they were no longer curable. Further investigation revealed low utilization of clinical breast exams and screening mammography, particularly among more recent immigrants. Cost did not appear to be a problem as free screenings were available for low-income and uninsured women.

To better understand why women were not being screened, the social worker contacted a community health nurse at a large multiservice agency serving the Arab American community for help in identifying potential barriers. The nurse, a second-generation Muslim American herself, had many insights that she was eager to share, and she offered to serve as a consultant in developing the program. Some of the key issues that she identified included a lack of education about breast cancer, the importance of regular screening in detection while the cancer is at a curable stage, and religious and cultural concerns about modesty. The nurse also noted that some women were reluctant to seek medical care because they had encountered religious discrimination or ignorance about their cultural beliefs on the part of healthcare providers. The nurse identified much strength in the Arab American community that could be built upon, such as strong extended family and community ties and religious beliefs that encouraged a healthy lifestyle.

With the help of the nurse, the social worker organized a task force to guide the development of the program. The members included influential community and religious leaders, health professionals, and survivors of breast cancer who were willing to share their experiences to help other women. At the recommendation of the task force, a local advertising agency was enlisted to develop Arabic-language educational brochures, billboards, and public service announcements. An imam encouraged men attending prayer services to take care of their families by seeing that their wives and mothers had recommended mammograms. A survivor volunteered to appear in a television spot and organized a "buddy program" to take women to screenings. Healthcare providers were educated about the importance of ensuring that examinations would be conducted by female healthcare workers. The result was a substantial increase in the number of women receiving breast exams and mammograms.

ROLE OF SOCIAL WORK IN COMMUNITY AND PUBLIC HEALTH

As noted earlier, social workers practice in all areas of community health, including prevention and health promotion, health education and community outreach, community organizing and advocacy, health program planning and administration, and research and evaluation (Otis-Green, 2008; Ruth & Sisco, 2008). Social workers are also active in public health. The Association of State and Territorial Public Health Social Workers (ASTPHSW, 2005) described the major characteristic of public health social work as an epidemiological approach to identifying health and social problems, with an emphasis on primary prevention and health promotion. **Public health social work** is typically practiced in a multidisciplinary setting and blends the roles of direct service provider, consultant, administrator, program planner, evaluator, policymaker, and researcher. Obviously, there is considerable overlap between social work practice in community health and social work in public health. As Ruth & Sisco (2008) observed, many social workers in healthcare settings engage in public health social work practice without fully recognizing how they are using knowledge and skills from both fields.

To increase awareness of public health social work and to ensure the competency of its practice, a Standards Working Group, including representatives and support from federal, state, and local public health agencies, academic institutions, the National Association of Social Workers, and the American Public Health Association, has developed a set of professional practice standards (ASTPHSW, 2005). These standards can be grouped into several overarching principles, as summarized below.

Social Epidemiology

- Assess and monitor social problems affecting the health status and social functioning of at-risk populations within the context of family, community, and culture. Health status of a population can be understood through the knowledge of mortality rates such as prevalence and incidence of disease.

- Identify and assess the factors associated with resiliency, strengths, and assets that promote optimal health. The community assessment provides information on the needs of a population while also identifying problems and discovering strengths and resources (Stanhope & Lancaster, 2012).

- Identify, measure, and assess the social factors contributing to health issues, health hazards, and stress associated with ill health. Health disparities and social determinants of health are present and must be acknowledged as barriers to optimal health. Ecological models that incorporate multilevel system change can be used to implement interventions that address the social inequalities that affect health behaviors of a community or population.

- Evaluate the effectiveness, accessibility, and quality of individual, family, and population-based health interventions. Ongoing evaluation of implemented interventions is necessary to monitor for improved quality. Process evaluation, impact evaluation, and outcome evaluation from the PRECEDE-PROCEED model provide a framework for continuous program evaluation (Green & Kreuter, 2005).

Social Planning, Community Organizational Development, and Social Marketing

- Inform and educate individuals, families, and communities about public health issues. Equipping a community with knowledge of specific increased risk of disease and illness is a responsibility of all healthcare workers. Without the knowledge of the existence of a problem, the community is helpless to change.

- Empower and mobilize individuals, families, and communities to become active participants in identifying and addressing public health concerns to improve individual, family, and societal well-being. Community members have input through focus groups and interviews into the concerns and health problems that exist. Through focus groups, a public health concern may come to surface that has not been addressed through statistical findings. Encouraging key community member to be stakeholders in the program allows for greater community participation.

- Promote and enforce legal requirements that protect the health and safety of individuals, families, and communities. All newly conceptualized health promotion programs should work closely with established state and national platforms. There are many agencies with existing programs that can be implemented within communities to increase access to healthcare such as the National Health Core and Federally Qualified Health Centers. County health departments can also be useful in planning health promotion activities.

- Ensure public accountability for the well-being of all, with emphasis on vulnerable and underserved populations.

- Develop primary prevention strategies that promote the health and well-being of individuals, families, and communities. Primary prevention strategies are aimed to provide protection against disease before occurrence as, for example, through influenza vaccinations.

- Develop secondary and tertiary prevention strategies to alleviate health and related social and economic concerns. Secondary prevention seeks out early detection of a disease process so that intervention can begin early. Mammography and prostate screenings are secondary prevention strategies. Tertiary prevention strategies are aimed at preventing further disability, such as with physical therapy following a stroke crisis.

Leadership and Advocacy

- Ensure the elimination of health and social disparities wherever they exist, such as—but not limited to—those based on community, race, age, gender, ethnicity, culture, or disability. Utilizing ecological models as a theoretical framework for health promotion allows interventions to be directed at health disparities and social determinants of health of a community as well as the individual.

- Ensure and promote policy development for providing quality and comprehensive public health services within a cultural, community, and family context. Advocating for policy development and health reform that provides quality healthcare services is a role for all providers.

Data Collection, Research, and Evaluation

- Ensure the competency of its practice in addressing the issues of public health effectively through a core body of social work knowledge, philosophy, code of ethics, and standards (ATPHSW, 2005).

EMERGING TRENDS

Emerging trends with important implications for social work in community health and health promotion include the rising socioeconomic inequality in the United States and its association with poor health, persistent and widening health disparities, and growing concern about environmental hazards and health (Centers for Disease Control and Prevention, 2011; Brender, Maantay, & Chakraborty, 2011). To illustrate, despite the availability of evidence-based smoking cessation treatments, including counseling and especially pharmacotherapeutic approaches, tobacco use remains the leading preventable cause of death and disease in the United States (Cox, Okuyemi, Choi, & Ahluwalia, 2011; Ranney, Melvin, Lux, McClain, & Lohr, 2006). Recent declines in tobacco use appear to have leveled off at approximately 20%, and rates of use are strikingly higher among racial/ethnic minorities, blue-collar workers, and the poor and uneducated (Cox et al., 2011; Orleans, 2007). Despite documented interest and willingness to participate in tobacco-cessation treatment, utilization among racial/ethnic minorities is low (Cox et al., 2011). Furthermore, little research has been done on barriers to access or effectiveness of treatment for underserved populations (Cox et al., 2011).

The problem of nonadherence to recommendations for preventive health behavior and to treatment recommendations constitutes a major area of concern. It is estimated that tobacco use, poor nutrition and lack of exercise, and alcohol use account for 40% of all deaths in the United States (Curry & Fitzgibbon, 2009). Medication nonadherence for patients with chronic conditions is estimated to result in 125,000 deaths per year and costs ranging from $100 billion to $300 billion per year (Bosworth et al., 2011). Most of the interventions that have been shown to be effective in promoting adherence to long-term medication treatment are complex and include elements such as accessible care and information, reminders and telephone follow-up, counseling and self-monitoring, and supportive care. However, even effective interventions have not led to large improvements in adherence or better clinical outcomes (Bosworth et al., 2011). One reason for this finding is that most existing adherence interventions fail to include patient perspectives and do not provide multifaceted, tailored approaches, including health literacy and behavioral interventions, shared responsibility between patient and provider, and ongoing evaluation. There is also a need for systems-based strategies, including financial incentives, electronic health records, and greater public awareness (Bosworth et al., 2011).

The effects of the physical and chemical environment on health are also emerging as a concern. A recent review demonstrated that residential proximity to environmental hazards had significant relationships with adverse health outcomes, including adverse pregnancy outcomes, childhood cancers, asthma hospitalizations, stroke, end-stage renal disease, and diabetes (Brender et al., 2011). These findings underscore the need for social work interventions that address the social determinants of health.

Multiple studies have proven that health disparities and social determinants are ever present and influence health outcomes. An emerging theme and opportunity now exist to explore health equity. **Health equity** is defined as the highest level of health for all (Srinivasan & Williams, 2014). "Several factors must be considered to shift the research agenda from a disparity model to an equity model in which the central theme is achieving the highest level of health" (Srinivasan & Williams, 2014, p. 73). Five initial steps are included in establishing a broader research agenda to investigate the influence of health equity. The steps include

- considering the role of population health in research and interventions;
- understanding complex, multidisciplinary, multilevel, and multi-factorial interactions;
- improving research methodologies and statistical analytical techniques;
- building on community resiliency and partnerships; and
- developing the research and professional workforce (Srinivasan & Williams, 2014).

Health promotion interventions must combine community-level interventions with needed individual behavioral changes. Patient education should always be considered an integral element aimed at individual change; however, change may not occur if community-level interventions are not implemented congruently. An example would include educating parents on the dangers of lead poisoning in older homes of a community and supplying the equipment, paint, and workforce to replace the lead-infested homes. Knowledge is needed at the individual level; however, change cannot occur without the community-level intervention of resurfacing the homes.

Efforts must be made to link knowledge of disease beyond biological to societal levels. The development of population-level assessment tools for multilevel research is needed for health equity based research. However, as noted by Srinivasan and Williams, there appear to be no active large-scale projects underway that aim to achieve health equity on a national scale" (Srinivasan & Williams, 2014, p. 129). Opportunities may be present in smaller projects that allow for the identification of common health equity themes and metrics to be used for evaluation (Srinivasan & Williams, 2014).

Community-based participatory research (CBPR) provides a method to build on community partnerships. Israel et al. noted that "CBPR is a partnership approach to research that equitably involves community members, practitioners, and academic researchers in all aspects of the process, enabling all partners to contribute their expertise and share responsibility and ownership (2010, p. 2094). Encouraging community input through interviews, identification of key stakeholders, and the involvement of the community in the research are crucial for health equity research.

Health equity research endeavors will depend upon the development of multilevel, multi-factorial, and multidisciplinary teams. Partnerships with state, national, and federal agencies as well as communities, academic settings, and healthcare facilities are needed to further prepare researchers who are knowledgeable on social determinants of health and their influence in health promotion and outcomes (Srinivasan & Williams, 2014).

An important and encouraging development is passage of **the Patient Protection and Affordable Care Act (PPACA)**, which includes an unprecedented dedicated funding stream of $15 billion for a "Prevention and Public Health Fund," to be administered over ten years. The PPACA also establishes a new National Prevention, Health Promotion, and Public Health Council to develop and coordinate a national strategy for prevention, wellness, and health promotion. The PPACA provides new funding for community-based preventive activities and interventions, and supports the development of workplace wellness programs (Cogan, 2011; Preston & Alexander, 2010).

CHALLENGES

Although social workers have much to contribute to community health and health promotion, there are also significant challenges. Deficit-reduction proposals have identified the $15 billion allocated for prevention in the Affordable Care Act as a potential target for cuts, and the PPACA itself faces ongoing legal challenges. Public health budget cuts have forced local health departments to reduce or eliminate preventive programs and employees and have threatened community health centers (Kuehn, 2011). Many community clinics have no social work services available, despite increasing recognition of the benefits of holistic care (Otis-Green, 2008). As Golden (2011) pointed out, social workers are critical to prevention and wellness programs, but social work services cannot be an unfunded mandate.

Another identified challenge is the need for a more explicit focus on prevention in social work practice and education. In a study documenting the low level of articles focused on prevention in the social work literature, Marshall (2011) and her colleagues observed there are likely many social workers who are engaged in health promotion and prevention whose work is not characterized as such and who may not consider their work as prevention oriented (Marshall et al., 2011). In addition to a greater emphasis on prevention, there is a great need for transdisciplinary training in social work and public health (Ruth & Sisco, 2008; Ruth et al., 2008). MSW/MPH programs, which have proliferated in recent years, are one model, but there is also need to infuse public health content into traditional MSW programs as well as into continuing education for social workers (Ruth & Sisco, 2008). There is also a need for increased recognition of and partnering with community health workers, who share social work's goals of pursuing social justice and providing culturally appropriate services (Spencer, Gunter, & Palmisano, 2011).

OPPORTUNITIES

Over the past several decades, the focus on individual lifestyle change in health promotion and disease prevention has broadened to include social and environmental factors, but often without adequate resources (Navarro, Voetsch, Liburd, Giles, & Collins, 2007). In response, the National Expert Panel on Community Health Promotion, convened by the Centers for Disease Control in 2006, has recommended federal support for new approaches to health and wellness that incorporate diverse community voices, including a focus on wellness that incorporates mental health, spirituality, and complementary and alternative medicine (Navarro et al., 2007). In addition, the panel recommended supporting interventions that focus on changing living conditions strongly associated with health, promoting culturally tailored interventions by incorporating cultural competency and health literacy, implementing evidence and practice-based interventions, and conducting evaluation and surveillance. The panel also recommended training and capacity-building for a "socio-ecological approach" to community health promotion, including competencies in "cultural competence, advocacy, policy development, evaluation, use of community indicators, development of partnerships, and use of new communication technologies" (Navarro et al., 2007, p. 4). These recommendations offer major opportunities for social workers, whose theoretical perspective, core values, knowledge base, and practice skills have the potential to play a key role in their implementation.

SUMMARY

Social work has had long professional involvement in the areas of community health and health promotion. This chapter identified the theoretical framework underpinning community health and examined the competencies necessary for professional social work practice in this arena as well as the values and ethics associated with such practice. Models were offered for considering health promotion and wellness. The emerging trends in public health have significant implications for social work practice and present both challenges and opportunities for the future.

KEY TERMS AND CONCEPTS

- Passive, active surveillence
- Epidemiology
- Primary, secondary, and tertiary prevention
- Universal, selective, and indicated prevention
- Eco-social theory

- Health Belief Model

- Social marketing

- PRECEDE-PROCEED Model

- Cultural competence, cultural targeting, and cultural tailoring

- Public health social work

- Health equity

- Community-based participatory research (CBPR)

- Incidence, prevalence

- Morbidity rates, mortality rates

- Social determinants of health

- Health disparities or health inequalities

- Trans-theoretical module

- Social production of disease theory

QUESTIONS FOR DISCUSSION

1. What are some of the *individual* risk factors for low birth weight and infant mortality? What are some of the *social determinants of health that may be present*?

2. Using the spectrum of preventive intervention, describe some *primary, secondary, and tertiary* preventive interventions that could help prevent poor pregnancy outcome.

3. Describe and give examples some of the individual and environmental *predisposing, reinforcing, and enabling* factors that can influence smoking cessation.

EXERCISES

1. You are a social worker in a community health center serving a large Hispanic population. A recent study found that women in this community, many of whom are immigrants, have a low rate of cervical cancer screening and a high rate of death from cervical cancer due to delay in diagnosis. You have been asked to plan a community assessment to understand why women are not getting screened. The assessment will be used to develop an outreach program. What are some of the strategies that you would use?

2. HIV/AIDS is one of the leading causes of morbidity and mortality for women in the United States, particularly among low-income women, Latinas, African American women, and transgender women. You are a social worker in a large urban health department and have been asked to help develop a two-page concept paper proposing a comprehensive program to prevent HIV infection among high-risk women. What are some of the steps that you would recommend the health department take to develop the program?

REFERENCES

Abroms, L. C., & Maibach, E. W. (2008). The effectiveness of mass communication to change public behavior. *Annual Review of Public Health, 29,* 219–234.

Association of State and Territorial Public Health Social Workers (ASTPHSW). (2005). *Public health social work standards and competencies.* Columbus, OH: Ohio Department of Health.

Becker, M. H., Drachman, R. H., & Kirscht, J. P. (1974). A new approach to explaining sick-role behavior in low-income populations. *American Journal of Public Health, 64,* 205–216.

Bosworth, H. B., Granger, B. B., Mendys, P., Brindis, R., Burkholder, R., Czajkowski, S. M., Daniel, J. G., Eckman, I., Ho, M., Johnson, M., Kimmel, S. E., Liu, L. Z., Musaus, J., Shrank, W. H., Whalley Buono, E., Weiss, K., & Granger, C.B. (2011). Medication adherence: A call for action. *American Heart Journal, 162,* 412–424.

Bracht, N. (1999). *Health promotion at the community level: New advances* (2nd ed.).Thousand Oaks, CA: SAGE.

Braveman, P. A., Kumanyika, S., Fielding, J., LaVeist, T., Borrell, L. N., Manderscheid, R., & Troutman, A. (2011). Health disparities and health equity: The issue is justice. *American Journal of Public Health, 101*(Supplement 1), S149–S155.

Brender, J. D., Maantay, J. A., & Chakraborty, J. (2011). Residential proximity to environmental hazards and adverse health outcomes. *American Journal of Public Health, 101*(Supplement 1), S37–S52.

Centers for Disease Control and Prevention. (2011). CDC health disparities and inequalities report— United States, 2011. *Morbidity and Mortality Weekly Review, 60*(Suppl), 1–124.

Chattopadhyay, A. (2008). Oral health disparities in the United States. *Dental Clinics of North America, 52,* 297–318.

Clark, N. M., & Houle, C. R. (2009). Theoretical models and strategies for improving disease management by patients. In S. A. Shumaker, J. K. Ockene, & K. A. Riekert, (Eds.). *The handbook of health behavior change.* New York, NY: Springer Publishing Company.

Cogan, J. A. (2011). The Affordable Care Act's preventive services mandate: Breaking down the barriers to nationwide access to preventive services. *Journal of Law, Medicine & Ethics,* 355–365.

Cox, L. S., Okuyemi, K., Choi, W. S., & Ahluwalia, J. S. (2011). A review of tobacco use treatments in U.S. ethnic minority populations. *American Journal of Health Promotion, 25*(5S), S11–S30.

Crosby, R., & Noar, S. (2011). What is a planning model? An introduction to PRECEDE-PROCEED. *Journal of Public Health Dentistry, 71, S7–S15.*

Cross, T. L., Bazron, B. J., Dennis, K. W., & Isaacs, M. R. (1989). *Towards a culturally competent system of care* (Volume 1). Washington, DC: The Georgetown University Child Development Center.

Curry, S. J., & Fitzgibbon, M. L. (2009). Theories of prevention. In S. A. Shumaker, J. K. Ockene, & K. A. Riekert, (Eds.), *The handbook of health behavior change.* New York: Springer Publishing Company.

Fisher, T. L., Burnet, D., Huang, E. S., Chin, M. H., & Cagney, K. A. (2007). Cultural leverage: Interventions using culture to narrow racial disparities in health care. *Medical Care Research and Review 65*(5S), 242S–283S.

Fisher-Owens, S. A., Barker, J. C., Adams, S., Chung, L. H., Gansky, S. A., Hyde, S., & Weintraub, J. A. (2008). Giving policy some teeth: Routes to reducing disparities in oral health, *Health Affairs, 27*(2), 404–412.

Flegal, K. M., Carroll, M. D., Ogden, C. L., & Curtin, L. R. (2010). Prevalence and trends in obesity among U.S. Adults, 1999–2008. *JAMA 303*(3), 235–241.

Golden, R. L. (2011). Coordination, integration, and collaboration: A clear path for social work in health reform. *Health & Social Work, 36*(3), 227–228.

Gordis, L. (2014). *Epidemiology* (5th ed.). Canada: Elsevier Saunders.

Gordon, R. (1983). An operational classification of disease prevention. *Public Health Reports, 98,* 107–109.

Gordon, R. (1987). An operational classification of disease prevention. In J. A. Steinberg & M. M. Silverman, (Eds.). *Preventing mental disorders* (pp. 20–26). Rockville, MD: DHHS,.

Grantham, S., Ahem, L., & Connolly-Ahem, C. (20010. Merck's *One Less* campaign: Using risk message frames to promote the use of Gardasil® in HPV prevention. *Communication Research Reports,* (25 Oct), 318–326. doi: 10.1080/08824096.2011.616243

Green, L., Richard, L., & Potvin, L. (1996). Ecological foundation of health promotion. *American Journal of Health Promotion, 10,* 270–281.

Green, L. W., and Kreuter, M. W. (2005). *Health program planning: An educational and ecological approach* (4th edition). New York: McGraw-Hill.

Healthy People 2020. (2014). *Disparities.* Retrieved from http:www.healthypeople.gov/2020/about/disparitiesAbout.aspx

Israel, B., Coombre, C., Cheezum, R., Schulz, A. McGranaghan, R., Lichtenstein, R., Reyes, A., Clement, J., & Burris, A. (2010). Community-based participatory research: A capacity-building approach for policy advocacy aimed at eliminating health disparities. *American Journal of Public Health, 100*(11), 2094–2102.

Kipling, R. (1992). *Just-so stories: The elephant's child (1902).* Reprinted by Everyman's Library Children's Classic. New York: Alfred A. Knopf.

Krieger, N. (Ed.). (2004). *Embodying inequality: Epidemiologic perspectives.* Amityville, NY: Baywod Publications, Inc.

Krieger, N., & Zierler, S. (1995). What explains the public's health? A call for epidemiologic theory. *Epidemiology, 7*(1), 107–109.

Kansas University Work Group for Community Health and Development. (2012). *Ethical Issues in Community Interventions* (Chapter 19, Section 5). Lawrence, KS: University of Kansas. Retrieved from the Community Tool Box: http://ctb.ku.edu/en/tablecontents/sub_section_main_1165.aspx

Kuehn, B. M. (2011). Public health cuts threaten preparedness, preventive health services. *Journal of the American Medical Association, 308*(18), 1965–1966.

Lathrop, J. (1919). Income and infant mortality. *American Journal of Public Health, 9,* 270–274.

Link, B., & Phelan, J. (1995). Social conditions as fundamental causes of disease. *Journal of Health and Social Behavior, 35,* 80–94.

Marshall, J. W., Ruth, B. J., Sisco, S., Bethke, S., Piper, T. M., Cohen, M., & Bachman, S., (2011). Social work interest in prevention: A content analysis of the professional literature. *Social Work, 56*(3), 201–211.

Moniz, C. (2010). Social work and the social determinants of health perspective: A good fit. *Health and Social Work, 35*(4), 310–313.

Mrazek, P., & Haggerty, R. (1994). *Reducing risks for mental disorder: Frontiers for preventive intervention research.* Washington, DC: National Academies Press.

National Association of Social Workers, (2008). *Code of Ethics of the National Association of Social Workers.* Washington, DC: NASW.

Navarro, A. M., Voetsch, K. P., Liburd, L. C., Giles, H. W., & Collins, J. L. (2007). Charting the future of community health promotion: Recommendations from the National Expert Panel on Community Health Promotion. *Preventing Chronic Disease, 4*(3), 1–7. Retrieved from http://www.cdc.gov/pcd/issues/2007/jul/07_0013.htm

Netto, G., Bhopal, R., Lederle, N., Khatoon, J., & Jackson, A. (2010). How can health promotion interventions be adapted for minority ethnic communities? Five principles for guiding the development of behavioural interventions. *Health Promotion International, 25,* 248–257.

Office of Minority Health, U.S. Public Health Service (2001). *National standards for culturally and linguistically appropriate services in health care. Final report.* Washington, DC: U.S. Department of Health and Human Services.

Ogden, C. L., Carroll, M. D., Kit, B. K., & Flegal, K.M. (2012). Prevalence of obesity and trends in body mass index among U.S. children and adolescents, 1999–2010. *JAMA, 307*(5), 483–490.

Orleans, C.T. (2007). Increasing the demand for and use of effective smoking-cessation treatments. *American Journal of Preventive Medicine, 33*(6S), S340–S348.

Otis-Green, S. (2008). Health care social work. In T. Mizrahi, & L. Davis, (Eds.), *Encyclopedia of social work* (20th ed). New York: National Association of Social Workers.

Preston, C. M., & Alexander, M. (2010). Prevention in the United States Affordable Care Act. *Journal of Preventive Medicine and Public Health, 43*(6), 455–458.

Prochaska, J. O., Johnson, S., & Lee, P. (2009). The transtheoretical model of behavioral change. In S. A. Shumaker, J. K. Ockene, & K.A. Riekert, (Eds.), *The handbook of health behavior change.* New York: Springer Publishing Company.

Ranney, L., Melvin, C., Lux, L., McClain, E., & Lohr, K. N. (2006). Systematic review: Smoking cessation intervention strategies for adults and adults in special populations. *Annals of Internal Medicine, 145*(11), 845–855.

Richard, L., Gauvin, L., & Raine, K. (2011). Ecological models revisited: Their uses and evolution in health promotion over two decades. *Annual Review of Public Health, 32,* 307–326.

Roberts, D. K. (2009). *Epidemiology.* In R. M. Mullner, (Ed.), *Encyclopedia of health services research.* Thousand Oaks, CA: SAGE. *SAGE Reference Online*

Rosenstock, I. M. (1974). Historical origins of the health belief model. *Health Education Monographs, 2,* 328–335.

Ruth, B. J., & Sisco, S. (2008). Public health social work. In T. Mizrahi, & L. Davis, (Eds.), *Encyclopedia of Social Work* (20th ed). New York: National Association of Social Workers.

Ruth, B. J., Sisco, S., Wyatt, J., Bethke, C., Bachman, S. S., & Markham Piper, T. (2008). Public health and social work: Training dual professionals for the contemporary workplace. *Public Health Reports, 123*(Supplement 2), 71–77.

Siefert, K. (1983). An exemplar of primary prevention in social work: The Sheppard-Towner Act of 1921. *Social Work in Health Care, 9*(1), 87–103.

Spencer, M., S., Gunter, K. E., & Palmisano, G. (2010). Community health workers and their value to social work. *Social Work, 55,*169–180.

Srinivasan, S., & Williams, S. (2014). Transitioning from health disparities to a health equity research agenda: The time is now. *Public Health Records, 129*(Supplement 2), 71–76.

Stanhope, M., & Lancaster, J. (2012). *Public health nursing: Population-centered health care in the community* (8th ed.). Maryland Heights, MO: Elsevier.

Williams, D. R. (1997). Race and health: Basic questions, emerging directions. *Annals of Epidemiology, 7(5),* 322–333.

World Health Organization. (2010). *Social determinants of health.* Retrieved from http://www.who.int/social_determinants/thecommission/finalreport/key_concepts/en/index.html

CHAPTER 11

Gerontological Healthcare Social Work Practice

William J. Spitzer

INTRODUCTION

If ever a field of human services practice has the potential (and responsibility) to come into its own, it is gerontological social work. Two factors affect this compelling prediction. One is the significant demographic shift occurring in the population of the United States. The second arises from the historic evolution and characteristic activities of the social work profession. This chapter will identify and consider the statistical trends associated with the phenomenon often referred to as "the graying of America." It will make the point that this trend has sweeping impacts not only on those citizens reaching their senior years but also on the adult children, caretakers, and the nation at large as the aging trend prompts profound psychological, sociological, and economic changes in our country. This chapter will also highlight the dimensions of social work that make it uniquely positioned to evolve as one of the most influential professions to address service issues evident among the most rapidly growing segment of our population. At the same time, it will be noted that the profession has yet to position itself for these undeniable future practice opportunities. As a consequence, the challenge lies ahead for social work to cultivate sufficient numbers of competent, energetic practitioners to address the psychosocial needs of a burgeoning elderly population.

OUR AGING POPULATION

At the time of the Declaration of Independence, the estimated total population of the United States was about 2.5 million and the estimated life expectancy at birth was 39 years (Lowy, 1979, p. 21). Between 2010 and 2050, the U.S. population is projected to expand from 310 million to 439 million, an increase of 42% (Vincent & Velkoff, 2010, p. 1). Whether considered in absolute numbers or as the percentage of the overall population, the particular demographic change among those aged 65 years and older is without precedent and profound. The more than 40 million individuals in that age segment now represent 13.1% of the U.S. population, or more than one of every eight Americans. Since 1900, the percentage of Americans older than 65 years of age has *more than tripled* (from 4.1% in 1900 to 13.1% in 2010) (*Figure 11.1*), and the number has increased *more than thirteen times* (from 3.1 million to 40.4 million). That number is projected to increase to 55 million in 2020—a 36% increase for the decade. By 2030, nearly one in five U.S. residents will be 65 years of age or older. By 2050, there will be about 88.5 million older persons, *over twice their number in 2010* (Vincent & Velkoff, 2010) (*Figure 11.2*). In that year, those 65 years of age and older will constitute 20% of the U.S. population—quite noteworthy when one considers that this age group comprised only 4% of the total population at the turn of the 19th century (U.S. Census Bureau [USCB], 1995).

Figure 11.1

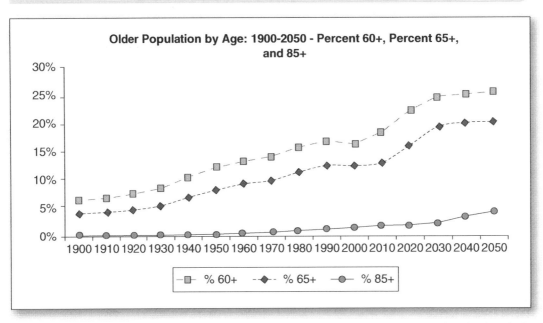

Sources: Projections for 2010 through 2050 are from: Table 12. Projections of the Population by Age and Sex for the United States: 2010 to 2050 (NP2008-T12), Population Division, U.S. Census Bureau 8/14/08; The source of the data for 1900 to 2000 is Table 5. Population by Age and Sex for the United States: 1900 to 2000, Part A. Number, Hobbs, Frank and Nicole Stoops, U.S. Census Bureau, Census 2000 Special Reports, Series CENSR-4, Demographic Trends in the 20th Century, 2002. Table compiled by the U.S. Administration on Aging (AoA) using the Census data noted.

Figure 11.2

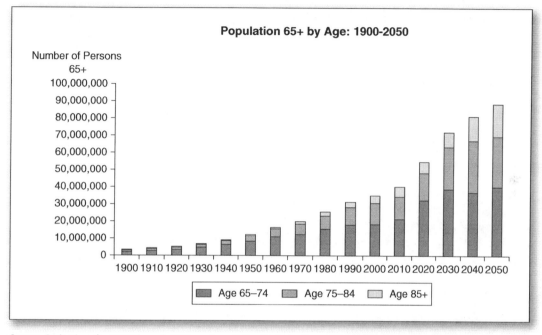

Sources: Projections for 2010 through 2050 are from: Table 12. Projections of the Population by Age and Sex for the United States: 2010 to 2050 (NP2008-T12), Population Division, U.S. Census Bureau; Release Date: August 14, 2008 The source of the data for 1900 to 2000 is Table 5. Population by Age and Sex for the United States: 1900 to 2000, Part A. Number, Hobbs, Frank and Nicole Stoops, U.S. Census Bureau, Census 2000 Special Reports, Series CENSR-4, Demographic Trends in the 20th Century. This table was compiled by the U.S. Administration on Aging using the Census data noted.

Reflecting the increasing ethnic and racial diversity in our aging population, 20.0% of persons 65 years of age and older in 2010 were minorities: 8.4% were African American, 6.9% were of Hispanic origin (who may be of any race), about 3.5% were Asian or Pacific Islander, and less than 1% were American Indian or Native Alaskan (Administration on Aging, 2011). The percentage of the population 65 years of age or more that is represented by Caucasians is projected to decrease by about 10%, whereas the percentages of all other races are expected to increase (Vincent & Velkoff, 2010, p. 4).

DEMOGRAPHIC INFLUENCES

Health is dependent on biologic factors (including one's genetic makeup) and the complex interaction of the individual with their environment (including physical surroundings, social factors, and personal lifestyle) (Banta & Jonas, 1995, p. 18; Berkman & Breslow, 1983;

Burnett, 1971). Health is characteristically reflected in measures such as birth rates, death rates (mortality), and **life expectancy** (defined as the average number of years a population of a certain age would be expected to live, given a set of age-specific death rates in a given year).

The aging of our population is the result of a decline in fertility and mortality rates, combined with increased life expectancy (Shrestha, 2006, p. i). The **infant mortality rate,** calculated to be nearly 100 infants per 1000 born in 1900, fell to a rate of 9.1 by 1990 (Banta & Jonas, 1995, p. 16). While a greater percentage of infants are surviving birth, *the U.S. birth rate has dropped to the lowest level since national data have been available*, falling from 15.9 in 1980 to 14.0 in 2008 (National Center for Health Statistics, 2010). The total fertility rate in the United States, which peaked after World War II at about 3.8 children per woman in the late 1950s, has fallen to 2.0 children in 1999.

Of equal significance, the number of overall deaths per 1000 population **(the crude mortality rate)** was slightly over 17 in 1900 but dropped to 8.6 per 1000 population by 1990 (Banta & Jonas, 1995, p. 16). Declining overall mortality rates reflect that life expectancy at birth (the expected number of years to be lived) is at an all-time high. We are living longer than ever before. In the late 1700s, the average American could anticipate living for approximately 35 years (USCB, 1995). That number reached 49 years in the period from 1900 to 1902 and nearly 78 years by 2003 (Shrestha, 2006, p. 2). The projection of life expectancy in the year 2020 is 79.5 years (U.S. National Center for Health Statistics, 2010).

Of note, the change in the life expectancy of males is impacting the male:female ratio among those who are 65 years of age and older. While more male births occur than female births (with 104.9 male births for every 100.0 female births in 2003) (National Center for Health Statistics [NCHS], 2005), male mortality exceeds female mortality in every age group, with the result that women have long outnumbered men in the older age groups. The 2010 Census reflected that there were over twice as many women as men at the age of 85 years or older (*Table 11.1*; also see: Howden & Meyer, 2011). Although that trend is projected to continue over the next four decades, the gap between the number of women and men is expected to narrow. The narrowing is due to the more rapid increase in life expectancy for men that is projected in the next several decades. In 2050, 55% of those 65 years of age or more are projected to be female, down from 57% in 2010 (Vincent & Velkoff, 2010, p. 8). The decline in the female share/increase in the male share of the population is even more dramatic among the oldest old. Among those 85 years of age and over, 61% are projected to be female in 2050, down 6% from 67% in 2010. Disconcertingly, in 2007, out of 33 countries within its peer group of Organization for Economic Co-operation and Development (OECD) countries, the United States ranked 27th and 26th for life expectancy at birth for females and males, respectively (U.S. Department of Health and Human Services [DHHS], 2011).

The substantial decrease in mortality and increase in life expectancy during the first half of the 20th century are thought to be largely attributable to increased food supplies and improved nutrition, which in turn reduced human contact with microorganisms like cholera or tubercle bacillus (McKeown, 1994, pp. 9–10). At the same time, evolution of the **germ theory of disease** led to the eradication and control of numerous parasitic diseases, especially among infants and children. That theory prompted greater emphasis on *preventative medicine* by both departments of public health and individuals. Increased attention to personal hygiene and public health led to development of water purification, sewage

Table 11.1   Number and Percentage of People Age 65 and Over and Age 85 and Over, by Sex, 2010

Age and Sex	Number (in thousands)	Percentage
65 and over		
Total	40,268	100.0
Men	17,363	43.1
Women	22,905	56.9
85 and over		
Total	5,494	100.0
Men	1,790	32.6
Women	3,704	67.4

Source: Federal Interagency Forum on Aging-Related Statistics. (2012). Older Americans 2012: Key indicators of well-being. Washington, DC: U.S. Government Printing Office. Data: U.S. Census Bureau, 2010 Census Summary File 1.

disposal and milk pasteurization measures along with greater emphasis on sanitary food preparation and hand washing (Shrestha, 2006, p. 3; McKeown, 1994, pp. 6–11).

The increased life expectancy since the mid-1900s is thought to be associated with improvements in the prevention and control of **chronic** (long-duration, recurring) **diseases** of adulthood, particularly heart disease (most importantly, coronary heart disease, hypertension, and rheumatic heart disease), cerebrovascular diseases (strokes), influenza, and pneumonia (Shrestha, 2006, p. 4). In addition to medical advances, personal decisions to embrace healthier lifestyles (such as smoking cessation, decreased cholesterol/fat intake, and decreases in blood pressure levels) and increased access to healthcare (whether through purchased health insurance or public programs like Medicaid) have further contributed to greater life expectancy.

PRESENT HEALTH STATUS OF THE AGING POPULATION

While life expectancy has improved, concerns prevail about the health status of aging Americans. In the United States, approximately 80% of all persons 65 years of age and older have at least one chronic condition and 50% have at least two (National Center for Chronic Disease Prevention and Health Promotion, 1999). In the period from 2007 to 2009, the most frequently occurring conditions among older persons were uncontrolled hypertension (34%), diagnosed arthritis (50%), all types of heart disease (32%), any cancer (23%), diabetes (19%), and sinusitis (14%). About 27.7% of persons 60 years of age and older report height–weight combinations that place them among the obese (Administration on Aging, 2011). Depression, a type of mood disorder, is the most prevalent mental health problem among older adults (Centers for Disease Control, 2008, p.2) Unfortunately depression is also frequently associated with suicide (National Alliance on Mental Illness [NAMI], 2009). The risk for late-life behavioral health problems, including social isolation, chronic illness, physical or mental disability and dependence, and other stresses, also increase with aging (American Geriatrics Society [AGS], 2005a, 2005b; NAMI, 2009; American Psychological Association [APA], 2012).

A strong relationship exists between age, disability status, and reported health status. In 2010, nearly four in 10 older persons reported some type of disability (e.g., difficulty in hearing, vision, cognition, ambulation, etc.) (Administration on Aging, 2011). In a 2005 survey, 56% of persons over the age of 80 years reported a severe disability and 29% reported that they needed assistance with **activities of daily living (ADLs)** such as bathing, ambulating, eating, or dressing. Among persons 65 years of age and older, 64% of those who had a severe disability characterized their health as fair or poor whereas only 10% of those who had no disability characterized their health as fair or poor. The presence of a severe disability is also associated with lower levels of income and educational attainment (Administration on Aging, 2011). Johnson, Toohey, and Wiener (2007) pointed out that "because the overall size of the older population will increase rapidly, the number of disabled older Americans will soar in coming decades. By one estimate between 2000 and 2040, the numbers of older adults with disabilities will more than double, increasing from about 10 million to about 21 million" (p. 12).

HEALTHCARE AND SOCIAL SERVICE NEEDS OF THE AGING POPULATION

With aging comes the prospect of declining health and, as a result, greater care needs and expenditures for health and social services. The rapid growth in the number of older persons, coupled with continued advances in medical technology, is expected to prompt increased pressure on health and long-term-care spending. Older Americans spent 13.2% of their total expenditures on health, more than twice the proportion spent by all consumers (6.6%). In 2009, the average annual healthcare expenditure for persons 65 years of age or older in the United States was over *seven* times the healthcare expenditure incurred by persons 25 years of age or less (U.S. Bureau of Labor of Labor Statistics [USBLS], 2009). The Administration on Aging (2011) reported that older consumers averaged out-of-pocket healthcare expenditures of $4,843 in 2010, an increase of 49% since 2000. In contrast, the total population spent considerably less, averaging $3,157 in out-of-pocket costs. In 2010, average health-related costs incurred by older consumers consisted of $3,085 (64%) for insurance, $795 (16%) for medical services, $805 (17%) for drugs, and $158 (3%) for medical supplies. Nearly a fifth of older people will incur more than $25,000 in lifetime out-of-pocket long-term costs before they die (Kemper, Komisar, & Alecxih, 2005/2006). These expenses become an issue when one considers that nearly 10% of older Americans (about 3.5 million) were below the poverty line in 2010 and that the median income of older persons in 2010 was $25,704 for males and $15,072 for females (Administration on Aging, 2011).

Long-term care becomes necessary when individuals are no longer able to perform everyday tasks or meet their own personal care needs. Along with heightened financial burdens, the prospect of contending with chronic illness and/or increasing disabilities introduces concern about the availability of appropriate caregiving and, ultimately, place-ment. In 2010, over half (55.1%) the older non-institutionalized persons lived with their spouse, whereas about 29.3% (11.3 million) of all non-institutionalized older persons (including 8.1 million women and 3.2 million men) lived alone (Administration on Aging, 2011). Significantly, Johnson and Wiener (2006) noted that 61% of frail older adults who did not live in nursing homes received help with basic personal activities or with household chores from paid and unpaid caregivers.

Johnson et al. (2007) noted that much of the long-term care received by the frail elderly is provided informally by family members, with adult daughters often assuming primary responsibility for parental care (p. 6). Of concern, the availability of family caregivers may decline over time because of rising divorce rates (Teachman, Tedrow, & Crowder, 2000), increasing childlessness (Bachu, 1999), declining family sizes (Bachu & O'Connell, 2001), and the rising labor force participation of women (Blau, 1998). The fact that the frail older population is growing faster than the younger population will in itself further reduce the availability of needed caregivers. It is estimated that, by 2040, there will be only nine adults between 25 and 64 years of age to support each frail older adult, down from 15 younger adults in 2000 (Johnson et al., 2007).

If family members are unavailable or unable to provide informal care in the coming years, many older adults may have to resort to paid services, either formal home care or some alternative living arrangement that offers needed services. Shrestha (2006) identified "one consequence of lengthening life expectancies is that the older population's needs for care—assistance with daily tasks to allow continued community-living for high-functioning seniors, institutions for those with more severe disabilities or cognitive impairments, train-ing of a specialized work force in geriatric care—are likely to increase, particularly for the oldest-old" (p. 2). To put a number on that demand, Johnson et al. (2007) projected that "rapid population growth will substantially boost the number of older people using paid long-term care services" to the extent that "the number receiving paid home care will more than double between 2000 and 2040, increasing from 2.2 million to 5.3 million" (p. v). At the same time, some estimates have suggested that the number of elderly requiring nursing home care will triple between 1990 and 2030 (Zedlewski & McBride, 1992).

THE OPPORTUNITY FOR SOCIAL WORK PRACTICE

In their *"Blueprint for the New Millennium,"* the Council on Social Work Education (CSWE) (2001) projected that

> As a result of the demographic changes (in the United States), there will be a greater need for social workers to use their skills to enhance the quality of life for older adults and their families and to assist them in navigating ever-changing and increasingly complex health, mental health, social service and community

environments. Social work offers a comprehensive approach to meeting an individual's physical, emotional, spiritual and social needs, and this perspective will be essential in providing services to older Americans and their families. (p. V)

CSWE is far from alone in its projections of a burgeoning need for social workers specializing in gerontological practice and its identification of the current insufficiency of such social workers who are prepared to meet even a portion of present demand. The National Institute on Aging (NIA) predicted that, by 2020, 60,000 to 70,000 social workers would be needed to provide services to the elderly. Notwithstanding social work having a historically prominent role in long-term care (Brody, 1974; Silverstone & Burack-Weiss, 1983), NIA prophesized that "it seems unlikely that the supply of formally prepared social workers will keep pace with anticipated growth in positions" (NIA, 1987).

Driven by the expanding senior population and its increasing use of home health services, residential care, and hospices, it has been estimated that growth in these industries will positively affect social work employment as well as other occupations (USBLS, 2003–2004), particularly nursing and social and human service assistants (U.S. DHHS, 2006). As shown in *Figure 11.3*, the number of professional social workers employed in long-term care settings was projected by the USBLS in the Occupational Employment Matrix (OEM)

Figure 11.3 Projections of the Number of Professional Social Workers in Long-Term Care

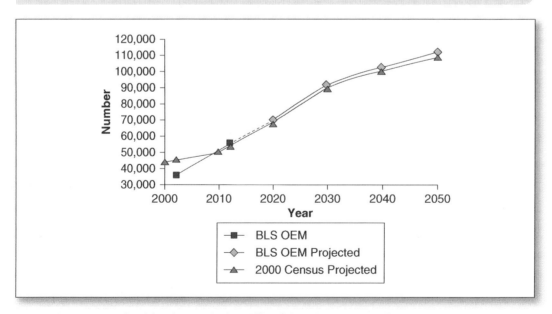

Source: U.S. Department of Health and Human Services, Office of the Assistant Secretary for Planning and Evaluation (2006). *The supply and demand of professional social workers providing long-term care services: Report to Congress.* Retrieved from http://aspe.hhs.gov/daltcp/reports/2006/Swsupply.htm#future

to increase from approximately 36,000 in 2002 to 55,000 in 2012. Significantly, by 2050, an estimated 110,000 social workers will be needed in long-term care services.

Comparison of social work education statistics, however, puts the USBLS projections into startling perspective. A 2000 report from the National Center for Education Studies (NCES) revealed that a total of 16,000 new MSWs and 15,000 new BSWs graduated from social work education programs that year, with the number of graduating BSWs increasing by about 50% between 1995 and 2000 and with the number of graduating MSWs increasing by about 25% during the same period (National Association of Social Workers [NASW], 2006). Consistent with the earlier NIA predictions (1987), however, Dawson and Santos (2000), in a major study of funding for the education and training of geriatric-care personnel, concluded that "there (were) national shortages of geriatric-care personnel in the medical, mental health, and social service professions who (were) prepared to provide effective services for the nation's older population" (p. 1). At the same time, Scharlach, Damron-Rodriguez, Robinson, and Feldman, (2000) found that the majority of both BSW and MSW educational programs offered students little direct or infused gerontology content. Not surprisingly, but certainly a parallel concern, Kane (1999) found limited interest among sampled BSW/MSW students in working with older adults experiencing dementia. Her study revealed that only 2.9% of students identified a desire to work in that area of practice.

Concern over insufficient student interest, enrollment, and professional preparation in gerontological practice is not new. A 1990 survey of members of the NASW found that 62% of respondents, regardless of specialty, indicated that they needed aging knowledge (Peterson & Wendt, 1990). In 1997, Damron-Rodriguez and Lubben warned that there were too few programs providing gerontology curriculum at the bachelor's (BSW) level or specialization at the master's (MSW) level. Their conclusion was consistent with the findings of a study by Damon-Rodriguez, Villa, Tseng, and Lubben (1996) in which 75% of social work schools reported that they had no gerontological field faculty and an earlier report by Lubben, Damron-Rodriguez, and Beck (1992) in which 80% of BSW programs reported offering no coursework on aging. The following year, investigation by Klein (1998) disclosed that only 5% of graduating MSW students had taken a course in gerontological social work. Still a unresolved concern, only 34% of MSW programs offered a concentration in Aging/Gerontology in 2013 and only 1,245 (4.8%) of 25,759 MSW candidates identified their field of practice as aging or gerontology (CSWE, 2013).

Concerted action by professional bodies such as CSWE, NASW, National Society for Social Work Leadership in Health Care, American Society on Aging, Association for Gerontology Education in Social Work, Gerontological Society of America, and myriad national, state, and local service providers affords the best prospect of addressing this pervasive issue. More vigorous education/marketing regarding the expanding needs of an aging population and burgeoning social work practice opportunities must be combined with additional faculty recruitment, expanded MSW/BSW aging curricula, increased availability of specialized aging training grants and demonstration projects, non-traditional public and private sector internships, practice-based research and ongoing practitioner training programs (CSWE, 2001; DHHS, 1987). Underlying all such effort must be a clear message that social work represents a proven value-added factor that is capable of impacting both individual and family quality-of-life issues as well as the ability of society to effectively, efficiently, and economically provide for the needs of the most rapidly growing sector of the U.S. population.

GERONTOLOGICAL SOCIAL WORK FUNCTIONS

Engagement of professional social work personnel with aging populations can occur in a wide range of contexts, require diverse technical skills, and potentially overlap with other disciplines' contributions (Spitzer, Neuman, & Holden, 2004, p. 33). The Hartford Foundation has engaged in a partnership with the CSWE to better prepare social workers for working with the elderly. The gerontological practice competencies identified by this partnership are found at the end of this chapter. NASW promotes the social work profession as uniquely qualified to serve older patients, families, and groups by performing these functions:

- Interdisciplinary and interagency collaboration
- Support before, during, and after transitions of care
- Expertise in navigating the continuum of care
- Enhancement of medication and treatment adherence
- Prevention, assessment, and treatment of elder abuse
- Advance care planning
- Advocacy
- Mediation and crisis intervention
- Case management and care coordination
- Counseling and psychotherapy
- Support and protection of client self-determination
- Culturally competent, strengths-based practice
- Client-centered assessment and intervention
- Program development, implementation, and evaluation

Source: National Association of Social Workers (2008). *Social work in long-term care and aging: Decreased health care costs, increased quality of life.* Washington, DC: NASW. Retrieved from http://socialworkers.org/practice/aging/2008/swLTChandout0808.pdf

The U.S. Department of Health and Human Services (1987) identifies the broad context for social work performing those functions as including

- Homemaking and home health programs
- Day programs
- Family service associations
- Community mental health centers

- Senior centers

- Respite programs

- Hospice programs

- Care management activities

- Information and referral programs

- Advocacy and legal service programs

- Protective social services

- Nutrition programs

- Nursing homes and homes for the aged

- Acute care and mental hospitals

- Discharge-planning activities

- Area Agencies on Aging

- State and local surveillance and licensure programs.

Source: U.S. Department of Health and Human Services (DHHS)(September 1987). *September 1987 Report to Congress: Personnel for Health Care Needs of the Elderly Through Year 2020.* Chapter III: Estimates of personnel and training needs. Washington, DC: DHHS.

INTERVENTION WITH AN AGING POPULATION

While the context may vary, there are recurring themes that underpin practice with aging populations. Getzel and Mellor (1983) perceive gerontological social work practice as inextricably tied to interdisciplinary collaboration (p. 2). The United States Department of Labor (2013) defined health care social work as "providing individuals, families, and groups with the psychosocial support needed to cope with chronic, acute, or terminal illnesses. Services include advising family care givers, providing patient education and counseling, and making referrals for other services. (Social workers) may also provide care and case management or interventions designed to promote health, prevent disease, and address barriers to access to healthcare."

In addition to acute care (inpatient) and outpatient clinic settings, the social work roles specified are consistent with those regarded as most relevant for addressing the needs of residents in nursing homes (Brown, 1999), home health (Dziegielewski, 1998) and assisted living communities (Spitzer et al., 2004; Spitzer & Neuman, 2003). Butler (2002) and Williams (2002) noted that the principles of resident independence, dignity, individuality, privacy, and choice that are the basis of the assisted-living milieu readily lend themselves to the integration of social work as they are congruent to the profession's values and practice.

To intervene with aging clients, one has to work on a premise about aging itself. Aging can be viewed as a continuous process whose cumulative effects are manifested at a later stage in the life cycle (Lowy, 1979, p. 2). If, like Erikson (1963), one perceives life to be one of developmental stages that include infancy, childhood, youth, middle age, and old age, then being old is a normal phenomenon. But, as Kropf and Hutchison (2000) pointed out, "people bring into their later years a wealth of experiences, varying health conditions and differing attitudes, behavior and levels of functioning that are different between people of similar ages" (p. 3). **Ageism** has been defined as bias against elder adults because of their age. In our Western culture, the elderly are not venerated and stereotypes persist about elderly people being unintelligent, difficult, asexual, unemployable, and unattractive (Varcarolis & Halter, 2010). Among social workers, many initially indicated a lack of desire to work with the elderly because of pre-existing attitudes, only to subsequently learn the rewarding and enriching benefits of gerontological social work.

In addition to the innumerable lifestyle patterns among the elderly, there are also great variations in their ability to function. These variations effectively determine where an individual resides on an aging continuum that potentially extends from having good health and spirits through contending with severely debilitating physical and mental conditions such as Alzheimer's disease. The practitioner can expect the prospect of having to address myriad complex issues—issues that have prevailed over the course of a lifetime or that have arisen more recently as inevitable outcomes of the aging process. Intervention may be complicated further by older adults' inability to recognize or reluctance to report problems that they experience (AGS, 2005b).

To effectively intervene with this population, social workers must be aware of their clients' positions on the aging continuum, including the unique expressions and experiences of aging as influenced by variables such as ethnicity, religion, culture, race, and socioeconomic status. Of equal importance, social workers must be cognizant of their own attitudes, beliefs, stereotypes, and prejudices as they affect their personal adjustment to aging and ultimately death. Lowy (1979) reminded us that any intervention that is put forth must be carried out with a fundamental sensitivity toward the central values of human worth and dignity, the uniqueness of the individual, and the client's self-determination (pp. 4, 53–60).

Just as the aging population's needs can be regarded as being on a continuum, Kropf and Hutchison (2000) have conceptualized *levels of intervention* by healthcare social workers to aging patients and their families. *Primary interventions* focus on preventing problems from occurring and are exemplified in health and wellness programs as well as targeted efforts to intervene with specific problems like alcoholism (p. 4). *Secondary interventions* begin with the onset of physical and/or social problems and attempt to contain any resulting functional impairments. Efforts focus on preventing temporary health conditions from escalating into chronic problems. Educational programs may aid patients in either self-care efforts and/or maintaining appropriate professional treatment. Counseling as a secondary intervention to patients with depression may serve to reduce the prospects that the individual will engage in substance abuse or other adverse behaviors as means to alleviate stress, loneliness, or anger at life circumstances. *Tertiary interventions* are employed with older patients and their caregivers when the patient experiences more profound functional impairments and support is needed for ongoing care. Examples of these interventions include supportive groups for caregivers and the use of resident councils or involvement in social activities by patients placed in settings such as assisted-living communities or nursing homes. The latter efforts are intended to assist cognition, motivation, reality orientation, and motor skills by actively engaging the resident in social participation, decision making, and creative expression.

Specialized assessment skills and approaches are critical in gerontological social work. The geriatric assessment serves as "the threshold between clients and needed services" and is one of the primary tools used by practitioners in the field of gerontology to make services for older people responsible, appropriate, and effective (Geron, 2006, p. 722). Various standardized instruments are available for clinicians to use in geriatric assessment (see Kane & Kane, 2000). A comprehensive geriatric assessment should consider the following dimensions:

- Physiological and health status, including healthcare utilization patterns, use of adaptive devices, and nutritional status

- Functional abilities

- Cognitive functioning and sensory deficits

- Emotions and mental well-being

- Social functioning

- Religiousness and spirituality

- Quality of life

- Overall satisfaction

- Personality styles and traits

- Family caregiving capacity and limits

It is essential to evaluate the whole person within the context of his or her social and physical environment. To build rapport with the elderly client, social workers should position themselves in front of the client to compensate for any visual field deficits; should speak slowly, clearly, and with the appropriate volume required; and should minimize distractions and monitor for fatigue.

One important assessment for social workers serving this population is to distinguish cognitive deficits that may be the result of delirium, depression, or dementia. **Delirium** is characterized by a disturbance in attention and a change in cognition (including memory deficits and disorientation) that develops over a short period of time" (APA, 2013, p. 596). It is common in hospitalized patients, particularly the elderly. Delirium can be present in 11% to 42% of the generalized hospitalized population, but may be as high as 60% for hospitalized seniors. Delirium occurs in conjunction with another physiological disorder and is transient. There are four common features to delirium: sudden onset and fluctuating course, inattention and inability to focus, disorganized thinking, and disturbances in consciousness (Varcarolis & Halter, 2010). Major conditions commonly associated with delirium include postoperative recovery; drug intoxication and withdrawal; inappropriate or over-medication; metabolic disorders such as dehydration and electrolyte imbalance;

neurological diseases such as head trauma and tumor; and severe psychosocial stress, particularly in the frail elderly. Because acute delirium will resolve, distinguishing it from other more permanent conditions affecting cognition is critical in order to provide necessary care to the elder and, in particular, to avoid decisions such as nursing home placement, which would confound the disorder.

Dementia is a loss of brain function that occurs with certain diseases. It affects memory, thinking, language, judgment, and behavior (National Institutes of Health, 2013). Alzheimer's disease is regarded as perhaps the most common form of dementia in the elderly (CDC, 2013). **Alzheimer's disease** is a progressive brain disease characterized by decreases in memory and cognitive functioning and is the most common reason for nursing home placement *(Table 11.2)*. By age 85 years and older, between 25% and 50% of people will exhibit signs of Alzheimer's disease. Up to 5.3 million Americans currently have Alzheimer's disease (Hebert, Scherr, Bienias, Bennett, & Evans. 2003). Although there is an early-onset form of the disorder, the incidence of Alzheimer's disease increases with age (Sadock & Sadock, 2008):

- At 65 years, the incidence is less than 1%.

- At 85 years, the incidence is between 11 and 14%.

- At 90 years, the incidence is between 21 and 25%.

- At 95 years and older, the incidence reaches 31% to 36%.

Table 11.2 denotes the four stages in the progression of Alzheimer's disease.

The second most common cause of dementia is vascular in nature, with decreased cerebrovascular flow resulting in decreased oxygen to the brain, impairing cognitive functioning. Vascular dementias account for approximately 15% to 30% of all dementias. Other conditions that can cause dementia include Parkinson's disease and alcoholism (Sadock & Sadock, 2008).

Screening for dementia in elderly patients can be conducted with use of an assessment tool called the Mental Status Exam (Folstein, Folstein, & McHugh, 1975). There are two versions used in practice, including a full version and the Mini Mental Status Exam. Full versions of the exam are easily obtained on the Internet, but most are administered and scored by psychiatrists or psychologists. Social workers and nurses typically use a modified version of the Mini Mental Status Exam to determine a patient's general orientation in the three "spheres" of orientation: person, place, and time. Patients are asked who they are, where they are, and the time of day, month, or year. If the patient is disoriented to time and place, clues may be offered in an effort to prompt recall; for example, patients may be asked if they know if it is morning or evening or if they know where they are (i.e., their own home, the name of the nursing home in which they reside, relative's home, etc.). Screening for orientation in the frail elderly is an important precursor before proceeding on to more specific assessment procedures.

When an individual is severely disoriented and/or in the moderate to advanced stages of Alzheimer's disease, social workers may be involved in procedures to determine if the patient is incompetent. Incompetency is a legal term that means that the individual lacks

Table 11.2   Stages of Alzheimer's Disease

Stage	Severity	Symptoms
Stage 1	Mild forgetfulness	• Short-term memory loss • Awareness of forgetfulness • Ability to compensate or cover • Depression may be common, which worsens symptoms • May be difficulty diagnosing
Stage 2	Moderate confusion	• Progressive memory loss • Social withdrawal • Declines in functioning • Difficulty functioning out of familiar environment • Depression, denial, and feeling frightened are typical • Commonly needs assistance or in-home care
Stage 3	Moderate to severe ambulatory dementia	• Further decline in activities of daily living • Personal hygiene and grooming effected • Frustration and agitation common • Difficulty communicating • May need institutional care
Stage 4	Late end stage	• Family recognition disappears • Non-ambulatory, no purposeful activity • Forgets to eat, swallow • Incontinent • Requires institutional care

Source: Hall, G.R. (1994). Caring for people with Alzheimer's disease using the conceptual model of progressively lowered stress threshold in the clinical setting. *Nursing Clinics of North America, 29*(1), 129–141.

the capacity to make personal decisions. Typically, a psychiatrist or a neuropsychologist will do a **competency** evaluation and make a clinical determination. If the individual has identified a patient advocate for healthcare, medical decisions can be made by that individual. If there is no patient advocate, it may be necessary to petition the court for a **legal guardian**. A legal guardian has the authority to make decisions regarding the patient's care and treatment, including signing the individual into a care facility. However, the legal guardian does not have the authority to handle financial affairs and a **conservator** must be appointed. Each state has different procedures, but all typically involve filing a legal petition for a guardian and/or conservator.

Reminiscence therapy is a common treatment approach for dementia that is used by gerontological social workers. This type of therapy involves recalling and communicating memories of past experiences and important life events. Reminiscence therapy can be done with an individual or in groups. The primary purpose of the intervention is to stimulate memory in order to make connections with the past and possibly provide an opportunity for conscious or unconscious resolution of unresolved grief or other issues. *Simple reminiscence* involves the pleasant recollection of past memories for the purposes of enjoyment. *Evaluative reminiscence* is more in-depth and may be used as part of a process of life review. Occasionally, unpleasant and stressful information is recalled, a type of reminiscence referred to as *offensive-defensive reminiscence*. This type of reminiscence can be the cause or result of behavioral or emotional issues, and dealing with these issues can provide an opportunity for resolution. The therapist provides a structured activity and then guides the process, often using visual aids such as pictures, auditory stimulation such as music, and tactile stimulation such as touching familiar objects (Jones, 1997). Other interventions in dementia care are evolving, including modifying the environment to offer smoothing and calming activities such as lighting effects as alternatives to psychotropic medication for the agitated patient (Avalon, Gum, Feliciano, & Arean, 2006). Medications such as Aricept that can help slow cognitive decline and stabilize mood and behavior are also routinely used in the management of dementia patients.

Geriatric depression is widespread, affecting at least one of six patients treated in general medical practice and an even higher percentage in hospitals and nursing homes (Reynolds & Kupfer, 1999). Although most of these individuals will have experienced depression at other points in their lives, initial onset late in life is not uncommon. Depression in the elderly is correlated with dependency, chronic illness, and loss of functioning and is exacerbated with grief over the loss of a loved one. Untreated depression in the elderly increases the risk of physical and mental decline and can be fatal. The highest rate of suicide in the U.S. is among elderly white males (National Alliance on Mental Illness, 2009). Tragically, most of these individuals saw a physician within a month before committing suicide, suggesting that the depression was undiagnosed and untreated. Typical symptoms of depression in the elderly include lethargy, fatigue, sleep and appetite disturbances, flat or irritable affect, and even paranoid ideation (Varcarolis & Halter, 2010). Depression in the elderly, however, can appear differently than that in younger populations and can be associated with memory problems and confusion. Furthermore, the elderly may *somatize* the symptoms, experiencing physical rather than emotional symptoms. Treatment with antidepressant medications can be effective in up to 80% of elderly patients with depression; however, clinicians need to be careful to assess for adverse drug interactions with other concurrently prescribed medications. Patient forgetfulness in taking medication can further complicate treatment.

Social workers can help identify patients who are depressed or at risk of depression through careful assessment or by commonly used depression screening tools. Two common depression screening tools used in healthcare are the Beck Depression Inventory (available through Pearson) and the Patient Health Questionnaire 9 (PHQ-9, available through Pfizer). The Geriatric Depression Scale (see *Table 11.3*) is publically available as its development was funded in part through federal grants and has proven a useful tool for social workers (Adams, 2011; Yesavage, Brink, Rose, & Leirer, 1983 as cited by Corcoran & Fischer, 2013, pp. 329–330).

Table 11.3   Geriatric Depression Scale

Question	Answer	Score* *(points)*
1. Are you basically satisfied with life?	No	1
2. Have you dropped many of your activities and interests?	Yes	1
3. Do you feel that your life is empty?	Yes	1
4. Do you often get bored?	Yes	1
5. Are you hopeful about the future?	No	1
6. Are you bothered by thoughts you can't get out of your head?	Yes	1
7. Are you in good spirits most of the time?	No	1
8. Are you afraid that something bad is going to happen to you?	Yes	1
9. Do you feel happy most of the time?	No	1
10. Do you often feel helpless?	Yes	1
11. Do you often get restless and fidgety?	Yes	1
12. Do you prefer to stay at home, rather than going out and doing new things?	Yes	1
13. Do you frequently worry about the future?	Yes	1
14. Do you feel you have more problems with memory than most?	Yes	1
15. Do you think it is wonderful to be alive now?	No	1
16. Do you often feel downhearted and blue?	Yes	1
17. Do you feel pretty worthless the way you are now?	Yes	1
18. Do you worry a lot about the past?	Yes	1
19. Do you find life very exciting?	No	1
20. Is it hard for you to get started on new projects?	Yes	1
21. Do you feel full of energy?	No	1
22. Do you feel that your situation is hopeless?	Yes	1
23. Do you think that most people are better off than you are?	Yes	1
24. Do you frequently get upset over little things?	Yes	1
25. Do you frequently feel like crying?	Yes	1
26. Do you have trouble concentrating?	Yes	1
27. Do you enjoy getting up in the morning?	No	1
28. Do you prefer to avoid social gatherings?	Yes	1
29. Is it easy for you to make decisions?	No	1
30. Is your mind as clear as it used to be?	No	1

*The total score is classified as normal (0 to 9), mild depression, (10 to 19), or severe depression (20 to 30).

Source: Adapted from: Yesavage, J.A., Brink, T.L., Rose, T.L., & Leirer, V.O. (1983). Development and validation of a geriatric depression screening scale: A preliminary report. *Journal of Psychiatric Research, 17*, 37-39 Corcoran, K., & Fischer, J. (2013). *Measures for Clinical Practice and Research: A sourcebook. (Vol. 1).* (5th ed.). New York: Oxford University Press.

CASE STUDY

Dementia Patient Assessment/Intervention

Mrs. Ryan is a 91-year-old, small, frail woman who recently lost her husband of 65 years. She lives alone in a senior citizen apartment. You are a privately hired case manager/social worker hired by the family to visit her weekly in her home and coordinate her care and home services. You have arranged for a companion/housekeeper for four hours daily in the morning who assists with meals, housecleaning, and personal care.

Mrs. Ryan has always been alert; is oriented in all three spheres (person, place, and time); is able to communicate and to solve problems; and is wise and reflective about her situation. She misses her husband but reflects that they "had a wonderful life together." Last week, she went to her doctor and received a good report, although he did adjust her medication schedule.

In the morning, you receive a frantic phone call from the housekeeper that Mrs. Ryan is very confused, hallucinating, and complete disoriented. You instruct the housekeeper to call 911 and transport her to the hospital, where you meet her. After an initial workup in the emergency room that rules out a stroke or head injury, Mrs. Ryan is admitted to the hospital. She has calmed down some, but is still very confused.

You talk over her care with the intern, who is convinced that Mrs. Ryan has dementia and that she probably had been covering up her cognitive problems at home. "She is," he says, "91 years old." He advises you that she will probably need a nursing home when discharged from the hospital.

Questions:

1. Do you think Mrs. Ryan has dementia?

2. Why or why not?

3. What information would you share with the intern to help him understand the patient?

4. What questions would you ask of the physicians in order to ensure that everything is explored?

Assessing for *elder abuse and neglect* is a critical function of gerontological social workers. In 2003, between 1 and 2 million Americans 65 years of age and older had been injured, exploited, or mistreated by a caregiver or family member (National Center on Elder Abuse, 2005). It has been estimated that 2% to 10% of elders experience some form of abuse in their lifetime (Lachs & Pillemer, 2004) although fewer than 1 in 14 incidents are actually reported to the authorities (Pillemer & Finkelhor, 1988). Financial exploitation is also a serious concern for the elderly, and it has been estimated that there may be as many as 5 million financial abuse victims each year (Wasik, 2000). Elder abuse occurs in home and institutional settings, but the National Incidence Study found that the most common abuser was an adult child (47%) or spouse (17%) (National Center on Elder Abuse, 2005).

Interviews of elders should be conducted privately and with direct questions about whether the elder had been hit, pushed, kicked, slapped, or inappropriately touched. Questions about elders' access to their funds and whether they are fed, clothed, and bathed adequately should also be asked. Beginning with an open-ended question such as "How are you being treated at home?" can open up a discussion on these concerns (Spangler & Brandl, 2007). Although it is critical to report suspicion of elder abuse, social workers must be sensitive that elders harbor fears about reporting caregivers as it may ultimate result in criminal proceedings and displacement of the elder.

CASE STUDY

Patient Abuse/Neglect Intervention

Mr. Smith is a 76-year-old veteran who lives on a VA pension of $1,100 a month and a Social Security benefit of $646 per month. He is alert and oriented but is somewhat frail. Because of long-term smoking and alcohol abuse, he is weak and has difficulty breathing during exertion. He has no family.

Mr. Smith worked primarily as a horse groomer and trainer. Up until last year, he was still working for the couple who own the horse ranch, where he currently lives Mr. Smith lives in the barn with the horses. He has a bed in a stall and a small dresser. The barn has a bathroom (but no shower) and running water. Mr. Smith tries to do chores around the farm, but this is growing increasingly difficult. The owners of the farm bring him leftovers from their family meals, take him to his doctor appointments, and make sure that his prescriptions are filled.

The owners of the farm present themselves as very devoted to Mr Smith. They say that he can stay on the farm as long as he likes and, in return for his room and board, they take all of his money. They have already petitioned to become his legal guardian and conservator.

Mr. Smith tells you that these people are his only friends, and although they yell at him and ridicule him at times, he has no one else. He says he has not ever been physically abused by the couple, but they do threaten to place him in a nursing home if he "can't get along." He says he doesn't mind living in the barn as he considers horses better than people. Mr. Smith is adamant that his situation not be reported to Adult Protective Services as he is certain this will result in nursing home placement. He does wish that the couple would at least give him a few dollars now and then, but they refuse, saying that they need it for his care and that he would only buy booze with it.

Questions:

1. Is Mr. Smith being subjected to abuse or neglect? If so, what kind?

2. How would you counsel Mr. Smith? How would you talk with the owners of the farm?

3. Would you report this situation? How would you make a report?

4. What are the ethical considerations and dilemmas in this case?

5. What alternatives and resources might be available to Mr. Smith?

SOCIAL WORK POLICY PRACTICE WITH AN AGING POPULATION

Beyond direct intervention designed to optimize individual patient/family outcomes, the continuing growth and compelling needs of the aging population make it crucial that the profession contribute to innovative program leadership and advocating, formulating, legislating, and administering policies that address the issues of growing older. Mickelson (1995) defined **cause advocacy** as arising when problems result from conditions beyond the client's ability to change or influence them as an individual. Such advocacy on the profession's part reflects social work's fundamental commitment to the person-in-environment perspective by attempting to modify those issues negatively impacting groups of people. In the instance of the aging population, Sheridan and Kisor (2000) identified examples of issues of importance to social workers in gerontological practice as including

- Healthcare and quality of life

- Housing, transportation, and other resources

- Attitudes toward aging and elder abuse

- Changing family structures

- Work and caregiver arrangements

- Special population (e.g., minority, disabled; Alzheimer's disease) needs

- Mental health, substance abuse, and suicide issues

- Long-term care (availability/sufficiency)

- Retirement and leisure planning concerns

Because of the far-reaching social significance of issues related to the aging population, support for gerontological social work research comes from many federal agencies, including several institutes at the National Institutes of Health (NIH), the Centers for Disease Control and Prevention (CDC), the Agency for Healthcare Research and Quality (AHRQ), the Centers for Medicare and Medicaid Services (CMS), the Administration on Aging (AoA), the Department of Veteran's Affairs (VA), and the Department of Housing and Urban Development (HUD) (Social Work Policy Institute, 2010).

Schneider and Lester (2001) underscore the importance of social work activism in legislative and administrative advocacy. The prospects for social work success in legislative advocacy are thought to be enhanced by the evolution of the "new Federalism," which affords states greater authority over benefits, rules, and priorities of clients (Schneider & Netting, 1999). Unprecedented opportunities lie ahead for the profession to engage on behalf of this rapidly expanding and influential voting constituency and its unique age-related needs.

SUMMARY

Driven by declining fertility and birth rates plus increasing longevity, the "graying of America" and its projected doubling of those 65 years of age and older by 2050 represents one of the most significant demographic trends experienced in the United States. The anticipated prevalence of chronic conditions and disabilities of an aging population, coupled with a predicted decline in availability of capable family caretakers and potentially insufficient numbers of healthcare professionals and care alternatives pose looming social concerns of historic proportions. The health and social service needs of the aging population will overtax the capacity of the service delivery system unless changes are introduced.

Over thirty years ago, Carol Meyer (1975) remarked that the field of aging contains in microcosm all of the elements found in the field of social work at large. Ample evidence exists of social work leadership in healthcare (Laurie & Rosenberg, 1995; Rosenberg & Weissman, 1995; Spitzer, 2004). The challenge for the profession, however, is to act on the 2001 CSWE proposition that "all social workers…have basic competence in aging" (CSWE, 2001, p. V) while responding to the BLS-projected demand for 109,000 social workers specialized in gerontological practice by 2050 (U.S. DHHS, 2006).

KEY TERMS AND CONCEPTS

- Infant mortality rate
- Crude mortality rate
- Life expectancy
- Ageism
- Activities of daily living (ADLs)
- Long-term care
- Germ theory of disease
- Chronic diseases
- Levels of intervention
- Cause advocacy
- Dementia, depression, and delirium
- Alzheimer's disease
- Competency
- Legal guardian and conservator
- Reminiscence therapy

QUESTIONS FOR DISCUSSION

1. What is the "graying of America"? Why are we experiencing this phenomenon?

2. What are the predominant health concerns of the aging population cohort?

3. What are the principal concerns regarding future care of those 65 years of age and older?

4. How do you perceive social work can impact on the issues associated with the "graying of America"?

5. What needs to be done to "ramp up" the social work profession's ability to prepare more future social workers with an interest and competence in gerontological practice?

EXERCISES

1. Go to your state government website and locate the forms and instructions for petitioning for a legal guardian or conservator. Where would you file these forms in your community?

2. How would you report a case of suspected elder abuse in your community? Go to your state and/or county website and locate the procedures for making a report. Where do you call? What forms need to be completed and where should they be sent?

3. Go to the website for "Out of the Shadows," an online course offered by SAMHSA (Substance Abuse Mental Health Service Association) on preventing, identifying, and intervening in cases of elder abuse. Review the statistics and identify those seniors who are most at risk of abuse and neglect.

4. Go to the Hartford Foundation's Partnership of Aging Education website and complete the Geriatric Social Work Competencies Scale to determine areas for your further growth and learning in order to work with this population. http://www.hartfordpartnership.org/index.php?/geriatric_competencies

5. As a class activity, rent the film "Elder Abuse: Five Cases" available from Fanlight Productions (http://www.fanlight.com/catalog/films/101_ea.php) and discuss the cases.

HARTFORD FOUNDATION GERIATRIC SOCIAL WORK COMPETENCIES

I. Values, Ethics, and Theoretical Perspectives

1. Assess and address values and biases regarding aging.

2. Respect and promote older adult clients' right to dignity and self-determination.

3. Apply ethical principles to decisions on behalf of all older clients with special attention to those with limited decisional capacity.

4. Respect diversity among older adult clients, families, and professionals (e.g., class, gender, and sexual orientation).

5. Address the cultural, spiritual, and ethnic values and beliefs of older adults and families.

6. Relate concepts and theories of aging to social work practice (e.g., cohorts, normal aging, life course perspective).

7. Relate social work perspectives and related theories to practice with older adults (e.g., person-in environment, social justice).

8. Identify issues related to changes, transitions, and losses over the life cycle in designing interventions.

9. Support persons and families dealing with end of life issues related to dying, death, and bereavement.

10. Understand the perspective and values of social work in geriatric interdisciplinary practice while respecting the roles of other disciplines.

II. Assessment

1. Use empathy and sensitive interviewing skills to engage older clients in identifying their strengths and problems.

2. Adapt interviewing methods to potential sensory, language, and cognitive limitations of the older adult.

3. Conduct a comprehensive geriatric assessment (biopsychosocial evaluation).

4. Ascertain health status and assess physical functioning (e.g., ADLs and IADLs) of older clients.

5. Assess cognitive functioning and mental health status of older clients (e.g., depression, dementia).

6. Assess social functioning (e.g., social skills, social activity level) and social support of older clients.

7. Assess caregivers' needs and level of stress.

8. Administer and interpret standardized assessment and diagnostic tools that are appropriate for use with older adults (e.g., depression scale, Mini-Mental Status Exam).

9. Develop clear, timely, and appropriate service plans with measurable objectives for older adults.

10. Re-evaluate and adjust service plans for older adults on a continuing basis.

III. Intervention

1. Establish rapport and maintain an effective working relationship with older adults and family members.

2. Enhance the coping capacities and mental health of older persons through a variety of therapy modalities (e.g., supportive, psychodynamic, etc.).

3. Utilize group interventions with older adults and their families (e.g., bereavement groups, reminiscence groups).

4. Mediate situations with angry or hostile older adults and/or family members.

5. Assist caregivers to reduce their stress levels and maintain their own mental and physical health. Provide social work case management to link elders and their families to resources and services.

6. Use educational strategies to provide older persons and their families with information related to wellness and disease management (e.g., Alzheimer's disease, end-of-life care).

7. Apply skills in termination in work with older clients and their families.

8. Advocate on behalf of clients with agencies and other professionals to help elderly clients obtain quality services.

9. Adhere to laws and public policies related to older adults (e.g., elder abuse reporting, legal guardianship, advance directives).

IV. Aging Services, Programs, and Policies

1. Outreach to older adults and their families to ensure appropriate use of the service continuum (e.g., health promotion, long-term care, mental health).

2. Adapt organizational policy, procedures, and resources to facilitate the provision of services to diverse older adults and their family caregivers.

3. Identify and develop strategies to address service gaps, fragmentation, discrimination, and barriers that impact older persons.

4. Include older adults in planning and designing programs.

5. Develop program budgets that take into account diverse sources of financial support for the older population.

6. Evaluate the effectiveness of practice and programs in achieving intended outcomes for older adults.

7. Apply evaluation and research findings to improve practice and program outcomes.

8. Advocate and organize with the service providers, community organizations, policymakers, and the public to promote the needs and issues of a growing aging population.

9. Identify the availability of resources and resource systems for older adults and their families.

10. Assess and address any negative impacts of social and healthcare policies on practice with historically disadvantaged populations.

REFERENCES

Adams, K. B. (2001). Depressive symptoms, depletion, or developmental change? Withdrawal, apathy, and lack of vigor in the Geriatric Depression Scale. *The Gerontologist, 41*(6), 768–777.

Administration on Aging. *A profile of older Americans: 2011*. Retrieved from http://www.aoa.gov/AoARoot/Aging_Statistics/Profile/2011/14.aspx http://www.aoa.gov/Aging_Statistics/Profile/2011/docs/2011profile.pdf

American Geriatrics Society (AGS). (2005a). *Substance abuse*. Retrieved from http://www.healthinaging.org/aging-and-health-a-to-z/topic:drug-and-substance-abuse/

American Geriatrics Society (AGS). (2005b). *Depression*. Retrieved from http://www.healthinaging.org/aging-and-health-a-to-z/topic:depression/

American Psychological Association (APA). (2013). Diagnostic and Statistical Manual of Mental Disorders (DSM-5). Washington, DC: American Psychiatric Publishing.

American Psychological Association (APA). (2012). *Elder abuse and neglect: In search of solutions*. Retrieved from http://www.apa.org/pi/aging/resources/guides/elder-abuse.aspx

Avalon, L., Gum, A. M., Feliciano, L., & Arean, P. Q. (2006). Effectiveness of nonpharmacological interventions for the management of neuropsychiatric symptoms in patients with dementia: A systematic review. *Archives of Internal Medicine, 166*, 2182–2188.

Bachu, A. (1999). Is childlessness among American women on the rise? *Population Division Working Paper No. 37*. Washington, DC: U.S. Census Bureau.

Bachu, A., & O'Connell, M. (2001). Fertility of American women: June 2000. *Current Population Reports*. Washington, DC: U.S. Census Bureau.

Banta, H., & Jonas, S. (1995). Health and health care. In *Jonas's health care delivery in the United States* (5th ed.). New York: Springer Publishing Company.

Berkman, L., & Breslow, L. (1983). *Health and ways of living: The Alemeda study*. New York: Oxford University Press.

Blau, F. (1998). Trends in the well-being of American women, 1970–1995. *Journal of Economic Literature, 36*(1), 112–165.

Brody, E. (1974). *A social work guide for long-term care facilities*. Rockville, MD: National Institute of Mental Health.

Brown, M. (1999). Psychosocial functions and training needs of social workers in nursing homes: A survey. *Continuum, 19*(1), 7–13.

Burnett, M. (1971). *Genes, dreams, and realities*. New York: Basic Books.

Butler, S. (2002). The case for assisted living. *Social Work Today*, 2, 5, 7, 21

Centers for Disease Control and Prevention. (October 2013). *Dementia/Alzheimer's Disease*. Retrieved from http://www.cdc.gov/mentalhealth/basics/mental-illness/dementia.htm

Centers for Disease Control and Prevention and National Association of Chronic Disease Directors (2008). *The state of mental health and aging in America. Issue brief 1: What do the data tell us?* Atlanta, GA: National Association of Chronic Disease Directors.

Centers for Disease Control and Prevention (CDC). (2006). *Understanding suicide*. Retrieved from http://www.cdc.gov/violenceprevention/pub/suicide_factsheet.html

Corcoran, K., & Fischer, J. (2013). *Measures for Clinical Practice and Research: A sourcebook. (Vol. 1).* (5th ed.). New York: Oxford University Press.

Council on Social Work Education. (2001). *Strengthening the impact of social work to improve the quality of life for older adults and their families: A blueprint for the new millennium.* Alexandria, VA: Author.

Council on Social Work Education. (2011). *2011 Statistics on Social Work Education in the United States.* [Internet]. Retrieved from: http://www.cswe.org/File.aspx?id = 62011

Council on Social Work Education. (2013). *2013 statistics on social work education in the United States.* Retrieved from: http://www.cswe.org/File.aspx?id = 74478

Damron-Rodriguez, J., & Lubben, J. (1997). The 1995 White House Conference on Aging: An agenda for social work education and training. In C. Saltz (Ed.), *Social work response to the 1995 White House Conference on Aging: From issues to actions* (pp. 65–77). New York: Haworth Press.

Damron-Rodriguez, J., Villa, V., Tseng, H., & Lubben, J. (1996). Demographic and organizational influences on the development of gerontological social work curriculum. *Gerontology & Geriatrics Education, 17,* 3–8.

Dawson, G. D., & Santos, J. F. (2000). *Combating failure: An investigation of funding for the education and training of geriatric-care personnel.* Notre Dame, IN: University of Notre Dame, Gerontology and Geriatrics Education Office.

Dziegielewski, S. (1998). *The changing face of health care social work.* New York: Springer Publishing Company.

Erikson, E. (1963). *Childhood and society.* New York: Norton.

Folstein, M. F., Folstein, S. E., & McHugh, P. R. (1975). Mini-mental state: A practical method for grading the cognitive state of patients for the clinician. *Journal of Psychiatric Research, 12*(3), 189–98.

Geron, S. M. (2006). Comprehensive and multidimensional geriatric assessment. In B. Berkman (Ed.), *Handbook of social work in health and aging* (pp. 721-727). New York: Oxford University Press.

Getzel, G., & Mellor, J. (1983). *Gerontological social work practice in long term care.* New York: Haworth Press.

Hebert, L., Scherr, P. A., Bienias, J. L., Bennett, D. A., & Evans, D. A. (2003). Alzheimer disease in the U.S. Population. *Arch Neurol.* 2003;60:1119-1122.

Howden, L., & Meyer, J. (May 2011). *Age and sex composition: 2010 Census Briefs.* Washington, DC: U.S. Census Bureau. Retrieved from http://www.census.gov/prod/cen2010/briefs/c2010br-03.pdf

Johnson, R., Toohey, D., & Wiener, J. (2007). Meeting the long-term care needs of the baby boomers: How changing families will affect paid helpers and institutions. *Urban Institute Retirement Project Series Discussion Paper 07-04.* Retrieved from http://www.urban.org/UploadedPDF/311451_Meeting_Care.pdf

Johnson, R., & Wiener, J. (2006). A profile of frail older Americans and their caregivers. *The Retirement Project Occasional Paper Number 8.* Washington, DC: The Urban Institute. Retrieved from http://www.urban.org/url.cfm?ID = 311284

Jones, G. M. M. (1997). *Caregiving in dementia: Research and applications* (Vol. 2). London: Routledge.

Kane, M. (1999). Factors affecting social work students' willingness to work with elderly with Alzheimer's disease. *Journal of Social Work Education, 35(1),* 71–85.

Kane, R. L., & Kane, R. A. (2000). *Assessing older persons.* New York: Oxford University Press.

Kemper, P., Komisar, H., & Alecxih, L. (2005/2006). Long-term care over an uncertain future: What can current retirees expect? *Inquiry, 42,* 335–350.

Klein, S. (1998). *A national agenda for geriatric education: White papers* (Vol. 1). Health Resources and Services Administration, Bureau of Health Professionals. Washington, DC: U.S. Government Printing Office.

Kropf, N., & Hutchison, E. (2000). Effective practice with elderly patients. In Schneider, R., Kropf, N., & Kisor, A. (Eds.). *Gerontological social work: Knowledge, service settings and special populations* (2nd ed.) (pp. 3–25). Belmont, CA: Brooks/Cole.

Lachs, M. S., & Pillemer, K. (2004, October). Elder abuse. *The Lancet, 364,* 1192–1263.

Laurie, A., & Rosenberg, G. (Eds.) (1984). *Social work administration in health care.* New York: The Haworth Press.

Lowy, L. (1979). *Social work with the aging: The challenge and promise of the later years.* New York: Harper & Row Publishers.

Lubben, J., Damron-Rodriguez, J., & Beck, J. (1992). A national survey of aging curriculum in schools of social work. In J. Mellor, & R. Solomon, (Eds.), *Geriatric social work education.* Binghamton, NY: Haworth Press.

McKeown, T. (1994). Determinants of health. In P. Lee, & C. Estes, (Eds.), *The nation's health.* Boston, MA: Jones and Bartlett Publishers.

Meyer, C. (Ed.) (1975). *Social work with the aging.* Washington, DC: NASW Press.

Mickelson, J. (1995). Advocacy. In *Encyclopedia of social work* (19th ed.) (pp. 95–100). Washington, DC: NASW Press.

National Alliance on Mental Illness. (2009). *Depression in older persons.* Retrieved from http://www .nami.org/Content/NavigationMenu/Mental_Illnesses/Depression/Depression_Older_Persons_ FactSheet_2009.pdf

National Association of Social Workers. (2006). *Assuring the sufficiency of a frontline workforce: A national study of licensed social workers.* Washington, DC: Author.

National Association of Social Workers. (2008). *Social work in long-term care and aging: Decreased health care costs, increased quality of life.* Retrieved from http://socialworkers.org/practice/ aging/2008/swLTChandout0808.pdf

National Center for Chronic Disease Prevention and Health Promotion (CDC). (1999). Chronic disease notes and reports: Special focus. *Healthy Aging, 12,* 3.

National Center on Elder Abuse. (2005). Elder abuse Prevalence and Incidence. Retrieved March 27, 2012 from: http://www.ncea.aoa.gov/ncearoot/Main_Site/Library/Statistics_Research/Abuse_ Statistics/Statistics_At_Glance.aspx/

National Center for Health Statistics. (December 2010). Births: Final data for 2008. *National Vital Statistics Reports (NVSR), 59,* 1.

National Center for Health Statistics (NCHS). (2005). Births: Final data for 2003. *National Vital Statistics Reports (NVSR), 54,* 2.

National Institute on Aging. (1987). *Personnel for health needs of the elderly through the year 2020.* Bethesda, MD: Department of Health and Human Services, Public Health Service.

National Institutes of Health (NIH). (2013). *Dementia.* Retrieved from: http://www.nlm.nih.gov/medlin-eplus/ency/article/000739.htm

Peterson, D., & Wendt, P. (1990). Employment in the field of aging: A survey of professionals in four fields. *The Gerontologist, 30,* 679–684.

Pillemer, K., & Finkelhor, D. (1988). The prevalence of elder abuse: A random sample survey. *The Gerontologist, 28,* 51–57.

Rosenberg, G., & Weissman, A. (1995). *Social work leadership in healthcare: Directors' perspectives.* New York: The Haworth Press.

Reynolds, C., & Kupfer, D. (1999). Depression and aging: A look to the future. *Psychiatric Service, 50* (9): 1167–1172.

Sadock, B. J., & Sadock, A. (2008). *Concise textbook of clinical psychiatry* (3rd ed.). Philadelphia, PA: Lippincott Williams & Williams.

Scharlach, A., Damron-Rodriguez, J., Robinson, B., & Feldman, R. (2000). Educating social workers for an aging society: A vision for the 21st century. *Journal of Social Work Education, 36*(3), 521–538.

Schneider, R., & Lester, L. (2001). *Social work advocacy: A new framework for action.* Pacific Grove, CA: Brooks/Cole.

Schneider, R. L., & Netting, F. E. (1999). Influencing social policy in a time of devolution: Upholding social work's great tradition. *Social Work, 44,* 349-357.

Sheridan, M., & Kisor, A. (2000). The research process and the elderly. In R. Schneider, N. Kropf, & A. Kisor, (Eds.), *Gerontological social work: Knowledge, service settings and special populations* (pp. 225–254). Belmont, CA: Wadsworth/Thompson Learning.

Shrestha, L. (August 2006). *CRS report for Congress: Life expectancy in the United States*. Washington, DC: Congressional Research Service. Retrieved from http://aging.senate.gov/crs/aging1.pdf

Silverstone, B., & Burack-Weiss, A. (1983). The social work function in nursing homes and home care. In G. Getzel, & M. Mellor, (Eds.), *Gerontological social work practice in long-term care* (pp. 7–33). New York: Haworth Press.

Social Work Policy Institute. (2010). *Understanding our aging society–social work contributions*. Retrieved from http://www.socialworkpolicy.org/research/understanding-our-aging-society-social-work-contributions.html

Spangler, D., & Brandl, B. (2007). Abuse in later life: Power and control dynamics and a victim centered response. *Journal of the American Psychiatric Nurses Association, 12,* 322–331.

Spitzer, W. (Ed.) (2004). *Leadership in health care social work: Principles and practice*. The National Society for Social Work Leadership in Health Care. Petersburg, VA: Dietz Press.

Spitzer, W., & Neuman, K. (2003). The evolution of assisted living and implications for social work practice. In W. Spitzer, (Ed.). *Selected proceedings–38th Annual Conference–National Society for Social Work Leadership in Health Care* (pp. 23–33). Petersburg, VA: Dietz Press.

Spitzer, W., Neuman, K., & Holden, G. (2004). The coming of age for assisted living care: New options for senior housing and social work practice. *Social Work in Health Care, 38*(3), 21–45.

Teachman, J., Tedrow, L., & Crowder, K. (2000). The changing demography of America's families. *Journal of Marriage and the Family 62,* 1234–1246.

U.S. Department of Health and Human Services (DHHS). (September 1987). *September 1987 report to Congress: Personnel for health care needs of the elderly through year 2020.* (Chapter III: Estimates of personnel and training needs.) Washington, DC: DHHS.

U.S. Department of Health and Human Services (DHHS) (2011). *General (US) health status*. Retrieved from http://healthypeople.gov/2020/about/GenHealthAbout.aspx#life

U.S. Department of Health and Human Services, Office of the Assistant Secretary for Planning and Evaluation (2006). *The supply and demand of professional social workers providing long-term care services: report to Congress*. Retrieved from http://aspe.hhs.gov/daltcp/reports/2006/Swsupply.htm#future

U.S. Bureau of Labor Statistics (USBLS). (2009). *Consumer expenditures in 2009, news release*, USDL-10–1390. October 2010. Retrieved from http://www.census.gov/compendia/statab/cats/income_expenditures_poverty_wealth/consumer_expenditures.html

United States Department of Labor, Bureau of Labor Statistics. (2013). *Occupational employment and wages: Health care social workers*. Retrieved from: http://www.bls.gov/oes/current/oes211022.htm

U.S. Bureau of Labor Statistics (USBLS). (2003–2004; Winter). *Occupational Outlook Quarterly*.

U.S. Census Bureau. (1995). *Statistical brief: Sixty-five plus in the United States*. Washington, DC: US Department of Commerce. Retrieved from www.census.gov/population/socdemo/statbriefs/agebrief.html

U.S. National Center for Health Statistics. *National Vital Statistics Reports (NVSR), Deaths: Final Data for 2007, 58,* No. 19, May 2010.

Varcarolis, E. M., & Halter, M. J. (2010). *Foundations of psychiatric mental health nursing* (6th ed.). St. Louis, MO: Saunders Elsevier.

Vincent, G. K., & Velkoff, V. (May 2010). *The next four decades: The older population in the United States: 2010 to 2050*. Washington, DC: United States Census Bureau, Administration on Aging.

Wasik, J. F. (2000, March/April). The fleecing of America's elderly. *Consumers Digest,* 31–34.

Williams, H. (2002). Social work skills in assisted living. *Journal of Social Work in Long-Term Care, 1*(3), 5–8.

Yesavage, J.A., Brink, T.L., Rose, T.L., & Leirer, V.O. (1983). Development and validation of a geriatric depression screening scale: A preliminary report. *Journal of Psychiatric Research, 17,* 37–39.

Zarit, S. (1980). *Aging and mental disorders*. New York: Macmillan.

Zedlewski, S., & McBride, T. (1992). The changing profile of the elderly: Effects on long-term care needs and financing. *The Milbank Quarterly, 70,* 247–275.

Pediatric Healthcare Social Work Practice

Sarah Power and Melinda Gronen

INTRODUCTION

This chapter provides an overview of pediatric social work—an area of specialty practice committed to providing a wide range of supportive services to children and families within healthcare settings. As members of the healthcare team, pediatric social workers join with children and their families to optimize the quality of medical care they receive, encourage healthy coping as they face illness or disability, and offer resources to enhance their well-being.

The services social workers provide are numerous and far-reaching. They represent the profession's unique appreciation for the **ecological perspective,** which recognizes the interactions between patients, families, and their environments. As a result, services fall within a range of care depending upon the unique needs of each patient, family, healthcare setting, and community. With this ecological perspective, pediatric social workers understand that illness or disability not only impact a child's development but also how a family functions, interacts with, and integrates into the community in which they live.

The passage of the **Patient Protection and Affordable Care Act of 2010 (PPACA)** has had implications for the manner in which pediatric services are delivered in the United States. With its focus on chronic healthcare and intent to integrate services across the continuum of inpatient and outpatient settings, the PPACA is prompting new models of care designed to enhance the quality and economy of service.

CHILD HEALTH IN THE UNITED STATES

The 74.2 million children under 18 years of age in the United States represented 24% of the total population in 2010 (Howden & Meyer, 2011). The 2010 findings of the National Health Interview Survey (NHIS) revealed that while 82% of children aged 17 years and under reported that their health was "excellent" (41 million, or 55%) or "very good" (20 million, or 27%), almost six million children (8%) had no health insurance coverage, 5% of children had no usual place of healthcare, and 2% of children were regarded as in fair or poor health (Bloom, Cohen, & Freeman, 2010).

Poverty influences both health condition and use of healthcare. Bloom et al. (2010) noted that about 42% of children in poor families reported being in excellent health, compared with 64% of children in families that were not poor. Children in poor families are five times as likely to be in fair or poor health as children in families that are not poor. Children in poor or uninsured families are more likely to use a health clinic (39%) or emergency room (4%) as their usual place of healthcare, whereas physicians' offices were used as the usual place of healthcare by 86% of children with private insurance and by 63% of children covered by Medicaid or other public coverage. Approximately 1.6 million children were unable to get needed medical care because the family could not afford it.

While the majority of children in good health may experience short-term, acute illnesses such as respiratory, gastrointestinal, or ear infections (Torpy, Campbell, & Glass, 2010), they recover with few adverse consequences. However, according to the U.S. Department of Health and Human Services (2008), 13.9% of children under 18 years of age in the United States, or approximately 10.2 million children, are estimated to have special healthcare needs. Overall, 21.8% of U.S. households with children have at least one child with **special healthcare needs**. The U.S. Department of Health and Human Services has adapted the definition of children with special healthcare needs (CSHCN) to be " . . . those who have or are at increased risk for a chronic physical, developmental, behavioral, or emotional condition and who also require health and related services of a type or amount beyond that required by children generally", as proposed by McPherson et al. (1998, p. 137). Furthermore, children who rely on supportive interventions to survive are included in this population because of the life-threatening consequences should their supportive technologies fail.

CHRONIC HEALTH

Chronic health issues are a particularly serious concern among pediatric patients, with the most prevalent and serious examples including the following.

Asthma

The most common chronic childhood illness, asthma is a chronic respiratory disease that impairs breathing. It affects 7.1 million U.S. children and, in 2008, school-aged children with at least one asthma attack in the previous year reported missing 10.5 million days of school in the prior school year (Akinbami, Moorman, & Liu, 2011).

Diabetes

The seventh leading cause of death in the United States (USDHHS, 2011), diabetes develops when the body fails to produce sufficient insulin or insufficiently uses its own insulin, prompting elevated blood glucose levels. There are two types of diabetes, Type 1 and Type 2. An estimated 215,000 people under 20 years of age had diabetes in 2010. Although Type-2 diabetes was previously known as "adult-onset" diabetes, children are increasingly being diagnosed with Type 2—a circumstance that may be linked to increasing rates of childhood obesity.

Obesity

Obesity is generally defined as excess body fat but, because excess body fat is not readily measured directly, obesity is more often defined as excess body weight as measured by **BMI** (body mass index). BMI reflects weight adjusted for height and is regarded as a useful indicator of overweight and obesity (U.S. Department of Health and Human Services [USDHHS], 2010). Occurring when a child has a high amount of extra body fat, childhood obesity rates have tripled in the last thirty years, with significant health risks to children (USDHHS, 2010), with obesity contributing to an estimated 112,000 preventable deaths each year (Ogden, Carroll, Ogden, & Curtin, 2010). While the prevalence of obesity did not change a great deal during the 1960s and 1970s, obesity increased from 5% to 17% among children during the period 1980 to 2008. Such a trend is an enduring concern as obese children are likely to become obese adults (Krebs et al., 2007; Wright, Pepe, Seidel, & Dietz, 1997). Being overweight (with high BMI levels) is associated with childhood development of atherosclerosis (Berenson, Srinivasan, Bao, Newman, Tracy, & Wattigney, 1998) and diabetes (CDC, 2008) with subsequent risks for cardiovascular disease, stroke, kidney disease, and blindness, among other risks. Inappropriate (high caloric) intake, insufficient physical activity, genes, metabolism, behavior, environment, and culture are contributing factors to being overweight and obese (USDHHS, 2010).

Cystic Fibrosis

This genetic disease involves mucus build-up that obstructs vital organs in the body and ultimately results in breathing problems when mucus clogs the lungs. An estimated 30,000 U.S. children and adults report having cystic fibrosis. Due to medical advancements, life expectancy rates for children with cystic fibrosis have increased, with the anticipated age of survival in 2009 being in the mid-30s (Cystic Fibrosis Foundation, May 2011).

Cancer

Cancer is a term used for diseases that occur when abnormal cells divide without control and invade other tissues (National Cancer Institute, October 2011a). Although the incidence of invasive cancer in children has increased slightly over the past 30 years, mortality rates have declined by more than 50% for many childhood cancers. In 2011, 11,210 new cases of pediatric cancer were estimated in children between the ages of 0 and 14 years (National Cancer Institute, October 2011b). The improvements in survival rates are regarded as largely attributable to improvements in treatment and the high proportion of patients participating in clinical trials.

MENTAL HEALTH

Nationally, increased attention is being directed at the mental healthcare needs of children. In part, this heightened awareness is due to incidents of gun violence perpetrated by children and a desire to identify, understand, and provide treatment to at-risk children and prevent such tragedies.

In 2013, the CDC released the report, *Mental Health Surveillance Among Children—United States, 2005–2011*, which estimates that 13% to 20% of children between the ages of 3 and 17 years experience a mental health disorder in any given year. Mental disorders are described as "serious changes in the way children typically learn, behave, or handle their emotions." It is important for pediatric social workers to understand that millions of children and their families are impacted by ADHD (attention deficit hyperactivity disorder), behavioral or conduct disorders, depression, anxiety, and other mental health challenges. Particularly concerning for adolescents are illicit drug and alcohol use as well as risk for suicide. In 2010, suicide was the second leading cause of death among adolescents aged 12 to 17 years (CDC, 2013). These numbers underscore the importance of pediatric social workers being competent in assessing the mental health needs of children and ensuring that their practice settings have the resources needed to respond to children experiencing symptoms, including acute crises. Correspondingly, The Joint Commission (2014) recognizes the identification of patients at risk for suicide as a national patient safety goal.

DEVELOPMENTAL DISABILITIES

Developmental disabilities can occur at birth through genetic mutations such as the abnormality that causes Down syndrome. Other disabilities may be acquired through childhood trauma, including head injuries and spinal cord injuries. Between 2006 and 2008, developmental disabilities were reported in approximately one in six children in the United States. The disabilities included attention deficit disorder, intellectual disability, cerebral palsy, autism, seizures, stuttering or stammering, profound hearing loss, blindness, learning disorders, and/or other developmental delays (Boyle et al., 2011).

On October 30, 2000, President Clinton signed into law the *Developmental Disabilities Assistance and Bill of Rights Act of 2000 (Public Law No.106–402)*. This legislation defines a developmental disability as a severe, chronic disability in a child that impedes the achievement of normally expected developmental milestones and capacities. A developmental disability must be manifested before the age of 22, involve mental and/or physical impairments, and be expected to persist indefinitely. The disability must result in substantial functional limitations in three or more of the following activities of daily living: self-care, receptive and expressive language, learning, mobility, self-direction, and the capacity for independent living and economic self-sufficiency (section 102[8]). Disability is regarded as a natural and normal part of the human experience that does not diminish the rights of individuals to make choices and direct their care and participate to the greatest extent possible in their communities.

The overall purpose of the Act is to ensure that individuals with developmental disabilities and their families are included and, in fact, direct the service planning for care (U.S. Department of Health and Human Services: Administration on Intellectual and Developmental Disabilities, 2000). This process is called **person-centered planning** because it places the individual at the center of all care planning. The Act also requires states to establish a protection and advocacy center to ensure that the rights of these individuals are protected.

The Individuals with Disabilities Act (IDEA) was originally enacted by Congress in 1975 and was most recently amended in 2004. It requires states, schools, and agencies to provide early intervention and special education services to more than 6.5 million children with disabilities who qualify for services. Individuals can qualify for special education from early childhood up until the age of 26, depending on their needs. School social workers and special education teachers work together through the development of an *Individualized Educational Plan or (IEP)* (National Dissemination Center for Children with Disabilities, n.d.).

Pediatric social workers in particular should be familiar with the legislation impacting children's health and services, including to their state's protection and advocacy centers. They should also be prepared to assist parents attain the necessary medical documentation to demonstrate service eligibility and need. The following case study portrays how a healthcare social worker can affect the care of a child and family in need.

CASE STUDY

Applying Resource Knowledge

Jason was a 17-year-old boy who had suffered a severe head injury in a motor vehicle accident. Although a senior, he had not yet graduated high school. After discharge from the hospital and rehabilitation center, the parents went to Jason's school to arrange for him to continue his education through special education services. The school originally denied services, stating they did not have the appropriate type of services to address this kind of impairment, and that Jason was "too old" and too close to graduation to begin special education services as this point. The parents came back to the rehabilitation social worker who knew the law and requirement that the disability must occur before the age of 22 to qualify. She connected the parents to the protection and advocacy group in their state, who sent a representative to the next IEP for Jason. Jason was ultimately approved for special education support until the age of 26.

ACCIDENTAL INJURY

Children are particularly prone to accident-related injuries. Over 30 million children visit hospital emergency departments each year, with 43% of those visits prompted by the child incurring an injury (Weiss, Mathers, Furjuoh, & Kinnane, 1997). Unintentional injuries are the number-one cause of death in children up to the age of 19 years in the United States (Borse et al., 2008). Among children from birth to 3 years of age, the leading major causes of injury in descending order were falls, poisoning, transportation, foreign body, and fires/burns. The overall rate of falls exceeded poisoning, the second leading cause of injury, by a factor of two (Agran et al., 2003). Three million pediatric hospital admissions yearly are often for planned tests, surgeries, and procedures or for continual treatment of chronic health condition(s); however, others are due to unexpected illness or injury (American Academy of Pediatrics, 2011).

PEDIATRIC CARE SITES AND SOCIAL WORK PRACTICE

Pediatric healthcare services are delivered in a broad and expanding array of settings. As discussed in Chapter 2, healthcare is delivered across a continuum of services. One form or another of social work practice is present in essentially all of these contexts. The diverse settings afford a range of specialized pediatric services:

Pediatric Primary Care Clinics

These sites offer routine medical care to pediatric patients during the course of their childhood. This care typically includes well-child visits, immunizations, sick visits, and health coordination for children with special needs. Passage of the PPACA in 2010 has focused attention on *how* primary care is delivered and on addressing poor health outcomes, in this instance involving children with complex medical needs. One operational result of the PPACA is the development of the **medical home model** within pediatric primary care.

The American Academy of Pediatrics (2002a) describes a medical home as "accessible, continuous, comprehensive, family centered, coordinated, compassionate, and culturally effective delivered or directed by well-trained physicians who provide primary care and help to manage and facilitate essentially all aspects of pediatric care" (p. 184). While the initial medical home models were targeted toward children with special needs, the philosophy has evolved as an ideal for all children.

A key component of the medical home model is its emphasis on teamwork. As such, social workers are key contributors to this care model, which may include serving as formal care coordinators. More than ever, collaboration and cooperation of all healthcare providers will be expected, to the point that transdisciplinary team models are being explored in which individual, providers function in multiple roles with input from other team professionals, are being explored.

Subspecialty Clinics

These settings offer focused expert care for children impacted by a specific illness or problem. Advances in pediatric medicine have increased the demand for subspecialty care. Healthcare social workers practicing in these specialty settings focus their training and work experiences on unique pediatric problems, such as cystic fibrosis. They characteristically contribute to interdisciplinary healthcare teams by responding to, and consulting on, psychosocial issues ranging from the child's and family's adjustment to the medical condition to addressing resource needs.

In the United States, the American Board of Medical Specialties (2012) identifies 20 board-certified pediatric subspecialties: adolescent medicine, child abuse pediatrics, developmental-behavioral pediatrics, hospice and palliative medicine, medical toxicology, neonatal-perinatal medicine, neurodevelopmental disabilities, cardiology, critical care medicine, emergency medicine, endocrinology, gastroenterology, hematology-oncology, infectious diseases, nephrology, pulmonology, rheumatology, transplant hepatology, sleep medicine, and sports medicine. Of concern, a growing national shortage of pediatric subspecialists is contributing to children having to experience long wait times before being seen. The National Association of Children's Hospitals and Related Institutions revealed in 2009, for example, average wait times of 9 weeks for appointments with pediatric neurologists and 13 weeks for appointments with developmental-behavioral pediatricians (Greenwood, 2010).

Social workers in these clinic settings typically focus their efforts on promoting compliance with treatment regimens, initiating community resource referrals, and coordinating care with outside agencies for needed medical and social service needs. Such effort may become more challenging in the future as changes in health insurance coverage are likely to increase the numbers of clinic cases with potential impacts on amount of time available per patient. As demands increase, attention must be on the sufficiency of available community resources.

Acute Care and Rehabilitation Hospitals

Approximately 250 children's hospitals exist, accounting for less than 5% of all hospitals in the United States. Due to their high level of specialization, children's hospitals often serve the sickest children and those with the most complex medical needs (National Association of Children's Hospitals and Related Institutions, 2007).

In pediatric hospital settings, social work roles are especially broad, varying from case management to patient and family counseling. The blend of these functions depends on the particular health provider's philosophies and staffing. In discharge planning roles, social workers focus on the safe transition of patients leaving the hospital and entering or re-entering the community. In other systems, social workers may focus solely on the psychosocial needs of patients while nurses or other trained staffs address discharge planning. Still other hospitals may utilize social workers in dual roles, but always in the context of interdisciplinary teams.

Home Health Agencies

These agencies provide medical care to children in their homes. An estimated 500,000 children in the United States receive home health services (United States Department of Health and Human Services, Agency for Healthcare Research and Quality, 2004). These services, some of which are life-sustaining, include skilled nursing visits for respiratory care, including ventilator and tracheostomy support, wound care, infusion therapy, nutrition support and enteral feedings, injectable medications, medical equipment and supplies, and end-of-life care.

In home health settings, social workers may focus on providing patients the psychosocial support and resources they need to remain safely at home. The emphasis on home healthcare is driven both by a sensitivity to have the child recuperate in his or her own familiar family surroundings and the significant cost savings inherent in avoiding prolonged and otherwise unnecessary hospitalization.

Long-Term Care Facilities

Twenty-four-hour care of children is often warranted for children with profound disabilities and correspondingly complex care needs, including those who are technology dependent. In long-term care facilities, social workers often partner with families to identify the training and resources needed to facilitate taking their children home. For other families, the focus of social work intervention may be to strengthen the family's relationship with the child when returning home is not possible. Central to all of these interventions is the goal of optimizing the child's quality of life.

End-of-Life Care

Hospice and palliative care represent two unique models of care that focus on affording end-of-life comfort. **Hospice care** typically serves patients whose life expectancy is less than 6 months and who are no longer pursuing curative therapy for their illness. Hospice care can be provided in patients' homes or in specialized facilities. Less defined, **palliative care** is directed at preventing or relieving pain and suffering. Patients receiving palliative care may be pursuing ongoing curative treatment and ultimately transition to hospice care. Palliative care services may be provided in hospitals as well as in patients' homes.

There is a growing utilization of hospice and palliative care for children, although the majority of the 53,552 children who died in the United States in 2005 did so in hospitals (Friebert, 2009). Pediatric social workers dealing with end-of-life care focus on understanding and representing patients' and families' desires as well as affording emotional support and resources that may range from arranging financial assistance through securing transportation, homemaker services, and pastoral involvement.

SOCIAL WORK PRACTICE KNOWLEDGE AND SKILLS

The unique circumstances of a child experiencing an illness, injury, or disability along with the associated treatment dictates that pediatric social workers possess specific knowledge in order to effectively practice. This knowledge includes understanding

- The *impact of illness* on children and families
- The use of *psychosocial assessment* as a social work tool
- *Interventions* to strengthen coping and ameliorate the negative effects of illness

- Effective *integration* onto the interdisciplinary team

- Meaningful *documentation*

- Knowledge of *child maltreatment*

The Impact of Illness on Children and Families

For parents and loved ones, illness of a child evokes a myriad of responses, including fear, anxiety, depression, anger, confusion, disbelief, and grief. If an illness is chronic, feelings of grief may be related to the loss of and hopes for the *healthy* child. If a child is disabled, parents may grieve the loss of their child's physical and/or cognitive abilities.

Parents must not only contend with these emotions but also learn how to communicate with medical providers, often in new and complex environments. They have to become aware of the current and future implications of their child's condition, the nature of necessary treatment, and the child's own response to their medical state. Additionally, parents must create new roles for themselves within these medically focused relationships, all the while continuing to provide ongoing love and care for their child. These new tasks can be arduous and may challenge even the most sophisticated, loving parent's ability to positively cope. It therefore is crucial for healthcare teams, including social workers, to recognize and understand the challenges faced by patients and families as well as their strengths and possibilities.

To gain this understanding, pediatric social workers characteristically employ **family systems theory** as the "lens" through which to view the patient and family. This theory views children as existing within complex, dynamic families, or systems. These systems are instrumental and often predictive of how children will cope with and adapt to illness (Bruce, 2006; Anthony, Gil, & Schanberg, 2003). In turn, the experiences of children contending with their medical condition impacts how family members respond. When a child is dealing with an injury, illness, or disability, it reverberates through the lives of everyone in the family system.

The **Family Adjustment and Adaptation Response (FAAR) Model** (Patterson, 1988) provides a framework for understanding the impacts of a child's condition on his or her family. Family systems strive to maintain normalcy and balance when faced with adversity and rely on resources and coping strategies to adjust to life's demands. When a crisis occurs, however, the demands of the situation can tax or exceed the family's coping abilities. For many families, having their child diagnosed with an illness or disability constitutes a major crisis—one for which they may not have anticipated, have no historical precedent, and have limited response capacities. In response to crisis, families strive to restore balance through adaptation by

1. Altering or expanding definitions and meanings, taking into account their changed circumstances,

2. Reducing pileup of demands,

3. Developing and acquiring new resources, and

4. Developing new coping strategies for dealing with demands.

Source: Patterson (1988, p. 229).

Patterson (1988) noted that families experience continual cycles of adjustment, crisis, and adaptation throughout their lifetimes. For families of children experiencing an illness or disability, these cycles include the stages of the child's diagnosis and treatment and the limitations associated with their health condition. Children and families may experience improvement, recovery, relapse, success, disappointment, and possibly even end of life.

Contending with these cycles while providing care to a child with illness or disability is a stressful experience. It requires additional time to care for the child, changing of previous life routines, altering family roles and creating new norms (Boebel Toly, Musil, & Carl, 2010; Rodrigues & Patterson, 2007). Family relationships are impacted and change, communication is altered, and increased financial burdens challenge family resources. Whether an illness is time-limited or chronic, children and family members must make adjustments and create new coping strategies. These strategies are unique to each individual, being affected by one's age, ethnicity, socioeconomic status, past crisis experience, environment, and access to support (Shudy et al., 2006). Some factors are specific to the illness and child, including the severity of the medical condition, the child's age and developmental stage at the onset of the condition, the course of medical treatment, and the type of impairment (Rodrigues & Patterson, 2007).

Although some children and families may be well adjusted in the context of their response to an illness or disability, others experience challenges that extend beyond the known health problem(s). Frequent hospitalizations and/or clinic visits may act to significantly disrupt the child's normal development. School-age children may experience lengthy or frequent absences, which negatively impact learning and detract from their peer relationships.

Children experiencing illness or disability are at risk for emotional and behavioral problems compared with their healthy peers (Barlow & Ellard, 2006; Pinquart & Shen, 2011; Anthony & Schanberg, 2003). These problems may manifest themselves in increased anxiety, depression, somatic complaints, disturbed peer relationships, delinquency, or other previously uncharacteristic behavior. Pinguart and Shen (2011) suggested that these may be the consequence of the child feeling out of control, experiencing symptoms of distress, having restrictions in activities, sensing rejection by peers, or simply feeling pain and discomfort. As children respond to these feelings and try to make sense of their circumstance, they need reassurance, support, and consistency from parents and family members. Parents, however, are often experiencing their own coping struggles and must balance meeting their child's needs while simultaneously addressing their own. More often than not, they focus their energies toward their child, leaving little in reserve for themselves.

Research provides evidence of the emotional challenges experienced by families when impacted by a child's illness. Both parents and siblings are at increased risk for mental health symptoms (Eiser, 1997), including acute stress disorder and post-traumatic stress disorder (Bruce, 2006; Shaw et al., 2009; Shudy et al., 2006). In particular, studies have identified the importance of maternal mental health, noting that the mother's psychological well-being typically impacts the overall health of the entire family (Boebel Toly et al., & 2010; Shudy et al., 2006).

Studies of families with children in pediatric intensive care units (PICU), where the sickest children are treated, provide crucial insight into understanding how parents are impacted when they lose primary control over their child's well-being. Role alteration has been found to be a significant parental stressor in the PICU setting. The parent may perceive that they are no longer the principal decision-makers; in fact, they may experience a sense of impotence based on their lack of familiarity with the child's medical condition, treatment circumstances, and prognosis. Other identified stressors to parents and children alike include observing changes in the child's physical appearance, equipment alarm sounds, nursing procedures, and the nature of staff communication (Shudy et al., 2006).

Parental stress resulting from communication problems underscores the particular importance of relationships between staff and parents. When positive, these relationships bring comfort and satisfaction to both families and staff. Confidence that staff care about the parent as well as the child and a sense that their questions are being answered honestly have been identified as fundamental needs of parents of children in PICUs (Shudy et al., 2006). Stress levels have also been found to decrease when parents are allowed to be involved in their child's care (Frazier, Frazier, & Warren, 2010; Shudy et al., 2006).

Having a sibling with a chronic illness can have adverse effects on the healthy child (Barlow & Ellard, 2006; Sharpe & Rossiter, 2002; Dauz Williams, 1997). These effects include deteriorating school performance, struggles in peer relationships, withdrawal, and isolation. Murray (1998) also noted that strengths in these sibling relationships can lead to increased appreciation for life, greater sensitivity, enhanced family closeness, and empathy for others.

Illness of a child may not be the greatest stressor in many families' lives, even when the illness is life-threatening. In 2010, 16.4 million children in the United States lived in poverty (U.S. Bureau of the Census, 2010); these families struggle to meet basic needs, including food and housing. In these circumstances, illness of a child may exacerbate an already fragile situation and prompt an immediate crisis, such as when parents are unable to afford gasoline to travel back and forth to the hospital to visit their child or attend clinic appointments. The impact of illness is exacerbated in the context of poverty and when other pre-existing stressors combine to tax the emotional capacities and financial/social resources of patients' families.

Pediatric social work practice demands technical competence, focus, compassion, flexibility, courage, and personal strength. In addition, however, it requires resilience. Walsh (2006) defined **resilience** as "the capacity to rebound from adversity strengthened and more resourceful" (p. 4). To sustain oneself in a setting fraught with the undeniable emotional dynamics of a child's illness, injury or disability, pediatric social workers must have the capacity to be sensitive in their introspection, but resolute in their ability to derive benefit for future practice from often heart-rending patient experiences.

Psychosocial Assessment

What psychosocial information will be helpful in order to understand the patient and family's current situation and anticipate their future needs?

Pediatric social workers respond to a variety of patient-care needs, ranging from concrete, problem-specific requests such as arranging transportation to clinically complex situations including end-of-life decision making. Dependent on the number and complexity of presenting issues, social work assessments may correspondingly range from being focused and brief to comprehensive and lengthy. While brief assessments typically retain a narrow focus, the in-depth comprehensive assessments afford a basis for developing viable post-hospitalization patient-care plans. Psychosocial assessments also represent an important mechanism for clarifying other healthcare professionals' understanding of unique patient and family needs. Consistent with fundamental social work practice canons, the psychosocial assessments highlight the role of patient and family strengths in contending with health circumstances (Spitzer, 2003). Social workers engaged with patients and families over extended periods of time continuously reassess circumstances and needs. While parents are the primary source of assessment information in instances of very young children, assessments should seek responses from the child at the earliest point that the child is able to contribute.

Since psychosocial assessments are the social worker's primary practice tool, it becomes crucial to understand the assessment process and its purpose with patients and families. Families also need to clearly understand why social work consultation is beneficial. While some referrals to social work are requested by patients and families, many others are the result of observations by and/or concerns among members of the medical team. Still other referrals are the result of high-risk screenings initiated upon admission (e.g., domestic violence or homelessness screening). After being informed of the reason for social work involvement, parents should be made aware that the basis for the psychosocial assessment is to identify needs and promote the best outcomes, including the optimized use of all involved healthcare personnel and resources. This dialogue is particularly crucial should patients and families harbor misconceptions or lack of knowledge about the role and intent of social work intervention.

Thoughtful, sensitive interview questions are at the heart of psychosocial assessment. Each social worker develops his or her own interviewing style and identifies what information is important to obtain. *Tables 12.1* and *12.2* outline a comprehensive psychosocial assessment and its use. An effective psychosocial assessment not only divulges useful information but also supports the engagement process, allowing the social worker to build rapport and trust with the patient and family. It provides the groundwork for the helping relationship.

Interventions

Based on my assessment, what is needed? What do I have to offer the patient and family?

Pediatric social work interventions range from simple to complex and can be most broadly described in two categories of providing psychosocial support and concrete resources, including post-hospitalization care planning (discharge planning). Often, these interventions are delivered in tandem, complementing one another. *Importantly, advocacy is the thread that runs through both, promoting patients' and families' access to needed care.*

In healthcare settings, social workers often serve as a healing presence when families and loved ones hear and attempt to cope with difficult news. They help patients and families make sense of situations by (1) promoting open and direct communication by medical teams and (2) promoting parental coping skills and identifying resources needed by families to support their adjustment to their new circumstances. Conveying basic but essential coping skills may include teaching families to be assertive with medical teams in order to obtain answers to questions. To that end, it often proves useful to encourage families to utilize notebooks so that they can write down important information such as names of care providers and pending questions.

Table 12.1 Psychosocial Assessment Components

Living Situation	What is your current address?
	Who lives with you?
	Do any other family members live in your building or nearby?
	Is your living situation stable or fragile?
	Do you feel safe at home? In your community?
	Do you enjoy living in your community?
	Has your family ever experienced homelessness?
Family Members and Roles	Tell me about your family.
	How do you share responsibilities (caring for children, taking children to school/doctor appointments, performing household chores, paying bills)?
	How do you make important decisions in your family?
	Who do you turn to for support in your family?
	What are the strengths of your family?
	If there is anything you would change about your family, what would it be?
Parental Work, School, or Vocational History	Do you work? Attend school? Practice a trade?
	What is your schedule?
	Do you have flexibility in your schedule, or is it rigid?
	Is your child's illness or disability impacting your job or education? If yes, how?
	Do you have protected sick time or vacation hours at work?
Financial Considerations	How do you financially support your family?
	Do you experience any financial challenges?
	Are your bills (rent, mortgage, utilities, etc.) up to date?
	Do you receive any government assistance, such as SSDI, SSI, TANF, food stamps, or WIC?
Parental Perception of the Child	Tell me about your child.
	What type of baby, toddler, teenager is s/he?Was s/he a planned pregnancy or a surprise? (for parents of young children)How did you feel when you learned you were pregnant? How did your partner respond?
	Describe your child's personality?
	What are your child's favorite things to do or to play with?
	What do you do to have fun with your child?
	How do you show affection to your child?
	Is there anything challenging about caring for your child right now (coping with crying, toilet training, tantrums, school performance, managing specific behaviors, etc.)?

(Continued)

Table 12.1   (Continued)

Social Support	Who helps you outside of your family?
	Are you involved in any community organizations that provide support to you?
	Do you believe you have adequate support?
	As a parent, do others help you care for your child or offer respite?
	Is there anything that our staff can be doing to support you?
Medical Needs and Access to Insurance or Healthcare	Do any other family members have medical needs?
	Does your family have health insurance?
	Do your family members have a relationship with a healthcare provider?
	Is there anyone who needs medical care right now?
Relevant Developmental and Cognitive History	How is your child's physical and emotional development?
	What things is s/he doing developmentally?
	What do you expect him or her to do next?
	Do you believe your child is similar or different than other children his or her own age?
	Do you have any worries about your child's development?
	Has anyone else shared worries with you?
	What school does your child attend?
	Does your child attend school regularly?
	How is your child's school performance?
	Does your child receive any special services at school?
Impact of Illness or Disability on the Child and Family	How has your child been impacted by the illness or disability?
	How is your child coping?
	What does your child know about the illness or disability? About the prognosis?
	How has your child's illness or disability impacted you and your family?
	How have any siblings been impacted? What are your hopes for your child's medical care and treatment?
Spirituality and Faith	Do you belong to a spiritual or faith community?
	If yes, how does it impact who you are?
	Is there anything about your spirituality or faith that you want our staff to know about?
	Would you like to have contact with our hospital chaplain?
Cultural Values and Beliefs	Does your family have any cultural traditions or rituals that are important to you and your family?
	Tell me what it's like being from xx? How has being from a different country shaped who you are?
	Do you have any cultural values or beliefs that you'd like the healthcare team to know about?

Marital/ Significant Other/Domestic Partner Relationship	Are you currently in an intimate relationship?
	How long have you been together?
	How do you describe your relationship?
	How are you supporting each other during this time?
	Are you experiencing any struggles in the relationship?
	What happens when the two of you disagree?
	Has there ever been pushing, hitting, kicking, or other physical or emotional harm between the two of you? If yes, tell me about it.
	Have the police ever been called to your home?
Perception / Understanding of Illness or Disability	Tell me about your understanding of your child's illness or disability?
	What are your greatest worries or fears?
	Do you feel comfortable asking medical staff questions about your child?
	Do you have any unanswered questions right now? If yes, what are they?
End-of-Life Considerations (if applicable)	Are there any medical interventions you wouldn't want for your child?
	When you think about quality of life for your child, what's important to you?
	Is there a point in your child's care that you may want to discontinue treatment?
	Who do you want here for support as you make difficult decisions?
	What additional medical information would you like to have to make decisions?
	Do you have any clergy or religious person you would like to discuss options with?
	How can we assist you in helping your other children cope?
Coping and Mental Health Functioning	How are you coping with your child's illness or disability?
	Where do you gain your strength?
	Are there times when you cope better than other times?
	Have you ever been diagnosed with depression, anxiety, bipolar disorder, or another mental health condition? If yes, tell me more about it. Were you prescribed medication?
	Are you currently experiencing feelings of anxiety or depression?
	After the birth of your child(ren), did you experience feelings of sadness or depression?
	When you're feeling overwhelmed, do you ask for help or hold your feelings in?
	What can healthcare staff do to support you?
	Does your family have past experience with illness? How did you make it through?
Substance Misuse	Have you ever experimented with drugs such as marijuana, cocaine, methamphetamine, or heroin?
	Do you currently drink alcohol? If yes, how often and how much?
	Have you ever been worried about your own drinking or drug use?
	Has anyone ever told you s/he is worried about your drinking or drug use?

(Continued)

Table 12.1 (Continued)

	Do you have any worries about alcohol or drug use by your spouse or partner?
	Are you prescribed any pain medication? If yes, for what?
	Have you sought treatment for alcohol or drug use in the past? If yes, tell me how you maintain sobriety now.
Legal/Criminal Issues	Have you ever been arrested? If yes, for what?
	Are you currently on probation or parole?
	Has your partner ever been arrested? If yes, for what?
History of Child Abuse and Neglect	Are you familiar with the child welfare system?
	Has your family ever been involved with it? If yes, what happened?
	Has your child ever been abused or neglected? If yes, what happened?
	Were you abused or neglected as a child? If yes, what happened and how did you cope?
Child Safety (injury prevention focus)	Are there any weapons in the home? If yes, are they locked? Is ammunition stored separately?
	Are medications locked and out of reach of children?
	Are there secure screens on all of your windows?
	Have you ever left your child unattended in the bathtub?
	Do you have a swimming pool or retention pond near your home? If yes, is there a locked gate around the perimeter? Do you have a pool cover?
	Does your child have a car seat in every vehicle s/he travels in?
Clinical Impressions	Was the family engaged in the social work assessment process?
	Did you identify any current or future needs? Family challenges?
	What are the strengths of the family?
	What is your understanding of the family's ability to meet the child's healthcare needs?
	What services are needed to optimize outcomes for the child and family?
Plan	What is the concrete action plan you and the family have agreed upon?
	Who is responsible for follow-up?
	Will you continue to follow this patient and family, close the encounter, or refer to another social worker?
	How are you communicating your assessment and plan with other members of the healthcare team and indicated community agencies?

Source: Authors.

Table 12.2   Pediatric Psychosocial Assessment Example

Reason for Referral	Social worker received a referral from Dr. xx, endocrinologist, for psychosocial assessment and support due to patient's new diabetes diagnosis. Patient is a 10-year-old girl, Jasmine, admitted 2 days ago after presenting to the Emergency Room with lethargy. She's been diagnosed with Type-1 diabetes mellitus. I met with patient's mother, Maria, alone in patient's room this morning while Jasmine engaged in play with Child Life. Jasmine's father, Enrique, spent the night at the hospital last night and returned home this morning to shower. The family's primary language is Spanish, and a Spanish-speaking interpreter was used for the interview. Mother shared the following information:
Living Situation	Patient lives with her mother, father, and 5-year-old brother, Emilio, at xx in Chicago. Their contact numbers are xx. The family rents the second floor unit of a two-flat building where they've lived for 3 years. Mother's father, Carlos, died 10 months ago and her mother, Rosa, is in the process of moving in with the family. Mother explained that Rosa is moving in to share rental costs. Mother states that patient and her brother are very close to their grandmother and are very excited. Mother states that she and Father believe this will be a good decision for their family, especially in light of Jasmine's new diagnosis. Mother states she's feeling a "little bit nervous" because they have not told the landlord about her mother moving in yet. They plan on doing this is in the next few days.
Parental Perception of Patient	When asked to describe patient, Mother smiled and said, "she's sweet and sinister." Mother went onto explain that patient is a really good child who has been getting into some trouble lately with older teenage girls who live downstairs in their building. When asked to give examples, Mother said, "they're going to people's houses when they don't have permission, staying up late, watching music videos they're not supposed to...that kind of stuff." Mother describes patient's personality as "outgoing and fun." She says patient's favorite things include listening to her I-pod, dancing, hanging out with the neighbor girls, and harassing her brother. Mother states that patient's room is adorned with Justin Bieber posters. Until this hospitalization, Mother perceived patient as a typical 10-year-old girl.
Relevant Developmental and Cognitive History	Mother states that patient is in the 4th grade at xx Elementary. Mother says that patient is in regular education classes and is a "B" student. Patient's favorite class is music. Mother says patient's school has already called to check on patient. Mother was told that she should call the school nurse to talk about how they can help with patient's diabetes. Mother is not sure how to do this.
Impact of Illness or Disability on the Child and Family	When asked how Mother believes patient is coping with the diagnosis, she replied, "I'm not sure it's hit her yet. I'm not sure it's hit any of us yet." Mother shared that she feels terrible because she thought patient was lying about feeling sick. Mother said, "Finally, I just looked at her and realized something was really wrong. She didn't look right. Thank God we brought her in." Mother states that she, Father, and patient are scheduled to begin formal diabetes education this afternoon. She says she's feeling a little nervous but hopes it will

(Continued)

Table 12.2   (Continued)

	go okay. When asked what she's most worried about, Mother says that she fears giving the insulin injections and blood draws. Mother says that she's never been able to handle shots herself, and has always avoided doctors. She says that Father is more confident than she is. Mother says that he is reassuring everyone that they can do this. Mother describes patient as seeming withdrawn. Mother became tearful as she talked about her long-term fears, wondering if patient will grow into a healthy woman and be able to have children of her own. Mother shared that Emilio came to the hospital last night and seems confused about what's going on. Mother said that Rosa will be bringing him back tonight after the teaching session.
Cultural Values and Beliefs	Mother identifies the family as Mexican American. She came to Chicago with her parents when she was 10 years old. Mother says that although she can understand some English, she prefers speaking in Spanish. Mother shared that a doctor came in to patient's room last night and spoke in English. She couldn't understand what was said and didn't feel comfortable interrupting him. Mother states that both patient and Emilio speak Spanish and English.
Parental Work History and Source of Income	Mother states that she runs her own cleaning business out of the home. She says the business is good right now but she sometimes struggles with consistent clients. Right now, a woman who works for her is doing the cleaning while patient is in the hospital. Father works for his uncle and manages a car repair shop. Mother says they both like their jobs but work long hours. Mother states that the family relies on their two incomes for support. Last year, Mother hurt her back and couldn't work. This caused some financial problems and prompted the decision to have grandmother move in. Mother states that they live paycheck to paycheck. Currently, they are a few weeks behind in paying their utility bills but Mother says they will catch up.
Medical Needs and Access to Insurance/ Healthcare	Both the patient and Emilio have state-sponsored health insurance and are cared for by Dr. xx at the xx Clinic. Mother states that they don't pay premiums or copays for medication. Mother says she's feeling anxious because she's not sure how they're are going to obtain the diabetic supplies, saying, "I hope the insurance pays for everything we need." Mother reports that she and Father do not have health insurance for themselves.
Parental Coping and Mental Health Functioning	Mother shares that neither she nor Father have a mental health diagnosis. She explains that she did experience symptoms of post-partum depression after Emilio's birth. She says that she started to take a medication but stopped taking it because she couldn't afford it. Since that time, she has not had any depressive symptoms. Mother describes current feelings of sadness regarding her daughter's illness. Her primary coping method right now is talking to her family members and medical staff, in addition to praying.
Substance Misuse	Mother denies any history of substance misuse by herself or Father.
Legal/ Criminal Issues	Mother states that she was ticketed for driving without a driver's license 2 years ago and has a suspended driver's license for failure to appear in court for a speeding ticket. She shared her embarrassment that this happened, and she relies on her family members or public transportation in order to work. She states that her license should be reinstated in one month.

History of Child Abuse and Neglect	Mother states that neither of her children has experienced abuse or neglect. She shares that this is one of her worst fears, and she is vigilant in making sure they are safe.
Clinical Impressions	Mother actively engaged in the social work assessment. While she expressed anxiety related to her ability to manage patient's daily diabetes regimen, she was also able to identify strong family support from patient's father and maternal grandmother. Mother expressed concerns about patient's adjustment to illness and appears to be motivated to manage patient's diabetes to promote patient's health and well-being.
	Mother was able to identify several areas in which social work can be of assistance, including helping to coordinate with the patient's school, requesting that all information be provided in Spanish (written and verbal), and ensuring that the family is aware of potential out-of-pocket costs related to patient's medicine and supplies. All of these questions demonstrated to social work Mother's ability to be proactive in her management of patient's disease.
	Mother identified potential areas of financial stress, but at this time appears to have a plan to meet the family's basic needs. Social worker encouraged Mother to communicate any financial needs so that social work can assist in problem-solving.
	Mother expressed much love towards patient and concern about her emotional response to the new diagnosis. Social worker talked with Mother about normal developmental responses to illness and provided Mother with written information on how to support patient's emotional health. Also discussed the possible emotional impacts of chronic illness on the family, including patient's brother.
Plan	1. Mother and Father are primarily Spanish-speaking. Please utilize Spanish interpreters and provide all written information in Spanish for every interaction with parents. Social worker provided information to Mother and Father on how to access interpreters. Discussed with patient's bedside nurse, xx, and Dr. xx. 2. Social worker, diabetic educator, and Spanish interpreter are scheduled to participate in a conference call with Mother and patient's teacher and school nurse at xx elementary school on Wednesday at 10:00 am. Social worker will help ensure that the school understands patient's medication administration and what to do if patient shows symptoms of a diabetic emergency. Mother signed a release of information. 3. Social worker made a referral to Child Life for support to patient during glucose testing and insulin administration. 4. Social worker will continue to meet with family throughout hospitalization to assess coping and concrete needs assistance. 5. Social worker is coordinating with the medical team to learn if patient's insurance will provide her diabetic supplies and coordinate with the family to ensure that delivery is set up prior to discharge. 6. Social worker will discuss patient's care with the outpatient diabetes social worker, xx, so patient's care needs can be followed after discharge. Please page xx for any questions or needs. Cecilia Sanders, LCSW Pager xx

Source: Authors.

Consistent with efforts to enhance communication, social workers typically play a key role in making sure that families and medical teams have the same understanding of the sick child's needs. This function can be traced to origins of healthcare social work practice, and its value remains unchanged today. In busy healthcare environments, it is not uncommon for communication breakdowns to occur. It can also be expected that families struggle to understand and integrate complex and potentially unsettling medical information. As a consequence, it becomes good practice to frequently verify the family understanding of changing health conditions and interventions. Recognizing the importance of clear and sustained communication between families, patients, and healthcare team members, social workers often facilitate interdisciplinary care meetings, which allow personal interaction of all parties (including pediatric patients if developmentally appropriate). By facilitating timely, accurate, and inclusive information flow, misunderstandings are avoided (as well as the prospect of unwarranted litigation by disgruntled families), and the stage is constructively set for both immediate and long-term compliance with healthcare directives.

Many family members are so focused on the care of the child that they neglect their own needs. The importance of the *family members'* basic needs, however, must not be overlooked. Families must be relied upon for clear thinking and an emotional frame of mind that constructively supports the pediatric patient in contending with potentially overwhelming circumstances. Family members benefit from reminders to practice self-care, including healthy eating and sleeping. Hunger and exhaustion are incongruent with healing. As many families lead lives with significant unmet basic needs, social workers frequently become the primary stewards of resources, determining the nature of such needs and orchestrating health system and community resources in response. In times of scarcity, this *often* proves a challenging role.

The depth of psychosocial support provided to patients and families is a function of their unique needs. A commonly used therapeutic technique includes helping patients and families reframe or expand the meaning of their situation while supporting their ability to cope and make their current circumstance as manageable as possible. Anticipatory guidance regarding the potential adverse effects illness can have on the mental health and well-being of patients and families is a component of offered support. For this reason, social workers routinely provide counseling resources, including those that target sibling adjustment. These resources may include support groups for various age groups that are led by health system social workers. As families determine how much information to share with their sick child and/or siblings regarding a diagnosis, treatment plan, or prognosis, social workers can further the parents' understanding of the developmental needs of their child(ren) and how to best support the healing and adjustment of the entire family. Some organizations employ child life specialists who partner with social workers in these circumstances. Social workers typically offer stress reduction and coping techniques through direct counseling, bibliotherapy, and/or referral to clergy or specialized therapists in the community.

The most fundamental intervention issue is to enhance family problem-solving capabilities and decrease the "pile-up of demands" that may be perceived as overwhelming (Patterson, 1988). When situations become too difficult for families to effectively cope, crisis-intervention techniques may be employed to de-escalate the effects of the immediate stressors. The crises experienced by the family may be directly related to the medical care of the child or related to pre-existing family dynamics. Just as social workers assist patients and families in reframing challenges, they also help medical staff reframe their perceptions of patient and family behaviors considered to be difficult, non-compliant, and litigious or otherwise challenging to both the child's adjustment and delivery of care. Rather than focusing on perceived shortcomings, social workers consistently advocate for patients and families to be viewed through a "strengths-based" lens and use interventions such as mediation techniques to promote healthy communication (Weick, 2003).

Social workers' expertise in community resources is instrumental in delivering effective care to patients and families, including discharge planning. This expertise serves as a bridge by which patients and families travel from healthcare settings to their communities. Community-based resources include referrals to home health agencies for durable medical equipment and skilled nursing, financial resources including government entitlements, counseling and bereavement services, respite, child care, and connections to agencies providing concrete resources such as food, clothing, and housing (see *Table 12.3* for a list of activities characteristic to pediatric social work practice).

Table 12.3   Pediatric Social Work: Characteristic Activities

- Providing adjustment to illness counseling with special attention to the mental health needs of the patient and family members, particularly siblings
- Promoting an understanding of a medical diagnosis and implications of treatment plan compliance
- Crisis intervention
- Advocacy for patient and family-centered care
- Post-hospitalization (discharge) care planning
- Participation in interdisciplinary team meetings and ethics consultations
- Psychosocial education and anticipatory guidance regarding care needs
- Provision of community resource information and referral, including connecting patients and families to government entitlements and financial resources
- Mediation of family challenges and conflicts
- Intervention regarding domestic violence and personal safety planning
- Substance abuse assessments and treatment referrals
- Child abuse and neglect assessments and mandatory reporting
- Helping parents understand and manage child behavior challenges
- Assistance coordinating adoptions
- Psychiatric assessments of children (and/or parents)
- Advocacy within the education system

(Continued)

Table 12.3   (Continued)

- Facilitation of psychoeducational support groups which may include caregiver distress, bereavement and disease-specific topics
- Basic needs assistance including food, lodging, and transportation
- Providing adjustment to illness counseling with special attention to the mental health needs of the patient and family members, particularly siblings
- Promoting an understanding of a medical diagnosis and implications of treatment plan compliance
  - Crisis intervention
  - Advocacy for patient and family-centered care
  - Post-hospitalization (discharge) care planning
  - Participation in interdisciplinary team meetings and ethics consultations
  - Psychosocial education and anticipatory guidance regarding care needs
  - Provision of community resource information and referral, including connecting patients and families to government entitlements and financial resources
  - Mediation of family challenges and conflicts
  - Intervention regarding domestic violence and personal safety planning
  - Substance abuse assessments and treatment referrals
  - Child abuse and neglect assessments and mandatory reporting
  - Helping parents understand and manage child behavior challenges
  - Assistance coordinating adoptions

Source: Authors.

Integration and Collaboration With the Healthcare Team

How can I integrate into healthcare teams and contribute to the overall understanding of the patient and family's unique needs? How do I optimize the care provided by the team?

Social workers in healthcare settings most often participate as members of teams. These professional teams may consist of any variation of physicians (at different stages of training), nurse practitioners, nurses, physician assistants, rehabilitation specialists (physical therapists, occupational therapists, speech pathologists), nutritionists, child life specialists, chaplains, psychiatrists, psychologists, patient advocates, and volunteers. Each team member has a different, yet interrelated, role, and the value of each member's contribution is derived from his or her specialized training, expert knowledge, and professional perspective.

In examining how the social worker fits within a team, there are times when the role may be well-defined and easily navigated. At other times, however, team members may not utilize social workers to the full scope of their knowledge and skills. As noted in Chapter 1, early in the history of healthcare social work, Ida Cannon faced significant obstacles in her efforts to professionalize the discipline. She overcame the challenges, and her efforts resulted in a strong collaborative social work identity in adult and pediatric medical settings. In contemporary practice, each social worker has a responsibility to continue Ms. Cannon's legacy, representing a strong consistent professional voice within the healthcare team.

Interdisciplinary teams pose challenges to the individual practitioner arising from the numbers of colleagues on a team, the complexity of issues under discussion, idiosyncratic personalities, and the prevailing oversight or supervisory modality. Integrating onto the interdisciplinary team can prove challenging as a result of

- limited health team knowledge regarding social work roles,

- perception a family will be offended by a social work consult,

- fear social work will "intrude" on the medical team's relationship with the patient and family,

- perceived overlapping or disagreement about responsibilities and roles on the team, and

- conflicts in training and/or disagreement on warranted intervention modalities among team members.

Social workers must proactively define their role while at the same time negotiate the fine line of a profession serving in a "host," and even potentially hostile, setting. Rather than assuming a stance that challenged the medical model and primacy of the physician in healthcare, Cannon instead attempted to accommodate social work within the prevailing hospital culture. Her tactic proved successful in establishing her role and that of social work in her setting.

In response to team integration challenges, it is useful for social workers to

- inventory their professional knowledge and skills, identifying opportunities for growth and development;

- develop expertise in their specific practice area to enhance competency and demonstrate credibility to the team;

- reflect on the role they play in team integration challenges and request feedback so as to gain an understanding of role perceptions and ways to improve collegial collaboration; and

- initiate open and honest discussions with team members to define and clarify roles and discuss team dynamics and serve as a role model for mutual respect and solution-focused problem-solving.

When social work is successfully integrated on a healthcare team, other disciplines stand to gain a more comprehensive understanding of patient and family strengths as well as the challenges that impact the adjustment to illness, treatment, and discharge planning. Social workers, in turn, become cognizant of the unique perspectives held by other team members. In order to optimize collaboration, patient-care discussions should be a routine component of practice. These discussions may occur during interdisciplinary care coordination meetings or bedside rounds. They serve to ensure that all team members are working together and making patient-care decisions based on the same information. Such communication not only supports teamwork and seamless care coordination but also enhances the confidence held by patients and families regarding individual practitioners and the overall quality of care.

CASE STUDY

Social Work Integration in a Pediatric Setting

Thomas was recently hired to be the social worker in a pediatric gastroenterology outpatient clinic. While Thomas had experience in other outpatient settings, he had no experience working with patients diagnosed with eosinophilic esophagitis (EE) who were receiving care in the main clinic where Thomas would be providing social work services.

Thomas was introduced to the group of physicians, nurse practitioners, and nutritionists who would make up the team and began to accompany the team into the patient appointments to better understand the team dynamics. While being welcomed, several team members mentioned feeling as though social work had "nothing new to add" to the interventions already being performed by the team.

After observing the medical team and listening to the patients and families for several weeks, Thomas made several observations. He noted that EE was rare and had only recently been identified in the literature. The patients had numerous symptoms with varying severity, including vomiting, trouble breathing, food aversion, and stomach pain. The treatments included use of a strict medical diet, an elemental formula diet, or long-term use of steroid medications. The only way to assess the progress of the treatments was to perform a biopsy under anesthetic every 6 weeks. Thomas also noted that each patient responded differently to treatment and that all patients seemed to struggle with different emotional and behavioral reactions to the treatment modality and frequent sedated biopsies.

In his observation of parental response, Thomas saw that the restrictive medical diets impacted the ability of the parent to send the child safely to school or daycare, created a tremendous amount of stress when siblings could eat a normal diet and the patient could not, led to high anxiety regarding whether the treatments would work, and caused fear regarding the side effects and risks of repeatedly sedating their child. Through observing patient and parent responses and research into the diagnosis, Thomas presented his ideas to the medical team. He created a comprehensive education packet for newly diagnosed children and their parents. The packets combined medical information already provided by the medical team along with resources that addressed the emotional aspects of the disease on patients and families across the developmental spectrum.

As he began to work with families separately at their frequent clinic visits, Thomas consistently heard parents talk about how isolating this disease was for the child and family. In response to these feelings, Thomas began gaining consent from families to be able to "pair" patients and families with others so that newly diagnosed patients were connected with patients and families who were further along in the treatment phase. This was met with much success, particularly among Spanish-speaking families, who expressed feeling as if they finally had the support they needed.

After establishing this informal mentoring program, parents began to express the desire to meet as a group to support each other and begin to raise money for research into the diagnosis. With the full support and participation of the medical team, Thomas successfully established a parent-led support and child activity group that became prominent in the organization and a model for other medical clinics.

Case Study Discussion Questions:

1. What specific social work skills did Thomas utilize to integrate into an unfamiliar healthcare setting?

2. How did Thomas's professional assertiveness impact the lives of his patients and families?

3. Name three ways in which you can bring your professional skill set into a challenging health-care social work position.

Documentation

How do I document in a manner that reflects my work and brings psychosocial meaning to the patient's care?

Thoughtful, well-articulated documentation contributes to social work's integration onto the interdisciplinary team while enhancing the team's understanding of and appreciation for the needs of the patient and family. Information provided typically identifies

- Patient and family understanding of medical condition

- Adjustment to current circumstances

- Available family resources and unmet resource needs

- Understanding of current and anticipated patient care

- Capacity to identify/execute an ongoing patient care plan

- Barriers to care collaboration and/or discharge

- Supplemental external resources being engaged to meet needs

Quality documentation is strengths-based and culturally sensitive. While concerns or issues in patient and family psychodynamics are noted, emphasis is made to document those positive functional characteristics that can be engaged to move treatment forward.

Using specific health system protocols, patient care documentation is entered in a timely, accurate manner so as to maximize its appropriate use by other healthcare team members. As patient conditions are suspect to frequent change, effort is made to continuously update documentation as appropriate. Effort is made to ensure that observations and comments are objective; hearsay comments (comments made by someone other than the immediate party) are regarded as unsubstantiated and therefore avoided. Documentation focuses on relevant issues pertaining to the patient condition and treatment; extraneous topics, including critiques of individual practitioners or healthcare systems, are precluded. (*See Table 12.2 for an example of a documented psychosocial assessment.*) The essence of establishing what to document in the medical/healthcare record is to record that information that other healthcare professionals would need to know in order to effectively intervene with the patient.

The process and expectations of documentation are rapidly changing as a result of both technological improvements in electronic medical (EMRs) and healthcare (EHRs) records as well as increased attention to the central role of patient care documentation in legislation such as the PPACA. Because electronic healthcare records hold the promise of making more complete data files available on immediate notice across the spectrum of settings in which the patient is receiving care, it becomes even more crucial that all healthcare professionals recognize the importance of accurate, timely, and care-relevant documentation.

Child Maltreatment

Child maltreatment is a broad term that is used interchangeably with "abuse and neglect" to describe the various ways in which children may experience harm. In the federal fiscal year 2012, an estimated 686,000 children were abused or neglected in the United States. Of these children, an estimated 1,640 children died. These numbers reflect a prevalence rate for unique child victims of 9.2 victims per 1,000 children. Notably, children under the age of 1 year are the most vulnerable for maltreatment, representing 21.9 per 1,000 victims. In addition, the youngest victims of abuse also have the highest fatality rates, with 70% of child maltreatment deaths occurring in children under the age of 3 years (USDHHS, 2013). To put these statistics into perspective compared to another serious childhood illness, there are nearly eighty times more victims of child maltreatment in the United States per year than all new pediatric cancer diagnoses (USDHHS, 2009; National Cancer Institute, January 2008). Furthermore, child maltreatment statistics represent only the children who come to the attention of child welfare authorities. It is believed that thousands of others suffer silently, never coming to the attention of child welfare systems.

In response to the problem of child maltreatment, the federal government passed the Child Abuse Prevention and Treatment Act (CAPTA) of 1974, which provides a minimum federal definition of child maltreatment (Child Welfare Information Gateway, 2011). However, each state is responsible for its own laws and response systems. As a result, there is no uniform national definition of what constitutes child maltreatment and variability exists across states. Despite differences in the legal definitions, it is possible to view child maltreatment within six main categories:

1. Physical abuse: inflicting injuries to a child including bruises, burns, fractures, abdominal trauma, and abusive head trauma

2. Sexual abuse: any form of sexual contact with a child, including fondling, penetration, oral or genital contact, exposing a child to pornography, or creating pornographic images of a child

3. Emotional abuse: demeaning behavior towards a child, including yelling, belittling, blaming, or humiliation

4. Neglect: failing to meet a child's basic needs, including food, clothing, shelter, healthcare, or education

5. Risk of harm: exposing a child to a situation that causes a risk to the child but has not caused actual harm (e.g., exposing the child to domestic violence, chemical dependency, or criminal activity in the home environment)

6. Medical child abuse (previously known as Munchausen syndrome by proxy): fabricating or producing medical symptoms in a child that result in a child receiving unnecessary and harmful or potentially harmful medical care (Roesler & Jenny, 2008)

It is critical for social workers in healthcare settings to possess comprehensive knowledge of their individual state's child welfare laws and definitions, including their professional roles as mandated reporters. This is due to the high prevalence of child maltreatment and also due to the unique roles healthcare professionals serve in identifying and responding to maltreatment. Children often present to healthcare settings for treatment of injuries or conditions that are the result of child maltreatment. In some instances, the child's condition causes immediate concern for maltreatment, whereas in other situations, concerns arise only after further medical evaluation.

Social workers responding to concerns for maltreatment must be prepared to offer crisis intervention and therapeutic support to parents and loved ones who experience feelings of shock and dismay upon learning there is suspicion that a child has been maltreated. These feelings serve to complicate coping and problem-solving abilities as well as family functioning. Concurrently, non-offending parents may be grappling with suspicions that someone they love and/or trust, including their spouse or partner, may have caused harm to their child. Furthermore, the offender may be present with the child in the healthcare setting, adding to the complexities of ensuring the child's safety and well-being, supporting the family (including the possible offender), and helping medical staff remain effectively focused. These dynamics require the responding social worker to hold a high degree of skill and comfort in managing highly emotive and volatile situations as well as the ability and commitment to withhold personal judgment and remain neutral.

Beyond providing crisis intervention and emotional support, the social worker's role includes the psychosocial assessment of the patient and family. This requires special attention to obtaining an accurate history of the events leading to the child receiving medical care as well as an assessment of the family's overall functioning, including risk factors for maltreatment. There are three important risk categories for maltreatment which social workers must understand: *parental* risk factors, *child* risk factors, and *environmental* risk factors. *Parental risk factors* include young age (chronological or developmental), cognitive or developmental disabilities, relationship conflict, custody issues, substance abuse, mental illness, history of violence or extensive law enforcement involvement, domestic violence, and previous or current child protective services involvement. *Child risk factors* include age (the younger the child, the more risk), difficult temperament (actual or perceived by the caregiver), physical or cognitive disability, and a chronic medical or mental health condition. *Environmental risk factors* include homelessness, limited or insufficient financial resources, recent or long-standing unemployment, inadequate or suboptimal child care arrangements, lack of access to affordable health insurance, and language, cultural, or religious barriers to accessing healthcare or supportive service (Myers et al., 2002). The presence of risk factors does not cause a child to be maltreated. It simply indicates that there exists increased vulnerability within the family system and interventions should be aimed at alleviating the risks. The correlation between neglect and poverty illustrates this point. Research indicates that children living in poverty are at increased risk for experiencing neglect. However, the majority of children living in poverty do not experience neglect. There are unique needs and vulnerabilities of some families experiencing poverty that lead to child neglect.

Social work assessments can be used to identify at-risk children and employ interventions to prevent maltreatment from occurring, often by helping families gain access to concrete resources. Specifically in healthcare settings, social work assessments are vitally important in assessing a parent's capacity to meet a child's medical needs through compliance with the treatment plan and preventing *medical neglect*. Medical neglect results from a parent failing to respond to obvious signs of serious illness in a child or failing to adhere to medical advice once it is given (Jenny, 2007). Social workers partner with medical teams and families to understand what is required to meet a child's medical needs and identify and overcome possible barriers in care. Furthermore, social workers help medical teams understand the context in which possible medical neglect has *already* occurred in order to support compliance moving forward. For example, a social worker may learn that a parent did not bring a child to a series of diabetic clinic appointments because of lack of transportation, or the social worker may learn that the parent is distracted from meeting the child's medical needs due to his or her own personal addiction challenges.

Regardless of the contributing factors leading to the maltreatment, social workers must fulfill their roles as *mandated reporters*. Although child welfare reporting laws often protect the identities of reporters, these authors recommend that social workers partner with medical teams to inform parents of child maltreatment concerns and reporting responsibilities whenever possible. Rare exceptions exist when there are concerns regarding the safety of the reporter or the parent is unable to be contacted. This clinical approach is intended to promote relationships of transparency, trust, and healing. By removing secrecy surrounding the reporting process, social workers and medical teams can strive to genuinely join with parents and child welfare authorities to therapeutically confront the challenges families are facing and focus on the health, well-being, and recovery of the child.

Due to the prevalence of child maltreatment as well as recognition of child abuse pediatrics as a board-certified medical subspecialty in 2009, there are increasing opportunities for social workers in healthcare settings, specifically hospitals, to specialize in the management of child maltreatment cases. In addition to providing direct practice to children and families within these environments, social workers can be instrumental in developing policies and procedures regarding the identification and management of child maltreatment cases consistent with evidence-based practices and national best practice standards.

PROFESSIONAL VALUES AND ETHICS

Professional social work values in action reflect the individual practitioner's pledge to service, pursuit of social justice, honor for the dignity and worth of the individual, promise of integrity, championing of the importance of human relationships, and strides for competence (National Association of Social Workers, 2008). These values serve as the ethical compass of social work practice.

Within the context of healthcare teams, social workers must know who they are and what they represent to the team. While team relationships are among the most satisfying within the work environment, the pediatric social worker is constantly challenged to find the balance of collaboration and negotiation within the team and adherence to one's own professional values and ethical principles. Self-awareness, grounded confidence in practice, and a balanced perspective become crucial. Ample opportunity to model these values *in action* for team members occurs during times of differing professional opinions, blurred roles, and ethical dilemmas.

The social work value most central to developing trusting relationships is that of honoring the dignity and worth of the patient and family (and/or other relevant decision-makers). Use of the **strengths-based** practice approach supports relationship development by focusing on patients' and families' internal and external competencies, resources, and assets. It is the social worker's skill in identifying and promoting the use of these individual and family strengths that opens the door to support and promote the ongoing health and well-being of the child and family. Saleebey (2010) provided the following framework for strengths-based practice:

- Believe the patient and family and believe *in* the patient and family.

- Affirm and show interest in the patient and family's view of things.

- Focus on the dreams, hopes, and visions of your patient and family in order to encourage them to begin thinking about what might be and how it might come out.

- Assess the assets, resources, reserves, and capacities that the patient and family have access to.

- Believe that there are forces for healing, self righting, and wisdom within or around the patient/family and begin to search for and employ these forces in the service of achieving the treatment goals (pp. 133–134).

There are times when the act of embracing professional social work values and focusing on patient and family strengths introduces challenges. Patient care decisions that are inconsistent with professional values may give rise to ethical dilemmas and potentially impact the patient and family. In pediatric practice, these dilemmas may involve

- End-of-life decisions, including when to forego life-sustaining treatment

- Participation of patients in clinical trials

- Consent, assent, and disclosure issues

- Disparities in access to quality medical care

- Integration of cultural beliefs and values into care

- Identification and assessment of child maltreatment

Social workers recognize the importance of supporting patients' rights to self-determination while contending with these issues. However, when working with children, this value has different meaning because of the role(s) parents assume in children's lives. For parents faced with making difficult decisions, including end-of-life decisions, these can be some of the darkest, most troubling moments of their lives. These are also precisely the moments when social work plays an integral role by ensuring that family members understand the medical information being provided to them, have an opportunity to share their personal values with the medical team, and have their questions sufficiently addressed. In some situations, issues related to the *quality* of life parents hope for their child and the *quantity* of life the medical interventions may provide become ethical considerations.

One of the most charged ethical issues in pediatric social work practice relates to end-of-life and quality-of-life decisions. Boebel Toly et al. (2010) noted that advances in science and technology, particularly in the areas of mechanical ventilation, intravenous nutrition and medication administration, nutrition support, and apnea monitors in the past two decades have dramatically increased the survival rate of chronically ill children. These advances have also promoted greater dependency on technology and intensive home care for the continued survival of the child, but with potentially negative impacts on the psychological health of the child's family and caretakers.

As professionals, social workers must continually be aware of how their own personal beliefs impact their engagement with families and the care they provide. This may be a difficult endeavor when complex ethical issues are involved and emotions are heightened. Sometimes, though, there is simply no clear "right or wrong" decision. In these cases, social workers should pursue supervision and consultation with colleagues for active reflection and support.

CASE STUDY

Addressing Values and Ethics in Pediatric Care

A 24-week-old preterm infant (micro-premie) was transferred to the neonatal intensive care unit (NICU) at a tertiary care hospital from an outside hospital 12 hours after his birth. His parents named him Noah, and because the birth was a cesarean section, his mother remained hospitalized at the birth hospital located 50 miles away. Due to Noah's extreme prematurity, he was critically ill and was in an isolette, required intubation for breathing, and had several brain hemorrhages (bleeds in the brain that may occur in premature infants).

The social worker was called to meet with Noah's father, Mr. Simpson, who had arrived at the hospital. Noah was the fourth child born to the Simpson family, and while his birth was happily anticipated, none of Noah's siblings had been born prematurely or had special needs. Noah's premature birth came as a devastating shock to his parents.

When the social worker met with Mr. Simpson, he stated that he and his wife "wanted Noah to die" and "to be taken off any support" because the family did not want a child with "any special needs." While Noah was critically ill and his chances for survival low, he was stable and being cared for by an advanced medical team.

The social worker and medical team provided support and information to Mr. Simpson and explained that while Noah was very ill, he had a chance for survival. Mr. Simpson was insistent that he and his wife "had already discussed it" and were ready to have Noah "die. . .right now."

The medical team and social worker were concerned that Mr. Simpson was having a crisis response and was feeling overwhelmed by the events of the last 24 hours. The medical team was also concerned that Mrs. Simpson was 50 miles away and therefore not present to represent her decisions related to Noah's care.

The social worker met with Mr. Simpson to perform a psychosocial assessment and better understand Mr. Simpson's request. Mr. and Mrs. Simpson were well educated, economically stable, and reported having multiple resources in helping to care for their three other children. Mr. Simpson was emphatic that it was unacceptable for Noah to have any "special needs." Mr. Simpson stated that he did not want a child who couldn't read, speak, see, hear, or was "slow." When the medical team stated that only time would show what kind of deficits Noah may have, Mr. Simpson responded that "no deficits" were acceptable as he and his wife did not want to raise a child who wasn't "normal."

While parents of premature infants often have to make decisions about end-of-life care, this type of response by a parent was unusual so shortly after Noah's birth. Mr. Simpson was emphatic that the NICU team "end Noah's life" immediately and repeatedly stated that he had made funeral arrangements in the past several hours.

In this situation, the role of the social worker and medical team was to assess Noah's medical status as well as consider the wishes of the family. Due to Mr. Simpson's concerning statements, the

(Continued)

(Continued)

primary medical team requested an Ethics Consult. The Ethics Team determined that Noah's care could not be discontinued, but his parents were able to make the decision not to escalate any of Noah's medical interventions and the team would not intervene should Noah's condition deteriorate.

Two days later, Noah began to show signs of distress. The family did not want the medical team to intervene. To provide the family with the ability to participate in Noah's end-of-life care, Noah was transferred back to the hospital where his mother remained hospitalized and died in his mother's arms with both of his parents present.

The social worker who was working with Noah and his family was 8 months pregnant during this intervention and had a strong emotional response to the values and beliefs of Mr. and Mrs. Simpson. She struggled personally to align with a parent who had financial and emotional resources to care for a disabled child but simply did not want to parent a child who was not "perfect." The social worker could not imagine making this choice if her own child was delivered prematurely and felt that the family was selfish.

Putting aside her own personal belief system, the social worker recognized that Mr. Simpson was realistic regarding the long road that faced Noah and the medical and developmental hardships the family may have faced due to his extreme prematurity. Noah's parents had the inherent right to make decisions about whether or not to escalate treatment but could not ask medical providers to remove any of the current interventions (nutrition, fluid support, respiratory support) at time of arrival in the NICU.

Case Study Discussion Questions:

Apply Saleeby's strengths-based framework (2010) to this family.

1. What is your opinion of Mr. Simpson's request of the medical team? Do you believe a parent can refuse to care for a child with special needs?

2. Who is your identified patient? How do the social work concepts of self-determination and advocacy present in this case example?

3. As the social worker, what would your response have been to Mr. Simpson and the medical team? How do you keep your own feelings from interfering with your relationship with a family?

PRACTICE CHALLENGES

Working in a pediatric setting provides an array of opportunities to intervene and effectively support family functioning. As in any field, however, there are inherent challenges. These roadblocks are not insurmountable but require social workers to employ fundamental social work values and creative problem-solving in order to affect change on both an individual and system level.

Passage of the PPACA is destined to have significant impacts on both healthcare consumers and service delivery environment. As not all states have accepted the opportunity to expand their Medicaid programs in conjunction with the PPACA rollout, disparities can be anticipated in terms of how poor families in particular are able to access and benefit from quality health and behavioral healthcare. Varying state laws will differentially impact the ability of low-income families as well as immigrant and/or undocumented families to attain affordable health insurance. This disparity in access presents ethical and practice challenges for the pediatric medical social worker. When a child or family is prevented from receiving the medical care and psychosocial support that they need to strengthen the health of the family, it undermines core social work values. Social workers must be diligent in researching state laws, government entitlement programs, and community agencies to be able to offer options and ameliorate barriers. Additionally, the PPACA emphasis on prevention, wellness and chronic health issues heightens the focus on ambulatory, outpatient services. Clinic social workers should anticipate the prospect of increased enrollments and shortened interventions with individual cases.

As communities become increasingly ethnically, religiously, racially, and financially diverse, social work interventions have correspondingly become more challenging. In order to effectively provide assessment, intervention, and advocacy to parents and children with medical needs, it is imperative to understand the cultural framework of the family. Having access to skilled medical language interpreters, possessing relevant knowledge related to diversity, and being able to acknowledge and address oppression due to bias are key challenges to developing intervention strategies that will be effective and supportive. Healthcare social workers must learn to use neutral language, be aware of their own personal biases and knowledge gaps, and be adept at comforting families from diverse backgrounds at times when there are healthcare needs or crises.

While child maltreatment is regrettably pervasive, the interventions are often challenging and present considerable ethical and moral dilemmas for the pediatric medical social worker. Social workers are trained to view individuals from a family system and strengths-based perspective. At times, this training can feel at odds when a social worker needs to advocate for the safety of a child that may result in the removal of that child from the care of his or her parents. In these cases, the potential risk and current harm to the child must be thoroughly assessed in relation to the strengths of the family system and the implications of such removal.

At a time when healthcare organizations face escalating costs and lower reimbursement rates, it becomes crucial that social workers identify ways to align their professional values and goals with the business goals and strategic plans of their practice settings. For social workers who traditionally see their roles as clinical in nature, this may pose a challenging paradigm shift. In comparison, for social workers routinely participating in hospital discharge planning, this may be a well-understood and embraced view. These practitioners have experienced increasing pressures to efficiently discharge patients in the fewest number of days while ensuring they have remained long enough in care for appropriate treatment and safe discharge. Whether social workers are primary discharge planners or act as psychosocial consultants to the medical team, they are crucial to the early identification of discharge barriers and successful, expedient bridging of patients and families to needed community resources. In addition to monitoring lengths of stay, social workers in both hospitals and clinics can play key roles in preventing avoidable readmissions and unnecessary emergency room visits, both of which can be very costly to hospitals and stressful for patients and families. Through quality discharge planning from hospitals and timely, comprehensive care coordination in clinic settings, social work interventions support patients and families in accessing the correct level of care in the most appropriate setting.

Driven by reimbursement pressures and increased attention to quality outcomes, healthcare organizations closely analyze the utilization patterns and medical needs of the patients they serve. A 2011 study found that 2.9% of patients with frequent recurrent admissions to children's hospitals consisted of 18.8% of overall hospital admissions and represented 23.2% of charges (Berry et al., 2011). These data are significant as they demonstrate the importance of understanding the needs of a small percentage of children who have a *large* impact on resource utilization. The example illustrates an opportunity for pediatric social work to join in critical discussions leading to improvements in both quality care delivery (such as expansion of medical home models) and prudent, economical hospital operations.

PRACTICE OPPORTUNITIES

Endless opportunities exist in pediatric services for social workers to improve delivery of care, contribute and lead program development efforts, and advance professional practice. Let's examine some specific opportunities in which social work can make particularly valuable contributions to patient and family care.

Healthcare has been evolving away from a disease-centered model and toward the *patient-centered models* promoted as crucial service-delivery components of the PPACA. In the older, disease-centered model, physicians make almost all treatment decisions based largely on clinical experience and data from various medical tests. In patient-centered models, patients become active participants in their own care and receive services designed to focus on their individual needs and preferences, in addition to advice and counsel from health professionals (USDHHS, Agency for Healthcare Research and Quality, 2002). In pediatric care, this model represents an approach to service delivery that recognizes the vital roles that family members serve in the care of children and promotes practices that optimize family involvement. The family is formally viewed as a member of the healthcare team with recognition that parents hold expert knowledge regarding what is best for their children.

While most healthcare settings agree with the premise of **patient-and-family-centered care**, the rollout of this philosophy may vary significantly in both form and outcome, depending on the organization and involved parties. Due to their empowerment orientation and characteristic relationships with families, social workers are well positioned to support these initiatives. Patient-and-family-centered care may include development of child and parent advisory councils where children and parents serve as formal advisors to the organization, shaping policies and practices ranging from visitation guidelines to architectural design of new buildings. Parent-to-parent support or mentoring programs also arise from this philosophy. Social workers may partner with parents who have children with special healthcare needs and who are interested in extending support to other parents in a formal capacity.

At the same time, social workers need to lobby within provider organizations that the acceptance of such practices increases patient/family satisfaction with care, enhances medical compliance, and reduces healthcare costs as cooperation with efficient, effective practices increases. With research indicating that parental stress decreases when parents are involved in hospital care (Frazier et al., 2010; Shudy et al., 2006), actively engaging parents in crucial decision making inherently represents "best practice." Beyond conventional day-to-day care, such involvement may range from allowing parents to be present during resuscitation attempts and invasive procedures to honoring diverse health practices of the family by allowing complimentary or alternative medicine approaches in the treatment plan. Potential roles for siblings in the care of patients may be considered as well as formally including families in bedside rounds as a component of a provider's patient and family centered care practice.

Although psychoeducational support groups represent an effective treatment option, many pediatric social workers struggle to find sufficient time for coordination and facilitation of such activities. As a result, the availability of support groups and families may become limited in the face of community need. Needs assessments that underscore patient interest and benefits to patients and the organization alike often prove the catalyst for successfully launching these groups. Support group topics typically include patient and family adjustment to a specific disease, caregiver distress bereavement, and sharing of techniques for providing ongoing care. Groups may vary in structure (open or closed) and duration (on-going or time-limited).

Medical needs predictably change over time, with few pediatric healthcare providers being able to sustain involvement as children with special needs or chronic illnesses become adults. For children whose conditions extend into adulthood, anticipating this change in care can be stress-inducing for both child and family. Although it is critical to implement strategies that facilitate the *transition from pediatric to adult medical services*, there continue to be significant gaps in these practices. A policy statement collectively endorsed by the American Academy of Pediatrics, the American Academy of Family Physicians, and the American College of Physicians and American Society of Internal Medicine (2002b) states

> . . . a consensus on the critical first steps that the medical profession needs to take to realize the vision of a family-centered, continuous, comprehensive, coordinated, compassionate, and culturally competent healthcare system that is as developmentally appropriate as it is technically sophisticated. The goal of transition in healthcare for young adults with special healthcare needs is to maximize lifelong functioning and potential through the provision of high-quality, developmentally appropriate healthcare services that continue uninterrupted as the individual moves from adolescence to adulthood. (p. 1304)

Unfortunately, the vision of this statement does not reflect universal practice. Many children transition into adult care settings without sufficient preparation. Pediatric social workers can be particularly valuable to this issue by identifying best practices related to transitional care and taking leadership of efforts by pediatric clinics and hospitals to integrate visionary changes.

Social workers have active roles in disseminating information and practice recommendations throughout the array of pediatric healthcare settings. Forums for such communication are numerous and include formal lectures, staff meetings, patient care rounds, grand rounds, brownbag lunches, and one-on-one sessions. The issues addressed in such forums are literally boundless but characteristically include techniques for conveying difficult news to patients and families, professional boundaries, child abuse and neglect, domestic violence, substance misuse, cultural competence, vicarious trauma/self-care, effective interdisciplinary collaboration, available resources, and effective methods for engaging resistant families. Topic competence, balanced perspective on patient/family and organizational needs, leadership in establishing educational forums, and ability to facilitate collegial dialogue make important, lasting impressions about the value-added contribution of social work to healthcare.

An exciting array of opportunities exists by which pediatric social workers can advance professional practice. Instilled commitment to field instruction and academia promotes the profession's ongoing growth through transfer of knowledge and facilitation of new ideas and critical reflection in the work environment (Mailick & Caroff, 1996; Spitzer & Nash, 1996; Rehr, 1983). The commitment that professional staff members make to social work education is consistent with a practice setting that is committed to excellence. This excellence extends to staff providing peers and colleagues with clinical supervision toward professional social work licensure, including group supervision.

In the spirit of embracing opportunities, pediatric social workers must embrace *informed* self-advocacy when requesting additional resources, including sufficient staffing levels, within their practice settings. It is essential for social workers to understand existing financial landscapes and climates to make timely and appropriate requests. Comprehensive needs assessments including gaps in existing services as well as the anticipated added value of any new resource will bring credibility to any advocacy effort. The Society for Social Work Leadership in Healthcare (2013) has recommended specific inpatient staffing ratios that can serve as a blueprint for adequate staffing; however, the underlying justification is critical in the context of each unique environment. Strategies to strengthen resource-related advocacy efforts include identification of medical provider champions, development of interdisciplinary workgroups focused on quality, and partnerships with the organization's philanthropic body.

SUMMARY

This chapter reviewed major child health issues in the United States and examined practice contexts in pediatric healthcare. It examined social work roles, professional challenges, and future opportunities. In doing so, it highlighted the value of the social work contribution to healthcare delivery and underscored the responsibility of the individual social work practitioner to both advance professional practice and education. Working in conjunction with the healthcare team, social work represents a significant professional resource to the pediatric patient and family as well as to provider organizations and ultimately the community at large.

The specialty of pediatric social work affords abundant opportunity to engage in stimulating, challenging practice in an increasingly diverse array of inpatient and outpatient healthcare settings. The professional rewards are significant, including the satisfaction of intervening with a vulnerable young patient population and influencing both the child's and family's health status and quality of life. Being ill, injured, or disabled at any age is often an overwhelming, debilitating experience, but contending with such circumstances as a child or parent of a young child can be particularly challenging. Adjustment is made more difficult when families have social, emotional, and/or financial limitations. These situations call for sensitive, competent, ethical practice from dedicated professionals who can apply their own skills and compassion while effectively orchestrating additional necessary resources.

KEY TERMS AND CONCEPTS

- Ecological perspective
- Special healthcare needs
- Primary care and subspecialty clinics
- Acute care and rehabilitation hospitals
- End-of-life care
- Family systems theory
- Family Adjustment and Adaptation Response Model
- Resilience
- Child maltreatment
- Strengths-based practice
- Patient-and-family-centered care
- Medical home model

QUESTIONS FOR DISCUSSION

1. Child maltreatment impacts many children and families. What skills do you need to develop in order to assess and intervene in these cases?

2. Pediatric healthcare presents complex ethical considerations that require the social worker to support a patient and family from a neutral perspective. Are there any decisions by medical teams, patients, or families you feel that you could never support?

EXERCISES

1. You are the social worker in an outpatient clinic located in a school-based health center. The nurse practitioner you work with has just informed you that a 14-year-old in the 8th grade has a positive pregnancy test. The patient is crying and does not want to tell her parents. You have been consulted to meet with the student to provide emotional support and help her understand the options.

   - Look up the laws regarding adolescent healthcare rights in your state. What confidentiality laws apply to pregnancy? Does she have the right to refuse to tell her parents?

   - What options would you offer this patient? If you offer the option of pregnancy termination would she be able to have the procedure without parental consent?

   - What actions would you recommend to her?

   - What are your personal feelings about this situation?

2. Read the following scenarios and consider your role as the social worker on the interdisciplinary medical team:

   - Max is a previously active and healthy 6-year-old boy who sustained a complex femoral fracture after falling out of a tree while playing at his grandparent's farm. His injury required surgery to fix the bone and he must wear a spica cast for 6 weeks. The spica cast is a rigid plaster cast that covers both Max's thighs and covers his stomach up to his chest. The cast prevents Max from being able to sit upright, walk, or use the bathroom for the next six weeks. Max will require special car restraints, a wheelchair, and be required to wear diapers.

   - Shante is an 8-month-old infant who was just diagnosed with spinal muscular atrophy (SMA) Type 2 after her parents and pediatrician noticed that she was not meeting her developmental milestones. SMA is a degenerative and incurable genetic disorder that manifests in general muscle loss and mobility impairment over time. Shante's parents were told that she may never be able to sit without assistance, stand, or walk. The physicians also told her parents that over time, some babies with this disease become unable to breathe and require ventilation support.

      i. Discuss possible psychosocial implications of each scenario, for the patients and family members.

      ii. What questions from *Table 12.1* do you regard as particularly crucial in a comprehensive psychosocial assessment?

      iii. What do you believe are important components of ongoing care in each scenario?

REFERENCES

Akinbami, L., Moorman, J., & Liu, X. (2011). Asthma prevalence, health care use, and mortality: United States, 2005–2009. *National Health Statistics Reports, 32,* Hyattsville, MD: National Center for Health Statistics. Retrieved from http://www.cdc.gov/nchs/data/nhsr/nhsr032.pdf

Agran, P., Anderson, C., Winn, D., Trent, R., Walton-Haynes, L., & Thayer, S. (2003). Rates of pediatric injuries by 3-month intervals for children 0 to 3 years of age. *Pediatrics, 2003, 111* e683. Retrieved 6/18/12 from http://www.pediatricsdigest.mobi/content/111/6/e683.full.pdf + html

American Academy of Pediatrics. (2002a). The medical home. *Pediatrics, 110,* 184–186.

American Academy of Pediatrics, American Academy of Family Physicians, American College of Physicians, American Society of Internal Medicine. (2002b). A consensus statement on health care transition for young adults with special health care needs. *Pediatrics, 110,* 1304–1306.

American Academy of Pediatrics. (2011). *Hospital care.* Retrieved from http://www2.aap.org/healthtopics/hospitalcare.cfm

American Board of Medical Specialties. (2012). *Specialties and subspecialties.* Retrieved from http://www.abms.org/who_we_help/physicians/specialties.aspx

American Hospital Association. (January 2012). *Fast facts on U.S. hospitals.* Retrieved from http://www.aha.org/research/rc/stat-studies/fast-facts.shtml

Anthony, K., Gil, K., & Schanberg, L. (2003). Brief report: Parental perceptions of child vulnerability in children with chronic illness. *Journal of Pediatric Psychology, 28,* 185–190.

Barlow, J., & Ellard, D. (2006). The psychosocial well-being of children with chronic disease, their parents and sibling: An overview of the research evidence base. *Child Care, Health and Development, 32,* 19–31.

Berenson, G., Srinivasan, S., Bao, W., Newman, W., Tracy, R., & Wattigney, W. (1998). Association between multiple cardiovascular risk factors and atherosclerosis in children and young adults. The Bogalusa Heart Study. *New England Journal of Medicine, 338*(23):1650–1656.

Berry, J. G., Hall, D. E., Kuo, D. Z., Cohen, E., Agrawah, R., Feudtner, C., Hall, M., Kuesser, J., Kaplan, W., & Neff, J. (2011). Hospital utilization and characteristics of patients experiencing recurrent readmissions within children's hospitals. *Journal of the American Medical Association, 305,* 682–690.

Bloom, B., Cohen, R., & Freeman, G. (2010). Summary health statistics for U.S. children: National health interview survey, 2010. *Vital Health Stat, 10,* 1–80. Retrieved from http://www.ncbi.nlm.nih.gov/pubmed/22338334

Boebel Toly, V., Musil, C., & Carl, J. (2010). Families with children who are technology dependent: Normalization and family functioning. *Western Journal of Nursing Research, 34,* 52–71.

Borse, N., Gilchrist, J., Dellinger, A., Rudd, R., Ballesteros, M., & Sleet, D. (2008). *CDC childhood injury report: Patterns of unintentional injuries among 1-19 year olds in the United States, 2000-2006.* Atlanta, GA: Centers for Disease Control and Prevention, National Center for Injury Prevention and Control. Retrieved from http://www.cdc.gov/safechild/images/CDC-ChildhoodInjury.pdf

Boyle, C. A., Boulet, S., Schieve, L. A., Cohen. R. A., Blumberg, S. J., Yeargin-Allsopp, M., & Visser, S. (2011). Trends in the prevalence of developmental disabilities in U.S. children 1997–2008. *Pediatrics, 127,* 1034–1042. Retrieved from http://pediatrics.aappublications.org/content/127/6/1034.full.pdf + html

Bruce, M. (2006). A systematic and conceptual review of posttraumatic stress in childhood cancer survivors and their parents, *Clinical Psychology Review, 26,* 233–256.

Centers for Disease Control and Prevention. (2008). *National diabetes fact sheet: Estimates on diabetes in the United States–2007.* Atlanta, GA: U.S. Department of Health and Human Services, Centers for Disease Control and Prevention.

Centers for Disease Control and Prevention. (2013). Mental health surveillance among children—United States, 2005–2011. *MMWR, 62*(Suppl; May 16, 2013), 1–35. Retrieved from http://www.cdc.gov/mmwr/preview/mmwrhtml/su6202a1.htm

Child Welfare Information Gateway. (2011). *About CAPTA: A legislative history*. Washington, DC: U.S. Department of Health and Human Services, Children's Bureau. Retrieved from http://www.childwelfare.gov/pubs/factsheets/about.cfm

Cystic Fibrosis Foundation. (May 2011). *Frequently asked questions*. Retrieved from http://www.cff.org/AboutCF/Faqs/

Dauz Williams, P. (1997) Siblings and pediatric chronic illness: A review of the literature. *International Journal of Nursing Studies, 34*, 313–323.

Eiser, C. (1997). Children's quality of life measures. *Archives of Disease in Childhood, 77*, 350–354.

Frazier, A., Frazier, H., & Warren, N. (2010). A discussion of family centered care within the pediatric intensive care unit. *Critical Care Nursing Quarterly, 33*, 82–86.

Friebert, S. (2009). Pain management for children with cancer at end of life: Beginning steps toward a standard of care. *Pediatric Blood Cancer, 52*, 749–750. Retrieved from http://onlinelibrary.wiley.com/doi/10.1002/pbc.21892/pdf

Greenwood, K. (August 2010). PPACA and the growing shortage of pediatric subspecialties. *Health Reform Watch, August 2010*. Retrieved from http://www.healthreformwatch.com/2010/08/22/ppaca-and-the-growing-shortage-of-pediatric-subspecialists/

Howden, M., & Meyer, J. (May 2011). Age and sex composition—2010: 2010 Census Briefs. Retrieved from http://www.census.gov/prod/cen2010/briefs/c2010br-03.pdf

Jenny, C. (2007). Recognizing and responding to medical neglect. *Pediatrics, 120*, 1385–1389.

Joint Commission. (2012). *About the Joint Commission*. Retrieved from http://www.jointcommission.org/about_us/about_the_joint_commission_main.aspx

Joint Commission. (2014). *2014 Joint Commission resources e-dition*. Retrieved from https://e-dition.jcrinc.com/MainContent.aspx

Krebs, N., Himes, J., Jacobson, D., Nicklas, T., Guilday, P., & Styne D. (2007). Assessment of child and adolescent overweight and obesity. *Pediatrics, 120*(Suppl. 4), S193–S228.

Mailick, M., & Carloff, P. (1996). *Professional social work education and health care*. New York: The Haworth Press.

McPherson, M., Arango, P., Fox, H., Lauver, C., McManus, M., Newacheck, P., Perrin, J., Shonkoff, J., & Strickland, B. (1998). A new definition of children with special health care needs. *Pediatrics, 102*(1):137–140.

Murray, J. (1998). The lived experience of childhood cancer: One sibling's experience. *Issues in Pediatric Nursing, 21*, 217–227.

Myers, J.E.B., Berliner, L., Briere, J., Hendrix, C. T., Jenny, C., & Reid, T. A. (2002). *The APSAC handbook on child maltreatment* (2nd ed.) London: Sage.

National Association of Children's Hospitals and Related Institutions. (2007). *All children need children's hospitals* (2nd ed.). Retrieved from http://www.upstate.edu/gch/pdf/allchildren.pdf

National Association of Social Workers. (2008). *Code of Ethics of the National Association of Social Workers*. Washington, DC: Author. Retrieved from http://www.socialworkers.org/pubs/code/code.asp

National Cancer Institute. (January 2008). *Fact sheet: Childhood cancers*. Retrieved from http://www.cancer.gov/cancertopics/factsheet/Sites-Types/childhood

National Cancer Institute. (October 2011a). *Dictionary of cancer terms: Cancer*. Retrieved from http://www.cancer.gov/dictionary

National Cancer Institute. (October 2011b). *Pediatric cancers: Incidence and mortality rate trends*. Retrieved from https://www.acco.org/LinkClick.aspx?fileticket = M5NeDHMG-u4 % 3D&tabid = 670

National Dissemination Center for Children with Disabilities. (n.d.). *IDEA–The Individuals with Disabilities Education Act*. Retrieved from http://nichcy.org/laws/idea

Ogden, C., Carroll, M., Ogden, C., & Curtin, L. (2010). Prevalence and trends in obesity among U.S. adults: 1998–2008. *Journal of the American Medical Association, 303*, 235–241. Epub 2010 Jan 13.

Patterson, J. (1988). Families experiencing stress: The family adjustment and adaptation response model. *Family Systems Medicine, 5*, 202–237.

Pinquart, M., & Shen, Y. (2011) Depressive symptoms in children and adolescents with chronic physical illness: An updated meta-analysis. *Journal of Pediatric Psychology, 36,* 375–384. Retrieved from http://jpepsy.oxfordjournals.org/content/36/4/375.short

Rehr, H. (1983). Introduction: Posing the issues. In G. Rosenberg, & H. Rehr, (Eds.), *Advancing social work practice in the health care field* (pp. 1–10). New York: The Haworth Press.

Rodrigues, N., & Patterson, J., (2007). Impact of severity of a child's chronic condition on the functioning of two-parent families. *Journal of Pediatric Psychology, 32*, 417–426.

Roesler, T. A., & Jenny, C., (2008). *Medical child abuse: Beyond Munchausen syndrome by proxy* (1st ed.). Elk Grove Village, IL: American Academy of Pediatrics.

Saleebey, D. (2010). Power in the people: Strength and hope. *Advances in Social Work, 1*, 127–136.

Sharpe, D., & Rossiter, L. (2002). Siblings of children with a chronic illness: A meta-analysis. *Journal of Pediatric Psychology, 27*(8), 699–710.

Shaw, R., Bernard, R., DeBlois, T., Ikuta, L., Ginzburg, K., & Koopman, C. (2009). The relationship between acute stress disorder and posttraumatic stress disorder in the neonatal intensive care unit. *Psychosomatics, 50*, 131–137.

Shudy, M., de Almeida, M., Landon, C., Groft, S., Jenkins, T., & Nicholson, C. (2006). Impact of pediatric critical illness and injury on families: A systematic literature review. *Pediatrics, 118*, S203–S217.

Society for Social Work Leadership in Healthcare. (2013). *National pediatric standards for social work practice update*. Retrieved from http://www.aposw.org/docs/StandardsCareAndStaffing.pdf

Spitzer, W. (Ed.) (2003). *The strengths-based perspective on social work practice in health care*. National Society for Social Work Leadership in Health Care Petersburg, VA: The Dietz Press.

Spitzer, W., & Nash, K. (1996). Educational preparation for contemporary health care social work practice. In M. Mailick, & P. Carloff, (Eds.), *Professional social work education and health care* (pp. 9–34). New York: The Haworth Press.

Torpy, J., Campbell, A., & Glass, R. (2010). Chronic diseases of children. *Journal of the American Medical Association, 303(7)*, 682–682. Retrieved from http://jama.jamanetwork.com/article.aspx?volume = 303&issue = 7&page = 682

United States Bureau of the Census. (2010). *Income, poverty, and health insurance coverage in the United States: 2009, Report P60–238*, (Table B-2, pp. 62–68). Retrieved from http://www.census.gov/prod/2010pubs/p60-238.pdf

United States Bureau of the Census. (2012). *State and county quick facts*. Retrieved from http://quickfacts.census.gov/qfd/states/00000.html

United States Department of Health and Human Services, Administration on Children, Youth, Families, Children's Bureau. (2013). *Child maltreatment 2012*. Retrieved from http://www.acf.hhs.gov/programs/cb/resource/child-maltreatment-2012

United States Department of Health and Human Services, Administration on Intellectual and Developmental Disabilities. (2000). *The Developmental Disabilities Assistance and Bill of Rights Act of 2000*. Retrieved from http://www.acl.gov/Programs/AIDD/DDA_BOR_ACT_2000/index.aspx

United States Department of Health and Human Services, Agency for Healthcare Research and Quality. (2002). *Expanding patient-centered care to empower patients and assist providers*. Research in Action, Issue 5. AHRQ Publication No. 02–0024. May 2002. Rockville, MD: Agency for Healthcare Research and Quality. Retrieved from http://archive.ahrq.gov/research/findings/factsheets/patient-centered/ria-issue5/ria-issue6.pdf

United States Department of Health and Human Services, Agency for Healthcare Research and Quality. (2004). *Medical expenditure panel survey: Household component, health systems research*. Rockville, MD: Author. Retrieved from http://meps.ahrq.gov/mepsweb/

United States Department of Health and Human Services. (January 2010). *The Surgeon General's vision for a healthy and fit nation*. Rockville, MD: U.S. Department of Health and Human Services, Office of the Surgeon General. Retrieved from http://www.ncbi.nlm.nih.gov/books/NBK44660/pdf/TOC.pdf

United States Department of Health and Human Services, Centers for Disease Control and Prevention. (2011). National diabetes fact sheet: National estimates and general information on diabetes and pre-diabetes in the United States, 2011. Atlanta, GA: Author. Retrieved from http://www.cdc.gov/diabetes/pubs/pdf/ndfs_2011.pdf

United States Department of Health and Human Services, Health Resources and Services Administration, Maternal and Child Health Bureau. (2008). *The national survey of children with special health care needs chartbook 2005–2006*. Rockville, MD: Author.

Walsh, F. (2006). *Strengthening family resilience* (2nd ed.). New York: The Guilford Press.

Weick, A. (2003). Being well: A strengths approach to health and healing. In W. Spitzer (Ed.), *The strengths-based perspective on social work practice in health care*. Petersburg, VA: The Dietz Press, 1–11.

Weiss, H. B., Mathers, L. J., Forjuoh S. N., & Kinnane, J. M. (1997) *Child and adolescent emergency department visit databook*. Pittsburgh, PA: Center for Violence and Injury Control, Allegheny University of the Health Services.

Williams, P. D. (1997). Siblings and pediatric chronic illness: A review of the literature. *International Journal of Nursing Studies, 34*, 312–323.

Wright, R., Pepe, M., Seidel, K., & Dietz, W. (1997). Predicting obesity in young adulthood from childhood and parental obesity. *New England Journal of Medicine, 37*(13), 869–873.

Co-occurring Psychiatric and Substance Abuse Disorders in Medical Patients

Karen M. Allen

INTRODUCTION

The intersection of physical health, mental health, and addiction is one of central importance to social workers in healthcare settings. The ecological framework of the individual within the context of their social environment is the essential foundation of most, if not all, approaches for understanding and addressing psychiatric and substance disorders. Almost half (46.4%) of the general population will develop a diagnosable mental illness at some point in their life. With the inclusion of substance abuse disorders, the rate of individuals who have experienced a psychiatric disorder in the past year skyrockets to 26.2% (Kessler, Berglund, Demier, Jin, & Walters 2005a). These conditions are often diseases of the young, with nearly half of all cases reporting onset by age 14 and three-quarters by age 24. Given this high rate of prevalence, it is reasonable to wonder if these conditions are serious or relatively mild and potentially over-reported. Kessler Chiu, Demier, & Walters, (2005b) explored the level of severity in those who reported a serious mental illness within the past year. They found that, in this sample, 60% rated their disorder as causing "serious" or "moderate" functional impairments during the past year. The extent of functional impairment was more debilitating for respondents with bipolar disorder (83%), drug dependence (56.5%), obsessive-compulsive disorder (50.6%), oppositional-defiant disorder (49.6%), and mood disorders (45%).

A review of studies by Booth, Blow, and Loveland Cook (1998) suggested similar prevalence rates of 50% for psychiatric illness in general medical and surgical inpatients. Significant portions of medical patients were found to manifest symptoms of psychological distress such as depression and anxiety that do not necessarily equate to the presence of a diagnosable psychiatric disorder. European studies have found similar results, with nearly 50% of hospitalized medical patients demonstrating general psychiatric and substance abuse disorders. Significantly, Owens, Myers, Elixhauser, and Brach (2007) determined that 5% of women seen for pregnancy and child birth have the presence of a co-occurring mental disorder. Yates et al. (2004) found that a high proportion (53%) of depressed patients had concurrent medical conditions that were correlated with age, low income level, unemployment, low education, and length of depression.

Individuals with psychiatric disorders experience significantly higher rates of medical disorders than those without psychiatric illness (Dickey, Norman, Weiss, Drake, & Azeni, 2002). The mortality rate for individuals with serious mental illness has been found to be significantly higher than that for the general population. Individuals with severe psychiatric disorders are likely to die at earlier ages than those without psychiatric disorders. In addition to death by suicide, individuals with chronic mental illness are more likely to die from heart disease, hypertension, and obesity (Miller, Paschall, & Svendensen, 2006). In a study of patients seen in the mental health agencies of eight states, Colton and Manderscheid (2006) noted that "in every case, public mental health patients had an elevated risk of death compared to general populations, representing lost decades of life and productivity" (p. 2).

PSYCHIATRIC CARE IN HEALTHCARE SETTINGS

Historically, the chronically mental ill were institutionalized in almshouses and, later, in asylums. Beginning in the late 1950s, the development of psychotropic medications such as thorazine permitted institutionalized psychiatric patients to be managed in the community. **Deinstitutionalization** describes both the policy and social movement of moving these patients out of large, inpatient state psychiatric facilities and into community-based care with the subsequent closing of inpatient psychiatric facilities (Torrey, 1997). The impact of deinstitutionalization has been profound. In 1955, there were 558,239 severely mentally ill patients were institutionalized in public psychiatric institutions, but by 1994 this number had decreased to slightly over 70,000. Deinstitutionalization is predicated on the **least restrictive principle** that individuals should be treated settings that maximize their freedom, autonomy, and self-direction. Unfortunately, funding for community-based mental healthcare has not kept up with needs and, over 2 million chronically ill individuals lack access to needed psychiatric care (Torrey, 1997). As a consequence, the mentally ill often are compelled to seek care in acute care hospitals that may or may not have mental health units.

Today, largely as a result of deinstitutionalization and the closure of public psychiatric hospitals, community clinics and hospitals are the primary source of psychiatric treatment or behavioral healthcare in the United States. In 1970, only 5% of psychiatric unit beds were located in general hospital psychiatric units, but by 2002 this number had increased to 30%. In 1980, 843 hospitals had psychiatric units, and by 1992 this number had increased to 1,571.

Approximately one in four hospital admissions (7.6 million hospitalizations in 2004) involve a mental illness and/or substance abuse disorder. For nearly 6% of all hospitalizations, a primary diagnosis of a mental health or substance-abuse disorder is the reason for admission. When psychiatric and/or substance-abuse diagnoses are seen together or concurrently with a medical condition, they are said to be **co-occurring disorders**. Eighteen percent of all medical patients in the hospital also have a co-occurring psychiatric or substance abuse disorder. The cost of these hospitalizations is approximately 9.9 billion dollars annually, and they also account for nearly 33% of all uninsured hospitalizations. The frequency and type of co-occurring disorders in hospitalized patients is as follows: mood disorders (1:10 hospitalizations), substance-abuse disorders (1:14 hospitalizations), delirium/dementia (1:20 hospitalizations) and to a lesser degree, anxiety disorders, and schizophrenia. The elderly account for a disproportionate share of hospitalizations related to psychiatric disorders. Although individuals 80 and older comprise slightly more than 5% of the population, they account for 21% of medical admissions related to psychiatric disorders, primarily dementia, delirium, and depression (Owens et al., 2007).

The type of psychiatric care provided in acute care hospitals has been an area of concern for several reasons. A review of research by Mark, Stranges, and Levit (2010) revealed that care provided to psychiatric patients in acute care beds varied from that provided on specialized units. Psychiatric patients in acute care beds were rarely attended by psychiatrists, less likely to receive antidepressant medication, and more likely to have more diagnostic tests including CAT scans and EEGs. Furthermore, patients who are admitted with primary or secondary psychiatric conditions are less likely to be discharged home. They are almost twice as likely as other patients to need placement in a non-acute care facility such as a psychiatric hospital, nursing home, or rehabilitation center. They are also five to eight times more likely to leave the hospital against medical advice (*AMA discharge*). Given that a significant number of these patients are uninsured, locating suitable placements can be challenging (Owens et al., 2007).

As managed care has evolved to include aggressive cost-cutting measures in behavioral healthcare, the amount of inpatient care covered by insurance companies has decreased by over 14% (Mark et al., 2010). One important role for social workers in mental healthcare is providing case management services for managed care companies. In this capacity, social workers screen psychiatric admissions and/or requests for treatment, help determine the level and intensity of care needed, and authorize payments for services.

Over 50% of patients with mental illnesses receive mental healthcare and medications from primary care clinics and physicians, with estimates that between 11% and 36% of primary care patients have a mental or substance abuse disorder. While the use of primary care to manage psychiatric and substance abuse conditions has grown, the consistency and quality of treatment is variable. Not all primary care physicians are adequately trained in or keep current in current standards of care for psychiatric conditions. However, when care is appropriate and optimal, positive results can be achieved. The coordination of medical and mental healthcare services in a comprehensive, holistic approach to the patient is called *integrated healthcare* or *integrated behavioral health* (Center for American Progress, 2010; Integrated Behavioral Health Project, 2009).

THE SOCIAL WORK ROLE IN BEHAVIORAL HEALTHCARE

Social workers in healthcare settings play a crucial role in working with patients with psychiatric and substance-abuse disorders (see *Appendix G*). One essential function is educating other team members about these conditions in a general way as to the specific needs and concerns of individual patients. Additional responsibilities of the social worker are listed below and then subsequently discussed:

- Screening and identification of patients with co-occurring disorders

- Ensuring that mental health needs are addressed

- Providing crisis intervention and lethality risk assessment

- Facilitating involuntary and voluntary transfers to psychiatric units

- Support, education, and assurance that patient rights are protected

- Coordination of mental and physical healthcare services

Screening and Identification of Patients With Co-occurring Disorders

Many psychiatric disorders such as depression and schizophrenia can be effectively managed and have a low potential for remission if treated appropriately. Recovery from alcohol and drug addiction can be facilitated with the appropriate management of withdrawal symptoms. Screening for these disorders using a variety of brief screening tools as well as more comprehensive assessment of the patient are necessary to improve outcomes. Screening and assessment are essential parts of the clinical management process for each patient and should result in the development of appropriate treatment goals and interventions to address mental health needs. These services may be provided directly by the healthcare facility if available; if they are not directly available, additional resources will need to be identified and collaborations supported (Sacks, 2008).

Nielson and Williams (1980) reviewed research regarding the incidence of depression in ambulatory care patients, which was indicated to be approximately 11% to 12.2%. They noted that it is not uncommon for individuals to visit a physician in the weeks preceding suicide, suggesting that for these patients depression was not diagnosed or adequately addressed. In a retrospective review of medical records, physicians were found to have failed to diagnose depression in about 50% of cases. If the depression was diagnosed and treated, the majority of patients reported a rapid and beneficial decline in symptoms. In comparison, those who were undiagnosed and untreated reported the persistence of depressive symptoms one year later.

Standardized screening is effective for identifying depression and other mental health conditions. Sacks (2008) identified three basic criteria for selecting screening tools: sensitivity, specificity, and overall accuracy. Screening tools should be short (not exceeding 40 questions) and easy to administer. Three commonly used instruments that can be used to assess for mental illness are the Mental Health Screening Form III (Carroll & McGinley, 2001), the Beck Depression Inventory–II (or BDI–II)(Steer & Beck, 1988), and the Brief Symptom Inventory (BSI) (Derogatis & Melisaratos, 1983). Standardized screening tools can be employed by any member of the clinical healthcare team and can be integrated into routine clinical assessments.

Once patients are preliminarily identified through screening, detailed **biopsychosocial-spiritual assessments** are performed to reveal psychosocial problems associated with mental health issues. In exploring medical histories, patients may report having sought treatment for mental health conditions, including prescribed medications. Genograms can be very helpful for identifying family histories and patterns associated with psychiatric and substance-abuse disorders. Inquiring about suicide, substance abuse and associated health conditions, legal troubles, and psychiatric hospitalizations in the family can help to determine familial patterns in psychiatric disorders. In interacting with patients, social workers may recognize behaviors, thought processes, and mood disorders that are indicative of a mental illness and should refer such patients to the appropriate healthcare team member for diagnosis. This may be a psychiatrist or, in some facilities, a *neuropsychologist*, which is a psychologist with advanced training in neurology.

Addressing Mental Health Needs

Once the presence of a mental health or addictive disorder is identified, the social worker assumes an important role in making sure that mental health needs are addressed. The primary care physician may need to request a psychiatric consultation, or, if symptoms are severe enough, a patient may need stabilization in an inpatient psychiatric unit. If the social worker has identified a substance-abuse disorder, detoxification protocols may need to be ordered by the treating physician. Social workers may additionally assist other treatment team members to understand a patient's psychiatric condition and how it may affect their progress with the patient.

One of the major provisions of the Patient Protection and Affordable Care Act of 2010 is an increased emphasis on the integration of care. This includes primary care and prevention, chronic disease management, mental healthcare, and substance abuse treatment. When this constellation of conditions occurs in patients, as it often does, it may be more accurate to use the term multi-occurring rather than co-occurring disorders, which often is thought to imply that only two conditions are managed. These requirements create exciting opportunities for social workers in physical and behavioral healthcare; however, cross-training, support, and supervision will be needed to ensure that workers are competent in addressing all domains.

Sterling, Chi, and Hinman (2011) identified four general models of care: (1) *serial treatment*, in which episodes of care are provided in separate systems of care; (2) *simultaneous/parallel care*, in which behavioral and physical care services are provided simultaneously but in different, uncoordinated systems of care; (3) *coordinated/parallel care*, in which care is received simultaneously in different, but formally linked systems; and (4) *integrated care*, in which care for all disorders are provided by cross-trained providers in a single program or system of care. Integrated care is being encouraged by the federal government in a number of ways including (1) creation of the "medical home" in which a primary care physician assumes responsibility for arranging for and coordinating all care, (2) the expansion of community health centers and federally qualified health clinics (FQHCs), and (3) the development and support of Accountable Care Organizations (ACOs). Furthermore, funding is provided through the act for expanded home and community-based services that include Community-Based Care Transitions Programs, in which social workers and case managers working for Medicare and Medicaid assume responsibility for coordinating post-discharge hospital care of high-risk patients (Centers for Medicare & Medicaid Services, n.d.).

Until new systems of care that provide integrated services for multi-occurring disorders arise, social workers will continue to provide services to these patients in traditional care settings. In smaller healthcare settings such as ambulatory care clinics that lack onsite psychiatric services, social workers are valuable in identifying community resources of potential benefit to patients. This may involve developing resource networks of private providers as well as private and community-funded clinics. The social worker should also identify where psychiatric crisis centers are available and understand the requirements for a referral or assessment. In addition, knowledge of inpatient psychiatric beds and admission criteria is also important.

Developing networks of community-based mental healthcare services is crucial in order to (1) prevent otherwise unnecessary admissions to inpatient psychiatric facilities, (2) connect patients with supportive services that can help sustain them in the community, (3) promote collaboration on initiatives to improve the continuum and quality of available care, and (4) protect the rights of the mentally ill, particularly with respect to self-determination and use of the least restrictive forms of care (Segal & Baumohl, 1981). A continuum of community mental healthcare services is described in a subsequent section of this chapter. In coordinating care with community mental health settings, social workers are often responsible for matching patients with appropriate agencies and levels of care, providing case management and/or integrating the psychiatric plan of care into the medical treatment plan, and assisting primary care physicians to monitor medications. Social workers, however, need to recognize that the principles of self-determination and least restrictive form of care create a "right to try" approach for the patient. In consultation with the physician, the role of the social worker may be to try to maximize safety, minimize risk, and provide backup plans if a patient refuses to consider a more intensive type of care (Segal & Baumohl, 1981).

Crisis Intervention and Lethality Risk Assessment

A crisis is a "perception or experiencing of an event or situation as an intolerable difficulty that exceeds the person's current resources and coping mechanisms" (James, 2008, p. 3). According to James (2008), crisis intervention involves the following:

- Developing an understanding of the problem, especially from the patient's point of view

- Ensuring client safety

- Providing support

- Examining alternatives including choices and treatment

- Making plans and arrangements

- Obtaining commitment from the client to take the actions that have been agreed upon

Two types of crisis are commonly encountered by social workers dealing with psychiatric patients in healthcare settings. The first involves psychiatric **decompensation,** characterized by the Social Security Administration (2008) as a temporary worsening of psychiatric symptoms; a loss of coping abilities and the inability to adapt to life changes and stress; and difficulty with normal activities of life, including concentrating, being persistent at tasks, pacing oneself, or maintaining social relationships. Decompensation occurs when medical treatments, including psychotropic medications, are no longer effective;

when patients elect to terminate or alter their psychotropic medications; and/or when life stresses and events exceed the individual's coping capacity.

A second form of psychiatric crisis is related to the potential of suicide. In 2007, 395,320 individuals were treated in hospital emergency rooms for self-inflicted injuries and almost 166,000 individuals were hospitalized in suicide attempts (Centers for Disease Control and Prevention [CDC], 2014). Nearly two-thirds of hospitalizations for suicide attempts involved poisoning, while 10% involved cutting and piercing, and only 1% involved firearms (Owens et al., 2007). The low rate of firearm-related attempts may be due to the fact that there is a higher rate of completion when a firearm is used for suicide. Although the completion rate for firearms is high, clinicians should be aware that less dramatic methods can be quite effective. Overdosing on over-the-counter medications such as Tylenol, for example, can result in permanent liver damage.

Brendel, Lagomasino, Pertis, and Stern (2008) reported 50% of all suicides are associated with affective disorders; 25% with drugs and alcohol; 10% with schizophrenia; and 5% with personality disorders. According to Sadock and Sadock (2008), in addition to mental illness, other risk factors associated with suicide include gender (males are four times more likely to commit suicide), race (white males commit two out of every three suicides in the United States), divorce (being married decreases the risk of suicide), and professional status (professionals are considered to be at higher risk for suicide, particularly if there is a loss of status or employment). According to the CDC, in 2011, suicide was the tenth leading cause of death in the United States, with nearly 40,000 deaths being attributed to suicide that year (almost 13 per 100,000). Firearms accounted for approximately 50% of these deaths, followed by hanging/suffocation and drug or alcohol overdoses (poisoning). Additional statistics from the CDC are provided in *Table 13.1* and *Figure 13.1*.

Table 13.1   Suicide Statistics (2011)

• Suicide was the tenth leading cause of death for all ages in 2010.	• Suicide rates for males are highest among those aged 75 and older (rate 36 per 100,000).
• There were 38,364 suicides in 2010 in the United States—an average of 105 each day.	• The rate of suicide for adults aged 75 years and older was 16.3 per 100,000.
• Based on data about suicides in 16 National Violent Death Reporting System states in 2009, 33.3% of suicide decedents tested positive for alcohol, 23% for antidepressants, and 20.8% for opiates, including heroin and prescription pain killers.	• The prevalence of suicidal thoughts, suicide planning, and suicide attempts is significantly higher among young adults aged 18-29 years than among adults aged ≥30 years.
	• Firearms are the most commonly used method of suicide among males (56%).
• Suicide results in an estimated $34.6 billion in combined medical and work loss costs.	• Poisoning is the most common method of suicide for females (37.4%).
• Suicide among males is four times higher than among females and represents 79% of all U.S. suicides.	• Among American Indians/Alaska Natives aged 15 to 34 years, suicide is the second leading cause of death.

(Continued)

Table 13.1   (Continued)

- Females are more likely than males to have had suicidal thoughts.
- Suicide is the third leading cause of death among persons aged 15-24 years, the second among persons aged 25-34 years, the fourth among person aged 35-54 years, and the eighth among person 55-64 years.
- Among 15- to 24-year olds, suicide accounts for 20% of all deaths annually.
- Suicide rates for females are highest among those aged 45-54 (rate 9 per 100,000 population).

- The suicide rate among American Indian/Alaska Native adolescents and young adults ages 15 to 34 (31 per 100,000) is 2.5 times higher than the national average for that age group (12.2 per 100,000).
- Of students in grades 9–12, significantly more Hispanic female students (13.5%) reported attempting suicide in the last year than Black, non-Hispanic female students (8.8%) and White, non-Hispanic female students (7.9%).

Source: Suicide Statistics. Centers for Disease Control and Prevention, 2011.

Figure 13.1   Trends in Suicide 1999–2007 by Race/Ethnicity/Age Group

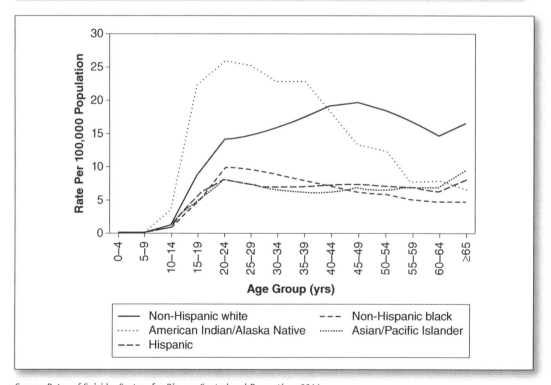

Source: Rates of Suicide. Centers for Disease Control and Prevention, 2011.

Optimally, healthcare providers encountering individuals in a psychiatric crisis should be able to offer timely and accessible aid, comprehensive assessment, initial stabilization, appropriate matching of patient needs to treatment options, and choice in options for continued crisis stabilization options. As part of the assessment process, social workers conduct a thorough risk assessment of **lethality** (or the potential for a client to inflict self-harm). The risk assessment is initiated by exploring the extent of **suicidal ideation**. Suicidal ideation is the presence of suicidal thoughts, which range in frequency and intensity and at times take on almost a fantasy-like quality about them regarding how others will feel when the person is gone. Sometimes the thoughts are intermittent; in riskier cases, the person will report persistent thoughts. When the thoughts involve consideration as to how and when the suicide might be carried out, the individual is said to have a *plan for suicide*. If the individual reports having access to the instrument of their planned suicide, such as a gun or poison, he or she is said to have the *means*. When ideation, a plan, and the means are acknowledged by the patient, the situation is considered very lethal and hospitalization should be considered. In less severe cases, the individual may be discharged home in the care of their family until psychiatric care is coordinated and provided a **safety plan.** The safety plan is a behavioral contract in which the patient promises not to harm himself or herself and the family agrees to provide round-the-clock direct supervision of the patient and to remove any and all possible means for self-harm, including prescription and over-the-counter medications (James, 2008).

In an earlier draft of this text, the authors had intended to include a suicide risk assessment tool entitled The SADPERSONS Scale (Patterson, Dohn, Bird, & Patterson, 1983), which is an instrument used to assess lethality by asking questions in 10 categories. However, in reviewing the current evidence supporting the use of this tool, we noted emerging research that questioned the reliability and validity of the SADPERSONS scale in accurately predicting the risk of suicide. Warden, Spiwak, Sareen, and Bolton (2014) conducted a meta-analysis of 148 studies that used the scale. As noted in chapter six, meta-analysis is an analysis of available research on a topic. Warden et al. located 148 studies, but only nine studies met the criteria for quality of design, control, and sample section established by the authors to be included their analysis. The nine studies reviewed were highly variable in their findings, causing the authors to conclude there is insufficient evidence for using the scale to predict suicidality. However, a recent study cited by the National Institute of Mental Health reviewed 17 common suicide risk assessment questions and found that four had high predictive value in assessing lethality when used in the emergency room (Horowitz et al., 2012; National Institute of Mental Health, 2013). Referred to as the Ask-Suicide Screening Questions (ASQ), the recommended questions are:

1. In the past few weeks, have you wished you were dead?

2. In the past few weeks, have you felt that you or your family would be better off if you were dead?

3. In the past week, have you had thoughts about killing yourself?

4. Have you ever tried to kill yourself?

Should an individual answer positively to these questions, the social worker should determine the means of suicide the individual considered and access to that means (such as a firearm). The response to these questions then determines interventions that are necessary such as hospitalization or developing a safety plan/contract with the client. Our decision to remove the scale from this book until further research is conducted and to incorporate the ASQ is presented as an example of how professionals continually use evidence and research to guide practice.

In some situations, social workers incur a **duty to warn** another individual who has been threatened with harm by a mentally ill individual. This duty was established in 1976 by the Tarasoff v. Regents of the University of California court ruling. In this case, a patient who was in counseling at a clinic operated by the University of California expressed his intent to harm another student named Tarasoff. Although the clinician took some action, the court ruled that he did not go far enough and that when a specific threat has been made regarding a named individual, clinicians are obligated to ensure that the person being threatened is informed (Appelbaum, 1994).

Facilitating Transfers to Psychiatric Facilities

Although the primary care physician and consulting psychiatrist (if available) will likely determine the plan of care, social workers often are the lead team member who facilitates transfers of patients to the psychiatric unit, to a psychiatric crisis center in the community for further assessment, or to a psychiatric hospital. As part of this process, social workers must understand state mental health codes. This involves making sure that all documentation is completed appropriately, that all procedures are explained to the patient and family, and that established protocols are followed. In addition, social workers must ensure that patient rights are protected during the process and that patients are treated with dignity and compassion. The National Alliance on Mental Illness (NAMI) was established in 1979 as the civil rights movement was expanded to include mentally and developmentally disabled individuals. This organization provides advocacy, support, and education to individuals and families coping with mental illness. In addition, each state and/or county must designate an office of *recipient rights* to assure that the recipients of public mental healthcare do not have their rights violated. Two important aspects of the rights of the mentally ill involve the right to be free from unnecessary restraints (including chemical restraints) and the right to be protected against inappropriate institutionalization or commitment.

Ideally, patients who are at risk of harming themselves will have been initially stabilized in the hospital and will consent to the transfer. If not, an **involuntary commitment** or **civil commitment** may become necessary. An involuntary commitment is a legal process in which an individual in psychiatric crisis (either decompensation or risk of suicide) is court-ordered into treatment at a psychiatric hospital. Criteria for commitment are established in each state's mental health code and vary. Typically, individuals can be committed if they are a *danger to themselves or others* and/or if the mental illness is so severe they *do not understand the need for treatment and are unable to care for their basic needs*. Typically, the necessary documentation involves a *petition for commitment*. The petition can be completed by a family member, a professional or a police officer. Following the petition, the patient is evaluated by a psychiatrist who will complete *a physician certificate* in which a diagnosis is made and justification for the initial commitment established. Some states require that two physicians or psychiatrists certify a patient as being in need of commitment. This permits an initial period of commitment for a relatively short period of time (e.g., 72 hours) in a treatment facility for evaluation and stabilization by mental health professionals. During this stage of treatment, the mental health team will determine if continued commitment is warranted. If additional hospitalization is necessary and if the patient still refuses to consent to treatment voluntarily, the case is presented to a judge, who will review the documentation and take testimony from the patient, family, and treatment team. Attorneys may or may not be involved in commitment procedures.

Patients in psychiatric crisis can be extremely anxious and agitated and may at times be hostile and aggressive. Of paramount importance is the protection of the patient, staff, and others. When chemical or mechanical restraints are found necessary, they are carefully regulated with detailed protocols for their use. Restraints are only used as a last resort and never as a convenience for staff or to intimidate and punish the patient. Staff who care for restrained patients should regularly receive special training to help ensure their physical safety as well as training in how to de-escalate crises. The following strategies suggested by the Substance Abuse and Mental Health Services Administration (Center for Substance Abuse Treatment, 2006, p. 28) are appropriate for deescalating aggressive behaviors:

Table 13.2   Strategies for De-escalating Aggressive Behaviors

- Speak in a soft voice.
- Isolate the individual from loud noises or distractions.
- Provide reassurance and avoid confrontation, judgments, or angry tones.
- Enlist the assistance of family members or others who have a relationship of trust.
- Request medication when appropriate.
- Separate the individual from others who may encourage or support the aggressive behaviors.
- Enlist additional staff members to serve as visible backup if the situation escalates.
- Have a clearly developed plan to enlist the support of law enforcement or security staff if necessary.
- Establish clear admission protocols in order to help screen for potentially aggressive/violent patients.
- Determine one's own level of comfort during interaction with the patient and respect personal limits.
- Ensure that neither the clinician's nor the patient's exit from the examination room is blocked.

Source: Substance Abuse and Mental Health Services Administration, 2006.

Throughout the process, social workers need to ensure that the patient and family are informed of the recommendations and procedures. It is important to educate patients and families on their rights and to reassure them that legal protections are available for them. Patients admitted on an involuntary basis will be encouraged at various points during the commitment to consent to treatment and to sign in voluntarily.

Coordination of Mental Healthcare Services

Mason and Auerbach (2009) concluded that social workers provide significant benefit by developing relationships with community mental health agencies and then connecting patients to these agencies when they seek emergency care. Although these patients may need brief periods of observation, psychiatric assessment, and medication management, the social worker's biopsychosocial assessment can match needs and resources for community-based care. Mason and Auerbach (2009) found that over 80% of the emergency room patients who were seen by social workers could avoid hospitalization and receive their care through community agencies, outpatient psychiatric services, home care, and nursing facilities.

Because the scope of psychiatric services may be limited in an acute care setting, development of relationships and a network of mental health providers is critical to supporting patients in the community. The services noted in *Table 13.3* can be provided through public community mental health funding or may be associated with private mental healthcare facilities and providers. Social workers should identify providers in each of the following service areas and cultivate relationships that promote the referral of patients to appropriate service providers.

Table 13.3 Continuum of Mental Healthcare Services

Level of service	Description
Prevention and education	Services that educate and encourage participants to avoid certain harmful activities or to engage in positive activities that promote their emotional and social functioning.
Early intervention	Recognizing warning signs for potential problems (substance abuse, developmental delays, violence) and taking early action to reduce the factors that put the individual or family at risk. Services to families with children with a diagnosed developmental delay (language, behavioral, cognitive, etc.) to include speech, behavioral, cognitive or other therapies, transportation services, etc.
Outpatient services	Mental health services provided in a clinical setting that is not residential in nature. Those served are able to use therapeutic relationships to maintain clinical stability and independent functioning between scheduled appointments. Can involve individual, family, and group treatment modalities. For the chronically mentally ill, will include a therapist, often a social worker and psychiatrist, who will oversee medication management.
Crisis intervention	Services that allow for immediate response to a situation involving imminent danger to ensure the safety of the individual involved. Psychiatric crisis intervention centers are designated in the community mental healthcare system and can stabilize a patient on medication and/or evaluate the patient for possible voluntary and involuntary commitment to a psychiatric facility.

Intensive outpatient care	Highly structured outpatient services for psychiatric or substance abuse treatment that involves programming for most of the day, allowing the patient to return home in the evening. For adolescents, educational programming will be included to permit students to continue their education.
Acute care hospitalization/ emergency room care	Provision of psychiatric and substance abuse interventions at acute care facilities or in the emergency room. Can be problematic if services are not covered by insurance and are inadequately developed to fully meet the patient's needs. May involve assessment, stabilization, and transfer to a more appropriate agency.
Inpatient psychiatric care	Services offered in a hospital setting. The inpatient setting may be a psychiatric unit in an acute care hospital or a designated psychiatric hospital.
Residential care facilities	Short-term recovery oriented services for individuals who have been part of treatment and seeking to re-enter the mainstream. Services for those who need structure, support, and reinforcement of a therapeutic milieu to reverse the course of behavioral deterioration.
Adult foster care and group homes	Homes in the community that provides long-term care for a small group of patients with similar conditions. Provides a community based, milieu therapy and residential care approach that includes 24-hour supervision and transportation to services.
Assertive Community Treatment (ACT)	A multidisciplinary, round-the-clock staffing approach for patient within the comfort of their own home and community. The ACT team provides these necessary services 24 hours a day, seven days a week, 365 days a year.
Support and advocacy	Interrelated services and resources that provide individuals with emotional informational and material sustenance. A structured ongoing series of meetings among people who share common issues and who give encouragement, information, and emotional sustenance to one another. Often led by patients and family members as part of a self-help approach.

Source: United Way Fox Cities. Definition of Service Categories.

Social workers should understand each of level of care, identify providers in the community for each level of care, and understand the criteria, eligibility, and funding requirements. This will permit the social worker to match each patient with the appropriate level of care.

SUBSTANCE ABUSE AS A CO-OCCURRING DISORDER

In 2004, 1 million hospital admissions were for substance-abuse disorders (Owens et al., 2007) and another 1.5 million patients sought help in the emergency room; 45% of these admissions involved drug dependency, 34% were for alcohol-related problems, and 22% involved both alcohol and drug dependency (Owens et al., 2007). In a retrospective review of 2,040 hospital records, Smothers, Yar, and Ruhl (2004) found that 40% to 42% of the records documented a diagnosis of alcohol-related problems.

The new edition of *Diagnostic and Statistical Manual of Mental Disorders* (DSM-V) (American Psychiatric Association, 2013) makes significant changes from previous diagnostic classifications in substance-abuse disorders. Now categorized as substance-related and addictive disorders, conditions are classified as **substance-use disorders** (previously abuse and dependency); *intoxication*, and *withdrawal*. Substance-related disorders are assessed along a continuum and are classified as mild, moderate, or severe, depending on eleven criteria. Criteria 1 through 4 reflect impaired control; 5 through 7 indicate impairment in social functioning due to substance use; 8 and 9 relate to risky use; 10 indicates withdrawal; and 11 indicates increased tolerance. Ten classes of drugs (alcohol, cannabis, opioids, etc.) are used to make a *substance specific diagnosis*. There is also increased recognition of the complexity of cognitive, behavioral, and biological conditions and co-occurring mental illnesses. The prevalence of substance-related disorders in individuals with major mental illness is also outlined (American Psychiatric Publishing, 2013, p. 482).

A critical feature of the new classification system is that individuals who are prescribed opioids to manage a chronic pain condition and who are taking them as prescribed and under medical supervision cannot be classified as having a substance-use disorder (American Psychiatric Publishing, 2013, p. 541). This was a controversial step and was intended to avoid stigmatizing individuals who relied on prescribed medical to manage a condition such as chronic pain. These patients are common in a medical social worker's caseload and while intervention to decrease reliance on opioids may be indicated, a diagnosis of substance-use disorder is excluded.

Alcohol abuse is the most common drug used and abused in our society. Two-thirds of adults in the United States drink regularly and, at some point, 18% will abuse alcohol and 13% will become dependent on alcohol. Approximately 60% of individuals with a substance-abuse disorder have a co-occurring psychiatric condition. Prolonged alcohol abuse can affect all organ systems, including the liver (cirrhosis), the central nervous system (alcohol-related dementia), and the gastrointestinal tract. Alcohol is also frequently associated with domestic violence, accidents, and homicide. Alcohol use during pregnancy can cause **fetal alcohol syndrome**, leaving a child with life-long disabilities (Hasin, Stinson, Ogburn, & Grant, 2007).

A number of alcohol abuse screening tools are available, including the Michigan Alcohol Screening Test (MAST) and the Alcohol Use Disorders Identification Test (AUDIT). Both of these instruments are easily located on the Internet. The **CAGE** is an acronym for four simple questions that can be incorporated easily into a biopsychosocial assessment, with two or more positive responses being indicative of a potential alcohol abuse problem. The questions are

- Have you ever tried to **C**ut down on your drinking?

- Have you been **A**nnoyed with someone who indicated concern about your drinking habits?

- Have you ever felt **G**uilty about your drinking?

- Have you ever had a drink first thing in the morning (**E**ye-opener) to steady your nerves or get rid of a hangover?

Other drugs present serious health concerns when abused and require management for withdrawal. Of special note are the increasing rates of prescription pain killer use and abuse (Oxycontin, Vicodin) and methamphetamine. *Figure 13.2,* from the National Survey on Drug Use and Health (NSDUH), describes current trends in the use of legal and illegal drugs.

Figure 13.2   Substance Use Patterns in Individuals Aged 12 and Over

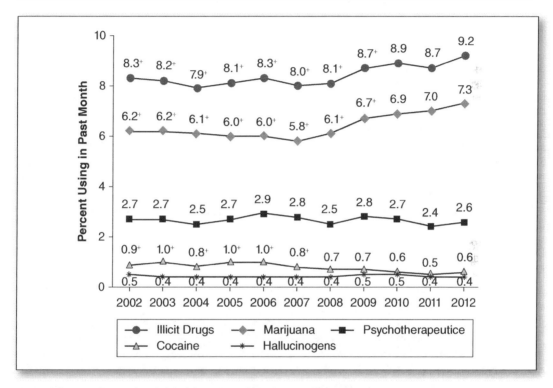

Source: Substance Abuse and Mental Health Services Administration, 2013.

Social workers can be an important resource to patients who undergo detoxification in healthcare settings. According to the Center for Substance Abuse Treatment (2006), **detoxification** is a set of medically supervised interventions aimed at managing acute intoxication and withdrawal. There are three stages to the detoxification process: evaluation, stabilization, and fostering readiness for treatment and recovery. Often, detoxification is initiated in the emergency department when patients are admitted for an overdose of drugs or alcohol. In some cases, withdrawing suddenly from certain substances, including alcohol, can be life-threatening. The purpose of medically supervised detoxification, which often includes medications such as benzodiazepine (alcohol withdrawal) and clonidine (opioids), is to prevent potentially life-threatening complications that might appear if the patient was left untreated. In addition, managing the detoxification process is a form of palliative care that reduces the individual's discomfort of withdrawal.

In addition, monitoring the detoxification process (either as an inpatient or outpatient) can help connect the patient treatment system and recovery network. As members of the treatment team, social workers can work with the patient and family to assess the readiness for treatment and to help connect the patient to the appropriate level of services. The Substance Abuse and Mental Health Services Administration (Center for Substance Abuse Treatment, 2006) has suggested the following strategies for engaging and retaining patients in detoxification and recovery: (1) educate the patient on the withdrawal process, (2) engage patient support systems (family, peer, and community) in the process, and (3) encourage the patient to maintain a drug/alcohol-free environment and avoid environments where these substances are present.

Tailoring treatment according to the patient's stage of readiness is important. DiClemente & Prochaska (1982) developed a **trans-theoretical model of change** which identifies the following stages of change that an individual experiences while considering making major changes in their behavior: pre-contemplation, contemplation, preparation, action, and maintenance. In the *pre-contemplation stage*, the substance abuser may or may not recognize the substance abuse problem but is not considering any change in behavior at present. Often in this stage, individuals have not experienced any serious health or social consequences associated with their substance abuse. In the *contemplation stage*, the individual has some awareness that the substance abuse is a problem. The individual may express a desire for sobriety but has yet to take any concrete steps towards that goal.

The goal of intervening in the pre-contemplation and contemplation stages is to try to move the patient into recognizing the problem and committing to taking steps toward sobriety. Once this is accomplished, the individual enters the *preparation stage*. During this stage, the individual recognizes that the substance abuse is a problem and expresses a sincere desire to change. This stage is characterized by setting goals and making commitments to stop using. The next stage is the *action stage,* when the patient takes actual steps and actions to stop using. The intervention at the preparation and action stages is to support the patient in his or her goals, contract with the patient to following through on his or her intentions, and monitor for follow-through. In the final stage, *maintenance*, the patient works to maintain the changes that have been achieved (DiClemente & Prochaska, 1982; Prochaska, DiClemente, & Norcross, 1992). This is not a linear model, and for many if not most patients, relapses are the rule rather than the exception. Individuals will progress through various stages as well as regress to earlier stages as they undergo the difficult process of changing behavior. As noted in previous discussions, some models consider relapse a sixth stage of change, which is especially important to consider when working with substance-use disorders. *Figure 13.3* presents the stages of change model.

The following strategies, based on motivational interviewing, are also suggested:

- Focus on patients' strengths.

- Show respect for patient decisions and autonomy.

- Treat relapse as a decision with consequences and explore the reasons the decision to use a substance again was made.

Figure 13.3   Stages of Change Model

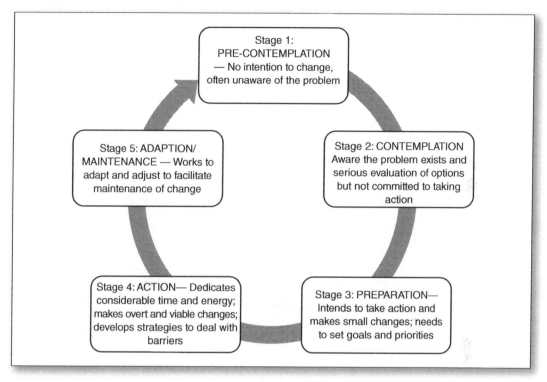

Source: Adapted from Prochaska, J. O. and C. C. DiClemente (1982). "Transtheoretical therapy: Toward a more integrative model of change." *Psychotherapy: Theory, Research and Practice* 19(3): 276–288.

- Avoid confrontation.
- Do not label the patient.
- Empathize, make an attempt to understand the patient's perspective, and accept the patient's feelings.
- Accept that treatment goals will require small steps in order to reach ultimate goals.
- Listen reflectively, ask open-ended questions, and help the patient identify and understand the discrepancies between the patient's ultimate goals and his or her behavior and/or choices (Center for Substance Abuse Treatment, 2006, p. 33).

Evidence is increasing for the effectiveness of motivational interviewing and the trans-theoretical model of change, which are increasingly being integrated into other cognitive behavior approaches in the treatment of addictive disorders (Burke et al., 2003, 2004). The Center for Substance Abuse Treatment of (CSAT) of the Substance Abuse and Mental Health Services Administration has extensive training materials and resources that are publically available to support the integration of this approach into clinical practice (2009).

CASE STUDY

Medical and Substance Abuse Issues in a Family

Mrs. Jones is a 38-year-old married woman with two children, ages 12 and 10. She is seen by the social worker on the rehabilitation unit, where she was admitted following a medical work-up to diagnosis what turned out to be a devastating, progressive neurological condition that would ultimately prove fatal. At the time of her admission, the disease was progressing rapidly and already had impaired her physical mobility and cognitive capacity.

The social worker asked to meet with the husband, who was a truck driver with a 10th-grade education. He was very hard-working and valued being a good provider to his family. His hours had limited his ability to be involved in his wife's care. Because his shift started at 6:00 A.M., the social worker met with him at the hospital at 5:00 A.M. At the meeting, it was apparent that the husband had been drinking and was intoxicated. The social worker pointed this out, and the husband stated he had been up all night and had "had a few beers." He denied alcohol abuse or addiction and did not feel he had any problem.

The social worker was troubled by this, and asked the patient's parents if they had any concerns about how the husband might be handling the situation. The parents then reported their concerns about his drinking, which was chronic and substantial. At the time of the patient's discharge, a family conference was arranged to discuss her needs. After this meeting, the social worker asked the husband and the patient's parents to stay behind and discuss a few concerns. An intervention had been staged, and the parents shared their concerns about the husband's drinking and how this would affect his ability to care for the patient and manage the family. He adamantly denied a problem and stated that "anyone would understand him drinking a bit right now because of the condition his wife was in." The social worker provided the patient her card, and offered assistance if ever he felt he needed it.

Two years later the husband called the social worker. He remembered the meeting and had kept his card in his wallet the whole time. He admitted his drinking was a problem and asked for her help. He explained at the time of their first meeting, he was aware that he had a problem, but was not willing to take any steps to doing anything about it. In fact, he said, he felt entitled to drink more because of his wife's illness. Gradually, though, he began to be afraid of what the drinking was doing to his health. He felt a great deal of shame when he blacked out in front of his children, noting that "It was like they were losing both parents instead of just one." He began to realize he needed to do something. He had kept the social worker's card in his wallet and decided to call her for help.

The social worker talked with the patient's rehabilitation physician, who agreed to admit him for three days of alcohol detoxification. She explained to the husband that this was necessary for his safety and would help set the foundation for continued recovery. The social worker then arranged for intensive outpatient treatment for the husband and coordinated adult day care for the patient, who could not be left alone while the husband was in treatment.

Six months later, the social worker was contacted again and asked for help in placing the wife in a nursing home, which was done. At that time, the husband was still sober and had returned to work. He reported that he was continuing to work on his sobriety, and had completed 90/90 (90 AA meetings in 90 days). He had a sponsor, a home AA group, and was doing service work by helping to set up the coffee and refreshments for the three meetings a week he attended. "And more if I need them," he said.

Although the social worker was pleased at the outcome, she was troubled by one aspect of her handling of the case. In retrospect, she realizes that should never had permitted the patient to leave the hospital and go to his job as a truck driver while he was clearly intoxicated, as was the case on their first meeting. A safer, more appropriate course of action would have been to contact the hospital's security department and request they intervene to preventing the husband from leaving and subsequently driving while intoxicated.

Questions for discussion:

1. In this case, the husband was not the patient. Was it appropriate for the social worker to intervene with him?

2. What does this case tell us about the stages of change?

3. What stages of change in the patient can you identify in the case study?

INTEGRATING CARE

The Patient Protection and Affordable Care Act of 2010 requires that health systems work to integrate medical and mental healthcare, creating the opportunity for improved, coordinated services for patients and an increased presence of social workers in primary and ambulatory care settings. While it would be difficult to capture all of the known and potential benefits for coordinating care between medical and mental health providers, Ai, Rollman, and Berger (2010) found that integrated care improved outcomes for patients with comorbid mental health symptoms (e.g., anxiety) and heart diseases by building patients' protective factors such as positive attitudes, social supports, coping mechanisms, and spirituality. Hine, Howell, and Yonkers (2008) examined ways to integrate medical and psychological treatment within primary care settings by using integrative, collaborative care approaches to reduce long-term-care costs and improve patient access. They found that co-locating mental health professionals with primary care teams improved the health outcomes for individuals living with serious mental health needs by destigmatizing mental health services and addressing medical conditions including side effects from psychotropic mediations.

The White River Model provides an example of a successful co-located, collaborative care model (Pomerantz et al., 2010). Begun in 2004, the model involved having the primary mental healthcare clinic at a Veterans Affairs Medical Center offer a full range of mental health services within the primary care clinic. Only patients with complex issues were referred out to specialty services. In this model, the clinic was staffed by a therapist (a clinical psychologist or master's level social worker) and a psychiatrist and was complemented by care management and health psychology staff (Pomerantz et al., 2010). The clinic in this model also incorporated a chronic disease management approach. By co-locating and collaborating across the health and behavioral health spectrum, this model reduced new referral wait times to just minutes rather than weeks. Access to mental health services was improved, with only 25% of the patients at this clinic needing referral to specialty mental health services. Importantly, there was improved adherence to evidence-based quality of care for the treatment of depression (Pomerantz et al., 2010).

Similar to the conceptual model by Coleman and Boult (2003) for assessing patient risk factors presented in chapter 8, the National Council for Community Behavioral Health Care (2009) has recommended a Four Quadrant clinical integration model to better link health and behavioral health services.

The model is applied to subsets of the population in which mental/medical healthcare services are integrated in particular ways to serve each group. The Four Quadrant Model addresses who is responsible for coordinating the services that are to be located in the clinic and those that are provided by other community partners and how emergency care is provided for patients experiencing crisis. It is a "bi-directional" model, meaning that behavioral services are integrated or "co-located into medical care and medical care is integrated into behavioral healthcare. A collaborative, interdisciplinary team that, at a minimum, comprises a behavioral health consultant (a nurse, social worker, or psychologist), a designated psychiatrist, and a primary care physician. Other requirements in the model are consumer choice, the use of standardized screening tools, measuring outcomes, patient tracking, and evidence-based care.

In the Four Quadrant Model, both behavioral and physical health risks are considered and patients are classified into one of four groups (quadrants). Patients in Quadrant I have low medical and low behavior health risks; those in Quadrant II have high behavioral and low medical health risks, those in Quadrant III have low behavioral and high medical risks, and those in Quadrant IV have high behavioral and high medical risks. This model can be used to determine the optimal integration and co-location of services. For example, patients in Quadrant II exhibit high behavioral healthcare needs and a lower need for medical care. The behavioral health clinician/case manager has responsibility for coordinating care with the primary care physician. For patients with high physical care needs and low mental healthcare needs, coordination of care is primarily accomplished by the primary care physician. The model is useful conceptualization of how to integrate care on the basis of patient needs, and it continues to be refined as healthcare policy, financing, and treatment innovations evolve.

Other ways of integrating care apart from the co-location of services are emerging. The use of technology for team members to communicate across distances, including phone applications, is being developed and piloted. A centrally located, easily accessed electronic medical record also creates possibilities, provided that the information is not too easily accessed. Healthcare teams are using FaceTime, multiple-user Skype accounts, and other live videoconferencing tools to connect virtually when providing community-based care. For example, technology permits a social worker who is visiting a mentally patient in his or her home to directly consult with the patient's primary care physician who is working in the office. Concerns about the security of these systems and patient confidentiality have not been fully resolved. The cost of a single, secure system continues to be a barrier to the widespread use of technology for team members to discuss sensitive patient care.

SUMMARY

This chapter focused on the delivery of mental health services in healthcare settings, including the extent and nature of psychiatric hospitalizations and the social work role in behavioral health. Particular attention was placed on co-occurring disorders, or when psychiatric and or substance-abuse diagnoses are seen together or concurrently with a medical condition. With 18% of all hospitalized medical patients having co-occurring psychiatric or substance-abuse disorders, we recognized the significance of intervening with this population.

The continuum of mental healthcare services was introduced, as were the fundamental interventions employed with patients manifesting co-occurring disorders. The value of integrated care in meeting patient needs was particularly emphasized. Social workers represent an important support to patients with co-occurring disorders. They are crucial members of the healthcare team, assessing patient status, collaborating with team colleagues, initiating referrals, providing direct intervention, and monitoring patient status. Because these patients can be particularly challenging to the medical team, the non-judgmental support of the social worker can be instrumental in setting the stage for eventual treatment compliance, motivation, and behavioral change.

KEY TERMS AND CONCEPTS

- Co-occurring disorders
- Deinstitutionalization
- Least restrictive principle
- Decompensation
- Lethality
- Safety plan

- Duty to warn

- Involuntary or civil commitment

- De-escalation

- CAGE

- Fetal alcohol syndrome

- Trans-theoretical model of change

- Substance-use disorder, substance specific diagnosis

- Duty to warn

- Detoxification

- Suicidal ideation

QUESTIONS FOR DISCUSSION

1. Why are patients with co-occurring disorders particularly challenging to the medical team? How can the social work help the team in understanding the patient? What approach can the social worker use to help lay a foundation for change in the patient?

2. Mortality in individuals with chronic mental illness and co-occurring disorders is less than that of the general population. Discuss reasons why this is the case.

3. Why is the DiClemente and Prochaska stages-of-change model called trans-theoretical? What types of behavior change are appropriate to address with this model? What problems might not be appropriate?

EXERCISES

1. Role play the stages-of-change model and motivation interviewing with the case study provided in the chapter.

2. Go to the Substance Abuse and Mental Health Services Administration website (http://www .samhsa.gov/) and review their available training materials and resources. Download one of their many publications on treating co-occurring disorders and present a PowerPoint to your class.

3. Obtain a copy of your state's petition for involuntary civil commitment. Create a role play of a suicidal individual admitted to the hospital in a drug overdose. Complete the form and explore where in your community further psychiatric care and screening could be obtained.

REFERENCES

Ai, A., Rollman, B., & Berger, C. (2010). Comorbid mental health symptoms and heart diseases: Can health care and mental health care professionals collaboratively improve the assessment and management? *Health and Social Work, 35*(1), 27.

American Psychiatric Association. (2013). *Diagnostic and statistical manual of mental disorders.* (5th ed.). [DSM-V]. Washington, DC: Author.

American Psychiatric Publishing. (2013). *Substance-related and addictive disorders.* Retrieved from http://www.dsm5.org/Documents/Substance%20Use%20Disorder%20Fact%20Sheet.pdf

Appelbaum, P. S. (1994). *Almost a revolution: Mental health law and the limits of change.* New York: Oxford University Press.

Booth, B. M., Blow., F. C., & Loveland Cook, C. A. (1998). Functional impairment and co-occurring psychiatric disorders in medical hospitalized men. *Archives of Internal Medicine, 158,* 1551–1559.

Brendel, R. W., Lagomasino, I. T., Perlis, R. H., & Stern, T. A. (2008). The suicidal patient. In T. A. Stern, J. R. Rosenbaum, M. Fava, Biederman, J., & Bauch, S. L. (Eds.), *Massachusetts General Hospital Comprehensive Clinical Psychiatry.* Philadelphia, PA: Mosby Elsevier.

Burke, B. L., Arkowitz, H., & Menchola, M. (2003). The efficacy of motivational interviewing: A meta-analysis of controlled clinical trials. *Journal of Consulting and Clinical Psychology, 71*(5), 843–861.

Burke, B. L., Dunn, C. W., Atkins, D. C., & Phelps, J. S. (2004). The emerging evidence base for motivational interviewing: A meta-analytic and qualitative inquiry. *Journal of Cognitive Psychotherapy, 18*(4), 309–322.

Carroll, J. F. X., & McGinley, J. J. (2001). A screening form for identifying mental health problems in alcohol/other drug dependent persons. *Alcoholism Quarterly, 19*(4), 33–47.

Center for American Progress. (2010, October). *Mental health care services in primary care: Tackling the issues in the context of health care reform.* Lesley Russell, Visiting Fellow. Retrieved from www.americanprogress.org/issues/2010/10/pdf/mentalhealth.pdf

Centers for Disease Control and Prevention, (2011). *Health disparities and inequities report.* Retrieved from http://www.cdc.gov/mmwr/pdf/other/su6001.pdf

Centers for Disease Control and Prevention. (2014). *National suicide statistics at a glance.* Retrieved from http://www.cdc.gov/ViolencePrevention/suicide/statistics/aag.html

Centers for Medicare & Medicaid Services, (n.d). *Community-based care transitions program.* Retrieved from http://innovation.cms.gov/initiatives/CCTP/?itemID=CMS1239313

Center for Substance Abuse Treatment. (1999). *Enhancing motivation for change in substance abuse treatment. Treatment Improvement Protocol (TIP) Series, No. 35.* HHS Publication No. (SMA) 13-4212. Rockville, MD: Substance Abuse and Mental Health Services Administration.

Center for Substance Abuse Treatment. (2006). *Detoxification and substance abuse treatment. Treatment Improvement Protocol (TIP) Series, No. 45.* Rockville, MD: Substance Abuse and Mental Health Services Administration. Retrieved from http://www.ncbi.nlm.nih.gov/books/NBK64115/

Coleman, E.A., & Boult, C. E. (2003). Improving the quality of transitional care for persons with complex care needs. *Journal of the American Geriatrics Society, 51*(4), 556–557.

Colton, C., & Manderscheid, R. (2006). Congruencies in increased mortality rates, years of potential life lost and causes of death among public mental health clients in eight states. *Preventing Chronic Disease, 3*(2), 1–10.

Derogatis, L. R., & Melisaratos, N. (1983). The brief symptom inventory: An introductory report. *Psychological Medicine, 13*(3), 595–605.

Dickey, B., Norman, S. T., Weiss, R. D., Drake, R. E., & Azeni, H. (2002). Medical morbidity, mental illness, and substance use disorder. *Psychiatric Services, 53*(7), 861–869.

DiClemente, C., & Prochaska, J. (1982). Self-change and therapy change of smoking behavior: A comparison of processes of change in cessation and maintenance. *Addictive Behaviors, 7*, 133–142.

Hasin, D. S., Stinson, F. S., Ogburn, E., & Grant, B. F. (2007). Prevalence, correlates, disability and co-morbidity of DSM-IV alcohol abuse and dependence in the United States. *Archives of General Psychiatry, 64*, 830–842.

Hine, C., Howell, H., & Yonkers, K. (2008). Integration of medical and psychological treatment within the primary health care setting. *Social Work in Health Care, 47*(2), 122.

Horowitz, L. M., Bridge, J. A., Teach, S. J., Ballard, E., Klima, J., Rosenstein, D. L., Wharff, E. A., Ginnis, K., Cannon, E., Joshi, P., & Pao, M. (2012). Ask Suicide-Screening Questions (ASQ). A brief instrument for the pediatric emergency department. *Archives of Pediatrics and Adolescent Medicine, 166*(12), 1170–1176.

Integrated Behavioral Health Project. (2009, October). *Partners in health: Primary care/county mental health collaboration.* Retrieved from www.ibhp.org

James, R. K. (2008). *Crisis intervention strategies* (6th ed.). Belmont, CA: Thomson Brooks/Cole.

Kessler, R. C., Berglund, P., Demler, O., Jin, R., & Walters, E. E. (2005a). Lifetime prevalence and age-of-onset distributions of DSM-IV disorders in the National Comorbidity Survey Replication. *Archives of General Psychiatry, 62*, 593–602.

Kessler, R. C., Chiu, W. T., Demler, O., & Walters, E. E. (2005b). Prevalence, severity, and comorbidity of 12-month DSM-IV disorders in the National Comorbidity Survey Replication. *Archives of General Psychiatry, 62*, 617–627.

Manderscheid, R., & Henderson, M. (2004). Highlights of organized mental health Services in 2000 and major national and state trends. In *Mental health, United States, 2002.* Rockville, MD: U.S. Department of Health and Human Services (publication number: SMA 3938).

Mark, T., Stranges, E., & Levit K. (2010). Using healthcare cost and utilization project state inpatient database and medicare cost reports data to determine the number of psychiatric discharges from psychiatric units of community hospitals. *U.S. Agency for Healthcare Research and Quality (AHRQ).* Retrieved from http://www.hcup-us.ahrq.gov/reports.jsp

Mason, S. E., & Auerbach, C. (2009). Factors related to admissions to a psychiatry unit from a medical emergency room: The role of social work. *Social Work in Mental Health, 7*(5), 429–441. doi:10.1080/15332980802545046

Miller, B. J., Paschall, C. B., & Svendensen, M. D. (2006). Mortality and medical comorbidity among patients with serious mental illness. *Psychiatric Services, 57*(10), 1482–1487.

National Institute for Health and Care Excellence. (2013, April). *Self-harm: longer term management: Evidence update.* Retrieved from https://www.evidence.nhs.uk/search?q = sad%20persons%20scale

National Institute of Mental Health. (2013, January 4). *Emergency department suicide screening tool accurately predicts at risk youth. Science update.* Retrieved from http://www.nimh.nih.gov/news/science-news/2013/emergency-department-suicide-screening-tool-accurately-predicts-at-risk-youth.shtml

National Council for Community Behavioral Health Care. (2009, April). *Behavioral health/primary care integration and the person-centered healthcare home.* Retrieved from http://www.allhealth.org/briefingmaterials/BehavioralHealthandPrimaryCareIntegrationandthePerson-CenteredHealthcareHome-1547.pdf

Nielson, A. C., Williams, T. A. (1980). Depression in ambulatory medical patients. *Archives of General Psychiatry, 37*, 999–1006.

Owens, P., Myers, M., Elixhauser, A., & Brach, C. (2007). *Care of adults with mental health and substance abuse disorders in U.S. community hospitals, 2004.* Agency for Healthcare Research and Quality Publication No. 07–0008. Retrieved from archive.ahrq.gov/data/hcup/factbk10/factbk10.pdf

Patterson, W. M., Dohn, H. H., Bird, J., & Patterson, G. A. (1983). Evaluation of suicidal patients: The SADPERSONS Scale. *Psychosomatics, 24*(4), 343–349.

Pomerantz, A., Shiner, B., Watts, B., Detzer, M., Kutter, C., Street, B., & Scott, D. (2010). The White River model of colocated collaborative care: A platform for mental and behavioral health care in the medical home. *Families Systems Health, 28*(2), 114–129.

Prochaska, J. O., DiClemente, C. C., & Norcross, J. C. (1992). In search of how people change: Applications to addictive behavior. *American Psychologist, 47*, 1102–1114.

Sacks, S. (2008). Brief overview of screening and assessment for co-occurring disorders. *Internal Journal Mental Health and Addiction, 6*, 7–19.

Sadock, B. J., & Sadock, V. A. (2008). *Kaplan & Sadock's concise textbook of clinical psychiatry.* (3rd. ed.). Philadelphia, PA: Lippincott Williams &Wilkins.

Segal, S. P., & Baumohl, J. (1981). Social work practice in community mental health. *Social Work, 26*(1), 16–24.

Smothers, B. A., Yahr, H. T., & Ruhl, C. E. (2004). Detection of alcohol use disorders in general hospital admissions in the United States. *Archives of Internal Medicine, 164*(7), 749–756.

Social Security Administration. (2008, Sept.). *Disability evaluation under Social Security.* Retrieved from http://www.ssa.gov/disability/professionals/bluebook/12.00-MentalDisorders-Adult.htm

Sterling, S., Chi, F., & Hinman, A. (2011). Integrating care for people with alcohol and other drug, medical and mental health conditions. *Alcohol Research & Health, 33*(4), 338-349.

Steer, R. A., & Beck, A. T. (1988). Use of the Beck Depression Inventory, hopelessness scale, scale for suicidal ideation, and suicide intent scale with adolescents. In *Advances in Adolescent Mental Health* (Vol. 3, pp. 219–231). Greenwich, CT: JAI Press.

Substance Abuse and Mental Health Services Administration. (2013, September). *Results from the 2012 National Survey on Drug Use and Health: Summary of national findings.* Retrieved from http://www.samhsa.gov/data/sites/default/files/NSDUHnationalfindingresults2012/NSDUHnationalfindingresults2012/NSDUHresults2012.pdf

Torrey, E. F. (1997). *Out of the shadows: Confronting America's mental illness crisis.* New York: John Wiley & Sons.

United Way Fox Cities. (n.d). *Mental health continuum of care-Definition of service categories.* Retrieved from http://www.unitedwayfoxcities.org/mental-health/definition-of-service-categories

Warden, S., Spiwak, R., Sareen, J., & Bolton, J. M. (2014, June 2). The SAD PERSONS Scale for suicide risk assessment: A systematic review. *Archives of Suicide Research.* Retrieved from http://www.ncbi.nlm.nih.gov/pubmed/24884399

Yates, W. R., Mitchell, J. R., Rush, A. J., Madhuker, H. T., Wisiewski, S. R., Warden, D., Hauger, R. B., Fava, M., Gaynes, B. N., Husain, M. M., & Bryan, C. (2004). Clinical features of depressed outpatients with and with co-occurring general medical conditions in STAR*D. *Psychiatry and Primary Care, 26*(6), 421–429. doi: 10.1016/j.genhosppsych.2004.06.008

CHAPTER 14

Supervision and Performance Evaluation

M. Carlean Gilbert and William J. Spitzer

INTRODUCTION

This chapter explores the history of supervision and its role in establishing and guiding competent practice. Terms, competencies, and the theoretical foundations of supervision are presented along with the ethical responsibilities of supervisors and trends in supervisory practice. As performance evaluation is a principal component of supervision and management, evaluation methodologies used in both **administrative and clinical supervision** are reviewed.

Evolving healthcare environments not only introduce change to clinical practice but also have implications for changing the nature of supervision and evaluation. Most recently, the emphasis of the Patient Protection and Affordable Care Act (PPACA) on integrated physical and behavioral healthcare, wellness, prevention, and chronic health will have an unquestionable impact on the practice locations and necessary skill sets of behavioral interventionists and their supervisors. The nature of supervision itself is anticipated to evolve, with the prospect of increased patient care team involvement. The contemporary emphasis on evidence-based practice is underscored.

IMPORTANCE OF CLINICAL SUPERVISION

Clinical supervision impacts one's professional development, certification, licensure, and execution of responsibilities. At a fundamental level, clinical supervision is consistent with the ethical duty of social work practitioners to continuously improve their professional knowledge and skills. The National Association of Social Worker's *Code of Ethics*, Section 1.04 (2008) specifies that social workers are responsible for meeting practice standards for interventions that they provide and taking responsible steps such as obtaining supervision to ensure competence in their work and to protect clients from harm. Providing supervision has significant legal implications. Supervisors are the individuals in the organization designated with the formal authority and responsibility to ensure the effective and efficient delivery of social work services. In this capacity, they retain **vicarious liability** and can be found liable for the actions or inactions of their supervisees (Reamer, 1998).

As social work education and professional identity have evolved, scholars have advanced a diverse array of theories, models, and terminologies of supervision. In the most recent meta-analysis of supervision, Mor Barak, Travis, Pyun, and Xie (2009) examined 27 published studies involving child welfare, social work, and mental health supervisees. Their analysis revealed that the task assistance, social and emotional support, and interpersonal interactions among supervisors and supervisees had statistically significant beneficial impacts on supervisees. These favorable characteristics were correlated with expressions of increased job satisfaction, worker effectiveness, feelings of psychological well-being, and commitment to the organization. Decreased anxiety, reduced depression, diminished stress, lessened burnout, and fewer job turnovers were further noted, as were decreases in role conflicts, ambiguities, and overload. These findings underscore the benefits of supervision to practitioners, organizations, and presumably recipients of healthcare social work services.

Evaluation of competence is an integral component of supervision and may have a clinical and/or administrative/operations focus. Competency is reflected in the performance of the tasks and duties associated with assigned professional roles. Contemporary emphasis in healthcare delivery centers on accountability, with optimal performance achieved through continuous quality improvement (CQI) activities, identification of best practices (benchmarking), and self-incorporation of benchmarked, evidence-based practice. While specific knowledge, skills, and abilities are necessary to successfully supervise personnel and evaluate performance, the personalities of both supervisee and supervisor also have a distinct influence on supervision and its outcomes.

Competence arises from the combination of formal academic preparation, sound judgment, and the knowledge and perspective associated with professional experience. Credentials are utilized to demonstrate that an individual has fulfilled a standardized set of expectations and therefore is thought to possess at least a baseline level of competence. Three distinct categories of credentials exist. Professionals may be credentialed by academia, their professional association or society, and/or by license conferred by the state(s) in which they practice.

Academic credentials are those conferred by educational bodies on completion of specified coursework, frequently including some experiential component (e.g., field placement, internship). In social work, these credentials most typically include the Bachelor of Social Work (BSW), Master of Social Work (MSW), and either the PhD or Doctor of Social Work (DSW) degrees. Variants of these degrees, such as the Master of Science in Social Work (MSSW), are conferred by some universities. At the bachelor's and master's degree levels, the perceived legitimacy of the degree is a function of it being granted by a university department or school accredited by the Council on Social Work Education (CSWE). Of the 40,237 social work degrees awarded for the 2012–2013 academic year, 42.8% were baccalaureate degrees, 56.4% were master's degrees, and 0.8% were doctorate degrees (CSWE, 2013).

Professional credentials are awarded by those associations, societies, or other bodies that are composed of individuals who are engaged in the same profession. Two examples of such social work organizations are the National Association of Social Workers (NASW) and the Society for Social Work Leadership in Health Care (SSWLHC). NASW confers a diverse array of credentials, including membership in the Academy of Certified Social Workers (ACSW) and their highest credential, the Diplomate of Clinical Social Work (DCSW). Specialty practice credentials may also be pursued, including such titles as Certified Social Work Case Manager, Clinical Social Worker in Gerontology, and Advanced Certified Hospice and Palliative Care Social Worker. Professional credentials are recognition from one's peers that the recipient has attained a level of expertise in his or her field and that the individual subscribes to the performance standards espoused by that professional body.

Professional credentials entail varying years of practice experience, referring letters of endorsement by peers, and passage of an examination. To illustrate, membership in the NASW's Academy of Certified Social Workers (ACSW), the most widely recognized national professional (non-license) credential, requires applicants to possess a master's degree from a school of social work accredited by CSWE, to complete 2 years of post-graduate social work employment with supervision from an MSW-credentialed supervisor, and to pass an examination (NASW, 2013). NASW also requires 2 or 3 years of supervision for MSW and BSW applicants, respectively, who seek advanced practice specialty credentials in fields of practice such as addictions, case management, clinical, education, gerontology, healthcare, hospice and palliative care, and youth and family.

Professional credentials differ from **professional licenses** in that the latter credentials are conferred by individual states and acknowledge that the holder is authorized in that specific state to engage in a particular practice that would otherwise be deemed unlawful were the individual not licensed. The requirements for licensure vary significantly from state to state, and the titles of licenses are also diverse and include such titles as licensed baccalaureate social worker, licensed master clinical social worker, licensed independent social worker, and licensed social worker with advanced standing (as an example, see http://www.socialworklicensure.org/state/social-work-licensure-texas.html). Whereas a professional credential generally distinguishes benchmark competence, a license only denotes that the individual has demonstrated the ability to practice at a minimum level of acceptable performance determined by a particular state.

Typically, professionals seeking a license for independent practice must complete 3,000 hours of professional clinical experience that is accompanied by weekly, one-hour sessions with a licensed clinical supervisor. These requisites are in addition to passage of the American Association of State Social Work Boards' examination. Thirteen states—Arizona, Florida, Kentucky, Louisiana, Maryland, Minnesota, Mississippi, Missouri, New Jersey, Oklahoma, Oregon, Texas, and Virginia—require that persons who represent themselves as clinical supervisors must complete additional training in the practice of supervision. It should be noted that some settings employ social workers but are exempt from requiring that they be licensed. The number of these settings is on the decline, however, as reimbursement is generally linked to possession of a license and agencies increasingly view possession of a license as a legal safeguard that staff have achieved some standard of competency. Supervisees in non-licensed settings who intend to apply for licensure must confirm that their supervision is provided by a supervisor who fulfills the state criteria for clinical supervision. That may necessitate securing private supervision external to their employment. Licenses and professional credentials are regularly renewed and to varying degrees require evidence of continuing formal education, active engagement in practice, passage of an examination, and submission of fees.

THE HISTORICAL CONTEXT OF SUPERVISION

Extending from the 1850s through the 1890s, the concept of supervision in the United States referred to the oversight of public and private programs and institutions rather than individual workers. Supervisors were accountable to public and private boards for confirmation that asylums and poor houses were run efficiently and effectively and that clients were treated humanely (Kadushin & Harkness, 2014; Munson, 2002). By the 1890s, "paid agents" were used to recruit, train, assign, and direct the case-related activities of volunteers known as "friendly visitors" of the Charity Organization Societies (COS). Forerunners of contemporary supervisors, the initial duties of these agents were primarily administrative, but educational functions were soon added (Tsui, 1997). Fledging in-service training programs offered by the COSs in the 1890s preceded the gradual transfer of professional education from agencies to universities. By 1910, five schools of social work were established (Kadushin & Harkness, 2014). Echoing the leadership role that agencies took in training workers, the Charity Organization Department of the Russell Sage Foundation, whose director was Mary Richmond, offered the first supervision course in 1911.

DEFINITIONS: FIELD EDUCATION, SUPERVISION, AND CONSULTATION

Established definitions of social work supervision have their roots in organizational models, education, and practices of the profession. Although the word "supervision" is often used interchangeably to describe supervision, clinical supervision, social work field education, and **consultation**, these terms each have important distinctions.

Field Education

The term field education is reserved to describe the distinct activities, roles, and functions of practitioners who instruct social work students. In social work, field education is the signature pedagogy (CSWE, 2012)—the central form of instruction and learning through which a profession socializes its students to practice. CSWE (2012) noted

The intent of field education is to connect the theoretical and conceptual contribution of the classroom with the practical world of the practice setting . . . the two interrelated components of curriculum—classroom and field— are of equal importance within the curriculum and each contributes to the development of the requisite competencies of the professional practice. Field education is systematically designed, supervised, coordinated, and evaluated based on criteria by which students demonstrate the achievement of program competencies (CSWE, 2012, Educational Policy 2.3).

Although both staff supervision and field instruction share historical roots in agency-based trainings and practice, they have branched into distinct areas of practice and scholarship. Attention is focused on supervision of practitioners, as a detailed discussion of field education is beyond the scope of this text.

Supervision

In the original lexicon of social work, supervision within the United States refers to agency-based functions. Kadushin's (1976, 2014) classic conceptualization of clinical supervision envisioned it as located in an organization and constructed around three inter-related functions: administrative, educational (clinical), and supportive.

The administrative function is based on authority delegated to supervisors by management to maintain supervisees' job performance. Supervisors are charged with facilitating staffs' abilities to deliver effective and efficient services to clients in ways that are consistent with professional practice standards and the policies, procedures, objectives, and structure of the employer (Kadushin & Harkness, 2014; Shulman, 1993, 2010; Tsui, 2005). Administrative functions are accomplished by organizing the work of supervisees through individual and service assignments and overseeing the staffs' assessments and interventions. Administrative functions include performance appraisals, which are evaluative functions often affecting salary increases and promotions. In performing appraisals, supervisors provide educational or clinical supervision to improve the knowledge and skills of staff within the mandate of the employing agency (Munson, 2002). As a third function, supervisors offer support to enhance staffs' self-awareness regarding their responses to job-related experiences and to foster their abilities to cope with associated stresses in any setting (Bogo & McKnight, 2005; Kadushin & Harkness, 2014; Tsui, 2005).

Clinical Supervision

Gibelman and Schervish (1997) maintained that the growing emphasis on clinical social work in the United States, including social workers entering private practice, has further distinguished the definitions of supervision and clinical supervision. In describing clinical supervision as focused on client-clinician dynamics, they viewed supervision as not inevitably agency-based. By decoupling the administrative connection between supervision and healthcare systems, clinical supervision can be provided directly by staff, purchased privately by supervisees, or subcontracted by supervisees' employing institutions. The American Board of Examiners in Clinical Social Work (ABECSW) described clinical supervision as a function that is provided by social workers with advanced training, years of practice experience, and mastery of competencies to supervisees who seek to acquire knowledge, skills, and identity as a clinical social worker (ABECSW, 2004).

Clinical Consultation

Although some may erroneously view consultation as a form of supervision, it is important to differentiate supervision from clinical consultation. Consultations typically are optional, short term, and requested by a practitioner rather than required by employers or licensure and certification boards. Consultants may offer suggestions or provide advice, but recipients are free to disregard their opinions. Importantly, consultation does not require an evaluative component as does most supervision.

THEORETICAL FOUNDATIONS

Theories are the overarching perspectives that function to organize, explain, and predict outcomes by guiding practitioners' assessments and interventions. These organizational frameworks enable individuals to select from and categorize potentially overwhelming amounts of data. Theories provide conceptual models that enable professionals to make inferences, develop "if-then" propositional statements, frame meaningful questions to explain phenomena, and create important practice directives (Lewis, 1982).

Social work supervision has no single, unifying theory that guides supervisors in their work (Kadushin & Harkness, 2014; Munson, 2009; Tsui, 2005). Some scholars have adapted theories from social scientists to explain the supervisory process. Shulman (2010) utilized the framework of William Schwartz, for example, to develop his interactional supervision model, which conceptualizes supervision as a continuous dynamic among three integrated subsystems of supervisors, patients, and staff. Based on a review of social work literature and empirical studies of supervisory tasks, Kadushin and Harkness (2014) defined supervision based on the functional tasks of administration, education, and support provided by agency-based supervisors. Munson (2002) presented supervisory processes in the context of tensions existing between authority and autonomy of organizations.

Many models of supervision can be clustered into overarching frameworks based on practice theories. Tsui (2005) noted several reasons for this adaptation, including the scarcity of supervision theory, the abundance of well-developed practice theories, and efficacy of therapy as a model for supervision. After examining clinical supervision models, Bernard and Goodyear (2014) identified three theoretical underpinnings to supervision: (1) psychotherapy, (2) developmental theories, and (3) social role models. Supervisors may integrate theoretical approaches to supervision with the models and techniques of practice specific to their client populations and settings. Bernard and Goodyear found evidence to conclude that theories affect the professional practices of both clinicians and supervisors. These findings underscore the need for supervisors to be cognizant of how their theoretical orientations influence their perception of supervisees' actions.

Psychotherapy Approaches

Supervision models incorporating psychotherapy include psychodynamic, person-centered, cognitive-behavioral, systemic, constructivist, and strength-based theories (Bernard & Goodyear, 2014). **Psychodynamic theory** has had a significant impact on social work practice and supervision since the late 1800s. Supervisors frequently rely on psychodynamic concepts such as transference, counter-transference, therapeutic and real relationships, ego functions and defenses, and interpretations. One application of psychodynamic theory to supervision is found in the *working alliance* (or *working relationship*), which refers to those prescribed aspects of clinician-client relationships that delineate the work each will do to alleviate clients' problems. Bordin (1979) wrote that this concept, originating in psychoanalytic theory, contributed to the effectiveness of psychotherapy and could be generalized to all forms of it. This view was later validated in a review of psychotherapy outcome research (Lambert, 1992) in which the author concluded that approximately 30% of treatment outcomes were associated with the therapeutic relationship.

Bordin (1983) broadened the conceptualization of the working alliance and its demands of the change agent and person pursuing change in psychotherapy and applied it to supervision. He identified three aspects of the working alliance in supervision: (1) *mutual agreement on goals* (e.g., advancing supervisees' competencies in interviewing or increasing their self-awareness), (2) *mutual understanding of tasks* (e.g., supervisors and supervisees participating in direct observation), and (3) *bonds* (e.g., developing mutual liking, caring, and trusting). Continued support for research, practice, and education of supervisors on the working alliance has been aided by the development of assessment tools such as the Supervisory Working Alliance Inventory (Efstation, Patton, & Kardash, 1990), which incorporates supervisor and supervisee versions.

Perhaps the most significant use of psychodynamic theory in supervision is the **parallel process,** which is regarded as a manifestation of transference and counter-transference. Labeling it the "reflective process," Searles (1955) was first to describe that "processes at work in the relationship currently between the patient and therapist are often reflected in the relationship between therapist and supervisor" (p. 135). This was subsequently referred to as "parallel process," in which supervisees unconsciously recreate the behaviors of their clients in their own supervisory sessions (Ekstein & Wallerstein, 1958; Doehrman, 1976; Frielander, Siegel, & Brenock, 1989). When the supervisors respond to the supervisees in a constructive manner, supervisees learn to respond therapeutically to their clients.

Let's consider a situation exemplifying the parallel process. In meeting with her supervisor, a supervisee presents a complex case in which she felt overwhelmed and powerless and then switches the subject to trivial matters. Further exploration reveals the client behaved similarly with the supervisee. By gently confronting the supervisee regarding what appeared to be her avoidant behavior, the supervisor redirected the discussion to the supervisee's feelings of helplessness. This subsequently enabled the supervisee to challenge the client's evasiveness in a similar manner.

Parallel process is considered an embodiment of *isomorphism*, a term used by systems theorists and family therapists to describe the one-to-one correspondence of processes among different systems, e.g., client, supervisee, supervisor, and supervisor's manager. Although evidence-based research on parallel process has been hampered by its subtle nature, its contributions to the development of supervisees' learning, personal growth, empathy, assessment, and intervention skills have been recognized by practitioners for over fifty years (Williams, 1997).

Developmental Approaches

Developmental theories are based on the assumption that supervisees progress through sequential stages of professional growth as they move towards competency. At the same time, their supervisors adapt their educational approaches as supervisees' learning needs change. While counseling psychologists have created many supervision models, extensive use of the **Integrated Developmental Model (IDM)** by Stoltenberg, McNeill, and Delworth (1998) warrants further discussion.

The IDM identifies three dimensions of assessment regarding supervisees (professional growth-motivation, dependence-autonomy, and self-other awareness) and prescribes associated supervisor interventions. These supervisee characteristics and supervisor responses vary among four developmental stages. Supervisees at *Level I* typically have limited training, have inadequate experience with an unfamiliar population, and/or are functioning in a new setting. They tend to be highly motivated but anxious about their practice competence. Autonomy is reflected in the extent to which the supervisee is reliant on the supervisor. Supervisees are inclined to be focused on the self and often harbor negative perceptions of their competencies (Stoltenberg, 2005). Supervisors are encouraged to respond to their supervisees by providing structure, positive feedback, and limited confrontation. Addressing parallel processes would be inappropriate in most cases as it is likely that novice supervisees are sensitive to criticism and have limited self-awareness.

Level II supervisees are transitioning from high dependence to autonomous functioning. In this phase, supervisees' motivation may fluctuate as they vacillate between feeling exceptionally confident or confused. With respect to autonomy, supervisees may manifest their independence by engaging in resistant behaviors with their supervisors. As supervisees increase their skill confidence, they may shift their focus from themselves to empathizing with their clients. Accordingly, Stoltenberg et al. (1998) comment that supervisors of Level II practitioners during this turbulent phase need "considerable skill, flexibility, and perhaps a sense of humor" (p. 87).

Level III is characterized by supervisees' developing confidence, use of "self," and a personal style of practice. Supervisees become increasingly able to focus on the client and monitor their own thoughts, emotions, and behaviors in relation to clients. The supervisory relationship becomes more collegial. In the final stage, *Level IIIi* (Integrated), supervisees have maturely integrated Level III competencies with an awareness of their strengths and limitations. Stoltenberg (2005) emphasized that supervisees may function in distinct domains of practice, e.g., individual versus couples work.

Social Role Approaches

Models based on social role theories conceptualize various roles of supervisors (most frequently as teachers and therapists) and view this as an essential aspect of supervision (Bernard & Goodyear, 2014). Bernard (1979) developed the *Discrimination Model,* so named because it postulates that supervisors will adapt their in-session responses to the specific needs of supervisees. As challenges arise, supervisors choose one of nine different responses based on a three-by-three matrix created by three foci and three roles. In this model, supervision focuses on supervisees' (1) intervention skills, (2) conceptualization skills (e.g., identifying patterns in clients' behaviors), and (3) personalization skills (e.g., management of countertransference issues). The supervisor serves in the roles of (1) teacher, (2) counselor, and (3) consultant. Referencing the developmental approach, Bernard and Goodyear (2014) noted that supervisors are more likely to use the teaching role with beginning supervisees and the consultant role with advanced supervisees.

SUPERVISION COMPETENCIES

One role of social work associations is to establish and promulgate expectations of the competencies required by clinical supervisors. The ABECSW (2004) recognizes the following competencies for clinical supervisors:

1. Proficiency in assessment and diagnosis

2. Capability to plan treatment

3. Knowledge of clinical supervision processes such as parallel process and self-awareness

4. Use of observational tools

5. Ability to evaluate practice

The NASW Standards for Social Work Practice in Health Care Settings (NASW, 2005) imply competency by stating that "A social work leader or supervisor shall be available to supervise healthcare social work staff on their responsibilities in practice, research, policy, orientation, and education. The purpose of supervision is to enhance the clinical social worker's professional skills and knowledge, to enhance competence in providing quality patient care" (Standard 19, pp. 32–33).

In effect, the challenge to the social work supervisor is twofold. The supervisor must be knowledgeable about supervisory techniques and be able to competently demonstrate the ability to translate theory into practice—that is, he or she must be able to develop harmonious relationships with supervisees that promote first disclosure and then individual professional growth through review of performance. The second professional challenge is that, like his or her supervisees, the supervisor must maintain a continuously updated level of competence in the skills necessary for effective and efficient practice. The supervisor must understand what technically must be done to accomplish the work and must also demonstrate sensitivity to the interplay of how doing work impacts the supervisee and how the personal makeup of the supervisee affects his or her work.

SUPERVISION MODALITIES

Dependent on the organizational context, structure, and resources in which patient care services are rendered, supervision may be provided to individual staff or extended to group, team, and peer modalities, with supervisors selected among one's colleagues. Each modality has unique characteristics and employs differing techniques in its delivery.

Individual Supervision

Individual supervision is typically provided through one-to-one, hourly meetings between supervisee and supervisor. Although individual supervision is generally regarded as the most widely used model of supervision (Bogo & McKnight, 2005; Kadushin & Harkness, 2014; Tsui, 2005), one study noted that individual supervision was infrequent and supplanted by a variety of supervision models (Kadushin, Berger, Gilbert, & de St Aubin, 2009). *Time-limited supervision* has proven to be popular in healthcare. Introduced by Wax (1963) following his experience at the Palo Alto Veterans Administration Hospital, this model challenged the then-prevailing practice of directionless, interminable supervision. Wax introduced a phase-based process of weekly supervision designed to orient supervisees to the philosophy and policies of the organization and then to help the supervisees to develop both professional judgment and required patient care skills. Wax believed that experienced staff in a new setting could achieve these objectives within 4 months, whereas inexperienced staff required 18 to 24 months. The time and effort required by this model, however, can prove challenging to hospital-based social work supervisors with corporate or other concurrent administrative responsibilities.

Group Supervision

Group supervision is the second most widely adopted model of supervision (Kadushin & Harkness, 2014). Characterized by the presence of a social work supervisor performing the functions of supervision in a group format, group supervision is a supplement to or a substitute for casework supervision. Group supervision is most successful when staff have discussed and agreed upon its use in a work unit. This modality conserves time and resources while facilitating lateral peer learning and the sharing and normalizing of job-related stress (Bogo & McKnight, 2005; Kadushin & Harkness, 2014; Sulman, Savage, Vrooman & McGillivray, 2004; Tsui, 2005). The very nature of group supervision suggests that a fundamental benefit derived from its use is the ability of supervisees to become aware of and learn from one another's experiences and approaches.

Team Supervision

Team supervision is an altered approach to group supervision in which social work supervisors assume an egalitarian role with supervisees, collectively making work assignments, designing performance checks, and contributing to professional development through educational and clinical guidance. Although supervisees have increased autonomy, the supervisor retains ultimate administrative accountability for team performance (Kadushin & Harkness, 2014; Tsui, 2005). As noted, patient care teams may have a physician, nurse, or other medical professional with supervisory authority over team members from other professions. Despite concerns about the efficiency and effectiveness of delivery systems dependent on team decision making (Faulkner & Amodeo, 1999), Abramson (2002) pointed out that teams remain at the center of service delivery in healthcare and, as such, obligate social workers to understand the principles and skills of team practice, including collaborative decision making.

The use of teams in healthcare has expanded significantly during the last several decades, and variations of such teams are now prevalent in nearly all practice settings. *Intra*disciplinary teams contain members with the *same* academic background and/or disciplinary practice, whereas *inter*disciplinary teams are comprised of personnel from *varied* disciplines or professions who routinely collaborate on issues or problems. Both are similar in that a number of individual experts work together to consider patient care cases or resolve issues. A **multidisciplinary team** is one in which members use their individual expertise to *first* develop their own answers to a given problem, and *then* come together—bringing their individually developed ideas—to formulate a solution (Kokemuller, 2012). Any and all of these teams are likely to have a designated leader or supervisor.

The prevalence of team supervision was furthered with the passage of the Patient Protection and Affordable Care Act. With its thrust on integration of physical and behavioral healthcare, the PPACA promotes collaboration across the continuum by expecting all professionals to be engaged in ongoing coordinated care. The importance of collaboration is further underscored by predictions that there will be insufficient healthcare professionals to meet burgeoning service demands. Necessity will likely dictate future shifts in where, when, how, and by whom services will be delivered. Use of **transdisciplinary teams** is expected to become prominent with this shift in professional roles. Unlike interdisciplinary teams characterized by groups of professionals working interdependently but with clearly defined disciplinary bounds and utilizing their own tools, the transdisciplinary team approach is based on the premise that one person can perform several professional roles by providing services to a patient *under the supervision of individuals from the other disciplines involved* (Spitzer & Davidson, 2013).

Peer Supervision

Peer supervision has been described in the field of psychotherapy for over 50 years (Todd & Pine, 1968; Counselman & Weber, 2004). The fiscally driven changes in healthcare that commenced in the 1990s emphasized self-managed work teams that empowered staff by conferring increased decision-making autonomy and team collaboration in lieu of earlier hierarchical organizational models that employed department directors and supervisors (Tally, 2006).

Successful engagement of this modality is contingent on (1) the practice competencies of the participants; (2) their willingness, experience, and capacity to assume responsibility for supervising and evaluating one another's practice; (3) the organizational sanctions that legally empower the team to render decisions that might ultimately affect practice approaches as well as staff "personnel actions" (promotion, demotion, firing, etc.); and (4) the clarity of, appropriateness of, and consensus about defined practice standards. Shifting to this form of supervision from the traditional supervisor/manager format can prove challenging as it places a significantly distinct set of new duties and responsibilities for judging one another on previously clinical (or non-management) personnel. Illustrating these concerns, Tally (2006) noted that "rooted in the self-management concept is the belief that team members will give true and constructive feedback to each other. This is definitely the most challenging aspect of peer supervision (as it) is tied to assigning colleagues (a performance score) . . . and this reluctance to confront performance needing improvement" can prompt implementation issues necessitating Human Resources involvement (pp. 79–80).

Peer Consultation

Because peer consultation is incorrectly termed peer supervision by some, it is included in the discussion of supervision modalities. Peer consultation may be provided in individual or group format, occur in spontaneous or formally scheduled meetings sanctioned by the institution, and offer support and guidance. Social workers or other healthcare professionals who occupy similar positions in the organizational hierarchy may serve as peer consultants, but they lack the authority of supervisors designated by the organization. This latter factor becomes important in the event of litigation or other formal challenge to a professional patient care decision.

TRENDS IN SUPERVISION

As noted in Chapter 2, the funding and delivery of healthcare services in the United States experienced far-reaching changes with the introduction of the Medicare capitated payment system for hospital care in the early 1980s. Private and public third-party payers soon followed suit and adopted managed care payment and delivery procedures. Because the prospective payment system transferred financial risk from payer to provider, hospital revenues were reduced. Hospital administrators responded to this challenge by merging with competitive institutions, creating multi-hospital healthcare systems, dividing functions among programs and teams, and decentralizing departments (Bazzoli, Dynan, Burns, & Yap, 2004; Weil, 2003). Not infrequently, the consequence of these cost-saving measures was the elimination of social work directors, middle managers, and supervisors (Kadushin & Harkness, 2014; Weissman & Rosenberg, 2002).

Despite reports by researchers in healthcare (Whitaker, Weismiller, & Clark, 2006) and behavioral health (U.S. Department of Health and Human Services, 2007) of increases in the severity and complexity of client problems, paper work and caseloads, the availability of supervisory positions *decreased*. In 2004 researchers conducted a stratified random sample of approximately 10,000 licensed social workers from 48 states and the District of Columbia who were members of the National Association of Social Workers (NASW). The study purpose was to profile primary areas of practice, roles, functions, and service settings (Whitaker, Weismiller, & Clark, 2006). When asked about their roles as supervisors, 7% of respondents indicated they spent "20 hours or more" per week providing supervision. Approximately 2.5% of study participants also acknowledged that a decrease in supervision, which was second only to reimbursement levels (approximately 4%), negatively impacted their work. Diminishment of supervision could be inferred as one of the reasons why 12% of study respondents revealed that they planned to leave the profession.

Three years later, social workers reported that the amount of time that they spent in supervision dropped from 7% to 5%. Although the findings of these self-selected participants cannot be generalized to the entire population of NASW members (who do not represent all degreed or healthcare social workers), they suggested a trend towards reduced supervision (Whitaker & Arrington, 2008). Expressing concerns about retention, Whitaker et al. (2006) conclude that "Although most social workers express satisfaction with their career choice and aspects of their practices, too many become discouraged by agency environments that are unresponsive to their needs for professional growth, respect and fair compensation" (p. 35).

The Annapolis Coalition, a not-for-profit organization charged with addressing the workforce crisis in the mental health and addictions sectors of the behavioral health field, raised similar concerns about the diminishment of supervision (U.S. Department of Health and Human Services, 2007). Following a two-year strategic planning process involving over 5,000 individuals, the Coalition reported that "erosion of supervision" (p. 1) of direct care staff contributed to problems in the recruitment, retention, training, and performance of the workforce. Of further concern, researchers found a lack of training in the management and leadership skills needed for successful succession planning as older leaders retired.

Changing Models of Supervision

A decline in social work supervisory positions in hospitals associated with the introduction of managed care was reported in a 4-year-long longitudinal study initiated in 1994 (Berger, Robbins, Lewis, Mizrahi, & Fleit, 2003). A later qualitative study of 17 supervisees found that as hospitals restructured, workers necessarily sought alternative innovative ways to address their educational and supportive needs (Kadushin et al., 2009). In contrast to existing literature that identified formal clinical supervision as the most widely used model of supervision (Bogo & McKnight, 2005; Kadushin & Harkness, 2014; Tsui, 2005), supervisees participating in Kadushin et al.'s (2009) focus groups indicated that individual formal supervision was infrequent. Instead, a critical finding was that supervisees used a combination of supervisory models, including (1) seeking secondary on-site supervisors (team leaders, senior workers or leads), (2) participating in group or team supervision, (3) engaging in peer supervision, (4) paying for private supervision, (5) relying on peer consultation for clinical and supportive supervisory functions, and (6) receiving supervision on a "PRN" (as-needed) basis.

Participants confirmed Bogo and McKnight's (2005) finding that supervision was opportunistically shaped by the "order of the day" (p. 56) rather than matched with the professional developmental needs of the supervisees. One explanation for the ad hoc provision of supervision was that shorter lengths of patient hospitalizations, high caseload turnover, and frequent crises demand immediate attention that is incompatible with traditional weekly scheduled meetings. Regardless of licensure status, focus group participants reported that the content of supervision centered predominantly on administrative issues. They perceived that supervisors' primary commitments were to hospital bureaucracy and did not believe that they received supervision that systematically matched their professional practice or personal development needs. While the study by Kadushin et al. (2009) was limited because it involved a small convenience sample that did not represent all healthcare supervisees, it offered unique insights from the perspective of supervisees from different geographic regions of the United States.

Interprofessional Supervision

As noted, flattened organizational structures that eliminated clinical supervisory positions contributed to social workers increasingly being supervised by other professionals such as nurses and members of interdisciplinary teams (Berger & Mizrahi, 2001; Gibelman & Schervish, 1997). In FY 1992, Berger and Mizrahi noted that only 13% of participants in a national sample received supervision from other professionals. By 1994, this percentage had increased to 16%, and, by 1996, nearly a fifth of those sampled were being supervised by someone outside their own profession. Bogo, Paterson, Tufford, and King (2011) determined that supervisees had mixed feelings regarding interprofessional supervision. Although they often valued supervision from others, practitioners expressed a need for supervision by someone from their own profession who supported the values, beliefs, language, ethics, and philosophies of their profession. Profession-specific supervision was especially important when the practitioner was the only member of a profession on an interprofessional team.

How supervision is perceived can vary depending on the profession (Bogo et al., 2011). Sampled nurse participants, for example, fearfully anticipated being criticized for an error when asked to see their supervisors—a reaction that could potentially be explained by the life-and-death nature of their work and the associated worries of facing risk-management issues. Occupational therapists and social workers, on the other hand, viewed supervision as an occasion to discuss their personal struggles as clinicians, e.g., counter-transference.

The evolving healthcare environment has implications for supervision. The PPACA is shifting the focus and modalities of healthcare delivery in the United States. To curtail costs, optimize use of healthcare resources, and achieve desired patient care outcomes, the PPACA promotes integrating service delivery along the continuum of healthcare settings and through continuous, coordinated interaction of practitioners. Teamwork is the vehicle for this approach and with it comes the prospect of increased inter-professional supervision.

As Little (2011) forecast that "social workers practicing in either medical or mental health settings will soon all be practicing in some version of an integrated model of care" (p. 1), the socialization process of other disciplines becomes particularly important for those who are providing or receiving interprofessional supervision. Little (2011) and Ehrlich, Kendall, and Muenchberger (2012) noted that the greater transdisciplinary coordination necessary with integrated care promoted by the PPACA will require an increased collegial understanding of what each discipline represents as a service provider. Professionals other than social workers will not necessarily share similar perspectives, values, and methodologies of patient care. In instances when clinical supervision is obtained from non-social workers, it may be warranted for supervisees to petition for supplementary group supervision, peer consultation, or contracted supervision offered by members of their own profession. Such contact serves the purpose of maintaining one's own professional identity and advancing individual professional growth.

Use of Technology

Few would disagree that technology has contributed to profound and rapid changes in their personal lives. The use of technology for clinical supervision in healthcare and mental healthcare has paralleled these transformations. Telecommunication technologies can benefit the provision of clinical supervision by enabling "real time" exchange of information, affording supervision to off-site workers, and providing access to isolated practitioners such as those in rural areas or overseas military bases. Electronically delivered supervision using Internet-based media such as Skype can be conveyed 24 hours a day, 7 days a week, and, by eliminating travel time, can reduce the expense of face-to-face sessions. Access to experts in specialized areas of practice can be accordingly made easier—a particularly pragmatic consideration when consultation is needed with little or no notice. The Patient Protection and Affordable Care Act of 2010 clearly promotes the use of electronic media such as electronic medical records to store and convey patient care information. Acknowledging forecasts that there will be insufficient numbers of practitioners available despite growing need for healthcare services, the Act endorses innovative means for healthcare personnel to maintain their expertise through the new electronic technologies that augment traditional face-to-face communication.

Patients, healthcare colleagues, supervisees, and supervisors may be expected to differ in their usage, comfort, and understanding of technology. One view is that individuals may be regarded as either Digital Natives or Digital Immigrants (Prensky, 2001). Often younger individuals, *Digital Natives* are born into a world of technology and are conditioned to access information quickly and continuously. They obtain instant gratification and multi-task using multiple technologies such as instant messaging and emailing. Digital Natives "think and process information fundamentally differently from their predecessors" (Prensky, p. 1). *Digital Immigrants*, in comparison, did not grow up in digital language environments and, like immigrants in a new country, may (or may not) have acculturated to it.

The distinction between these two groups is relevant because at the same time that the relative percentage of supervisees who are digital natives increases, supervisors (many of whom are likely digital immigrants) may find themselves challenged to understand the ethical, legal, and treatment implications of using new technologies for supervision. These technologies may range from mobile telephones, e-mail, iPhones, and text messages to iChat, Skype, teleconferences, videoconferences, Google Chat, and Dropbox. While these technologies can be advantageous to the supervisory process, caution is urged that both supervisors and supervisees consider the following critical issues:

1. Can confidentiality be breached through the use of unsecured equipment?

2. What legal and malpractice issues occur when state or national boundaries are crossed by multisite healthcare systems?

3. What state regulations pertain to acceptance of clinical supervision administered through technology in fulfillment of criteria for licensure application (Gilbert & Maxwell, 2011)?

4. Are the supervisor and supervisee competent in the use of the technology (Powell & Migdole, 2012)?

One important source of information on the use of technology is the publication entitled *Standards for Technology and Social Work Practice,* which was a collaborative effort of the National Association of Social Workers and the Association of Social Work Boards (2005).

ETHICAL RESPONSIBLITIES OF SUPERVISORS

Healthcare social workers regularly confront multifaceted cases in complex organizational settings, navigate among different values, ethics, and priorities of transdisciplinary team colleagues, and cope with the implications of cutting-edge biotechnologies. Perhaps these factors account for healthcare social workers ranking the desire for more education and training in professional ethics highest (22.8 %) in contrast to social workers from all other fields of practice (Whitaker et al., 2006). This need for additional education and training in healthcare ethics affects not only a sizeable number of self-identified health practitioners, but their supervisors as well. Ethical concerns are a primary reason why supervisees, especially seasoned ones, seek clinical supervision.

An ethical concern arises when there is uncertainty or conflict about values. Values are those strongly held ideals, principles, and standards that inform decision making or actions. Munson (2002) noted that "values relate to what one believes, and ethics relate to how one behaves" (p. 102). In a therapeutic relationship, ethical concerns can be viewed as an integral part of the helping relationship and can facilitate the therapeutic process. In the spirit of the parallel process, ethical dilemmas can also facilitate the supervisory process and can actually be a "teachable moment"—a golden opportunity for personal insight and professional growth (DeWane, 2007).

The NASW *Code of Ethics* (NASW, 2008) maintains that "social workers who provide supervision or consultation should have the necessary knowledge and skill to supervise or consult appropriately and should do so only within their areas of knowledge and competences" (Section 3.01). Fundamental expectations for ethical supervisory practice include setting clear, appropriate, and culturally sensitive boundaries with supervisees and refraining from engagement in any dual or multiple relationships that may serve to exploit or potentially harm supervisees. A dual relationship exists when a relationship other than a professional one develops. This situation can occur not only between staff and clients but also between supervisors and staff. One illustration of a dual professional relationship could be seen in a situation in which a staff member has a side service business that the supervisor would like to use.

Munson (2006) emphasized that supervisors need to apply ethical standards to each technique that practitioners utilize in patient care situations and that "techniques that have not been subjected to empirical analysis, or are not subject to regular and consistent monitoring, should be considered unethical under current practice standards" (p. 8). The ethical delivery of supervision is predicated on communication that (1) reflects the canons of professional practice; (2) conveys accurate, appropriate, and timely information in a manner comprehensible by the supervisee; and (3) is afforded by a supervisor consistently interacting in a responsible, constructive manner that promotes professional development and practice competence.

PERFORMANCE EVALUATION

Purpose

As previously noted, supervisors fulfill educational, supportive, and administrative functions for staff and organizations (Bogo & McKnight, 2005; Kadushin and Harkness, 2014; Tsui, 1997). Administrative functions include conducting performance evaluations, arguably one of the most important supervisory roles as it affects staff (supervisee) development and presumably patient care outcomes. Munson (2002) distinguished between *administrative evaluations,* which examine a wide range of competencies, occur at intervals, and can result in "personnel actions," and **practice evaluations.** The latter are characterized by ongoing discussions of organization-sanctioned practice behaviors that are changed immediately, are assessed promptly after being modified, and typically are confined to the supervisory relationship. Because the performance evaluation is a universally important function in healthcare settings, it is discussed in detail.

Every organization, regardless of size, type, or mission, engages in some form of staff performance evaluation. **Performance evaluation** is a process to assess how individual staff members are performing and how they can improve their job performance and contribute to overall organizational performance. Performance is evaluated in order to make decisions on wage and salary levels and to determine promotions, terminations, disciplinary actions, recognition and rewards, or training needs. While performance appraisal processes may vary, Gibson, Ivancevich and Donnelly (1973) observed that the anticipated end results are essentially the same:

- Improved staff contribution to the organization

- Improved morale and attitudes of staff

- Reduced staff anxiety resulting from ambiguity as to where they stand with their superiors

Awareness of performance is crucial to maintaining the credibility of staff, programs, and the organization at large. Consistent, quality performance contributes to patient satisfaction and to the achievement of patient and organizational goals, and, in the process, enhances external perceptions of staff and organizations as competent, "preferred providers." Documentation of sustained quality performance also reduces the prospect of malpractice, breach of contract, failure to perform, and other litigation being initiated based on a perception that staff (and therefore the organization) is not fulfilling service expectations. Yet other implications of failure to appropriately perform include loss of service contracts by an organization or, in the instance of direct patient care such as therapy, misguided actions by patients that endanger the patients themselves or others or that otherwise negatively impinge on service delivery.

Staffs can be evaluated informally through judgments rendered by others in the organization and/or formally through the use of a rating mechanism. While some evaluations may be very informal (e.g., a compliment by a colleague), most methodologies are much more formal, utilizing a proscribed process entailing both written and verbal elements. Beatty and Schneier (1977) noted that evaluations are typically predicated on three measures of performance: (1) personal traits (such as leadership ability or interpersonal skills), (2) job performance behaviors, and (3) job results. These variables are the basis for comparing the individual staff to some established expectation. Expectations may be promulgated through organizational policies and procedures, by contractual stipulations and law, and/or by standards and guidelines issued by regulatory/accrediting bodies such as the Joint Commission or the Commission on Accreditation of Rehabilitation Facilities or by a profession. Importantly, there is a predominant expectation that the individual practitioner will concurrently engage in *self-evaluation* so as to practice only in an ethically responsible, "professional" manner. The National Association of Social Workers underscored the fundamental relationship of ethical behavior to competent practice in their revised Code of Ethics (2008) Section 1.04 (Competence):

a. Social workers should provide services and represent themselves as competent only within the boundaries of their education, training, license, certification, consultation received, supervised experience, or other relevant professional experience.

b. Social workers should provide services in substantive areas or use intervention techniques or approaches that are new to them only after engaging in appropriate study, training, consultation, and supervision from people who are competent in those interventions or techniques.

c. When generally recognized standards do not exist with respect to an emerging area of practice, social workers should exercise careful judgment and take responsible steps (including appropriate education, research, training, consultation, and supervision) to ensure the competence of their work and to protect clients from harm.

Methodology: Management Evaluation

Workers typically are evaluated on their performance in discharging responsibilities to both patients **and** the organization. While professional clinical competence is an integral component of "benchmark" performance, staff must also responsibly function in the organization. Staffs are expected to subscribe to established policies, procedures, guidelines, and norms that may specify everything from how to assume "on-call" duties, initiate referrals to colleagues, and recognize the expectation for their presence at specified meetings through employing the proper steps for requesting leave and using the organizational credit card. Failure to demonstrate acceptable "organizational behavior" can result in staff being construed as unrepresentative of the organization and/or unreliable as a "team player." In contemporary environments touting integrated healthcare and transdisciplinary team-delivered services, being identified as non-cooperative to shared performance expectations can have career-devastating implications.

The success of performance evaluations depends primarily on the (1) system and measures (criteria), (2) culture, and (3) the perceived attitudes and needs of the participants—that is, the degree of their "engagement" with their jobs (Vance, 2006). The evaluation system should be uniformly applied and predicated on clear, relevant criteria. The organizational culture must be one that regards systematic, continuous staff evaluation as crucial to enhancing service quality by identifying and promoting "benchmark" performance. The success of evaluations is also contingent on the work attitude maintained by staff; staffs who regard their activities as valuable, meaningful, and professional will respond to appraisals more constructively than staffs who hold their position and/or the organization in disdain.

Methodology is crucial in performance evaluations. W. Edward Deming (1986), for example, once commented that inappropriately conducted supervision and appraisals could end up only nourishing short-term performance, while annihilating long-term planning, building fear, demolishing teamwork, nourishing rivalry, and, in the end, leaving staff bitter, dejected, and feeling inferior to the point of being unfit for work. To avoid such perils while garnering optimal performance, Peters (1987) in his well-known treatise, *Thriving on Chaos*, emphasized that every opportunity should be taken with staff to celebrate, recognize, communicate, and teach.

Fundamental to constructive performance evaluation is a clear, mutual understanding by management (supervisors) and staff about the nature of the work involved, its importance (or contribution), processes expressed in policies and procedures, expected outcomes, and steps that can be taken to improve performance. Included is a shared understanding of why the staff member is suited to performing the involved work. Staffs need to have an understanding of the specific tasks associated with their work and both what constitutes expected performance and, importantly, *why*. Clarifying why a certain performance is expected (why selected outcomes are relevant) provides the basis for appreciating the value-added contribution of that position in the organization—it underscores the individual importance of the staff member. Objectives should be mutually agreed upon, unambiguous, sufficiently supported with appropriate resources, and accomplishable; importantly, they should be meaningful to both clients and the organization.

Although the emphasis in performance evaluations is on the achievement of objectives, it should not be at the expense of *how* the objectives are attained (Beatty & Schneier, 1977). Managers should confer recognition on the efforts expended by staff as well as their creativity and ethical motivation in pursuing their work. What is crucial is the genuineness of the interaction between management and the staff; the foundation for a constructive, relevant performance appraisal is the conveyed sense that the organization regards the individual staff, the impacts of the staff's contributions to date, and the staff's potential for further professional development. The appraisals should be conducted in an atmosphere of respect, courtesy, and appreciation for those efforts to achieve desirable outcomes. Constructive criticism is used when remedying situations with undesirable outcomes or when performance does not fully meet expectations.

Following a review of previously established goals or desired outcomes, the supervisor should commence the evaluation with a request for the staff to reflect on what has transpired during the evaluative period by focusing initially on perceived accomplishments. Doing so provides an opportunity to convey Peters's (1987) point of sharing and celebrating positive outcomes and the energies expended by staff in pursuit of competent service. Interest should be shown in what work elements staff found to be satisfying and rewarding. It contributes to the supervisor being seen as supportive, an advocate, and a developmental resource. The stage is then constructively set for the necessary second-step discussion on difficulties, shortcomings, or failures experienced in pursuing desired service goals.

Large-scale studies (Meyer, Kay, & French, 1965) showed that criticism in evaluations has a negative effect on performance, whereas mutual goal setting has a positive effect in reducing anxiety and defensive behavior (Beatty & Schneier, 1977). Having initially recognized and honored the capabilities of the staff, supervisors' subsequent disclosure of concerns or problems becomes comparatively less threatening and instead affords the opportunity for meaningful, in-depth discussion about factors thwarting goal accomplishment. Instead of conveying blame, discussion focuses on constructively identifying specific steps that can minimize or eliminate the recurrence of service delivery problems. This may include retraining, enrollment in expanded education, provision of needed equipment, and/or revision of policies, procedures, personnel assignments, and/or work schedules. If one presumes that staffs do not *intend* to have negative outcomes in their work, but in fact *experience* them, then the outcome can more likely be thought to arise from lack of experience, insufficient training or equipment, faulty processes, and/or an otherwise unanticipated variable that was not controlled. If one further presumes that the staff member attempted his or her best performance at the time and the result was an unwanted outcome, one can also anticipate that the effect on the staff member is such that he or she feels diminished or otherwise inadequate. To the extent that supervisory intervention at this moment explores the circumstance and affords constructive alternatives, the impact of such direction will be longer lasting and will positively contribute to the supervisory relationship.

Clear documentation is a necessary component of performance appraisals. It provides a legal basis for both employer and staff to acknowledge the substance of the appraisal, any established goals, and future implications. As with the appraisal itself, documentation should strive for a balanced view of the staffs' efforts by noting their successes, failures, and causative factors; the positive concrete steps taken to enhance future staff performance; and a statement of goals established for the forthcoming evaluation period. In instances in which staff performance is questionable and continued employment may be at issue, it is crucial that (1) staff be encouraged to promptly convey any ongoing support needs (additional supervisory time, further training, etc.) to the supervisor, (2) the work expectations be clearly reiterated, and (3) the implications of continued substandard performance be specifically identified (including time frames established for "corrective actions"). Evaluators of staff should seek to ensure that their comments on staff performance are as factually based as possible; performance verification is enhanced when data-gathering is by "triangulation" from multiple reliable sources. Potential information sources on staff performance include, but are not limited to, supervisor self-observation, staff self-report, team/work unit colleagues, incident and CQI reports, review of staff-prepared materials, client service complaints/compliments or other correspondence, organizational critiques, and documentation of accomplishments (awards, secured grants, appointments, etc.).

Staff comfort with evaluations and ultimately the positive impact of evaluations on performance is determined by staff confidence in the process. Staff members must trust that the intent is to enhance their performance and therefore their contribution to the organization rather than to assign blame and to castigate. Evaluative processes must be predictable in form and consistent in their application across all staff. They should center on celebrating achievements and identify constructive, non-diminishing remedies to unachieved personal and work unit goals and inefficient systems that result in underperforming organizations and unmet client needs. Evaluative discussions must be conducted in a confidential manner at all times.

Methodology: Clinical Practice Evaluation

Clinical practice, while unique in its focus, is not unlike any other work endeavor—enhanced performance arises from continuous evaluation of outcomes and the subsequent modification of technique to improve results. The fundamental challenge of supervision is to constructively engage with competent technical knowledge and administrative direction aimed at enhancing the performance of individual professionals, while benefiting the pursuit of organizational, programmatic, and/or individual client goals (Spitzer, 2006).

The outcome measure of supervision is the ability of supervisees to transfer the intervention techniques explored in supervision into daily practice (Shamai, 1998). Munson (2006) observed that this relationship historically has been perceived to be crucial to intervention outcomes. Intervention outcomes essentially relate to client change; that is, whether the client's circumstances have changed as a result of the therapeutic intervention (Jacobson & Traux, 1991) Evaluation of clinical competence therefore typically placed greatest focus on the extent of the clinician's

1. skill in identifying and understanding the client's circumstances,

2. ability to relate to the client's responses to events in his or her life,

3. ability to convey appropriately supportive responses to the client, and

4. capacity to formulate, with the client, relevant and realistic (achievable) goals leading to the client's satisfactory adjustment to his or her life circumstances and adversities.

That historic focus, however, became tempered by economic pressures of the 1990s that prompted dynamic shifts in the business aspects of healthcare and mental healthcare delivery. Whether a proprietary private sector or public non-profit service model, emphasis was (and continues to be) placed on practice efficiency and effectiveness as means to achieve quality patient care, cost reduction, and revenue maximization. At the same time, and influenced at least in part by these external pressures, the clinical focus shifted from primarily relationship to one incorporating a behavioral and task orientation. Ironically, as Munson (2006) pointed out, managed care organizations utilized earlier problem-solving and task-oriented interventions dating to Mary Richmond and adopted them as concrete, measurable means of evaluating the effectiveness of mental health interventions and reducing service costs. The effects of this approach to practice can be stressful as professional counseling ethics become juxtaposed with financially driven business practices. Munson observed that perhaps managed care might be better termed "managed cost."

The PPACA places principal focus on the integrated delivery of physical and behavioral healthcare, while concentrating on wellness, preventive care, and chronic health concerns. Increased emphasis will accordingly be placed on service delivery in primary care settings. Horevitz and Manoleas (2013) pointed out that because social workers are trained as generalists using a biopsychosocial perspective, they will be well positioned to assume positions in these contexts. Although their sample of practitioners perceived the competency areas most important in primary care practice as knowledge of psychotropic medication, interdisciplinary collaboration, psychoeducation, knowledge of chronic illness, and cultural competence (p. 766), the researchers also cautioned that use of evidence-based practice will increasingly become prevalent. For supervisors, it becomes crucial that they possess an understanding of these competencies, presumably guided by their own practice expertise.

Munson (2002) regarded clinical evaluation not as a process for judging the effectiveness of clients' treatment or as a performance review, but rather for evaluating clinicians' practices to enhance learning and, therefore, effectiveness in practice (p. 241). Munson, like Shulman (2010), viewed clinical evaluation as an opportunity to promote staff proficiency. A number of reasons, however, may contribute to unease with the evaluation experience, despite the stated desire by staff to receive feedback. Evaluation activates status and power differentials between supervisors and staff that may have been quiescent during regular day-to-day interactions. Kadushin and Harkness (2014) observed that the supervisor's organizational position and clinical expertise create a social distance between the supervisor and his or her supervisees. They also noted that if supervisors must make negative assessments, they may (1) feel guilty because the supervisee's inadequate performance suggests the supervisor's own failure to perform adequately as a supervisor, (2) fear hostility from the supervisee, or (3) as Shulman (2010) commented, have apprehension that a negative recommendation in the supervisor's role as professional "gatekeeper" may trigger litigation. Kadushin and Harkness (2014) and Shulman (2010) provided similar guidelines for favorable evaluation processes; Shulman's work is summarized in seven steps:

1. Present an evaluation guide at the beginning of supervision.

2. Refer to elements of the guide periodically during supervision.

3. Build periods of assessment into supervision prior to formal evaluation.

4. Review collaboratively the guide and prepare preliminary assessments.

5. Document supervisors' and supervisees' views on performance.

6. Meet to discuss the two versions of the preliminary assessment.

7. Document agreements and disagreements in the final evaluation.

Given this perspective, the evaluation process begins with the practitioner being asked to rate his or her own practice. Those responses are then utilized as a baseline upon which subsequent progress is considered. The assessment continues with an analysis of the clinician's current skill level, the approaches employed by the clinician, and the outcomes experienced by clients.

The same mutual understanding of roles and performance goals sought in *non*-clinical evaluations was articulated by Munson (2002) in the clinical context as achieving a "congruence of perceptions," noting that "mutual sharing of questions, concerns, observations, and speculations . . . aids in select(ing) alternative techniques to apply in practice" (p. 11). As with any evaluation, the clinician must sense that the evaluator is fairly and uniformly employing ethical, clear, and appropriate criteria. The evaluator must also be capable of demonstrating his or her technical competence (including capacity to apply theory to clinical material/ practice) and ability to use insightful analysis in considering the clinician's actions.

Increasingly, the interventions and outcomes of any one clinician are evaluated in contrast with the experiences of other practitioners in similar circumstances. This arises from belief that, whenever possible, practice should be grounded on prior findings that demonstrate empirically that certain actions performed with a particular type of client or client system are likely to produce predictable, beneficial, and effective results (Chambless et al., 1998; Woody & Sanderson, 1998). Cournoyer and Powers (2002) noted that a host of contemporary factors have combined to promote use of **evidence-based practice:**

1. The evolution of managed care systems rewarding interventions based on known effective techniques

2. The NASW Code of Ethics states that "social workers should base practice on recognized knowledge, including empirically based knowledge, relevant to social work and social work ethics." (NASW, 2008, §4.01[c])

3. Increasingly empowered consumers who expect practitioners to maintain relevant practice competencies

4. Council on Social Work Accreditation Standards (2.1.6) that expect "social workers (to) use practice experience to . . . employ evidence-based interventions, evaluate their own practice, and use research findings to improve practice, policy, and social service delivery" (CSWE, 2010, p. 5)

5. The emergence of state laws and court decisions holding practitioners accountable for their professional actions

6. Shifts to service funding contingent on demonstrable outcomes

7. The proliferation of malpractice and negligence lawsuits

Two resources for evidenced-based practice are *The Cochrane Collaboration,* which focuses on health interventions, and *The Campbell Collaboration,* which focuses on social welfare issues. They can be found at www.cochrane.org and www.campbellcollaboration. org, respectively. The significant role of evidence-based practice in the future is clearly visible in the stipulations of the Patient Protection and Affordable Care Act of 2010. The Act expects that evidence-based practice will be used as the basis for examining, refining, and delivering patient care services.

Clinical evaluation focuses on how patient care is rendered and the outcomes of any intervention. Central issues are the dimensions of the therapeutic relationship and the extent to which the clinician was able to evoke change in the patient. Outcomes are evaluated on the basis of their constructive impact on patient functioning and the subsequent modification of their life circumstances. Assuming use of evidence-based practice, clinicians should be able to explain, justify, and document existing research that supports the choice of interventions. The value of practice evaluation is enhanced when sensitivity is demonstrated toward the perspectives and experiences of the clinician, while at the same time effort is taken to provide education and support toward the goal of continuously improving the clinician's practice.

SUMMARY

The contemporary healthcare environment places the highest value on accountability, collaboration, and promotion of competent, evidence-based practice, regardless of profession. Supervision and performance evaluation are fundamentally important to achieving positive patient care outcomes and efficient, effective service delivery. Proper execution of these functions relies on the supervisor possessing knowledge, technical skills, and, importantly, the ability to consistently demonstrate ethically responsible, compassionate, and yet pragmatic behavior as a model for staff. As numerous modalities of supervision exist, care must be exercised that the manner of supervision is consistent with the organizational mission and service culture.

The future affords both challenge and opportunity. Evolving care models, particularly those promoted by the Patient Protection and Affordable Care Act of 2010, shift the venue and manner of service delivery by emphasizing earlier engagement, continuity of care across multiple service settings, interdisciplinary collaboration, and teamwork. These models include the increasing prospect that supervision will be offered by those other than in one's own profession. Practitioners and supervisors alike will be challenged to gain the broadened knowledge and collaborative perspective requisite for success in these scenarios. Regardless of supervisory or administrative model however, success will be defined by the extent that collaboration improves patient care, cultivates a positive work environment, and enhances individual professional development of staff.

KEY TERMS AND CONCEPTS

- Academic credentials
- Clinical and administrative supervision
- Consultation
- Ethical issues in supervision
- Evidence-based practice
- Inter- and intra-disciplinary, multidisciplinary, and transdisciplinary team concepts
- Parallel process
- Professional credentials
- Professional licenses

- Supervision theories/models (e.g., psychodynamic, IDM, discrimination model)
- Vicarious liability
- Working alliance

QUESTIONS FOR DISCUSSION

1. What factors would impact the selection of a supervisory model in healthcare settings?

2. What issues may arise when shifting from individual to group supervision or from receiving supervision from a professional in your own discipline to one from another profession?

3. What factors make giving and receiving a professional evaluation potentially difficult?

EXERCISES

1. Role-play a situation in which a supervisor provides an evaluation to a staff member who is a relatively new professional and, while earnest, has made a number of clinical misjudgments in patient care. Practice the steps for assessing his or her job performance capabilities and difficulties, while maintaining sensitivity to ethics, being pragmatic and yet compassionate.

2. Consider the situation of Evelyn, who, at 55 years of age, is a first-time supervisor in adult oncology. She highly values autonomy and self-reliance. After three weeks of supervising Liz, who is also 55 years of age and a recent MSW graduate after a career change, Evelyn finds herself dreading weekly supervision with Liz. She avoids her between meetings because Liz asks many questions about what to do. Consider the sources of strain between the supervisor and supervisee, and propose recommendations on how the supervisor should respond.

REFERENCES

Abramson, J. S. (2002). Interdisciplinary team practice. In A. R. Roberts & G. J. Greene (Eds.), *Social workers' desk reference*. New York: Oxford University Press.

American Board of Examiners in Clinical Social Work. (2004). Clinical supervision: A practice specialty of clinical social work. A position statement of the American Board of Examiners in Clinical Social Work [Electronic Version]. Salem, MA: author.

Bazzoli, G., Dynan, L., Burns, L., & Yap, C. (2004). Two decades of organizational change in health care: What have we learned? *Medical Research and Review, 61*, 247–331.

Beatty, R. W. & Schneier, C. E. (1977). *Personnel administration: An experiential skill-building approach.* Reading, MA: Addison-Wesley Publishing Company.

Berger, C., & Mizrahi, T. (2001). An evolving paradigm of supervision within a changing health care environment. *Social Work in Health Care, 33,* 1–18.

Berger, C. S., Robbins, C., Lewis, M., Mizrahi, T., & Fleit, S. (2003). The impact of organizational change on social work staffing in a hospital setting: A national, longitudinal study of social work in hospitals. *Social Work in Health Care, 37*(1), 1–18.

Bernard, J. M. (1979). Supervisor training: A discrimination model. *Counselor Education & Supervision, 19,* 60–68.

Bernard, J. M., & Goodyear, R. K. (2014). *Fundamentals of clinical supervision* (5th ed.). Upper Saddle River, NY: Pearson.

Bogo, M., & McKnight, K. (2005). Clinical supervision in social work: A review of the research literature. *The Clinical Supervisor, 24*(1/2), 49–67.

Bogo, M., Paterson, J., Tufford, L., & King, R. (2011). Interprofessional clinical supervision in mental health and addiction: Toward identifying common elements. *The Clinical Supervisor, 30*(1), 124–140.

Bordin, E. S. (1979). The generalizability of the psychodynamic concept of the working alliance. *Psychotherapy: Theory, research and practice, 16*(3), 252–260.

Bordin, E. S. (1983). A working alliance based model of supervision. *The Counseling Psychologist, 11*(1), 35–42.

Chambless, D. L., Baker, M. J., Baucom, D. H., Beautler, L. E., Calhoun, K. S., Crits-Christoph, P., Daiuto, A., DeRubeis, R., Derweiler, J., Haaga, D. A., Johnson, S. B., McCurry, S., Mueser, K. T., Pope, K. S., Sanderson, W. C., Shoham, V., Stickle, T., Williams, D. A., & Woody, S. R. (1998). An update on empirically validated therapies, II. *Clinical Psychologist, 51*(1), 3–16.

Council on Social Work Education. (2012). *Educational policy and accreditation standards (revised 2010; updated 2012).* Retrieved from http://www.cswe.org/File.aspx?id = 13780

Council on Social Work Education. (2013). *2013 statistics on social work education in the United States.* Retrieved from http://www.cswe.org/File.aspx?id = 74478

Counselman, E. M., & Weber, R. (2004). Organizing and maintaining peer supervision groups. *International Journal of Group Psychotherapy, 54,* 125–143.

Cournoyer, B., & Powers, G. (2002). Evidence-based social work: The quiet revolution continues. In A. R., Roberts & G., Greene (Eds.), *Social workers' desk reference* (pp. 798–809). New York: Oxford University Press.

Deming, W. E. (1986). *Out of the crisis.* Cambridge, MA: MIT Center for Advanced Engineering Study.

DeWane, C. J. (2007). Supervisor, beware: Ethical dangers in supervision. *Social Work Today, 7*(4), 34.

Doehrman, M. J. (1976). Parallel processes in supervision and psychotherapy. *Bulletin of the Menninger Clinic, 40(1),* 1–104.

Efstation, J. F., Patton, M. J., & Kardash, C. M. (1990). Measuring the working alliance in counselor supervision. *Journal of Counseling Psychology, 37*(3), 322–329.

Ehrlich, C., Kendall, E., & Muenchberger, H. (2012). Spanning boundaries and creating strong patient relationships to coordinate care are strategies used by experienced chronic care coordinators. *Contemporary Nurse,* 2012 Jun 9. Retrieved from http://www.ncbi.nlm.nih.gov/pubmed/22680935

Ekstein R., & Wallerstein, R. S. (1958). *The teaching and learning of psychotherapy.* New York: Basic Books.

Faulkner S. R., & Amodeo, M. Interdisciplinary teams in health care and human services settings: Are they effective? *Health and Social Work, 24*(3), 210–219.

Frielander, M. L., Siegel, S. M., & Brenock, K. (1989). Parallel process in counseling and supervision: A case study. *Journal of Counseling Psychology, 36,* 140–157.

Gibelman, M., & Schervish, P. H. (1997). Supervision in social work: Characteristics and trends in a changing environment. *The Clinical Supervisor, 16*(2), 1–15.

Gilbert, C., & Maxwell, C. F. (2011). Clinical supervision in health care in the Internet era. *Social Work Today, 11*(2), 24–27.

Gibson, J. L., Ivancevich, J. M., & Donnelly, J. H. (1973). *Organizations: Structure, processes, behavior.* Dallas, TX: Business Publications.

Horevitz, E., & Manoleas, P. (2013). Professional competencies and training needs of professional social workers in integrated behavioral health in primary care. *Social Work in Health Care, 52*(8), 752–787.

Jacobson, N., & Traux, P. (1991). Clinical significance: A statistical approach to defining meaningful change in psychotherapy research. *Journal of Consulting and Clinical Psychology, 59,* 1, 12–19.

Kadushin, A. (1976). *Supervision in social work.* New York: Columbia University Press.

Kadushin, A., & Harkness, D. (2014). *Supervision in social work* (5th ed.). New York: Columbia University Press.

Kadushin, G., Berger, C., Gilbert, C., & de St Aubin, M. (2009). Models and methods in hospital social work supervision. *The Clinical Supervisor: An Interdisciplinary Journal of Theory, Research, and Practice, 29*(2), 180–199.

Kokemuller, N. (2012). *What is the difference between a transdisciplinary team and a multidisciplinary team?* Retrieved August from http://smallbusiness.chron.com/difference-between-transdisciplinary-team-multidisciplinary-team-18762.html

Lambert, M. J. (1992). Implications of outcome research for psychotherapy integration. In J. C. Norcross & M. R. Goldfried (Eds.), *Handbook of psychotherapy integration.* New York: Basic Books.

Lewis, H. (1982). *The intellectual base of social work practice: Tools for thought in a helping profession.* New York: The Lois and Samuel Silberman Fund and The Haworth Press.

Little, V. (2011). Integrated care: Where we've been and where we need to go. In W. Spitzer (Ed.), *The evolving practice of social work within integrated care* (pp. 1–9). National Society for Social Work Leadership in Health Care. Petersburg, VA: The Dietz Press.

Meyer, H. H., Kay, E., & French, J. P. (1965). Split roles in performance appraisal. *Harvard Business Review, 43*(1965), 123–129.

Mor Barak, M. E., Travis, D. J., Pyun, H., & Xie, B. (2009, March). The impact of supervision on worker outcomes: A meta-analysis. *Social Service Review, 83*(1), 3–32.

Munson, C. (2006). Contemporary issues and trends in social work supervision. In W. Spitzer (Ed.), *Supervision of health care social work: Principles and practice.* The National Society for Social Work Leadership in Health Care. Petersburg, VA: The Dietz Press, pp. 1-28.

Munson, C. E. (2002). *Handbook of clinical social work supervision* (3rd ed.). New York: The Haworth Press.

Munson, C. E. (2009). *Handbook of clinical social work supervision* (3rd ed.). New York: Routledge. (Reprinted from Munson, C.E. [2002] *Handbook of clinical social work supervision* [3rd ed.]., New York: The Haworth Press)

National Association of Social Workers and the Association of Social Work Boards. (2005). *Standards for technology and social work practice.* Retrieved from http://www.socialworkers.org/practice/standards/naswtechnologystandards.pdf

National Association of Social Workers. (2005). *Standards for social work practice in health care settings.* Retrieved from http://www.socialworkers.org/practice/standards/NASWHealthCare Standards.pdf

National Association of Social Workers. (2008). *Code of Ethics.* Retrieved from http://www.social workers.org/pubs/code/code.asp

National Association of Social Workers. (2013). *Academy of certified social workers.* Retrieved from http://www.socialworkers.org/credentials/credentials/acsw.asp

Peters, T. (1987). *Thriving on chaos*. New York: Harper and Row Publishers.

Powell, D., & Migdole, S. (2012, June). *Can you hear me now? New frontiers of clinical supervision*. Presentation at the International Interdisciplinary Conference on Clinical Supervision, Garden City, NY.

Prensky, M. (2001). Digital natives, digital immigrants. *On the Horizon, 9*(5), 1–6.

Reamer, F. G. (1998). Ethical standards in social work: A review of the NASW Code of Ethics. Washington, DC: NASW Press.

Shackelford, J. R., Sirna, M., Mangurian, C., Dilley, J. W., & Shumway, M. (2013). Descriptive Analysis of a Novel Health Care Approach: Reverse Colocation—Primary Care in a Community Mental Health "Home." The Primary Care Companion for CNS Disorders, 15(5) PCC.13m01530. doi:10.4088/PCC.13m01530

Searles, H. F. (1955). The informational value of the supervisor's emotional experiences. *Psychiatry, 18*, 135–146.

Shamai, M. (1998). Therapists in distress: Team supervision of social workers and family therapists who work and live under political uncertainty. *Family Process, 37*, 245–259.

Shulman, L. (1993). *Interactional supervision*. Washington, DC: NASW Press.

Shulman, L. (2010). *Interactional supervision* (3rd ed.). Washington, DC: NASW Press.

Spitzer, W., & Davidson, K. (2013). Future trends in health and health care: Implications for social work practice in an aging society. *Social Work in Health Care, 52*(10), 959–986.

Spitzer, W. (2006). Preface. In W. Spitzer (Ed.), *Supervision of health care social work: Principles and practice*. The National Society for Social Work Leadership In Health Care. Petersburg, VA: The Dietz Press.

Stoltenberg, C. D. (2005). Enhancing professional competence through developmental approaches to supervision. *American Psychologist, 60*(8), 857-864.

Stoltenberg, C. D., McNeill, B. W., & Delworth, U. (1998). *IDM: An integrated developmental model for supervising counselors and therapists*. San Francisco: Jossey Bass.

Sulman, J., Savage, D., Vrooman, P., & McGillivray, M. (2004). Social group work: Building a professional collective of hospital social workers. *Social Work in Health Care, 39*(3–4), 287–307.

Tally, P. (2006). Social work peer supervision: One department's experience. In W. Spitzer (Ed.), *Supervision of health care social work: Principles and practice*. The National Society for Social Work Leadership in Health Care. Petersburg, VA: The Dietz Press.

Todd, W. E., & Pine, I. (*1968*). Peer supervision of individual psychotherapy. *American Journal of Psychiatry, 125, 780–784*.

Tsui, M. S. (1997). The roots of social work supervision: An historical review. *The Clinical Supervisor, 15*(2), 191–198.

Tsui, M. S. (2005). *Social work supervision: Contexts and concepts*. Thousand Oaks, CA: SAGE.

U.S. Department of Health and Human Services, Substance Abuse and Mental Health Services Administration. (2007). *An action plan for behavioral health workforce development: Executive summary*. Washington, DC: SAMHSA.

Vance, R. J. (2006). Employee engagement and commitment: A guide to understanding, measuring and increasing engagement in your organization. *Society for Human Resource Management (SHRM) Foundation effective practice guidelines*. Retrieved from http://www.shrm.org/about/foundation/research/Documents/1006EmployeeEngagementOnlineReport.pdf

Walker, R., & Clark, J. (1999). Heading off boundary problems: Clinical supervision as risk management. *Psychiatric Services, 50*(11), 1435–1439.

Wax, J. (1963). Time-limited supervision. *Social Work, 8*(3), 37–43.

Weil, T. (2003). Hospital downsizing and workforce reduction strategies: Some inner workings. *Health Services Management Review, 16*, 13–23.

Whitaker, T., & Arrington, P. (2008). *Social workers at work. NASW Membership Workforce Study.* Washington, DC: National Association of Social Workers.

Whitaker, T., Weismiller, T., & Clark, E. (2006). *Assuring the sufficiency of a frontline workforce: A national study of licensed social workers. Executive summary.* Washington, DC: National Association of Social Workers.

Williams, A. B. (1997). On parallel process in social work supervision. *Clinical Social Work Journal, 25*(4), 425–435.

Weissman, A., & Rosenberg, G. (2002). Health care and social work: Dilemmas and opportunities in R. Patti (Ed.), *The handbook of social welfare management* (pp. 511–520). Thousand Oaks, CA: SAGE.

Woody, S. R., & Sanderson, W. C. (1998). Manuals for empirically based support treatments: 1998 update. *The Clinical Psychologist, 51*(1), 17–21.

Cultural Competence in Healthcare Social Work

Karen M. Allen

INTRODUCTION

With the increasing diversity in the United States populations, social workers and other service providers have been challenged to develop culturally competent skills that meet the "social, cultural and linguistic needs of patients" (Georgetown University Health Policy Institute, 2004). **Culture**, as defined by the National Association of Social Workers (2000) describes "the integrated pattern of human behavior that includes thoughts, communications, actions, customs, beliefs, values, and institutions of a racial, ethnic, religious, or social group" (p. 61). These patterns are passed on through generations. Although culture has historically emphasized race and ethnicity, increasingly broader conceptualizations include class, gender, religious and spiritual orientation, sexual orientations, age, and physical and mental abilities (National Association of Social Workers [NASW], 2006). Recognizing cultural and ethnic differences in healthcare should encompass three general domains: practice approaches, access to services, and healthcare disparities across populations.

In the process of defining cultural competence, we examine the impact of culture on our emotions, behaviors, and values and recognize the particular relevance of culture as it impacts health, healthcare use, and effective intervention. The focus is primarily on practice approaches in the delivery of culturally competent social work services in healthcare settings, although healthcare disparities and access will be briefly addressed. Spiritual and religious orientations are similarly acknowledged for their influence and impact on patient interaction.

DEFINING CULTURAL COMPETENCE

Cultural competence is "the process by which individuals and systems respond respectfully and effectively to people of all cultures, languages, classes, races, ethnic backgrounds, religions and other diversity factors in a manner that recognizes, affirms, and values the worth of individuals, families and communities and protects and preserves the dignity of each" (NASW, 2001, 2006). **Linguistic competence** is an essential feature of culturally sensitive services and refers to providing readily available, culturally appropriate oral and written language services to individuals with limited English proficiency (Agency for Healthcare Research and Quality, 2003). Linguistic competence is a particularly important aspect of cultural competence in healthcare. Social workers play a key role in ensuring that patient education materials are translated to meet the needs of the service population and in ensuring that translation services and resources are available to the institution and patient (Farrar & Kirkpatrick, 2010).

Health literacy is defined as "the degree to which individuals have the capacity to obtain, process, and understand basic health information and services needed to make appropriate health decisions" (Nielsen-Bohlman, Panzer, & Kindig, 2004, p. 32). We take an expansive view of health literacy and understand it to be directly influenced by the client system's culture—that is, their worldview, beliefs about health and illness, and traditional healing practices. Further, this perspective on health literacy is expanded to include the interactional dynamics of the patient–provider relationship. That is to say, the medical care is at least as influenced and directed by the health literacy (worldview, beliefs, and values about health) of the physician, team, and healthcare system as it is by that of the patient (Neuman, Matto, Hutchison & Singleton, 2005).

Cultural competence is not static and requires frequent relearning and unlearning about diversity. Practitioners must acknowledge the implications of their own "cultural lens" and continuously reflect on their own assumptions, biases, and stereotypes. This requires practitioners to adopt an attitude of open-mindedness and respect for all patients, including those who differ from them socially or culturally; to utilize interventions that recognize that effective clinical relationships may be constructed differently across cultures; and to understand the impact of healthcare disparities and inequalities that contribute to unequal access and treatment. Although definitions of cultural competence continue to evolve, Niemeier, Burnett, and Whitaker (2003) observed that the common elements of cultural competence include

- the adjustment or recognition of one's own culture in order to understand the culture of the patient;

- appreciation and respect for cultural differences and similarities within, among, and between groups; and

- the development of a set of attitudes, behaviors, skills, and policies that help providers to work effectively in cross-cultural situations.

Cultural humility as proposed by Tervalon and Murray-Garcia (1998) describes a life-long commitment to self-evaluation and self-critique in exploring cultural biases. It acknowledges the power differential between providers and patients in order to develop non-paternalistic partnerships for care. Ideally, we should maintain an awareness of and sensitivity to the cultural groups with whom we are working. However, although culture is shared among members of the group, each individual constructs his or her own meaning and interpretation. Using a non-judgmental attitude, being open-minded, and reflecting a sincere curiosity about the cultural experiences and beliefs of patients are crucial when working with individuals from different cultures. We acknowledge our limited understanding about the patient's culture and validate the patient as an expert in his or her own life and culture. We can then respectfully ask the patient to introduce us to his or her culture so that we might arrive at a shared understanding of his or her health condition, its meaning, and its treatment (Anderson, 1997; White, 1995).

Culture provides a framework in which individuals understand the causes, treatment, and meaning of disease, illness, and disability. In the United States, our science and technology-oriented culture promotes understanding disease as a function of bacteria, virus, or genetic mutation. Correspondingly, treatment is technology-based, including medication, surgery, radiation, and so on. In comparison, other cultures often perceive disease as a function of evil spirits or an imbalance in the body. Kleinman, Eisenberg, and Good (1978) stressed the importance of negotiating these kinds of discrepancies between patient and physician explanations of illness. The authors developed eight culturally sensitive assessment questions that are now familiar from many discussions of cross-cultural medicine:

1. What do you call the problem?

2. What do you think caused the problem?

3. Why do you think it started when it did?

4. What do you think the sickness does? How does it work?

5. How severe is the sickness? Will it be a short course or a long course?

6. What kind of treatment do you think the patient should receive and what are the most important results you hope are received from this treatment?

7. What are the chief problems the sickness has caused?

8. What do you fear most from the sickness?

Congress (1994; 2005) adopted the genogram and eco-map used in social work practice to create a **culturagram,** which identifies common themes, practices, and events in culturally diverse groups. Congress acknowledged that developing cultural competence in each of the many cultures, religious groups, and ethnicities represented in a diverse community can be daunting. It is important to note that approaching individuals and families with a generic or simplified understanding of their culture and background can lead to stereotyping and making assumptions. Illustrating the point, a refugee from the Sudan who has fled the trauma of civil war is very different from an individual from West Africa who immigrated to attend college. Use of a culturagram is valuable in assessing culturally diverse family systems. Ten areas are significant in forming culturally appropriate assessments:

- Reasons for relocation

- Legal status

- Time in community

- Language spoken at home and in the community

- Health beliefs

- Crisis events

- Holidays and special events

- Contract with cultural and religious institutions (including religious beliefs, practices, and customs)

- Values about education and work

- Values about family—structure, power, myths, rules (including roles and gender norms)

Figure 15.1 updates Congress's original culturagram. For example, we include a recognition of the impact of trauma, the importance of immigration narrative (which is often a story that is passed down through generations), rituals, and gender roles, which are often culturally determined.

It is important to contemplate the factors that shape an individual's **worldview,** or, in the original German, *Weltanschauung.* A person's worldview is "the overall perspective from which one sees and interprets the world" (Altman & Rogoff, 1987, p. 8). A person's

Figure 15.1   Culturagram

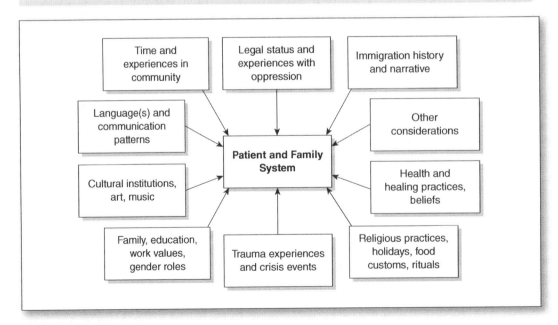

Source: Adapted from Congress (1994, 2005).

worldview incorporates that person's fundamental beliefs about whether or not the world is safe and predictable, whether people are inherently good or evil, and whether we can control our destiny. People who are refugees from wars or political persecution, for example, are likely to have developed a worldview in which they regard the world as unsafe and unfair. As a consequence, they may have difficulty trusting people in authority, such as physicians and other healthcare providers. Of particular relevance, beliefs about science, medicine, and the causes and treatments of disease are included in a person's worldview.

The African American experience of racism and discrimination in this country extends into healthcare, with African Americans continuing to struggle for equal access to care and equal standards of care. The Tuskegee syphilis experiment, which began in 1932 and continued until 1972, was one of the most horrific examples of inappropriate and immoral healthcare provided to African Americans. These types of experiences have contributed to shaping the worldviews of many African Americans such that the largely white medical establishment is frequently approached with a degree of suspicion.

Understanding an individual's worldview is fundamental to understanding that individual and optimizing treatment (Galanti, 2008; Leininger, 1991; 1996). Failing to appreciate the influence of past experiences, religious beliefs and customs, and health can have profound consequences. The use of native plants, for example, can cause adverse drug reactions, and customs of fasting can complicate diabetes care. In some Asian countries, the practice of "cupping" or "coining" is done to draw out evil spirits. This practice can leave red welts, which could potentially be used as the basis for a referral to protective services. Social work can serve an important role in promoting greater awareness of individual and cultural understandings of, and preferences for, health and healthcare as well as how these conditions interact with typical healthcare practices in the United States. Social work functions in a bridging role between patients and healthcare providers to facilitate a mutual understanding of each other's culture, customs, health beliefs, and practices (Neuman et al., 2005). With such shared awareness, healthcare interventions can be designed with the knowledgeable participation of all parties.

SPECIFIC CONSIDERATIONS IN CULTURALLY COMPETENT HEALTHCARE

The degree to which traditional cultural norms are expressed depends on the extent of assimilation and acculturation. **Assimilation** is the process by which individuals of two or more cultures who have come into contact with each other lose their unique cultural identities and become fused into a single homogeneous cultural unit different from any of the original component cultural units. This is a two-way process in which both the minority and dominant group are modified. It is an evolving process that includes both individual and group identities and, as such, can cause challenges. **Acculturation** describes the process whereby the traits of a new culture are adopted and incorporated into an existing culture. In this process, two or more cultures in contact with one another each become modified, but without much evidence of their fusing into a single homogenous culture (see www.sociologyguide.com).

Both acculturation and assimilation are affected by factors such as the length of one's residency in a country, the degree of social isolation or integration, and the extent to which English is a second language. Health outcomes and health status have been found to be poorer where acculturation and assimilation are limited, as in the case of Mexican immigrants who continue to primarily rely on Spanish as their dominant language (DuBard & Gizlice, 2008). Of note, in many cultures there is heightened acceptance for expression of physical pain or distress rather than emotion. This contributes to **somatization**, or the experience of emotional conflict and anxiety in the body (Galanti, 2008).

Two general approaches exist in developing cultural competency in healthcare. The first, involving a review of commonly encountered ethnic, cultural, and religious groups, runs the risk of potentially stereotyping or overgeneralizing certain cultural traits to patients. In comparison, Galanti (2008) developed a second approach, which considers common dimensions of experiences that may vary according to culture. Social workers taking a position of cultural humility and engaging with patients and families in an exploration of culture, ethnicity, and religion are more likely to reach an understanding of how best to meet identified needs (Anderson & Goolishian, 1992; Anderson, 1997).

Our text interjects information on specific cultural groups to illustrate the themes of this section. While case examples and references to specific cultures are provided, caution must be exercised that every individual and family be regarded as unique. The therapeutic approach of being initially unaware, curious, and culturally humble is recommended; social workers should not make *assumptions* nor rely on *stereotypes* based on assumptions or over-simplifications (Jenks, 2011). The following themes (adapted from Galanti, 2008) commonly vary by culture:

- Family structure, roles, and gender
- Communication patterns and time orientation
- Pain
- Religion and spirituality
- Customs around daily living and life stage events
- Beliefs and practices about physical and mental health and illness

Family Structure, Roles, and Gender

The provision of healthcare services necessitates effective communication with the patient, with the family, and, when the patient is incapacitated, with designated family spokespersons. This has the prospect of becoming complicated depending on the way kinship is structured. In many cultures, family identity and affiliation is determined unilaterally through the father's line or, in the instance of the Jewish culture, by the mother's lineage. Generally speaking, contemporary American society is marked with bilateral identification drawn from both parental lines. *Family structure* describes how a family is organized, how power and authority are distributed, and how roles and tasks are determined.

Gender roles are typically an important consideration in working with people from other cultures. In many patriarchal cultures (such as Muslim cultures), the individual with the most authority is the oldest male. Direct conversations with female family members can be interpreted as inappropriate and even insulting. Female patients may defer to their husbands in decision making and may even refuse to sign surgical consents and other forms. In some strict Muslim, patriarchal cultures in which the modesty of women is highly valued and protected, assigning same-sex caregivers may be helpful. Generally, it is important to include the female patients in discussions but to accept the cultural expectations of the family.

The term *Latino* is used to designate people in the United States whose origins can be traced back to the Spanish-speaking countries of Latin America as well as the Caribbean, Mexico, Central America, and South America. The term *Hispanic* was created by the federal government as a classification system for those individuals who speak Spanish. Latino is considered to be a more encompassing term and is what we have chosen to use for this text. Both terms are used to describe individuals from a wide array of countries, and there is great variation in language and cultural traditions between the groups (Flores & Vega, 1998). Latinos highly value the extended family and use the term *familismo* to describe this intense sense of belonging and pride in the family. Although it may be difficult to establish trust with Latino families, there is also a high degree of respect for authority and status (*respecto*). Patients may be hesitant to ask questions and may indicate agreement with a treatment plan in order to avoid disagreeing and being disrespectful to the physician. Reciprocal demonstration of respeto by healthcare providers is expected, particularly by Latino males.

Latino families tend to be hierarchical and patriarchal. The older generation is respected and revered, with the oldest male typically holding the greatest power in the family. Males in Latino culture are expected to be the head of the household, to be good providers, and to uphold the integrity of the family (machismo). Women are socialized to and take great pride in being dedicated, nurturing, and loving spouses. There is a strong value placed on motherhood and having children. This is characterized by the term *marianismo*. In addition, people of Hispanic origin may expect *personalismo,* or a warm, personal regard with people with whom they are interacting. Taking time to inquire about children and elders in the family can demonstrate concern and personalismo.

Other family systems that tend to be patriarchal are those of Asian and Middle Eastern families. In Middle Eastern families, the family spokesperson is likely to be the oldest and most educated male. Husbands may defer to fathers and uncles. When a female patient is being assessed, the husband may answer for her. Sexual segregation may be expected, and women may not be involved in decision making. Asian cultures vary by country and by degrees of education and assimilation. In general, they are patriarchal and revere elders. Both Asian and Middle Eastern families have high-context communications styles (as described below), although Asians tend to be more reserved and indirect, whereas Middle Eastern individuals frequently are more expressive.

Communication and Time Orientation

The anthropologist Hall (1976) identified two general styles of intercultural communication patterns that vary by culture: **high-context** and **low-context communication**. These styles are delineated by how much individuals from the culture rely on other cues besides words to understand the message being conveyed. Hall believed we receive many more verbal, non-verbal, and contextual cues in an encounter than we can consciously acknowledge or have been taught to be aware of by our culture.

In low-context cultures (as in the United States and particularly within the medical profession), communication is largely determined by the words selected as well as by voice inflection and tone. Communication tends to be precise, logical, linear, and factual; there is a literal interpretation of what is spoken. The broader aspects of low-context cultures are that they tend to be individualistic, to be action-oriented, and to seek quick solutions to problems. Feelings and intuition are not emphasized. The purpose of communication, especially around healthcare issues, is to reach a decision. The culture of medicine places considerable value on low-context communication (Neuman et al., 2005).

In contrast, high-context cultures rely on social and behavioral cues beyond verbal language to interpret messages. These cues can involve sitting arrangements, gestures, posture, and other subtle forms of communication that may or may not be recognized by individuals from low-context cultures. High-context cultures such as those of many Middle Eastern, Asian, and Hispanic cultures are not individualistic but rather value the collective and group. As they are relational, time is needed to develop the trust and relationship essential to providing care. Individuals in these groups value harmony and want to avoid conflict or any signs of disrespect. They may agree in order to be polite, without truly agreeing or even understanding any requests made of them. Communication emphasizes process and will not be directive and action-oriented. As discussions may include many family members, it can prove challenging for healthcare providers seeking to identify *the* family spokesperson. Communication may be reserved and polite, as in Asian cultures, or demonstrative, as in Italian culture. Recognizing whether one is dealing with a high- or low-context culture is an important starting point for engaging with patients and families from different cultures.

In general, providers are wise to avoid the use of colloquialisms and idioms that may be easily misinterpreted by those from another culture. An example could be made of a patient visiting the United States who is anxious to return home and asks his physician when he will be discharged from the hospital. His light-hearted physician jokes that the patient is going to have to stay another week. Seeing the patient's distressed look, the physician replies he "was just pulling the patient's leg." Not understanding the phrase, the patient becomes entirely confused as the physician was not in fact, pulling his leg. For reasons like this, the use of slang terms, especially referencing anatomy, should be avoided. Even specific words can be misconstrued, and they can have different meanings in the same language. Consider that when a patient is informed of "positive" test results, he or she might assume that he or she is receiving good news, when the term "positive" results in fact might be indicative of an abnormality, such as a malignancy.

The formality of communication will also vary by culture. Older African Americans often use a more formal tone when dealing with healthcare providers and typically should not be addressed by their first names unless given permission to do so. Importantly, naming varies by culture. In some Middle Eastern cultures, the first name is followed by the individual's father's name and then by the individual's grandfather's name. It is correct to address this individual as Mr. and then his first name (Galanti, 2008).

Non-verbal communication patterns also vary by culture. Americans value prolonged eye contact and interpret this as indicative of honest and forthright communication. However, in Native American and Asian cultures, it is generally disrespectful to look directly at someone. In Middle Eastern cultures, direct eye contact between the sexes is considered inappropriate. Similarly, touching a patient during conversation is not usually condoned in the Asian culture, and public displays of affection are considered in poor taste. In comparison, Hispanic patients and families may feel comfortable hugging and kissing a nurse or social worker as part of an enthusiastic greeting. Gestures, however, can prove problematic, such as the hand gesture for "OK," which has a sexual connotation in many cultures. The "universal" thumbs up gesture, is not universal at all, and in fact in Great Britain constitutes an insult.

Time orientation is yet another experience that varies by culture. In the United States, we monitor time by a clock and a calendar. In contrast, Hispanic cultures are more likely to organize time around daily activities and routines. For example, Maria had an appointment to be seen in a health clinic. She arrived an hour late because she needed to take her young son to preschool. She lingered at the preschool, enjoying and participating in the children's activities. On arriving at the clinic, she was upset to learn that her appointment would need to be rescheduled. She understood that she had an appointment in the morning but did not think an hour delay would matter that much. She also expected the clinic staff to understand that spending time with her child was more important than being on time for an appointment. Native Americans value listening over talking and believe that things will happen when they are ready to happen. In their culture, time is relatively flexible and generally is not structured to the clock. Other cultures, such as that in India, regard the calendar by seasons rather than months. While healthcare workers are unlikely to change cultural differences in time orientation, compromises can be usually be reached when flexibility is granted while explaining the need to be on time.

Experience of Pain

The subjective experience of pain is difficult to assess, and the outward expression of pain varies across individuals and cultures. In general, highly expressive Hispanic, Italian, and Jewish cultures tend to be less reserved and more open in acknowledging pain and discomfort and asking for assistance. In comparison, Asian culture values stoicism and correspondingly discourages demonstrations of pain. Although there may be some cultural tendencies, individual responses to pain vary. As Galanti (2008) noted, failing to appreciate individual and cultural differences in pain behavior can have tragic results. An elderly Asian gentleman was admitted to the emergency room for sepsis, which caused cardiac problems from which the patient nearly died. He had just seen his physician, where he had complained of "jageun," or small pain while urinating. The physician prescribed medication and scheduled a recheck appointment for three months. The patient appeared satisfied at that time. The physician was unaware that on the previous day, the patient had been found by his wife crying in the bathroom. She later stated that the patient's discomfort appeared to be severe and had been occurring for three weeks. The patient was culturally conditioned to avoid talking about himself with much detail and to accept a certain amount of pain. The patient was particularly uncomfortable discussing the details of an intimate body function with someone of "high" respect.

Cultural perspectives on the use of pain medications are important as they can affect treatment compliance and clinical outcomes. This can be particularly relevant when analgesics are prescribed to prevent the onset of severe pain, such as post-surgical pain. Individuals harboring suspicions of the healthcare and pharmaceutical system may avoid what they perceive as "unnecessary" pills and resort to medication only when pain becomes severe.

Religion and Spirituality

Religion and spirituality are fundamental elements in the lives of many people and can impact their health and use of healthcare. The term *religion* refers to a formal identification and typically some, or at least minimal, participation with an organized religious group, whereas *spirituality* is used to describe an individual's constellation of attitudes and beliefs about the human spirit, or soul, and its place and relationship to a higher power and the universe. According to Tanyi (2002)

> Spirituality is an inherent component of being human, and is subjective, intangible, and multidimensional. Spirituality and religion are often used interchangeably, but the two concepts are different. Spirituality involves humans' search for meaning in life, while religion involves an organized entity with rituals and practices about a higher power or God. Spirituality may be related to religion for certain individuals, but for others, such as an atheist, it may not be. (p. 500)

Although the findings are somewhat inconsistent, there is some evidence to suggest that spirituality can have an effect on mortality, success in coping with chronic illness, and recovery. Research by Yates, Chalmer, James, Follansbee, and McKegney (1981) found that cancer patients who are spiritual have a better quality of life and better outlook than those without such beliefs. Other studies have found that spirituality can enable people to enjoy life, even when experiencing severe pain, and that many find prayer to be helpful in controlling pain (Brady, Peterman, Fitchett, Mo, & Cella, 1999). Spirituality is important in helping people contend with illness and the prospect of facing death. In one study of 108 women with advanced gynecological cancer, 75% said that religion and spirituality played an important role in helping them cope with their disease and 49% said they had become more religious since being diagnosed (Roberts, Brown, Elkins, & Larson, 1997). Heart transplant patients who identify themselves as spiritual and who participate in religious activities complied better with follow-up treatment and had a higher return of physical function, less anxiety, and fewer health worries than other patients (Harris et al., 1995). Some studies have suggested that individuals who are religious may live longer, and researchers have speculated that decreased levels of stress hormones may be involved (Koenig et al., 1997; Strawbridge, Cohen, Shema, & Kaplan, 1997). Exploring the intersection of religion, spirituality, and health is an essential dimension of a comprehensive biopsychosocial-spiritual assessment and can be introduced with simple open-ended questions such as "Has this illness affected your faith or spirituality in any way?"

Acknowledging and supporting prayer activities is important to many hospitalized patients. Although some families may seek the comfort of a chapel, others may not want to leave the patient and prefer to pray at bedside. In some cultures, prayer may be expressive and enthusiastic whereas in others it will be quiet and private. Sensitivity should be accorded and accommodations made wherever possible. Social workers fulfill a valuable function by offering to connect patients and families with pastoral services in the hospital and/or with the family's religious leader. In the absence of pastoral care services or a patient preference, typically networks of volunteers exist in communities to engage in offering spiritual support to patients.

A major underpinning of one's religion or spirituality is the patient's belief as to whom or what exactly has the power to cause and cure disease. In a number of U.S. religions, including Pentecostalism and Christian Science, only God has this power. American Baptists similarly believe this but may view physicians as being empowered by God and/or Jesus. Many of the Jewish faith believe that only God has the power to heal, but Jewish culture also places a high value on science, technology, and education. Many members of the Jewish faith believe that physicians are the "hand of God" and therefore are typically accepting of modern American medicine. Depending on culture or faith, illness can be seen as punishment for sins or, as it is for the Hmong, the result of evil spirits. In one specific instance, a woman with breast cancer was asked about whether her faith and spirituality were helpful to her in coping with the disease. Breaking down in tears, she shared that she believed the cancer was a punishment from God for an affair she had had 35 years earlier. Tearfully, she said that the man involved had loved her body and, in particular, her breasts.

Other cultural considerations include traditions about blood and body integrity. In some cultures, notably, conservative and Orthodox Judaism, the human body must be buried whole following death, and neither autopsy nor organ transplant can be considered. Although Jehovah Witnesses will accept contemporary medical care, including surgery, a religious prescription prevents the use of blood products and transfusions. In some traditional Asian cultures, the drawing of blood can be problematic as this is associated with *"soul loss"* and the belief that the soul can become detached from the body and left to wander. Caesarean sectioning may be refused by the Hmong and other traditional Asians cultures because of the belief that the soul is attached to all of the body, and cutting the body cuts the soul from it. A similar belief held by Native Americans makes it taboo to cut a child's hair, which is seen as a sign of a health.

Customs of Daily Living and Life Stage Events

Every one of us has preferences and customs that are part of our routines. Some of these preferences, such as diet and personal hygiene, are culturally influenced. Fasting during Ramadan and Yom Kippur are required in most Muslim and Jewish traditions. This can cause complications for patients who are already nutritionally compromised. Other groups, such as Seventh Day Adventists, Buddhists, and Hindus, are forbidden to eat meat. The eating of pork is taboo in many cultures. Many Jewish individuals keep kosher, with restrictions on mixing meat and dairy products. Filipinos eat rice with every meal and perceive that something is missing if it is not served. Rice consumption is considered essential to their well-being and health (Galanti, 2008).

Insensitivity to the temperature and serving of hot and cold items to patients can prove problematic. In some cultures from tropical and hot climates, only cold foods are eaten during the summer months. Among Mexicans, disease may be viewed as the product of an imbalance between the "hot" and "cold" elements of the body. From that perspective, consumption of food that is too hot or cold contributes to the imbalance. Patient preferences will also drive behavior, and innumerable examples exist of patients who ate poorly in the hospital until family members were permitted to bring in foods that were part of the patient's cultural traditions or habit.

Customs of bathing and personal hygiene vary, and many cultures, even Western cultures, do not share the American preoccupation with daily showering or bathing. In many African cultures, fresh water is not easily available and a full bath is considered a waste of a precious resource. A layer of dirt can sometimes be seen as either a source of protection or means to hide from evil spirits. In some countries, hospitalized patients may be bathed weekly or less. Toileting customs also vary, with water cleansing preferred over the use of toilet paper in some countries. The custom in some traditional Asian cultures is for both men and women to squat over the toilet—even if this means standing directly on the seat (Galanti, 2008).

All cultures have practices and customs associated with major life stage events, such as birth, coming of age, marriage, and death. Pregnancy taboos and customs have been studied since the late 1800s by early anthropologists. Because pregnancy and birth is a particularly dangerous time for the mother and baby in many parts of the world, it gives rise to numerous customs and taboos. Galanti (2008) noted one common belief shared among Asians, Latinos, African Americans, and many Anglo Americans is proscription against a pregnant woman raising her arms above her head. The fear is that this gesture will wrap the umbilical cord around the baby. In many cultures, special customs surround miscarriages, with full burials and services expected for very early term miscarriages.

Prenatal care is highly valued and is expected by Anglo American women in the United States, where pregnancy is viewed as a medical condition that should be managed with a physician. African American women and those from other cultures may view pregnancy as a natural state that does not warrant medical intervention. Among African Americans, mothers, aunts, and other women provide support, consultation, and advice to the pregnant woman.

Culture may affect how the pains experienced with child birth are expressed. Asian and Filipino cultures that value stoicism have a tendency to be reserved, whereas the African American culture, which is highly expressive, contributes to women being more demonstrative in communicating their labor pains. Who is expected and allowed in birthing rooms varies. It is an increasing custom for Anglo American fathers to not only be present, but to videotape the happy event. Other cultures would find this practice incomprehensible. In Orthodox Judaism and other cultures, pregnancy is seen as an unclean state and husbands may not wish to be involved in any part of the birth process. This is also true of Muslim cultures and may present a difficulty if healthcare staffs have relied on the husband to translate. In Mexican cultures, presence in the labor room is seen as women's work, whereas the job of the male is to be strong for the family outside of the delivery room. Members of many cultures, including Muslims, Southeast Asians, and Africans, bury the placenta after childbirth. In Ann Fadiman's book "*The Spirit Catches You and You Fall Down*," (1997) about the Hmong culture, the placenta is regarded as the "jacket" of the soul. It is buried in a place that will lead the soul to the place of its ancestors when it departs from the individual. In Vietnamese culture, the umbilical cord is dried for a good luck charm.

Many Latino cultures, including Mexican, perceive it as very inappropriate to talk about bad things in the future, such as an impending death. This perception arises from a strong belief in fate and in tempting fate, called *fatalisimo*. One implication of this belief is that individuals from these cultures are less likely to complete advance directives. Kagawa-Singer and

Blackhall (2001) found that 65% of Korean Americans and 52% of Hispanic Americans prefer not to be informed of a terminal prognosis. In China and other Asian countries, it is customary for the physician to inform the family but not the patient of a terminal prognosis. This presents legal challenges in the American medical system as it contradicts the values of informed consent and right to self-determination. Galanti (2008) recommended that healthcare personnel be aware of whether state law permits patients (even competent ones) to assign their medical decision-making authority to their preferred decision-maker. She suggested encouraging patients to sign such forms in advance, thereby providing documentation designed to serve the desire of the patient as well as protecting the hospital and staff.

The intent of hospice care is to provide sensitive, minimally intrusive attention to physical and emotional needs that patients and families have toward the end of life. Consenting to hospice care in some cultures, however, can be viewed as "giving up" or denying the power of God to heal and cure, and making decisions regarding the withdrawal of life supports or implementation of "do not resuscitate (DNR)" orders can have cultural influences as well. In many cultures and religions (Buddhism, Catholicism, Orthodox Judaism, Korean), life is considered sacred in all forms and the withdrawal of life supports can be viewed as a violation of this sacred belief. African Americans are more likely than their Caucasian counterparts to want life support measures continued. For some, this is a product of the experience of racism and discrimination; for others, it is rooted in their religious beliefs. In contrast, Galanti (2008) describes the Chinese valuing of the family over the individual, such that withdrawal of life supports may be permitted if circumstances have transcended into a burden to the family.

Given the nature of healthcare practice, social workers must be aware of the customs, values, and beliefs that surround the end of life, death, mourning, and burial. Compassionate understanding can help to ensure that the wishes of the culture and family, with respect to the body, are honored by the healthcare team. Autopsies and organ donations can be taboo practices. In some cultures, it is unacceptable to leave the body of the deceased individual. In American culture, it is important for many families to be present at the bedside at the moment of death. Talking to the patient and assuring the individual that the remaining family members will be all right after the individual's departure is thought to free the individual from languishing at the end of life. In some cultures, a candle is lit or shoes are placed nearby to guide the departing individual on his or her journey.

Embalming and interment customs vary, and many cultures, including among those of the Jewish faith, have prohibitions about who can handle the body. Although cremation is an increasing practice in the United States, generally Jews and Muslims oppose this practice, as the body must be interred whole. The Catholic position on this practice is mixed, historically believing that a whole body is necessary for resurrection, but cremation is common for Hindus and Buddhists. As a number of cultures (e.g., Mexican, Muslim) regard it as unlucky to discuss funeral wishes in advance, it is not unlikely that all arrangements will need to be made once the patient has died. In American culture, laying out of the embalmed body is common and an open casket is not usual. In contrast, for those practicing Judaism, the body is not embalmed and is buried as quickly as possible. Following a memorial service or mass, Irish Americans commonly hold a wake, which might take on the appearance of a celebration to outsiders. For the Chinese, much of the funeral and burial rites will be determined by the individual's status or place in the family. Younger sons may have smaller, less ostentatious funerals as it is considered inappropriate for elders to demonstrate too much respect to those who are younger. Many cultures will remove or cover mirrors in the house, and the wearing or prohibition of certain colors is observed. In American culture, the customary color of mourning is black; the Chinese do not wear the color red, as it is seen as the color of happiness.

In Mexican, Puerto Rican, some Muslim, and African American cultures, there is a tendency for visible and noticeable demonstrations of grief, which can include wailing or "keening." Anglo American culture values a more reserved, even private expression of grief, as do Asian cultures. It is taboo for the Hmong to appear distressed at the passing of a loved one as there is joy in reincarnation. In China and other Asian countries, although stoicism and reserve are valued in mourning, elaborate customary rituals honoring the dead must be performed exactly as prescribed. The purpose of these rituals and all other funerary rites is not only to honor the deceased but also to assist family members to cope with the loss of a loved one. Jews commonly sit *shiva,* during which the grieving family is not left unattended for a period of 7 days. In the United States, the period of mourning may last for at least a year (permitting the passing of all four seasons and associated holidays). During this time, a reserved decorum is expected with dating and remarriage is strongly discouraged. The Chinese period of formal mourning is 100 days.

Cultures around the world believe that the spirits of the dead are present in this world and interact with us on a regular basis. The Chinese believe that the spirit will visit the home within 7 days, and a red plaque is placed outside the door so the spirit does not get lost. Mexicans and other Latin Americans maintain a strong belief in the presence of spirits, and, similar to the Catholic tradition of All Saints Day, the Day of the Dead (El Dia de los Muertos) is celebrated as a holiday on November 2. Families may attend the ceremony, leave food and presents for the deceased, and construct altars in the home in hopes of inviting the dead to visit. The Shonas of Zimbabwe maintain a strong belief in the presence of spirits, feeling that the spirits interact regularly with the community and serve as protectors to the family. Sensitivity to cultural beliefs and practices is crucial, and social workers can help other healthcare team members who might be concerned when individuals from other cultures report believing they were visited by a deceased loved one.

Beliefs and Practices: Physical/Mental Health and Illness

Mental health and mental illness are relatively new concepts in our history. For much of history, mental illness was thought to be caused by evil spirits, the "evil eye," and curses, or by an imbalance in body humors. In much of the world, it still is. The range of "normal" behavior varies by cultures as well. For example, in an Anglo American funeral, excessive wailing and fainting would cause concern for the individual's mental health. At African American funerals, this would be customary. There may be a stigma associated with seeking professional help or even in talking about emotional and mental health concerns (Jang, Chiriboga, Herrera, Tyson, & Schonfield, 2011). Individuals may seek solace from family members, the extended family, elders, or the church. When support is sought, it very important to not "pathologize" the presenting problem; talking about stress and nerves may be entirely adequate for counseling. In many Asian cultures, the stigma against mental illness is so strong that individuals commonly somatize their pain into physical illnesses, thereby authenticating the need for supportive counseling by the physician (Nicolaidis et al., 2011; Saechao et al., 2001).

All cultures have their traditions of healing. In the United States, the dominant form is a medical, scientific model, although beliefs about the healing power of God are common. Folk-healing traditions include coining and cupping to draw out evil spirits; sweat lodges and other practices to break a fever or to exude negative energy; exile and quarantine; fasting; medicinal use of plants, foods, tonics, and teas; the use of psychoactive substances; exorcism; acupuncture; use of traditional healers, called *shamans* in many cultures; the sacrifice of animals; prayer; and the performance of healing ceremonies. In Fadiman's book *The Spirit Catches You and You Fall Down,* (1997) progress is made in the care of a severely epileptic Hmong child when the traditional healing practices are understood and accepted and an alliance is formed between the healthcare providers, the family, and the shaman.

The use of plants and dietary supplements can be cause for concern. Forty percent of Americans take some form of dietary supplement. One quarter of Asians and about 10% of African Americans use herbal remedies and supplements as an important part of their self-care. These can interact with prescription drugs in a number of disadvantageous ways. In some instances, the supplement and a prescribed drug may be chemically similar and the combination may result in too strong of a dose. Particular foods can also interact with medicines. To illustrate, individuals taking blood thinners are often advised to avoid cranberry juice and to limit their intake of green, leafy vegetables. Exploring traditional healing practices and customary supplements, foods, and herbs should be incorporated into comprehensive psychosocial-spiritual assessments and shared with physicians for evaluation (American Council on Science and Health, 2000; Arcury, Grzywacz, & Bell, 2007).

The Gay, Lesbian, and Transgendered Population

Although much progress has been made in recognizing and accepting gay, lesbian, bisexual, and transgendered (GLBT) individuals in many aspects of the "mainstream" U.S. culture, significant barriers persist in access to care and adequacy of care for this population. As Krehely (2009) noted, particularly high levels of healthcare disparities and poor outcomes can be found when GLBT status occurs in conjunction with minority or ethnic status. When compared with their heterosexual counterparts, GLBT individuals are less likely to have health insurance and are more likely to delay care, to fail to fill prescriptions, or to get care in an emergency room. They are also less likely to rate their health as excellent and experience higher rates of certain cancers, psychosocial distress, and suicide attempts. These disparities are attributed in part to the presence of persistent stigma, lack of healthcare insurance or plans that address the specific healthcare needs of the GLBT, inadequate data and research on GLBT health, and the lack of specially trained providers (Krehely, 2009). In addition, according to SAMHSA (2001), nearly one-third of this population may have problems with substance abuse and are less likely to seek treatment than their counterparts. Finally, although accurate estimates of the incidence of interpersonal violence in this population are difficult to attain, Friedman, Marshal, Stall, Cheong, and Wright (2008) found that same-sex couples report interpersonal violence as their most serious health concern after HIV/AIDS.

As much of the healthcare related research in the GLBT population has historically focused on sexually transmitted diseases and HIV/AIDS, a pressing need exists for comprehensive and inclusive studies that address the full scope of psychosocial stressors, stigma, and obstacles to health encountered by this population. Although overall incidence rates have stabilized for most groups in the years between 2008 and 2010, the estimated rates for males having sex with males (MSM) has increased 12%. Furthermore, the age of incidence decreased and now these diseases disproportionately affect people between the ages of 24 and 35. African Americans, particularly young African American males, are most at risk (Centers for Disease Control and Prevention [CDC], 2013). Cultural and religious stigmas in the African American community regarding males having sex with males are factors that inhibit safe-sex practices, early diagnosis, and treatment. Barriers to healthcare, including access, lack of insurance, and a shortage of primary care providers, are also factors. Because early identification and treatment with antiretroviral therapy have been shown to slow the progression of HIV to the disease AIDS and reduces transmission from one person to another, social workers must become educated and comfortable addressing this issue with at-risk clients. In practice, social workers should encourage individuals to be tested and referred to the appropriate specialists and clinics for care (CDC, 2013). *Figure 15.2* reveals the 2010 incidence rate of new HIV infections and how MSMs are disproportionally affected. Once a patient has been diagnosed, in addition to providing emotional support, social workers can assist the patient in obtaining and maintaining the required drug regimen.

Figure 15.2   Estimated New HIV Infections—2010

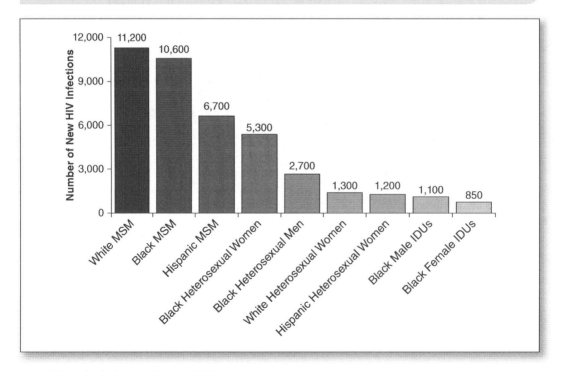

Note: MSM = males having sex with males; IDUs = intravenous drug users

Source: Estimated New HIV Infections (2010). Centers for Disease Control and Prevention, 2013.

The limited failure to recognize gay marriage and support the rights of same-sex couples places a significant burden on American's 2.5 million GLBT elders, who are twice as likely to live alone and four times less likely to have children to assist in their care (Krehely, 2009). Even when the couple is recognized and supported by the healthcare team, persistent legal barriers can prevent disclosing medical information and block medical decision making of the same-sex partner of a patient, thereby preventing his or her full engagement in the care of his or her loved one. Along with offering supportive and inclusive care that encourages patients to disclose their gender/sexual orientation and identify issues of concern, social workers involved with this population can intervene by

- encouraging healthcare team members to recognize and address their own feelings and attitudes about working with GLBT individuals;

- contributing to training that enhances the competency/sensitivity of care,

- becoming familiar with and identifying the particular healthcare challenges and problems faced by GLBT patients,

- providing an opportunity for patients to explore and heal from the stigma and negative experiences associated with homophobia and heterosexism,

- assuring the inclusion of GLBT patients in appropriate medical studies and the protection of their rights as human subjects in those studies,

- helping patients assert their rights to competent care, and

- advocating for the inclusion of GLBT partners in medical decision-making processes (SAMHSA, 2001).

CULTURALLY COMPETENT HEALTHCARE ORGANIZATIONS

Culturally competent practice is enhanced when there is an organization commitment to providing culturally competent care. In fact, the literature on culturally competent social work practice states that the efforts of the individual practitioner will not have much impact *unless* expectations for culturally competent practice is woven into the fabric of the healthcare (Bankhead & Erlich, 2005). According to Nybell and Sims (2004), cultural competence in social service organizations requires that staffing management and leadership is congruent with the diversity of the client population served. This necessitates reviewing policies and practices related to recruiting, hiring, training, and retaining a diverse work force as well as assessing the organization within the context of the community it serves. Further, programs and services must be evaluated to determine the extent to which resources are allocated fairly and appropriately so that all groups are served. Agency-wide cultural competence training initiatives should be implemented, specifically targeting the needs and demographic makeup of the community served. At the level of interaction between professionals and clients, written materials must be translated and resources made available for translation if necessary (Ludwig-Beymer, 2008).

The following guidelines are suggested for culturally competent organizations (Green, 1999; Hutchison, 2003; Lum, 2003; Mor Barak, 2000):

- Diversity should be reflected in all levels of the organization from clients to the board of directors.

- The organization should conduct and support ongoing training and communication about diversity issues and multicultural communication.

- Staff should be actively engaged in learning about the community, its norms, values, and formal as well as informal resources. Particular attention should be paid to preferences for care giving and care receiving.

- Staff should engage in active outreach, attending local functions, giving presentations at community organizations and so on, particularly when a targeted population is suspicious of Western bioscience.

- Staff should maintain working relationships with other organizations that serve the targeted population, such as ethnic agencies (NASW, 2006).

Cross, Bazron, Dennis, and Isaacs. (1983) conceptualized the cultural competence of organizations as falling along a continuum. Beginning with the least level of competence, organizations may be *culturally destructive,* with extreme insensitivity to patients' cultural identities, health practices, and beliefs. *Cultural incapacity* is reflected when organizations have failed to develop any capacity to respond to patients of different cultures. Organizations that believe that good practices in and of themselves are culturally appropriate are seen as *culturally blind.* Organizations that recognize and attempt to rectify weaknesses in serving those from different cultures are regarded as *culturally pre-competent.* A **culturally competent organization** accepts and respects differences between cultural groups, continually assesses their policies and practices regarding cultural sensitivity, has an ongoing commitment to expand cultural knowledge and resources, and promotes cultural competence in hiring and developing staff.

Social workers have much to contribute to organization-wide efforts that enhance cultural competence. Our knowledge of the community, its resources, and formal and informal leaders can be a distinct asset in creating supportive networks of concerned individuals with cultural expertise for guiding the process. Our macropractice skills can lead and facilitate the change effort and ensure appropriate responsiveness to the community at large. Finally, we have the capacity to work at mezzo and micro levels with groups, families, and individuals to ensure that cultural beliefs about health and illness are understood and reflected in care. The following checklist *(Table 15.1)* is adapted from work by Goode (2006) and the National Center for Cultural Competence. Originally designed for assessing agencies working with children, the checklist has been adapted by others for assessing the cultural sensitivity of healthcare organizations and social service agencies serving a variety of client age groups.

Table 15.1 Checklist for Culturally Competent Organizations

PROMOTING CULTURAL DIVERSITY AND CULTURAL COMPETENCY

This checklist is intended to heighten the awareness and sensitivity of personnel to the importance of cultural diversity and cultural competence in human service and health settings. It provides concrete examples of the kinds of values and practices that foster such an environment.

Directions: Please select A, B, or C for each item listed below.

A = Things I do frequently

B = Things I do occasionally

C= Things I do rarely or never

PHYSICAL ENVIRONMENT, MATERIALS & RESOURCES

_____ 1. Pictures, posters and other materials are displayed that reflect the cultures and ethnic backgrounds of patients and families served by the program or agency.

_____ 2. Magazines, brochures, and other printed materials in reception areas are of interest to, and reflect the different cultures of patients and families served by the program or agency.

_____ 3. When using videos, films, CDs, DVDS, or other media resources for mental health prevention, treatment or other interventions we insure that they reflect the cultures of patients and families by the program or agency.

_____ 4. When using food during an assessment, we insure that meals provided include foods consistent with the cultural and ethnic backgrounds of patients and families served by the program or agency.

_____ 5. We insure that toys and other play accessories in reception areas and those used during assessment are representative and inclusive of the various cultural and ethnic groups of the community we serve.

COMMUNICATION STYLES

_____ 6. For children and youth who speak languages or dialects other than English, staff attempt to learn and use key words in their language so that they are better able to communicate with them during assessment, treatment or other interventions.

(Continued)

(Continued)

_____ 7. Staff attempt to understand any cultural or familial colloquialisms used by patients and families that may impact on assessment, treatment or other interventions.

_____ 8. The organization has appropriate visual aids available to use with patients and families who have limited English proficiency.

_____ 9. Bilingual or multilingual staff are identified and trained/certified as interpreters for assessment, treatment, and other interventions for patients/families w/limited English Proficiency.

_____ 10. Bilingual staff or multilingual trained/certified interpreters are available and used during assessments, treatment sessions, meetings, and for other events for patients and families who require this level of assistance.

11. Staff have been trained to keep in mind that:

_____ a) limitations in English proficiency are in no way a reflection of an individual's level of intellectual functioning.

_____ b) limited ability to speak English has no bearing on an individual's ability to communicate effectively in their language of origin.

_____ c) patients may or may not be literate in their language of origin and/or English.

_____ 12. Patient education materials and other written communications are translated into the patient's and family's language of origin.

_____ 13. Staff understand that it may be necessary to use alternatives to written communications for some patients and families, as word of mouth may be a preferred method of receiving information.

14. Staff understand the principles and practices of linguistic competency and:

_____ a) apply them within their programs and services.

_____ b) advocate on behalf of patients and families when appropriate.

_____ 15. Staff understand the implications of health/mental health literacy within the context of the patient/family's culture or origin.

VALUES AND ATTITUDES

_____ 16. Staff use alternative formats and varied approaches to communicate and share information with patients and families who experience illness and/or disability.

_____ 17. Staff avoid imposing values that may conflict or be inconsistent with those of cultures or ethnic groups other than their own.

_____ 18. Staff discourage others from using racial and ethnic slurs and other derogatory terms by helping them understand that certain words can hurt others.

_____ 19. Books, movies, and other media resources used by the agency have been screened for negative cultural, ethnic, or racial stereotypes.

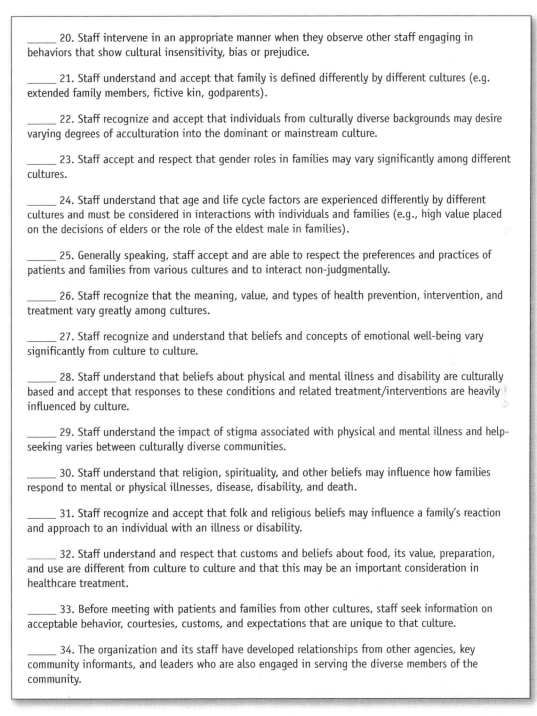

_____ 20. Staff intervene in an appropriate manner when they observe other staff engaging in behaviors that show cultural insensitivity, bias or prejudice.

_____ 21. Staff understand and accept that family is defined differently by different cultures (e.g. extended family members, fictive kin, godparents).

_____ 22. Staff recognize and accept that individuals from culturally diverse backgrounds may desire varying degrees of acculturation into the dominant or mainstream culture.

_____ 23. Staff accept and respect that gender roles in families may vary significantly among different cultures.

_____ 24. Staff understand that age and life cycle factors are experienced differently by different cultures and must be considered in interactions with individuals and families (e.g., high value placed on the decisions of elders or the role of the eldest male in families).

_____ 25. Generally speaking, staff accept and are able to respect the preferences and practices of patients and families from various cultures and to interact non-judgmentally.

_____ 26. Staff recognize that the meaning, value, and types of health prevention, intervention, and treatment vary greatly among cultures.

_____ 27. Staff recognize and understand that beliefs and concepts of emotional well-being vary significantly from culture to culture.

_____ 28. Staff understand that beliefs about physical and mental illness and disability are culturally based and accept that responses to these conditions and related treatment/interventions are heavily influenced by culture.

_____ 29. Staff understand the impact of stigma associated with physical and mental illness and help-seeking varies between culturally diverse communities.

_____ 30. Staff understand that religion, spirituality, and other beliefs may influence how families respond to mental or physical illnesses, disease, disability, and death.

_____ 31. Staff recognize and accept that folk and religious beliefs may influence a family's reaction and approach to an individual with an illness or disability.

_____ 32. Staff understand and respect that customs and beliefs about food, its value, preparation, and use are different from culture to culture and that this may be an important consideration in healthcare treatment.

_____ 33. Before meeting with patients and families from other cultures, staff seek information on acceptable behavior, courtesies, customs, and expectations that are unique to that culture.

_____ 34. The organization and its staff have developed relationships from other agencies, key community informants, and leaders who are also engaged in serving the diverse members of the community.

(Continued)

(Continued)

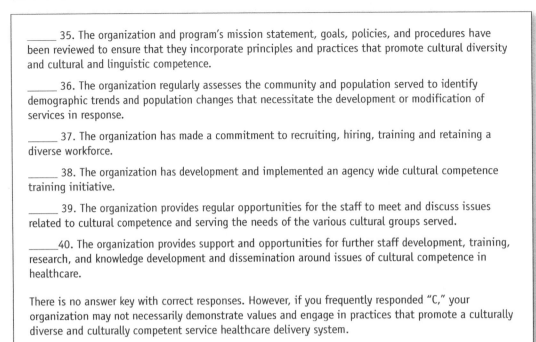

_____ 35. The organization and program's mission statement, goals, policies, and procedures have been reviewed to ensure that they incorporate principles and practices that promote cultural diversity and cultural and linguistic competence.

_____ 36. The organization regularly assesses the community and population served to identify demographic trends and population changes that necessitate the development or modification of services in response.

_____ 37. The organization has made a commitment to recruiting, hiring, training and retaining a diverse workforce.

_____ 38. The organization has development and implemented an agency wide cultural competence training initiative.

_____ 39. The organization provides regular opportunities for the staff to meet and discuss issues related to cultural competence and serving the needs of the various cultural groups served.

_____ 40. The organization provides support and opportunities for further staff development, training, research, and knowledge development and dissemination around issues of cultural competence in healthcare.

There is no answer key with correct responses. However, if you frequently responded "C," your organization may not necessarily demonstrate values and engage in practices that promote a culturally diverse and culturally competent service healthcare delivery system.

Source: Adapted from Goode (2006).

SUMMARY

Culture as reflected in the thoughts, communications, actions, customs, beliefs, values, and institutions of a racial, ethnic, religious, or social group has a pervasive impact on individual health and use of healthcare services. This chapter has examined these impacts and the importance of developing sensitivity to the cultural nuances of patients and families seeking healthcare. Religious and spiritual orientations have significant roles affecting an individual's persona, including how the individual envisions his or her health condition, the acceptability of treatment, and the manner in which he or she interacts with the healthcare team. Attention to gay, lesbian, bisexual, and transgendered (GLBT) individuals includes the impacts of historic discrimination to this group and the manner in which care is sought out and received.

Individual practitioners and healthcare organizations alike are accountable to maintain a level of cultural competency that reflects their awareness and appreciation for the uniqueness of the individual. Social work in particular has a responsibility to be proactive in assisting the healthcare team to understand patient and family member beliefs and values about one's health condition and the treatment of presenting problems. Respect and accommodation to patient needs and preferences will enhance the likelihood of positive interventions and outcomes. Sensitivity and compassion based on such respect is fundamental to healthcare social work practice.

KEY TERMS AND CONCEPTS

- Culture
- Cultural competence
- Linguistic competence
- Health literacy
- Cultural humility
- Culturagram
- Worldview
- Assimilation
- Acculturation
- Somatization
- High-context communication
- Low-context communication
- Culturally competent organizations

QUESTIONS FOR DISCUSSION

1. How does cultural humility and the clinical position of "not-knowing" assist us in working with people from different cultures? Are there limitations to this approach? What would be an alternative?

2. Gender roles, power, and authority in families vary by cultural traditions. How might you work with a woman from the Middle East who will not talk with you directly and insists that you speak with her husband?

3. What cultural groups are strongly represented in your community? What do you know about them? How much interaction do you have with them? How well prepared would you feel to work with them in a healthcare setting? What steps could you take to develop some familiarity with other cultures in your community?

EXERCISES

1. Create a list of ten open-ended questions that you could use as part of a biopsychosocial assessment to explore a patient's culture.

2. Go to the website for the Provider's Guide to Quality and Culture (http://erc.msh.org/mainpage.cfm?file = 1.0.htm&module = provider&language = English) and select one of the cultural groups that are described there. Prepare a brief presentation on the cultural beliefs and practices and present it to your class.

3. Create a culturagram for your family of origin and its culture of origin. If you need to, interview someone to learn about how your family came to America and other religious, cultural, and health beliefs and practices.

REFERENCES

Agency for Healthcare Research and Quality. (2003). *Planning culturally and linguistically appropriate services: A guide for managed care plans.* Retrieved from http://www.ahrq.gov/populations/plan clas.htm

Altman, I., & Rogoff, B. (1987). World views in psychology: Trait, interactional, organismic and trans-actional perspectives. In D. Stokols & I. Altaman (Eds.), *Handbook of environmental psychology,* (Vol. I, pp. 7–40). New York: John Wiley.

American Council on Science and Health. (2000, November 1). *What's the story? Drug supplement inter-action.* Retrieved from http://acsh.org/2000/11/whats-the-story-drug-supplement-interaction/

Anderson, H. (1997). *Conversation, language and possibilities: A postmodern approach to therapy.* New York: Basic Books.

Anderson, H., & Goolishian, H. A. (1992). The client is the expert: A not knowing approach to therapy. In S. McNamee & K. Gergen (Eds.), *Therapy as social construction* (pp. 25–39). Newbury Park, CA: SAGE.

Arcury, T. A., Grzywacz, J. G., & Bell, R. A. (2007). Herbal remedy use as health self-management among older adults. *Journals of Gerontology Series B: Psychological Sciences & Social Sciences, (62B)*2, 142–149.

Bankhead, T. & Erlich, J.L. (2005). *Diverse populations and community practice.* Thousand Oaks, CA: SAGE.

Brady, M. J., Peterman, A. H., Fitchett, G., Mo, M., & Cella, D. (1999). The case for including spiritual in quality of life measurement in oncology. *American Journal of Obstetrics and Gynecology, 16,* 121–128.

Centers for Disease Control and Prevention. (2013, May 3). *HIV incidence.* Retrieved from http://www.cdc.gov/hiv/statistics/surveillance/incidence

Congress, E. (1994). The use of culturagrams to assess and empower culturally diverse families. *Families in Society, 75,* 531–540.

Congress, E. (2005). Cultural and ethical issues in working with culturally diverse patients and their families. *Social Work in Health Care, 39*(3–4), 249–262.

Cross, T. L., Bazron, B. J., Dennis, K. W., & Isaacs, M. R. (1989). *Toward a culturally competent system of care: A monograph on effective services for minority children who are severely emotionally dis-turbed.* Washington, DC: Georgetown University, Child Development Center, Child and Adolescent

Service system Program, Technical Assistance Center. Retrieved from: http://www.mhsoac.ca.gov/meetings/docs/Meetings/2010/June/CLCC_Tab_4_Towards_Culturally_Competent_System.pdf

Dubard, C. A., & Gizlice, A. (2008). Language spoken and difference in health status, access to care, and receipt of preventive services among U.S. Hispanics. *Research and Practice, 98*(11), 2021–2033.

Fadiman, A. (1997). *The spirit catches you and you fall down: A Hmong child, her American doctors, and the collision of two cultures*. New York: Farrar, Straus and Giroux.

Farrar, A., & Kirkpatrick, W. (2010). Opportunities to demonstrate leadership in language access services. In W. Spitzer (Ed.), *Immigration: health care social work policy and practice issues* (pp. 83–94). National Society for Social Work Leadership in Health Care. Petersburg, VA: Dietz Press.

Flores, G., & Vega, L.R. (1998). Barriers to health access for Latino children: A review. *Family Medicine, 30*, 196–205.

Friedman, M. S., Marshal, M. P., Stall, R., Cheong, G., & Wright, E. R. (2008). Gay-related development, early abuse and adult health outcomes among gay males. *AIDS and Behavior, 12*, 891–902.

Galanti, G. (2008). *Caring for patients from different cultures*. (4th ed.). Philadelphia: University of Pennsylvania Press.

Georgetown University Health Policy Institute. (2004, February). *Cultural competence in health care: Is it important for people with chronic conditions?* Washington, DC. Retrieved from https://hpi.georgetown.edu/agingsociety/pubhtml/cultural/cultural.html

Goode., T. A. (2006). *Promoting cultural competence and cultural diversity in early intervention and early childhood settings*. Retrieved from http://www.azdhs.gov/bhs/pdf/culturalComp/self_assess.pdf

Green, J. (1999). *Cultural awareness in the human services: A multi-ethnic approach* (3rd ed.). Boston: Allyn & Bacon.

Hall, E. T. (1976). *Beyond culture*. New York: Anchor Books.

Harris, R. C., Dew, M. A., Lee, A., Amaya, A., Buches, L., Reetz, D., & Coleman, C. (1995). The role of religion in heart-transplant recipients long-term health and well-being. *Journal of Religion and Health, 34*(1), 17–32.

Hutchison, E. (2003). Formal organizations. In E. Hutchison (Ed.), *Dimensions of human behavior: Person and environment* (2nd ed., pp. 471–505). Thousand Oaks, CA: Pine Forge Press.

Jang, Y., Chiriboga, D. A., Herrera, J. R., Tyson, D. M., & Schonfeld, L. (2011). Attitudes toward mental health services in Hispanic older adults: The role of misconceptions and beliefs. *Community Mental Health Journal, 47*, 164–170.

Jenks, A. C. (2011). From "list of traits" to "openmindeness": Emerging issues in cultural competence education. *Culture, Medicine and Psychiatry, 35*, 209–235.

Kagawa-Singer, M., & Blackhall, L. J. (2001). Negotiating cross-cultural issues at the end of life. *Journal of the American Medical Association, 286*, 2993–3001.

Kleinman, A., Eisenberg, L., & Good, B. (1978). Culture, illness and care: Clinical lessons from anthropologic and cross-cultural research. *Annals of Internal Medicine, 88*, 251–258.

Koenig, H. G., Cohen, H. J., George, L. K., Hays, J. C., Shema, S. J., Larson, D. B., & Blazer, D. G., (1997). Attendance at religious services, interleukin-6, and other biological parameters of immune function in older adults. *International Journal of Psychiatry and Medicine, 27*, 233–250.

Krehely, J. (2009, December 21). *How to close the LBGT health disparities gap*. Center for American Progress. Retrieved from http://cdn.americanprogress.org/wp-content/uploads/issues/2009/12/pdf/lgbt_health_disparities_race.pdf

Leininger, M. (1991). *Culture care and universality: A theory of nursing care*. New York: National League for Nursing Press.

Leininger, M. (1996). Founder's focus: Transcultural nursing administration: An imperative worldwide. *Journal of Transcultural Nursing, 8*(1), 28–33.

Ludwig-Beymer, P. (2008). Creating culturally competent organizations. In M. M. Andrews & J. S. Boyle (Eds.), *Transcultural competence in nursing care* (pp. 197–225). Philadelphia PA: Wolters Kluwer/Lippincott Williams & Wilkins.

Lum, D. (2003). *Culturally competent practice: A framework for understanding diverse groups and justice issues* (2nd ed.). Pacific Grove, CA: Brooks/Cole.

Mor Barak, M. (2000). The inclusive workplace: An ecosystem approach to diversity management. *Social Work, 45*(4), 339–352.

National Association of Social Workers. (2000). Cultural competence in the social work profession. In *Social work speaks: NASW policy statements 2000–2003* (5th ed.). Washington, DC: author.

National Association of Social Workers. (2001). *Standards for cultural competence in social work practice*. Washington, DC: Author.

National Association of Social Workers. (2006). *Indicators for the achievement of the NASW standards for cultural competence in social work practice*. Retrieved from http://www.socialworkers.org/practice/standards/NASWCulturalStandardsIndicators2006.pdf

Niemeier, J. P., Burnett, D. M., & Whitaker, D. (2003). Cultural competence in the rehabilitation setting: Are we falling short of meeting needs? *Archives of Physical Medicine and Rehabilitation, 84*, 1240–1245.

Neuman, K., Matto, H., Hutchison, E., & Singleton, K. (2005). The spirit catches you: A transactional model of cultural competence and health literacy. In W. Spitzer (Ed.), *Cultural diversity and health care social work* (pp. 17–35). National Society for Social Work Leadership in Health Care. Petersburg, VA: Dietz Press.

Nicolaidis, C., Perez, M., Mejia, A., Alvarado, A., Celaya-Alston, R., Gallan, H., & Hilde, A. (2011). "Guardarse Las Cosas Adentro" (Keeping things inside): Latina violence survivors' perceptions of depression. *Journal of General Internal Medicine, 26*(10), 1131–1137.

Nielsen-Bohlman, L., Panzer, A., & Kindig, D. (Eds.). (2004). *Health literacy: A prescription to end confusion*. Washington, DC: The National Academies Press.

Nybell, L. M., & Sims, S. S. (2004). Race, place, space: Meanings of cultural competence in three child welfare agencies. *Social Work, 49*(1), 17–26.

Peterman, A., George, F. D., Brady, M. J., Hernandez, L., & Cella, D. (2002). Measuring spiritual well-being in people with cancer: The functional assessment of chronic illness therapy-spiritual well-being scale (FACIT-Sp). *Annals of Behavioral Medicine, 4*(1), 49–58.

Roberts, J. A., Brown, D., & Larson, D. B. (1997, January). Factors influencing views of patients with gynecologic cancer about end-of-life decisions. *American Journal of Obstetrics and Gynecology, 176*, 166–172.

Saechao, F., Sharrock, S., Reicherter, D., Livingston, J. D., Aylward, A., Whistnant, J., Koopman, C., & Kohli, S. (2001). Stressors and barriers to using mental health services among diverse groups of first-generation immigrants to the United States. *Community Mental Health, 48*, 98–106.

Strawbridge, W. J., Cohen, P. D., Shema, S. J., & Kaplan, G.A. (1997). Frequent attendance at religious services and mortality over 28 years. *American Journal of Public Health, (87)*, 957–961.

Substance Abuse and Mental Health Administration. (2001). *A provider's introduction to substance abuse treatment for Lesbian, Gay, Bisexual and Transgendered Individuals*. HHS Publication No. (SMA) 09-4104. Retrieved from http://kap.samhsa.gov/products/manuals/pdfs/lgbt.pdf

Tanyi, R. A. (2002). Toward clarification of the meaning of spirituality. *Journal of Advanced Nursing, 39*(5), 500–509.

Tervalon, M., & Murray-Garcia, J. (1998). Cultural humility versus cultural competence: A critical distinction in defining physician training outcomes in multicultural education. *Journal of Health Care for the Poor and Underserved, 9*(2), 117–125.

Yates, J. W., Chalmer, B. J., James, P., Follansbee, B., & McKegney, F. B. (1981). Religion in patients with advanced cancer. *Medical and Pediatric Oncology, 9*, 121–128.

White, M. (1995). *Re-authoring lives: Interviews and essays*. Adelade, Australia: Dulwich Centre.

CHAPTER 16

The Future of Healthcare and Social Work Practice

William J. Spitzer

INTRODUCTION

Our text has explored both the evolution and current state of health, healthcare, and social work healthcare practice in the United States. We have examined the characteristics of our healthcare delivery system and the technological, economic, sociopolitical, and professional factors shaping that system. Our study has addressed the impacts on patients and families as they attempt to access and utilize healthcare services. What lingers is the question of what the future holds for both consumers and providers of healthcare in the United States. What challenges lie ahead as we seek effective, yet economical means of reducing health risks and enhancing our quality of life? What roles can social work anticipate as it strives to bring its professional competence to bear on behalf of needy patients, families, and communities?

ON THE HEALTHCARE POLICY HORIZON

The healthcare environment is clearly in a state of flux. Is this state likely to continue? In a word, yes. As we look ahead, we see a myriad of conditions that suggest robust winds of change prompted by escalating healthcare costs, greater numbers of aging consumers requiring more and expensive care, growth in the extent of public financing for healthcare, heightened decision-making expectations by patients, an increasing number of previously uninsured Americans accessing needed healthcare, and remarkably sophisticated technologies that are altering how and where care is provided. These factors influence public opinion and legislation at national and state levels targeting cost, quality, and access to healthcare.

The Patient Protection and Affordable Care Act of 2010

The coverage provisions in the Patient Protection and Affordable Care Act (PPACA) built on a piecemeal insurance system that left many Americans without affordable coverage. Historically, most people in the United States obtained health insurance coverage as a fringe benefit through a job. However, many people were left out of the employer-based system, and the availability of employer-based coverage has eroded over time (Majerol, Newkirk, & Garfield, 2014). The impact of the PPACA will be particularly significant as its broad provisions range from extending eligibility for healthcare and improving quality to supporting innovation and better aligning healthcare expenditures with provider costs (United States Department of Health and Human Services [USDHHS], 2011). Consumer participation has steadily increased in the "Marketplaces." Additionally, the Congressional Budget Office projects that the law will decrease the number of uninsured people by 12 million in 2014 and by 26 million by 2017 (Blumenthal & Collins, 2014). Prior to the PPACA, federal law mandated coverage for the following principal eligibility groups:

- pregnant women and children under 6 years of age with family incomes at or below 133% of the Federal Poverty Level (FPL),

- children 6 through 18 years of age with family incomes at or below 100% of the FPL,

- parents and caretaker relatives who meet the financial eligibility requirements for the former Aid to Families with Dependent Children (AFDC) (cash assistance) program, and

- those elderly and disabled who qualify for Supplemental Security Income benefits based on low income and resources.

Prior to the PPACA, federal law excluded non-disabled, non-pregnant adults without dependent children from receiving Medicaid unless states obtained waivers to cover them (Kaiser Family Foundation, August 2011). As one step in broadening healthcare access, the PPACA expands eligibility for Medicaid to lower income individuals under the age of 65 years at 138% of the poverty level ($15,415 for an individual and $31,809 for a family of four) and assumes federal responsibility for much of the cost of this expansion. If adopted by all states, the Medicaid expansion could provide health insurance to as many as 12.3 million people by 2022, with corresponding reductions in state uncompensated care costs and in spending for some state programs (Holahan, Buettgens, Carroll, & Dorn, 2012). To fund this expansion of Medicaid coverage, the PPACA provides that the federal government will cover 100% of the states' costs of the coverage expansion in 2014 through 2016, gradually decreasing to 90% in 2020 and thereafter. This new financing translates into an infusion of federal dollars into states to the tune of $800 billion through 2022 (Holahan, Buettgens, & Dorn, 2013).

The PPACA also enhances federal support for the Children's Health Insurance Program, simplifies Medicaid and Children's Health Insurance Program (CHIP) enrollment, improves

Medicaid services, provides new options for long-term services and supports, improves coordination for dual-eligibles (those who qualify for both Medicare and Medicaid), and improves Medicaid quality for patients and providers. Between 2014 and 2016, the federal government will pay 100% of the cost of covering newly eligible individuals. In 2017 and 2018, states that initially covered less of the newly eligible population will receive more assistance than states that covered at least some non-elderly, non-pregnant adults ("Expansion States"). States were required to maintain the same income eligibility levels through December 31, 2013 for all adults, and this requirement has been extended through September 30, 2019 for children currently in Medicaid. Six months after the launch of the coverage provisions of the PPACA, 6 million people had enrolled in Medicaid or CHIP (Blumenthal & Collins, 2014). That number had increased to 10.8 million individuals as of December, 2014 (Wachino, 2015).

A significant series of unanswered questions relate to consumer participation. How many individuals will ultimately enroll in the PPACA? At what level will they enroll? Will enrollees be younger and possess such good health that their demands on the system are limited, or will they be "higher risk" individuals, whose participation will prove more costly in needed services? Initial efforts to launch the enrollment website for PPACA were plagued by major implementation problems that delayed consumer signups, contributed to a wariness among those not yet enrolled, and absolutely made for political difficulties as opponents to the legislation took the problematic rollout as a sign that the program was ill-conceived and not ready for implementation. Considerable effort was invested to overcome logistical issues and regain stature in the public eye. For the program to be successful, the PPACA will need to demonstrate that it truly is affordable to the individual consumer, delivers on its promises to enhance the quality of healthcare, and is easily accessible from the point of enrollment. As of February 2015, over 11 million Americans selected health care plans or had been re-enrolled through the marketplace. This included approximately 8.6 million through the federally run HealthCare.gov marketplace and another 2.8 million through the state marketplaces (Wachino, 2015).

State Participation Decisions

An equally major question on the healthcare policy horizon is whether and how the states will participate in the expansion of Medicaid. For the states currently expending 16 cents of every dollar in state general funds on Medicaid, it is a balancing act. The advantages of infusing new federal dollars into state budgets by acceptance of the new act must be weighed against concerns about loss of control and potential burdens on state budgets occurring after the federal match starts to decline in 2017. In sum, to receive the new funds, the states must

- Accept new eligibility guidelines, including elimination of resource tests

- Extend newly eligible adults a benchmark benefit package consistent with those available through the new health insurance exchanges

- Improve their outreach and enrollment efforts in conjunction with the health insurance exchanges (which must be operational by 2014)

- Anticipate that the Medicaid disproportionate share hospital allocations will be reduced, primary care provider payments will be increased for a 2-year period, and state options for home and community-based services will be expanded. *Disproportionate share hospitals (DSH)* are those that treat high numbers of indigent patients; 3,109 hospitals receive this adjustment. Medicare DSH payments are highly concentrated. Ninety-three percent of total DSH payments go to large hospitals in urban areas, and about 65% of all DSH payments go to teaching hospitals (Fishman & Bentley, 1997).

In addition to these conditions, implementation will require substantial changes to state policy; extensive enhancement, if not replacement, of state IT systems; the production of new application and enrollment materials; the establishment of new outreach methods; the potential reorganization of state eligibility personnel; and unprecedented coordination between state organizations (Camillo, 2013). The Supreme Court allowed states to opt out of the Medicaid expansion. Using that determination, as of March 2014, twenty-four states are not moving forward with Medicaid *(Figure 16.1)*. Idaho, Montana, Wyoming, South Dakota, Nebraska, Kansas, Oklahoma, Texas, Louisiana, Alabama, Mississippi, Georgia, Florida, North and South Carolina, Tennessee, Maine, Alaska, and Wisconsin have declined to participate, while Utah, Missouri, Indiana, Virginia, and Pennsylvania continued to debate expansion. States that choose to reject the Medicaid expansion can set their own Medicaid eligibility thresholds, which in many states are significantly below 133% of the poverty line. In addition, many states do not make Medicaid available to childless adults at any income level, and this may create unequal coverage compared with that in participating states. If the 24 states do not change course and elect to not participate in the PPACA, researchers at the Urban Institute estimate that 5.7 million individuals will be deprived of healthcare coverage in 2016 (Council of Economic Advisors, 2014, p.2). As many of these states have high rates of uninsured residents and lower health status, the PPACA may have the paradoxical effect of increasing disparities across regions, even as it reduces disparities between previously insured and uninsured Americans as a whole (Radley, McCarthy, Lippa, Hayes, & Schoen, 2014).

Many of the states declining to participate have pointed to a potential negative impact on their budgets, although research has shown that the costs of expanding Medicaid are thought to be less than 1% of state budgets and that no state would experience a positive flow of funds by choosing to reject the Medicaid expansion (Glied & Ma, 2013; Holahan et al., 2012). In fact, as the federal share of the Medicaid expansion is so much greater than the state share, taxpayers in non-participating states will end up bearing a significant share of the overall costs to expand the Medicaid program through federal tax payments while not having the opportunity to appreciate any benefits (Glied & Ma, 2013). If the 24 states that have not yet expanded Medicaid had done so as of January 1, 2014, those states and their citizens would have received an additional $88 billion in federal support through calendar year 2016. States that have already expanded Medicaid will receive $84 billion over that period (Council of Economic Advisors, 2014, p. 5).

The extent of ultimate state participation in the program will be important as program operations and funding assumed states would elect inclusion. Non-participation and the prospect of non-equivalent levels of healthcare also challenge the question of whether more robust levels of healthcare should *or can* universally exist in the United States.

Predictably, most states have responded to this decision in partisan ways, with all 14 states in which Democrats control the governor's office and both houses of the state legislature choosing to move forward with plans to expand Medicaid, as have seven of 12 states in which control of state government is split between Democrats and Republicans. Conversely, of the 24 states in which Republicans control the governor's office and both chambers of the state legislature, only three—Arizona, North Dakota, and, most recently, Michigan—have approved plans to extend Medicaid eligibility (Holahan et al., 2013).

Figure 16.1   Current Status of State Medicaid Expansion Decisions, 2014

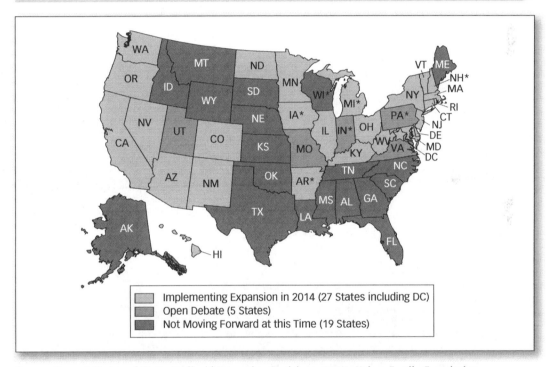

Implementing Expansion in 2014 (27 States including DC)
Open Debate (5 States)
Not Moving Forward at this Time (19 States)

Source: Current Status of State Medicaid Expansion Decisions, 2014. Kaiser Family Foundation.

Past experience has shown that the availability of federal funds has served as an effective incentive for states to provide coverage to meet the health and long-term care needs of their low-income residents despite state budget pressures. More than half of states implemented a Medicaid program within the first year federal funding became available (1966), and nearly all states were participating in Medicaid within four years, even though participation required substantial state investment. Over time, states have met new federal requirements to extend Medicaid coverage and expanded beyond minimum coverage levels at the regular federal matching rate. States have also expanded Medicaid and CHIP coverage for children at an enhanced federal matching rate (Kaiser Commission on Medicaid and the Uninsured, August 2012).

With the Supreme Court upholding the PPACA, planning began on designing the state-based health insurance exchanges that would serve as the marketplaces for citizens to purchase qualified health plans and gain access to premium tax credits and cost-sharing reductions (Kaiser Family Foundation, 2011). The ruling allowed states to opt out of creating these exchanges, realizing that the default action would be a federal exchange or federal–state partnership model. For states, this constitutes another major policy issue—whether to accept new federal funds to design insurance exchanges or decline that revenue and yield control to federally established exchanges.

ON THE HEALTHCARE SERVICE DELIVERY HORIZON

The future focus of healthcare is on *wellness, prevention, and intervention with chronic diseases and conditions prompted by social problems,* such as poverty and violence. One hundred and seventy-three million Americans from birth to the age of 64 years were enrolled in private health coverage in 2011, with an estimated 71 million Americans receiving expanded coverage of one or more preventive services in 2011 and 2012 due to the PPACA (Skopec & Sommers, 2013). Additionally, an estimated 34 million Americans in traditional Medicare and Medicare Advantage plans have received at least one preventive service, such as an annual wellness visit at no out-of-pocket cost because of the healthcare law. Taken together, this means about 105 million Americans with private health plans and Medicare beneficiaries have already utilized the PPACA's prevention coverage improvements (USDHHS, March 2013b).

Notwithstanding newly legislated mandates and priorities, how future healthcare is actualized in practice will be influenced by

- advances in medical technology,
- availability of physicians and other providers,
- consumer changes (behavior/numbers), and
- an evolving "provider marketplace" resulting from reimbursement changes, increasing costs, capital access, greater provider competition, and changes in employee insurance (coverage) programs.

The Impact of Technology

Now more than 10 years into the new millennium, the healthcare delivery environment is already characterized by a spectacular array of expanding medical advances, particularly in the areas of preventive services, wellness, and interventions for chronic health conditions. These range from new developments in imaging, surgical procedures, and pharmacology to discoveries in genetic engineering and nanotechnology. **Genetic engineering** (Collins, n.d.) alters the DNA of a cell for purposes of research, manufacturing animal proteins, correcting genetic defects, or making improvements to plants and animals bred by humans. **Nanotechnology** involves the manipulation of matter on an atomic and molecular scale and may lead to advances including new drugs that could identify and incapacitate certain viruses or create molecular surgical tools guided by computers and injected into the blood stream that could find and destroy cancer cells or invade bacteria, unclog arteries, or provide oxygen when circulation is impaired.

Prompted in part by increased consumerism and a "patient-centric" approach in healthcare, the practice of **personalized medicine** will emerge, leading to the development of particular therapies for people with specific gene sequences and focusing on use of medicines and interventions that best meet individual genetic, lifestyle, and environmental differences. Using molecular tests to identify patients' susceptibility to disease will concentrate healthcare on preventive as opposed to disease-management strategies.

Other remarkable technological breakthroughs have led to wearable robots or mechanical exoskeletons already in development that enable people with spinal cord injuries to walk again and to IBM's "Watson" question-answering computer that is being transformed into a physician's smart assistant by being able to read and understand 200 million digital pages and deliver a suggestion, recommendation, or probability to a physician within 3 seconds (Lohr, 2012). It is also likely that the United States will track the Japanese government's lead in providing financial assistance to companies for the production of personalized care robots for the elderly to lower nursing home costs. To serve the elderly in nursing homes, four types of robots are being developed, including motorized robot suits that can lift or move non-ambulant people, ambulatory robots that can assist the elderly who have difficulty walking, self-cleaning robotic toilets, and monitoring robots to track wandering dementia patients (Japan Daily Press, 2013). The catalyst for this development in Japan is the same found in the United States: reduction of escalating healthcare costs and insufficient projected nursing care workforce. Japan anticipates a need for *4 million* such workers by 2025.

The $10 billion market in 2010 for home health monitoring devices is anticipated to grow about 26% annually with innovative technologies allowing caregivers of elderly patients to enlist the help of "digital pill boxes" that monitor whether necessary medications have been taken and home in on the exact location of the patient. While these devices are not yet available, they are not far off as Intel has already developed a personal telehealth "Health Guide" system, and GE is working on "Quiet Care," a remote monitoring system for people with disabilities and aging adults (Comstock, 2013). Technologies capturing body and procedural images for patient education contribute to better informed patient decision making and medical compliance (Collins, 2012). These technologies also allow data to be transmitted to health professionals for rapid analysis. One such application, "AirStrip," connects various hospital bedside devices — an EKG machine, a ventilator, or a fetal heart monitor, for example—to its server and then transmits the data to a smartphone or tablet. It can also transmit data from monitors in an ambulance to the emergency room, allowing a physician to be aware of patients' conditions via his own smartphone while preparing staff so that they are ready to treat patients as soon as they arrive at the hospital (Zimmerman, 2012).

The seemingly infinite promise of **bioinformatics** is increasingly evident in an array of technological advances that impact consumers' focus and behavior toward healthcare. In addition to engaging in healthier behaviors, including diet and exercise, technologically savvy consumers in unprecedented numbers are using blogs, Facebook, and Twitter along with e-mail and text messaging to obtain patient information and to answer health questions. In contrast to traditional sick care encounters, there is growing emphasis for patients and healthcare providers to be "partners" as they collaborate on both health and sickness. Wireless broadband has already been a game-changer in this regard, with wireless health portals allowing use of personalized bio-data templates to conveniently obtain real-time feedback and self-evaluation of select health status variables, including heart rates, blood pressure, electrocardiograms over extended periods of time, blood glucose, and weight. Such monitoring is achieved in part through the use of nearly 15,000 currently available mobile telephone applications. Cell phone systems allow clinicians to get timely data from patients using a familiar possession, respond in near real time, ask questions of patients, and alert physicians if warranted. In one medical group of 1,000 physicians serving 800,000 patients in northern California, Morrissey (2013) noted that 76% of the adult patient population signed up for Palo Alto's personal-health portal, including 71% of people in their 60s, 58% in their 70s, and 37% in their 80s.

The impacts of electronically monitoring patient health conditions can be significant. In a study cited by Morrissey (2014) of one health system's discharged congestive heart failure patients, patients who fed data back to a health system *in addition* to being followed by nurses had a readmission rate of 6.7%, whereas those who were contacted by visiting nurses alone had a readmission rate of 36.4%. Oss (2013a) cited a major Veterans Health Administration study that included 4 years of data on almost 17,000 patients in which the Care Coordination/Home Telehealth (CCHT) program utilized home telehealth technologies, gave required training to patients and caregivers, reviewed telehealth monitoring data, and provided active care or case management. Program outcomes included an average Medicaid savings for diabetes ($4,533,812), congestive heart failure ($7,243,184), chronic obstructive pulmonary disease ($4,286,265), and mental health ($547,722), totaling $16,610,984 (assuming average price of an inpatient stay of $20,858). The VHA also estimated potential annual savings of $379,873,488 based on the assumption of a 19% reduction in hospitalizations and that 60% of all Medicaid/Medicare readmissions were telehealth appropriate.

Evolving national healthcare policies and pursuit of enhanced business practices are prompting adoption of **electronic medical records (EMRs)** and **electronic health records (EHRs)**. These technologies further enhance the conveyance of continuously updated patient data between service providers. EMRs allow physicians to electronically maintain files of lab results, visit notes, diagnostic test results, insurance information, demographics, health histories, and other medication information within their offices, while EHRs facilitate the electronic exchange of EMRs between providers, thereby allowing the medical record to "follow" patients among providers (American Medical Association [AMA], n.d.). These systems aid physicians and other healthcare providers with managing scheduling, patient registration, health histories, insurance status, and medication lists. Professionals can electronically preview patients' medical histories, prescribe medication, order tests and labs, initiate billing, submit claims, and facilitate coding as well as electronically communicate with their consulting providers, payers, labs, and pharmacies. In some cases, patients may view their results through a patient portal (AMA, n.d.).

"Telemedicine" can be expected to evolve as a principal tool for cost-savings and as a demonstrated service delivery option when the availability of practitioners is limited, time is of the essence in decision making, and/or case complexity warrants greater professional input. The potential utility of telemedicine is particularly evident when considering mental healthcare. With nearly 80 million Americans already living in designated mental health professional shortage areas (Novotney, 2011), forecasts that *behavioral health disorders will surpass all physical diseases as a major cause of disability* (Bloch, 2011), a looming physician shortage, and legislated emphasis on coordinated multidisciplinary care, *telemental health* technologies are anticipated to expand significantly in the future. Telemental health systems use interactive telecommunication technologies to integrate comprehensive services within a specified region (Smith & Allison, 1998). Given evidence that differences between Internet-based therapy and face-to-face interventions are **not** statistically significant (Barak, Hen, Boniel-Nissim & Shapira, 2008), further deployment of telemental health services is inevitable.

Physician Services

Current problems in physician–patient communication are well known, including the use of incomprehensible medical "jargon," failure to fully share knowledge of medical conditions, and reliance on complex, impersonal telephone answering systems (Friedman, 2012). These communication barriers, along with physicians' historic reluctance to use e-mail communication with patients, are expected to be gradually overcome with the result being both *expedited personal health information transfer* between patients and physicians or other healthcare providers and *enhanced consumer knowledge* of health issues. Coupled with heightened personal interest in physical fitness, wellness, and preventive medicine, an increase in individual and high-deductible health plans will force consumers to be more active in their own healthcare. Sixty percent of U.S. adults report that they track their weight, diet, or exercise routine, and 33% track health indicators or symptoms such as blood pressure, blood sugar, headaches, or sleep patterns. Additionally, 46% of trackers state that this activity has changed their overall approach to maintaining their health or the health of someone for whom they are a caregiver. Forty percent say that tracking has led them to ask a physician new questions or to get a second opinion from another physician, while 34% indicate it has affected a decision about how to treat an illness or condition (Aegis Health Group, 2014).

With greater consumer involvement in healthcare decision making, physicians and other healthcare providers will be obligated to adapt to increasing demands for evidence-driven medicine by providing greater data and transparency. To improve patient–practitioner communication, recently introduced services provide contracting physicians with a suite of tools that enable the easy creation of a web site where patients can complete intake forms, schedule appointments, ask for weekly medication reminders, and track symptoms for chronic conditions. Patients and physicians decide together which metrics they will track—blood sugar, blood pressure, or frequency of asthma attacks, for example—and that information is shared (Zimmerman, 2012). Use of these services will expand as Tanner (2012) observed that "physicians are realizing that patients want more than a fifteen minute office visit and callback at the end of the day."

The future is likely to hold other changes for physician practices. Concerned with the prospect of decreased reimbursement rates versus steadily increasing practice costs,

Schimpff (2011) has forecast that more physicians *with financially established patients* will convert to "retainer-based" (or "concierge") practices, in which patients pay a flat fee each year, often $1500 to $2000, in return for their primary care physician (PCP) being available by cell phone at all times, being responsive to e-mail, and being capable of guaranteeing appointments within 24 hours. In this scenario, a physician would see you in the emergency room, attend to you during your hospitalization, and then do home or nursing home visits as needed at no extra charge. Patients, however, would still need insurance (and likely incur additional charges) should they require specialists, tests, or hospitalization.

Concern about reimbursement for patient care is already prompting disconcerting shifts of practice among physicians, with implications for the future accessibility of healthcare to those reliant on the two major public programs—Medicare and Medicaid. In 2012 alone, physician reimbursement was scheduled to be reduced by nearly 30% (Smith and Ricci, 2012). The growing disparity between Medicare and Medicaid and commercial rates is perceived as a threat to physician income, with Medicare payments averaging about 80% of private health insurance and Medicaid payments averaging 58%. The negative impact of this wide disparity in reimbursement is evident in a 2014 physician practice survey which showed that the rate of Medicare acceptance among physicians surveyed was considerably higher than the rate of Medicaid acceptance (45.7% Medicaid versus 76.0% Medicare) (Merritt Hawkins, 2014). The implication is that physician access becomes much more difficult for patients obligated to rely principally on Medicaid as their source of healthcare coverage. Concern over decreasing physician availability will undoubtedly trigger political debate regarding overall spending, particularly in light of the existing national deficit.

Changes in Consumer Behavior

There is increasing evidence of changes in consumer behavior as it relates to their personal health. These changes in turn impact the frequency and nature of healthcare utilization. Fundamental to a shift toward healthy behavior is a growing confidence among older Americans that they can maintain a high quality of life throughout their senior years (National Council on Aging [NCOA], 2014). The 2014 United States of Aging Survey, conducted under the partial auspices of the NCOA (2014), found that 85% of sampled seniors 60 years of age and older believed that they were prepared for any health changes as they age. Bolstering their confidence about their health in future years, survey findings noted that seniors are taking more proactive steps to improve their health, with 53% indicating that they set health goals in 2014, such as eating better, losing weight, and increasing their exercise. More than one-third of seniors (37%) said that they exercise every day, compared with 26% in 2013, and 39% said they rely on themselves for the motivation to live a healthy lifestyle (NCOA, 2014). Those who set health goals were found to be more than twice as likely to think that their overall quality of life will improve compared with those who did not set health goals (38% vs. 16%) and were found to be more than three times as likely to be confident that their health will be better in future years (28% vs. 9%). The top three health goals set by seniors this year are eating healthier (37%), losing weight (30%), and living a more physically active lifestyle (24%).

The NCOA study revealed that the top services anticipated to be needed by an aging population include home maintenance, transportation, and long-term care. These services are significant given that 77% of those sampled indicated that they intended to remain in their current homes for the rest of their lives and over half stated they would prefer to live independently for as long as possible. The clear implication for the future is that community services will need to be enhanced to meet looming needs. Only 48% of those 60 to 64 years of age believed that their communities were sufficiently addressing senior care needs (NCOA, 2014, pp. 2–3). Reconceptualized health and social service delivery systems will need to be implemented to meet these burgeoning needs. One important implication is that demand for the services of care providers and health professionals will correspondingly increase.

The Advent of Integrated Care

As previously noted, the Patient Protection and Affordable Care Act of 2010 is providing a major impetus for change in healthcare service delivery. Reflecting the move to personalized medicine, attention will be on the individual patient and his or her unique needs while efforts are made to constrain service delivery costs through the efficient and timely (early) use of only needed health resources. Here, the focus on wellness and prevention in particular can be efficiently addressed through *primary care*. As defined by the Institute of Medicine (IOM) (1996), primary care is . . . the provision of integrated, accessible healthcare services by clinicians who are accountable for addressing a large majority of personal healthcare needs, developing a sustained partnership with patients, and practicing in the context of family and community." (p. 31) "**Integrated**" refers to "the provision of comprehensive, coordinated, and continuous services that provides a seamless process of care" (IOM, 1996, p. 32). Simultaneous to the emphasis on primary care is that on patient-centered care. **Patient-centered care** establishes a partnership among practitioners, patients, and their families (when appropriate) to ensure that decisions respect patients' wants, needs, and preferences and that patients have the education and support that they need to make decisions and participate in their own care (IOM, 2001, p. 3).

Consistent with patient-centered care, the pursuit of cost accountability and enhanced quality, the future is destined to feature greater emphasis on **transdisciplinary research** in public/private partnerships involving advocates, social scientists, and "hard" scientists as well as other stakeholders in coalitions to work on basic and applied research for the public good (Coalition for Health Communication, 2010). Exemplifying this trend, the PPACA establishes a non-profit *Patient-Centered Outcomes Research Institute* to identify research priorities and to conduct research comparing the clinical effectiveness of medical treatments. With one in four Americans having *multiple* chronic health conditions, attention will increasingly be directed toward the growing prevalence of diseases such as diabetes, cancer, asthma, substance abuse, heart disease, obesity (defined as a body mass indexes of over 25), Alzheimer's disease, and musculoskeletal disorders. These conditions profoundly impact individual lifestyles of our aging population while posing significant cost burdens to patients, families, and the nation as a whole. To focus attention on this issue, the PPACA makes provision for the Centers for Disease Control to confer grants to states and large local health departments to conduct pilot programs in the 55- to 64-year-old population to evaluate chronic disease risk factors, conduct evidence-based public health interventions, and ensure that individuals who are identified with chronic disease or who are at risk for chronic disease receive clinical treatment to reduce risk.

Federal emphasis will increasingly focus on systems integration, a broader span of proprietary and community providers, an emphasis on least-intrusively delivered services, and decreased inpatient care. The primary delivery mechanism will be not only the much-heralded Accountable Care Organizations (ACOs) (as discussed in Chapter 2) but also the expanded use of existing **Federally Qualified Health Centers (FQHCs).** FQHC designation from the Bureau of Primary Healthcare and the Centers for Medicare and Medicaid Services is conferred to nonprofit public or private clinics located in medically underserved areas or who provide care to medically underserved populations. FQHCs must provide a detailed scope of primary healthcare as well as supportive services to all patients, regardless of their ability to pay. They must be governed by boards primarily composed of local community members. The concept is for states to foster connections between FQHCs and other private primary care providers, thereby connecting Medicaid beneficiaries with services needed to help them manage their health and reducing costly visits to hospitals. At the same time, by entering into collaborative relationships with states and private practices, FQHCs should be able to strengthen their own financial position, advance their quality goals, improve their staffing mix, enhance the continuum of care and the kinds of services available to their patients, and further their mission.

Looming on the healthcare delivery horizon is the **backward (reverse) integration** of insurers with service providers (Oss, 2013b). Previous efforts in **forward integration,** including creation of managed care entities, risk-based contracts, and other mechanisms to control healthcare spending have had mixed results, with some successes and many failures. ACOs are the most recent examples of forward integration as they are essentially payer-like collaborations of providers that manage health insurance dollars. In comparison, reverse integration can be illustrated in the 2013 acquisition of the West Penn Allegheny Health System by the insurer Highmark. In this case, the insurer will offer a preferred (less costly) plan to its 3 million subscribers if they use the services the insurer now acquired. The integration was triggered by competition in the same market with the University of Pittsburgh Medical Center, which operates 19 hospitals and its own 1 million-plus subscriber health plan. In 2010, Humana, one of the largest health insurers in the United States, bought Concentra, a privately held healthcare company with 300 medical centers in the United States. Legislative changes and other constraints that increasingly limit profits on the health insurance side are prompting these acquisitions in an effort to explore generating profits on the delivery side.

One intriguing example of backward integration, dubbed "Oscar," is unfolding in New York State. Focusing on function, ease of use, and design, Oscar seeks to redesign insurance by making consumers seek out their healthcare insurers *before* their physicians (Fisher and Liebman, 2013). It expands the role of the health insurance company to one of physical, mental, and behavior healthcare provider, not only covering costs but also serving as the primary place to obtain medical care at any time. While continuing to utilize copays and deductibles for patient visits, Oscar will feature free telemedicine with 24/7 access to physicians, free generic pharmaceuticals, and online price comparisons. Subscribers will be *paid* to answer questions about their health and care preferences, information that will then be used to develop individualized, proactive healthcare plans. In contrast to the prevalent practice of discussing prescription refills in person with physicians, subscribers will have "one-click refills" using a health records feed similar to a "Twitter" timeline. With 83 affiliated hospitals in New York, Oscar is designed to make the telehealth-to-in-person relationship seamless. Further, in the spirit of transparency promoted by the Patient Protection and Affordable Care Act, Oscar subscribers will be able to look up and compare prices of physicians and healthcare services.

Offering yet another example of the impact that changing reimbursement patterns have on shaping an integrated service delivery system, increasing numbers of physicians dissatisfied with their private practice income are selling or otherwise disengaging from sole ownership of those practices and becoming employees of larger provider systems. For the physician, such a shift not only affords a dependable salary but also removes the frustration and cost of service billing and other operating overhead while offering the prospect of defined working hours. At the same time, hospitals are encouraging this trend as it not only bolsters their ability to control the entirety of patients' healthcare needs but also lends itself to better containment of service delivery costs. Realizing mutual benefits, physicians and healthcare providers have now partnered to form 106 of the 250 ACOs in Medicare (USDHHS, January 2013a).

ON THE HEALTHCARE SOCIAL WORK PRACTICE HORIZON

To forecast the future of social work practice in healthcare, one needs to consider (1) those populations likely to be in highest need of health services by virtue of sheer numbers, life impacts, and/or projected healthcare cost, (2) initiatives prompted by legislation, technology, and service delivery issues in healthcare provider systems, (3) evolving trends such as consumerism, focus on healthy lifestyles, and the corporatization of healthcare services, and (4) the strengths of the profession itself. For social work, the critical issue is where the profession can be best applied to (1) positively impact on individual quality of life, (2) enhance the effectiveness and efficiency of healthcare service delivery efforts, and, in so, doing (3) contribute to both overall public health and cost containment (Spitzer and Davidson, 2013).

Evolving Environment; Evolving Opportunity

Overall employment of social workers is expected to grow by 25% from 2010 to 2020, nearly TWICE as fast as the average for all occupations (Bureau of Labor Statistics [BLS], 2013). Increasing demand for healthcare services and practitioner shortages afford significant future opportunities for social work. Growth in healthcare practice is projected as being the greatest of all social work fields, increasing 34% (with more than 51,000 anticipated new positions) from 2010 to 2020. The largest predicted increases in social work employment are in ambulatory healthcare services (health practitioner offices, outpatient care centers, and home healthcare services), social assistance (individual and family services agencies, community services, vocational rehabilitation, and child day-care services), and nursing, residential, and community care facilities for the elderly (USDHHS, 2006).

An aging American population and the heightened care needs among the elderly will particularly affect demand for social work services. Chronic diseases will be a priority focus of future healthcare delivery as they account for 70% of all deaths in the United States (Centers for Disease Control and Prevention, 2012) and over 75% of national health expenditures. Nearly two of three members of our aging population (65 years of age or older) are affected by chronic diseases. Crucial in future service delivery will be coordinated interventions (including social work) that effectively integrate acute care (hospital), nursing home, inpatient rehabilitation hospital, long-term acute care hospital (LTAC), ambulatory care, assisted living community, and home care settings as a means of concurrently addressing physical and psychosocial patient care. Given the prospect of increasing demand for senior housing and services, abundant calls have already appeared for ramped-up social services in the long-term-care arena (Dziegielewski, 1998; Michelsen, 1989; Butler, 2002; Feinberg, 2002; Franks, 2002; Harrington, 1999; Williams, 2002; Spitzer, Neuman, & Holden, 2004; Stahlman & Kisor, 2000; Dhooper, 1997).

Emphasizing service integration and primary care, the Patient Protection and Affordable Care Act promotes use of patient-centered "**health homes**" and home health services in particular to address chronic health concerns prevalent among the increasing numbers of elderly. Health homes are defined (PPACA [HR3590] §2703) as a designated provider operating in coordination with a team of healthcare providers or a health team selected by individuals with chronic conditions to provide home health services. Health homes represent a strategy for helping these individuals better manage their chronic health conditions and characteristically feature comprehensive care management, care coordination and health promotion, comprehensive transitional care from inpatient to other settings, patient and family support, referral to community and social support services, and use of health information technology (HIT) to link services as feasible and appropriate (Paradise & Nardone, 2014).

The homes become responsible for managing and coordinating all the health services that a patient receives from multiple providers, help to promote good health, and offer support to patients and families, including referrals to community and support services. Along with enhancing the health of the individual patient, overall cost savings derived from health home use can be significant. Using the state of Rhode Island as an illustration, Oss (2014) cited statistics that health homes have produced a reduction in that state's hospital spending such that from 2010 through 2013, inpatient and residential expenses fell from $22.1 million per year to $14.8 million per year and the average length-of-stay (LOS) dropped from 12.4 days in 2010 to 6.85 days in 2013. In a recent 50-state survey of Medicaid directors conducted by the Kaiser Commission on Medicaid and the Uninsured, 21 states indicated that they planned to adopt or expand their use of health homes, evidence of the popularity of this new state plan option with enhanced federal financing (Paradise & Nardone, 2014).

Significantly, as defined in the PPACA, the term "team of healthcare professionals" may include "physicians and other professionals such as a *social worker*." Of note, the interventions specified for delivery in health home context are consistent with the activities and functions that have traditionally characterized social work healthcare practice: "comprehensive care management; care coordination and health promotion; comprehensive transitional care (including follow-up from inpatient to other settings); patient and family support; and referral to community and support services" (PPACA HR3590–203/204). The PPACA's emphasis on cost control and community care may well serve to highlight social work's brokerage role.

Changes in the availability of crucial healthcare personnel will impact on how services will be delivered and by whom. The Association of American Medicine Colleges (AAMC) cites U.S. Department of Health and Human Services estimates that the physician supply will increase by only 7% in the next ten years. In some specialties, including urology and thoracic surgery, the overall supply of physicians will actually *decrease*. At the same time, the Census Bureau projects a 36% growth in the number of Americans over the age of 65 years, *the very segment of the population with the greatest healthcare needs*. Further, the PPACA was expected to make health insurance coverage available to more than 30 million previously uninsured Americans by 2014. As a result, by 2020, a serious shortage will exist of both primary care and specialist physicians to care for an aging and growing population. The AAMC's Center for Workforce Studies determined that there will be 45,000 too few primary care physicians and a shortage of 46,000 surgeons and medical specialists by the year 2020 (*Table 16.1*). Existing physicians are also aging, with nearly one-third of all physicians anticipated to retire in the next decade, just as more Americans seek their expertise for care (AAMC, 2010).

Schimpff (2011) noted that the anticipated shortages of physicians will necessarily mean more reliance on others to deliver crucial healthcare services. He stated these professionals are likely to include nurse practitioners and physician's assistants for primary care, *social workers,* and psychologists for mental healthcare, and optometrists for vision

Table 16.1   Projected Supply/Demand-Full-time Equivalent Physicians Active in Patient Care Post Healthcare Reform, 2008–2025

Year	Physician Supply (All Specialties)	Physician Demand (All Specialties)	Physician Shortage (All Specialties*)	Physician Shortage (Non-Primary Care Specialties)
2008	699,100	706,500	7,400	None
2010	709,700	723,400	13,700	4,700
2015	735,600	798,500	62,900	33,100
2020	759,800	851,300	91,500	46,100
2025	785,400	916,000	130,600	64,800

Source: Association of American Medical Colleges, 2010. *Total includes primary care, surgical, and medical specialties. (See https://www.aamc.org/download/158076/data/updated_projections_through_2025.pdf)

care. With the advent of these specialized practitioners, physicians will need to change their attitudes to the extent of involving them more in care decisions and embracing their full value to the care team. While the prospect for broadened and more visible social work deployment is enticing, new challenges will be present within these relationships as each of the disciplines will need to demonstrate even greater collaboration and coordination in practice.

Regardless of the legislative climate and political administration, the emphasis on collaboration, coordination, and use of professionals beyond physicians will undoubtedly continue. As one illustration, Oregon created *Coordinated Care Organizations* (CCOs) for individuals covered under the Oregon Health Plan (Medicaid). The Oregon Health Policy Board (http://www.oregon.gov/oha/ohpb/pages/health-reform/ccos.aspx) defines CCOs as networks of healthcare providers that will have the flexibility to support new models of care that are patient centered and team focused and that will reduce health disparities. CCOs prioritize working with individuals with high healthcare needs, multiple chronic conditions, mental illness, or chemical dependency. They involve those members in accessing and managing appropriate preventive, health, remedial, and supportive care and services to reduce the use of avoidable emergency room visits and hospital admissions. The unfolding opportunity for social work lies in its intent to have patients receive assistance in navigating the healthcare delivery system and in accessing community and social support services by using community health workers and personal health navigators whose defined competency standards include those already established by the State Board of Licensed Social Workers (see http://www.oregonlaws.org/ors/414.665).

Another venue for amplified engagement of social work services exists in the context of inpatient care, particularly driven by increased numbers of patients with complex health conditions. While much of the future attention on wellness and preventive services corresponds to primary care that is often delivered in outpatient settings, more serious illnesses will translate into a need for more hospitals, more beds (especially intensive care unit [ICU] beds), and more operating rooms with highly sophisticated technologies. Schimpff (2011) observed that this marks a departure from recent decades, when the mantra has been "too many hospitals and too many beds." He projected that as smaller hospitals have difficulty accessing the credit markets to finance expensive technology and facilities, the result will be a wave of hospital mergers and fewer stand-alone hospitals.

The implications for the individual healthcare social worker of the PPACA-prompted service delivery changes are many and significant. The emphasis on prevention and primary care comes with greater acknowledgement of the social determinants of health and healthcare use. As such, social workers will need to accurately screen and respond to such variables. They will need to adopt evidence-based interventions for disease management that minimize the effects and cost of chronic illnesses. With the focus on patient independence (and reduced use of high-cost service options), home-based primary care teams will assume greater significance in care delivery. With more serious illnesses being treated in the hospitals and the prospect of more beds being made available comes the challenge to social work (and other practitioners) of dealing with higher caseloads, making faster assessments, and being more expedient by being more accurate in care planning.

Patient Care Planning

Patients with more serious illnesses predictably have more extensive post-hospital care needs, with the result that discharge planning correspondingly becomes more complex. In 2012, the Department of Health and Human Services authorized a demonstration project under Title XIX of the Social Security Act to evaluate integrated care around hospitalization. Project requirements stipulate that "hospitals participating in the demonstration project shall have or establish *robust discharge planning programs* to ensure that Medicaid beneficiaries requiring post-acute care are appropriately placed in, or have ready access to, post-acute care settings (HR3590–205, Section 2704, (a)(5); see http://democrats.senate.gov/pdfs/reform/patient-protection-affordable-care-act-as-passed.pdf). Consistent with other recent initiatives, the intent behind calling for "robust discharge planning programs" is a desire to engage the patient, family, and involved healthcare professionals in a collaborative effort to identify the most therapeutically appropriate *and* economical post-discharge care options and then actualize an efficient, expedient, safe movement of the patient to such settings from the hospital. Patient education and information and referral will become increasingly important. Along with the ready availability of community-based health and social support services, patients' awareness of their health conditions, ongoing care needs, and the implications arising from their compliance with medical advice are implicit to the success of these discharge planning efforts.

At the federal level, in 2010, the Department of Health and Human Services announced that it was funding nearly $4 million in grants for Patient Navigator Outreach and Chronic Disease Prevention Programs to develop and operate **patient navigator services** that improve healthcare outcomes for individuals with cancer or other chronic diseases, with specific emphasis on health disparity populations. On June 6, 2014, the Centers for Medicare and Medicaid Services (CMS) announced the availability of funding totaling $60 million to support Navigators in Federally-facilitated and State Partnership Marketplaces in 2014–2015. Such initiatives reflect the increasing importance attached to expediently bringing to bear any and all existing system resources to resolve patient-care needs. Importantly, they underscore activities entirely consistent with the historic, central role of healthcare social work services in "boundary spanning," "resource brokering," and serving as both care coordinator and patient advocate.

The term *navigator* refers to individuals who are employed by Assistance Programs that contract directly with the CMS to provide free outreach and enrollment assistance services to consumers in Federally-facilitated Marketplace (FFM) and in Consumer Assistance Partnership Marketplaces (FPM) states (Pollitz, Tolbert, & Ma, 2014). Navigators provide unbiased information to consumers about health insurance, the Health Insurance Marketplace, qualified health plans, and public programs, including Medicaid and the Children's Health Insurance Program. Under the PPACA, navigators must conduct public education and outreach, help consumers apply for subsidies, facilitate enrollment in qualified health plans (QHPs), and provide consumers with fair and impartial information about their QHP options. In addition, navigators must refer consumers to applicable state ombudsman or Consumer Assistance Programs (CAPs) for help with any grievance, complaint, or question about coverage once enrolled. Navigator program grant recipients recruit, train, and employ patient navigators with direct knowledge of the communities they serve to coordinate care for patients with chronic illnesses. Eligible applicants included federally qualified health centers, health facilities operated through Indian Health Service contracts, hospitals, rural health clinics, and academic health centers . All state marketplaces are required to have navigators and other similar Assister Programs to help consumers understand their coverage options, apply for assistance, and enroll (Pollitz, Tolbert, & Ma, 2014).

Based on findings from the April–May 2014 Kaiser Family Foundation survey of Health Insurance Marketplace Assister Programs, more than 4,400 Assister Programs, employing more than 28,000 full-time-equivalent staff and volunteers, helped an estimated 10.6 million people during the first open enrollment period (Pollitz, Tolbert & Ma, 2014). Certified Application Counselor (CAC) Programs, which generally receive no marketplace funding, and programs sponsored by federal health centers funded by grants from the Health Resources and Services Administration (HRSA), together represent 71% of all Assister Programs and account for more than 60% of people who received help.

Over 80% of Assister Programs reported that most or nearly all consumers who sought help did not understand the PPACA or the coverage choices offered them or simply lacked confidence to apply on their own. Almost 90% of programs reported that the majority of consumers whom they helped were uninsured. Prior to the first open enrollment, 30% of Assister Programs had no prior experience helping consumers and just 16% had experience helping consumers enroll in private health plans. Because so many Assister Programs expect to continue operating, the level of experience will likely increase going forward. If marketplaces continue to invest in resources to support Assister Programs, it is projected that a profession of expert Assisters could develop who understand consumer needs and how PPACA rules and coverage options apply to them (Pollitz, Tolbert, & Ma, 2014). The opportunities for social work are apparent.

Behavioral Healthcare

In 2014, nearly 1,300 health centers operated more than 9,200 service delivery sites that provided care to over 21.7 million patients in every state, the District of Columbia, Puerto Rico, the U.S. Virgin Islands, and the Pacific Basin. In 2013, health centers saw over 1.2 million behavioral health patients (USDHHS, July 2014). Recognition of the escalating need for behavioral healthcare services contributed to an additional $55 million in Affordable Care act funding being provided in July 2014 to establish or expand such services for over 450,000 people nationwide (USDHHS, July 2014). The funding is expressly intended to facilitate hiring of new mental health professionals, adding mental health and substance use health services, and employing integrated models of primary care.

The Health Resources and Services Administration (HRSA) reported that, as of June 2014, nearly a third of the American population (96 million people) were living in areas with reported shortages of behavioral health care professionals, including social workers (HRSA, 2014). The National Alliance on Mental Illness reports that *more than half* of all U.S. rural counties have *NO* practicing psychiatrists, psychologists, or social workers (Butcher, 2012). With the treatment capacity for behavioral services in critically short supply, telemedicine is becoming an increasingly attractive, cost-effective option for enhancing patient access to mental health services. The introduction of new technologies will alter the traditional manner of service delivery and provider roles, including social work. To illustrate, Butcher (2012) noted the successful telemedicine project launched by South Carolina, in which more than 9,700 tele-psychiatric consults occurred via videoconferencing available around-the-clock in hospital emergency departments. One major impact was to address the widespread problem of psychiatric patients who were boarded in emergency departments while difficult-to-locate inpatient beds were sought. Using telemedicine, patients can be connected quickly to a psychiatrist for a visit that typically lasts 30 to 45 minutes. After the session, the clinician electronically transmits notes about the diagnosis and a signed consultation recommendation to the emergency department physician, allowing the patient to be discharged, admitted to an inpatient bed, or transferred to another facility. The Veterans Affairs Department anticipated conducting more than 200,000 telemental consultations in 2012, up 30% from 140,000 in fiscal 2011 (Brewin, 2012). Recent research has revealed that the use of technology decreased psychiatric hospital admissions of VA mental health patients by 25% (Godleski, Darkins, & Peters, 2012).

Increased use of telemental health practices directly with patients will require social workers and other interventionists to revisit long-held beliefs about client-practitioner interaction, including the manner and context of such contact. Practitioners may have to relinquish their insistence on face-to-face sessions in deference to recognizing that some clients may be unable to participate due to distance, lack of transportation, or the urgency of the presenting situation. The practitioners' apprehension about relying on these evolving therapeutic mediums may be diminished with research findings that differences between Internet-based therapy and face-to-face interventions have been determined to not be statistically significant (Barak Hen, Boniel-Nissim, & Shapira, 2008).

At the same time that telemedicine represents a less expensive and more expedient intervention, it also enhances the prospect that a practitioner may be able to effectively reach more clients with ease, thereby enhancing overall access. The prospect of clients comfortably using such technologies may be seen in the dramatic popularity of electronic mediums like Facebook, Twitter, and Skype. If anything, there may be a curious paradox that, because of the extensive use of these indirect communication mediums, therapeutic intervention may need to increasingly be focused on how to *re*-establish client competency in *direct* interpersonal communication. Two considerations requiring further attention include effectively ensuring communication confidentiality and addressing licensing issues that arise from practitioners interacting with patients across state lines.

Whether one looks at the direction of healthcare policy as affected by current and proposed legislation, rapidly evolving healthcare technologies, and/or the new concepts of healthcare service delivery, the future holds promise for the creative use of social work. The three-stage challenge is one of determining which dimensions of the profession are congruent with the unfolding healthcare directions, generating increased interest in healthcare practice, and then providing a sufficient supply of skilled practitioners. With employment opportunities for future social work practitioners expected to grow by 25% overall and 34% specifically within health care (BLS, 2013) such remarkable growth is, however, proving to be a challenge for the profession. This is particularly true in senior services. Notwithstanding the expansive growth in the numbers of older Americans, social workers identifying health or aging as their primary practice areas currently account for less than a quarter of all practicing social workers; only 12% report that they are practicing in either an inpatient or outpatient health setting (Whitaker & Arrington, 2008). Not only is this number insufficient to address needs, in 2012, only 25% of Council on Social Work Education

(CSWE)-approved MSW programs offered healthcare as a field of practice and only a third of the schools offered aging/gerontology as practice field (CSWE, 2012). As a consequence, only 2,225 MSW candidates, or a combined 8.9% of all MSW students, were enrolled in these practice areas—a number that *dropped* from 11.1% in 2011 (CSWE, 2012, 2011). The number of students self-identified as concentrating in "health and mental health" also declined from 7.2% to 5.5% (CSWE, 2012, 2011). Impacting these circumstances will be the efforts of the National Association of Deans and Directors of Schools of Social Work (NADD), in conjunction with CSWE, in producing research-informed curriculum on competencies and promoting the roles of social work in integrated behavioral health and primary care settings. With funding from the SAMHSA- and HRSA-funded Center for Integrated Health Solutions, the intent is creation of master's-level curriculum materials for courses in advanced clinical practice, policy, and services (Spitzer & Davidson, 2013).

As Taylor (1992) emphasized, the value of social work is reflected in its empowering of patients, in balancing financial costs with psychosocial costs as it assists patients negotiate systems, and, ultimately, in contributing to the creation of caring communities (pp. 662–664). The knowledge, skills, and abilities that characterize the social work profession are precisely those that are called for in the future healthcare environment and include

1. an understanding of human dynamics that can be utilized in analyzing the extent to which patients are leading healthy (or unhealthy) lives, the factors influencing such behavior, and how patients are or are not appropriately using healthcare services;

2. ethical sensitivity and commitment to social justice in putting forward patient and family issues, needs, and concerns regarding their health and healthcare;

3. familiarity with healthcare provider systems such that social workers can effectively juxtapose advocacy for services responsive to patient/family healthcare needs with their recognition of the philosophic and/or pragmatic constraints of provider organizations;

4. commitment to advocating for the needs of patients (and on an extended basis, families and communities) as they attempt to access and utilize needed healthcare services;

5. foresight, ingenuity, and a sense of drive in exploring how existing resources may be maximized for needy patient populations or developed in their absence;

6. technical skill to competently ameliorate the psychosocial dynamics associated with being ill, injured, or disabled and patient/family secondary adjustments to hospitalization and/or other medical interventions;

7. extensive experience in collaboration, service coordination, and teamwork designed to expedite efficient, effective healthcare delivery;

8. demonstrated leadership of healthcare programs based on successful outcomes, including optimal patient health and fiscal responsibility in operations;

9. capacity to energize communities to identify and address unfolding health and healthcare needs with the goal of actualizing user-friendly provider response systems; and

10. sustained contribution both to the intervention literature, thereby promoting use of "best practices", and to advancing legislation focused on health promotion and timely, effective provider response to patient/community need.

ENVISIONING THE FUTURE

Based on the past and present, we may look to the future as having potential for even greater utilization of the social work profession and engagement of intervention modalities that even more efficiently and effectively address patient needs. We have seen that the future is filled with seemingly unending technological advances that hold the promise of enhancing public health. At the same time, there are fundamentally unresolved issues as to how health should be addressed as public policy, including whether there is an American "right" to health and the extent to which support of public health and intervention for needed healthcare should be legislated and budgeted.

We have further seen an evolution in social work practice that has both reflected and impacted changes in the healthcare delivery system. Patient care interventions have shifted to embrace new technologies, delivery priorities, and consumer needs and preferences. What has *not* changed over the years is the fundamental commitment to the core values of social work, although it would appear that the future may afford ample challenge to those values. It will be the strength of the profession and the individual commitment of its practitioners that will determine the leadership role the profession will hold in effecting constructive change in the next decades and beyond. The future is exciting, and the opportunities are there. It is our professional responsibility to anticipate and rise to the challenge.

KEY TERMS AND CONCEPTS

- Genetic engineering
- Nanotechnology
- Personalized medicine
- Bioinformatics
- Telemedicine
- "value approach" to healthcare
- Transdisciplinary research/practice
- Accountable Care Organizations (ACOs)
- Health homes
- Federally Qualified Health Centers (FQHCs)

- Physician shortage
- Patient navigator services
- "Forward" and "reverse" integration

QUESTIONS FOR DISCUSSION

1. How would you develop public health policy balancing patient access, equitability, and cost of service for development (research) and implementation?

2. What do you perceive as the primary factors likely to influence the shape of future healthcare services? What would be the priority services and why?

3. How would you envision social work services in future healthcare environments? What are the drivers determining the configuration of these services? What would be the range of needs and what would characterize social work intervention? What efforts might be necessary to introduce social work services into these situations?

EXERCISES

1. Contact a legislator in your area and seek out his or her perspective on the principal issues in providing healthcare services. What are the primary factors being considered in promoting legislation? Pay attention to access, equality, and cost.

2. Interview a healthcare administrator and invite him or her to comment on the directions of health services in your community and those factors driving the program planning for specific healthcare provider organizations.

3. Compare the formal policy statements of the national and state political parties on the issue of healthcare, especially in terms of access, equality, and cost. Consider how these differ and their potential short- and long-range impacts on consumer populations.

4. Analyze and contrast the social work services presently available in healthcare settings compared with your identification of existing consumer needs. What steps, if any, would you take to implement cost-efficient responses to those needs?

REFERENCES

Aegis Health Group (2014). *Population health 2.0: The age of the consumer.* Thought Paper Series, Volume 6, Issue No. 1. Brentwood, TN: Author.

American Medical Association. (n.d.). *Electronic Medical Records and Electronic Health Records.* Retrieved from http://www.ama-assn.org/ama/pub/physician-resources/health-information-technology/health-it-basics/emrs-ehrs.page?

Association of American Medical Colleges (AAMC). (June 2010). *The impact of health care reform on the future supply and demand for physicians: Updated projections through 2025.* Retrieved from https://www.aamc.org/download/158076/data/updated_projections_through_2025.pdf

Barak, A., Hen, L., Boniel-Nissim, M., & Shapira, N. (2008). A comprehensive review and a meta-analysis of the effectiveness of internet-based psychotherapeutic interventions. *Journal of Technology in Human Services, 26,* 109–160.

Bloch, C. (2011). *Addressing behavioral health.* Retrieved from http://telemedicinenews.blogspot.com/2011/04/addressing-behavioral-health.html

Brewin, B. (2012). VA to boost telemental health services by 30% this year. *Nextgov Newsletter,* June 20, 2012. Retrieved from http://www.nextgov.com/emerging-tech/2012/06/va-boost-telemental-health-services-30-percent-year/56385/

Bureau of Labor Statistics, U.S. Department of Labor. (2013). *Occupational outlook handbook 2012-13 edition.* Retrieved from http://www.bls.gov/ooh/community-and-social-service/social-workers.htm

Butcher, L. (2012). The mental health crisis. *Hospitals and health networks, May 2012.* Retrieved from *http://www.hhnmag.com/hhnmag_app/jsp/articledisplay.jsp?dcrpath = HHNMAG/Article/data/05MAY2012/0512HHN_Coverstory&domain = HHNMAG* http://www.hhnmag.com/display/HHN-news-article.dhtml?dcrPath = /templatedata/HF_Common/NewsArticle/data/HHN/Magazine/2012/May/0512HHN_Coverstory

Butler, S. (2002). The case for assisted living. *Social Work Today,* 2,7,5,21

Camillo, C. (2013). *Implementing eligibility changes under the Affordable Care Act: Issues facing state Medicaid and CHIP programs.* Retrieved from http://www.mathematica-mpr.com/publications/PDFs/health/eligibilitychangesstateissues_brief1.pdf

Centers for Disease Control and Prevention. (2011). Rising health care costs are unsustainable. Retrieved from http://www.cdc.gov/workplacehealthpromotion/businesscase/reasons/rising.html

Centers for Disease Control and Prevention. (2012). *Chronic disease prevention and health promotion.* Retrieved from http://www.cdc.gov/chronicdisease/index.htm

Coalition for Health Communication. (2010). *Future directions of health communication.* Retrieved from http://www.healthcommunication.net/CHC/research/future.htm

Collins, F. (2012). The real promise of mobile health apps. *Scientific American,* July 10, 2012. Retrieved 7/12/12 from http://www.scientificamerican.com/article.cfm?id = real-promise-mobile-health-apps

Collins. (n.d.). Genetic engineering. *Collins English dictionary—complete & unabridged* (10th ed.). Retrieved from Dictionary.com website: http://dictionary.reference.com/browse/genetic engineering

Comstock, J. (2013). Intel-GE's Care Innovations gets 510(k) for QuietCare. Retrieved from http://mobihealthnews.com/27024/intel-ges-care-innovations-gets-510k-for-quietcare/

Council of Economic Advisors. (2014). *Missed opportunities: The experiences of state decisions not to expand Medicaid.* Washington, DC: Author.

Council on Social Work Education (CSWE). (2011). 2011 *statistics on social work education in the United States.* Retrieved from http://www.cswe.org/File.aspx?id = 62011

Council on Social Work Education (CSWE). (2012). *2012 statistics on social work education in the United States.* Retrieved from http://www.cswe.org/File.aspx?id = 68977

Dhooper, S. (1997). *Social work in health care in the 21st century.* Thousand Oaks, CA: SAGE.

Dziegielewski, S. (1998). *The changing face of health care social work: Professional practice in an era of managed care.* New York: Springer Publishing Company.

Feinberg, R. (2002). The increasing need for social workers in assisted living. *Journal of Social Work in Long Term Care, 1*(3), 9–12.

Fisher, N., & Liebman, S. (2013). Say hi to Oscar: The new kid that may change health insurance. *Forbes Magazine* Retrieved from http://www.forbes.com/sites/theapothecary/2013/08/19/say-hi-to-oscar-the-new-kid-that-may-change-health-insurance/

Fishman, L., & Bentley, J. (1997). The evolution of support for safety-net hospitals. *Health Affairs, 16*(4): 30–47.

Franks, J. (2002). Social workers need to know more about assisted living and vice versa. *The Journal of Social Work in Long Term Care, 1*(3), 13–15.

Friedman, E. (2012). The sounds of silence: Are patients getting the information they need? *Hospitals and Health Networks.* Retrieved from http://www.hhnmag.com/hhnmag/HHNDaily/HHNDailyDisplay.dhtml?id = 9760001275

Glied, S., & Ma, S. (2013). *How states stand to gain or lose federal funds by opting out of the Medicaid expansion.* Washington, DC: The Commonwealth Fund.

Godleski, L., Darkins, A., & Peters, J. (2012). Outcomes of 98,609 U.S. Department of Veterans Affairs patients enrolled in telemental health services, 2006–2010. *Psychiatric Services*; doi:10.1176/appi.ps.201100206.

Harrington, D. (1999). New horizons for social work: Assisted living. *Social Work Leader, 25*(7), 1, 3-4.

Health Resources and Services Administration (HRSA). (2014). Data Ware House Shortage Area Summaries, Designated Health Professional Shortage Area Statistics, August 2014. See: http://datawarehouse.hrsa.gov/topics/shortageareas.aspx.

Holahan, J., Buettgens, M., Carroll, C., & Dorn, S. (2012). *The cost and coverage implications of the ACA Medicaid expansion: National and state-by-state analysis.* Washington, DC: The Kaiser Commission on Medicaid and the Uninsured.

Holahan, J., Buettgens, M., & Dorn, S. (2013). *The cost of not expanding Medicaid.* Retrieved from http://kff.org/medicaid/report/the-cost-of-not-expanding-medicaid/

Institute of Medicine of the National Academies. (1996). *Primary care: America's health in a new era.* Retrieved from http://www.nap.edu/openbook.php?record_id = 5152&page = 31

Institute of Medicine of the National Academies. (2001). *Crossing the quality chasm: A new health system for the 21st century.* Retrieved from http://www.iom.edu/ ~ /media/Files/Report%20Files/2001/Crossing-the-Quality-Chasm/Quality%20Chasm%202001%20%20report%20brief.pdf

Japan Daily Press. (2013). *Japan pushing for low-cost nursing home robots to care for elderly.* Retrieved from http://japandailypress.com/japan-pushing-for-low-cost-nursing-home-robots-to-care-for-elderly-2927943/

Kaiser Commission on Medicaid and the Uninsured. (2012). *A historical review of how states have responded to the availability of federal funds for health coverage.* Retrieved from http://kaiser-familyfoundation.files.wordpress.com/2013/01/8349.pdf

Kaiser Family Foundation. (2011). *Focus on health care reform*: Summary of the Patient Protection and Affordable Care Act of 2010. Retrieved from http://www.kff.org/healthreform/upload/8061.pdf

Lohr, S. (2012). *The future of high-tech health care—the challenge.* Retrieved from http://bits.blogs.nytimes.com/2012/02/13/the-future-of-high-tech-health-care-and-the-challenge/

Merritt Hawkins. (2014). *Physician appointment wait times and Medicaid and Medicare acceptance rates.* Retrieved from: http://www.merritthawkins.com/uploadedFiles/MerrittHawkings/Surveys/mha2014waitsurvPDF.pdf

Michelsen, R.(1989). Hospital based case management for the frail elderly. In T. Kerson (Ed.), *Social work in health settings: Practice in context.* New York: The Haworth Press.

Majerol, M., Newkirk, V., & Garfield, R. (2014). The uninsured: A primer – key facts about health insurance and the uninsured in America. Retrieved from http://kff.org/report-section/the-uninsured-a-primer-what-was-happening-to-insurance-coverage-leading-up-to-the-aca/

Morrissey, J. (2013). Connecting the continuum. *Hospitals and Health Networks.* Retrieved from http://www.hhnmag.com/hhnmag/jsp/articledisplay.jsp?dcrpath = HHNMAG/Article/data/06JUN2013/0613HHN_FEA_ATTGate&domain = HHNMAG

Morrissey, J. (2014). A three-way strategy to use technology to improve home care after discharge. *Hospitals and Health Networks*. Retrieved from http://www.hhnmag.com/display/HHN-news-article.dhtml?dcrPath = /templatedata/HF_Common/NewsArticle/data/HHN/Magazine/2014/Jul/fea-mobile-health-improve-home-care

National Council on Aging. (2014). *The United States of Aging Survey results 2014.* Retrieved from http://www.ncoa.org/improve-health/community-education/united-states-of-aging/2014/usa-survey-results-2014.html

Novotney, A. (2011). A new emphasis on telehealth. *American Psychological Association. June 2011 monitor on psychology.* Retrieved 7/1/12 from http://www.apa.org/monitor/2011/06/telehealth.aspx

Oregon Health Authority. (n.d.). *Coordinated care: The Oregon difference.* Retrieved from http://www.oregon.gov/oha/OHPB/Pages/health-reform/ccos.aspx

Oss, M. (2013a). *Home telehealth potential.* Retrieved from http://www.openminds.com/market-intelligence/executive-briefings/121013-telehealth-potential.htm.

Oss, M. (2013b). *Integration at a whole new level.* Retrieved from http://www.openminds.com/market-intelligence/intelligence-updates/071511-integration-insurance.htm

Oss, M. (2014). *Are health homes working? The payer perspective.* Retrieved from http://www.openminds.com/market-intelligence/executive-briefings/health-home-updated-payers.html/

Paradise, J., & Nardone, M. (2014). *Health homes: A profile of newer programs.* Retrieved from http://kff.org/medicaid/issue-brief/medicaid-health-homes-a-profile-of-newer-programs/?utm_campaign = KFF%3A + The + Latest&utm_source = hs_email&utm_medium = email&utm_content = 13707259&_hsenc = p2ANqtz-8NEBzClfR730cSMSPcSBXIiYrKdDrBK5HVH9WU7XM3vKDTzG5lUNnioaKDXt8ZYPDBGevpMefLoX0GlxHVoWEzpO1dfg&_hsmi = 13707259

Pollitz, K., Tolbert, J., & Ma, R. (2014). *Survey of health insurance marketplace assister programs.* Retrieved from http://kff.org/health-reform/report/survey-of-health-insurance-marketplace-assister-programs/?utm_campaign = KFF%3A + General&utm_source = hs_email&utm_medium = email&utm_content = 13464436&_hsenc = p2ANqtz-9VyxBXr6zAfEBHfJz0HQH561KloXZkkou4jOZZrPNdS0RK29cYTM2VF99ebRMv_5vFtbdM2I4ERmFhaxPTtg9USU3b6Q&_hsmi = 13464436

Radley, D., McCarthy, D., Lippa, J., Hayes, S., & Schoen C. *Aiming higher: Results from a scorecard on state health system performance.* New York: The Commonwealth Fund, May 2014. Retrieved from http://www.commonwealthfund.org/Publications/Fund-Reports/2014/Apr/2014-State-Scorecard.aspx

Schimpff, S. (2011). *The future of healthcare delivery.* Retrieved from http://www.medicalmegatrends.com/disruptive-changes-medical-care.html

Smith, D., & Ricci, C. (2012). *Top ten healthcare trends—2012.* Retrieved from https://www.besmith.com/thought-leadership/white-papers/top-10-healthcare-trends-%E2%80%93-2012

Smith, H., & Allison, R. (1998). *Telemental health: Delivering mental health care at a distance. A summary report.* Rockville, MD: U.S. Department of Health and Human Services, Substance Abuse and Mental Health Services Administration, Center for Mental Health Services, Health Resources and Services Administration, Office for the Advancement of Telehealth.

Spitzer, W., & Davidson, K. (2013). Future trends in health and health care: Implications for social work practice in an aging society. *Social Work in Health Care, 52*(10), 959–986.

Spitzer, W., Neuman, K., & Holden, G. (2004). The coming of age for assisted living care: New options for senior housing and social work practice. *Social Work in Health Care, 38*(3), 21–46.

Stahlman, S., & Kisor, A. (2000). Nursing homes. In R. Schneider, N. Kropf, & A. Kisor, (Eds.), *Gerontological social work: Knowledge, service settings and special populations* (pp. 225–254). Belmont, CA: Wadsworth/Thompson Learning.

Skopec, L., & Sommers, B. (2013). Seventy-one million Americans are receiving preventive services coverage without cost-sharing under the Affordable Care Act. *ASPE Issue Brief*. Washington, DC: U.S. Department of Health and Human Services. Retrieved from http://aspe.hhs.gov/health/reports/2013/PreventiveServices/ib_prevention.pdf

Tanner, L. (2012). Some doctors are embracing social media. *Richmond Times-Dispatch*, June 20, 2012, p. A2.

Taylor, P. (1992). New wave social work: Practice roles for the 1990s and beyond. In M. Holosko & P. Taylor (Eds.), *Social work practice in health care settings* (2nd Edition). Toronto: Canadian Scholars' Press.

United States Department of Health and Human Services (2006). *The supply and demand of professional social workers providing long-term care services: Report to Congress*. Retrieved from http://aspe.hhs.gov/daltcp/reports/2006/Swsupply.htm#future

United States Department of Health and Human Services. (2011). Medicare program; Medicare shared savings program: Accountable care organizations. *Federal Register, 76*(2), 67802–67990.

United States Department of Health and Human Services (2013a). *More doctors, hospitals coordinate care for people with Medicare*. USDHHS Press Release. Retrieved from http://www.hhs.gov/news/press/2013pres/01/20130110a.html

United States Department of Health and Human Services. (2013b). *Affordable Care Act extended free preventive care to 71 million Americans with private health insurance*. USDHHS Press Release. Retrieved from http://www.hhs.gov/news/press/2013pres/03/20130318a.html

United States Department of Health and Human Resources. (2014). *HHS awards $54.6 million in Affordable Care Act mental health services funding*. USDHHS Press Release. Retrieved from http://www.hhs.gov/news/press/2014pres/07/20140731a.html

United States White House. (2013). *Twenty-four states refuse to expand Medicaid: Here's what that means for their residents*. Retrieved from http://www.whitehouse.gov/share/medicaid-map?utm_source = healthcare-email&utm_medium = email&utm_content = 110713-graphic&utm_campaign = healthcare

Wachino, V. (2015). *Nearly 10.8 million additional individuals enrolled in Medicaid as of December 2014*. Retrieved from: http:..www.hhs.gov/healthcare/facts/blog/2015/02/medicaid-chip-enrollment-december.html

Whitaker, T., & Arrington, P. (2008). Social workers at work. NASW Membership Workforce Study. Washington, DC: National Association of Social Workers.

Williams, H. (2002). Social work skills in assisted living. *The Journal of Social Work in Long-Term Care, 1*(3), 5–8.

Zimmerman, E. (2012). *Vital signs by phone, then, with a click, a doctor's appointment*. Retrieved from http://www.nytimes.com/2012/04/12/business/smallbusiness/start-ups-use-technology-in-patient-doctor-interaction.html?_r = 2

Appendix Log

APPENDIX	CHAPTER	INFORMATION
A	4	Title: Inpatient healthcare social work position description Author: William Spitzer (original)

Inpatient Healthcare Social Work Position Description
XXX Healthcare System

POSITION OVERVIEW/RESPONSIBILITES

- Rapidly and accurately identifies and appropriately intervenes to address the psychosocial needs of patients, families, and significant others on the (medical) unit/service

- Consults, educates, and supports other professionals regarding patient/family adjustment to condition and treatment as well as present and anticipated psychosocial care needs/barriers

- Advocates for the appropriate utilization of patient, family, health system, and community resources in establishing safe, timely, ethical, and effective plans for ongoing care

PATIENT CARE ACTIVITIES

High-Risk Screening

Accurately and rapidly engages in high-risk screening of patients admitted to assigned unit(s) to systematically identify those with psychosocial needs, including issues related to adjustment to health condition/treatment, domestic violence, legal (including citizenship, custody and guardianship, patient rights, and advance directives issues), suicide potential, and ongoing care. Through patient and/or caregiver interview(s), consultations, rounds, and/or medical record reviews, completes screening documentation within 48 hours of admission. Records findings and recommendations in healthcare record; initiates appropriate referrals and consults with other disciplines as warranted.

Psychosocial Assessment

Performs accurate, focused, and culturally sensitive psychosocial assessment of patients' circumstances, strengths, and needs. Meets with patients, family members, caregivers, and other involved parties consistent with needs preliminarily identified in high-risk screening. Provides particular attention to patient/family adjustment to illness, injury, or disability; adjustment to treatment/hospitalization; availability and appropriateness of emotional support and resources (finances, housing, transportation, etc.); and capacity to engage in realistic, timely care planning.

Psychosocial Counseling

Provides crisis intervention, short- and long-term counseling as warranted to patients, families, caregivers, and other significantly involved parties using individual, family, and/ or group methodologies. Develops an effective age-appropriate working relationship with patients and/or caregiver(s) through engagement, collaboration, advocacy, decision-making and problem-solving activities. Uses self in a differential, therapeutic manner to remedy case-related conflicts. Demonstrates knowledgeable, culturally sensitive use of effective interventions as measured by achievement of realistic outcomes and feedback from patients, colleagues, and other involved parties. Recognizes principles of patient rights, privileged communication, and confidentiality.

Patient/Family Education (Information and Referral)

Addresses patient and/or caregiver(s) understanding of, and adjustment to, the medical diagnosis and the treatment process to as to maximize benefits of medical intervention and enhance patient/caregiver functioning. Provides such information in a clear and timely manner, updating as warranted and appropriately documenting such intervention in the healthcare record.

Patient Post-Hospitalization Care Planning

Develops focused, accurate, timely care plans relevant to (medical) unit/service patient/ family psychosocial needs and concerns. The plan should consider appropriate developmental stages of patients. The plan should include clinical/diagnostic impressions, with goals consistent with overall medical treatment plan. Post-hospitalization care plans should address, but not necessarily be limited to, medical equipment, housing, ongoing professional care, financial assistance, transportation, and child care arrangements. Documents intervention promptly and concisely in healthcare records and other pertinent venues. Clarifies patient/caregiver(s) understanding of discharge instructions, obtains consultations as warranted, and provides contact information for post-discharge questions and issues.

INTERDISCIPLINARY ACTIVITIES

Program Development

Contributes to planning for programs on the medical unit/service or within the health system that address current and potential future patient/family psychosocial needs.

Collaboration

Actively serves on medical unit/service healthcare team, offering information regarding psychosocial needs of patients/families and functions of healthcare social work. Participates in interdisciplinary team meetings, patient care rounds, and specialized staffing. Develops effective staff relationships, including contribution of staff support as warranted.

Quality Improvement

Recognizes the principles and importance of continuous quality improvement in patient care service delivery. Identifies opportunities for enhancement of services in the assignment area(s).

Education/Training/Committees

Shares relevant information and conducts education for patients, families, involved decision-makers, and healthcare staff on interventions, community resources, and role of social work. Participates on health system and community committees/task forces addressing patient care.

PROFESSIONAL DEVELOPMENT

Knowledge Base

Maintains thorough understanding of healthcare social work practice related to assigned patient population and health system care unit/service. Establishes, continuously reviews, and modifies practice goals. Reviews practice-related literature and participates in ongoing education and professional organizations as appropriate to update knowledge base. Contributes as feasible to knowledge base through research and publication.

Supervision

Participates and utilizes supervision to assess level of competence, identify areas for professional growth, and establish mutually agreed-upon development goals. Demonstrates commitment to enhancing practice. Assists with or supervises graduate/undergraduate students and volunteers. Regularly attends and participates in service unit/area meetings with the goal of identifying and addressing patient care issues.

CQI Focus

Identifies opportunities for practice-based quality improvement through self-assessment efforts. Constructively incorporates supervision and input from colleagues so as to enhance practice. Contributes toward development of patient care monitors as appropriate in assigned areas.

ACCOUNTABILITY

Documentation/Statistics

Completes timely, accurate, and comprehensive documentation in patient care records and other health system communications. Maintains timely and accurate statistics; prepares reports as requested for the purpose of enhancing service delivery, evaluating service programs, identifying resource needs, or responding to regulatory or other legal obligations.

Professional Ethics

Understands and subscribes to the canons of ethical social work practice as outlined in the NASW Code of Ethics and as demonstrated in performance of patient care. Emphasizes practice canons in educational and community activities.

Regulatory Compliance

Understands and adheres to the health system's, patient care service unit's, and social work profession's policies, procedures, and guidelines pertaining to patient care and social work practice. Recognizes and responds appropriately to federal, state, and local statutes governing patient care.

REPRESENTATIVE ACTIONS AND DECISIONS

- Initiates patient/family intervention based on self-assessment of service need
- Initiates community/facility referrals based on identified patient/family needs
- Initiates consultation with health system staff regarding psychosocial issues
- Develops intervention plans with patients, families, involved significant others
- Participates in education and research activities with health system staff
- Contributes to CQI activities through self-analysis of services and needs
- Participates in service area meetings, training, and patient care conferences

APPENDIX	CHAPTER	INFORMATION
B	4	Title: Computerized Inpatient High-Risk Screening Form Source: W. Spitzer; also see: Spitzer, W. (1997). Psychosocial high-risk screening: Enhancing patient care through rapid social work engagement. *Continuum: An Interdisciplinary Journal on Continuity of Care, 17,* 1, 3–9.

MEDICAL COLLEGE OF VIRGINIA HOSPITALS
Virginia Commonwealth University
Richmond, Virginia 23298

Patient Identification (Patient Plate)

PATIENT/FAMILY PSYCHOSOCIAL SCREENING

The factors evident **at the time of initial screening** by Social Work Services are noted below with the date(s) of any service referrals appropriate at that time. Documentation of service following such referral will be noted elsewhere in medical record. Issues not apparent during, or arising subsequent to, the initial screening will be recorded elsewhere in the medical chart at the time they occur.

PATIENT AGE / HEALTH ISSUES
( )   <18 years
( )   >65 years
( )   New diagnosis of _____
( )   Concurrent diagnoses
( )   First hospitalization
( )   Recurrence of condition
( )   Multiple hospitalizations within last six months
( )   Marked change in functional or cognitive status
( )   Known physical disabilities
( )   Patient and/or family manifests emotional, behavior, or cognitive response(s)
          potentially impacting medical treatment.
( )   Patient/family manifests limited understanding of, or adjustment to,
          condition, treatment and/or prognosis
( )   Patient and/or family manifests discharge related teaching needs

PATIENT/FAMILY SOCIAL ISSUES
( )   Unknown prior address or homeless
( )   Pt unable or unwilling to communicate
( )   Citizenship and/or guardianship issue
( )   Patient and/or family advance directives issue
( )   Absence of family or other social/emotional support system
( )   Non-English speaking
( )   Sociocultural factor influencing patient family service need
( )   Issue regarding patient legal status including incarcerations
( )   Issue regarding patient and/or family literacy
( )   Protective/preventative Services Referral (Adult/Child)
( )   Significant concurrent life changes
( )   Issue regarding caregiver availability for discharge planning
( )   Issue regarding caregiver willingness/availability to provide post discharge care
          (physical and/or emotional support)
          SOCIAL WORK SERVICES WILL BE INITIATED (check box)   _____

SUBSTANCE USE
( )   Suspected/actual patient/family history of substance abuse
( )   Withdrawal management issues
          SUBSTANCE ABUSE CONSULTATION TEAM REFERRAL   REFER DATE: _____

PSYCHIATRIC ISSUES / HISTORY
( )   Evidence of psychiatric history (retardation, illness, disability)
( )   Competency issue
( )   Potential/actual patient risk to self or others
( )   Patient refuses medical treatment
( )   Patient has confusion/disorientation potentially affecting treatment
          CLINICAL NURSE SPECIALIST OR PSYCHIATRIC LIAISON PROGRAM REFERRAL   REFER DATE: _____
          MCVH REHAB PSYCHOLOGIST/TEAM REFERRAL   REFER DATE: _____

Form H-MR-445 (8/95)
Social Work

White-Medical Records/Yellow-Department

Patient Identification (Patient Plate)

MEDICAL COLLEGE OF VIRGINIA HOSPITALS
Virginia Commonwealth University
Richmond, Virginia 23298

PATIENT/FAMILY PSYCHOSOCIAL SCREENING

INHOME PATIENT CARE NEEDS
( )   Actual/potential need for in-home *skilled* care
   COMMUNITY HOME HEALTH PROGRAM REFERRAL   REFER DATE: _____

( )   Actual/potential need for in-home *non-skilled* care
   SOCIAL WORK SERVICES WILL BE INITIATED (check box)

PHYSICAL REHABILITATION
( )   Actual/potential need for in-/outpatient rehabilitation
   MCVH REHAB CONSULT SERVICE REFERRAL   REFER DATE: _____
   COMMUNITY REHAB CONSULT REFERRAL   REFER DATE: _____

SPIRITUALITY
( )   Patient and/or family spiritual/religious issue or need
   PASTORAL CARE SERVICE REFERRAL   REFER DATE: _____

PAIN MANAGEMENT
( )   Patient experiences uncontrolled pain
   PAIN MANAGEMENT CLINIC REFERRAL   REFER DATE: _____
   MCVH REHAB PSYCHOLOGIST/TEAM REFERRAL   REFER DATE: _____

PATIENT PLACEMENT NEEDS
( )   Concern regarding availability/appropriateness of previous or existing residence for placement
( )   Concern regarding patient recognition of placement need
( )   Patient geographic residence a potential discharge factor
( )   Actual/suspected presence of others dependent on patient for care
( )   Actual/potential need for placement:
   ( )   Adult/Child Foster Home
   ( )   Nursing Home Care
   ( )   other (specialized shelters/program, residential care, etc.)
   SOCIAL WORK SERVICES WILL BE INITIATED (check box)   _____

OTHER ONGOING PATIENT CARE NEEDS
( )   Actual/potential need for medical equipment/supplies
( )   Transportation (to/from MCVH: immediate and/or ongoing)
( )   Potential/actual financial concerns (disability, Medicaid, commercial insurance, Medicare, etc,)
( )   Actual/potential need for ongoing community program
      (counseling, support groups, workshops, employment/education)
   SOCIAL WORK SERVICES WILL BE INITIATED (check box)   _____

( )   Cancer rehab counselor referral   (REFERRAL DATE: _____)
( )   Child Life referral   (REFERRAL DATE: _____)
( )   Hospital School Teacher   (REFERRAL DATE: _____)

( )   **NO PSYCHOSOCIAL NEEDS IDENTIFIED AT TIME OF SCREENING**

COMMENTS/OTHER NEEDS/ISSUES: _____
_____
_____
_____

Social Worker Name/pager: _____   **Admit Date:** _____/ _____/ _____

                              Screen Date: _____/ _____/ _____

Form H-MR-445 (8/95)
Social Work

White-Medical Records/Yellow-Department

APPENDIX	CHAPTER	INFORMATION
C	4	Title: Computerized Patient/Family Discharge Information Form Source: Spitzer, W., Burger, S., & Farley, B. (1998). Promoting inpatient/family education through use of automated interdisciplinary discharge information. *Continuum: An Interdisciplinary Journal on Continuity of Care, 18,* 1, 3–7.

HANNIBAL, Susan
650 Triumph Street
Richmond, Virginia

Telephone: (804) 555-0000

Zip code: 23298

DISCHARGE INFO FORM

Medical Record Number: 131490000   Financial Acct Number: 12340000
Nursing Unit: M11C

For medical questions, call the *Medical College of Virginia Physician Hotline at 1–800–762–6161*

Referring Physician: LEE, Robert L.
Responsible Attending Physician: JEFFERSON, Thomas
Discharging Service: Neurology
Reason for Hospitalization (in layperson terms):   Injury to the brain
Allergies: Drug Allergy to Captopril

The following information will help you care for yourself after your discharge from the hospital:
Restrictions:
      Restrictions: USE CANE FOR WALKING

      Person(s) instructed: Mother, sister and yourself
      Patient may return to work/school after clearance by Dr. Jefferson

Diet and Nuitrition:

      Discharge Diet: LOW SALT DIET

      Please call the dietitian with any questions about your diet.

      DIETITIAN: Marci Patton   TELEPHONE: (804) 828 – 9999
      AS A REMINDER: PLEASE REFER TO HANDOUTS PROVIDED BY THE DIETITIAN
      FOR YOUR LOW SALT DIET.

Medication Instructions:

      IF YOUR PRESCRIPTION WAS FILLED AT MCVH PLEASE CALL THE PHARMACIST IN THE EMERGENCY ROOM PHARMACY AT
      828-1234 FOR QUESTIONS ABOUT YOUR MEDICATIONS.

Prescriptions:

      Get From: Medication:
      MCVH Pharmacy   CLOMIPRAMINE CAP 50MG
                                                              CAPS/TABS TAKE 1 CAP OR TAB AT BEDTIME

Followup Appointments:

      YOU HAVE AN APPOINTMENT SCHEDULED WITH THE BRAIN INJURY CLINIC, WITH DR. KOSNER, NORTH HOSPITAL, ON
      THURSDAY, 3/26/98 AT 10.00A.M

HANNIBAL, Susan
650 Triumph Street
Richmond, Virginia

Telephone: (804) 555- 0000

Zip code: 23298

DISCHARGE INFO FORM

Social Work:

YOUR MCVH SOCIAL WORKER WAS JANE ADDAMS AND CAN BE REACHED AT (804) 828-0212.

WHILE AT MCVH, INFORMATION ABOUT RESOURCES WAS GIVEN TO YOU AND TO YOUR MOTHER. YOUR FUTURE TRANSPORTATION WAS ARRANGED THROUGH EDWARDS CARE SERVICE (804-555-5555). PLEASE CONTACT THEM IF YOU HAVE A QUESTION ABOUT GETTING TO AND FROM THE MEDICAL COLLEGE OF VIRGINIA FOR YOUR CARE.

AN APPOINTMENT HAS BEEN ARRANGED FOR YOU AT SOCIAL SECURITY ADMINISTRATION FOR 11:00AM ON APRIL 1, 1998. THE ADDRESS IS 718 EAST FRANKLIN STREET. IF YOU HAVE QUESTIONS, PLEASE CONTACT THEM AT 1800-772-1213. IF YOU HAVE A PROBLEM WITH THESE RECOMMENDATIONS OR NEED MORE HELP, PLEASE CALL JANE ADDAMS OR THE SOCIAL WORK MAIN OFFICE (7.30AM-5.00PM, Monday-Friday) AT (804) 828-0212. IF YOU HAVE AN EMERGENCY, PLEASE CALL THE HOSPITAL OPERATOR AT (804) 828-0999 AND REQUEST THE ONCALL SOCIAL WORKER.

Occupational Therapy:

PLEASE CONTACT YOUR OCCUPATIONAL THERAPIST WITH ANY QUESTIONS.
NAME: Jackie Nesvig   Telephone: (804) 828-2222

ASSISTANCE WAS PROVIDED ABOUT GROOMING AND ENERGY SAVING TIPS USE THESE ACTIVITIES TO HELP YOU GET BETTER: HANDBOOK & LOG BOOK

Nursing:

Person(s) instructed: Mother, sister and yourself

CALL YOUR DOCTOR IF YOU HAVE LIGHTHEADEDNESS

CLEAN YOUR WOUND WITH HYDROGEN PEROXIDE AND APPLY RESTORE TO YOUR BACK EVERY OTHER DAY FOLLOW THE INSTRUCTIONS THE NURSE HAS GIVEN YOU CARING FOR YOUR WOUND AT HOME.

Your Primary Nurse was: Clara Barton, RN   Telephone: (804) 828-7777

I understand the information given to me.   _____ YES   _____ NO

I have received all my personal belongings   _____ YES   _____ NO

PATIENT/Caretaker: _____   Date: _____
                                    (signature)

Nurse: _____   Date: _____
                                    (signature)

Social Work Services
Inpatient Statistical Information Record

POLICY

Social work personnel will promptly complete statistical reports detailing their intervention and outcomes with health system in- and outpatients, families, and other involved parties.

The intent is to systematically and comprehensively collect relevant information about patients, interventions, and outcomes. Total volumes of patients seen, the rapidity and extensiveness of engagement, and the complexity of patient needs can be calculated for purposes of staff supervision and performance evaluation, intervention monitoring and enhancement (CQI), and program planning.

Specific sections include patient-identifying information, service dates, presenting issues and patient care needs, problems and barriers encountered by staff extending service, rendered social work services, extent of goal accomplishment, issues related to extended length of hospitalization, discharge disposition, patient acuity (complexity), and authorizing signature of the attending social worker(s). One form is utilized per patient, reflecting any and all unit transfers following admission.

PROCEDURE

Patient Background/Admitting Data

Enter patient last name followed by first name. Include age/birthdate, medical record number, address from which patient was admitted (note if different than permanent residence, including any facility name), date of admission and the medical service (medicine, surgery, pediatrics, etc.) and medical unit/floor to which the patient was initially admitted. Enter date of the high-risk screening.

Section I: Social Work Services Rendered

Identify all social work services provided to the patient and/or family by noting the appropriate service. If "other" is checked, specify the nature of service.

Section II: Service Outcomes and Goal Accomplishment

For each medical service or unit patient received care, enter up to four of the most important social work services rendered (use numbers found in Section I).

Enter number reflecting extent to which service was accomplished: FULLY (1), PARTIAL (2), NOT ACHIEVED (3).

Section III: LOS Extension/Barriers to Care (Extended Hospitalization Monitor)

In the box, enter the number of days of discharge delay from date physician indicates patient is dischargeable. Then, in the spaces provided, briefly note the categorical factor(s) contributing to a discharge delay.

Examples:

Patient delay: unanticipated deterioration of condition. *Family delay:* family may be unavailable for decision making. *Community resource:* appropriate placement may not be available. *Health system:* needed procedure was not completed.

Section IV: Discharge Disposition

Reflects the patient disposition upon hospital discharge. Note the number corresponding to the discharge target (entering name/address of discharge target in space provided). *Check box if patient had been readmitted to health system within the preceding 30 days.*

Section V: Authorizations, Patient Acuities, and Form Completion Date

Social worker enters initials and patient care service/unit. Enter patient acuity level using established criteria.

DEPARTMENT OF SOCIAL WORK SERVICES
POLICY AND PROCEDURE

Policy Number:
Approval Date:
Revision Date:
Effective Date:

TITLE: INPATIENT SOCIAL WORK SERVICES INPATIENT STATISTICAL INFORMATION RECORD

POLICY:

Social work personnel will promptly complete statistical reports detailing their intervention and outcomes with health system in- and outpatients, families, and other involved parties.

The intent is to systematically and comprehensively collect relevant information about patients, interventions, and outcomes. Total volumes of patients seen, rapidity and extensiveness of engagement along with complexity of patient needs can be calculated for purposes of staff supervision and performance evaluation, intervention monitoring and enhancement (CQI) and program planning.

Specific sections include patient identifying information, service dates, presenting issues and patient care needs, problems and barriers encountered by staff extending service, rendered social work services, extent of goal accomplishment, issues related to extended length of hospitalization, discharge disposition, patient acuity (complexity) and authorizing signature of the attending social worker(s). One form is utilized per patient, reflecting any and all unit transfers following admission.

PROCEDURE:

Patient Background/Admitting Data:
Enter patient last name followed by first name. Include age/birthdate, medical record number, address from which patient was admitted (note if different than permanent residence, including any facility name), date of admission and the medical service (medicine, surgery, pediatrics, etc.) and medical unit/floor to which the patient was initially admitted. Enter date of the high risk screening

Section I: Social Work Services Rendered:
Identify all social work services provided to the patient and/or family by noting the appropriate service. If "other" is checked, specify the nature of service.

Section II: Service Outcomes and Goal Accomplishment:
For each medical service or unit patient received care, enter up to four of the most important soc wk services rendered (use numbers found in Section I).
Enter number reflecting extent to which service was accomplished: FULLY (1); PARTIAL (2); NOT ACHIEVED (3)

Section III: LOS Extension/Barriers to Care (Extended Hospitalization Monitor)
In the box, enter the number of days of discharge delay from date physician indicates patient is dischargeable. Then in the spaces provided, briefly note the categorical factor(s) contributing to a discharge delay.

Examples:
Patient delay: unanticipated deterioration of condition; *Family delay:* family may be unavailable for decision making; *Community Resource:* appropriate placement may not be available; *Health system:* needed procedure was not completed.

Section IV: Discharge Disposition:
Reflects the patient disposition upon hospital discharge. Note the number corresponding to the discharge target (entering name/address of discharge target in space provided). *Check box if patient had been readmitted to health system within the preceding 30 days.*

Section V: Authorizations, Patient Acuities, and Form Completion Date
Social worker enters initials and patient care service/unit. Enter patient acuity level using established criteria.

Department of Social Work Services Inpatient Statistical Information Record

Patient Name: _____ Med Record #_____ Admit Med Serv / Unit _____/_____

Age: _____ Admit Date: _____ First SW Contact Date: _____ Admitted From: _____

I. Social Work Services Rendered

1. High-risk screening (DATE: _____)
2. Psychosocial assessment
3. Financial assistance
4. Consult-w/l health system
5. Consult-community agency
6. Case conference
7. Supportive pt. adjustment counseling
8. Court appearance
9. Routine transportation (bus; wheelchair transp.)
10. Special transportation (including aircraft)
11. Advance directives / Ethics consultation
12. Placement (ex: SNF, ALF, Rehab)
13. Post-discharge follow-up
14. Guardianship
15. Housing assistance
16. Substance abuse tx arrangements
17. Crisis Intervention
18. OB options counseling
19. Domestic violence counseling
20. Family counseling
21. Citizenship issue/Interpreters
22. Other: _____

II. Service Outcomes / Goal Accomplishment

Med Srv/Unit	SWer	SW Srvs Rendered				Srv. Accomplishment (1-full; 2-part; 3-not achieved)			
		1st	2nd	3rd	4th	1st	2nd	3rd	4th
_____	____	____	____	____	____	____	____	____	____
_____	____	____	____	____	____	____	____	____	____
_____	____	____	____	____	____	____	____	____	____

III. Service Barriers – LOS Extension Monitor   Estimated Days of Delayed Discharge: _____

Contributing Factors:
Patient: _____
Family: _____
Community: _____
Health System: _____

IV. Discharge Disposition:

____	Own home	____	Relative home	____	Assisted Living Facility
____	Skilled Nursing Home	____	D/C with personal care	____	D/C with equipment
____	Intermed. Nurs. Home	____	Psychiatric program	____	Substance Ab. Tx.
____	Shelter	____	Adult/Child Foster Care	____	Inpatient Rehab.
____	Expired	____	Against Medical Advice	____	Unknown
____	Other (Specify: _____				

Discharge Target Address: _____

V. Authorizations and Patient Overall Psychosocial Acuity Level (based on need and rendered services)

Social Worker Name	Med. Serv/Unit	Patient Acuity (Refer to Acuity Scale)	Date
_____	_____	_____	_____
_____	_____	_____	_____
_____	_____	_____	_____

APPENDIX	CHAPTER	INFORMATION
E	8	Home Healthcare Patient Referral Form. Author: William Spitzer (original)

PATIENT REFERRAL FORM

NAME: _____   S.S.#: _____ / _____ / _____

ADDRESS: _____   D.O.B: ____ / ____ /_____

_____   PHONE: (_____)_____-_____

INSURANCE

Plan #1: _____ Policy No: _____ (eg, Medicare)

Plan #2: _____ Policy No: _____ (eg, AARP)

EMERGENCY CONTACT

Name: _____   Phone: _____

Address: _____

PRIMARY DIAGNOSIS: _____

MEDICALLY NECESSARY HOME CARE SERVICES:

☐ Skilled Nursing   ☐ Physical Therapy   ☐ Home Health Aides

☐ Occupational Therapy   ☐ Speech Therapy   ☐ Medical Social Work

---

IF PATIENT'S PRIMARY INSURANCE IS <u>TRADITIONAL MEDICARE,</u>
PLEASE COMPLETE THIS SECTION

DATE OF LAST FACE TO FACE ENCOUNTER: ____ / ____ / _____
Traditional Medicare patients are required to have a face to face encounter with a MD, APRN or PA within 90 days prior to, or 30 days following, the start of home care.

CLINICAL FINDINGS TO SUPPORT NEED FOR HOME CARE: _____
_____

REASON PATIENT IS HOMEBOUND: _____

PHYSICIAN SIGNATURE: _____ DATE ___ / ___ / _____
                       MD MUST SIGN HERE

PHYSICIAN NAME PRINTED: _____

PLEASE CALL TO CONFIRM OUR RECEIPT OF THIS FAX
☐ CHECK BOX IF NEXT DAY VISIT NEEDED

<u>FAXLINES:</u> 203.458.4388 OR 1.866.862.0999 (toll free)

<u>INTAKE LINES:</u> 203.458.4257 or 1.866.862.0888 (toll free)

APPENDIX	CHAPTER	INFORMATION
F	8	Sample Position Description-Nursing Home Social Worker. Author: William Spitzer (original)

Nursing Home Social Worker Position Description

GENERAL DESCRIPTION

Provision of social services to residents and families that enhance the admission, adjustment to placement, sustained quality of life during residency, and resident discharges when appropriate. Areas of focus include emotional, behavioral, financial, and social dimensions of the resident's life. Priority is also attached to establishing and maintaining a positive, constructive working relationship with family members and other involved parties so as to maximize the understanding of and collaboration with resident care. The social worker actively participates in establishing and updating resident information through a continuous care planning process.

DUTIES AND RESPONSIBILITIES

1. Engagement in "pre-admission planning" with acute care (hospital) personnel and/or other involved parties regarding potential admission to the nursing facility. Requesting, securing, and reviewing appropriate documents providing needed admission determination data.

2. Meeting with resident, family, and other involved parties to establish relationship, and to confirm resident care needs and health status on admission. Conduct resident assessments and psychosocial histories within 5 working days of admission. Create resident file in advance of admission and update as material is available.

3. Assess and discuss psychological, emotional, and behavioral issues with resident and other involved parties as available and appropriate. Establish action plan for addressing identified issues; monitor and update record on continuous basis.

4. Address financial issues with resident and other involved parties. Assist in identifying available options (including social security, VA benefits, Medicare, Medicaid, etc.) and assist in application process where appropriate.

5. Arrange to meet with resident as appropriate to individually respond to identified psychosocial needs and monitor quality of life during placement.

6. Contribute input (including leadership when appropriate) to resident groups. Respond to and advise resident council as warranted regarding concerns, interests, and needs of residents.

7. Actively contribute to scheduled and impromptu care conferences by providing assessment of resident status, ongoing and potential future needs, family issues, and any legal or other community-related dynamics that would influence care and resident quality of life.

8. Complete accurate, timely, comprehensive, and relevant ongoing documentation of psychosocial status and needs. Complete appropriate sections of the MDS 2.0.

9. Schedule conferences with family members and/or other involved parties to address identified issues, solicit any additional relevant resident information, and respond to concerns or requests.

10. Collaborate with Activity Director(s) regarding resident involvement consistent with resident capabilities/interests and designed to enhance quality of life.

11. Collaborate with community agencies to continuously update knowledge of resources/events while advocating for maximized appropriate resident involvement

APPENDIX	CHAPTER	INFORMATION
G	13	Position Description: Primary Care Social Work Behavioral Health Counselor. Source: Integrated Behavioral Health Project, 2009

Sample Position Description
Social Work Behavioral
Healthcare Counselor in Primary Care

- Assists the primary care provider in recognizing, treating, and managing mental health and psychosocial issues and acts as a contributing member to the primary care team;

- Conducts client intakes, focusing on diagnostic and functional evaluations, then makes recommendations to the primary care provider concerning the clients' treatment goals and plan;

- Provides consultation and training to the primary care providers to enhance their skill and effectiveness in treating mental health problems;

- Provides brief, focused intervention for clients who are in need of mental health services;

- Gives primary care providers timely feedback about the client's care, treatment recommendations, and progress via documentation in the client's record and verbal feedback;

- Advises the primary care provider about which clients are better served at the primary care setting and which should be referred to specialty mental health facilities or elsewhere;

- Initiates follow-up to ascertain how clients are doing and to determine if any changes in treatment approaches are indicated;

- Develops, where indicated, relapse prevention plans and helps clients maintain stable functioning;

- Assists in the detection of "at risk" clients and in the development of plans to prevent worsening of their condition;

- Monitors and coordinates the delivery of health services for clients as related to behavioral healthcare, including linking with other treatment providers not only within the primary care setting but also, with the clients' permission, outside it as well;

- Assists, to the extent feasible, in the client's community functioning by helping with public benefits, vocational rehabilitation, social support, housing, etc;

- Documents the client's progress and diagnostic information in the treatment chart;

- Keeps the primary care providers fully informed of the client's needs and progress, and works with providers to formulate treatment plans;

- Works, where indicated, to effect behavioral changes in clients with, or at risk for, physical disorders and helps them make healthier lifestyle choices;

- Provides clients with self-management skills and educational information needed so they can be full participants in their own treatment and recovery;

- Helps the clients, where indicated, to cope with chronic conditions like pain and diabetes;

- Provides consultation to clinic management and other team members about behavioral services and suggested areas of outcome and program evaluation; and

- Assists the clients in complying with any medical treatment initiated by the primary care provider, such as offering strategies to cope with medication side effects.

Source: Integrated Behavioral Health Project, 2009.

Glossary of Terms

The following select terms appear throughout the text.

Academic credentials: Conferred by educational bodies on completion of specified course-work, frequently including some experiential component (field placement; internship).

Accountable Care Organizations (ACOs): Health care organizations that assume responsibility for the cost and quality of patient care by focusing on prevention, wellness, and intervention with chronic conditions; patient-centered primary care; and the use of integrated services. ACOs evolved as an integral component of the PPACA of 2010.

Active surveillance: An investigative technique in public health for determining the incidence of disease that uses trained individuals to collect data using an approved process for gathering the information that is needed to evaluate a current health threat.

Activities of Daily Living (ADLs): Routine personal tasks that include bathing, toileting, dressing, cleaning, and meal preparation and which are assessed to determine an individual's level of independence.

Acute care: Services, emergency care, hospitalization, and more involved outpatient or speciality care, typically provided through or in collaboration with a hospital.

Adaptation: The psychological process of successfully accepting and incorporating a new diagnosis and effectively addressing problems or concerns created by a change in health status.

Adjustment to illness counseling: designed to help the patient adjust to an illness or health condition.

Adverse outcomes or occurrences: Unexpected negative outcomes from an intervention.

Advocacy: An activity or process designed to secure or enhance needed services, resources, or entitlements.

Almshouse: An early form of institutional care that typically contained the sick, mentally ill, elderly, disabled, and vagrant together, making little if any distinctions between the circumstances and needs of their residents. By the mid-1700s, however, the sick began to be segregated from the other inhabitants of almshouses—a trend leading to the evolution of hospitals.

AMA: A hospital discharge of a patient that occurs "Against Medical Advice."

Ambulatory care: Healthcare services provided at clinics, urgent care, out-patient surgery centers, and other settings to patients who are not in a bed at the healthcare institution.

Acculturation: The process of adopting and incorporating the traits of a new culture into an existing culture.

Assimilation: The process of blending and fusing the traits of two cultures into a single homogeneous cultural unit that is different from either of the original component cultural units.

Assisted living: A form of congregate living that provides individuals with assistance in activities of daily living.

Autonomy: An ethical principle that supports the patient's right to participate in all aspects of, and decisions related to, his or her treatment.

Basic care: A form of long-term or extended care provided in nursing homes that is essentially custodial and that is not covered by Medicare but that may be covered by Medicaid.

Benchmark: A minimum threshold for performance that is established to evaluate quality of care.

Beneficence: An ethical principle that directs the professional to place the interests of the patient first in making any recommendations for intervention and care.

Best practice: Standards and published protocols or steps for care with research and evidence to support their use with particular problems and diagnoses.

Biomedical ethics: A form of ethical reasoning developed by Beauchamp and Childress (2001) that identifies four essential principles to consider when faced with a healthcare-related ethical dilemma: patient autonomy; beneficence, nonmaleficence, and justice.

Biopsychosocial assessment: An in-depth, detailed evaluation of the patient that gathers information in three primary domains: biological, psychological, and social as well as the spiritual.

Bureaucracy: A form of organizational structure characterized by high degrees of specialization, clear divisions of labor, authority and chain of command, and well-defined policies, procedures, and protocols.

Care coordination: Similar to case management, a person-centered, assessment-based, interdisciplinary approach to developing a comprehensive, cost-effective care plan that integrates healthcare and social support services and which is coordinated by a lead member of the healthcare team.

Case management: A primary function of healthcare social workers which involves the ongoing assessment of patient and family needs and arranging, coordinating, monitoring, evaluating, and advocating for a set of services necessary to meet to address complex problems.

Centers for Disease Control and Prevention (CDC): An agency in the United States government that confronts global disease threats and epidemics; tracks diseases and implements prevention programs; improves medical care and promotes public health.

Charity Organization Societies (COS): An early form of social relief, which was prominent in the Victorian era using "friendly visitors" to provide moral and spiritual uplifting to the poor.

Clinical supervision: A function that is provided by social workers with advanced training, years of practice experience, and mastery of competencies to supervisees who seek to acquire knowledge, skills, and identity as a clinical social worker.

Clinical trials: The progressive process of conducting and overseeing research in three phases to test the effectiveness of drugs, treatments, and other interventions while limiting and controlling risks for human subjects participating in the studies.

Cognitive-behavioral therapy: An approach to psychotherapy that addresses cognitive distortions that influence behavioral choices.

Community-based participatory research (CBPR): A research methodology used in public health and other disciplines that uses a partnership approach to equitably involve community members, practitioners, and academic researchers in all aspects of the research process.

Community hospitals: Facilities offering in- and out-patient routine, acute and secondary care, surgical procedures, and specialized outpatient services to a designated community.

Competency: Possessing and demonstrating the required knowledge, skills, and abilities to perform a role and task.

Concurrent monitor: A variable that is part of a concurrent evaluation or research study that is studied during the time that services are being provided to the patient.

Consequentialist perspective: States that ethical decisions are may consider the expected outcomes of a decision in the determination of whether the decision is morally acceptable.

Continuous Quality Improvement (CQI): Methodology/technique for continuously evaluating individual professional and overall program patient care efforts to determine their efficiency, effectiveness, and desirability of outcome.

Continuum of care: A conceptualization of the array of health and mental health services by purpose, complexity, and intensity as progressing from prevention, primary, acute, and secondary care to tertiary and end-of-life care.

Co-occurring disorder: Psychiatric and/or substance-abuse diagnoses occurring concurrently with a medical condition and affecting approximately 18% of all hospitalized medical patients.

Crisis: An event or situation that is experienced as intolerable and that exceeds the person's current resources and coping.

Critical pathways: A treatment protocol that is standardized and implemented with chronic, complex, and/or high-cost diseases that sequences critical steps in patient care, thereby increasing consistency of care by reducing variations between providers.

Crude mortality rate: The number of overall deaths per 1,000 population.

Culturagram: An adapted genogram and eco-map used in social work practice which identifies common themes, practices, and events in culturally diverse groups.

Cultural competence: The ability to respond respectfully and effectively to people of all cultures, languages, classes, races, ethnic backgrounds, religions, and other diversity factors in a manner that recognizes, affirms, and values their worth and dignity.

Cultural humility: A way of working with diverse client systems that demonstrates a life-long commitment to self-evaluation and self-critique in exploring cultural biases and which acknowledges the power differential between providers and patients.

Culturally competent organization: An organization that is committed to accepting and respecting differences between cultural groups; continually assesses their policies and practices regarding cultural sensitivity; has an ongoing commitment to expand cultural knowledge and resources; and promotes cultural competence in hiring and developing staff.

Culture: The integrated pattern of human behavior that includes thoughts, communications, actions, customs, beliefs, values, and institutions of a racial, ethnic, religious, or social group.

Data mining: A research and evaluation method that involves reviewing records and data already collected to answer research questions.

Decompensation: Condition characterized by a temporary worsening of psychiatric symptoms.

Deinstitutionalization: The policy and social movement of moving patients out of large, in-patient state psychiatric facilities and into community-based care often with the subsequent closing of in-patient psychiatric facilities.

Delirium: A deterioration in cognitive functioning, often transient and due to an occurrence such as an adverse reaction to a medication or a high fever characterized by four common features: sudden onset and fluctuating course; inattention and inability to focus; disorganized thinking; and disturbances in consciousness.

Dementia: A progressive deterioration of cognitive functioning and global impairment with no change in the level of consciousness, which is associated with an underlying medical disease such as Alzheimer's disease.

Deontological perspective: An ethical framework that holds that ethical rules are self-evident and should be upheld under all circumstances.

Detoxification: A set of medically supervised interventions aimed at managing acute intoxication and withdrawal. There are three stages to the detoxification process: evaluation, stabilization, and fostering readiness for treatment and recovery.

Developmental disabilities: A classification of medical syndromes and disabilities that typically occur at birth through genetic mutations such as the abnormality that causes Down's syndrome but which may be also acquired through childhood traumas including head injuries and spinal cord injuries.

Diagnostically Related Groupings (DRGs): A basis for of prospective payment implemented by Medicare that pays hospitals a pre-established amount per case treated using a patient classification system of 23 major diagnostic categories (MDCs) and more than 470 diagnostic groups (DRGs).

Disability: A physical or mental impairment that substantially limits one or more of the major life activities of an individual.

Discharge (continuity-of-care) planning: Term used to describe the process or arrangement for patients' care and services when they move from one level of care to another, such as from the hospital to home. Also see **transitional care planning**.

Disease: A pathological, biomedical condition that interferes with the body's capacity to regulate itself and perform essential functions.

Distress: An unpleasant emotional experience of a psychological, social, and/or spiritual nature that interferes with the ability to cope effectively and which extends along a continuum ranging from common normal feelings of vulnerability and sadness to problems that can be disabling such as depression, anxiety, and social isolation.

Distress risk screening: The assessment process for evaluating the potential impact of a cancer or other serious condition on a newly diagnosed patient.

Dorothea Lynde Dix: A social reformer in the mid-1800s who documented the abuse and maltreatment of the mentally ill in asylums and who advocated for more humane forms of treatment, including care in institutions specializing in the care of the mentally ill.

Dual-eligible beneficiaries: Those individuals who are qualified to receive benefits from both the Medicare and Medicaid programs.

Duty to warn: A legal obligation to report and warn an individual who has been threatened with harm by a mentally ill individual, established in 1976 by the Tarasoff v. Regents of the University California court ruling.

Ecosystem crisis: A natural or human-caused disaster that overcomes an individual, group, or community's capacity to cope.

Electronic health records (EHRs) and Electronic medical records (EMRs): A digitized version of the patient medical record that permits providers, usually limited to those working in the same healthcare system, to enter data and directly access patient information.

Entitlement program: A social welfare program that must be funded by the federal government and made available to people who meet the criteria for services (are entitled). Medicaid and Medicaid are entitlement programs.

Epidemiology: The study of how disease is distributed in populations and the factors that influence or determine this distribution.

Epigenetic crisis: In Erikson's human development model, the stage-specific challenges that must be resolved for healthy development to continue; also called a development crisis.

Ethical dilemma: A situation in which practitioners question the right thing to do when confronted with a moral question in which there are competing ethical principles, values, duties, rights, and obligations.

Ethics committee: A multidisciplinary group of healthcare professionals that has been specifically established to address the ethical dilemmas that occur within an institution.

Ethics-of-care perspective: Proposes that decisions include consideration and promotion of the relationship needs of all the parties involved in the dilemma.

Equilibrium: A concept from systems theory that describes a system in a balanced or steady stage.

Evaluation process: The process used to conduct practice or program evaluation studies which includes the following seven steps: designing, planning, implementing, data analysis and interpretation, reporting, data utilization, and follow-up.

Evaluation target: The focus of an evaluation study and which can be an individual patient, a caseload, a service or program, the facility as a whole, a community, or specific policies.

Evidence-based practice: A process of inquiry that utilizes published scholarly research to answer questions about the interventions shown to be most effective with a given patient population or problem. Research is conducted on an issue or problem; it is then critically evaluated, an assessment is made of its applicability, the new approach or procedure is integrated into practice, outcomes are evaluated, and modifications made as warranted.

Existential crisis: A state of disequilibrium and distress rooted in inner conflicts and anxieties around the issues of life's meaning and purpose.

Existential therapy: A philosophically based approach to psychotherapy that is premised on the belief that an individual's emotional and psychological distress is a result of an inability to cope with the realities of existence.

Extended-Care facility (ECF): A form of long term patient care provided by facilities traditionally considered a nursing. Levels of care include skilled and rehabilitative care as well as basic custodial care.

Family and caregivers: The network of individuals engaged in the healthcare process with the patient, typically assisting with decision making and at times providing care.

Family systems theory: A theoretical framework that recognizes the mutual influence of family members upon each other within the context of the broader social environment.

Federally Qualified Health Centers (FQHCs): A designation from the Bureau of Primary Healthcare and the Centers for Medicare and Medicaid Services that is conferred to non-profit public or private clinics located in medically underserved areas or who provide care to medically underserved populations.

Food and Drug Administration (FDA): The agency in the United States government responsible for patient safety by approving and regulating drugs and certain medical devices used in medical treatment.

Formative evaluation: The collection of evaluation data concurrently during the time of service used to measure how a service is being delivered and received.

Friendly visitors: Modeled after English almoners, these individuals visited the poor, investigated living conditions to determine the causes of destitution, and encouraged better nutrition, sanitary hygiene, and abstinence.

Functional ability: An assessment of the patient made by evaluating a variety of conditions including the patient's physical capacities, behavioral/psychiatric characteristics, and social/environmental conditions.

Futility: The use of life-sustaining or invasive interventions for patients in persistent vegetative state or who are terminally ill with no prospect of recovery.

Gatekeeper: A health care professional with the responsibility to ascertain patient acuity, diagnoses, the rationale for services, and patients' insurance benefits before authorizing services.

Genetic engineering: The process of altering the DNA of a cell for purposes of research, as a means of manufacturing animal proteins, correcting genetic defects, or making improvements to plants and animals bred by man.

Genograms: A tool useful in guiding patient assessments, they depict patients' "family trees," describing relationships between individuals and generations.

Gerotranscendence: An additional stage of development extending Erikson's original life cycle model in which the old-old achieve a form of self-realization by maintaining supportive relationships, sustained reflection, and introspection that helps an individual accept and prepare for death.

Global Burden of Disease (GBD): An indicator that measures disability and losses from a healthy life combined with premature death and which is represented by Disability Adjusted Life-Years (DALYs).

Guided care model: A team-based approach to managing chronic diseases that emphasizes the principles of chronic care, disease management, self-management, case management, lifestyle modification, transitional care, caregiver education and support, and geriatric evaluation and management.

Health: According the World Health Organization, a state of complete physical, mental, and social well-being and not merely the absence of disease or infirmity.

Health Belief Model (HBM): A framework for explaining how health beliefs and attitudes influence treatment adherence, which is improved depending on the perceived severity of illness, the belief that adherence will improve health, and that barriers to following recommendations are low or manageable.

Health disparity: A difference in health status that is closely linked with economic, social, and or environmental factors.

Health equity: A principle based in social justice which advocates for a shift from the current disparity model to an equity model in which the central theme is achieving the highest level of health for all.

Health literacy: The capacity of individuals to obtain, process, and understand basic health care information and services needed to make appropriate health decisions.

Health promotion and disease prevention: Strategies and services that intervene before an illness or disability occurs. Includes educating and supporting individuals in making lifestyle choices that promote health and wellness.

Health status: An individual's or community's state of health, wellness, and risk factors at a given point in time.

Healthcare disparities: Variations in health and disease in diverse populations, attributed in part to an unequal distribution of healthcare resources.

Healthcare social work: A field of specialized social work practice as well as the activities, services, roles, and functions of a social worker who is employed by an agency at any point in the healthcare continuum (prevention, primary care, acute care, long-term care, and end-of-life care).

Healthcare team: The multidisciplinary, interdisciplinary, or transdisciplinary team of healthcare providers, typically led by a physician, providing care to the patient.

Helping process: A conceptualization of the social work helping process consists of the following phases: (1) identification, engagement, assessment and care planning; (2) implementation and goal attainment; and (3) evaluation and termination.

High-risk screening: The process of identifying and prioritzing patients most in need of social work intervention due to conditions and characteristics that could negatively affect the provision of healthcare services, outcomes and costs.

Homemaker/home health aide: Individuals who provide personal care and assistance with bathing, grooming, meal preparation, transportation, shopping, and those tasks that do not warrant trained healthcare professionals.

Homeostasis: The property of a system in which components are regulated so that internal conditions remain stable and relatively constant.

Hospice and palliative care: A form of end-of-life care which promotes comfort and quality of life rather than aggressive treatment for individuals with an anticipated life expectancy of less than six months.

Host setting: An organization, such as a hospital, in which the primary purpose is something other than the provision of social work services. Social work services in host settings must contribute and be of benefit to the host setting accomplishing its primary mission.

Ida Maud Cannon: Widely credited with establishing the first organized social work department in the United States, defining the role of medical social work and negotiating the role of social work in what was regarded as a *host environment* in which social work and social issues were not the primary focus.

Illness: An individual's subjective experience of disease that includes social and emotional dimensions in addition to biomedical components.

Incidence: The number of new cases of a disease that occur during a certain time frame within a population of people who are at risk for developing the illness.

Indian Health Services (IHS): A bureau in the United States government charged with improving the health states of the American Indian and Alaskan Native peoples by providing comprehensive primary care services and disease prevention programs.

Indicators: Important performance variables that are monitored and studied to assess quality of care.

Individual mandate: A requirement of the Patient Protection and Affordable Care Act of 2010 for most U.S. citizens and legal residents to maintain a minimum level of health insurance coverage for themselves and their tax dependents or pay a tax penalty.

Individual Practice Associations (IPAs): A model of primary care composed of physicians who are paid on a discounted "fee-for-service" basis from a managed care organization rather than the salaried reimbursement characteristic of the staff-model physician group practice.

Indoor relief: Historic term for care provided to those residing in an institution.

Informed consent: Permission obtained by patients or subjects for their participation in research or evaluation studies and which requires that they be fully informed of any risks and benefits to participating, the voluntary nature of their participation, and how data from the study will be protected and used.

Integrated care: The provision of comprehensive, coordinated, and continuous services in a seamless process of care including inpatient and outpatient services as well as both physical and behavioral healthcare.

Interdisciplinary teams: Work groups comprised of personnel from *different* disciplines or professions who routinely collaborate on issues or problems.

Intradisciplinary teams: Work groups comprised of members with the *same* academic background and/or disciplinary practice.

Involuntary (or civil) commitment: A legal process in which an individual in psychiatric crisis (either decompensation or risk of suicide) is court-ordered into treatment at a psychiatric hospital.

Justice: A principle that the professional treat all patients equitably and is attentive to the just allocation of resources.

Least restrictive principle: An ethical principle and social policy that individuals should be treated settings that maximize their freedom, autonomy, and self-direction.

Lethality: Part of a crisis or suicidal risk assessment evaluating the client's potential to inflict self-harm.

Life expectancy: The average number of years an individual of a certain age who is a member of a given population would be expected to live, given a set of age-specific death rates in a given year. The life expectancy for a particular person or population group depends on several variables, such as their lifestyle, access to healthcare, diet, economic status, and the relevant mortality and morbidity data.

Linguistic competence: An essential feature of culturally sensitive services; refers to providing readily available, culturally appropriate oral and written language services to individuals with limited English proficiency (Agency for Healthcare Research and Quality, 2003).

Logo therapy: A form of existential therapy which stresses that life has meaning under all circumstances; people have a will to make meaning, and people have freedom under any condition to find and create meaning.

Long-term care: A range of services provided over an extended period of time, to meet the physical, emotional, and social needs of people with chronic illnesses or disabilities that interfere with their independence and ability to perform activities of daily living. Services may be provided in the home, through community programs, or in care facilities.

Managed care: A broad term that encompasses a variety of organizational interventions and reimbursement strategies designed to control healthcare costs and service utilization.

Mary Richmond: A prominent friendly visitor in the Baltimore Charity Organization Society who developed an organized curriculum for training volunteers, including a detailed system for documenting case records that led to the formal assessment and intervention procedures adopted by the emerging profession of social work.

Mary Stewart: Known as the "Lady Almoner" and widely viewed as an early pioneer of medical social work, Stewart referred patients to the appropriate Poor Law authority and local church parish while also administering the Royal Free Hospital's Good Samaritan Fund in London, England.

Matrix management: Defined by the "the existence of both hierarchical (*vertical*) coordination through departmentalism and the formal chain of command and simultaneously lateral (*horizontal coordination*) across departments (in a) patient care team" (Neuhauser, 1983).

Medicaid: Provides health insurance coverage for poor individuals who must meet stringent eligibility requirements established by each state. Considerable variation exists among the states as to participant eligibility. Although administered at the state level, it is a federal entitlement program and funded through a combination of federal and state dollars.

Medical complexity: A determination made on the basis of current diagnoses, prognoses, impact, and treatments required.

Medical home model: A model of primary care that focuses on longitudinal care in which the physician coordinates care and helps patients navigate complex healthcare delivery systems.

Medical model: A general orientation of physicians and their assumptions about patients, diseases, and treatment that espouses that a patient is someone who is sick or diseased and requires the interventions of a physician to diagnose, treat, and, if possible, cure disease.

Medicare: A health insurance program approved by the federal government as Title XVIII of the Social Security Act in 1965 and which took effect in 1966, initially providing coverage to individuals 65 years of age and older but later expanded to include disabled individuals. Considered a social insurance program, individuals qualify for Medicare by being employed and contributing through payroll taxes.

Mental health: A state of well-being in which every individual realizes his or her own potential, can cope with the normal stresses of life, can work productively and fruitfully, and is able to make a contribution to her or his community.

Mental hygiene movement: A movement in the mid-1800s, pioneered in the United States by social reformer Dorothea Dix, which advocated for more humane forms of treatment, including care in institutions specializing in the treatment of the mentally ill.

Meta-analysis: A form of research that synthesizes and evaluates the findings of multiple research studies that address a particular problem using established criteria for judging the quality of the studies included in the analysis.

Minimum Data Set (MDS): An interdisciplinary patient-assessment form that is required by the federal government for each nursing home resident.

Morbidity rates: Report how often a disease occurs within a population.

Mortality rates: Report the cause of death for all individuals in a given population and are instrumental for measuring the severity of disease processes and the success of treatment of diseases.

Motivational interviewing: An approach to psychotherapy that explores an individual's motivations in decision making and for making changes using stages of change model.

Multidisciplinary teams: Work groups in which members use their individual expertise to *first* develop their own answers to a given problem, and *then* come together—bringing their individually developed ideas—to formulate a solution.

Multi-payer healthcare system: Currently used in the United States and characterized by a significant array of health insurance companies vying against one another in a highly competitive marketplace.

Nanotechnology: Involves the manipulation of matter on an atomic and molecular scale and may lead to advances including new drugs that could identify and incapacitate certain viruses or create molecular surgical tools guided by computers and injected into the blood stream that could find and destroy cancer cells or invade bacteria, unclog arteries, or provide oxygen when circulation is impaired.

Narrative therapy: An approach to psychotherapy that assists patients in making sense out of life by creating a story or narrative in which events are linked together by themes, beliefs, and understandings.

National Institutes of Health (NIH): An agency of the United States government which conducts research and oversees a variety of programs and services to improve the health of the population. It evolved from an early epidemiological laboratory operated by the Public Health Services in 1887.

Nationalized healthcare system: A healthcare system in which the providers are public sector employees who receive their salary from or are reimbursed directly by the government for their professional services.

Nonmaleficence: A principle that guides professionals to actions that will prevent or avoid harm coming to a patient or another involved party.

Non-normative loss: A loss that is not expected within the context of the human life cycle, such as the death of a child.

Normative loss: A loss that can be expected when considering the context of the human life cycle, such as the death of one's grandparents.

Oncology: The medical speciality that addresses cancer and cancer-related conditions.

Organization: A macro system that is goal-directed, consisting of units that are deliberately structured with coordinated activities and processes. Organizations are connected to, and interact with, their external environments or communities.

Organizational climate: Describes the general atmosphere of an organization that includes expectations of employee morale and attitude. Organizational cultures and climates can differ widely, depending on factors such as ownership, mission, staff composition, and geographic locale.

Organizational culture: Reflected in the norms, values, customs, and behaviors with which employees are expected to comply. Members of organizations are also expected to observe and follow the ways that others typically act.

Organizational design: The process for determining how tasks and authority will be delegated. Consists of organizational structure; processes, and outcomes.

Outdoor relief: Historic term for care delivered to individuals outside of institutions.

Palliative care: A form of medical care that may be provided at the end-of-life or to patients with serious illnesses that are incurable and that provides medical treatments that address symptoms and pain.

Parallel process: Regarded as a manifestation of transference and counter-transference in which supervisees unconsciously recreate the behaviors of their clients in their own supervisory sessions.

Passive surveillance: An investigative technique in public health to determine the incidence of disease that includes the use of data that have been previously collected.

Patient: A traditional term for any individual who receives healthcare services.

Patient-centered care: A model of health care that establishes a partnership among practitioners, patients, and their families (when appropriate) to ensure that decisions respect patients' wants, needs, and preferences and that patients have the education and support they need to make decisions and participate in their own care.

Patient-focused health homes: A model of care emphasizing early integrated intervention by physicians and other practitioners collaboratively addressing both physical and behavioral health needs of patients with a focus on preventive care and wellness.

Patient navigation: The process of guiding patients through complex health systems and assisting them in overcoming logistical, financial, communication, medical system, psychological, cultural, and other kinds of barriers to care.

Patient Protection and Affordable Care Act (PPACA): Landmark healthcare legislation passed by Congress in 2010 and subsequently upheld by the Supreme Court. The Act addressed escalating healthcare costs, concerns regarding quality care, and difficulties in access and affordability by changing healthcare reimbursement and introducing significant changes in the healthcare delivery system. Most notable of these changes were the development of health insurance exchanges (marketplaces) and creation of Accountable Care Organizations.

Payer: An entity that pays for care, typically an insurance company that may be public or private, profit, or non-profit.

Performance evaluation: A process to assess how individual staff members are performing and how they can improve their job performance and contribute to overall organizational performance.

Person-centered planning: A model of care in which the patient's preferences and instructions are primary in designing and implementing services and the treatment plan.

Personalized medicine: Predicated on developing particular therapies for people with specific gene sequences, it focus on use of medicines and interventions that best meet individual genetic, lifestyle, and environmental differences.

Practice evaluation: Integrating basic research methodologies and evaluation strategies into professional practice to determine the effectiveness of interventions.

Pre-admission planning: The identification and assessment of patient needs prior to admission to the hospital or before treatment is provided and arrangements for services are in place.

PRECEDE-PROCEED Model: A comprehensive, multistepped, participatory educational and ecological model for health promotion and wellness that has been used successfully in communities, schools, workplaces, and healthcare settings for more than 30 years.

Preferred Provider Organizations (PPOs): Typically third-party payers such as a self-insured business or union that contracts with selected physicians, hospitals, and other healthcare providers. In return for the payers guaranteeing a certain volume of patients and assured payment, the providers will discount their conventional fees for service and establish utilization review mechanisms to control costs.

Prevalence: The number of individuals with a specific disease in a population at specific point in time.

Primary healthcare: Services usually provided at a patient's first contact with the healthcare delivery system and involving the diagnoses of illnesses and diseases and provision of initial treatment. In addition, these outpatient, clinic, and physician-based services afford episodic care for common non-chronic illnesses and injuries; drug prescriptions for treating common illnesses or injuries; and routine dental care, such as examinations, cleaning, or repairs.

Problem-oriented assessment and intervention: Clinical work that focuses on immediate problems that directly affect patients' health and well being. Although the assessment is limited in scope to variables and conditions that intersect with a problem, the social worker still assesses the problem by identifying the fundamental biopsychosocial conditions that impact it. Intervention plans then directly address the problem and its related concerns.

Professional credentials: Awarded by associations, societies, or other bodies comprised of individuals engaged in the same profession and are recognition from one's peers that the recipient has attained a level of expertise in their field and that the individual subscribes to the performance standards espoused by that professional body.

Professional license: Authorization conferred by individual states to professional practitioners authorizing the holder to engage in a particular scope of practice that would otherwise be deemed *unlawful* were they not licensed.

Prospective Pricing System (PPS): An alternative to traditional models of paying for healthcare with a fee-for-service basis by using predetermined reimbursement limitations for specific procedures, conditions, and Diagnostically Related Groupings (DRGs) in an effort to contain costs.

Provider: An individual who provides healthcare services to patients. This term broadly includes physicians, nurses, social workers, and literally all other members of the healthcare team who provide direct patient care and services.

Psychoeducational group: A form of group work common in healthcare social work practice that combines emotional support with providing disease and treatment-related information, sometimes using a structured curriculum or outline of topics.

Public health: Implies a focus on the health of populations and correspondingly emphasizes disease prevention; promotion of health; reporting and control of communicable diseases; responsibility for environmental factors, such as air/water quality, that affect health and collection; and analysis of data identifying the state of public health.

Public Health Service: A division of the United States Department of Health and Human Services (DHHS) that consists of the Centers for Disease Control (CDC), the Food and Drug Administration (FDA), the Health Resources and Services Administration, the National Institutes of Health (NIH), the Substance Abuse and Mental Health Services Administration, the Indian Health Services, and the Agency for Healthcare Policy and Research. Operating 10 regions and a uniformed corps of 6,000 service members in addition to the Office of the U.S. Surgeon General, the PHS does not focus on direct service delivery, but on shaping the national public health system to promote health and prevent disease

Qualitative research: A type of research that typically involves a small sample to explore common themes, beliefs, perceptions, knowledge, or impressions of an issue, service, or problem.

Quantitative research: A type of research that typically involves a large sample to gather objective, numerical data including surveys; test scores; and recidivism, relapse, and drop-out rates to measure the relationships between variables or the impact of interventions.

Rebecca Cole: An African-American physician who, as a "sanitary visitor," visited the homes of women and children served by the New York Clinic. In 1889, increasing appreciation for the significant influence of social conditions on individual and community health status motivated Johns Hopkins Hospital to incorporate sanitary visitation into the training of some medical residents.

Referral: The process of requesting patient services from another provider. A referral system may be "open" which permits the social worker to initiate services without a specific request from the physician or "closed" which requires a physician's order to initiate care.

Regulatory agencies: Government organizations at state and federal levels that regulate care and ensure that healthcare organizations, providers, and payers meet regulatory standards, laws, and administrative policies.

Reminiscence therapy: A common treatment approach for dementia that involves recalling and communicating memories of past experiences and important life events. Reminiscence therapy can be done with an individual or in groups. The primary purpose is to stimulate memory in order to make connections with the past and possibly provide an opportunity for conscious or unconscious resolution of unresolved grief or other issues.

Resilience: The capacity to rebound from adversity strengthened and more resourceful.

Retrospective audit: The collection and analysis of service data performed after a service has been rendered. May involve the research technique of data mining.

Richard Cabot: Physician and reformer in the early 1900s who is widely regarded as prompting the evolution of social work practice in healthcare by hiring first Garnet Pelton (a nurse) and then Ida Cannon to investigate social conditions affecting individual health and use of healthcare. He contributed to the development of the first social work department in a hospital by funding such work at Massachusetts General Hospital.

Safety plan contract: A written, behavioral contract enacted to protect potentially suicidal patients in which the patient promises not to harm himself or herself and the family agrees to provide round-the-clock direct supervision and to remove any and all possible means for self-harm, including prescription and over-the-counter medications.

Scaling: In cognitive behavioral therapy, an intervention using a 10-point scale by patients to describe and chart the severity of their emotional distress before and after interventions.

Secondary care: Characterized by routine medical or surgical unit hospitalization and specialized outpatient care. In contrast to primary care, secondary care is continuing care for sustained or chronic conditions and, in addition to being delivered by hospitals, may be provided in a wide range of specialty centers, including ambulatory surgery centers, radiology centers, urgent care centers, and renal dialysis centers.

Self-management and **stress management** strategies: Used in cognitive behavioral therapy to help clients regulate emotions and reduce anxiety levels.

Sentinel event: An unexpected occurrence involving death or serious physical or psychological injury, or the risk thereof.

Single-payer system: Government-sponsored and administered health insurance for all citizens. The insurance entity reimburses providers for services, but the providers do not necessarily have to be public employees. In both single- and multi-payer systems, the government pays for covered services, either directly or indirectly (through the single payer), with tax revenues and/or "premiums" by individuals and businesses.

Situational crisis: An uncommon and extraordinary event that can be foreseen and prepared for by an individual.

Skilled care: A form of long term or extended care provided in nursing homes to patients needing physical therapy or skilled nursing care and which may be covered by Medicare for up to 100 days.

Social determinants of health: Social, economic, political and environmental conditions that affect health status and which encompass a variety of factors such as: social gradient (a shorter life expectancy with more disease processes occurring as an individual moves down the social ladder); social exclusion (resentment and discrimination); and social support (lack of social support systems) which accumulate to further separate an individual from health.

Social marketing: The process that uses information about a population to promote the adoption or acceptability of ideas or practices in that population and which has been adapted by public health services to create campaigns featuring well-designed messages to that target audience with sufficient frequency that they are seen, heard, and remembered.

Social production of disease theory: Proposes that one's social and economic position (e.g., gender, race/ethnicity, and social class) determines one's exposure to health-damaging risk factors as well as the presence or absence of health-protective factors.

Somatization: The experience of emotional conflict and anxiety in the body (Galanti, 2008).

Staff-model physician group practice: A model in which physicians are regarded as staff and are prepaid for services rendered to enrolled members of Health Maintenance Organizations (HMOs).

Strengths perspective: A practice approach that builds on patients' strengths (talents, knowledge, capacities, resources) as they work toward an enhanced quality of life.

Substance Abuse and Mental Health Services Administration (SAMHSA) The agency in the United States government that tracks the use of alcohol, tobacco, and legal and illegal drug use in the population. The agency also funds prevention and intervention research as well as promotes education.

Substance-use disorders: The new diagnosis category in the DSM-V comprised of substance-use disorders (previously abuse and dependency); intoxication, and withdrawal and which are classified as mild, moderate, or severe.

Suicidal ideation: The presence of suicidal thoughts, which range in frequency and intensity and at times take on almost a fantasy-like quality about them regarding how others will feel when the person is gone.

Summative evaluation: Evaluation that is done at the conclusion of services and used to judge the aggregative or "sum" of the results of the intervention.

Survivorship care planning: A supportive psychosocial intervention that prepares cancer and other patients with serious illness for the potential for surviving treatment and living with the disease as a chronic, rather than terminal illness.

System: A set of related or interrelated elements or units that function together as a whole in order to achieve a purpose.

Tertiary care: Regarded as the "apex" of healthcare services. It represents the most complex diagnostic and therapeutic services, including organ transplants, burn treatment, and cardiac or other organ surgery. These services are provided by large, regional healthcare centers that are most often teaching hospitals affiliated with universities (also referred to as academic medical centers/systems).

Transdisciplinary teams: A form of interdisciplinary care that is based on the premise that a team member can perform several professional roles and provide various kinds of services when supervised by other team members from other disciplines.

Transfer form: A document that is employed by hospitals to provide patient information and physician's orders for care upon institutional transfer from the hospital to a nursing home or other type of care center.

Transitional care planning: The collaboration between the patient, family, and treatment team and any other key decision-makers to facilitate the patient's transition from one level of care to another or to move in and out of various types of care.

Trans-theoretical model (TTM): The stages of change model in which the patient progresses through various stages (pre-contemplation, contemplation, preparation, action, and maintenance) in pursuing behavioral changes. Considered transtheoretical as it can be integrated into many clinical and theoretical approaches to address multiple behavioral problems.

Unworthy (undeserving) poor: Historic term for those able-bodied individuals impoverished as a result of moral failings.

Values: The preferences, perceptions, and evaluations of worth.

Vicarious liability: The legal risk incurred by supervisors with the formal authority and responsibility to ensure the effective and efficient delivery of social work services to be potentially held liable for the actions or inactions of their supervisees.

Waiver: A provision provided to a state by the federal government that approves variation from federal requirements and criteria established for entitlement programs.

Wellness: An optimum state of health that permits a maximized quality of life and social functioning. As an integrated and holistic approach to living, it requires balance and purpose in order to enable an individual to reach his or her potential. It involves a conscious and deliberate approach to advancing physical, psychological, and spiritual health.

Worthy poor: Historic term referring to disabled, elderly, children, and widows in need of relief.

Index

Made in the USA
San Bernardino, CA
22 March 2018